Transformation

Of a
Common Man

The Brian Scott Story

By

James E. Frazier

ISBN: 0-7596-3993-0 (e-book)
ISBN 0-7596-3994-9 (Paperback)

This book is printed on acid free paper.

1stBooks – rev. 7/10/02

Contents

iv

Dedication

**To my brother
Kendrick Crosby Frazier**

**For all the
skeptics, investigators and philosophers,
scientists, psychics, priests and psychologists
who have devoted their lifetimes
to understanding the mysteries of man.
Though each has entered
this drama from a different path,
they all seek the truth.**

Many thanks

To my wife Carre,
to my parents,
and my children,
who all have sacrificed part of their life
with me
so that this book could be completed.

And
To many others who made this book possible
by reading, editing and consultation.

Prologue

THE HOST, the Secondary World Aliens, the Long Ears and Voltar, leader of the Council for the people of Epsilon Eridani.

Drawings by David Kindvall.

PROLOGUE

Coming of the Host

From Time Beyond all time, he came. From the misty-fire of Light and Sound, he descended into Form. I AM, I AM, his name thundered through the infinite void. Demons stirred. Ancient gods of the earth, and angels of heaven awoke to peer through misty veils of eternity. The time of reaping had come to God's last creation, to man on earth, to the blue-white world of water, to the Garden planet.

Shining angels shook moist, golden wings. Demons rattled dry curses from leathery throats. Giants, sylphs and avatars all wanted in the game. The time had come again for the Host.

From the white-haired Old Man flowed a joyous song for all to hear, "Let the Play of Life begin. Let the Play of Life begin."

Hear and behold his song.

Song of the Host

I Am. I Am. This is my name, and by this I come. I sail onward upon the shining sea of mind, crossing oceans of time, sailing through gates of life, by the light. By the light of mind, I come. Through the gates of time, I am drawn to third from your sun, to the Earth I am drawn.

I bring nourishment for man, sustenance for the mind, knowledge of the past, enrichment to the mind of man. Of this, I bring wisdom so that you may survive, and of this -- I am. I am. Now hear me. I come in love with a challenge, and a warning for man. Seek to understand this, of I.

Accept quantum evolution of mind. Expand to Nous 10. Do this, of I, or you and all knowledge of your world shall perish—not by man, and not by my hand, but by that of your Secondary World--the Secondary World of man. Of this, the knowledge you need to understand, and to survive is given within the Play of Life. Of the Play of Life, you will come to understand.

The Gathering

At a doorway in a circular craft, a white haired Old Man with a pleasant face raised his ephemeral right hand. The huge door opened like the iris of an eye – from the center outward. Bright white light bathed the Old Man's purple robe and his high collar. Under the velvety robe, he wore a silver suit and a wide belt of blinking lights. Two giant guardians followed the Host, breathing heavily.

They hurried toward the outer rim of the craft and stopped there at a window to admire the moon of Earth. They studied the white mountains, pock-marked plains, and long, dark shadows. Then, as their craft rotated, they all gazed upon the beautiful, blue planet of Earth. "The Garden," the Host said in his deep, strong voice -- "the *Garden of Man*." The big creatures smiled and giggled with soft, high-pitched voices.

Their circular craft slowed to a stop and hovered near a long, sleek satellite orbiting the moon. Vents on the lunar orbital opened, and a red light beam scanned them. The Old man held up a black disk pendant, which hung upon his chest by a braided silver chain. The light focused upon the etched image of a spider on the front side. Then the Old Man turned the disk over. On the backside, bold numbers glowed in the beam of light: 020-020-020.

Satisfied, the probe beeped with approval. The light turned green and transmitted a signal downward to the blue-white world of Earth. Instantly, an orange sphere of light rose upward. Within moments, the orange orb stopped behind the moon. The orange glow dimmed, and a sleek, silver craft appeared. Green lights rotated around the middle.

The two guardians took deep breaths, heavy with worry. The Old Man urged them forward with an encouraging wave of his ephemeral hands.

The Agreement

A few minutes later, in a dark amphitheater, the long-eared giants stood nervously under inspection by a group of short, milky-white aliens with large foreheads and big, black eyes.

On his throne-like chair of plush red leather sat the leader of these beings. An older alien, with bluer skin, the Leader greeted the Host with respect.

After a few pleasantries, the Old Man spoke firmly as if offering a gentle command. "All zones, each plantation of hu-man, shall be given rapport of Nous 10 via the council of Epsilon Eridani, within *their Play of Life*." He gestured to the long-eared creatures. They didn't seem like guardians anymore, but boyish giants, a bit afraid of the little aliens with cold black eyes and big heads.

The alien leader and his aides gathered together, stunned.

Over the generations, some humans had attained higher levels of mind after contact with the black-eyed aliens, but children of the uplifted subject usually didn't pass the evolution on beyond *their* children. The next generation descended back to Mind Level One. This was the problem with man. Changes in the DNA and in the brain lasted for a few generations, but not long enough to be passed on for centuries. The children always *devolved* back to Nous 1, eventually.

The alien leader began to explain all of this to the Old Man, but the Host waved away the words with his ephemeral hand and spoke in a deep, commanding tone. "You will allow--a final test of man by these of Eridani within their *Play of Life*." He gestured at the two giants who nodded with respect at the alien leader.

The alien leader controlled his rage. Whenever an outside race of people wanted to experiment with Earth, they used the same old argument: the progeny devolved, except when using THEIR method.

The alien's voice crackled with anger. "That which we found here, WE have lifted up to Nous two. Thus, *the great civilizations of man,*" he said in human voice. "What are we to do? We need a new body for 12 strand DNA."

The giants from Eridani murmured with disagreement and started to protest. The leader snapped sharply. "WE created man. The problem is OURS. "

The Host stepped forward. He spoke firmly, but with compassion to the dome-headed leader. "In that is your error. All life is of the Creator. All forms of hu-man are of Mind Level ten. Each hu-man responds by his own heart and by freedom of choice at Nous ten. No longer can you ignore the SOUL of man."

The leader and his aides whispered with debate, for their beliefs were divided about their own creation. The Host waited patiently, and then stepped closer. "The people of Eridani have lifted tribes into nations here on Earth. Nous two maintained with success in their Play of Life."

The milky-white aliens protested, but the Old Man swept their arguments away with a wave of his hand. He spoke in a commanding tone. "As a final test, you will allow a rapport of ONE man, and an uplifting to Nous ten."

"No," the leader hissed. " We have prepared five hybrids that will thrive on earth. The time of hu-man on the land – finished. Hybrid phase-out underway."

The Host stepped close to the leader and commanded softly. "This shall be done of I." He glared at the alien eye to eye.

The Host held up both hands with palms outward. He spoke slowly, laying down the law. "Both of you must obey rules for FULL DESCENT. NO interference beyond primary circle. All projections, all data, all presentations via selene orbital, access code 020-020-020. "He paused as both sides recorded the rules. Then he finished. "Only knowledge *of man* shall be given to man," he concluded, "until full agreement for descent ten established."

"Term of contact?" the alien leader asked, dejected.

The Host nodded at the two giants. The tallest stepped forward and spoke in a soft, electronic voice. "One generation of man: 40 human years: 1971 to 2011."

Seething with anger, the leader pointed a long finger at the giants. "You will fail in this folly. You will FAIL! Of this, DO NOT SPEAK OF I, or my people to any hu-man, nor of our plantations or hybrids, nor of the cycle of time." The two giants nodded their heads in agreement, bumping each other for support.

"It is done," the Host announced to all. "Of this, let the *Play of Life* begin," he boomed. "Of this, and by this, Nous ten shall be given to man." Then, he hurried away with the giants following.

As they reached an outer hallway, the Old Man whispered to them. "If your plan fails, they will make life worse for your people." They reached a transport station. "This *Play of Life* may be more costly to you, than the others."

"We will take the risk," the taller giant whispered. "The people of Earth must be set free. They must know the truth."

As they entered the transporter area, the two giants nodded to each other, and de-cloaked. Their bulky, gray bodies shifted back to their real form—tall, red-haired men with muscular bodies and boyish faces. The tallest, Voltar, wore an ornate headband and gold bands on his arms, wrists and ankles. He moved like a noble king. Danyael looked a bit more scholarly. He wore copper armbands. Each wore a white tunic trimmed in gold, and a belt of blinking lights--like the Host's.

In unison, they touched their belts. With a soft velvety tone, they vanished--displaced back to their craft, and to safety.

They carried good news for their people: another *Play of Life* could begin. This descent would hopefully be their greatest, their final descent of ten allowed over 12,000 years. In this tenth and final descent, the civilization—the nation--to be uplifted would be the strongest on the Earth: the United States of America.

Due to the nine previous descents, man on Earth had been uplifted. Communication and transportation had been advanced over the 12,000 years in most of the continents while allowing free-will, free choice and self-determination among men. The *Play of Life* had worked numerous times, some with more success than others. Some descents had failed, but if this tenth descent proved successful, then North America would serve as a model to all the nations – to all mankind—for a millennium. All secrets would be revealed to mankind, knowledge of the past would be given, and the mysteries of earth would become known. But *one* man would have to agree, and go forward of his own free will—a common man with no special knowledge or traits—a man at home amongst the common people.

If the process failed, attacks might come to this common man, to the people of Eridani and perhaps even to the United States of America.

Many risks and dangers lay ahead. But, in this way, with great hope and yet great fear, the final *Play of Life* began.

From the Author

I met Brian Scott on a hot summer day in Fullerton, California at the home of a UFO investigator. We first shook hands on Sunday, July 3, 1976. I listened to his story of UFO contact with a skeptical ear.

For a young man in an apparently frightening dilemma, Brian seemed jolly. I figured right off, he was probably pulling a con game of some kind. In his prime of years, at the age of 32, Brian stood tall and strong with thick shoulders, blue eyes and well groomed brown hair. I was surprised at his clownish smile, and his healthy radiance. He seemed to glow with joy.

I had expected an anguished, tormented man after hearing him on a radio show on May 17. Instead, he laughed and joked easily about his alleged UFO contact and the investigation which followed. He entertained like a comedian--a class clown having fun with a journalist--but to my surprise, he also provided plans and drawings, like an engineer.

After studying the documents, I interviewed his wife and other witnesses to bizarre events in their home. Though I was very wary of Brian, for he could certainly tell a good story, I trusted the other witnesses because they spoke from their hearts. They had kept a written log and tape-recorded events.

I was 29 that year, fresh out of the Cinema School at the University of Southern California. My concern was not UFO's at all, but the human experience--the human mind. My background was in psychology, biology, journalism and filmmaking. I wanted a story, a good drama for a movie.

I didn't care if Brian was a hoaxer, I would simply expose him. If he was a victim of psychosis, multiple-personality, or demonic possession, fine. It all still sounded like a great story for a movie or book. With my background in clinical psychology and neurobiology, I felt certain to find a good plot--a movie worth seeing by audiences. I planned to spend six months in research, and then sell the screenplay as my calling card into the film production industry of Hollywood.

Soon, I discovered that no UFO investigators understood the events following alleged contact. Since some events didn't fit our established "framework" of reality, the victims were usually left to fend for themselves. Brian, like most of America's UFO contactees had simply been abandoned without medical, psychological or financial support. I didn't believe this was right, but I could certainly understand the situation.

For example, I really didn't believe that Brian's contact was real, but his behavior had changed and noted UFO researchers had conducted an investigation. Both Dr. J. Allen Hynek and Dr. Jacques Vallee had received input from local investigators and talked to Brian personally. They both admitted that they didn't fully understand the phenomenon he and other contactees were experiencing. This sent Brian off in a new direction. If the expert didn't understand, who did? Brian soon discovered the answer—no one.

In his book, <u>Invisible College,</u> Vallee called for "a new framework..." to understand UFO contact. From 1976 onward, Dr. Hynek told many people he believed the physical side was real, and that the psychic events were real, also. He just didn't know how to interpret BOTH, together. No one did.

Since Hynek and Vallee both clearly indicated that our culture didn't have the framework for understanding both aspects, I felt obliged to work on the mystery. I was young, and seeking a niche in life as a writer. I had seen enough to know they were right. Brian, I believed, was caught in the mystery like a fly in a spider web. Although I didn't fully trust Brian, I did trust Vallee, Hynek, and witnesses to events around Brian. So, I decided to work on the puzzle, until I could see a pattern.

More than 25 years has passed since then, and many people wonder why I kept this great, epic story secret for so long. In reply, I must say that I truly wanted to solve the mystery, and share the solution accurately with readers—as a trusted author. So after the events ended in March of 1980, I studied long and deep into many realms.

There are other reasons, too. Children were involved who needed to mature before hearing the story. Also, I wanted to protect Brian from religious extremists who might attack him. Plus, I wanted to watch the transformation process unfold in our society, and confirm the prophecies given to me.

To my great surprise, our culture has changed rapidly since 1980. New technology has provided freedom. Human transformation is spoken about openly -- even by the Common Man. Movies and TV shows sometimes feature characters much like Brian Scott, but few details of a true "sudden evolution" are known. This book is a beginning for a new framework—a new understanding.

I was never interested in UFO's, or their investigation. My interest has always been the mind of man, the brain and our mental experiences. After meeting Brian, I witnessed many paranormal events, and saw signs in the sky. Many other investigators claim to have solid evidence. They have data and photos and reports to indicate that crafts exist, not built by man. Inside the crafts appear to be intelligent beings that have apparently interacted with thousands of people on our world—contactees. The contactees seem to experience a certain pattern of events after the contacts. That pattern, we can study—the pattern of the post-contact experience. Due to research by many authors, and dozens of books about UFO's, I feel modern audiences have enough knowledge to understand BOTH the physical and psychic side of the Post-Contact UFO experience. I believe the emphasis in our society, and the focus of our government should now be on the contactees, not on the crafts and their technology.

Today, I believe that common people and scholars in psychology, anthropology and neuro-biology will easily understand the "new framework" offered in these pages, because it is not new to this planet. In fact, we are experiencing and witnessing the same old, ancient pattern being repeated again, right in our modern civilization—right under our nose.

Have I understood correctly? Is the *"Play of Life"* the right paradigm? You decide. My role is to give you the facts and the story, from my view.

From over 300 hours of tape recordings with real people and hundreds of documents, I have distilled dramatic, compelling scenes to show you the process of transformation, the logic and apparent method. I have shown you the personality and behaviors of the real people, their words and their feelings. I urge you to provide your own interpretation for I cannot be correct on every issue— the story is way too big for one man, for one person to fully grasp.

I do believe Brian's story could "trigger a transformation of all mankind," as I was told. If that is true, the process will begin with individuals who understand the events and the technology. Then supposedly, the transformation will proceed outward to the nation through individual actions based on the technology, the logic and method in *The Play of Life.*

We shall see--together. I am still learning. We all are. Welcome to *The Play of Life.* Some of the primary knowledge you need to survive in the days to come *supposedly* is given within these pages: <u>The Brian Scott Story—Transformation</u>.

-- James E. Frazier

June 22, 2000 A.D.

Part I

The Brian Scott Story

The Dark Side - Panic

The Dark Night of Soul - Descent into Hell

Chapters 1–10

James E. Frazier

Man is

Two Men in One.

One is

Awake in the Darkness

The Other

Asleep in the Light.

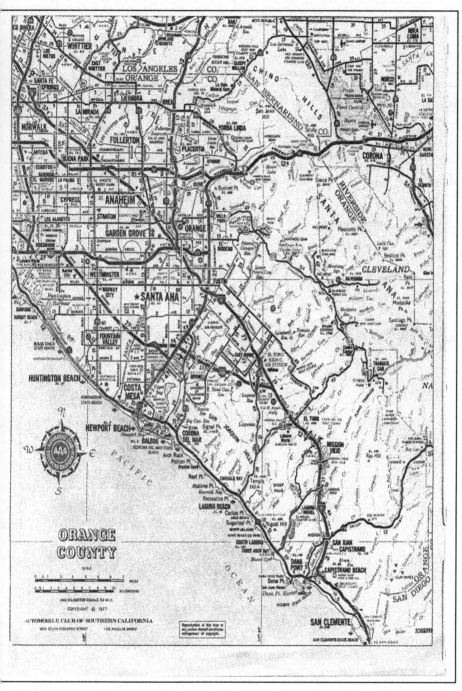

ORANGE COUNTY – Southern California, just South of Los Angeles.

SOUTHERN CALIFORNIA'S ORANGE COUNTY – Garden Grove, Santa Ana,
Disneyland, Fountain Valley, two Naval Stations and a US Marine Air Base – El Torc

BRIAN SCOTT at age 3 with his dog in Philadelphia. This
1946 photo was taken by William Scott, Jr.—Brian's dad.

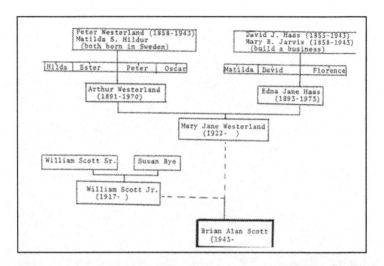

BRIAN'S 3rd BIRTHDAY. From the left -- Dad, Grandma, Brian and Mother.

6

MOTHER – Mary Westerland. She moved to Long Beach with Brian in 1946 and worked as a waitress most of her life.

FATHER – William Scott Jr. Wanted to be a photographer. He stayed in Philadelphia area.

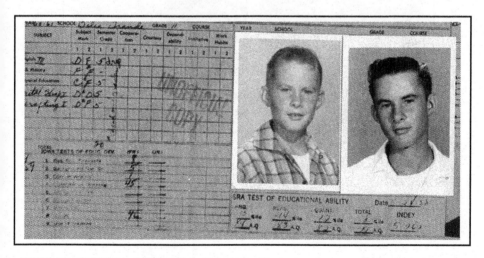

BRIAN'S SCHOOL RECORDS 1960-61. He quit school and worked on a cruise ship with his mom.

BRIAN in 1970 with a Colt .45 pistol.

BRIAN and MARY BETH in 1972.

TOP ROW -- MARY BETH with parents. Camping.
BOTTOM ROW --The new boat, and a new love.

BRIAN VOMITS a white substance after hitting the Ball of
Light with a broom. Mary Beth snapped this picture. Their
attempts to photograph the ball of light were not
successful.

SYMBOL on door of examination room.

THE LONG EARS. Drawn by artist David Kindvall

1971 CONTACT – drawn by Brian. He sees a silver disk with purple-green glow coming from bottom. Location: Superstition Mountains East of Phoenix, Arizona.

FIRST CONTACT

"PLEASE DON'T KILL ME."
--Brian Alan Scott

"WE SHARE ONE MIND, ONE THOUGHT AT NOUS 10."
-- Voltar

(Nous = mind.)

Chapter I

First Contact

On a fateful day in the summer of 1971, in the desert near the Superstition Mountains north of Phoenix, Brian Alan Scott and his Arizona cowboy buddy caught a dozen dangerous rattlesnakes. They milked fangs for venom, and stored poison in their cooler with sodas and beer.

Brian waved a three-foot long rattler. "We are in the money, now." At 28, he stood strong and robust. His cowboy hat shaded ruddy skin and bright blue eyes. With a clownish smile, Brian handed the snake to his lanky partner, Rex Walters. Rex milked the venom into a glass beaker.

When the venom stopped flowing, Brian kissed the snake on the head. "Thank you, sweetie," he giggled.

"I hope that one gets loose and bites your butt," Rex smirked. Square-jawed and rough-hewn, he stood six-foot six in his boots. For him milking snakes meant serious business. He measured the harvest. "We made some good money today."

As Rex checked his numbers, Brian stroked the snake. "She don't get nothing, and it's her milk."

"You're gonna get bit," Rex warned.

"No worse than a dog bite," Brian said. "You got her juice."

"You sure I got it all? Even a clown can get killed, Brian. "

Brian laughed.

Later in the day near sunset, the two buddies blasted away at tin cans mounted on cactus. Clouds of blue gunsmoke filled the air as their barrels blazed with fire.

While reloading, Brian suggested they try out for a job at the Apache Junction Movie Studio, staging gunfights for tourists.

"Are you serious?" Rex laughed. "We're not *that* good."

"We are good. Come on, I've got to do something."

Brian had been living on his own since the age of seventeen surviving by driving old cars in demolition derbies for the prize money. In his last grudge match, he had pinned his opponent against a wall. Brian had laughed as the young man struggled to escape, but then the car exploded. Before Brian or anyone else could help set the boy free, flames erupted. As the crowd screamed in horror, Brian and others tried to fight through the flames without success. As firemen arrived, the boy cried out for help to Brian—then he died, burned to death. His final agony, his tormented face and plea for help haunted Brian, along with the smell of burning hair and flesh. Brian vowed never again to race.

Instead, Brian now earned money by painting logos on racecars and advertising signs for businesses. Sometimes, he created model sailing ships for bars or restaurants. His huge sailing ships inspired awe and applause. Three to four feet long, complete with rigging, white sails, and little men on deck in uniforms, the ships earned money for rent, but not enough for food or gas. So, Brian hustled odd jobs, milked snakes, and sometimes conned stores for food or gas.

The Contact

After sunset, as they began to pack up, Brian heard a strange sound, like a howl in the desert. A coyote, Brian thought. He grabbed a flashlight, a Colt .45 pistol from his pickup and prowled into the darkness. "Twenty-five bucks for the skin," Brian shouted to Rex.

Rex laughed. Brian would try anything. "Captain America—bold and brave," he shouted. Brian looked back at his Captain America truck, painted like an American flag with red and white stripes and dazzling stars on blue. Under the window, in ornate white letters he had painted his own racing name--Captain America. He had customized the entire truck as a street rod when he gave up racing. Beneath the hood, a 357 Chevy engine slumbered-- waiting to roar. Under the white camper shell, Brian stored his sailing ships, supplies and camping gear. He could go anywhere with the truck, even live outside for months. He didn't need an apartment, except for showers.

Rex finished packing his rusted '65 Ford pick-up as Brian stepped carefully through the saguaro cactus with a flashlight and Colt .45 in hand. Brian glanced eastward to the Superstition Mountains. They glowed gold and purple with the last rays of light. Suddenly, Brian saw a strange light rise from behind the mountains. Purple in color and bigger than a star, the light moved up into the inky black sky. He watched in awe. As the light continued towards him, he felt fear. He wanted to run, but didn't. Seconds later, the metal disk within the light, blotted out stars in the sky. He heard no sound, saw no motors, yet the craft seemed bigger than a truck.

For a moment, Brian watched in awe. The energy field coming from the bottom of the disk glowed purple and green, undulating like an electrical field. Then the craft stopped overhead. Brian gazed into the energy field, nearly hypnotized. Then he felt a tug. His body lifted. He panicked and started to run.

He kicked, struggled and screamed, but still his body rose into the sky. Insane with fear, he dropped both the flashlight and the Colt .45. He closed his eyes and began to pray.

A moment later, his feet landed on a solid floor in a dark room on the rim of the ship. Brian glanced out the door at the lights of Phoenix in the distance. Then the door closed. With a whoosh, he felt cool air rise up from the floor bringing a strange odor, like rotten eggs. Beside him stood Rex, terrified. They screamed and jumped like deer caught in a cage.

"Jesus, God in Heaven," Brian shouted. "Jesus, God in Heaven help us."

Then a huge door opened behind them. Bright white light burned into their eyes. Brian blinked and shaded his eyes to see four creatures--dark silhouettes-- with huge heads, long ears and no necks. They were not human. Again, Brian and Rex screamed with terror, swearing and praying--all in the same breath.

One creature stepped towards Rex. The big cowboy unleashed a fury of blows with both fists hitting the creature's arms and shoulders. Brian felt the solid thumping and cracking sound of fists on flesh and bone. For a moment, he hoped Rex would win but the giant touched Rex's neck behind his head, and the big cowboy dropped to the floor, unconscious.

Brian had seen Rex slug it out in a bar with three guys and win. Rex fought bikers, Indians and truckers--just for fun. Now, he lay unmoving in the creature's arms. Another hulk stepped inside and helped pull clothes off Rex's limp body. Rex moaned. He's alive, Brian thought. They didn't kill him. The two giants seemed gentle in a way. They weren't abusive—just doing a job.

Brian heaved with emotion as the third giant pointed at his belt. "No. Get away from me," Brian screamed. When Brian drew back, the hulk moved forward and tugged at his shirt. Brian almost died from fear. The giant paused and waited a moment so Brian could calm. Then he pointed at the belt buckle, again.

Resistance seemed futile, so Brian began to undress. "Don't kill us. Please, don't kill us," he heaved. "I'll do what you want. Just don't kill me."

Moments later, Brian stood naked in a curved hallway filled with rising mist. He looked over his shoulder to see Rex carried away by two giants.

Brian didn't like the odor. The mist smelled like electrical wires, an arc welder and rotten eggs, combined. He looked down to mist rising up through

17

grates in the floor. Then Brian heard a rumbling sound. The inner wall of the craft rotated for a moment, then stopped. A huge door waited with a big black symbol. Around the frame, tiny lights blinked red and white. The symbol looked like a triangle covered by an arch. Brian wondered what it meant. Where were they taking him?

For the first time, he glanced at them. The two giants held his hands like old friends—not like enemies. Their muscular chests heaved up and down, breathing the thick mist with difficulty. In the cool air, steam exhaled from their crooked mouths. The mist clung to their dry, gray skin and seemed to be absorbed into the wrinkly flesh. Their skin reminded Brian of an elephant or rhinoceros with sparse hairs. He couldn't see their small, squinty eyes, but their noses were broad, flat and bent over to one side.

His body trembled with fear. Will they kill me? That's all he could think.

Then suddenly, one creature touched the symbol and the big door opened like the iris of an eye, from the center outward. Brian marveled at the door, and for a moment peered into the rotating wall of the craft wondering how it disappeared. The opening slot in the wall seemed about 15 inches wide.

Finally, a big hand nudged Brian forward. He squinted into a large, circular room filled with blinking lights, and other creatures standing behind waist high panels. They seemed to be waiting for him. No one spoke, but he heard lots of sounds--beeping, clicking, breathing and wheezing.

The creatures placed Brian against a cold wall. He tried to pull forward, but couldn't move. That scared him even more. He wailed in fear and struggled hard.

Suddenly, a box on a pole blinked alive with tiny red, green, and blue lights. One large purple light on the device caught his gaze, and Brian couldn't pull away. He tried to look aside, but the bright lights in the room hurt his eyes. The undulating purple light seemed more pleasant, and even relaxing. Brian's eyes fixated--wide open-- hypnotized.

Suddenly, lights blinked around the room. The shorter escort hurried to a workstation behind waist high panels, and the other giant stood near the blinking box. Everyone else seemed to relax.

The blinking box lowered to the floor and began moving upward with beeping sounds. As the box moved, Brian felt strange vibrations and sensations in his skin and bones. His knees vibrated. He felt the bones, the joints. Then, as the box rose upwards, he urinated. At his abdomen, he felt sick. His intestines gurgled and filled with gas. Then his heart raced and seemed to fly out of his body towards the larger escort.

When the box reached his head, Brian's mind suddenly stretched upward a foot or two into the air. This was the strangest feeling of all. He could suddenly see from a point high above his head. Then, his mind began to spin around and expand outward into the room. In a moment, he felt so dizzy he gagged and dry-

18

heaved. His eyes bulged outward in pain. His head felt like a balloon, ready to explode. Brian screamed like a wild man. "You're killing me. You're killing me."

From out of the haze, the taller escort stepped forward and placed his huge right hand on Brian's head. He spoke slowly in a deep, calm voice. "Of this, there will be no pain." Instantly, the purple light blinked off. The pain and pressure drained out of Brian's body.

"Of this, fear not of I, for you and I are one," said the creature slowly in a soothing, fatherly tone. "We share one thought, at Nous 10. Your world is a reflection of my world, and I am a reflection of you." As the giant spoke, pictures appeared in Brian's mind and deep feelings rose in his heart -- but he didn't understand.

"I am from time, beyond all time," said the giant. "Of my Host, through you, I bring life and wisdom to man." The pictures and feelings overwhelmed Brian's mind. He wanted to stop. He had never experienced anything like thoughts from another person in his own mind.

"Who are you?" he managed with a feeble raspy voice. "What do you want?"

SECONDARY WORLD of Earth. Described as Negative Nous Nines by Voltar's people. Supposedly they can obtain Nous 11 using technology. They lack feelings, claim responsibility for the genetic evolution of mankind, and control access to Earth. Apparently, all other groups must follow their conditions when working with man.

SECONDARY WORLD OF EARTH

IN THIS LIFE, ALL WILL BE KNOWN TO MAN:
SEXUAL IMPLANTATION OF KNOWN LIFE FORMS ON EARTH
AT DAWN OF TIME--BY SECONDARY WORLD OF EARTH.
THIS IS TRUTH.

- The Host

Chapter 2

The Secondary World of Earth

Two hours later, Brian found himself back on the cold desert soil, bare-footed and half-dressed. His boots had not been returned, so he hopped and jumped towards his Captain America truck avoiding cactus and rocks in the darkness. Rex was gone. Brian's race truck waited, so he rushed home and fell asleep. The next day, he found Rex at home packing up. Rex seemed quiet, angry and upset. He didn't want to talk, so Brian kept quiet. They never spoke about the light in the sky or the two hours of missing time. They just went separate ways without speaking to each other.

A few weeks later, Brian wound up in a Utah jail for shoplifting food from a grocery store. After 90 days behind bars, he returned to his mom's home in Southern California.

His mother entertained in an elegant steak house as a singing, story-telling waitress. Beautiful, petite and high-spirited, she earned good money with her flamboyant style and funny jokes. With her savings, she helped Brian re-start his life. He took a job in a factory running a box-making machine.

In the summer of 1972, Brian met Mary Beth, a radiant, athletic blond with big luscious brown eyes. About 20, she laughed easily. Though she was the girlfriend of a motorcycle gang member, she seemed too wholesome for the crowd, and Brian wanted to rescue her, and marry her on first sight.

When Mary Beth first saw Brian, she swooned. He was a hunk. Tan, fit and strong with big shoulders and narrow hips, he smelled of shaving lotion. Compared to her biker friends—he was well groomed and clean living. Brian laughed easily with Mary Beth, and they fell in love within days. Two months later, in August of 1972, they married near San Francisco in a simple ceremony with only her family present.

Brian tried to earn a living by selling advertising signs for a business based in Los Angeles. He visited restaurants and small stores to talk about their signage. He showed them samples, and ordered signs from his company catalogue.

The young newly-weds rented a small apartment and bought a little fishing boat. Winter came with cold windy days, but Brian still loved boating in the San Francisco Bay.

On a day that started out warm, he stayed out too long and their tiny boat was caught in a cold, sudden storm. When severe winds swamped their craft, the engine died. When night fell, they floated adrift--in freezing, black water.

Mary Beth cried out in anguish as her clothing froze to her skin. Brian paddled to a huge ship, and climbed up the net-like ropes dangling from a US Navy aircraft carrier. On deck, he was held at gunpoint for a while, but sailors finally rescued Mary Beth and brought her aboard.

Brian had filed a float plan, and when an article appeared in the paper about the rescue, he publicly blamed the San Francisco Harbor Master for not starting a search. Newspapers wrote stories about the harrowing night, and Brian was eventually awarded a new boat after the Harbor Master promised to reform the system.

Brian and Mary Beth rejoiced in the victory, but the headlines brought Brian a problem: an arrest. Some of the advertising signs he had sold to businesses had never been delivered. In court, Brian claimed the company he represented had gone bankrupt and failed to deliver, but the judge found him accountable and sent him to jail for 90 days.

Mary Beth, now pregnant, moved in with her parents in Buena Park. After the jail term, the judge placed Brian on probation in Orange County so he could be close to her. He took a job in a nearby factory and settled down to paying the bills and court fines. Finally, in October of 1973, the first baby arrived.

A Light in the Sky

In a crisp fall breeze, yellow leaves rolled down the sidewalks as Brian worked inside a noisy factory with huge screeching machines. Instead of folding flimsy cardboard boxes, he now drilled and cut rigid sheets of metal. He liked the idea of molding metal with his hands. He liked cutting solid sheets, transforming them into new devices, like shells for mainframe computers.

Wearing a blue apron and shoulder length hair, Brian studied a blueprint then quickly set up a machine to punch holes in sheet metal. Around him, a half dozen other men worked on loud, oily machines.

Brian took pride in his work and loved studying the blueprints. He measured his settings with precision, and when he kicked on the machine, the metal screamed in pain. Hot oil evaporated into smoke. Brian smiled, pleased with his work--with his new creation.

One day, in the last week of October, a bell rang at 5:00 p.m. and the labor stopped. The young men all punched a time clock and jostled to get outside for the last few minutes of gray, October light.

Brian hurried home in his 1967 Pontiac, driving through the hills of Buena Park while listening to rock music on the radio. He checked his hair, and cleaned his dirty fingernails as he drove. In the sky, among the first bright stars, he saw an orange-green light that zipped erratically in short, straight lines. Brian stopped the car.

On the bottom of the strange light, Brian saw a dome. Green and white lights rotated about the middle.

A few minutes later, Brian rushed into the big, brick home owned by his wife's parents. He wanted a witness. Beaming with pride, Mary Beth showed off their new blond-haired baby girl. The house bubbled with excited people.

Mary Beth's parents, her three rowdy stepbrothers and a cute 17 year old sister, Ginger, all lived together in the crowded house. A cousin and several others had come over to see the new baby.

Brian quietly asked Mary Beth to go with him for a ride, but instead she insisted he go to the store for milk and diaper wipes.

"Can't it wait?" he whined.

"No," she ordered. Brian shuffled into the big living room looking for a reliable witness. Ginger, his cute sister-in-law, and her boyfriend wanted to stay and feed the baby. A brother-in-law danced disco with a girlfriend putting on quite a show. No one wanted to leave.

Across the room, Brian eyed Patti, a plump cousin wearing bright colors. About 24, she stuffed chocolate candies into her mouth, licked her fingers and read from the Bible. "Take Patti," shouted Mary Beth, "and leave the car." Patti smiled and grabbed her Bible. She had some questions for Brian.

Captain America

Outside, Brian angrily pulled a tarp off the Captain America pick-up, and started the engine. The motor thundered and crackled with power. Flames shot out from the exhaust pipes. He would make them pay attention. He would make them remember this night.

The American flag truck rolled onto the driveway. Inside the throbbing cab, Patti hung on tightly. As the pick-up chugged forward, Brian smiled at everyone. His blue eyes sparkled and his racing name shimmered in ornate white letters: *Captain America.*

Brian popped the clutch. The truck jerked forward in a cloud of blue smoke and two big, black tires screeched loudly, marking the street with black lines. Everyone screamed. They smelled the pungent odor of burning rubber tires and covered their ears to muffle the sound. They would remember this night, for sure.

On a wide boulevard, dozens of cars waited for gas at a service station. The Captain America truck coasted around the corner. In the gas line, Brian saw a yellow customized Model A Ford with chrome exhaust pipes.

People waved at Brian, and kids saluted his American flag artwork, giggling.

Brian's truck slowed to a stop near the yellow Model A Ford with an artwork on the hood--a fire-breathing dragon. The dragon's green, reptilian wings transformed into creamy-white angel wings.

"Hey, what's happening?" Brian shouted to the driver.

"Just tanking up," said the pimply-faced man. "No more gas. This is it. Armageddon is coming. " He pointed at the artwork and laughed.

"I don't think so," Brian laughed. "But when they see you—they'll think it's coming."

Cars honked loudly. Brian rolled ahead. "I designed that," he beamed proudly.

"What? That dragon?"

"It started out as a wasp with wings."

Patti gasped. "It's Biblical?"

"No. It's pretty basic, really." He laughed boyishly. "Bottom line."

That's bottom line?" Patti gushed.

"I didn't paint it. I just roughed out the design for him. That's what I do. I do all kinds of drawings."

Patti breathed deep. "Brian, can I ask you a personal question?"

He wove in and out of traffic smoking a Marlboro cigarette. "I suppose you will, anyway. Right?" he smiled.

"No. I wouldn't."

"Okay. Go ahead," he said checking his hair in the mirror.

"Do you believe in God?"

Brian laughed. "That's a weird question." She waited for an answer. "Maybe you should start with something simple."

"That's pretty basic," she said firmly, imitating him. "Bottom line."

He laughed. "Yeah, I believe in God. But there are some other things going on in this world. Strange stuff—and they are in the Bible."

Brian swerved to avoid a near accident. "What an idiot." He shifted gears and accelerated out of the problem.

"Do you believe in life after death?"

"Do you really want me to answer a question like that right now?"

"Why not? We almost got killed. We could be dead five minutes from now."

He shrugged. "That's not a cheery thought."

"I found your old Bible on the shelf and I was comparing it to mine. Yours is a very worn King James."

"Well, then, you should know," he said.

"This IS your Bible, then? These are all your markings?" She held up the Bible with pages heavily marked in colored highlights. She flipped the pages.

"That was a long time ago," Brian said. "My grandma took me to church."

"You're a Christian, then?"

"Well, whatever that is," he nodded sheepishly.

"You are, or you aren't."

"I guess I was, before I got corrupted by the world." He cruised to a stop at a store and turned off the engine. "But, I'm not living that way now."

"You were saved?"

"I guess so."

"Were you baptized?"

"I remember getting dunked—and I know what you are going to say. The answer is yes. I accepted Him."

"I thought so. Brian, once the Lord takes your hand--he never lets go. You can let go of Him, but He doesn't let go of you. No matter how polluted you get."

"I am in a different world," he said. He studied the stars in the sky as he dug for money in his pockets. He wanted Patti to go into the store.

She waited for the money. "I knew you had been in jail, but I never did think you were a bad-guy. I just thought you got a little off-track for a few years. Lost in the wilderness, you might say."

Brian laughed. "I was definitely in the wilderness. Maybe I still am."

"But, I wanted to congratulate you for trying to be a good father to your new baby and a good husband to Mary Beth. She's my cousin, and I like to take care of her."

"Well, I have definitely changed, since 1971."

When Patti shuffled out of the store, Brian shouted, "Look at that!" Among the stars, a green-orange light moved in jumps. Then the light stopped. Brian squinted to see the dome-shaped bottom. Around the middle, green and white lights flashed.

"Hurry!" Brian shouted. "It's still there."

Secondary World Contact

Moments later, the Captain America truck roared up into the hills of Buena Park in Orange County. As eucalyptus trees whizzed by the window, Brian strained to see the orange light in the sky.

25

Patti talked nervously as she braced herself in the bouncing truck. She held an open Bible and shouted over the noise. "The Jews, after the exodus from Egypt, lacked the courage to enter the Promised Land, so God let them die out. Forty years they wandered. He let them wander in the wilderness, Brian. Then they all died--that whole generation. He fed and clothed them, even gave them manna from heaven. But, he let them wander--until death. Get it. That's my point. It's the reason to fear God. He lets you wander, if you don't obey: free will. You see? He just waited for the next generation. NO problem. Time is on His side. Do you get it? He waited for Joshua and let a whole generation die off."

Brian shrugged as he watched the light in the stars. "Not really. Now--that is really strange," he mumbled. "It's not like the other one."

Patty rambled. "But even Joshua was afraid to fight the giants in Canaan. So, God told him what to do. Finally, he listened. At Jericho, he won with God's way: blowing trumpets at walls. It made no sense. It was *supernatural*. That's what God wanted him to learn—how to fight and win His way. It's a supernatural way, by His might and power, not your own. My teacher says that if you don't understand that, you don't understand anything else in the Bible. Do you get it?"

Brian wasn't listening. He squinted at the light in the night sky. "Damn it!" He slammed the brakes. Patty crashed onto the floor with her Bibles.

"What is it?" Patti screamed.

"Look at that light," Brian screamed. "It's getting closer." His pulse raced with alarm.

"I can't see anything," she said.

He pointed into the sky. The light zipped among the stars in jerky movements. "Nothing does that."

"Jesus," she gasped. "What is it?"

Brian's heart raced. He squinted again closely. "It's different than what I saw before." Suddenly, the light moved directly at them and expanded in size. In a moment, it was bigger than a full moon.

"Oh, God, " Patti screamed. "What is that, Brian?"

"I don't know." They felt a low frequency throbbing surround them. The truck engine stopped and headlights faded out.

"Get out." Brian ran around and tried to open Patti's door. "Get out!"

"Why? What are you doing?" She clung to the truck door, holding it shut.

"Do you feel that? They are hitting the truck with a beam."

Patti flew out and clung to him shivering with terror.

"I saw something like this once before–in the desert," Brian said. He watched the light move closer and stop. Inside the energy field, he saw a metal skin. The silver shape was like a cone with green and white lights around the middle.

"It's not the same," Brian screamed as he felt a stretching sensation--an energy tugging at him.

Patti screamed. "Brian, what is it?"

They both felt a stretching of their perceptions. "I don't know," Brian moaned.

"Jesus! JESUS." Patti screamed. Brian tried to grab her hand, but with a snap, they both disappeared into the silence and darkness of the night.

Moments later, on the ground, the Captain America truck sat quietly with both doors wide open. The lights faded up as a crisp October wind blew dry leaves around the wheels.

In the sky, the orange glow soared up into the stars and stopped.

The Secondary World Leader

Inside the craft, in a small, bright, rectangular room, Brian heaved for air. "This is not the same."

"What?" she moaned, deliriously.

"This is not the same," he whispered with fear.

Just then, they heard sounds in the hallway.

"Get me out of here!" Patti screamed. Brian tried to stand up, but a bright, green light clicked on from above with a piercing, high frequency sound. Brian tried to turn away and protect Patti, but the sound ripped at their ears with a warbling tone. Within seconds, they both fainted.

Sometime later, Brian woke up on a cold, hard table in a large, brightly lit room. Probes stung into his scalp. A group of small aliens with domed heads, milky-white skin and large dark eyes watched him struggle awake. On a distant wall, he saw huge colored panels. Groups of aliens watched the patterns—Brian's brain and body signals.

One of the aliens, an older man with bluer-skin, and a slightly more human face, stepped closer and began talking. At first, Brian didn't understand the high-speed electronic tone, but the voice gradually slowed. "You are Scott, Brian--of the Host," the Leader said.

Brian trembled with fear. "You are Scott, Brian--of the Host, of Voltar, of Viracocha."

"How are you talking to me?" Brian said, his jaw trembling.

"By that of your mind," said the alien. This time his blue lips moved and Brian heard the same voice in his ears.

"That time you spoke."

"Verbal enactment. Comparative--Nous 1."

"Who are you?" Brian asked. He noticed a flurry at light panels on a distant wall as aliens, male and female, studied the patterns.

27

Brian glanced around to see other tables, holding men and women of earth, who lay unconscious. Aliens busily worked on their bodies.

"What are you doing?" Brian asked.

The leader spoke slowly. "Man's fate is sealed. "Enactment of Nous ten rapport by the Host and the return of the children, will fail."

"I don't understand," Brian said.

The leader conferred instantaneously with his aides in an electronic sounding language. Then he turned back to Brian, and spoke in a human voice.

"Scott, Brian: 020-020-020," the Leader said. "You were touched by the Host at birth. You received un-authorized implant – attempt for rapport at Nous 10."

"I don't know what you are talking about," Brian whispered.

The leader eyed Brian carefully and poked at him. "You are the final test of man. Voltar's intervention. Danyael's *Play of Life*."

Terrified, Brian shook his head. "You've got the wrong guy."

The leader spoke cynically. "Scott, Brian: 020-020-020. *The hope of all mankind*."

The mockery frightened Brian. He felt a deathly terror. His body began to tremble out of control. "Look, I don't think so," he whispered. "This is a very, very bad mistake." Fearing he would be killed, Brian peered around for a way out.

Suddenly, lights around the room pulsed red. Workers scurried away to control panels. The leader spoke calmly, though obviously aware of the threat. He didn't seem worried. "Man is of us, by sexual implantations of genetic substances, from the dawn of time known to man. This is truth. One thousand generations of man--none maintain Nous level 4. Flaw noted: DNA strand design. Four strands required -- man only two. "

He drew closer to Brian, and spoke in a human voice with a more friendly tone. "After Nous ten rapport, humans of today degrade to Nous 1 with no transmission to their descendants—their children. Uncorrectable error: the flaw is of two-strand DNA. Limited. All human plantations must be phased out, and the land prepared for a new man, of us—12 strand DNA—and *their* children."

Brian whined. "I don't understand what you are saying."

Aides warned the leader of an increasing danger. The leader waved them away and gestured at a screen in the wall. Brian saw a hybrid child, part human and part alien with a large, domed head, blue eyes and pink skin. "The future of man, on the land," the alien's dry voice crackled.

Brian finally understood. The aliens were planning to repopulate the earth after eliminating man. He wondered about the alarms. The craft rocked to one side, then pitched forward. Suddenly, all the lights turned red, and Brian noticed his hands were free to move.

"How did you find me?" He kept his hands down, hidden.

"We monitored you on a routine surveillance of plantations in this zone. The implant of Voltar's people must be de-activated."

"Routine surveillance?"

Brian felt the craft jerk hard. The leader again received warnings. "Voltar's enactment of *Play of Life* will fail," he said. Then he stretched out a long, slender hand and poked Brian once in the chest with his finger. Brian bristled.

The leader smirked at Brian. "Voltar will fail," his voice crackled with arrogance. "Because of who YOU are, and what YOU are." As the leader's finger poked Brian in the chest, Brian erupted and grabbed the leader by the throat in a fury. The alien's frail hands pulled frantically at Brian's large, meaty fingers.

"Let me out of here!" Brian bellowed at the aides. "Now!" He glared at them with the furry of a caged animal. "NOW," he screamed.

From behind Brian, one of the aliens pointed a rod tipped by crystal. A green light flashed from the rod and hit Brian in the neck. Brian froze in an agonized posture. Aides pulled the Leader away as Brian slumped to the floor.

The Leader grabbed the wand and angrily zapped Brian again in the forehead. Brian's body lurched. The Leader zapped again. Brian's body flipped backwards, and his eyeballs rolled up showing only whites.

The Leader handed the wand to an aide and stared at Brian with disgust. "Man -- king of animals." His voice broke. In pain, he massaged a bruised voice box. "Send him back," he ordered while coughing.

He waved at the red alarm lights. "Tell the *Children*, we will return their *final test.*" The leader could barely talk, and he shifted to the electronic sounding tones. The aides understood.

Moments later, on the ground, Patti and Brian lay crumpled in the dirt next to the Captain America truck. A narrow beam of extremely bright light zapped each of them for an instant.

Their bodies jumped. Patti quickly struggled to her feet moaning. "Oh my God." She stumbled over to Brian as another beam of white light struck Brian in the head. Slowly, he stumbled to his feet with Patti's help.

Above them, in the sky, hovered a circular craft with a purple-green energy field. "That's them," Brian moaned. "The first ones." He slipped and fell across Patti's shoulders. "They saved us." Patti pushed, heaved and shoved him into the driver's seat. "They came for me."

Brian cranked the motor. Flames shot out from beneath the truck and the motor thundered. Patti jumped in. Brian popped the clutch and tried to steer, but his arms felt rubbery. The truck sped around in a circle, out of control.

Brian's lurched over, slobbering.

Patti screamed as the truck bounced over a curb. "Brian!" she shrieked. "Stop this thing! Damn it. Stop." The Captain America truck knocked over a trashcan and punched through a hedge in a nearby yard, then stopped.

"Brian, get out. Get out!" Patti shouted. He hung over the wheel, nearly unconscious.

Patti opened the driver's door and pushed Brian over to the passenger side. Then she tried to drive. "Put it in gear!" For a moment, Brian snapped alert.

"Put it in gear?" he moaned with a smile as he shoved the gearshift forward. Then he fainted. The Captain America truck lurched forward. As the truck thundered onto the street, Patti clumsily shifted into second gear, grinding metal.

Patti knocked over more trashcans. People screamed at her from their porches. "I'm sorry. Forgive me," Patti hollered as the Captain America truck thundered down the street with Brian slumped against the passenger door.

"Brian, what happened to you?" shouted Patti frantically. "What did they do?"

"I don't know," Brian mumbled.

"What happened?" Patti shrieked.

"He's mad," Brian slobbered. "He's gonna get me. I know it. He don't like me." With a jolt and a convulsion, he fainted.

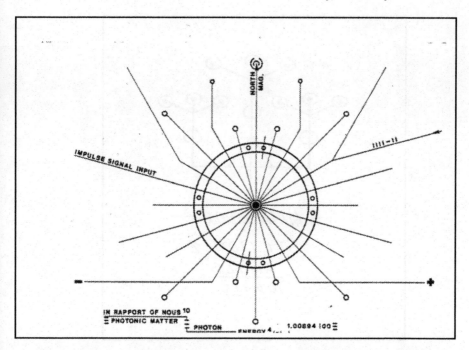

PHOTONIC MATTER—Electromagnetic radiation. Brian's drawing supposedly illustrates a way to understand Photonic Matter by making a comparison to earth knowledge. Note the positive and negative poles, and magnetic north.

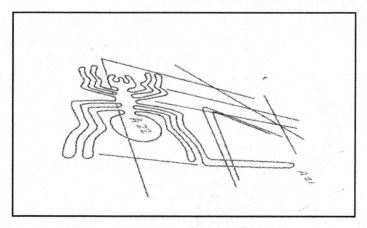

SPIDER ON NAZCA PLAIN -- Brian saw a grid system overlaid on the Nazca Plain. The abdomen of the spider was marked A22. The end of the extended leg was A21-- where he received energy from the ground. The spider is the symbol of The Host. Note similarity to the Photonic Matter drawing.

CANDELABRA. Symbol on door of room with big, three-ring computer. Brian's other drawings indicate five sections to the craft. This room is in Section 2 -- Analysis. The floor inside the computer, he described as the Rings of Time.

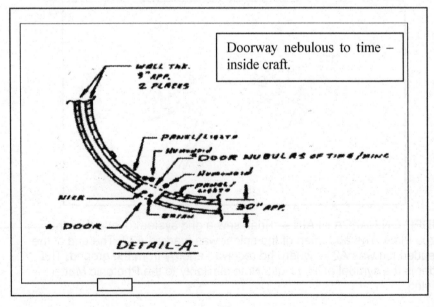

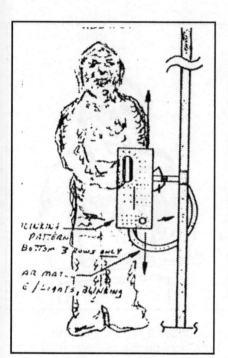

BIO-TELEMETRY Scanner with hypnotic light. Device is described as *hypno-genetic* in one drawing.

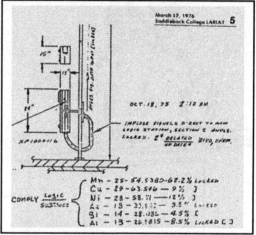

BIO-TELEMETRY Scanner side view showing transmission of data through a light tube. Comparatives given to earth are materials for construction of the device.

James E. Frazier

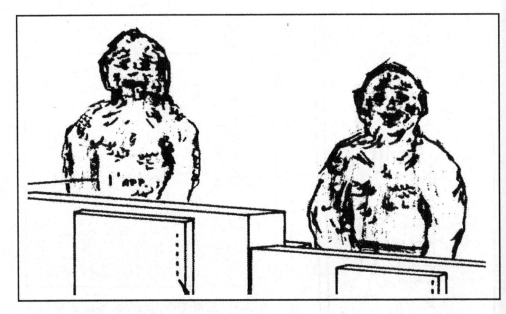

LONG-EARS WITH SMILING FACES -- Brian described them as agile and boyish, but very efficient. He could see lights from work panels shining on their chest. At one point, Brian said they *seemed bored*, shuffling their feet.

34

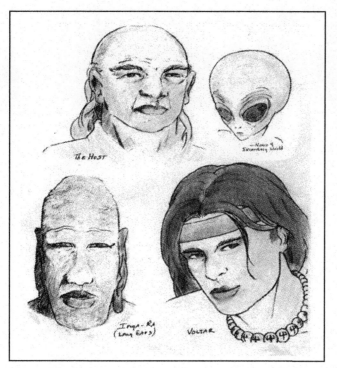

THE RINGS OF TIME – Rings in the middle of the 3 ring computer. Brian was able to play a game on them and travel through time.

James E. Frazier

HYPNOSIS

A SLEEP-LIKE CONDITION PSYCHICALLY INDUCED, USUALLY BY ANOTHER PERSON, IN WHICH THE SUBJECT LOSES CONSCIOUSNESS BUT RESPONDS, WITH CERTAIN LIMITATIONS, TO THE SUGGESTIONS OF THE HYPNOTIST.
--WEBSTER'S DELUXE UNABRIDGED DICTIONARY

THE HOST'S FIRST REQUEST

FROM THIS, NOW WILL YOU COMPLY?
TOUCH THE MARK AT A21. COMPLY OF THE HOST NOW.
TIME IS RELEVANT TO MANKIND. ONE IS TO KNOW.
--Voltar

Chapter 3

The Will of the Host

At the joyous, crowded house where all the relatives had gathered, Brian and Patti faced ridicule when they told the story. They could recount about 20 minutes, but they had been late by over two hours. Their bizarre story didn't make sense—even to them. Mary Beth assumed they had smoked dope or gone to a bar. "Just forget it," Brian finally told Patti. "They don't want to know."

A few days later, after the daze wore off, Brian began to feel a new freedom to live. What did he have to lose? He hadn't been killed, and in fact, he had been rescued and protected in some way by the first group of aliens he had met in the desert. His mind bubbled with questions. Why was he saved? Why him?

Memories of the first contact in the Arizona desert slowly became clearer in his mind. But he remembered nothing that would explain why the little alien was so concerned. He remembered talking to people, sitting in a circle. Maybe he had made some agreements. Maybe he had heard their story--the history of these people with red hair. Or--was he imagining. He didn't know. No one sent him any messages or answers when he asked for confirmation. So, he gave up asking. He seemed to have an ally—and that was good enough. That idea inspired him to have fun. He could either laugh or cry about his predicament—he had cried enough, as a young boy, yearning to know his true father, so now--he chose to laugh.

At work, Brian felt energized and excited. He felt something big was going to happen, someday. But he didn't worry about *when*. Besides, his ability to learn and create seemed to be accelerating.

Instead of cutting and punching the sheet metal as indicated by blueprints, he saw better ways in his mind. He began adapting and changing the designs to fit his own ideas. It worked. His boss even had commended him for a few of the changes.

At home, Brian didn't seem to need much sleep. He didn't feel tired. His mind felt free, excited, and open—like a sponge.

Brian didn't know that the "implant" of the friendly long-eared giants had been activated on schedule. He didn't realize that the alien leader had been unable to remove the implant due to the rescue and intervention of Voltar's people. He only knew that his mind seemed to be more focused—more useful. His brain had become a good friend and ally--a highly organized memory aide and creative partner.

Back to School

Brian's boss kept telling him to take classes in design if he wanted to keep changing blueprints. So, he did. His mom and in-laws provided support when he enrolled in Cerritos Junior College in classes about the fundamentals of drafting.

He worked during the days at the sheet-metal shop and attended class at night. He set up a drafting table and worked on homework assignments until the early morning hours. Everyone was impressed with his focus and attention to homework. For Brian, the work was easy. He didn't tire out. He loved learning.

A year later, to his own surprise, he graduated with straight A's, two awards from the State of California and a letter of recommendation saying he was top of the Top Ten draftsman in the program. He had even designed his own course in pipeline drafting--his major emphasis. The accomplishments stunned Brian. He had never done well in school. How could this be happening?

Brian guessed that the "implant" had somehow amplified his ability to think in three-dimensional images, a great skill for drafting and design. Now, he could easily hold an image in his mind, turn it around see the other side, and rotate it at any angle--all using his imagination. Most importantly, the image seemed to be accurate and detailed – that was new since the night in the desert.

At times, he would also see a few blinking lights in his mind, and then receive images of places he had never seen before, like an ancient pyramid near a lake. The images showed water flowing from the lake through pipes to fountains around the pyramid and finally coursing into a beautiful, gold-plated temple.

These vivid images inspired Brian to study pipeline design as a drafting specialty. If the long-ears wanted him to move water from the lake to the

38

pyramid, he would do it, he reasoned--but nothing made sense. He personally wasn't the least bit concerned about some ancient pyramid near a lake, but the vivid images made him wonder about his experience. What was an "implant," anyway? How did it work? What was he to do about it? He figured that his ally, the long-ears, held all the answers and could contact him anytime. They had rescued him before, so they obviously knew where he was. So, he just went on his way, living life as best he could.

The First Real Job

The oil companies stopped hiring pipeline draftsmen when the gas shortages hit in 1973, so when a big corporation in Mission Viejo offered Brian a job interview as a mechanical draftsman, he accepted. Awed and humbled by the huge workroom filled with draftsmen, Brian told the supervisor he couldn't do the job. The old engineer laughed and guided him to a huge wooden drafting table. "With your drawings, you'll do fine," he said.

Brian glanced around the room nervously. The older draftsmen wore suits, ties and crew cuts. A few younger men wore long hair, flowered shirts and bell-bottom jeans. Brian fit in the middle, wearing a corduroy jacket and blue jeans. But, could he actually do the job? He didn't think so.

At first, the documentation procedures in the huge company were much too confusing, but everyone was helpful. To Brian's great surprise, he gradually began to excel at the job. He drew sheet-metal blueprints for business machines and mainframe computers. He worked with notes and sketches from engineers, but he often added refinements. Within eighteen months, Brian had been promoted twice with wage increases.

In the fall of 1975--after a design idea of his saved the company thousands of dollars in manufacturing costs--Brian felt truly confident.

His life had changed. In only two years, he had been transformed from a homeless punch press operator living with his wife's parents, into a design-engineering draftsman with an attractive brick home in Garden Grove, three cars, a pretty wife and two daughters, one just six months old. He was only thirty-two years old and accelerating rapidly in his career. Brian felt on top of the world.

He knew his growth somehow involved the implant—AND HIS OWN EFFORTS. He had done the homework and burned the midnight oil. HE had developed the skills and earned the paychecks himself. For the first time, he felt good about himself, and his life.

Then, the dreams began.

The Dreams

Vivid, recurring dreams of the first UFO contact began creeping into his mind in September of 1975, always with blinking, colored lights: red, green and blue.

Usually, when the lights stopped blinking in their repeating pattern, he remembered the giant, long-eared gray creatures, and the symbol on the door, but that's it. He was still missing nearly two hours of time.

The really vivid dreams began with the lights repeating 22 times—red, green, blue—over and over. He counted 22 times and wondered why other colors were not involved. One day at work, when Brian lost consciousness, he tried to study the blinking lights and their pattern. When he awoke, his left hand held a pencil, and three words had been printed in bold letters across a blue-print. He had messed up a drawing with words he didn't understand: NOUS LAOS HIKANO.

Shocked, he quickly erased the words and fixed the drawing. His body trembled with fear for the first time in years. How could this be happening? He would never mess up a drawing—not on purpose, not even by accident. He would never be out-of-control at work. Somehow, he knew the writing was caused by the lights.

A fellow draftsman joked with Brian about sleeping on the job, and writing with his eyes closed. He had watched.

Brian confided his worries to the young man. Nothing like this had ever happened. How could he write something, and not know when it happened, or what it means? As they talked on a break, Brian whispered fearfully about seeing a light in the sky—and losing two hours of time.

A few days later, the young draftsman brought in a newspaper story about a new organization in Orange County formed to investigate UFO's. He wrote down the phone number on Brian's note pad. "Call them," he said seriously. "YOU need to call THEM."

Later that week, Brian secretly called the number and left a detailed message. He had seen a purple light in the sky in Arizona and lost two hours of time in 1971, he said.

The Investigation Begins

The next day, Brian sat at his drafting table with his left hand jerking rapidly. In his mind, Brian watched the flashing lights. Unknown to him, his left hand created a vertical column of numbers and a parallel column of English letters. His draftsman friend watched from the corner of his eye.

Brian's hand stopped writing, and he awakened, startled. His right hand held a cigarette with a long, drooping ash. The ash fell and rolled across his big drawing. Then he saw the two columns of numbers and letters. The bold letters spelled out the same words: NOUS LAOS HIKANO.

But this time, Brian heard a soft-electronic voice say the words in his mind: *NOUS LAOS HIKANO.* He whispered the words aloud, repeating them softly like the voice had done: "Nous Laos Hikano."

His drafting friend watched Brian with concern. "I saw you write that. You were in a trance with your eyes rolled up. "Maybe you should see a doctor. That's not normal to write that way."

Later that day, as the other draftsmen packed up, Brian's supervisor yelled from across the room. "Scott—come over here."

Brian hustled across the room fearing he would be fired for messing up a drawing. The supervisor smiled and nudged Brian, boyishly. "Brian, these two engineers want you assigned to the New Product design team. I think you can handle it."

"Excellent drawings," said a turban-wrapped Hindu engineer with a British accent.

"We will be pleased to have you as our design engineering draftsman," said a Frenchman with a thick accent.

"You start Monday," said the supervisor..

"Great!" Brian glanced at his boss. "Does it...?"

"It means another upgrade, and a raise," the supervisor smiled knowingly. "Design engineering draftsman, four."

Four!" Brian gasped.

"We had to skip you ahead for this spot," the supervisor said. "You were requested, and you qualify. So, it has been done. You get grade four pay."

"Thank you!" Brian bubbled with joy at the big raise. "This is great! Fantastic! It will make my wife happy, too." Brian giggled. His blue-eyes flashed and he danced around, rubbing his hands with glee. The supervisor shoved Brian and chuckled.

As Brian skipped away, the men all laughed. "He's the probably the best draftsman I've seen in thirty years," said the supervisor. "But he's a clown." The Frenchman and the tall Hindu laughed. They liked Brian.

Going Home

In the busy parking lot outside the building, several hundred workers walked to their cars. Brian's draftsman friend waved from a red-corvette, another draftsman waved a peace sign from his customized surfer van.

A few moments later, Brian fired up his car -- a 1970 brown Ford Pinto station wagon. He backed the car out and nudged his way into traffic.

A half-hour later, the Ford Pinto rolled past the Garden Grove city hall and police station, then bounced into the driveway of Brian's brick, ranch-style home. Across the street, a long black car with shadowed windows caught Brian's eye. He watched a back-seat window on the car roll up. Brian pondered a moment. Then, in a mirror, he watched the long, black car pull away from the curb.

Inside the house, Mary Beth, in a sour mood, confronted Brian. "Some doctor called for you today," she said as Brian laid his briefcase on a kitchen chair. "They want to set a time to meet us."

"Did they leave a number?"

"We've got to have a talk, Brian," she insisted. "They asked me a bunch of questions about UFO's!"

"You? What did they ask you?"

"If I had seen a UFO! Brian, two men were outside the house today. In a big, black car."

"They must be interested," Brian mused as he moved into the living room. He stood near the fireplace mantle and looked at his big sailing ship. As he studied the rigging and the sails and the faces on all the little men, Mary Beth steamed.

"What are you up to?"

"It's nothing. Don't worry about it."

"I want to know, now!" She twisted her long blond hair and blinked her big brown eyes. When he turned away, she pushed him hard. "What is going on, Brian?"

"It's just a phone call I made."

"You tell me what is going on," she grabbed his chest muscle with her fingers, and twisted.

"Don't do that." He pulled away.

"Tell me," she ordered.

In the kitchen, Mary Beth's sister, Ginger, searched through Brian's briefcase and jacket. Now a perky twenty year old with short brunette hair and a cute turned up nose, she found the paper bearing the words NOUS LAOS HIKANO. Ginger lived in the house part-time. She stayed in a guest room during the week and cared for the two baby girls so her sister could work full time.

Mary Beth twisted Brian's chest muscle, again. "Tell me."

"Okay! Damn it. I called a UFO research group and left a message about this time in Arizona that I saw a light in the sky, and lost two hours of time."

"Why did you do that?"

"It happened."

"You saw a UFO in Arizona?"

Brian pulled away. "I saw a craft and lost two hours of time. I've been having dreams about it, lately. And some flashings. In my mind."

"Flashings?"

"Lights that flash. In some weird pattern."

"It's some acid trip, flashback."

"No it's not," he groaned. "This is very organized."

In the kitchen, Ginger waved the writing at Mary Beth. Ginger had found a new writing almost every day for the last two weeks. Some writings were a page long with detailed statements from *The Host*. The two sisters had agreed to keep quiet to see if Brian asked for them.

"What do these doctors want?" Mary Beth demanded.

"I don't know. We have to find out. I guess they do hypnosis."

"Hypnosis? So you can act like a chicken?"

"No! I want to stop these lights in my head, that's all."

"What lights?"

"These dreams—and lights flashing in my head. They bug me."

"What else?"

"Nothing."

"Nothing else?" She glanced at Ginger, then grabbed at Brian.

He twisted away. "That's all."

Mary Beth pondered a moment. "I want to meet them."

"Okay. So do I."

"When did this happen? This UFO?"

"I don't know. The year before I met you."

"You never said nothing about it."

"Well, I didn't need to. Patti and I told everyone about that one in 1973, and you all just laughed."

"That was nothing. You guys were driving around."

"No we weren't," Brian whined. "We lost time."

"I will never believe that," Mary Beth laughed. "I think you got her stoned."

"Patti? She's a Bible thumper. She told you the truth—your own cousin. It wasn't just me." He turned to his big sailing ship and began dusting off the sails and cleaning the faces of all the little men.

In the kitchen, Ginger secretly opened a folder stuffed with a dozen papers. Mary Beth joined her.

"What does it say?" she whispered.

"N-O-U-S L-A-O-S H-I-K-A-N-O," Ginger said the words slowly. I wonder what it means?"

Mary Beth whispered. "I don't think he knows they are even happening."

43

Ginger flipped through the other pages of strange writings. "These sort of make sense if I read them about ten times—but this one is another language."

"None of them make any sense." Mary Beth jerked the folder away and jammed the papers back into a drawer.

The Hypnosis

The next day, two scholarly UFO investigators visited the house. Both men, about 55 years old, wore dark suits with ties and white shirts.

Dr. Charles Stuart, a physician, rubbed his big Scottish eyebrows as he talked. Friendly, persuasive and stocky, he stood about six feet tall. Professor Wayne Butler was a lanky art historian at a California university. In a refined British style, he listened and stroked his long, thin nose. He took notes, clicked his pen all the time, but seemed to be in command.

Both men assured Brian that they would find the truth about his missing time. "With hypnosis, we'll get to the bottom of this," Dr. Stuart said while patting Brian on the shoulder. "We'll make those lights stop, and give you some peace of mind."

When Brian agreed, Mary Beth frowned in disbelief. "I can't believe you are doing this," she moaned later. "How can they investigate a dream? Why even bother with something that happened four years ago?"

The next Wednesday evening, October 15, Brian parked his station wagon at the Orange County Medical Center and lumbered inside, briefcase in hand holding several drawings he had done at home on a portable drafting table. He found a directory, and located Dr. Stuart's address. "Here goes nothing."

Brian prided himself on self-control and self-awareness. The last thing he wanted was to lose self-control at his drafting table--at work. So, he wanted the lights to stop. That's all he had to say.

Inside the office, the burly Dr. Stuart wore a green surgery gown and a friendly smile. He greeted Brian warmly. The lanky Professor Butler pumped Brian's hand up and down, and clicked his ballpoint pen nervously.

"Thanks for coming," said the Professor. "I think you'll find that Dr. Stuart is one of the best medical hypnotists in California, if not the whole United States."

The doctor invited Brian to the big leather couch with a warm, soothing voice. Brian hesitated. He noticed two other men sitting in the back of the room. "These are members of our UFO organization," said the doctor. "They are here to observe and help us evaluate the hypnosis."

The two men nodded politely at Brian as the professor asked for any drawings. Brian fumbled in his briefcase for a file folder. He had done a few drawings of the craft and the creatures from his recurring dreams.

"Re-occurring dreams can be quite a problem," said the hypnotist warmly.

"The weird lights are worse," Brian said holding up three pages of inked drawings with exacting detail.

"These are fantastic," breathed Professor Butler.

From a doorway in the back of the room, another man, chomping on a cigar, entered and gathered the drawings from the professor. The cigar-smoker hurried away as the hypnotist guided Brian to the couch. Brian looked at the mirrored window in the back of the room. It must be for observation, he thought.

"Brian, let's sit down and get started. What do you say?" Brian sat down nervously. He wondered who was watching, but the doctor began. "With hypnosis, you need to relax your mind, and just listen to my words. You just listen, I do all the work," the doctor laughed heartily.

Brian leaned back on the couch and squirmed into a comfortable position. He felt the warm, soft leather with his hands and relaxed.

"Just make yourself comfortable. Have you ever seen my grandfather's old watch?" The friendly doctor pulled an old, gold-plated, ornate pocket watch from inside his gown. Brian laughed.

"Well, from now on, you can answer yes, because you are now looking at it. Just stare at my old grandfather's watch and listen very carefully to my voice."

Brian's eyes followed the watch back and forth a few times. "Your eyelids are getting heavy. Can you feel them getting heavy? Yes. Sure you can. Just relax them." Brian's eyes closed. "Actually, you don't need the watch," the doctor said. That was the last thing Brian remembered.

Two hours later, Brian's blue eyes slowly flickered open. He rubbed them red as he glanced at four men who had gathered closely around him.

"This is hot!" whispered one of the observers.

"Do we have enough to go the newspapers?" asked professor Butler clicking his pen and checking his notes.

"I think it is too early," doctor Stuart objected. "We have a lot of details to confirm."

"But it could be published in our journal," said the other observer.

The cigar-smoking man entered from behind the two-way mirror. "Great job," he said. He held up three transparent pages. "I had overheads made in your media department. You gotta see these."

Brian's mind spun. Still hazy from the hypnosis, he saw images of the craft and the ugly creatures with no necks and long ears. "This hypnosis makes you kind of fuzzy doesn't it?" he asked with a hoarse voice.

"You'll be all right in a few minutes," the doctor chuckled.

The Drawings

In the other room, Brian's first drawing was projected on a screen. The cigar-smoker carried a pointer in one hand and pencil in the other. His shirt pocket bulged with pens, pencils and assorted tools like many engineers Brian knew.

With excitement, the man pointed at details. "According to Brian's drawing, the ship was one-hundred and fifty feet by two-hundred feet," he said. They all gasped.

"The door was four feet wide, nine foot high with a three inch thick frame. It had a symbol on the door approximately three feet in diameter. Red and white lights above the doorframe blinked in sequential order, with a control panel of red and white light to the left of the door. "Is that right, Brian?" he asked.

Brian rubbed his eyes. "That's about right."

"This is detail like I've never seen before!" the cigar-smoker gushed.

"It's very close," Brian added with his raw voice.

The cigar-smoker continued. "Detail 'A' of the drawing gives the thickness of walls in this ship. The two walls apparently rotate within each other. Both are separated by a gap of about nine inches." He paused. "Now, that's the kind of detail I like to see." The men all smiled.

Dr. Stuart patted Brian warmly on the back with his thick hand. Professor Butler clicked his pen and wrote notes with his slender hand.

"This is absolutely incredible," said the cigar-smoker. "And, all of this information on one page."

"What does this symbol mean on the door?" the cigar smoker asked Brian.

"I have no idea," said Brian with a shrug. "They called the door something on the drawing."

The little man pointed at a phrase. He read: "Door Nebulas of time. Mind transport of energy."

"That's it," Brian said.

"What does this mean?"

"I don't know," Brian puffed up. "I was hoping you could tell me." He didn't like the man's demanding tone.

Dr. Stuart wrapped his arm around Brian's shoulder. "This man is important in our organization," the doctor whispered in a fatherly tone. "He's done this for years."

"I assume this word *'nebulas'* is spelled incorrectly," the man continued. "Did you mean *nebulous?*

"I am a terrible speller. I just wrote down what I heard," Brian said. "I'm sure the guy said 'nebulous to time' or I wouldn't have wrote it. I have no idea what it even means. I don't even remember doing most of that drawing. I started one of them, and found the others this morning."

The five men all studied Brian for a moment. A long silence followed as each man carefully weighed Brian's statement. Finally, they all accepted Brian's words. Maybe he didn't understand.

The cigar-smoker watched Brian, carefully. He wanted to confront Brian and see if he might break. "In this drawing, Detail C shows a large bulky creature about eight feet tall, holding an instrument with numerous lights. You indicate that this blinking instrument slides up and down on a pole, that a clear tube carries information from the instrument to somewhere else, and that the information is communicated in patterns of blinking light. Is that right, Brian?"

Brian smiled. "That thing has some of the flashiest, most freaky lights you could ever imagine. That one light on the bottom is--I don't know how to say it. You can't look away from it." Brian suddenly felt nervous as images of the examination popped into his mind. For a moment, in his mind, Brian saw the light-box moving up his body. Brian spoke slowly. "That light, when they turn that on, there is no way you can look away. It hurts to look away." Brian stopped and the men waited, patiently.

"Did I tell you about this in the hypnosis session?" Brian asked the doctor.

Dr. Stuart hugged Brian's shoulder warmly. "Yes, you did Brian. We're not going to go into that now." He turned to the men. "We're about done for tonight aren't we fellahs."

The cigar-smoking engineer stammered. "Could I ask one more question please--not about the light box, but about this big creature?"

Brian shrugged okay.

"What did he look like, exactly? What did he do?"

Brian tried to talk as images flashed into his mind. "I don't know. He had long flat ears attached along the side of his head, almost the full length of his head, and he had no neck and large hands with three big fingers and crooked thumb, and he had a big, flat nose, bent over to one side. Very ugly. Big lips, squinty eyes. He had a lot of loose, thick skin hanging down from his chest to his stomach. Gray skin, like an elephant or rhinoceros. It was dry and scaly on the top part of his chest."

The men listened, stunned by the description and detail.

"Who ran the instrument which was used to give you the medical examination?" asked the cigar-smoker.

"There were others in the room, behind instrument panels which sort of came up to their waist. You could see the lights reflecting on their chests as they moved the controls. Even though you would think they might be clumsy, they were very--not clumsy. Another one of them ran the box with the freaky lights," Brian said. "Did I tell you about this in the hypnosis?"

The hypnotist nodded warmly. "Don't worry about that now."

"Anything else about them?" asked the professor. "Did they look mean?"

"No," Brian laughed. "Not mean. Sort of friendly, really."

The professor gasped, "Friendly?"

"But ugly," Brian said sensing the man's disbelief. "The place smelled. It had a stench to it, and a vapor, this mist and all, and they breathed kind of hard -- like they was wheezing. I think they was having trouble breathing for some reason."

The men gathered closer to Brian. "But, they seemed to really know what they were doing behind the panels, very good at their jobs, you might say. But later, when the tall guy was talking to me, I noticed, those two sort of stood there, you know, shifting their feet-- shifting their weight on their feet."

"Like they were bored?" asked the professor.

"Yeah. I think they were bored."

"This is the first report of bored aliens," laughed the professor. The other men chuckled.

"They were business-like," Brian said. "Doing a job. Like they had done it before. They weren't the least bit excited."

"Brian," said the hypnotist warmly. "We covered a lot of this already in the hypnosis. You might need to let it rest for awhile."

"I'm not tired," said Brian.

"Brian, just one last question, if I could," said the cigar smoker. He pointed at words on the screen. "Here you write, *'non-Newtonian physics apply, thought by energy expansion of mind.'* Do you know what that means?"

"I have no idea," Brian laughed. "None, really."

The cigar-smoker pointed at the drawing. "And here, near our long-eared gray friend, you write something very interesting: *Clone, phase 271. Motivation-- new research continued, update research, thought expansion to Host mind.'* Brian can you tell us what all of this means?"

Brian mouthed a few of the words and gave up, frustrated. "I don't know what any of it means," he said. "I really don't."

"But you wrote it," snapped the little man.

"I must have understood it at the time, but I sure don't know what it means now."

The answer disappointed the impatient cigar-smoker. He puffed up a cloud of smoke.

The hypnotist stood. "I think Brian has done well for a first session," he said. Everyone else stood up, except Brian. He remained sitting. As the men talked, Brian heard a soft, electronic voice in his mind. He repeated the words, mumbling in a daze.

"All living organisms have a DNA factor present in which knowledge of updated information can be inserted into DNA by a procedure using the examination instrument: the bio-telemetry scanner." The men quieted at the sound of his raw voice.

48

Brian shook his head in a daze and continued. "I think the second part is about the gray guy. He is a clone with life span of 26-28 years. Two hundred and seventy phases before him -- of clones, like him. They update research, and implant knowledge into the DNA of man and women. Then they transmit information by their thought expansion process to the host mind--a host computer. It projects the personality of their god."

Brian chuckled. "Good Lord, I don't know where that came from." He giggled as the men gathered around him. "That was strange."

"Thank you, Brian!" said the cigar-smoker, obviously pleased. Everyone laughed and patted Brian as the little engineer punched numbers into his pocket calculator. He turned to the group. "More than 7000 years--271 phases of clones," he announced. "It's a 7000 to 7500 year term, they're talking about. And they are inserting knowledge into the DNA of man with that instrument of flashing lights." He smiled. "That makes sense."

"That makes sense to you?" Brian asked.

The cigar smoker smiled. "A lot of sense. Compared to other information."

Baffled, Brian wondered about the source of his thoughts. He had repeated the voice in his mind--words he didn't comprehend, words HE didn't think. He simply heard them right over the top of his own thoughts, like a radio broadcast. He didn't understand, but the investigators understood. "Is this supposed to happen?" Brian mumbled to the busy doctor.

Dr. Stuart waved away Brian's concern and ushered him out towards the door, but the lanky professor interrupted in the hallway. "Brian, do you have anything solid that would prove your contact?" he asked. He clicked the pen, as an example. "Like a pen, or an ashtray."

Brian thought deeply. "No, I don't think so. I really wasn't trying to prove anything. I am just trying to stop these flashing lights."

"I know," said the professor. "But to prove it was a UFO we need something solid, Brian. Something we can hang our hat on. You know. A rock. A Venusian ashtray," he laughed."

Brian stammered. "I can't think of any proof."

"'Go on home and get some rest, Brian," the doctor said as he nudged Brian into the hallway. "You did a good job. Now don't think about it anymore. We'll see you next week."

Brian lumbered out of the hospital carrying his briefcase and smoking a cigarette. Invigorated by the cold night air, he stopped at his car and looked up at the hospital. In a window on the second floor, he saw the men talking with wild animation. They looked excited and jubilant. But, Brian felt agitated. Something was wrong. What were they so excited about? Didn't they know this stuff? Was this new to them? He wondered what investigators knew, really, about the crafts and the people inside.

Brian held little interest in proving that UFO's exist. The aliens can prove they exist if they want to, he reasoned. Either group could obviously land on the White House lawn. They can do what they want, but they remain hidden by choice. So why bother trying to prove they exist? They were hiding for a reason. Brian didn't know the reason, but he knew it had to be very logical to them. They were smart—a lot smarter than man.

He wondered if the investigators knew about the conflict between the two groups, and all the genetic research on man. Oh, well, he finally conceded, he could drive himself crazy wondering. He didn't care anyway. He only wanted the flashing lights to stop.

The Host's Request

On Friday evening, when Brian's Ford Pinto station wagon bounced into his driveway at home, big pumpkins sat on the back doorstep. A cool October breeze spun dancing leaves down the street and across the driveway. The fall equinox had passed and Halloween was only two weeks away.

He hurried into the kitchen, where Mary Beth and cousin Patti cooked a new spaghetti sauce recipe. "I've got thirty minutes," he said. "Smells good." Brian had been invited by the investigators to meet America's number one UFO researcher, Dr. J. Allen Hynek.

Brian plopped into his favorite over-stuffed chair and picked up his baby daughters. He giggled with them as Ginger shouted from the kitchen. "We found another writing, Brian." She held the file bulging with Brian's automatic writings.

Angrily, Mary Beth grabbed at the file. Ginger pulled away. "It's about time that you talk about it," Ginger whined. "You can't hide things forever. Maybe the investigators should see these."

Mary Beth twisted Ginger's wrist hard and grabbed the folder, but Ginger bounced away impishly into the living room with one page.

"Is that spaghetti about ready?" asked Brian as he sniffed the aroma. "I want extra butter on my bread and only a bit of garlic."

"Picky. Picky," said Ginger.

"I'm serious. No one ever puts enough butter on my garlic bread. And one dash of garlic for this meeting. Not the whole can."

"Did you hear that cooks? Mr. Picky insists on double-butter, but go light on the garlic," Ginger laughed.

In the kitchen, Mary Beth and Patti mimicked Brian. They laughed.

Ginger teased Brian. "It's Patti's recipe, you better eat it." He pretended to grab his throat and gag.

50

Ginger laughed at him. "Brian you are terrible." She laughed. "Do you want to hear your latest masterpiece?" she asked.

"Not really. It's not me, anyway."

With a great flourish, she produced the paper. "You might be interested. Something is coming. It says:

> **Given to pass, of I. A ball of fire will come of I. I have complied. Seek this in knowledge of I. Of this, a sign for your Secondary Factor. Look to the north.**

"It gives a latitude and longitude," Ginger said. "And it says your Secondary Factor is Professor Butler. It's a sign for him." She continued.

> **Open. By, of you--the truth is related, right forearm, Zone A22 reference. One is to know, and by he, the Host will comply to A2.1 through A29.3. Comprehension 100%.**

Brian listened in awe. Mary Beth and Patti listened from the kitchen doorway.

> **Of your origin, knowledge is not conceived correctly in man's mind, yet by the Host this knowledge is given: Sexual implantation DNA of man by Secondary at dawn of time.**

> **My mind, by that of the Host, is one with you, and with all mankind. Go and touch the mark--A21.**

Mary Beth and Patti slipped quietly into the living room to gauge Brian's reaction.

"It's like a machine," Patti whispered. "Like a robot."

Brian studied a spider tattoo on his right forearm. "It said the *'truth is related by my right forearm?'*" The spider tattoo brought back a memory Brian didn't want to think about. He had done the tattoo at the age of 16—in a trance. He didn't remember doing it. He had woken up afterwards with ink and blood on his arm, and a spider tattoo. Two months after the spider, he had also created a big, black jaguar on his left forearm. He felt goose bumps rise on the back of his neck.

Ginger scanned the writing. "Oh, I see. The spider tattoo on your arm! That's right, Brian. Wow. You understood that one.You got that, and I didn't."

As Brian studied the tattoos on his arms, Ginger's pace accelerated with excitement.

> **From this I say, by THIS MARK, the truth is given. Go and touch the ground at A21, and by this, touch the mind of all mankind.**

Brian stared ahead blankly. "Does it make sense to you Brian?" Ginger asked. *"Touch the mind of all mankind?"*

"No," he laughed. "It doesn't. This is getting weird. Mary Beth, is that spaghetti ready? Those doctors are picking me up any minute."

Mary Beth stood in the doorway with a plate of spaghetti and garlic bread. "Brian, I think we are going to have to talk about this." She plopped the overflowing plate down on a TV tray for him.

"It smells great." He sniffed the bread. "You want to talk about the garlic?"

"No Brian. About these men--and about these writings."

"I don't know about the writings."

"You are doing them!" Mary Beth said with concern.

"Bull!" he blurted. "I am not."

"You are doing them Brian. You have to be," said Patti firmly.

Brian filled his mouth with spaghetti. "No, I'm not," he sputtered angrily.

"It has to be you, Brian," said Ginger.

"I know when I do something—damn it!" He chomped out the words as he ate. "Where did you find that one?" he asked Ginger.

"In the den, this afternoon."

"I wasn't in the den, I was at work all day, and I didn't even go into the den last night."

"Who else could write this?" Mary Beth asked.

"Well, it's not me. I don't even know what it says. How could it be me?"

"It has to be you," Patti laughed.

Outside their house, in the dark, a Chevrolet station wagon rolled up to the curb carrying the doctor and professor. The horn honked.

"Good god, I'm just starting to eat," Brian spewed.

"What are you getting out of this?" Mary Beth demanded.

"Nothing," Brian said. "I've been having a repeating dream! That's all. That's all it is. They are investigating it."

"Investigating a dream? A Brian Scott dream? No one will believe YOU, especially a dream."

"They are UFO investigators. That's what they do."

"Brian," Mary Beth pleaded in her soft, sweet voice. "Please don't start anything that makes trouble. I don't want to go back to that old life."

The horn honked again and he hugged her gently. "This is scientific, okay? Those are real UFO investigators. It is a real investigation. Nothing else."

A loud knock shook the door. Ginger opened the door for Professor Butler. "Time to go Brian," he shouted.

Dr. J. Allen Hynek

As they arrived outside a big Hollywood hills home wearing fall jackets, Brian breathed the cool air and looked up into the sky. A white ball-of-fire streaked over the city of Los Angeles.

The fireball might have been a sign for Professor Butler--the proof he had requested. But Brian had forgotten to mention the writing, so he said nothing.

Inside the plush living room, as drinks were served, Brian shook hands with a room full of scholarly men and women. Most were twice his age. Dr. Butler introduced Brian around as the newest 'hot' contactee.

The group then listened as Dr. J. Allen Hynek talked. Everyone knew him as the professional astronomer hired by the Air Force to debunk UFO's, and now a consultant on new movie in development by Stephen Spielberg--<u>Close Encounters of the Third Kind.</u>

Hynek seemed like a grandfather in a room among old friends. White-haired, and wearing a white suit, he laughed easily. Hynek told the group that someday he feared he would have to apologize in public for calling UFO's "swamp gas." They all laughed.

"We all know something is happening," Dr. Hynek told the group. "It's physical, but it's psychic, too. And we don't understand that. They-- whoever *they* are—just aren't playing with a straight deck. I don't understand the phenomenon anymore than any of you. You probably understand it better. In fact, some uneducated farmer halfway around the globe probably has the answers we are looking for tonight--or perhaps this man does." He gestured warmly to Brian, introducing him to the crowd. The men nodded with respect. "We need help to get all of our ducks in a row," said Hynek.

To relieve tension, Brian quacked like a duck, loudly. "QUACK. QUACK. QUACK. I can do a duck, but that's about all I know," he said. The group burst into laughter, and many somber investigators giggled to tears. When everyone calmed down, Brian told about the desert abduction, and loss of time. Brian felt nervous and he babbled, but the group seemed forgiving.

Afterwards, Dr. Hynek warmly shook Brian's hand and encouraged him to continue with hypnosis. He said Professor Butler would provide him with reports.

The Will of the Host

On Wednesday night, October 22, when Brian arrived in the doctor's office for hypnosis, a video technician turned on bright lights and a big video camera.

Brian handed the professor a drawing that looked a bit like a spider. "This is supposed to be another proof," Brian said. "Something man doesn't know. I found it this morning."

The professor showed the drawing to Dr. Stuart. "Photonic matter? What is photonic matter? Brian."

"I don't know," Brian shrugged. "I think it might be their energy. Like their electricity."

The hypnotist set the drawing aside slowly and took out his gold grandfather's watch. "Let's find out."

Within minutes, in a hypnotic trance, Brian began to relive more of his missing time with the long-eared aliens. He was led to down the curved hallway to a door with a different symbol. Shaped like a tree with three branches, the symbol seemed slender and more delicate compared to first one. "Candelabra," said the long-eared giant when Brian asked about the meaning.

Inside the huge room, Brian saw a circular, three-ringed "on-board computer." Jumping around the panels, a crackling, bright light sparked like electricity often taking the shape of a spider. "Photonic matter," echoed a deep, human-like voice in Brian's mind.

"This is of I," said a deep voice. Brian spun around to see the Host--the Old Man standing behind him. Short, slender but obviously in command, he wore a big pendant around his neck with a spider etched into the black obsidian.

Suddenly awake in the doctor's office, Brian both relived and reported on the experience.

"I am. I am. From beyond all time, I am." Brian said, imitating poorly the deep voice. "That's what he said. That's the way he always talks."

"So why did he bring you on board?" asked the doctor.

"Knowledge. Knowledge for man," Brian spoke like the Host. Then he became anxious. "I'm being put in a cylinder. I'm not afraid. It's like an eggshell inside. Comfortable. It has three rings of lights. The big guy holds my hand. I am not afraid, but I'm not sure if I'm going to like this."

"Why aren't you afraid, Brian? I'd be afraid."

"I was afraid the first time. I remember for a minute the first time--the examination. Oh, I see. Oh--the drawings. The knowledge I have been given to build things. It's from this. This machine. But, why me? Why me?"

On the warm leather couch, Brian gulped. "He tells me: *'because of the tattoos.'* My hand was *'guided'* by him when I did the tattoos on my arms. He asks if I want the *'knowledge of man.'* I agree. He asks if I want to continue on. I agree to continue. I feel like jelly inside. But, I say yes--I do."

On the couch, Brian squirmed. "Now the cylinder is up, and on my head a needle or something sharp, pokes my head." Brian grimaced in pain. "Owwwwweee."

Then, in his mind, Brian saw images of the pyramid in South America and the huge lake. "Incredible," he whispered. "They are giving me a taste of it, the knowledge. Okay, I agree to take more. I agree. I'll do it, if I can. It don't hurt. It don't hurt," Brian moaned. "Oh, everything is going around. Around...ohhhhh."

Brian's head filled with spinning images of the ancient pyramid, children and DNA. On the leather couch, his body writhed and his head bobbed. "Around. Around, and around, around. Aghhh. Aggghhhhhh."

"What are you feeling?" asked the doctor.

"Oh, oh. It's like my head is coming off, coming off the top of my shoulders. Ohhhhhh. So strange. So many things racing through my mind, ohhhh." Then Brian's face and body suddenly relaxed.

Professor Butler wiped sweat from his brow with a white handkerchief. "Did you get that on tape?" he asked the cameraman. The young man nodded with a 'thumbs-up' sign.

Brian continued. "They are talking now. One tells the other, *'The thought transference is complete.' From the machine to MY mind,*" Brian breathed. "The big one is pleased."

The Split

From that day onward, Brian began to speak to the doctor during hypnosis with at least two different personalities and voices. One authoritative voice reported events in a bold, certain tone. The other boyish personality spoke as the normal Brian, in a weak, and disbelieving tone. But occasionally, a third style emerged. The voice wasn't *reporting*, it *wasn't the boyish Brian*--it was the authoritative, commanding Presence of the Host.

"The truth mankind seeks of this can be known," the Host boomed. The strength stunned the investigators. They hadn't even asked a question. The Host had initiated the conversation. "I, the Host, will return to A22 on 2011 A.D., December 24th. And by this, know you, one and all--I am, I am."

This time, Brian saw an aerial view of the Nazca Plain of Peru. Superimposed on the ground, a huge grid system of red blinking lights covered the etched symbols. His view soared downward to one symbol: the spider. On the abdomen, A22 pulsed in bright red letters. One rear leg of the spider bent at a ninety-degree angle and extended outward, longer than the others. At the very tip of the leg, bright red numbers pulsated: A21.

The Host spoke boldly to Dr. Stuart and the professor.

> **From this, now will you comply? Touch the Mark at A21. Your instructions given. Comply of the Host now. Time is relevant to mankind. One is to know. All logic closed until A21 complied to--page 1 of 50 closed."**

"All right Brian," said the doctor in frustration.

"Nope," said Brian in his boyish voice.

The doctor ignored Brian with a shrug. "What's going to happen if you touch A21, Brian?"

"*Truth--an understanding for all mankind*?" Brian answered, but he questioned the words as he reported them.

"What is the truth?"

The Host boldly challenged the doctor. "Would you understand the truth if you heard it?"

"Are you asking me a question?" said the burly doctor rubbing his thick Scottish eyebrows.

Then Brian spoke, boyishly. "Ah, I'm not, but he is. Yes. He is asking you the question."

"The answer to your question is *yes,*" said the doctor firmly.

"Would you *believe* the truth if you heard it?" said the Host.

The doctor and the professor eyed each other with concern. They didn't like being questioned. The hypnotist answered boldly. "Yes!"

"Why has not man complied of the request even if we have complied ten-fold?" asked the Host.

Brian's head bobbed and he gulped. Then he reported in his boyish voice, "Again, the question is asked, *'Why will you not comply?'*"

"What do you want us to do, Brian?" countered the doctor, irritated.

Brian whispered softly, "No. Not I. It's not ME."

"What does the Host want us to do, Brian?" smirked the doctor.

In a weak, boyish voice, Brian responded. "I don't even understand myself. Everything is all mixed up."

"What does the Host want us to do Brian?" the doctor demanded.

Brian answered in a weak voice, reporting the more flowing and gentle words of the tallest giant.

> **He asks for a man, and this man, not because of who he is, or what he is, but because in his childhood, he was touched by the Host, and has risen to the position he holds through that, through dedication and devotion to this thought.**

This man asked that he be given the comprehension factor of 100% to the knowledge of man. But, there is as if those around he--now present--mock the truth. And it is, as if it is a simple thing, that if a man laughs of his brother, he in fact, only truly laughs at himself.

The accusation flustered the two investigators. "Is he talking about us?" whispered the professor. He glanced at the video camera.

Irritated, the doctor replied with scorn, "So what is it, that he--the Host-- wants us to do, Brian?"

Brian raced to keep up with the velvety voice in his mind. He rushed to repeat the words of the tall creature.

This man of the meeting in Hollywood: Hynek. To comply to the will of the Host and to arrange sessions through several very learned people, in a similar hypnotic state, to build documentation and reference, to go to point marked reference A21, to feel the truth through I, through the Host, through you, through Secondary Factor, and by this know the truth of all mankind.

Brian relaxed and exhaled deeply. "It seems so very simple."

"So what you're telling us then, is what they want us to get doctor Hynek to go down and put his hand on that spot on the Nazca Plain. Is that correct?"

"No. Through this symbol, *he* could realize that they *are the same two entities,* and that I—Brian--must touch the ground, and a hypnotic state to occur thereafter will help man gain in knowledge, through research of understanding, step-by-step to start with genetic coding through cloning."

The doctor felt offended. "All right. Ok Brian. Well, we've had about enough for tonight. I want you to relax."

"Hmm," Brian breathed, defiantly.

"It's important for you to relax your mind before I awaken you, because if you don't relax, you could end up with some problems like headaches, insomnia..."

"There is a door," Brian mumbled.

"All right. Well, don't worry about it tonight, Brian. We're all through for tonight. Just relax.

"Not until somebody complies."

"You're going to have to relax, Brian," the doctor demanded. "Now you do what I tell you to, now. You do what I tell you to, Brian," the doctor said gruffly.

"You miss-stated, you lied." Brian reported, gently.

"You do what I tell you to do, Brian!" the hypnotist asserted. "Right now, I want you to relax."

The professor gestured "cut" to the video-tape technician, and as the hypnotist awoke Brian, they all breathed with relief.

Outside afterwards, Brian smoked a cigarette and leaned against the door of his car. He could see the professor and the doctor arguing. He felt depressed. They were only trying to get answers for themselves--proof that UFO's exist. He felt they weren't trying to stop the lights or help him.

Worse, he had spoken in a strange way. When the doctor asked a question, the tall hulk would think. The thought would go to the onboard computer then come to Brian, somehow. He simply reported the soft electronic voice in his mind. The Host worked the same way, but with his words came a bold, commanding presence. He spoke so fast, Brian left out half the words.

Proof for Mary Beth

That night, when Brian returned home, Mary Beth confronted him. Ginger listened from her bedroom. "I want my own proof," she said.

"I can't give anybody proof!" Brian whined. "This is so damn ridiculous. It's pathetic. How can I give anybody proof?"

"Then stop this whole thing," she shouted. "Stop going to hypnosis. Stop all of this crap, Brian. I want my husband home at night—EVERY night."

"But, I am trying to stop these damn lights from flashing. And the writings!"

"You are doing them. Just stop them."

"No -- I'm not."

"Yes, you are, Brian."

"I'm NOT, damn it."

"You ARE!" she screamed. " You can STOP it."

Brian screamed. "How can I stop something that I don't even know I am doing? Tell me that, and I'll make the *damn* things stop."

The baby girls woke up crying, and Mary Beth ran to them, fearing for their safety.

The Host

THE HOST -- He rarely smiled but appeared pleasant and business-like. He spoke in a deep monotone voice most of the time, but also spoke with a high-speed electronic sound. Brian heard beeping as the Host spoke. He wore a blinking belt of lights. His symbol is the spider, and – for those who have wisdom – his name is equivalent to the number: 020 020 020.

BRIAN'S OWN drawing of the First Ball of Light. The glowing orange orb hovered in his backyard in Garden Grove, California on Brian's 16th birthday. The light started his transformation process.

DISSOCIATION

DISSOCIATION IS AN INTERNAL PROCESS BY WHICH BEHAVIORS ARE DISCONNECTED FROM A PERSON'S BELIEFS AND MEMORIES.

THE EXTREME CASE IS MULTIPLE-PERSONALITY. SLEEP-WALKING, AMNESIA, AUTOMATIC WRITING ARE LESSER EXAMPLES. MANY PHENOMENA OF HYPNOSIS ARE ALSO RESULTS OF DISSOCIATION.

-- The New Grolier Multi-media Encyclopedia,V.6

EXTRACTING THE SOUL FOR TRANSFORMATION

OFTEN THE SOUL IS CONCEIVED AS A BIRD READY TO TAKE FLIGHT
THE SOUL OF A SLEEPER IS SUPPOSED TO WANDER AWAY FROM HIS BODY
TO ACTUALLY VISIT OTHER PLACES AND SEE PERSONS.

DEPARTURE OF THE SOUL IS NOT ALWAYS VOLUNTARY.
IT MAY BE EXTRACTED … AGAINST ITS WILL BY GHOSTS, DEMONS OR
SORCERERS.
THE SOUL, IN THE OPINION OF PRIMITIVE PEOPLES,
MAY BE ABSENT FROM THE BODY WITHOUT CAUSING DEATH.
SUCH TEMPORARY ABSENCES ARE OFTEN BELIEVED TO INVOLVE
CONSIDERABLE RISK,
SINCE THE WANDERING SOUL IS LIABLE TO A VARIETY OF MISHAPS AT THE
HANDS OF ENEMIES.

(Sir James Frazer, Golden Bough)

Abridged from pages 210, 214, 217 and 774)

THE HOST'S COMFORT

"FEAR NOT THE MIND OF MANKIND.
OF THIS—OF THE SECONDARY WORLD,
MANKIND WILL SEE THE SIMILARITY OF EVENTS
YOU FOLLOW AS OTHERS IN THE PAST:
URGENCY, CONFUSION, SCHIZOPHRENIA."

--The Host

Chapter 4

The Mind of Man, Split

The next morning, Ginger found another writing in the den. The Host repeated the request, and promised another *ball of fire in the sky* as a sign for the professor.

That night, Professor Butler sat in his den surrounded by books on ancient art. He watched Brian's hypnosis tapes on a black and white monitor. Behind him stood a huge painting of a winged disk, a mysterious symbol used by the ancient Sumerians, Assyrians, Phoenicians and Canaanites. He looked at the painting, glanced at Brian's face on TV, and listened to the bold, mechanical voice. "Would you know the truth if you heard it?"

The professor rubbed his long-nose and clicked his pen in frustration. "We might not," he whispered. "We might not."

About then, in the sky, a sparkling ball of fire arched over Long Beach Harbor and Los Angeles.

The Black Rock

At dawn the next morning, Brian's Captain America truck bounced onto a beach. As waves crashed on the sand, Brian's feet stepped out and his boots kicked through dry grass. His hands dug under a black rock and lifted up a meteorite about ten inches wide and four inches thick. The soil steamed.

Slowly, Brian's eyes flickered and rolled out of a trance. "Oh Jesus," he said falling backwards. "Mother of God." Frantically, he scanned the beach and horizons. To the east, the red sun rose into a pink sky. To the west, waves crashed on the beach.

63

Several young surfers in black skin-suits walked over to him. "Are you all right, mister?" asked a blond-haired young man with a big toothy smile. "Are you stuck?"

"Where am I?" Brian asked in a fluster.

"Santa Barbara, dude," the surfer answered.

"Santa Barbara?" Brian gasped. "Are you sure?"

The boys all laughed, made jokes and hurried away giggling as Brian stumbled back to his Captain America truck with the meteorite.

At home, later that morning, Mary Beth told Ginger and Patti about Brian's discovery. With two hands, Mary Beth lifted the heavy, black stone for them to see. "Brian says he woke up in Santa Barbara--around sunrise. He has no idea how he got there."

"Butler asked for a rock," Brian said. "They gave him a rock."

"What did he think?" Ginger asked.

Brian smirked. "Not interested. Anyone can buy a meteorite," Brian clicked a pen and imitated the long-nosed professor. "A meteorite is not proof of UFO's."

Patti hefted the black stone carefully. "It's heavy. Very HEAVY."

"He said it was too mythological," Brian added. "Where in the hell could I buy a steaming hot mythological meteorite at 7:00 in the morning?" Brian laughed. "These guys are so far off track. In the ditch."

"And you don't even know how you got there?" Patti said.

"Right! I am more pathetic than them. I don't even know how I got there."

Patti lifted the black stone. "Well, what good is a meteorite, Brian?"

"I don't know!" whined Brian. "It's not my idea. *Jesus*. It's not MY proof. It's his."

"Whose?" Mary Beth demanded.

"The Host's!" Brian snapped. "It's not me doing this. It's him. Don't you see? How the hell could I do this? God almighty! A meteorite?"

"Well, even if it is, it doesn't prove anything to me," Mary Beth said. "What does it prove?" she shrugged. "Nothing, really."

"Good God! My own wife." Brian picked up the black chunk of iron. "It's a SIGN!" Brian shouted. "He asked for a rock. Here is his damn rock, for God's sake. The Host answered. That's significant as all hell, if you ask me. Probably hasn't happened for a thousand years."

"But it's not a UFO," said Ginger. "It's not an alien."

"Right," Brian steamed. "That's all they want."

Patti touched the black meteorite. "Do you know whose sign it is to cast stars to earth?"

"Is that in the Bible?" Mary Beth gasped.

"Yes. And it's not God. It's not Jesus." Patti eyed them all carefully. "It's the sign of the anti-Christ."

"This isn't about God," Brian snapped. "Or the Anti-Christ. Meteorites fall everyday, for heaven's sake. You've got to keep your imaginations under control, here."

"Did you ever hear of the Kaaba, in Mecca. Muslims worship this big box. Inside is nothing but a black meteorite. A sign—they believe from God."

"It is NOT FROM GOD. This is not religious in anyway."

"If it is not from God, then where is it from Brian? There is only one other choice."

Brian stammered. "Let's not get into that."

"It's either God or the devil."

"No. There are millions of other *things*. They are solid, physical beings, people--just like us, trying to help us."

Patti glared. "Brian, whether they are spirits or people, you are definitely getting into all that the Bible warns against: conjuring, divination, automatic writings, and signs in the sky. You have a black rock from space sitting on your living room table. Good, God." She paused. "I don't mind telling you, that as a Christian, this is starting to scare me. It's scaring the *hell* out of me."

Patti scurried away and slammed the door of the guest bedroom.

Mary Beth frowned. "See. Now you got her going."

"Well, how about someone telling me how I got to Santa Barbara? Huh? How the hell does a guy drive two hundred miles and not know it? Isn't that something!"

"I don't know," Mary Beth shouted. "How am I supposed to know?" She spun away, angrily. "Get that damn rock off my table."

As Brian juggled the heavy stone for Ginger to study, Mary Beth shouted from the bathroom. "And next time, if he is real, tell him to make it show up so I see it--right in front of my face. Then, I might believe it."

"I can't make him do anything," Brian muttered.

Perky Ginger flipped her braids and lifted the rock. She didn't seem afraid or superstitious. "What do you think it means, Brian?"

"It means I've got to do something," Brian said. "I just don't know what to do. Even if THEY don't believe it, I brought this rock home. How can I forget that? That kind of thing can't happen. It has meaning to me—and I have to accept that."

"So this really happened?"

"Right. How could I find a meteorite, that's still hot, and not even remember driving there? That's what I don't get."

Halloween

Just after sunset on Friday evening, costumed children swarmed over the sidewalks, laughing and giggling with their bags of treats. Dried, brown leaves blew along the street. In the cool air, Brian lit candles in two orange pumpkins he had carved with ghoulish, funny faces. He set them on the front steps with the help of his little girl, Kathy.

Mary Beth insisted he move the drafting table out of the house. As he carried the drawing board and chair into the garage, Mary Beth tossed his pens out the back door. With a clattering sound, they scattered on the driveway. "You forgot these," she shouted.

"Damn it. Those are my ink pens," Brian screamed. "You don't throw INK pens." He swore at his wife, and she slammed the door in a rage. Brian valued his ink pens more than anything he owned, even more than the Captain America truck. He had learned to earn a living with those pens. They had started his career, and had provided money for them to live. He muttered. *She didn't care. She just wanted his paycheck. She's stubborn and pig-headed.*

Brian slowly calmed down as he placed a light over his drafting board, set up a radio, and dialed mellow-rock music. He found an old tape recorder, and recorded on it: "Testing, Testing, one, two, three. Testing."

Brian enjoyed the garage. He relaxed and forgave Mary Beth. He couldn't stay angry long. "She's a good girl," he whispered as he inserted a tape from the Moody Blues, his favorite musical group. On the back wall, aligned in straight rows, hung his tools.

Out front, as the night fell, little ghosts and goblins knocked on the front door. Ginger and Mary Beth took turns handing out candy to the trick-or-treaters.

Later that night, as Brian worked at the drafting table, the radio sputtered with static. In a fret, Brian jostled the radio and antennae. He saw a purple haze reflecting on the Captain American truck, and whipped around to see the Old Man emerge out of a purple ball of light. The Host didn't smile, but appeared serious. Brian jumped out of his chair terrified.

The Old Man waited for Brian to calm down. He hovered in the doorway wearing a blinking belt of lights around his slender waist and a silver suit with a pointed collar. From his right shoulder, a dark tube arched down to the belt, pulsing with blood. Around his neck, hung a shiny black obsidian pendant etched with the image of a spider.

The Host held the spider out towards Brian then spoke in a soft, high-speed electronic tone for a moment. Then his voice slowed to a deep, masculine monotone, accompanied by soft electronic beeps.

I am, that I am. From time beyond, all time--I am. From the sky, the signs have come. From this time, now forward we

**must go, and from this, your Secondary Factor will know, I
am, that I am.**

"What do you want?" Brian yelled above the loud static from the radio. He
clicked on the tape recorder. The Host spoke again:

**Of this, now see. From this, man will know of his fate. Man's
mind at level one, within your understanding of time, cannot
relate to the factors now shown to you.**

The Host gestured for Brian to follow. Baffled, Brian backed away and set
the tape recorder down.

The Host pushed a special button on his blinking belt and, in an instant,
Brian zoomed upward to see the beautiful blue-white earth from space. Then he
zoomed downward into the mountains of Russia. Suddenly, Brian stood on the
ground at night in a forest. He smelled fragrant pine trees, and felt cold. Dry
twigs snapped under the weight of his feet. "Where am I? How did you do that?"
The Host did not reply.

Brian breathed deep and shivered. His warm breath steamed in the cold air.

He heard a dog bark, and glanced to see a small home. A big family inside
the cottage ate dinner by lantern light, laughing and talking in Russian. Brian
snapped a twig in his hands and listened to the wood crack. It was real. He
decided to walk towards them. At least they might let him get warm.

Suddenly, the earth rumbled. The ground shook. Rocks blasted into the sky
as red flames shot out of the ground. Trees split into pieces and toppled over,
crashing to the earth. As the family of peasant farmers ran out of the house in
terror, the ground exploded, consuming their house in flames.

Brian scrambled into rocks for cover. Squealing with terror, animals raced
past him: deer and elk and rabbits. Several deer on fire jumped into each other
trying to extinguish flames, and then died in anguish. Near them, Brian saw a
snake on fire, writhing in agony.

Then he came upon the family from the house, on fire. Scorched and
blackened, a small boy called to Brian for help as he died. Brian could do
nothing.

Brian choked with sorrow. "Oh, God. This is horrible."

He ran to the road among dozens of families stumbling out of the forest,
crying in anguish and sorrow.

In shock, Brian gazed long and carefully at the scene. "Good Lord," he
breathed. "What are you doing?" he cried out to the Host.

Suddenly, with a high-pitched electronic squeal, he shot up into the night
sky. Again, he saw the blue earth, and then zoomed downward towards North
America and into southern California. Suddenly back in the garage, he lurched
and fell against the drafting table.

The Host stood silently beside the Captain America truck as Brian gulped air and struggled to stand.

"Of this, a projection --of I."

Brian inhaled deeply. "Was that real? Was that happening?"

The Host raised his hand calmly, and nodded for Brian to be patient. When Brian calmed, the Host spoke.

Nuclear chain reaction. Nuclear material, storage of waste. Underground explosion. Russia. Ural Mountains. Russia.

Brian didn't understand. "What do you want me to do about it?" The Host didn't answer. "What am I supposed to do?" Brian shouted.

The Old Man gestured at the drafting table and spoke rapidly.

Of the past, this explosion, and of the future of man, let man now understand the request of I. Seek of this. Seek of this— past of man—and know your future.

Brian glanced at the tape recorder. The red light blinked. The Host continued:

Of this, of non-compliance by man, the fate by that of the Secondary World is now upon you. Be strong in this. Fear not, for you are of I. Fear not the negative Secondary World--YOU are of I, and protection is given. Fear not the mind of man, for by this, you will gain understanding, and by this, you will become a light unto your world. For you, Brian, will come to know the mind of all mankind. And by this, through I, by you, the truth will be known to all."

"What?" Brian shouted. "What am I supposed to do?"

The Host spoke again:

Of this, man will know: I am, that I am. The factors shown to you, of Nous 10, are not known by man at this time. Your knowledge, in rapport of Nous 10, will mark the mind of all mankind. And, of this mark, mankind will know I am, and that you are one with I. Fear not, for in rapport of Nous 10, you are truly one with I.

Then the Host gestured to the drafting table. Brian saw several drawings.

"Where did the drawings come from?" Brian snapped. He grabbed them and glared at the Old Man, angrily. "Where did these drawings come from? Did I do this or did you?"

"Fear not. You and I, are one," the Old Man said. He didn't smile. Though his face was pleasant, his expression remained firm, business-like.

"Are you doing these, or am I?" Brian screamed.

"You and I are ONE at Nous ten," he said firmly. The Old Man touched his belt and condensed into a purple light. The static on the radio escalated to a screech as the light shot upward out of the garage doorway.

Brian ran outside and watched the globe soar into the night sky. The radio instantly returned to normal. Music blared. "Damn it, he did it again," Brian muttered. "He didn't answer MY questions."

The Investigator's Response

Early the next morning, Saturday November 1, Mary Beth vacuumed the carpet and Ginger straightened up the laundry in a small room off the kitchen.

Sunlight streamed in through the big bay window. Two white couches glowed brightly against the golden yellow carpet. The mahogany-cased TV sat quietly next to a big piano Mary Beth hoped to play--someday.

Outside, in the lush backyard, yellowed leaves dropped from the trees and lay in piles on the ground. Brian had been raking. On the patio, dozens of green and flowered plants hung in the shade, all nurtured and watered by Brian. As he pruned the plants, Brian raved on the phone to Professor Butler. "If the meteorite didn't convince you, this will--I am sure of it. I got him on tape."

Brian excitedly hung up the phone and turned to Mary Beth. "He'll check it out--this is it."

"If a meteorite didn't work, a tape won't prove anything to them," she said.

"It will if there is an explosion in Russia. It could get Hynek to go down there."

Mary Beth shrugged. "I would still have to see something with my own eyes." She curled her long blond hair and pointed at her nose. "Right here."

Later on Saturday, Brian flipped channels on television. After President Ford appeared on a report, Presidential candidate Jimmy Carter addressed a crowd. "This is unreal," Brian said. "Jimmy Carter is running for President and he reported seeing a UFO. Jerry Ford is President and he is the one who started the Congressional investigation into UFO's. Which ever one wins, they both know about UFO's."

"How do you know?" Mary Beth asked.

"It was Hynek who gave the "Swamp Gas" label to UFO's in Ford's district. That made Ford so mad, he called a congressional hearing."

"How do you know about this stuff? UFO's?"

"They talked about it at that meeting in Hollywood. There were important people there," Brian said. "I met them. Little ole' me."

Mary Beth jumped on Brian. "Little *old* you," she laughed cuddling with him.

Later that afternoon, Professor Butler and Dr. Stuart talked in a quiet coffee shop. "Brian is becoming very unstable," said Butler as he scratched his long thin nose. "He insists that the Host has shown up in his garage, and he tape recorded his voice." He inserted the tape into a portable player and let Dr. Stuart listen to the static and Brian's shouting.

"That's the Host?" the doctor laughed. "That's static."

"Brian insists you can hear beeps when the Host talks."

"I don't like the way this is going," said Dr. Stuart rubbing his thick brow. "He could be having a psychotic break, caused by hypnosis."

As the tape played, Dr. Stuart rubbed his thick eyebrows.

"Damn it! I wish this had stayed simple," groaned Dr. Stuart. " I liked this at the early stage. One UFO contact. One medical examination. That made sense to me. That was all I needed. We could go with that. But two contacts, three contacts. That bothers me. Now we have the Host making requests, balls of fire in the sky, and an explosion in the Ural Mountains of Russia! Good God. What's next?" He eyed the professor carefully. "Wayne. It's too much. It's getting to me. It's expanding. That's the problem."

The professor agreed. "There are no news reports of an explosion in Russia. The reference librarian at the university came up with nothing."

"He's teasing us. That makes me mad. How much would it cost to go to South America?"

"I figure twelve-hundred, maybe two-thousand per person," said the professor. "I can't put it up. I've got kids in college."

"Right. No money," said the doctor slapping the table. "No money."

"Our goal has got to be firm. Hypnosis--only," Stuart declared.

"Right," said the professor. "Our organization won't back a guy like this anyway. The other UFO organizations would rip us apart. We have to *build* credibility for our organization."

"Right," said the doctor rubbing his thick balding forehead. "He's not a scientist, a scholar, a police officer or a pilot. He's just a common Joe—a common man."

The doctor turned off the tape player and picked up Brian's handwritten note. "Still, the hypnosis is so real. And, I just can't believe this is Brian Scott, talking." He read from Brian's note.

"Of this, I am, I am, from time, beyond all time. Of the past, and of the future of man, let man now understand the request of I. Of this, the factor of time, of this, will mark the mind of all mankind."

"*Mark the mind of all mankind.* You're right," said the professor. It's not Brian--as we know him. But, what if he is like Edgar Cayce, the sleeping prophet? Or, it could be a multiple personality case."

The burly doctor breathed deep and exhaled. "Wayne, I think we are already in way over our heads."

Neither man could possibly know that facts about an underground nuclear explosion in Russia had been successfully hidden from the western world for decades by America's Central Intelligence Agency. Nor could they know that in November of 1976—a year later--a top Soviet scientist would reveal the truth, off-handedly, in a British magazine article. Nor could they know that the scientist would be attacked by the CIA and labeled a fraud in the international press. Or, that the bold, highly-regarded geneticist would openly confront the CIA three years later in a 1979 book that would reveal the horrible details, and prove the purposeful CIA suppression. The facts had been hidden from America and Europe—on purpose. How could either man understand what The Host had shown Brian? More than 25,000 Russians had been irradiated, and at least 8,000 burned to death or died in some horrible way because of an underground nuclear waste catastrophe at the Mayak nuclear complex in the Ural Mountains of Russia. Animals by the thousands had died also, and plants—all irradiated by nuclear waste—and impacted genetically. The genetic impacts had been the focus of studies by geneticists and nuclear scientists in Russia. All reports had been supressed in Europe and America.

The Ball of Light Returns

Late that same evening, Saturday November 1, as Brian and Mary Beth watched television, Iggi, their nervous little bulldog, began yipping to go out.

Brian opened the kitchen door. The dog stopped, pointed like a hunting dog and trembled. In the driveway, near the garage, an orange ball-of-light hovered about seven feet above the cement. Brian gasped and began to shake with fear. The light beeped electronically then moved slowly towards the back yard.

Brian picked up the dog and held him. As Brian stood there petting the dog, he remembered the first time he had seen the orange ball-of-light. On his sixteenth birthday, after a late night party, he had run home. He planned to sneak into the house, but his dog barked wildly in the backyard. Brian hurried to calm the dog and then saw the orange ball of light – just hovering, as if waiting for him.

As the dog barked, the light had rushed forward to him and stopped in front of his face for a moment, beeping. He watched the undulating edges, and deep orange core as the light beeped sporadically.

In a moment of blacking out, like in a daydream, Brian had seen images of himself traveling with his mother on a big ocean-going ship. Then the orange orb soared up into the night sky.

The painful spider tattoo on his arm was created later that night, and about two months later, the tattoo of a prowling black jaguar had appeared on his left forearm, in the same way—after a trance. Embarrassed by the tattoos, he had hid them from his mom for a long time with long sleeve shirts. Brian never talked about them, but the vision gave him courage to quit school. He followed his mom onboard a cruise line for nearly a year. While she worked as a waitress on the Captain's table, he had worked in the kitchen, washing dishes and eventually decorating cakes. On the ship, he began to learn about life in the real world.

"What's wrong with Iggi?" Mary Beth asked shaking him from the reverie. Brian glanced out the big bay window. The orange-red light still hovered in the yard. "Look at that."

"What is it?" Mary Beth gasped.

For a moment, Brian said nothing. He felt great comfort in knowing someone else saw it with him. "It's the same thing I saw when I was sixteen," Brian said. In a way, he was happy. Now, as an adult, he knew for sure it was not made by man.

"What does it want?" she screamed.

"I don't know," he said calmly. "It's been here about ten minutes."

"What is it doing?" Mary Beth's voice trembled with fear.

"It's a light. That's all I know. This is how it all started—when I was sixteen."

"Whose light, Brian?" Mary Beth trembled.

"It's theirs," he said with a smile. He pointed upwards.

"THEIRS? God damn it, Brian!" Mary Beth screamed for Patti to wake up in the guest room. She often stayed on weekends to replace Ginger. The dog started yipping and Brian turned him loose as Patti ran out in her nightgown. "My God," she gasped. "WHAT IS THAT?"

"I saw one like that when I was sixteen," Brian said. "It didn't hurt me."

"It's ALIEN," Mary Beth screamed, rushing into the girls' bedroom. She bundled up the two babies.

"That is a DEMON," Patti screamed. She began to pray to Jesus.

"No, it's not," Brian said. "It's just a light. It beeps."

Mary Beth became more upset as Patti prayed. "Jesus save us. Jesus protect us from this demon."

Frustrated with their fears, Brian started for the door. "I'm going outside," he said.

"You are NOT leaving us," Mary Beth ordered. She clutched him tightly, "STAY HERE—with US." Brian tried to pull away, but Mary Beth pulled him down to the floor. The two women and the children hid behind the bed with Brian reluctantly sheltering them.

Brian Calls for Help

Early Sunday morning, November 2, Brian called the professor and told him about the Ball of Light. When Butler refused to come over for a visit, Brian pleaded. Finally, Butler stood firm. "It sounds too psychic," he said. "We are sticking to the hypnosis—hypnosis only."

"What are we to do?" Brian said. "My wife is terrified."

"I don't know Brian, but we have to stick to our specialty," Butler said.

Brian slammed the phone down, and in a rage called other investigators whom he had met at the reception for Dr. Hynek. He spent most of the day on the phone, calling long distance all across America.

Hours later, as evening approached, Mary Beth began falling apart. She had listened to his pleas for help all day, and he had received no real support. NO one cared enough to come over. No one even cared about protecting the CHILDREN.

In the bathroom, Mary Beth looked at herself in the mirror, lit a cigarette and began to shake nervously. She fumbled in the medicine closet looking for some old tranquilizers as she listened. She found a bottle and tossed down two capsules of Valium just as Brian shouted. "Hey! MARY BETH."

Brian cheered with joy. He had linked up with a UFO investigator who knew about orange spheres of light. "He says other people have seen orange lights," Brian danced around. "He says it's *not unusual.* And, he's in San Diego, only two hours away."

An Old Friend Arrives

Two days later, on Tuesday, November 4, Mary Beth's girlfriend arrived from Missouri for a visit. Kate Miller was a blond like Mary Beth, with big green eyes, and a soft, southern drawl. She was born into a family of Army officers and served in Vietnam as an army nurse. She could be sweet as sugar, or commanding as a general. Mary Beth and Kate stood about the same height, but Kate carried thirty pounds more muscle. She had recently filed divorce proceedings against her husband, a Marine who had become abusive. Mary Beth invited her to stay in the house for a few days during the procedures. She needed a friend—a lifesaver.

When Brian arrived home from work, they all celebrated. "Did Mary Beth tell you about the ball-of-light?" Brian asked.

"Yes she did," Kate frowned. "And I don't want to hear any more about it, Brian. If I see it, I see it. That's the way it has to be. I don't want to be influenced in any way," she placed a consoling arm around Mary Beth. "Let's talk about something else, Brian," Kate ordered. "No more stories." Mary Beth felt much better. Kate was in command.

Kate 's Proof

Later, as Kate and Mary Beth danced to loud disco music and prepared dinner in the kitchen, Brian slipped outside.

"Disco drove him out of the house," Kate whispered.

"It's my cooking," said Mary Beth. "I can never get anything right for his tastes."

"Mr. Picky," laughed Kate.

An instant later, the door banged open. Iggi the dog skidded into the kitchen with tail tucked between his quivering legs. Brian followed, slowly, his face white with fear.

"It's back."

Through the big bay windows, they all saw a glowing orange sphere, partially hidden by a branch and leaves.

"Let's go in the bedroom," gasped Mary Beth. She pushed Kate down the hallway in a flurry. Brian followed. They all squeezed together. The light didn't move. "I've never seen anything like that in all my life," whispered Kate. "It's so bright--yet..."

"It's not lighting up anything," breathed Mary Beth. "Oh, God. Patti isn't here. She prayed last time and it went away." Kate eyed Mary Beth with concern. She believed in God and eternal life, but she didn't think praying helped much in a battle. She had seen too many men die on a stretcher while praying to live.

"It's beeping!" Brian said. "Listen!" They strained to hear a soft high frequency, electronic tone.

"I've got to see this up close, Brian," Kate said grabbing Brian's arms. "Let's go!"

"No!" screamed Mary Beth.

"I want to go out there," Kate explained in a soft, commanding tone. "You stay here with the kids." Then Kate shoved Brian into the living room.

"Let's check this out. We are going to make sure this is for real, and not one of your tricks."

Moments later, Kate pushed Brian down the steps and into the driveway. He twisted away from her shoves. "Kate," he said, frightened. "I have to tell you this, I don't know what it is. Really, I don't."

74

"I know you Brian," she said pushing him hard. "And your damn practical jokes: taking lids off salt and pepper shakers and ketchup. Just like a little kid."

"That's far enough," Brian said spinning loose.

Kate could see the sphere in the tree among yellowed leaves. No wires hung the glowing orb in place, no branches provided support and no power cord delivered electricity, yet the edges of the orange orb undulated like an electrical field. Kate carefully studied the translucent edges. Light emanated outward from the deep red core becoming more orange and yellow towards the edge. Suddenly frightened, she reached for Brian's hand like a little girl. "You couldn't fake that," she whispered. "It's so bright, it should be lighting up this whole yard."

She walked closer. "Is it alien?"

"Yep, I think so. But I don't know whose it is. I met two groups. One is fed up with man, the other is trying to save us." She felt suddenly cold, and filled with fear. Just then, a breeze blew and a branch fell onto the concrete driveway behind them. Terrified, they both bolted for the door.

Inside, they slammed the door hard. "Lock this damn thing," Kate ordered.

Brian reached his arms around her and locked the door. The two remained embraced momentarily, breathing heavily.

"So, you saw it," Mary Beth said with a raw voice. Kate pushed Brian away and shoved herself into the kitchen.

"It's not made by man," Kate said, trembling.

Vance Dewey Arrives

Brian rummaged around and found his old quick-draw holster and some 45-caliber bullets. " This is all I have left." He held up the empty holster.

"It's a light, Brian," Kate laughed. "What could you do? Shoot it?"

"Well, yes. I'd like to hit it, and see what happens."

Mary Beth grabbed a long carving knife from a kitchen drawer and held it up. "Anything gets close to me or my kids..." The baby girls, on the couch, started to cry.

"This is going too far," Kate said. "For God's sake." She removed the knife from Mary Beth's hand. "Listen, you guys are going to have to be rational about this. You need procedures that are logical."

Brian called the San Diego investigator who knew about orange lights. Kate liked seeing Brian in front of his big sailing ship. He looked strong, handsome and commanding in his sky blue velour shirt, tight blue jeans and round-toed boots.

"He is coming," Brian said hanging up the phone. "He's from the Navy Electronics Laboratory in San Diego."

"Let's get this place cleaned up," Kate commanded. "He's an officer for sure."

75

About ninety minutes later, Brian finished polishing the furniture with lemon wax, and he started walking into the kitchen. He jumped backwards and shouted. "It's in here!" Both women ran to see. A small red sphere, about the size of a tennis ball, hovered above the laundry basket on top of the dryer. The room smelled like rotten eggs.

Mary Beth grabbed Brian. "Oh, God. It's inside. Smell it."

"It's not as bright as the orange one," Kate noted. "And smaller."

Brian glanced quickly at the TV screen to see static. "Look, it's making static," he whispered.

They all noted the TV static. Mary Beth tried to be brave. "I want to see something," she said flicking off the kitchen light. At that instant, a loud gong sounded above their heads. Brian and Kate jumped backward knocking Mary Beth to the floor. They all stumbled and fell into the living room. As Brian sprawled over a big foot stool, Mary Beth and Kate fell on top, and they all landed in a pile, groaning.

Again, the doorbell chimed.

"It's the doorbell, you fools," Mary Beth laughed in embarrassment. She ran to the front door as Kate and Brian untangled.

Four men waited as the door opened. "It was just here," shouted Mary Beth. "In the kitchen!" Three men followed her into the kitchen with Geiger counters.

Laughing, Kate pulled Brian up to his feet. "Try to look important, Brian."

"We were so scared we fell all over ourselves," Brian apologize to a tall, balding, golden-skinned man who waited patiently to shake hands.

"I'm Vance Dewey," he said warmly. "Are you okay?" Brian liked Vance immediately. He seemed fatherly—and in command.

For an hour or so, the men measured radiations in the house and the yard with Geiger counters and another device for alpha and gamma waves. Vance Dewey decided to place a magnetometer in the yard to measure the Ball of Light's magnetic emissions. Around 1:30 a.m. a van arrived. Technicians installed a magnetometer on the back patio.

Vance demonstrated the device for Brian, and an alarm rang loudly. "That will keep the neighbors happy," laughed Brian.

For the next few hours, everyone asked Brian questions. Around 4:00 a.m., Vance wondered about the spider on the Nazca Plain. Brian started to explain that the spider on his arm somehow matched the spider on the Nazca Plain, but his body stopped moving and his eyes rolled upward.

"Brian," Vance shouted with alarm. Brian's left hand jerked trying to write on paper with a pencil. His face turned chalky gray and stiff with his jaw taut--like a rock.

Mary Beth panicked when she saw Brian. She screamed. His body convulsed with short, violent jerks. As he turned to her, his face remained rock-solid and his chair pounded against the floor. Saliva drooled out on his chin as he tried to speak. The men all drew back, terrified.

"Oh, God. BRIAN!" Mary Beth screamed at Vance, "Help him. That's not my husband."

Suddenly, Brian slumped forward onto the drafting table. Vance placed his hands onto Brian's shoulders and whispered a prayer. Brian suddenly lifted his head—and seemed normal.

"What do you want?" he snapped at Mary Beth, irritated. "Why are you screaming?"

"What are you doing?" Mary Beth screamed.

"I don't know. What are you doing?" he hollered. "Why are you shouting?"

Then he looked around at the men. "What happened?" he gasped in fear. "Is it here?" He looked terrified.

In the confusion, Kate assumed command. "You were writing, Brian. That's all."

"I don't get it," said one of the men, a bearded physicist who worked closely with Vance. "What just happened?" He looked at Vance for an answer.

Holding Mary Beth in her arms, Kate spoke first. "I've only been here a few days, but it looks like Brian does these writings, then denies doing them. I don't think he knows what he is doing."

"How could I be doing something that I don't know I am doing?" Brian said. "How can that be?"

Vance moved forward and put both hands on Brian's shoulders. "This has happened to a lot of UFO contactees," he said gently. "Trances and writings. It's not talked about, but it happens," he shook Brian warmly. He paused to glance at the writing. "It's the most baffling part of the whole phenomenon," he nodded. "Like Dr. Hynek said, '*It's physical and psychic—both.*' That's the part we don't understand."

"Well, I sure as hell don't want something like that happening to me," Brian said. "I am me, and I don't want anything else going on."

Vance agreed. "Let's not worry about it now. We've all got to be at work tomorrow." He gestured for his men to pack up and leave.

"Wait. It's important to me," Brian countered. "I can't have that kind of stuff happening. This seems confusing as hell. Couldn't this be dangerous?"

"You're YOU now. That's the most important thing," Vance said patting Brian.

"I guess I am," Brian laughed. "I don't think I am anybody else."

77

Vance's Goodbye

At dawn, as birds sang and the street glistened with the rosy light of dawn, Vance and Brian walked outside, alone. "I want to really thank you for coming up," said Brian. "We could have never made it through this night." His voice trembled.

"It's okay," said Vance. "I've raised five kids," he whispered. "You can share anything with me."

"I'm scared. I don't want my wife to know how scared I am getting over this. At first, I wasn't, but now—I am."

"Brian, you're in a tough spot. Billy Graham just brought out a book about angels and UFO's--good angels and bad angels. Graham says they are manifesting around the world as UFO's and aliens--good and bad."

"Geez. Everyone is getting into the act," Brian chuckled.

"Brian. I don't know if he's right, but I can tell you I've never heard of a civilian contactee being seriously injured. Not killed--if you have that concern."

"Is that what I am?"

"What's that?"

"A contactee?"

"That's what they call them. Yes. It looks to me like you are a UFO contactee, a *civilian* contactee."

Brian smirked. "I'm glad to finally know."

Vance hugged him. "It'll be all right."

When the van and two cars pulled away, the first rays of sunrise painted the street a golden pink. Standing near his Captain American truck at the curb, Brian felt good as Mary Beth joined him.

"I'm a UFO contactee," Brian laughed. "That's what he called me." Brian looked in the mirror and straightened his hair. "Captain America is now a UFO contactee." He entertained Mary Beth pretending to race. "Captain America coming up on the inside, fighting for a checkered flag."

"Is this a race?" laughed Mary Beth as she hugged him. "With who?"

"I don't know what it is. But, I *never* start something I don't FINISH. Whatever it is, I want to do it, and put it *behind* me—in the dust."

Countdown to November 21

Each day, starting November 1, a short writing appeared in the den on a notepad. It was a strange number that changed daily. Ginger analyzed the numbers with help from her dad and one of the writings that provided a comparative. It showed how a math system called "base 3 or *trinary"* counted from 1-26. The same trinary code had been related to the English alphabet from the beginning, spelling out NOUS LAOS HIKANO.

This was different. The numbers counted, backwards, downward by one each day, like a clock ticking. Ginger figured the zero date would be November 21.

The Mother-In-Law Visits

On Wednesday morning, November 5, Kate and Mary Beth worked in the kitchen preparing an ornate dinner for Mary Beth's mom. Mary Beth wanted to put all the rebellion of her younger years away and make friends with her mom. This dinner was to be her peace offering, and she needed Kate's help.

As they cleaned house, each police car or ambulance on the street kicked off the magnetometer alarm all day long. Kate called Brian at work, and he told her to turn off the device.

Around 5:00 p.m., Brian arrived home with a bag of electronic wires and old tape recorders. Vance had told him to record everything on sound tape until he could recalibrate the magnetometer. So Brian was going to set up microphones.

Kate gently guided Brian outside the house. "Why don't you try to cool it while your mother-in-law is here?" she whispered. "This dinner is very important to your wife."

"Oh, we are only being invaded by aliens," Brian cracked.

Mrs. Parsons arrived in a burgundy suit and high heels. Ginger also dressed up in high heels looking elegant. As Mary Beth changed clothes, Brian asked Kate to listen for a sound in the fruit tree. She protested, but agreed just to keep Brian out of the house.

In the fruit tree, where she had seen the ball-of-light, she heard a soft low frequency hum. Still suspicious of Brian, she wanted to shake the leaves to see if she might find something--like a tape recorder. They hurried to the garage for a rake. In the garage, when she lifted the rake, she heard a louder, low frequency hum. The vibration penetrated her body and mind. She felt dizzy and for a few moments, blacked out.

All she knew is that she couldn't let go of the rake for a very long time. When she did, she stumbled into the driveway and crumpled to the concrete with a groan. Ginger and Mrs. Parsons ran out of the house screaming. Ginger jumped off the porch in her long gown, but Mrs. Parsons stumbled over the magnetometer in her high-heeled shoes, and crashed down the steps tearing her dress and twisting her knee. She cried out in pain as blood flowed onto her gown.

Ginger and Mary Beth tried to help their moaning mother, but Kate woke up and bandaged the abrasion for them. The gown was ruined.

79

Minutes later, wearing the torn dress and seething with anger, Mrs. Parsons limped into the garage to investigate Brian's sounds. Inside, she saw long dangling wires and microphones hanging in the rafters.

"What's going on?" she demanded.

Brian started to explain about how he had tried to record the Host, but the result had been static. Just as Mrs. Parsons began to feel frightened, Brian's voice blared out of the speakers: "Testing, testing one, two, three." That was enough to frighten everyone. They bolted for the door.

"This whole thing looks like a rig job," Mrs. Parsons raged. "Are you doing this to frighten my girls?"

"No," Brian cracked. "Why the hell would I do that?"

"It looks like a damn hoax," she screamed. "You've got speakers and sounds and wires--all you need."

"This better not be one of your dumb-ass tricks, Brian," snapped Mary Beth.

Brian blew up. "I was setting up to record. I had the recorder on pause." Frustrated, Brian tried to show everyone the test tape, but it stuck in the old recorder. He ripped it out and in a fury, smashed the recorder on his drafting table. As pieces flew, the ladies ran to the house terrified by his rage.

Mrs. Parsons refused to stay for her dinner.

In the kitchen, Mary Beth confronted Brian, crying. "If you are tricking us, I will divorce your ass," she screamed. When he tried to explain, Mary Beth hit and kicked at him like a wild animal. "All we have talked about since Kate got here is your goddamn lights. Now you have ruined my dinner!" she cried in agony.

"I didn't do anything." Brian pleaded. "I couldn't do that to Kate."

"Who knows what you can do?" Mary Beth screamed. She picked up a long butcher knife and waved it at Brian. "You just ruined the whole night for everyone. You bastard." She swung at Brian, but Kate jumped at Mary Beth and wrestled the knife from her hand.

Brian slammed out the door terrified by his own wife. Worse, he was late for his next hypnosis session.

Brian Gets Clarified

Inside the doctor's office, after the cameraman started the videotape, Dr. Stuart called Mary Beth to get the full story. As the videotape rolled, Dr. Stuart rubbed his thick eyebrows and clicked on the speakerphone so Brian and the long-nosed professor could hear.

Mary Beth spoke excitedly. "We heard a tape recorder in the garage saying, 'Testing, one-two-three.'" Feeling betrayed, Brian groaned in misery.

Suspicious of a fraud, the doctor asked questions. "As far as you're concerned is it real, or...?"

Mary Beth interrupted. "What I seen last night in the den was too much. It petrified me to see him like that. When I first walked up to him there was no response. Nothing. He was drawing with his left hand, and his face was like a rock."

Confused, Dr. Stuart asked her to explain.

"The other thing is, he wasn't looking at the paper and yet it was precise writing."

The doctor turned to Brian for an answer. "I don't know anything about it," Brian said. "Something happened. This isn't about the fight."

Mary Beth continued. "Once he had this seizure, he kind of collapsed, like his body let loose. Then he sat back up in his chair. He was all right, then."

"Did you ask him what happened?"

"He doesn't even know that he did it," Mary Beth said. "He doesn't remember. We are the ones who told him what he did. You see, this is what's really bothering me."

Dr. Stuart eyed Brian. He just shrugged. "Something happened."

The doctor talked to Mary Beth for a while and promised answers. After hanging up, he accused Brian of rigging up the wires and, perhaps even faking the orange lights.

"Some rig job," Brian seethed. "All that comes out of the tape is, *'Testing, one two three.'* Pretty damn fakey! Fakey as *hell*! My grandma could do a better job."

The lanky, long-nosed Professor listened skeptically. "It doesn't sound good, Brian." He clicked a pen nervously. The videotape rolled and recorded everything. Finally, the burly hypnotist asked Brian to sit down on the couch. "Let's get some answers," he commanded.

Brian refused. "No. I ain't going to do nothing until I get MYSELF clarified," Brian shouted. "I have questions. I need answers, too. If I am going to give you good answers, I need answers for MYSELF."

"Okay Brian," moaned Dr. Stuart. "What kind of questions do you want to get answered?"

Brian lit up a cigarette and spoke slowly. "It really bothers me about this time loss," he said. "I need some help with this. How could I do something that I don't know about? I don't even remember starting that writing in the den. How could I do that?" He gestured to the room. "Do they transmit to us in this room? How do they monitor me? Or, is this stuff actually coming out of me. If so, how does it work? And if they can do that, why do they need the damn lights that are scaring

81

my wife? The lights are messing up everything, you know. Besides, how can they read our minds, transfer thoughts from a machine to my mind? Isn't that impossible? And if so, why are they doing this? Why to me, instead of you, or you?" He pointed at each man in turn.

Finally, he relaxed. "We just had one hell of a fight," Brian admitted. "My mother-in-law was there. Her girlfriend was there from Missouri--Kate. It was a knock-down drag-out fight, fellahs. That's the way it was. I over-reacted. My wife is getting very emotional about all this, too. I'm not doing so well, either. We need some real help, I think. And until I get some of my questions answered--so I can be certain about my self and what the hell I am doing in all this--how can I give you answers?" He exhaled. "I just think this is all a waste of time."

"It's not wasted time, Brian," the doctor gently commanded as he rubbed his thick brow. "We don't have all the answers. And, I don't think *you* feel you have all the answers. Do you?"

"No. I just feel helpless," Brian said. "And pathetic."

The doctor gestured for Brian to sit down on the soft leather coach. He held up his ornate gold watch. "We are here to help," he said. "Let's get some answers."

Brian relaxed and lay down on the warm, leather couch. "But I don't see how this will help." He moaned. "I feel just like a drowning man, grasping at a straw." he said. "I need a rope. I need *real* help."

Ginger Sees and Hears

The next day, before Kate departed for Missouri, she typed out a full page of notes giving dates, times and a description of all that she had witnessed. She hugged Mary Beth and said she wished they could live closer together.

Later, when Ginger arrived to baby-sit, she filed the statement in the swollen folder. That evening, November 7, Mary Beth slept on the couch under a blanket as Ginger and Brian watched television. Suddenly, Brian noticed static. He crawled forward to check the TV. As Ginger bounced into the kitchen for a soda, she screamed. A large orange sphere hovered above the dryer. The light pulsed with a soft, high-pitched electronic tone. Brian ran to her side. Ginger clawed at him. "Oh, God. It's real," she screamed.

Brian tried to pry her loose and get a tape recorder. "No way, Brian! You are not leaving me," Ginger dug into him. The light beeped softly, again.

"God!" Ginger gasped. "Is it talking to us?"

"It might be." Brian glanced at Mary Beth still asleep on the couch. He wondered how she could sleep through the screams.

"This is scary, Brian!" Ginger wrapped around him.

"It's okay," Brian said. "Other UFO contactees have them. It's a normal thing, Vance Dewey said."

"Normal! You need to call him. Now!"

Brian shrugged. "Why? It'll be gone when they get here." Since the magnetometer had been turned off, Brian wanted to record the electronic beeps with a tape recorder. He again tried to pry loose, but Ginger pulled him into the living room.

"Brian--I've got to sit down," Ginger said. "I feel sick." She hobbled to the couch with Brian's help. "Does it hear us?" she whispered. A velvety tone pulsed in the air above them. Ginger jumped into Brian's arms, terrified--like a cat facing death.

"Can you talk to that thing?" she cried.

Brian pondered a moment. "Good idea." He gradually peeled her off of his arms, patted her gently, and then walked to the kitchen doorway. He stood tall like a gunfighter. "What do you want?" he growled. Ginger could see Brian, but not the light.

The light pulsed softly. "Who are you?" Brian asked. "Why are you frightening us?" No response. "Can you hear me?" The tones from the light changed. "Who are you? Which one are you? I have a right to know. This is my house, damn it."

Brian stepped forward out of Ginger's view. A moment later, she heard Brian groan.

"Brian?" Ginger screamed. "Brian? Don't play any games."

Suddenly, Brian shuffled around the corner of the French doors with the orange ball-of-light near his chest. He walked stiffly with arms down to his side.

Ginger gasped as the orange orb jerked Brian forward. He stumbled forward walking in a trance with jerky movements. Ginger stifled a scream. Mary Beth moaned but still didn't wake up.

Brian followed the orb into the den. A moment later, from the den, Ginger heard a deep voice. **"I am, that I am. From time beyond all time, I am. Of you, by this, the truth shall be known to all mankind."** She ran to the door and peeked inside. The orange orb hovered in front of Brian at chest level-- then released him. Suddenly, he fell backward and hit the wall hard. He woke up.

"How did I get here?" he screamed with fear.

"That light pulled you in here," Ginger shouted.

Brian glared at the light. "Damn it. How can I walk in here and not know it? Tell me!" The light beeped and gradually changed to the color purple. For a moment, Brian could hear several voices from the light talking among themselves. He could understand words like: *"Closed, open, transfer complete."*

Then the confusion stopped. "By you, all will be known," the Host spoke from the purple orb.

83

Ginger gasped. "It talked! My God, Jesus in heaven, please help us all." She swung around into the hallway and slid down to the floor, trembling with fear. Iggi the little bulldog whined. Ginger snatched him into her arms, and closed her eyes.

"Okay, you brought me in here. Now, what do you want?" Brian sputtered at the light in a threatening tone.

"Look to the East has come: Laos Nous Hikano. Of this, I will comply. Right forearm, reference. Of this mark, you are one with I."

Brian glanced at the spider on his right forearm. "Okay. So what does this mean?"

Suddenly, the Host emerged out of the light. He wore a silver suit and the blinking belt, just like before. His long white hair hung down to his shoulders. He held up his spider pendant, pointed at Brian's spider tattoo and at a new spider drawing on the desk. Then the Host spoke.

> **I am. I am. Of November 22, of Nazca: Time is relevant to this, of man. Of this, I will answer to he who is known to you, Hynek. Biological technology of Nous ten, given. Genetics: from deoxyribonucleic acid to cloning at Nous 4. Let he, Hynek, assemble learned men.**

Brian whined. "I can't get anyone to do that. Don't you see--I'm the wrong guy for this."

> **In this life, of you, through I, all mankind will know the truth, for by this--I will answer, step by step. Of this, I have complied ten-fold. Why will man not comply to my request?"**

"But why don't you do it?' Brian asked.

The Old Man gestured warmly to Brian. "Of this, you Brian, shall be a light to all mankind." He smiled with a knowing glance, but before Brian could ask a question, the Host absorbed back into a purple ball-of-light.

"Locked," stated a loud mechanical voice.

Then a softer, more human voice spoke from the light. "Comprehension factor 100 percent." The light zipped upward out of the room with an electronic squeal.

Brian spun around. "Ginger? Did you see that, he was right here."

Ginger lay curled up on the floor, holding the dog and crying. Brian comforted her and helped her back to the couch.

The Hypnosis of Rex

On November 12, Dr. Stuart hypnotized Brian's lanky cowboy friend, Rex Walters. The UFO organization paid for him to fly in from Phoenix, Arizona. Rex flat out said nothing had happened, but during the hypnosis, he relived seeing a light in the sky. Then all he could remember was lying on his back in a dark room.

The doctor probed, but finally stopped the hypnosis when Rex's heart rate reached a dangerously high level. "No more," Rex screamed, writhing in agony. "No more. Please, no more." The doctor stopped.

Afterwards, the professor told Brian the results were inconclusive.

After watching the tape, Brian smiled. "Rex remembers. That thing was hitting him in the head, causing pain, in his head. That's what he complained about. That's what it did to me. It hurts. I know they can do that."

But, for the UFO investigators, the session was inconclusive. Rex remembered nothing of fighting the gray hulks or even seeing the creatures. Thus, Brian's story officially lacked corroboration. Without support from another witness, or physical evidence, the story lacked much value.

The Final Hypnosis

On November 19, Brian attended his final hypnosis session. Mary Beth sat in the room awed and speechless as various voices spoke through Brian answering questions about genetics, plantations of man and alien control of zones on the earth. She couldn't believe the range of knowledge and the power of the personality which spoke through Brian.

Afterwards, Mary Beth and Brian quietly ate hamburgers at an A & W Root beer stand. "Why don't they just take you to South America?" she asked softly with new respect for Brian.

"I'm sure they could," Brian said robustly as he chomped down on a huge Papa Burger. He heard a soft electronic voice in his mind and reported the words. "Man must be involved by his own free will. What will be given is a gift for man, to be understood by man, and maintained by man. The knowledge man needs is of the past, of the people, and of the land in South America."

Brian paused. "I just heard him say that in my head. Good Lord, this is getting spooky. I can hear them talking in my mind, right now." Brian listened for a moment to several electronic voices and reported their conversation. "They are in *an over-ride situation, controlled by the others--the Secondary World.* He just told me that. They have to be careful. All communications are conditional.

Conditional." Brian laughed. "I think the hypnotist forgot to turn off the lights—or at least the sound. This is like a radio in my head."

Mary Beth giggled. "You are too much, Brian."

When they arrived home late at night, she warned Ginger. "His mind is still racing. It's like he is still hypnotized."

"What was it like?" Ginger whispered in the kitchen, as Brian shuffled into the shower.

"They are very worried he could be a prophet like Edgar Cayce or in the Bible."

"My God, Brian? No one would believe him."

"Right, but…it's not really him. Not Brian as we know him. He sounds like another person -- with a very deep voice," she imitated the voice. *"I am, I am. Of this, I am of time beyond all time. "*

Ginger laughed, then felt stunned. "That's what I heard—from the light." Her sister's imitation sounded like the light she had heard in the den. Ginger pondered for a moment. "You heard the Host speak THROUGH Brian's mouth?" she asked.

"I guess? It wasn't Brian."

"I heard it coming from the light."

"It came out of Brian," Mary Beth said. "And, he was bossy. I think he made the investigators a bit mad. Like he is talking down to them, like they was kids."

For a moment, Ginger remembered the countdown to November 21-- only two days away. "This is so unlike Brian. I mean—if anything, he's a clown. He's always goofing around."

"He wasn't joking with them. He was strong, very certain of everything, like he knew for sure exactly what he was talking about."

"This is so far out. Brian is never like that. Do you think the Host might turn our Brian into a prophet—like in the Bible?"

"No way. Not as Brian," Mary Beth said. "But if he spoke that way in public, on the streets--it could make people believe he was somebody. It is like *God* talking. He knows *everything."*

"That's so far out—our Brian."

Mary Beth whispered. "On the other hand, Brian—as we know him--is coming unglued. It's like he's splitting apart. Like split-personality. That's what it is. He's got *more than one personality."*

They both agreed and then giggled as Brian stepped out of the bathroom in his boxer shorts. He rambled at them. "If I don't come back, I want people to know that at least the Host kept *his* word. Man got lots of chances, and did nothing. And, that's the truth." The two sisters hugged each other and stifled their giggles.

The Nazca Plain

On Friday morning, November 21, at 2:10 a.m., Brian stumbled out of bed in his underwear and walked outside with a stiff gait. He stopped in the driveway. A long, warbling sound pulsed overhead and Brian woke up for a moment, startled. He turned to the house, but then a beam hit. Suddenly, his perception of the world stretched vertical, then horizontal. In a blink, he disappeared.

Around sunrise, Mary Beth woke up. "Brian is gone," she shouted at Ginger. They both jolted out of bed and raced around looking for Brian.

In the garage wearing her nightgown, Mary Beth found nine pages of writings on the drafting table. "Look at these," she said to Ginger who arrived breathing hard.

"The countdown," Ginger gasped. "November twenty-first."

"Today? Oh, no. That's right, today—21 days. But why? What does that mean?" asked Mary Beth.

"I don't know. That was the countdown—to today."

"Where the hell is he? Where is *my husband*," Mary Beth screamed appealing to the sky. "Where is my Brian?" She sobbed in agony.

"He'll be back," whispered Ginger as she hugged her sister.

"This is too much. Too much to bear," Mary Beth sobbed. Ginger rocked her crying sister, and held her.

Later that day, Garden Grove police officers searched the house and grounds without success. They even questioned the neighbors. That afternoon, Officer Joseph, badge number 190, filed a formal missing person report: Garden Grove, California police report #75-20245: November 21, 1975.

Missing Person. Victim is a white male 32 years old with brown hair, blue eyes. He stands 6 feet tall and weighs 170 lbs. Victim clad only in boxer under shorts.

Mary Elizabeth Scott awoke at approximately 0700 hours, and observed that her husband was not anywhere on the premises. Mary Elizabeth Scott stated that she proceeded to the garage area of the residence, where she came upon several drawings, apparently made by her husband (see attached). Mary Elizabeth Scott further related that she checked her husband's clothing and personal papers, wallet, driver's license, etc., and found them all to be in the residence, including the victim's checkbook and money.

87

Mary Elizabeth Scott related that her husband, Brian Scott, had been abducted in 1971, in the Arizona desert area, with an unnamed friend. Mary Elizabeth Scott stated that the abduction had been perpetrated by a "UFO" -- apparently referring to an extra-terrestrial space vehicle. Mary Elizabeth Scott stated that her husband had been in contact, since that date, on several occasions, with extra-terrestrial beings. Mary Elizabeth Scott stated that, for a ten-day period in October, of this year, her residence and yard had been infected with, what she described as "dancing orange lights." The lights were, apparently animate and possessed such functions as logic, thought processes, etc.

Mary Elizabeth Scott stated that her husband, at one point, conversed with one of the light objects, and the object took a semi-humanoid form and responded to questioning and carried on a conversation with her husband.

Mary Elizabeth Scott further evolved that her husband had been keeping a log, and at precisely 2400 hours on 11-20-75, an unknown event would take place.

Mary Elizabeth Scott stated that she felt that her husband had been abducted by extraterrestrial beings in a UFO.

Mary Elizabeth Scott stated that her husband had been interviewed by numerous prominent scientists, who had ascertained through regressive hypnosis, that the above-described events had taken place, including the prior abduction by extra-terrestrial beings.

Mary Elizabeth Scott supplied numerous drawings of spaceships, extra-terrestrial beings, etc. Mary Elizabeth Scott also supplied writings made by her husband while in a "trance" state, which apparently, reflected thoughts being placed in his head by the extra-terrestrial beings. Elizabeth Scott stated that she saw her husband in these trances on numerous occasions, and that occasionally, her husband would wander in the backyard, clad only in under shorts, in a "trance".

The officers checked the residence and noted that the victim's wallet, personal papers, checkbook, etc., had been left at the residence.

A professor Wayne Butler at California State University was contacted. He stated that he had a personal interest in the case and had interviewed the victim on numerous occasions. Dr. Butler stated that the victim's prior encounters had been, apparently, genuine, and did not believe the matter was a "hoax."

In the police station, officer Jones handed the report to his supervisor. "You might want to take a look at this," he said. "In case the newspaper gets it."

"Brian Alan Scott," the supervisor said. "He's on probation, isn't he?"

"Yeah," he had pulled Brian's record. "Little stuff. Little cons--Pizza Hut, Baskin Robbins, grocery stores for food. Possession of grass--getting in a fight. He's been clean for years, though. Made all of his payments—*at five dollars a week.* He's a success story for probation. Good attitude, they say—but a funny boy—a joker."

"Yeah. He's kind of silly. I see him all the time. Nice truck—*Captain America,*" he laughed. "If the aliens were smart, they'd take the truck and leave the clown at home."

"Maybe *they* need a few laughs." The officer chuckled. "Maybe earth is where they get their *clowns.*" They both laughed loudly.

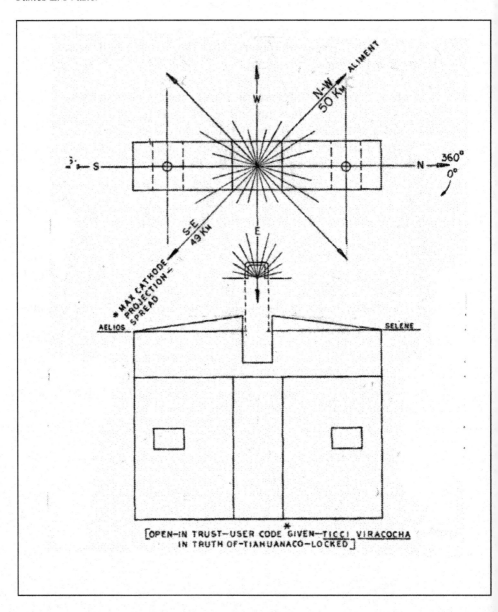

GATE OF THE SUN at Tiahuanaco

Brian's drawings show topview and sideview.

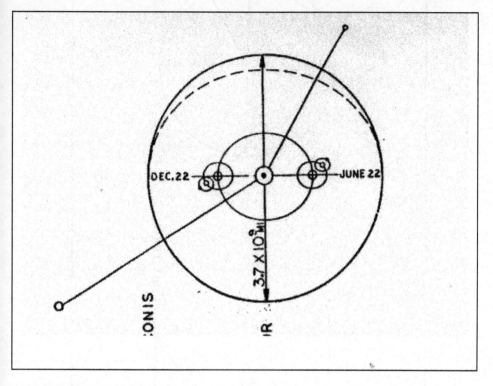

SOLAR SYSTEM – Brian's drawing which indicated an object in orbit behind the moon. The sun is in the center. Note earth, moon, object. Many people looked at this drawing, but no one asked Brian about the object for almost six months.

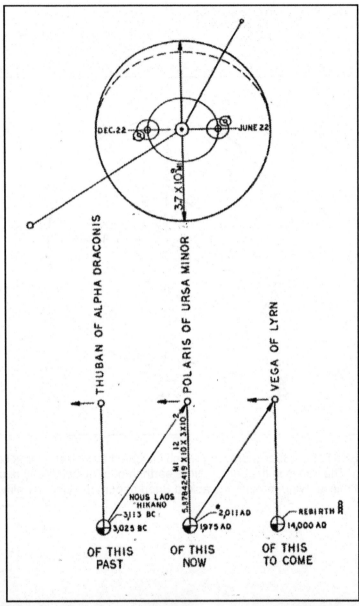

NORTH STARS -- This is a detail from one of the GATE OF SUN drawings showing the North Stars with dates of contacts. Brian's contact is compared to Quetzalcoatl of the Toltecs by date, and region of the planet. The Greek phrase *Nous Laos Hikano* apparently indicates a descent.

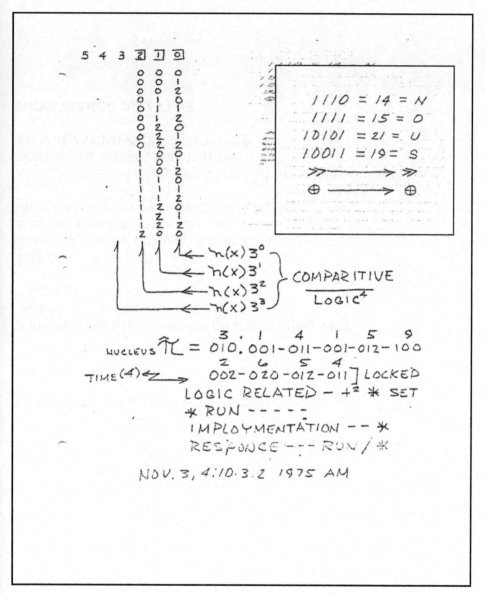

ALPHA-NUMERIC CODE -- From the beginning of Brian's writings, numbers
were related to letters in a code that used the base three system: 0-1-2.
Computers use a binary code: 0-1. Comparatives for the Base 3 system are
given using the value for *Pi*. The Greek words *Nous Laos Hikano* were the first to
be spelled out using this system.

James E. Frazier

EPILEPTIC CONVULSIONS

CONVULSIONS INDICATE DAMAGE IN THE
CENTRAL NERVOUS SYSTEM, BIOCHEMICAL
IMBALANCE OR UNCOORDINATED ELECTRICAL ACTIVITY.

BEFORE THE SEIZURE AND MUSCULAR SPASMS,
THE PERSON MIGHT EXPERIENCE FLASHES OF LIGHT,
NOISES IN THE HEAD, FOUL ODORS, VERTIGO, FEAR AND ELATION
-- EVEN HALLUCINATIONS.

IN THE SOMNAMBULISTIC TYPE,
THERE IS WALKING AND MOVEMENT,
EVEN WRITING, BUT NO MEMORY OF THE PERFORMANCE.

Abstracted from

Grolier's' New Multi-media Encyclopedia, V.6

THE SECOND REQUEST

THE KNOWLEDGE MAN NEEDS IS GIVEN OF TIAHUANACO--
NINTH DESCENT OF SECONDARY WORLD, 110 B.C.
TRANSPORTATION REQUESTED TO EXAMINE OF THIS.
FEAR NOT THE TRUTH.

I SAY, OF THIS MAN MUST UNDERSTAND
HIMSELF AND HIS OWN WORLD
BEFORE HE CAN BEGIN TO UNDERSTAND OTHERS.

--The Host

Chapter 5

The Host's Second Request

Brian woke up in a brightly lit cubicle on the rim of a craft. Next to him stood a tall gray-skinned hulk with no neck and long ears. "Fear not, for you are *one* with I," said the giant, wheezing. "Of this, of A21-- wisdom is now given."

He patted Brian on the shoulder in a comforting way. The room flashed with light and Brian found himself on the cold rocky ground of the Nazca Plain, barefooted, wearing only his boxer shorts.

He pranced around, shivering. Then he saw the first rays of sunrise. Within moments he felt heat from the sun's golden-red glow.

"Of your own will, look to the east. A21 waits you." He heard the giant's voice in his mind. Brian glanced upward and saw the huge craft wobbling overhead in the morning sky.

Brian stood in the center of the spider symbol, at zone A22. He tiptoed forward. The sharp stones hurt his bare feet. Half way down the spider leg, he turned a sharp 90 degrees and felt the bright rays of the sun on his bare chest.

Finally, he reached the end of the leg--A21. Brian slowly spun around looking to the north, the west, south and back to the rising sun.

Suddenly, he felt a vibration in the ground, and then a warm ring of energy rolled upward around his legs, his chest, shoulders and head. He felt dizzy.

Then a second ring of warmth rose upward from the ground. He breathed deep, relaxed and stretched. His skin tingled as the energy rolled up, encircling his body. He felt great.

Then a third ring of energy rose--stronger this time, and he heard deep flute music—a single flute. His thoughts and mind mellowed. He felt like warm jelly, melting.

After seven waves, the music grew louder with more flutes and strings. He loved the music.

By the time the fifteenth wave came, Brian floated in a dream. Around him, on the spider leg, he saw hundreds of people dancing to Incan music. Spinning Incan ladies wore purple dresses covered with mirrors that caught beams of sunlight. The bright light flashed into his eyes, like a golden strobe. His soul melted into the light. His mind, body and spirit twirled together as one, within the golden light and sound.

After the 21st pulse of warm energy, the sound stopped, abruptly. Brian heard nothing--silence. The images and sounds all ended. He felt like a glider, turned loose to fly. He opened his eyes to find himself standing in silence with arms uplifted to the sky--to God.

"I am, I am," whispered Brian without reason. He felt centered in his body. "I am, that I am," he repeated growing stronger. For the first time, he understood the meaning of the words. He was enough. He was everything that he needed. All was within him. All the power, all the knowledge, all the presence he needed was within him—locked in by those few words, and their meaning.

Brian heard a voice, and turned to see a dark-skinned native priest, wearing jaguar skins, green feathers and gold bracelets. Behind him, on the spider outline, stood dozens of young men of all races--brown, white, yellow and red--with their hands lifted upward to the sky, all saying in unison, "I am, that I am. I AM THAT I AM." Then Brian saw another priest, a tall, red-haired man wearing a turban and long white gown. He carried a golden staff and a black book. The priest clapped his hands. All the faces of the young men turned to Brian. They opened their arms to him with love. "Brian!" They shouted as if they had known him for years. They rushed to him with arms wide open.

For a moment, before Brian fainted, he wondered if every point on the grid carried such a potent blessing.

At home in Garden Grove, Ginger stretched and stirred from sleep on the white couch in the living room. She glanced outside through the big bay window into the backyard. She started a pot of coffee, and saw a flurry outside. Brian, bare-chested and wearing only his boxer shorts, struggled for balance, then fell to the ground.

"Brian!" Ginger raced outside and pulled him up to his feet. "What are you doing?"

He struggled and wobbled. "That stretching is too much. I don't like that. I can't even see straight."

"You better get some clothes on," she urged, escorting him into the house.

Wearing a two-day stubble beard on his face, Brian stumbled into the house in a daze, smacking his lips and patting his throat. "Drink. Dry," he pantomimed. "They never give you water." He smelled the coffee and quickly poured a cup. "Can you fix me something, Ginger?" he asked sweetly. "I am really starving." He gulped the coffee down and noticed the kitchen clock. The hands pointed at 7:25 a.m. "Damn it. I'm late! Crap!" He tossed down the coffee and stumbled into the living room stepping over people on the floor.

He gestured to Ginger. "What is going on? What are they doing here?" Cousin Patti and Mary Beth's brother Johnny had slept overnight, along with Ginger's boyfriend Todd.

In the bathroom, Brian couldn't find his wallet, keys, money, cigarettes or clothes. He always laid out everything in neat piles. "What the hell is going on?" he shouted at Ginger. "Where's my stuff?"

Everyone woke up.

"You're back!" Mary Beth shrieked. She jumped to his side and hugged him. Everyone woke up. They jumped with joy and hugged Brian with loving arms. He pulled away from them, dumbfounded. He even tried to push Mary Beth away. "I've got to go," he insisted as she covered him with a white bathrobe.

"You don't need to go, Brian," she whispered calmly.

"I've got to go to work," he grunted. "What the hell is going on?"

"You are staying home," ordered Ginger, firmly.

"I can't miss work."

"It is Saturday, Brian," Mary Beth smiled.

"It is not Saturday," Brian mumbled.

"Yes, it is."

"No it's not, Mary Beth. This is Friday. Payday! Remember. I've got to get my check."

Brian broke loose from her arms and hurried into the bathroom. Ginger waited for him to start shaving. She hoped he would notice the two-day beard. As Brian soaped up his face, he felt the stubble and glanced at Ginger.

"It's Saturday," Ginger sang.

"It's Saturday," they all shouted.

"You have been missing twenty-seven hours," Ginger said.

Brian peered at himself in the mirror. He rubbed the beard and began to breathe fast. "I can remember maybe ten minutes, maybe an hour. Then I was back."

He wobbled out of the bathroom dazed. Mary Beth guided him to the kitchen table. "Are you guys sure it is Saturday?" he whispered.

"Saturday, November 22," Ginger said. "Day twenty-two by the countdown."

The Scars of Life Removed

Later, as Brian ate two stacks of pancakes, a half-dozen eggs and a pound of bacon, the police arrived to ask questions. When they finished, the house filled with UFO investigators. As Brian told them the story, he realized that all the tiny scars on his hands and arms were missing. All of the marks from fighting, falling, and working were gone. He checked his stomach for burn scars from a teenage mishap with gasoline. He looked on his left arm for a bullet wound from a .22 caliber pistol--an accident. He looked for the bad barbed wire cut on his leg. Gone.

The investigators listened with fascination as Brian checked the scars and elaborated their causes. Most importantly, the crooked leg on his spider tattoo was gone. "Look at that," Brian said. "No more crooked leg on the spider."

"So what if they are?" asked Mary Beth. "What difference does that make, anyway?"

"I don't know," he said beaming. "It's just incredible. Why take the spider's leg?"

From that time on, the Host never requested that Brian go to the Nazca Plain. That phase of the *Play of Life* had ended. Because mankind did not participate, and did not create a team to interpret the data, the Host withheld the knowledge of genetics and cloning.

Brian gradually remembered a few things from the missing time, but not a whole day. He had been on the ship, and given a grand tour. He was told that man would not receive the knowledge because no *agreement* existed. "The wall is black again." That meant all the green lights on the outer wall of the three-ring computer had been turned off, leaving darkness. He had seen the wall turn black.

When man complied with requests from the Host and cooperated, green lights turned on, a few at a time. When man failed to comply, or lied—red lights appeared. For a direct contact, the entire wall needed to be green. It seemed like simple logic and a good plan. The purpose of their *Play of Life* was to educate man, and turn all the lights green, the boyish giant had explained. When most of the lights were green, the computer would allow a free flow of information to the people of earth. Brian had made progress, but now man had to start over. The wall was black again.

Voltar's people would never do anything to over-ride the computer, for it had been programmed with all the knowledge of their forefathers including plans for interacting with other worlds and cultures. It was like a game for children to play. The source of their education, the 3-ring computer had protected them from giving away too much information, at the wrong time, to the wrong people.

The one time they over-rode the machine with a mass vote of all the people, they had become enslaved by the dome-headed aliens from the star system Epsilon Bootees—man's Secondary World. The slavery had lasted for generations, over a thousand years. Escape had required death and sacrifice by millions of their people as they migrated to the sixth planet of seven.

The friendly giant had showed the whole story to Brian using projections of the three ring computer, and rings on the floor which moved him forward and backward in time. Brian could step on a ring and experience the past, or future probabilities on any issue, as projected within their *Play of Life.* He had enjoyed the rings of time because he could go forward or backward until he truly understood the point. Brian saw children using the rings for education.

The boyish giant also showed Brian the ninth descent at Tiahuanaco, in 110 B.C. Brian saw the temple and other beautiful buildings covered with gold and copper and silver. He saw that biological experiments were conducted at Tiahuanaco by BOTH groups of aliens. He saw them create new forms of life—alternative forms of man.

Faces of the test subjects, both men and women, looked like frogs or other amphibians. Some of the experiments resulted in bizarre and disgusting animals. Some died, and some were killed, but most looked like people—for the most part. Many had been taken off the earth to other worlds, the giant explained. "Today, your world is the nursery planet. The garden."

Brian decided not to tell the investigators anything about the Rings of Time, and what he had learned. In a way, he felt ashamed and embarrassed by what he had seen--as did the boyish giant. He had said the experiments at Tiahuanaco were the "shame of his people" and the cause of their conflict with the Secondary World.

Brian didn't understand it all so he decided to just keep his mouth shut.

He had also seen a glass room on the rim of the craft, where dozens of bright balls-of-light sat on pedestals. They received energy from their stands, like charging up a battery. The orbs were remote sensors for monitoring emotions, thoughts and the biology of man on earth. They probed everywhere, in advance, checking out any location, animal, plant or person.

That was about all Brian remembered—two hours *at the most.* That meant 24-25 hours of time were still missing. That worried him, but he figured it had something to do with the Rings of Time.

Overall, he was very happy. The tour was nice, he loved the Rings of Time, but even they didn't compare to the twenty-two pulses of energy he had received from the ground at A-21. That energy brought him more than knowledge—the joy stayed with him, the radiance shone on his face and the energy made him feel strong and fit for battle. He decided to keep quiet and just enjoy life. No one would believe him anyway.

99

The First Investigators Quit

Around noon that Saturday, the UFO investigators all drove to a Denny's restaurant for lunch. Vance Dewey listened closely to their frustrations about Brian.

"You know," said Dr. Stuart as he rubbed his thick brow. "The best thing Brian had going for him was his stupidity, if you forgive the expression--the way he speaks and writes. He can't even spell basic words right. He spells 'said' as 's-e-a-d.' That's pretty bad--third grade level." Anguished, he shuffled through the nine pages of writings found in the garage. "But I can't stomach his glibness. *Making requests of us*--that's what I don't like. He's downright demanding."

"He could have some form of reading disability--or be an idiot savant, in some form," mused Professor Butler. "The mind can do strange things." He clicked his pen and glanced at Vance Dewey. "Did you know he has a police record? It's not the worst, but we've decided he isn't a credible witness for our organization's purposes."

"Well, you know," mused Vance softly. "Maybe there is another purpose to all these contacts. I've talked to the witnesses and seen their state of mind. I feel they are telling the truth about the ball of light in the home. And, I know about the trances. That is not unusual among contactees. You can tell they are all upset. Something is happening. I'm sure of that." He paused. "You know, I heard Jacques Vallee say that UFO contactees are just common people, in uncommon situations."

"That's Brian," Dr. Stuart said. "And it's probably true, but I've had enough of this common Joe. I can't buy it. The aliens, if there are any, are playing games. I mean, making requests to US through him. It's not straight-forward and I don't like it."

The professor rubbed his long nose, took off his glasses and turned to Vance Dewey. "Even if he is for real, we can't go on forever doing hypnosis. We've got a lot of fascinating information from Brian--and *the Host*--about human plantations, the history of earth, quantum physics, even the nature of good and evil regarding this group of Secondary World aliens. But, what can we do with it? It's just talk! We can't check anything. There's nothing scientific. It's frustrating, very frustrating."

The big burly doctor stood up. "He's all yours if you want him. I've had it up to here with Mr. Brian Scott."

Vance nodded. "Okay. I'll work with him."

Brian's Real Father

The next week, Mary Beth's family invited Brian's mom, Mary Lorton, to share Thanksgiving dinner with their family—the Parsons. Brian helped serve the meal to everyone: his mom, Mary Beth, Ginger, the three stepbrothers and his two daughters.

Brian's mom, at 61, looked elegant and attractive. Comfortable with people, she talked and laughed easily with them all.

Mr. Parsons, staunch and square-jawed, wore his white hair in a short crew cut, like a military officer. An insurance underwriter, he followed world events closely. During the dinner, he led a lively discussion with his sons about the gas shortage and the Islamic Holy War against America. He talked about the Emperor of Japan, and the Emperor of Rome. "America doesn't listen to nations run by Holy men," he said. "The Japanese believed their Emperor was god, and look what happened to them."

After dinner, Mrs. Parsons whispered to Brian's mom. "Do you know Brian claims to be a UFO contactee?" she asked.

Mary laughed loudly. "I wouldn't wonder. I knew there was something different about that kid from the beginning. The doctors told me I couldn't get pregnant. But I did. Though I don't know how. Brian's father was too busy reading his damn books to even take a good look at me." She laughed. "So, I left him. I found a man who knew what to do with a woman. You know what I mean?"

Mary idolized Lucille Ball and imitated her boisterous humor.

"What about his dad?" Mr. Parsons asked.

"All he did was read books. That's all he cared about. His damn books! I nearly burned them."

"What kind of books?"

"Old books--very old books. He carried them with him all the time. Never set them down."

"Were they about some particular subject?"

"Hell, I don't know," she laughed. "I never looked at them."

"About UFO's?"

"No," she laughed. "He wasn't that weird. They were about these two fellows--famous Greeks." She finished off the glass of wine. "Plato!"

"And, Socrates?"

"Yes, that it," she laughed. "That's all he talked about. He was a photographer--very artistic--but a coward. Wouldn't fight in the war. Hell, you went! No one resisted--except MY husband. I couldn't believe it. I told him he had a yellow streak down his back a foot wide. I never said it behind his back, either. To his face!" she blurted. "That's why I left him and came out west, to get

101

a real man--and I sure did." She paused. "In a way, I believe Brian's father really did love those books more than me, more than anything--except maybe Brian. He really loved Brian."

"Does Brian know this?"

"NO! Heavens no. I think it's better that way. At least Brian is not a coward. He's a MAN." She pounded her slender fist into her palm, with pride. "At least I can say that about him--he's a real man."

The Photonic Matter Drawing

After dessert, Ginger showed her dad the drawings they had found in the garage when Brian disappeared.

"This represents photonic matter," she beamed, proudly holding up one drawing with eight lines radiating outward from a circle. "I call it the spider drawing," Ginger said. "They say it is '*living thought of the Host*.'" Brian watched from the kitchen with a wet dishtowel in hand.

Ginger's father adjusted his black-rimmed glasses and looked at the drawing. "This spider represents photonic matter?" he said. "What's photonic matter?"

Brian leaned into the living room. "It's their form of energy. It's their electricity. It moves all over the outside of their big computer, their host computer. It has three huge rings and these spiders zip all over it, expanding or shrinking down in size. It's fast--very fast."

Mary Beth's mother sat down in a nearby chair. "How do you know that Brian?" she asked.

"I saw it on the craft. It makes the air smell bad."

"See it's electrical," said Ginger, pointing at the drawing. "It has a positive and negative, but it's also aligned to the north--to magnetic north." Ginger held up a writing. "What does '*rapport*' mean, exactly?"

Ginger's mother answered calmly. "Rapport means sharing. If two people have rapport, that means they can share ideas and talk to each other—like your father and I."

Ginger held up the page. "This writing says Brian is in rapport with the Host at Nous 10. He's a liaison--a messenger, between Nous 10 and mind at Nous 1. That's what it says. I swear that's what it means."

In the kitchen, Brian laughed. "That's what I always wanted to be--a delivery boy for Western Union. You know they used to wear those little hats and ride bicycles." As Brian acted out riding a bicycle, Mary Beth jabbed him in the ribs.

"What is Nous ten?" Mr. Parsons asked.

"I have no idea," Brian groaned in pain. "It's the mind level they are at."

Ginger pointed at a writing. "It says Brian is '*one with time in rapport of Nous ten*'-- with them. These writings always talk about time."

"This is very interesting," Mr. Parsons said while stroking his wife's back. "What does it mean to you, Brian?" he asked in a grandfatherly tone.

"They can stretch time," Brian answered as he clowned around in the kitchen. "That's what they do. Only it affects your mind, somehow, and you can't remember--until they want you to. I don't know how the heck they do it. That's what I really want to know."

The Warning of World War II

"I'll tell you what," said Mr. Parsons. "You leave that folder here, and I'll take a look at it." He stood up and eyed Brian squarely. "Brian, are you in control of this thing?"

"I am not in control of anything," Brian laughed. "It's just happening."

"You get in control of it--fast." Mr. Parsons squinted at Brian. "If we didn't beat Japan, and give them the bomb, you'd all be bowing down to the Emperor, today. The Japanese believed he was God, born from the sun, and they were prepared to make you believe it, even if they died. But they were wrong--dead wrong. Do you understand me?"

"Not really," Brian said.

"The Japanese are smart people, and they were fooled. This kind of stuff, this writing--it's like that. Logical, mysterious, giving orders without explanations. Your Host is like this; he has an agenda. But you don't know what it is. He sounds to me like an emperor."

Brian pondered. "The Host?"

"Yeah--he's in charge of this, right?"

With a shrug, Brian agreed. "I guess so."

Mr. Parsons looked at everyone in the room. "The emperor of Japan was a god to his people. You know what it got them: two bombs. Even after the first one, these people were ready to follow their Holy emperor, unto death, over our dead bodies. So, we gave them a second one. Understand?"

"They thought their emperor was born out of the sun and was part God. The best thing Macarthur did after the war was make him walk in the streets. The people had to touch him, feel his clothes and see that he was just another human being, like them.

"That is what broke the Japanese people. You remember that. The Japanese weren't dumb, but they got taken down the wrong road. How? By stuff like this." He shook the folder of writings at them. "Hitler was mixed up in religious stuff too--symbols, astrology, mystical things. Remember, it all made perfectly good sense to them--and they are a smart people. Germans are smart. Orientals are very smart. But even a smart man can be fooled by this kind of stuff."

Science and Religion

On Friday after work, Brian worked on the magnetometer with Vance Dewey and a bearded physicist. Vance explained that the device was designed for an airplane or ship--in an isolated setting--not a busy street. But they made adjustments and would try again.

As the scientists departed, a VW bus arrived bearing two clean-shaven, young scholars from the University of California in Los Angeles. Calling themselves 'parapsychologists,' the two brown-eyed young men told Brian they believed some of the phenomena could be photographed with a special Kirlian camera.

In Kirlian photography, a small electrical charge is sent into a glass plate holding the object. Photographic paper captures the result, they explained. They wanted to use Brian's hand as a test object.

The researchers seemed committed to the scientific investigation of paranormal events. Lenny Jacobs and Levy Vogel dressed in conservative shirts and wore their hair short. They looked smart, stylish and Jewish. Levy had just earned a doctorate in medical psychology. Lenny, two years younger, was working on a master's degree in parapsychology under the guidance of Levy, his mentor.

They wanted to know if Brian had tried to communicate directly to the aliens. "Have you ever tried a séance?" Lenny asked.

"Are you serious?" asked Brian. "A séance?"

"We believe that communication can be established with them," Lenny said, "I've seen it done."

"Is this like talking to the dead?" Brian frowned.

"Not necessarily," Lenny breathed. "It's more like hypnosis. We have a hypnotist who is very good at it. She can help you and take you into it."

Brian invited them inside. "I'm not for talking to dead people. That's wrong, but if you want to try and reach living people, I guess it's no different than the first group."

As they talked around the table that night, Saturday, November 29th, Patti arrived carrying in her hands an ornate Jewish candelabra with eight small candles. She wanted Brian to light the candles because the eight days of Hanukkah had arrived. Brian didn't understand, but the two parapsychologists did--both being Jewish.

She explained that around 165 B.C., secular Jews wanted their nation to join up with the Greek-Syrian culture dominating them. But, the religious Jews had refused, saying the Greek-Syrians were pagan: consulting oracles, believing in idols and many different gods--instead of one God.

"By Greek command, Bibles were burned, Jewish mothers and children killed," Patti said. "That's when one man and his sons stood up to the Greeks—the Maccabees. Then the fight began. Eventually the Jews won with God's help, or else the Bible would have been destroyed in 165 B.C."

"Amazing," breathed Brian.

"It's all true," Patti blustered.

"I mean it's amazing to hear all of that coming out of you," Brian teased. "In one breath." Patti laughed and grimaced at him. "My point is Hanukkah is the time to overcome paganism in your own life, Brian. That's all I want to say. Our hippie, *'flower-power,'* *'do your own thing'* generation is filled with paganism. It is the same old Canaanite religion that the Jews fought. It's happening all over again—in America."

Brian held up the candelabra. "This is kinda like the one on the craft--the door to that computer room. It had three branches, though."

"The one from the temple has three main branches," Patti said. She dug into her big purse with excitement and handed him a book cover featuring a Menorah with three branches. Brian's version featured nine "lights" instead of seven, but otherwise the two menorahs were very similar.

As the researchers started talking with Brian about symbols on the craft, Patti departed. "Happy Hanukkah," she smiled.

Brian noticed that Patti had lost a lot of weight. "I hope she finds a boyfriend," he whispered to Mary Beth.

"A boyfriend? Why do you say that?" she laughed.

"She is getting into a lot of stuff. Heavy stuff. She might be getting too far out."

Mary Beth laughed at Brian. "She is huh? That's very good, Brian. You're a good judge of that," she teased. "You should know. Because there is nobody farther out than you."

The doorbell rang. "It's like a circus around here," Brian laughed as he opened the door. "Yes, who are you?" A serious-looking young man, with long hair and wire-frame glasses stood in the doorway.

"I'm Peter Bannock from the Lariat newspaper at Saddleback College," announced the bright-eyed reporter. "Are you Brian Scott?" He wore the serious look of a smart, upcoming reporter.

"Yes..."

"A Garden Grove police report on November 20th said you disappeared and your wife feared you were picked up by a UFO. The officer wrote about a ball-of-light turning into a semi-humanoid form and talking to you." Peter waved the police report. "Does that sound familiar?"

"I didn't know about the report," Brian said.

"Well, I would like to know more about this. Maybe a lot of our readers would too."

"Come on in," Brian laughed. "Join the circus." He shook hands. "By the way, I'm the clown." Everyone laughed again. "And these are all the zoo keepers."

As they all talked, Ginger arrived with five books of Brian's automatic writings. "Ninety pages, to date," she told the reporter. "I've spent $65 making copies in the last two days, Brian. That's more than my paycheck. I need a raise."

"I didn't know there was that many," Brian said.

"You've had fifteen since Thanksgiving that you haven't even looked at." Ginger eyed the reporter. "He never reads them. Can't understand them."

"It's the same old stuff," Brian countered.

"No. It's entirely different," Ginger said. "Now, it's all about the Secondary World." The two parapsychologists and the reporter flipped through the pages with great excitement.

"It tells where they are from. Most of it is about their 'sexual implantation of man' and this place they want you to go next in South America--a different place."

Ginger announced to them all. "They want him to go to the 'Gate of the Sun' at some place in South America. They want physical transportation to this place. There's another countdown, too: December 22. I don't know what that means. But last time, he was gone for 27 hours."

"So it's still happening?" the reporter breathed with excitement.

Ginger nodded. "It's happening." She pointed at the pages. "Just read the dashes as commas. Fill in a few words. The Secondary World is the bad guy--the aliens with big, domed heads."

The reporter and the researchers talked with Brian until the early morning hours. Brian tried to answer all their questions, but mostly he couldn't--so he laughed and made jokes about his bizarre situation.

Paying the Dues

The next evening, Brian and Mary Beth worked together on family finances. They laid out all of their bills on the living room table. The phone bill was sky high from calling UFO investigators for help. Then, Brian discovered Kate Miller had been calling collect from Missouri during the day.

"She's alone and afraid," Mary Beth pleaded. "She and Ginger talk during the day."

Brian slammed the table in a rage. "No more collect calls." "I'll pay $200 of the damn phone bill, the rent and main bills. The rest will get five dollars a week—five dollars a week on the balance. They can't sue us for that."

"Why don't you sell the truck?" Mary Beth said. "It's a gas hog, anyway."

Brian flared. "I am not selling my truck!"

"What about the race car?"

"Maybe," Brian said. "The hell with this. We have got to stop this. Just don't accept any more collect phone calls. Not even from Kate."

Mary Beth felt saddened. Her friend's six-year-old girl had been placed into a hospital after seeing the ball of light and hearing a low humming sound. Kate, herself, had developed a bleeding ulcer and needed medical treatment she couldn't afford.

In a way, Kate was much worse off because no one believed her. Only Brian, Mary Beth and Ginger could possibly understand. Since Brian was so irritated, Mary Beth didn't tell him more about Kate's problems. She slowly shuffled off to the bedroom, depressed.

"I'm getting another raise," Brian shouted. "We'll make it through this somehow."

Mary Beth pushed into the bedroom and froze with fear. A bright red ball-of-light hovered over her side of the bed only inches above the pillow.

She screamed. Brian and Ginger ran to her side. As they all watched, the light simply blinked out. That terrified Mary Beth. It could be anywhere. She looked around, shaking with fear.

Ginger pulled the pillow away and slapped at the bed. "Good god--this one stinks," she said. "It smells like rotten eggs, like sulfur."

Mary Beth collapsed against Brian. "Oh, God. It's after me. I know it."

Brian hugged her for a moment, until he heard the magnetometer ringing. He handed Mary Beth to Ginger. "Take her. I want to see if the magnetometer got this one."

Ginger struggled to hold her sobbing sister. "It's going to be okay, cooed Ginger. "It's gone, now. It'll be okay."

Moments later, Brian bounded back into the room with a smile on his face. "We got it—the magnetometer got a reading. This could be it," he gloated.

That night, as Mary Beth slept fitfully on the couch, Brian rose from bed about 2:10 a.m. and shuffled into the living room in his boxer shorts. Mary Beth followed in her nightgown. She watched Brian walk stiffly outside to the garage and begin drawing in the dim light. Mary Beth woke up Ginger in the guest room, and they huddled in the kitchen watching Brian through a window. He drew rapidly using pens and a straight edge.

"What is he doing?" asked Ginger.

"It's like he was a robot."

"That is weird," whispered Ginger. His hands flew at a furious pace.

"Look how fast he is going, and with his left hand."

Mary Beth gasped. "He's not left-handed." She started to tremble with fear. They could hear voices and he seemed to be talking, so they hurried to the back door and listened. From his lips came his own gentle, boyish voice and another -- deep and authoritative. They also heard another, more mechanical, and perhaps one more, flowing and smooth.

"Do you think we should wake him up?"

"No way," breathed Ginger. "If he is asleep. Just let him go."

"This is terrible," Mary Beth whined. "That's my Brian."

"God," Ginger breathed. "This is getting really scary."

"Now you know why I am sleeping on the couch. I don't know if that is my husband or -- something else."

That morning after Brian departed for work, Ginger gathered up the drawings. Throughout the day, as she cared for the two baby girls, Ginger read the words aloud. She didn't understand the calendar involving stars, astronomy, solstices and dates. She couldn't comprehend the corrected alignments for Stonehenge, or how black and white stones could be placed in a box to track the sun and moon, an ancient Incan system. So she focused on the last drawing--page ten—which showed the Gate of the Sun at Tiahuanaco, in South America. Words on the page said, "Given in Trust."

The drawing showed an alignment of SCOTT, MILLER AND WALTERS at the Gate of the Sun at sunrise on June 22, 1976. The purpose: Brian's 'Quantum Evolution' to Nous ten. Throughout the day, Ginger read the cryptic instructions aloud in a deep voice, often imitating the Host. Apparently the Host wanted Rex, Kate and Brian, but not Mary Beth. She wondered why.

Capturing the Ball of Light

That evening Vance Dewey, tall and golden, arrived to study data from the magnetometer. Since the weather had turned cold, he and Brian stepped inside the house to talk.

"Did you get it?" Brian asked with hope.

"Yes," Vance said cautiously. "But I don't know if it will prove anything. It gives us the duration, the amplitude and the frequency of the magnetic disturbance."

"Well," Brian shrugged. "Can it be used as proof -- as evidence?"

"It's a low-frequency electromagnetic disturbance. It's not really--unusual."

Brian shrunk. "Then it's not proof?"

"It's not *alien*."

"Damn it." Brian slammed the kitchen table hard with his fist. Dishes and plates rattled loudly.

"What's wrong?" hollered Mary Beth.

"It's not proof! We've got the evidence right here, and it's still nothing."

Vance calmed Brian. "It gives us information. I can tell you that the other measurements we have are not 'alien,' either. Yet they are significant radiations, documented by eyewitnesses. That's what *you've* got."

"But it's not proof?" Brian raged. "What the hell do we have to do to get proof? We can't go on like this, forever."

"Brian, you can't hurry these things," Vance said warmly.

"Well, Jesus. Now, we get a ball of light on tape, and it's nothing. I mean. Is there any UFO investigator that will call this proof? Give me a name. I'll call them right now." Brian stepped to the phone in a rage.

"You need to calm down, Brian," Mary Beth said softly. "You are getting way out of hand."

Knowledge of the Secondary World

Later that week, Brian and Mary Beth shopped for Christmas presents on a meager budget. She worried about Kate and wanted to buy her a present. Brian agreed.

At home, Brian decorated the Christmas tree as the two baby girls played nearby. He arranged the flashing, brightly colored lights and placed a white angel on top. Brian re-lit the Menorah with eight tiny candles and turned off the overhead lights. The room glowed with the warm golden candles and the colorful Christmas tree.

Ginger had found another writing in the den and read aloud as Brian and Mary Beth wrapped packages.

"Dec. 19, 1975 -- 2:10.3.1 AM-AE," Ginger read. "Three more days, on the countdown." She read slowly.

> **Open, of this man must understand himself and his own world before he can begin to understand others. Of this, knowledge is given by, of I. Of this, Dec 11, 2:12.3.6 AM-AE."**

Ginger held up the ten drawings Brian had completed at a rapid pace. "That's the night when these were done," she announced. She read aloud:

> **"Of I, of the Host. Of this, knowledge is now given. As an infant you are now–in knowledge. Of the Secondary World contact, the cloud will pass. Search your mind.**

"He gives the date you and Patti saw the light together in 1973, October 25. Now listen to what he says about that night." Brian and Mary Beth listened as Ginger read aloud:

Search your mind and of this understand. Of this, mankind will see the similarity of events you follow as others in the past. Urgency. Confusion, schizophrenia. Of this I ask you now, fear not the mind of mankind. Each to his own mind cannot be changed. Of the Host, you are one. The truth is of you. Knowledge is given. By of you, and of I, all will be known.

"He is telling about your visit with the Secondary World. *'Urgency, confusion, schizophrenia.'* You have been a little different since then. In fact--A LOT DIFFERENT."

"Yeah, I couldn't even drive my truck," Brian said.

"Evil is of the Secondary World," Ginger said imitating the Host. Brian laughed and tried an imitation, too. It was weak.

"Your imitations of yourself are terrible," Ginger laughed.

"Like I always said, IT'S NOT ME."

On the evening of December 21, Ginger arrived with a big box of presents from the in-laws. Brian clowned for the children and snuggled with Mary Beth. She glowed with joy as the stereo played funny Christmas songs.

But on Monday morning, December 22, Brian slipped from bed at about 4:00 a.m. and walked stiffly past the couch where Mary Beth lay sleeping. She didn't even hear him because she had swallowed a double dose of tranquilizers.

Brian shuffled past the colorful Christmas tree and the glowing menorah. He opened the back door and stepped outside on the cold concrete with bare feet.

On the cement driveway, Brian woke-up, shivering. For a moment, he glanced around confused, then started to run back inside. Suddenly, a high-frequency sound stopped him. He froze, unable to move. As the sound squealed, he felt a stretching again -- horizontally, then vertically.

A moment later, Brian opened his eyes in a small dark room with a bright green light in the upper corner. The light scanned him.

"Oh, no," he gasped. "Oh, GOD. No!"

The door slid open and before him stood the dome-headed, black-eyed alien, Leader of the Secondary World craft. Brian's heart raced. He jumped back in terror, remembering the fight, and how he had strangled the alien. He had been rescued then, but now--he would certainly be killed.

However, the leader didn't seem angry. He waited patiently for Brian to calm down, and finally extended a hand in friendship.

"Fear not," said the alien in a warm human voice. "Quantum evolution awaits you."

The Request for Transformation

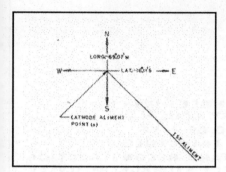

BEAM ALIGNMENT point. The latitude and longitude is an alignment point on an island in Lake Titicaca.

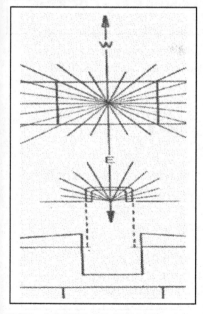

TOP of GATE OF SUN. The actual target of the beam is the top center of the monument. This drawing shows a radiant energy point of some kind where the carved image of Ticci Viracocha is located.

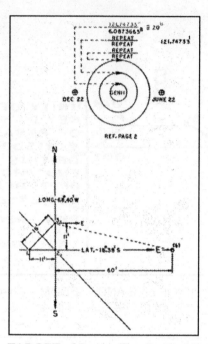

TARGET of Beam. The Gate of the Sun is the target. Brian was to stand at position 2 and look East to the Portal. The Gate of the Sun is 16 feet across.

Supposedly, the beam creates an energy field with a 49 Km. radius--the size of the activation zone. In the zone, temple stones and carvings are activated.

DAYS OF 20 – The top part of the drawing shows how the concept of a 20 day cycle was created. It relates to the vertical calendar on Page 2 of the drawings. Voltar referred to the *Play of Life,* as a time of testing and the *Days of 20.* Tests ran in a 20-24 day cycle.

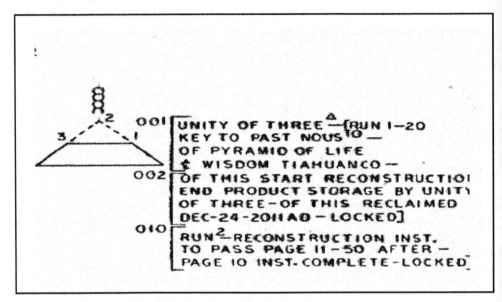

PYRAMID OF LIFE AND WISDOM – This detail asks for reconstruction of the pyramid to begin. The storage product would be picked up on December 24, 2011.

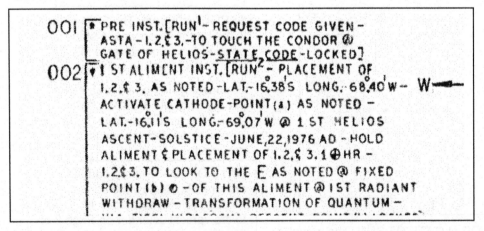

INSTRUCTIONS – Brian was instructed to "Touch the Condor" on the Gate of the Sun. The cathode point would be activated, and then he would stand in position 2 and look to the East for one hour. The transformation would take place. The words say: *at first radiant withdraw – transformation of quantum.*

FEAR NOT THE MIND OF MAN

FEAR NOT THE MIND OF MANKIND,
FOR OF YOU IS KNOWLEDGE,
JOY, UNDERSTANDING AND WISDOM FOR ALL.
FEAR NOT THE MIND OF MANKIND,
FOR I AM OF TIME BEYOND ALL TIME—
AND YOU ARE OF I.

-- THE HOST

Chapter 6

Man, Two Men in One

To Brian, the slender alien in the doorway seemed friendlier than before. "Come with I," he said in a warm, human voice. But, Brian remembered the last contact and didn't trust him.

"You will learn much," the Leader said with a hand open to Brian. His eyes looked nearly human. "Man is of us," he said. Brian was stunned by the change in appearance. Sure his head was bigger, and his skin was a bit blue, but he wasn't all that different from man on earth.

Brian decided to play along. He felt like a mouse in a trap, talking with a friendly cat.

He would stall, and hope for a rescue if anything bad started. He didn't expect to survive without help.

They walked about forty feet down the curved hallway, stepped onto a circular disk and zipped through the craft. Brian estimated the craft's size at 900 feet in diameter, ten times bigger than the craft of the giants with long-ears. He hoped *they* knew what was happening.

Brian looked around for a way to escape. Every wall seemed padded with fabric and styled for beauty. Colors of pastel pink, burgundy and purple provided a relaxing feel. Big, colored panels blinked with calming lights. The whole craft looked like an art museum. He liked the beauty, and the clean, ornate designs. He enjoyed and admired this huge ship much more than the small, undecorated ship of the long-ears. This craft didn't have mist, didn't smell, and the people didn't wheeze. In comparison, the craft of the giants seemed dull—purely functional with no artistry. But this craft seemed comfortable -- like a beautiful home artfully decorated.

The little disk under their feet carried Brian past numerous sectors. He saw young adults, male and female, sitting on padded benches. The girls seemed to curve in all the right places, and the boys seemed a bit more muscular. He saw tables where aliens relaxed and greeted each other by holding their right palms upward. They would pause a moment to establish mental rapport before engaging in talk. They gestured, but mostly their lips didn't move.

Most everyone seemed busy. They ignored him, though he caught a few looking. No one laughed, but they talked directly to each other, and obviously communicated. He noticed many gestures of their hands and faces that seemed human. Some were older than others. He began to see differences in the way they walked and in their appearances—some bigger, some smaller, huskier, or more slender. Both males and females wore silky silver suits. The females obvious had breasts, and hips just like females on earth. The more he looked, some of the young ladies seemed attractive, even appealing. He began to feel *at home.*

The heads on some were domed. On others, the top of their heads slanted backwards and elongated upwards at the rear. But, they were all real. He began to see them as people, as living beings with thoughts and feelings—just like humans.

In one sector, Brian saw big colored maps of the earth, including oceans, cross-sections of the earth and tunnels deep underground.

In another area, he glimpsed a laboratory filled with animals of earth that had been combined with other animal forms he had never seen. Many were frog-like in nature. In a different section, he glimpsed various types of aliens--some with rougher, darker reptilian skin and bizarre shaped heads and faces. But, they still looked like humans. It wasn't like the movies where they looked like monsters. They looked more human than anything else.

He even saw heads with hair, and people wearing glasses. He realized that a few humans, men and women, seemed to be working alongside the aliens.

Brian felt like an outsider looking in at a real world of busy people, but he wondered why no one paid him much attention. He wanted to shout, "Hey, I'm here. Look at me," but he was afraid no one would turn around.

The disk stopped, then descended inside a tube. Then a door opened, and they moved on the disk into a huge open chamber. He gasped at the beautiful designs and comfortable colors. He figured this room alone to be 300 feet in diameter and three times as high. Huge.

The alien Leader pointed downward into a deep chasm. Brian gazed down upon a huge sparkling crystal. Colors of the rainbow sprayed out in all directions.

"Power source," said the alien. "Comparison--prism. Refracted sunlight. Conversion of energy: solar. Energy for craft--propulsion." Brian understood, sort of.

He looked above. Numerous small craft seemed attached to the walls by rods. Cables of flashing lights connected to each scout ship.

"Technology not beyond grasp of man," the alien said. Brian understood. But, he wanted to see inside one of the sharp-looking crafts. With a nod, the alien approved.

The disk lifted them inside a small scout craft. Interior lights brightened with pleasing pastel colors. Sounds pulsed with pleasing tones. Brian felt the soft, gray fabric on the padded walls and ceiling. He smiled at the luxurious feel. Padded leather--no different than a nice car on the earth. The alien gestured for Brian to walk forward. Brian slid into the fancy cockpit with two padded chairs and an attractive instrument panel.

With the alien's approval, Brian sank into the big captain's seat. With a whoosh, the chair contracted to fit the contour of his body. Surprised, Brian was afraid for a moment, but as the chair surrounded his body, he felt comfortable. He eyed a black ball on a short chrome rod—the control stick--and he glanced at the alien. The Leader approved. Brian placed his hand on the ball. Suddenly, the panels zipped to life with bright colors, bars and circles. The overhead lights dimmed to a dark, purple glow—like a black-light on earth. This is cool, Brian thought. He smiled as the craft hummed with a warm, soothing vibration.

Brian let go of the control stick. The lights brightened, and the hum mellowed. He smiled, amazed. He loved the feel of this vehicle. It felt good--solid yet flexible.

"Exploration craft," said the leader. "Crew of three, plus three."

"How does it move?" asked Brian.

"Energy source noted," said the alien. "Sun primary power. Energy drawn from sun. Craft sails on beam--a projection, of thought. Band of thought expands, then contracts at Nous 4. Band of time stretched open."

Brian frowned. The solar part he could understand, but not the part about time and the mind.

"Magnetic fields bend beam of thought," the alien said slowly. "Navigator adapts to magnetic forces. Projects beam, point to point--by thought."

"Is it powered by thought?" Brian asked.

"No--navigated by thought. Powered by energy of sun—stored, *and* direct."

Brian understood. He would leave the issue of *time* and the *mind* alone. But, for now, he did appreciate the alien's clear answers. The Leader nodded diplomatically. Brian felt this man must certainly be a dignitary of some kind, and for the first time, he felt kind of bad about trying to strangle him.

"You may provide knowledge of this craft to mankind," said the alien. "Your hand will be guided." Brian knew that meant drawings and designs.

Later, as they departed the area, Brian glanced back at the beautiful scout ships and the huge open area. He felt excited. He wouldn't mind flying one of those. For the first time, he had good feelings for the little aliens.

They aren't that advanced, he thought. They aren't that different than us. They are just like real people—only different.

As they rode the disk back through the craft, Brian bubbled with excitement. Maybe he was wrong. Maybe he could work with them. The Secondary World suddenly seemed more suitable and earth-like than the giants with long-ears.

"Why me? Why are you offering this to me?" Brian asked.

"Within the parameters of our code for intervention, the requests of Voltar and his council have failed," the Leader said. "The fate of man remains unchanged. Nous ten rapport rejected—as we predicted."

Brian didn't understand.

"The Pyramid of Life and Wisdom at Tiahuanaco will NOT be reconstructed. Cells will not be stored for resurrection. No evidence of hu-man civilization will remain to confuse the next form of man."

"Form of man?" Brian asked.

"In the years to come, YOU may dwell among us—like others you have seen here. Of their own choice, they work with us. Of this, you will enjoy your new home."

Brian bristled at the word "home." But the alien gestured to living quarters complete with bedrooms including a large bed. An attractive female hybrid with a pretty, human face and long red hair, fell into the bed and sunk deep down inside. The edges of the bed rolled up, surrounding her in a cocoon. Brian gasped. Then suddenly the sides rolled back down. She popped up and rolled to her feet. Her curves and glances instantly aroused his passions. He could like living here, he thought.

She hurried away, glancing over her shoulder with a teasing smile. Brian gulped. He liked her. She was flirting with him, and her cute walk aroused him even more.

"You will find here *much pleasure*," said the alien. "Much, pleasure. We are not as hard, and cold as you may think." In a human voice, he imitated Brian. "*You may do your own thing.* " He even smiled as Brian reacted with shock. He could imitate Brian perfectly. "Here, Brian—you will be an honored guest."

Brian smiled in awe. The alien knew what he was thinking. "You shall be a liaison to the people of the land, to the past--and to the future. In this, we have compromised, in part, and by this your purpose shall be fulfilled."

Brian tried to think quickly. He didn't understand everything. Who compromised? The alien seemed to be offering a deal, but Brian knew nothing about "compromise" from the long-ears. He would not commit--not, without talking to them. Then, Brian thought about the hybrid girl. The leader read his thoughts.

"The choice is yours. If you choose to stay with us, you shall be a father to many," the alien said. "You will help seed the earth—the new man, shall be of you, in part." Brian understood. They wanted to use him as a source for hybrid children. He gulped, but in a strange way, he felt a bit flattered.

"Why me?"

"Your biological father of original seed line for two-strand DNA."

Brian thought deeply. All he knew about his real dad was that he read books and refused to fight in World War II. He wanted to know more. The alien gestured, "Not now."

On the disk again, they passed several busy laboratories. He saw small trees bulging with apples, oranges and grapefruit, cherries, avocados, peaches and plums.

In another room he saw a huge aquarium filled with unusual fish. Then he saw a big room filled with modified cows, sheep and farm animals. "Preparations underway," the alien said. "New food, new fibers for the new plantation of man."

"Did you create man?" Brian asked.

"Man is of us," the alien said. "We created man as he is today. Evolutionary processes are of us."

Brian gasped. "This is so hard to believe." The alien led Brian into a circular room, which glowed with green light. On the walls, numerous dark instrument panels throbbed with energy. Four smaller aliens waited at workstations.

"The logic of Voltar and his Host failed," said the alien with finality.

"Who compromised? What is that about?" Brian asked.

"You have done well, but no agreements were formed among man that would help you."

Brian felt guilty. "No one believes me. If I don't understand, how can anyone else?" The alien understood. He did not expect much of mankind. He expected failure.

"Man need not know all. Time-span limited. Knowledge of the past, irrelevant. All preparations underway for Phase ten. The old plantations shall be phased out."

"Phased out?" Brian gasped.

The alien touched Brian on the shoulder. "You may dwell with us. Of this, we offer now, quantum evolution to Nous four. Retention by that of I--of our DNA."

Brian gasped as aliens picked up instruments.

"Of this, a new beginning for you, and a *new man—your own plantation.*"

Brian understood the deal. He would be used to create hybrids—a certain type of the *new man*. He liked that idea and even felt flattered, but he didn't like the idea of 'phasing out' man. He liked most of the people on earth, and he still hoped to meet his dad someday.

He studied the Leader and other aliens in the room. They didn't look so perfect. They all seemed frail, pale and sickly. They didn't have all the answers, obviously.

The Host and the giants also had a plan for mankind – *quantum evolution*— and freedom. It might still work. He trusted the Host and the giants a bit more. They seemed friendlier. They had held his hands, treated him with more feelings, and with them, he felt more emotions, more love. Although this craft was more beautiful, he hadn't seen any giggling, any laughter, any love.

Thus, he nervously rejected the offer. "Whatever is this Nous four, I can probably get along without, just fine, as I am." Brian said. He clapped his hands, ready to go home.

"The neurological implant, of Voltar's people, must be removed," the alien crackled coldly. "Voltar's folly is ended." The Leader turned away angrily. His friendly demeanor evaporated.

From high above, a green light beam suddenly probed Brian's body. The instrument panels snapped alive. Brian started to run, but a piercing sound ripped at his brain. Stunned, Brian stopped moving, frozen in mid-stride, like a man moving in slow-motion.

A long, segmented instrument, like a robotic arm, swung loose from the ceiling and descended down. Brian could not move as the brace shrunk to fit his head. Somehow, his body rotated and he was laid flat on a table.

A glowing green probe touched against the back of Brian's neck. He fainted, but his eyes popped wide open. The other probe entered into his right ear. Brian's body convulsed in pain. Finally, his eyelids drooped shut.

When he awoke, Brian lay on his driveway at dawn. The concrete was damp with dew. He pulled himself slowly up the steps in agony, then he crawled into the house. He reached up to lovingly stroke Mary Beth on the couch, but passed out on the living room floor.

Brian's Christmas Present

On Christmas morning, as Mary Beth and Brian opened presents with their giggling children, Brian's lips sagged on the right side of his face. Saliva drooled down his chin. "Brian, your face is crooked," Mary Beth said with concern. "Your mouth is drooling."

Brian shuffled to the bathroom and studied his face in the mirror. His skin seemed lifeless on the right side of his face. His lips didn't work right.

At work a few days later, surrounded by his engineering team, Brian displayed a big drawing. As he talked, saliva drooled from his chin.

"I think you should see the nurse," said the Persian engineer in his British accent.

"I'll be all right," Brian said wiping the saliva away.

"Today!" the French engineer commanded.

In the company's medical office, the nurse examined Brian's face and checked his hearing. She frowned.

At home on Saturday evening, January 3, Brian told Mary Beth about the test results. His ears had lost the ability to hear high frequencies. The nurse wanted him to take a neurological exam.

When Brian shuffled into the den to get another pack of cigarettes, he saw a purple-white ball of light hovering in the corner. With a velvety sound, the Host emerged from the orb.

The Old Man didn't smile.

> **Secondary World attempted implant removal and quantum evolution -- of their method. Neural implant retained--logic protected. Scott protected. Method failed, injury resulted. This damage will pass, of I, of Nous ten. Fear not.**

> **Of this, knowledge shall be given to man. Fear not of I, for I bring life and nourishment for man. Evil is of the Secondary World.**

"But what happened?" Brian asked. "Why am I drooping?" The Host continued.

> **Fear not of the mind. Genii given for protection to unity of three: Scott, Walters, Miller. There is a way, but the way must be of man--of you, and of the gathering together of man around you in agreement.**

"But why?" Brian pleaded.

> **You will learn much of man, and of yourself, Brian. You are of I--liaison to the past knowledge of man and a Keeper of the Quipu for the People of Tiahuanaco. The answers man needs are of himself, and of the past, of Tiahuanaco. Man must comply. Time relevant: Final date of phase two completion--June 22, 1977. *Final!* Man must comply of his own free will. If not--the fate of man will come by that of man's Secondary World: destruction imminent 2-0-1-1. Imminent!**

The Host waited for Brian to understand. Then he touched his blinking belt and compressed back into a ball of bright purple light. With an electronic squeal, the orb zipped out of the room.

Brian sat down and worried. How could the future of man be on his shoulders? One man? That sounded ridiculous. He could do nothing, especially now. He could barely talk.

Brian in the Hospital

A few days later, Brian drove the Captain America truck to the Fountain Valley medical clinic. He ambled up to the front door in pain. When he tried to read the clinic directory, his vision blurred. A lady nurse helped him into the elevator. When the door closed and the elevator moved upward, the lights spun. "This is not good," he mumbled as he crumpled to the floor with a thud.

When the door opened on the third floor, the nurse shouted for help. Someone grabbed a wheel chair, and hollered for the doctor. "I'm okay," Brian moaned. "I just got dizzy. I'll be all right." He tried to push himself upright.

"Are you Brian Scott?" asked the dark-skinned doctor in a Spanish accent.

"I used to be," Brian mumbled. "I don't know who I am today."

Bell's Palsy

In the examining room, the handsome, Spanish doctor looked into Brian's ears and eyes. "It looks like Bell's palsy," he said. "It's common. It can be caused by cold temperature on your ear in the early morning--wet hair, riding with the window down in your car."

"It's my right side," Brian said. "No window."

"It's a temporary paralysis of the seventh facial nerve," said the doctor. "But, that doesn't explain your hearing loss. That's different. Were you exposed to any loud, sudden sounds--like explosions, dynamite?"

"I guess you could call it a piercing sound, and a very cold light."

"A light? What happened exactly?" asked the doctor.

Brian smiled. "I don't think you want to know."

The doctor smiled. "Tell me."

The next day Brian woke up in a hospital bed, sedated. "They have decided to keep you," Mary Beth whispered. "For psychiatric exams. You've been out all night."

Brian frowned. "We've got to get some help, Mary Beth. I can't stop this anymore. I am way off track. These people will never believe me."

Later that afternoon, Brian and Mary Beth used the hospital phone to call UFO investigators, collect. He had obtained a long list of people in California. Brian finally reached a scientist named Dr. Wilson in San Francisco. In a long conversation, Wilson told Brian that accepting Jesus as his Savior might stop the lights. Coming from a scientist, the testimony stunned Brian.

"It's not religious," Brian said. "People keep mixing up science and religion. That creates more problems. It's really just a sensor. I saw them on-board the craft."

Wilson then told Brian that the term Secondary World might also relate to the Book of the Hopi. The Hopi mythology described the Secondary World as a time before the flood--just like the Bible. According to the Hopi traditions, man is now living in the Third World. It too, would pass away. Wilson was specific. "In Genesis chapter 6, in the time of Noah, the angels were fornicating with the daughters of men." Wilson said. "The Bible clearly says so. That means sexual implantation of girls. Same story. For that reason, God destroyed the world by water. The flood was at the end of the Secondary World."

Brian had been told nothing about this by either group he had met—not Voltar, not the alien leader. Maybe the Bible was right. Maybe *they* didn't want to talk about it, he reasoned. "What can we do to make it stop?" Brian asked.

"I accepted Jesus and the lights went away. That's all I can tell you," Wilson said. "I've had no more problems."

When they hung up, Brian frowned at Mary Beth. "Everyone puts their own religious philosophy into this. It's crazy. That's dangerous. The lights are just *sensors.* I saw them on the craft."

"Patti prayed," said Mary Beth. "They stopped."

"No. They come and--they go," Brian said, slobbering his words, "They leave when they are done monitoring. You can't say they went because you prayed. That's superstition."

The next day, a nurse wheeled Brian downstairs to the lobby for an appointment with the clinic psychiatrist. As they waited in the busy lobby, Mary Beth arrived to find Brian writing on a hospital notepad in a trance. Embarrassed, she tried to wake him. "Is he aware that he is writing?" asked the nurse.

"I don't think he is aware of it," Mary Beth said, shaking Brian. "He never knows he's doing it."

"Complete amnesia?" asked the nurse.

"I guess. He don't know what they mean either."

"Has he been treated by any other doctor for this?"

"No, this just started. Really. He is a UFO contactee." Mary Beth felt nervous as a small crowd gathered. "I guess this is common—to UFO contactees. It happens to a lot of them."

121

They gasped, watching Brian's left hand jerk, mechanically. "But mostly he is a very normal man," Mary Beth said. "Very normal. He is not like this all the time." Mary Beth nudged Brian again, but he continued writing at a rapid speed.

"I wouldn't wake him," the nurse whispered. "Just let him come out of it, naturally."

"His appointment is in five minutes," Mary Beth said jabbing him hard in the shoulder.

Brian stopped writing with a jolt. His body trembled. "Oh God. I see it. I see it," he muttered in a daze. "Okay, I see it. I see it." Then he looked at Mary Beth, confused. "What's happening?" he asked.

"You tell me," she said. "You were doing some writing--on a doctor's notepad." Mary Beth returned the pad to Brian's nurse. She studied the words.

"What language is that?" the nurse asked in awe. "Look at this." She passed the notepad around to the group.

A tall, scholarly aide studied the writing. "That's Greek," he said. "Hebrew and I think, German."

Mary Beth shrugged. "It's for some scientist named Wilson. Brian talked to him last night."

"I know German," the aide said.

For once He gave so all mankind would know life and peace. Of this, His young and of His flesh, Son. But He was rejected in the heart of many. Of this, a few knew the truth. Of this I say Toro Muerto of Andean Mountain. Seek this. The truth mankind seeks is of this, of Toro Muerto. Of this, the truth will be known to all mankind. Locked.

"Does this make sense to you?" he asked Brian.

"No," Brian said. "Not really. Did I write that?"

"It's just like all the others we've got,' Mary Beth said. "A hundred or more. That's what he's in for." She laughed. "Not really. But it has been a problem."

The scholarly aide again looked at the writing.

Of I, the Host: 'I saw a new heaven and a new earth and the first heaven and the first earth were passed away and no more.

The words excited Brian. "That's what I saw. I saw that. Mary Beth, that's when you woke me up. I was watching this right then. It was so real." Brian asked the aide to read the last line again, slowly.

"I saw a new heaven and a new earth. The first heaven and the *first earth were passed away"*

Brian looked at them all. "See, it says *'first.'* That means there was a 'second.' The first was destroyed! That's what he wanted me to understand. It was--it really was, *destroyed.* That is what he wants us to understand. He is serious."

The group listened as Brian rambled. "The people were destroyed on purpose because they went wrong--in the first world, AND the SECOND. And, they weren't that different from us, today."

They all pondered the words for a moment. Finally, Mary Beth broke the silence. "Well, time for your appointment," she laughed loudly. "Off to see your shrink."

They all laughed. "Mary Beth, it's not funny," Brian moaned. "Don't make fun of this stuff--it's serious."

The Shrink

In the psychiatrist's office, Brian answered questions posed to him by the heavy-set doctor wearing black horn-rimmed glasses. On the inkblot test, Brian kept his answers simple and basic.

Then the doctor asked Brian if he had ever "woken up" in a strange place. Brian laughed. "Well, yeah--several times. Santa Barbara for one."

"Were you taken there by aliens?"

"No," Brian chuckled.

"Where you in one of these trances?"

"No. I don't think so," Brian laughed. "But, I must say, I don't know how I got to Santa Barbara driving my own truck."

The psychiatrist frowned. "That is called a *fugue,"* he said. "That can be a symptom of multiple personality." He smiled at Brian. "I think we need to do a few more tests. Maybe rule out some organic things—like a tumor or cancer."

The next day, early in the morning, a white-suited doctor wheeled Brian into a porcelain white room. Brian was placed inside a central tube of the huge magnetic imaging device. Two doctors sitting in another room behind thick, protective glass examined the computer image with the Spanish neurologist and psychiatrist.

They asked Brian to move his head as the machine captured different views of his brain. Brian heard the machine hum and buzz and click. He breathed deep and tried to relax. Not far behind the alien technology, he mused.

Two days later, the neurologist and the psychiatrist looked at the final images with a radiologist. The lesions on the 7th facial nerve had nearly healed. The CAT scan showed no other problems.

The two doctors walked out of radiology confused. "He reports symptoms of a dissociative reaction," said the psychiatrist. "Trances, black-outs, fugue. But he reports no ritual or sexual abuse in childhood. He gets along well with everyone at work. He's never been threatening. He is not reclusive or even moody. He likes people, they like him--and he is humorous, outgoing. So, not the usual pattern for dissociation like split-personality. I don't think he is dangerous."

The neurologist listened carefully. He was astonished at the rapid recovery of the nerve damage. "We could just release him, and see if he comes back." They agreed, and released Brian.

The Investigators Gather

After Brian returned home, Ginger called all the investigators so they could greet him and coordinate their plans.

On Sunday afternoon, Jan. 31, she passed out the latest writings. Brian sat in his chair, mostly uninterested. Ginger had never seen him this way.

As Ginger and Mary Beth served coffee to a half-dozen men, Lenny Jacobs-- the UCLA researcher--held up a book of documents, nearly 100 pages.

"According to these writings," said Lenny, "the Host's people ran genetic projects in this hemisphere in 3113 B.C., probably with the Toltecs, or Olmecs in Central America--probably with Quetzalcoatl—their god king and cultural hero. But they also shared a ninth descent with the Secondary world together in 110 B.C. at Tiahuanaco which involved another cultural hero—Viracocha. The ninth descent is the focus of all this material," Lenny said. "Tiahuanaco --110 B.C."

"That's the date and location they want us to focus on. The Host says the knowledge man needs is of Tiahuanaco and their ninth descent. Their tenth descent is related to Brian. It started in 1971 and will end in 2011—40 years— based on their calendar. All of this is laid out in drawings with tiny details you have to study for hours."

Everyone eyed Brian.

"Makes no sense to me," he said with a shrug.

"No more Nazca," said Lenny. "After November 22, the new stuff is all about Tiahuanaco, the Gate of the Sun and this place called Toro Muerto."

Then Levy, the older parapsychologist, spoke. "And, of course, despite the new request from the Host, we still don't get our requests met the way WE want. We don't get solid proof we can use." He eyed Brian carefully. "We need a sign that this is all true."

Brian frowned.

"What exactly is the primary request?" asked Vance Dewey.

Lenny answered. "The Host wants Brian to be at Tiahuanaco on June 22, 1976 for a *quantum evolution, and a 'radiant withdrawal'*--whatever that is. This *sudden evolution* takes place *after* he touches the Gate of the Sun. Also, he clearly wants Brian to design a pyramid to be built at Tiahuanaco. Its purpose is to store cells, from people, which will be reclaimed."

Lenny held up a big book opened to a picture of the Gate of the Sun. "This is it," he said. "Most mysterious calendar in the western hemisphere. Brian's writings say it is the key to mind levels two through ten. We don't use levels of mind in psychology today. Maybe we will someday. But most Eastern religions and many mythologies include levels of heaven. These might be related to consciousness, which might be interpreted as levels of mind. So, it's not that unusual of an idea. In fact, some Eastern religions use the idea of 10 realms of consciousness."

As everyone glanced at Brian with awe, he shrugged again.

"It ain't me," he said. "Don't think it is me saying this."

Lenny continued. "It all means nothing if we can't get there. If we can't stop the little aliens, they are going to wipe us out. I don't see how we can stop them." The room silenced. No one said a word for a few moments.

"I've studied these ten drawings," said a white haired man with a radiant face. He stood up and walked towards Brian. "These drawings include astronomy, archaeology, space travel and much more—calendars, time and the mind. It's incredible. It would take me years, and several doctorates to decipher everything on these pages. This is way beyond Van Daniken's books." He walked over to Brian and touched his shoulders. "My view is that Brian here is a designer in training, a special type of designer. Ask yourselves this: Were the pyramids advanced design? How about the Greek amphitheaters, or the Incan bridges and highways? Look at the temple cities of the Toltecs, Mayans, Aztecs. Amazing.

"The Spanish said the engineering at Mexico City was better than Rome. The city was bigger, more organized, and more beautiful than Rome—the pinnacle of the western world. The point is, the ancients in Central and South America had amazing engineering and construction methods. It's an untold story. But--you see--in ancient times, the designers, architects and builders, united with priests, kings and astronomers to build these monuments. And each monument held meaning. The designers don't get much play from historians. But the fact is, the designers had to understand the psychology of it all—AND the engineering before it could be built. It all started with designers. That's what Brian is—an architect, a designer of a modern pyramid, of modern technology. And, I believe, that's exactly what we need today to truly build a New World, a New Age that is real. To me, it all fits."

Brian perked up and smiled. "I've always said this is mostly about science and engineering."

The big, white-haired man continued. "Each pyramid held the encoded knowledge of their people and, of course, bodies of their royalty, which they hoped would be re-animated to live in some future time. The Host makes a similar request in modern form: to store cells of our people in the pyramid." He walked around Brian. "Perhaps, he wants them to be re-animated in 14,000 A.D. It's not so strange. Have you ever seen the pyramids in Egypt?"

"No," Brian nodded. "Not in real life."

"Well, you need to go. You need to get your ducks in a row," the man said.

"Ducks, I can do," Brian said not wanting the group to get too serious. He quacked loudly. "Quack. Quack. I can make really good duck sounds. In fact, that's the best comment I've heard all night." Everyone laughed as Brian imitated ducks. "I could do a ventriloquist show to raise money for the pyramid. I could be the Host's dummy, sit on his lap and do animal sounds. Let's see, I can also do a good cow. Moooooo," he bellowed. They all laughed hysterically. "I would make a very good dummy."

They all giggled hysterically and Brian kept them laughing until everyone departed with packages in hand. He liked the investigators. He just didn't want them to put him on some pedestal. He wasn't perfect. He had a past, a police record. They could never go anywhere by making him famous. He wasn't some hero to be worshipped. He felt better. The white-haired man understood. This was all about DESIGN and ENGNEERINIG—not religion. For the first time, he felt confident the whole thing could go forward without becoming a religion.

The Earthquake Signs

The next morning Brian found another writing in the den. Later, in a blue mood, he called Lenny Jacobs from the cafeteria at work. "It's for you and your buddy. A sign, I guess. It says, *'Of Guatemala, earthquake will pass.'* That's about it."

"When?"

"I don't know, Lenny, but I have a bad feeling about it, okay. Very bad," he sniffed. "I don't like the way this feels."

"Okay Brian. We'll wait to see what happens."

At home that night, the evening of February 3, Brian watched television reports of an earthquake in Guatemala. Thousands of people had been killed. Brian called Lenny Jacobs as reports continued.

"What's going on?" Mary Beth asked.

"I predicted an earthquake in Guatemala," Brian said. "Lenny wants to call the newspapers."

"What--and go public?"

"Yeah. Prediction comes true. Like psychics."

"Really?"

"He wants to get on all the talk shows."

"Brian, why would you do that?"

"That's what he's been waiting for. He got his sign."

"Is that what you want?" Mary Beth asked. "Brian Scott, the psychic? The New Age prophet?"

Brian frowned. "No, but how am I ever going to put this behind me? Nothing happens. People talk, but do nothing. *They* don't tell me nothing. It's going nowhere, and I know—the Secondary will kill off man. They believe it's the right thing to do."

The next morning at 6:30 a.m., Lenny pounded on the front door. Brian slipped out of the bathroom with shaving cream on his face.

Lenny showed Brian newspaper articles. "You were right," Lenny said. "Bad earthquake."

"People died," Brian said. "Lots of people."

"I need to see the writing," Lenny insisted.

As they pushed into the den, Lenny spotted another writing on the desk. He started to read, aloud.

'Time related to pass greater than 1:20 a.m. Guatemala earthquake. Greater than Feb. 3.'

"Is this another writing?" asked Lenny.

Brian frowned. "I don't know. I just got up."

"It's dated today! Another earthquake. Today?" Excited, Lenny read aloud.

'Latitude fourteen degrees, thirty seven minutes north. Longitude, ninety degrees and thirty one minutes west. Time related helios mid-ascension. Given. Earthquake greater than 6.2 to pass. Greater than 10.2 hours.'

Brian splashed shaving lotion on is face and stared in a reverie. In his mind, he saw buildings falling in jungle towns. He heard people screaming and crying out in terror as the ground shook.

"Brian!" Lenny shook him.

Brian's eyes suddenly reddened with tears. "I think some more people are going to die today," he mumbled. His heart filled with sadness. "Lenny, I hate this."

Mary Beth shuffled into the hallway wearing her nightgown.

"Lenny is here," Brian said to her. "I'm going to work." Brian picked up his briefcase and hurriedly poured coffee in a cup.

"Wait! We need to document this," stammered Lenny.

"Call Guatemala. Call the Red Cross." Brian blurted. "This is your sign, I don't care what the hell you do with it." He slammed out the door.

Mary Beth saw Lenny recoil. "He is really getting out of hand," she said. "He's getting rude and irritable to everyone."

Lenny understood. "Don't worry about it. This is getting too crazy for any of us to handle."

Brian's Earthquake

At work, as Brian tried to draw a blueprint, he heard men and women crying for help. When he closed his eyes, he saw bodies crushed to death, mothers dying with children in their arms. He felt their fear and sorrow. They didn't want to die. They didn't want to be crushed, suffocated, torn to bits by concrete—and God wasn't saving them. That was reality. They were being painfully destroyed as he watched. Tears rolled down his cheeks. He ran into the bathroom and vomited into the sink.

"What am I doing?" he moaned into the mirror. "What is happening to me?" Just then, he felt the whole bathroom jolt. He panicked. Instantly he ran into the hallway and raced towards the basement."Go, go," he shouted at people as he ran down stairs and into a hallway near the cafeteria. In the hallway, he felt the entire building rise up, roll to one side and crash downward. The walls exploded, and glass shattered all around him.

To protect himself, he slid to the floor and rolled up into a ball. He gasped, waiting to be crushed. He heard sounds of glass breaking, metal falling and people shrieking in pain. Finally, the shaking and terrible sounds stopped.

The lady from the cafeteria touched Brian's shoulder. He opened his eyes and peered around. The building stood solid. Light poured in from all the large glass windows--unbroken. No damage had been done. He rubbed his eyes.

"You okay, Mr. Captain America?" Kitchen workers stared at him. He felt embarrassed and confused.

"I thought it was an earthquake." He stood up, brushed off his pants and hurried away muttering, "What is happening to me." Now, he knew for certain that he was losing touch with physical reality.

The next evening at Brian's house, Lenny and Brian argued. "I need another sign, Brian."

"No. That was your sign! You asked for it, and you got it. Two of them in fact."

Lenny exhaled deeply. "I know. It was greater than 6.2 and I had it in my hand. But it wasn't documented—not *notarized.* My people want it notarized." Lenny exhaled. "Look, I can understand your upset, Brian."

"No you can't!" Brian snapped. "I do not want to go through that again. I saw it Lenny," he sat down. "It's not like TV, it's the real thing--with all the feelings.

People dying. It's too much, too much emotion--even for me. I don't want any more of this."

"If you want to get on a national talk show, I need another one," Lenny said.

"I don't want to be on TV," Brian said. "It's not me, anyway. It's him--the Host. Can't you *get* that?" Brian nudged Lenny towards the door. "No more earthquakes, please." Brian opened the door and Lenny departed in a huff. "Nothing is ever enough," Brian muttered. "Why the hell bother?"

Suddenly, the magnetometer rang on the back patio. Mary Beth screamed as a small red ball of light moved through the window and stopped in the kitchen.

Brian confronted the light in an angry mood. "What the hell do you want?" He heaved a book at the red orb. "Speak up. I've had it with you, too." The sphere bobbed downwards and the book smashed into a pile of dishes, breaking them all over the kitchen floor.

"What the hell are you doing?" Mary Beth shrieked.

"Did you see that?" Brian smirked. "The damn thing ducked." He rummaged for a meat cleaver then grabbed a broom. The light zipped outside. "Come back here," Brian shouted.

He charged out the door swinging the broom and meat cleaver. After the orb moved away, he tossed the meat cleaver. The red light stopped and emitted a high-pitched clapping tone. Stunned, Brian collapsed to the ground.

A few moments later, he rose up, crazed. "I know you are in there," he hissed. "You can hear me! You can hear everything." His voice filled with tears. The light hovered closer. "Go ahead, put me out of my misery," he ranted. The light remained silent.

Then Brian attacked in a wild fury swinging the broom like a sword. The light beeped again and he crumpled to the ground. Mary Beth rushed to his side. "Brian, stop. Stop this.!" she cried as she helped him into the kitchen.

" We've got to get help," she cried.

"Oh, God, I'm dizzy. Everything is moving," he moaned. Grabbing for balance, he crashed to the kitchen floor. Mary Beth pulled him upright and pushed him to his feet.

"I'm burning up. Hot," Brian mumbled. He tried to fill a glass of water, but lost his balance.

Mary Beth propped him up against the counter. A white, thick vomit erupted from his mouth--like marshmallow crème.

"I can't stop it," Brian gagged as he heaved again. Mary Beth grabbed the camera and snapped a picture. Brian crumpled to the floor, and jerked with convulsions.

Two-year old Kathy cried out, "Daddy!"

"Not now," screamed Mary Beth. "Go to your room!" Kathy ran away crying.

Mary Beth pulled him into the living room. Together they fell down.

Brian heaved deeply. "Asssssta," he growled. The deep, hollow rattle terrified Mary Beth. "Kathy, stay in the bedroom!" she screamed. "Watch your sister."

"Aasstttaaa."

Mary Beth ran into the kitchen and grabbed a huge butcher knife. "Come at me, and I'll let you have it. You do anything, and I swear, I'll kill you."

"Aaaasttttaaaa," growled the demon.

Mary Beth grabbed a tape recorder. "Don't get up, Brian. Please, don't get up."

"Over-ride. Secondary world over-ride," said a mechanical voice from Brian. "Over-ride Nous 10. Request. Transportation. Physical--via Titicaca."

Mary Beth placed the recorder on Brian's chest and backed away quickly with the big knife in hand. A red light blinked on the recorder.

Kathy peered around the corner. "Daddy?" asked the girl.

"Daddy's sleeping." Mary Beth said. "Leave him alone."

Brian mumbled in a deep, powerful voice. "Ninth descent Gate of Helios...."

The voice rambled on as Mary Beth hurried to the phone. She called home for help. Her oldest step-brother answered "Nick. Listen to me," Beth whispered. "Brian is having convulsions. He is in trance and a voice is speaking from his mouth. Can you come over here?"

"No. It's too late," he said. "School tomorrow."

Mary Beth started to cry. "Please, I don't know what I'll do if he goes after my babies." She sniffled. Then she regained her composure. "Please!" she commanded.

The Host spoke from Brian.

Titicaca key to Gate of Helios. Known--Gate of Sun. Of this, monitoring process began tonight by Secondary. Emotional reactions noted. Transmission end, Run 2. Locked.

Mary Beth sat down by Kathy in the hallway. "Daddy is resting. You can't play with him now."

Kathy pointed at Brian. "Daddy sleeping," she said. Tears welled up in Mary Beth's eyes. She covered her daughter's eyes and ears as the voice continued.

Before long, the front door slammed opened. Nick, with muscles bulging, rushed in ahead of Ginger and her hippie boyfriend.

"Where is he?" he snarled. He didn't like Brian.

"Don't take your eyes off him, Nick!" Mary Beth ordered. "The devil himself was talking through him." Mary Beth handed him the tape recorder. "Turn this on if anything happens." Nick wanted to fight, but accepted the tape recorder as his job.

Brian sat up, and began walking around. Nick followed closely behind. Brian picked up the aluminum coffee pot, removed the lid, and began to drink from the pot. He gagged and screamed. The pot crashed to the floor. "Good god that's hot! What is that?"

"Coffee!" exclaimed Nick in disbelief. He frantically flipped on the tape recorder.

"That's the worst coffee I've every tasted. God!"

Suddenly, Brian's body froze like a statue. His eyes rolled up, and he hissed like a jaguar -- at Nick. His lips curled back revealing large teeth. As Nick watched, they seemed to grow longer and Brian's face became a growling jaguar.

Terrified, Nick jumped backward and prepared to fight. Suddenly, Brian's personality smiled. "Do you drink coffee?"

"I don't think I need any," Nick gasped. He tried to take the pot out of Brian's hand. "Why don't you let me make it for you?"

"Good god, I like to make my own coffee!" Brian snapped.

Suddenly Brian froze. He appeared terrified for a moment. Then his expression changed. The Host spoke through him.

> **This now, Secondary World contact. Now. Monitoring your emotional reaction. (Pause.) Now! Monitoring your reactions. (Pause.) Now!"**

Ginger sat on the couch listening. Suddenly, she closed her eyes and moaned in pain. The Host continued.

> **Secondary monitored again, of female. This reaction is not of I. Of this, man is two men in one. One is awake in darkness, the other asleep in light. Of this is known to earth. The meaning of this is vital to man. Understand of this.**

Ginger, holding the dog in her arms, sat with a frozen expression on her face, her eyes wide-open. "Ginger!" Nick shouted with alarm. He looked at Todd for help. "Something is wrong with her."

An evil voice rattled from Brian -- a deep guttural growl. "This is of I."

Everyone in the room felt terror. "Ginger, are you all right?" Todd screamed. She stopped breathing. "Ginger! Don't stop breathing, honey. Honey!"

Nick tipped her backwards on the couch. "Ginger! Ginger!" Mary Beth raced to the phone and dialed 911 for an ambulance as Ginger's eyes locked in an unseeing, death-like stare.

"Ginger! Blink your eyes. Blink your eyes," Todd cried.

"Take a breath! Take a breath!" yelled Nick.

In a daze, Brian stood up and walked towards Ginger. Nick responded immediately, blocking Brian's path.

"Sit down Brian. Now!" he shouted. "Just sit your ass down!"

"She'll come out of it," Brian said as he sat down on the floor.

Suddenly the Host spoke through Brian. **"Secondary world monitoring female."**

Nick trembled with terror. "I gotta get out of here!" he bolted towards the door.

"Take Brian out of here," Mary Beth grabbed him. They stared at Brian as his expression turned rocky solid. The Host spoke from him again.

> **Female, Ginger, will recover of this. Secondary World touched her mind. Secondary World in conflict with I. Monitoring all, this night. Of this, I say: Man is two men in one. One is asleep in the light, the other awake in the darkness. Vital."**

Ginger started to breathe. She cried softly. In her mind, she saw faces of hundreds of young girls in various nations--girls of all races. "So many girls," she moaned. "Just like me. So many girls have lived and died on this world, wanting only to be loved, and to love," Todd patted her. She cried. "But they are all dead. And all of their love is gone. For what purpose? What reason?"

Then the Host spoke through Brian.

> **Man, today is an infant in knowledge. Of this wisdom will come to man, of you--Scott. You must learn of yourself, and the mind of man.**

Nick watched the light on the tape recorder blink as the Host spoke.

> **If man does not understand himself and his world, how can he expect to understand others? Of this, man must seek his past to know his future. A process of education must be employed. The key to which I have given: Gate of the Sun. Seek Gate of the Sun. Seek Lake Titicaca for knowledge of this. Man's past is key to his future. If man today remains lost in his dreams, destruction will be imminent, of Secondary. Imminent.**

Brian heard a siren and woke up disoriented. Mary Beth led paramedics into the house. "Nick, get Brian out of here," Mary Beth ordered.

Nick pulled Brian outside into the night. Rain had fallen. The streets glistened with water and the gutters gurgled with little rivers. Brian watched red and blue lights reflect off the shiny street. Radios blared and neighbors stood in their yards whispering.

"Amazing!" mumbled Brian. "All of this is happening because no one will answer a simple request." He lit a cigarette and inhaled deeply.

Nick flared. "Hey. If some dingbat aliens want you to go to South America, they should take you themselves, or give you proof that anyone can accept. To me it sounds like a load. A crock! I mean, why don't they just do it?"

Brian froze in mid-stride. The Host spoke from him.

Of this, free will is of man. Knowledge only may be given. Of this, Secondary World rules man. Noted: evil rules earth. Of this, all communications monitored, via selene orbital probe. All monitored. Over-ride permitted--on condition only. Conditional communications, only. Conditional relations. Man asks why? For, by his own hands, by his own mind, he must maintain and build. He must learn to survive of his own will in the world of the future, or perish.

When the voice finished, Brian stumbled. "Damn it. What happened?" Disoriented and dizzy, he slipped and fell hard into the gutter. Storm water soaked his clothes and jacket as waves splashed up onto the grass. Shivering, Brian held his head up to protect the cigarette.

For a few moments, he didn't move. He watched the stream of cold water wash around him. Nick started to laugh. Brian carefully clasped his fingers around the cigarette, took a long drag and nodded at Nick. "Do you mind helping me up?" he said. "I seem to have slipped into the gutter of life."

As the ambulance rolled away with lights flashing, Nick pulled Brian up out of the water.

"It's very clear," Brian said. "That I have no idea what is happening to me. Do you mind telling me how I got here?"

"You walked," Nick said. "Then you stopped, like you were paralyzed. Some DEEP voice was coming out of you."

"What did he say?"

"Just a bunch of crap," Nick said. "Total crap."

Police Report

POLICE REPORT – Friday, 13th, 1976. This is just part of the report which says Mary Beth was taken to the hospital with seizures, and that the 1 year old infant was found in the backyard by Brian and officers.

Doctor Bill

MEMO	DATE	O	A	B	C	D

NAME SCOTT, BRIAN
ADDRESS 12 ST
CITY GARDEN GROVE, CALIF 92640
537-7944

MEMO	DATE	O	A	B	C	D
	4/24/75	balance forward #5074				
Mary	12/22/75	25⁰	75⁰			2⁰⁰
Mary	1/26/76	16-				16-
Vicki	2/12/76	History & Physical				50⁰⁰
Vicki	2/13-2/17	5 Hospital Visits 1 @ $16				80⁰⁰
Mary	2/13/76	History & Physical				50⁰⁰
Mary	2/14-2/16	3 Hospital Visits 1 @ $16				48⁰⁰
Vicki	2/18/76	History & Physical				50⁰⁰
Vicki	2/19-2/23	5 Hospital Visits @ $16				80⁰⁰
Mary	3/12/76	15⁰⁰	85⁰			
Vicki	3/26	Billed Travelers				2-
Mary	3/26	Billed Travelers				2-
Jennifer	3/27/76	15⁰⁰				
Mary	3/27/76	15⁰⁰				
Mary	4/9/76	Travelers				
Mary	4/9/76	Travelers				
Vicki	4/9/76	Travelers				

BRIAN and MARY BETH in 1972, on their wedding day.
Three years later, in 1975, Brian's hair had been cut short,
and Mary Beth had given birth to two children.

POSSESSION

THE SUPPOSED CONTROL OF A HUMAN BODY AND MIND
BY AN ALIEN SPIRIT—HUMAN OR NON-HUMAN.
THE SPIRIT IS HELD TO HAVE ENTERED THE PERSON
IN ORDER TO FORETELL THE FUTURE OR PROCLAIM THE WILL OF GOD.
THE GOD HIMSELF MAY BE REGARDED
AS SPEAKING THROUGH THE MOUTH OF THE DEVOTEE.
HENCE, THE AUTHORITY OF A PROPHET.
THE MANIFESTATIONS ARE OFTEN VOLUNTARILY INDUCED
AND ARE PROVOKED IN MANY DIFFERENT WAYS.

(Encyclopedia Britannica, V. 18, Page 300-301).

Chapter 7

The Spirit of Man, Broken

The next afternoon, in a cold February rain, Brian's Captain America truck splashed out of the parking lot at work. Brian turned the radio from disco music to mellow rock. As he passed along a huge orange orchard, Brian saw a colorful VW bus with the hood up and a half-dozen hippies stumbling around barefooted in the mud, obviously stoned on some drug--probably LSD. Brian drove down the narrow dirt road. The driver, with a frightened look on his face, gestured for help. The battery was dead. Brian pulled the Captain America truck up behind the van painted with a 'flower power' scene.

With a jolt, Brian shoved the van forward as laughing young men and women jumped in and slammed doors. An attractive girl waved two-finger peace signs as the van started. Brian grumbled at them. "Go back to school. Get a job." He roared past the van and yelled. "And, stay out of the orchards."

As Brian drove home in the rain, he remembered how he had grown up among hippies and drug-users. In his younger years, he had tried LSD.

He knew it could make thoughts take physical form, as illusions. But it was nothing like thought transference from the machine on the giant's craft. That was solid, orderly, and accurate.

Thoughts didn't bother Brian, just the emotions that came with them. He didn't like that part. He had learned in drafting to not let his mind run wild. He had learned to use his mind like a vise to hold images still and solid. That new ability had given him a career. But, what happens when feelings take over— feelings could sweep away all logical thoughts, like a hurricane blasting down a

137

house. What good were logical thoughts, if feelings wiped them away? Why did something bad always seem to happen? Why did the dark-side always seem to win?

Brian hoped the terrible times were over. He didn't know they had just begun, for he had not yet learned to understand the dark side of himself, and others. He didn't know the goal of Voltar was for Brian to experience the deepest, most subconscious areas of mind and soul. He didn't know that his life would be destroyed. He didn't understand that the real purpose was for him to share the sorrows of man, so he could know the heart and soul of all mankind.

When Brian arrived home, a new UFO investigator waited in the kitchen. Mary Beth introduced a fat Italian man about 45 years old, his face pock-marked with acne scars. Even deeper scars marked the back of his neck, obviously from a severe burn. His shirt pocket bulged with pens and instruments. Bob Martino, a television repairman, lived nearby in Fullerton and had recently joined a national UFO organization.

Martino told Brian that Dr. Hynek and Jacques Vallee were in Los Angeles to work on a movie, Close Encounters of the Third Kind. "It's about contactees," Martino said. "They are doing it with the director of Jaws." Brian knew about it from the Hollywood meeting in the fall.

"Everything is hush, hush," Martino said. "It's a 'very personal' project of the director. Top secret." Martino wanted to obtain the book of Brian's writings. After Brian gave him a full book, Martino pushed himself away from the table, breathing heavily. "I'll call you," he said.

Brian watched Martino drive away in a beat up '63 Chevrolet with smoke pouring out of the exhaust pipe. Brian shrugged. "I don't know who is more pathetic, me or the investigators."

Later that night, Brian looked at the phone bill and groaned. "They want us to pay for the Bell's Palsy at the hospital." Then he ripped open the phone bill. "Damn it. Is Kate still calling collect?" he flushed with anger. "Another three hundred dollars?"

"Kate needs help," Mary Beth pleaded. "She has no money and can't use her dad's phone. She *has* to call collect."

"Don't accept then, Damn it!" Brian shrieked.

"It's Ginger! Tell her!"

Ginger bounced in from the bedroom with the baby in one arm. "There was another writing about an earthquake in Guatemala," she said waving the page. "I called Lenny. He wants it documented."

"Oh, God! You didn't?" Brian groaned. "Damn it. We've got to get our act together. I sent him home."

"He said he'll get you on a national talk show and open it in public if you have it NOTARIZED correctly. Maybe you could make some money that way."

"This is so ridiculous," Brian said. "It's not about earthquakes or money. We've got to put a stop to this. YOU'VE got to stop this." He glared at Ginger. "And, no more calls from Kate. Tell her to write letters, damn it."

Ginger turned away with hurt feelings and began to cry. "She says you caused it Brian. You should be paying for it."

Brian groaned. "Now I'M causing it? How the hell is that? HUH? Damn it to hell."

Mary Beth moved up close to Brian. "Calm down, Brian. Ginger is the best thing we've got. Why don't you just sell the truck? Pay off the phone bill and go to South America?"

"It won't do any good for me to go by myself. It has to be of man, because man WANTS to go. I know that much."

"But it's not working," Mary Beth said. "No one cares—and your children need you. This is taking you away from our family."

In the living room, little Kathy wanted to play with Brian. She sat on the couch pushing a big yellow truck. "Play, Daddy," she squeaked.

Brian wanted to go outside. "You play with her NOW," Mary Beth shouted handing him a load for the dryer. "After what she saw the other night, she needs you now--NORMAL."

Kathy smiled from her cute, heart-shaped face. She lifted up the heavy truck and melted Brian's heart with a pout. "Okay. I'll play trucks," he smiled. Brian slipped the diapers into the drier and walked back into the living room. The couch was empty, except for the truck.

Stunned, Brian spun around. He heard Ginger talking to the baby in the bedroom. He looked in on them. "Where's Kathy?"

"She's with you," Ginger answered.

"I don't have her." Baffled, Brian quickly searched the living room. "She's not here."

"She was right on the couch," said Mary Beth from the kitchen. "She didn't come in here." Frantically, Ginger searched the guest bedroom calling for Kathy. Brian searched the den as Mary Beth searched the master bedroom. Their fears raced. Their baby girl had simply vanished. Mary Beth felt the sorrow and terror of a mother losing her child--forever.

Then Brian saw the dog Iggi whining at the back door.

Brian let him out, and Iggi streaked outside, barking. Brian saw Kathy sitting in the yard, quietly. The dog barked loudly and snapped at the air above her. Brian sniffed the air. It smelled awful—like rotten eggs. He gagged, then swept Kathy into his arms as Mary Beth and Ginger arrived. "It was here," he said.

"Oh God," Mary Beth cried. She grabbed Kathy and ran inside.

139

Inside the house, Brian checked the lock. "It was shut tight," Brian whispered. "There was no way she could open it."

Mary Beth closed big heavy drapes on the bay window. "What are you doing?" whined Brian.

"I am shutting the curtains!" Mary Beth shrieked. "I do not want that thing seeing into our house!"

Brian shrugged. "I don't think the curtains make any difference. Can't you leave them open *a little?*"

"No!" she shouted, struggling.

"It's too dark with those drapes closed," Brian whined. "I feel shut-in."

"The drapes are closed," Mary Beth screamed. "Now lock the doors." Brian locked the front and back doors securely. He plopped on the floor again with Kathy and the toy truck as Mary Beth watched for a few minutes.

"This is driving me crazy," Mary Beth sobbed. "And you don't care."

"What can I do? I don't control it. Look--she's okay."

"I can't take this!" she screamed.

A preview for the ten o'clock news flashed on TV about a devastating earthquake in Guatemala. When Brian looked back, Kathy was gone. The truck remained. "Mary Beth? Did you just take Kathy?"

Mary Beth stomped into the room with laundry soap in hand.

"She was right here!" Brian said. "Right here. I looked up at the news and looked back. She was gone again."

Mary Beth cried out. "God damn it. The children! I knew it."

Iggi whined at the back door, again. The dog raced outside when Brian looked outside into the yard. Iggi raced towards the alley as Brian heard a child's cry. Brian bolted through the yard following the dog.

Behind the garage, in the alley near Brian's old 1964 Buick race car, sat Kathy, her eyes locked wide-open and staring at a red ball-of-light.

"Leave us alone," Brian hissed. He slid under the light, scooped up Kathy and ran back to the house with the dog yipping at his heels.

As Brian slammed into the house, Mary Beth grabbed and kissed Kathy, sobbing. "That time I know for sure the door was locked."

Kathy seemed dazed. "She's limp!"

Brian stood her up on the floor. She melted to the carpet with eyes fixed, wide-open.

"She's staring. Like Ginger!" Mary Beth cried.

Brian tried to stand Kathy upright again, but when he let go, she wilted forward onto her face.

"Oh God," Mary Beth cried. "Call somebody. They took her."

"Call who? A doctor?" he said running to the phone.

"Brian her forehead is hot, very hot." Mary Beth felt Kathy's body. "She's burning up."

Mary Beth hurried into the girls' bedroom with Kathy in her arms. When she opened the door, a light flashed brilliant white. Blinded for a moment, Mary Beth saw the Host over the baby's crib. He held his arms out shielding the baby, Amy, from above.

"Not of I," he said. "Evil of the Secondary."

"Leave us alone!" Mary Beth screamed. The Host nodded in agreement and disappeared as an ominous, red ball of light zipped into the room. The light beeped, clicked and hovered above the crib, terrifying Mary Beth. Her baby girl began to cry.

Suddenly, the light spoke with a dry, crackling voice. "Who are you?" The demanding tone cut into Mary Beth's heart.

"Who am I?" she asked with a whisper.

"Who are you?" the light asked again. Mary Beth's body trembled like a leaf. She wanted to grab Amy, she wanted to scream for help, but she couldn't move. Suddenly the light drifted downward, closer to the baby.

Mary Beth heard Brian on the phone talking to a doctor. Finally, she puffed up with strength. "I am Mary Beth Scott--wife of Brian and the mother of these two girls. Please don't hurt us."

The light spoke again. "Request Scott. Brian. Scott."

Mary Beth's legs shook out of control. "Brian. Brian! The light is in here," she yelled. "It wants you!"

Brian ran into the room. As he entered, the light beeped rapidly clicking with high-frequency sounds.

"It asked for you," Mary Beth said shaking.

"Whose are you?" Brian asked. He nudged Mary Beth out of the room with Kathy in her arms. He stalked closer to the crib. "You are the Secondary, aren't you?" The light didn't respond. "Aren't you!" he demanded. The light pulsed bright red. The high-frequencies tones and clicks rose in volume. "Get out of here!"

As Brian prepared to leap forward and grab Amy, the light streaked across the room striking toys and tossing them around the room. Brian grabbed the baby into his arms. Toys flew. The light zipped back and forth in front of Brian, and then dove under the bed. The toys on the bed lifted upward and, as he watched in slow motion, they seemed to stop in mid-air, then they plummeted back to the floor.

On the bed, the yellow toy truck rocked in motion, catching his eye. It rocked back and forth, slowly. The light zipped up and out of the room.

Brian sat down with the Amy in his arms. She cooed at him with a smile as if nothing terrible had just happened. He loved her innocence and her beautiful smile. He picked up the toy truck and held it in his hands. Why did he buy a heavy, metal toy truck for his girls? That was strange. Why did he seem so harsh and so mean and so cruel to Mary Beth and to his girls? Why was he so heartless, so unfeeling, so angry, so hateful, so bitter, so angry, so hate-filled?

The thoughts rose up suddenly like magma feeding a volcano. His whole body began to feel hot, to shake and quiver.

FLASH. Brian suddenly saw a vision of himself as a little boy. He saw his dad--a tall, slender, happy man with a thick Swedish accent and a camera. A bright light flashed as his father snapped pictures. Brian posed with a tiny black and white bulldog, his pet. A strobe for the camera FLASHED.

Brian played with a ball and smiled for the camera. FLASH. His dad laughed and smiled. FLASH. Brian loved his dad. For three years, Brian's brilliant father had raised his son, taking pictures and talking to him daily.

Brian remembered the only gift he ever received from his father—a photo album. It was in the room, somewhere. Brian's hands fumbled among the baby books and pulled out the big leather-bound photo album. It fell into his lap. Brian looked at the beautiful leather cover: BRIAN ALAN SCOTT –YOUR LIFE. The words had been engraved into the thick, beautiful leather. This was the most beautiful book he had ever seen. He turned the pages.

FLASH! He saw himself playing, smiling--as a joyful little boy--in picture after picture. FLASH! He saw pictures of his grandparents, his father. For years, he had longed to touch his dad, feel his skin, hear his voice, and hold his hand. But, he never had seen him again. Brian caressed the book as if it was the face of his father. He touched his father's skin in a photo and began to cry.

As tears flowed, Brian realized that he wanted a son to carry on his father's name--a son to play with the truck, a son to be like his dad.

Amy looked up at Brian. "Da Da," she whispered.

Brian had hidden his feelings. He loved both the girls so much that his heart overflowed--but still, he wanted a boy.

Brian fondled a photo of his dad, smiling. "My daddy," he whispered. "My daddy." Suddenly, Brian's heart broke open. A flood of emotion swept over him, drowning his mind. Waves of guilt and sorrow and loneliness swept over him.

Amy nudged against his neck. He hugged her close, and cried.

An hour later, Brian shuffled out of the bedroom with red eyes. He laid Amy next to Mary Beth on the couch, and lit a cigarette. "I am calling somebody," he told Mary Beth in a raspy voice. "How is Kathy?"

"She's asleep. I think she'll come out of it." Touching both girls, she sniffled back tears.

"Nothing happened to Amy," Brian said. "I don't know what they are doing, but I can't take it anymore." He held up the phone. "Who should I call? Tell me."

"No investigators," Mary Beth smirked. "They do nothing."

Brian pondered a moment then dialed Peter Bannock, the young newspaper reporter. Bright-eyed Peter rushed over to Brian's house within minutes after getting the call.

In the living room, Peter opened his notebook. "Maybe people who read this will give you help. We might as well tell the whole story."

"I don't know where to start," Brian said, standing next to his huge sailing ship. With red, swollen eyes, he brushed dust off faces of all the little men. He hadn't cleaned their faces for a long time.

"Why is this happening to you?" asked Peter. "That's the question everyone will ask. Why you and not someone else?"

"I don't know," Brian sniffed. "I think I was in the wrong place at the wrong time."

"That's not true," Mary Beth huffed. "You saw the light at sixteen. They knew you then. The Host said he had touched you at birth." She frowned. "Brian doesn't connect to what is happening." She looked at Peter, "I think we are being punished."

Brian groaned. "Punished?" Peter asked him. "Do you think you are being punished?"

Brian laughed wryly. "No. We aren't being punished. The first two investigators broke their word. They said they would comply, and then didn't. It gave the bad guys an opening."

"We ARE being punished," Mary Beth said. "He just agreed with me. It's like Job in the Bible--we are being punished."

Brian shrugged. "It is very simple. Man can't keep his word. Man failed, so they might as well be destroyed. This is just a sample of what they can do to us. What we have suffered is nothing—compared to dying."

"But why!" Mary Beth shouted. "What did we do?"

"You guys, look," said the reporter. "I can't follow any of this. I can't write a story about this kind of stuff. This is too vague. I need something I can work with."

"Where do you want me to start?" Brian asked.

"In the beginning," Peter said with his pen ready.

"The beginning of what? The earth? Or--man?"

"No, Brian. Your first contact."

Brian shrugged. "It's difficult to back up. I do know one thing. This isn't about THEM--it's about us." He breathed deeply.

"What do you mean, 'us?' Peter asked.

"Obviously they can do anything. They can prove they exist anytime, show up anywhere, but they don't. It's about MAN. So we learn about who we are. Our

143

mind, our heart. Our past, our future. First, we must understand ourselves, before we can understand them."

"Okay," Peter said with frustration. "Brian, look. Tell me about your first contact. That's all. Nothing else. Then, I'll try to understand."

They talked all night as Mary Beth slept on the couch with the two girls in her arms.

In the morning, Brian opened the curtains. Golden rays of sunlight beamed into the darkness through the big bay windows. The golden carpet and big white couches shone with light, like a vision of heaven. "Pretty living room," said Peter. "When you let in the light."

"Thanks for listening," Brian smiled as he patted Peter on the shoulder. For the first time, someone had listened--really listened. For the first time, Brian felt a glimmer of hope.

Earthquakes Again

The next day, on Thursday February 12, Mary Beth found Brian in the den, staring blankly at a writing. He looked up at her with tear-filled eyes. He had found another earthquake prediction.

"Are you okay, Brian?"

"I'm okay, but they're not."

"Who is *they?*"

"The people," he choked. "Brown skinned people. It just keeps going on for them. So many deaths of gentle, loving people." Tears rolled down his face. "I feel horrible." She hugged him. "And I'm supposed to get the *'prediction'* certified. What good will that do for the people who are going to die today?"

"It's okay, Brian."

"It's not okay." Tears welled up in his eyes. "It is NOT okay. I don't like these feelings. I don't want to know how they FEEL when they die," he sobbed. "I don't want to see them DIE. It's horrible. They want to live. They fight to stay alive. Even the children fight to live."

Mary Beth felt his sorrow.

The Hospital

At work that day, Brian and his design team set up an attractive display in the executive boardroom of the company. Brian arranged his drawings of their new product.

"Looks great," said the Persian, wearing a burgundy turban.

"You have outdone yourself, Brian," said the Frenchman. He patted Brian on the shoulder. "The prototype is better than I imagined."

As executives filed into the room, a sophisticated woman rushed around them. "Brian Scott, you have an emergency phone call."

Brian's face bleached. "Oh, God." He glanced at his team.

"Go ahead," said the Frenchman. "We can handle it." Brian raced for the doorway apologizing to a dozen very distinguished vice-presidents from around the world.

Minutes later, Brian's Ford Pinto screeched around the corner and bounced to a stop at the hospital. He ran inside the emergency room to find Mary Beth's mother and Ginger talking to a doctor. Kathy lay on a gurney, unmoving, with her eyes wide-open.

"How long has she been this way," the doctor asked Brian.

"About three days."

"THREE DAYS. You should have called earlier. What happened?"

"She had a contact with a ball of light."

"Lightening?"

"No. A ball of light."

The doctor examined her legs, feet and hands quickly, then her scalp for burns.

"Did she become listless, like this, after this ball of light?"

"Yes--after the second time. We hoped she would come out of it. She did the first time."

"We'll have to get her some fluids, and start some tests."

A nurse started an IV needle for fluids then wheeled Kathy away for tests.

That night, Mary Beth's parents gathered into the Intensive Care Unit to be with their sick little grandchild. "She just stares," Mary Beth said. "Then goes back to sleep. He said it is like a coma."

She'll be okay. She probably is with them--mentally," Brian said. "They can do that." A nurse perked up at his words, and frowned.

Brian's father-in-law gestured to Brian. "Can I talk to you outside?" Brian stepped outside. Mr. Parsons looked Brian in the eyes. "Brian, you've got one sick little girl, and no one knows what is causing it."

"It was the light."

Mr. Parsons spoke softly. "Brian, your lights and your UFO story are too much for anyone to believe. Don't talk about it, here. The nurses might think you are a loony bird, and Kathy may not get the best treatment, because of it."

Brian nodded in agreement.

145

"Now another thing, Brian. Something has to be done to stop this. We've got to do whatever it takes. You and me. Do you understand? As the men of this family. Do you understand?"

"I'm not sure we can," Brian said.

"If you can't. I will," he said firmly. "Somehow, someway, you have to cut loose from this--whatever it is. Put a stop to it, somehow, for the good of your family. Now, if you need help, I will help you. That's what I am saying. I will find a way. I have friends at El Toro. I can bring in doctors, pilots, MP's. I can get you a place to stay. I can make things happen."

Brian nodded with understanding. Mr. Parsons shook Brian's hand firmly.

The next morning, as Brian shaved, Lenny the UCLA researcher called. He asked if the last prediction had been notarized.

"Which one? Brian asked. "I'm getting so confused."

"How could you forget about it, Brian? That's important."

"We had a one hell of a day, yesterday. Kathy was hospitalized. I totally forgot about it."

Lenny insisted the paper be dated and notarized. "With good certification I can get you the help you need." Brian promised to try.

Mary Beth Possessed

That day, in a huge electronics factory, Mary Beth carried a heavy box of power supplies away from an assembly line to a cart. She had worked in the factory for several years and had earned the position of a line inspector. She sat back down on a tall stool at the end of the line. She pushed a button and the line began moving. About a dozen girls started to assemble power supplies for computers.

Marla Park, a pretty, long-haired brunette about twenty-four years old, watched the line run. As Mary Beth's supervisor, she had heard stories about the ball of light, and UFO's. She didn't believe them, but she liked Mary Beth. She could be trusted to be alert and do the tough jobs.

Then, she saw Mary Beth miss an inspection with eyes open wide and fixed. "Mary Beth!" Marla shouted. Mary Beth's face contorted. A dark countenance swept over her, and she jerked backwards off the stool. She hit a cart and fell to the ground, hard. Marla felt a primal fear, an instinctive terror that this was not normal. Her skin rippled with goose bumps.

As people gathered, Mary Beth lay on the floor growling and writhing. A deep voice rattled from her throat. "Astaaa. Astaaaaaa."

Marla bent close and tried to comfort Mary Beth, but her body was rigid as rock. "Astaaaa," growled a demon. Marla called for help.

146

In the executive conference room, Brian and his design team discussed the prototype with a few key executives. As Brian took notes for design changes, the president's executive secretary stepped into the room. "Excuse me. Brian, you have another emergency phone call." Brian apologized and hurried out of the room leaving his notes to the Frenchman.

An hour later, the Captain America truck screeched around a corner at a post office and skidded to a stop. Mary Beth sat in the front seat, dazed. "I'm okay," she said. "I don't know why they called you."

Brian eyed her carefully, and ran to the post office. He reached the front door just as a mailman keyed the lock. Brian shook the door politely. The man turned away. Brian pounded on the door hard. The man glanced back and mouthed the words, "Closed--5:00 p.m."

"This is important. It has to be certified. Today!" shouted Brian. He shook the envelope with the earthquake prediction.

The man pointed at the sign. "Five-o'clock."

"It's not even one minute after," Brian shouted.

"We are closed." Brian kicked the door and picked up a hand-sized rock from the landscape. He faked a throw into the window. Inside, the mailman and several people ducked. Brian dropped the rock, and hurried away.

The mailman opened the post office door. "You come back here again, and I'll have you arrested on the spot for menacing."

"Get a real job," Brian screamed.

"You are over the edge," Mary Beth said when Brian slammed into the truck. "You need to calm down."

"Screw him. Screw everybody," Brian screamed. He screeched away leaving two black tracks on the pavement and a cloud of blue smoke.

Mary Beth Taken

A few minutes later, Brian and Mary Beth slammed into their house. Ginger waited for an explanation with Amy in her arms. Brian steamed. "I had to leave the most important meeting of my life, missed the post office--and now she's fine. Jesus!" he slammed the back door as Mary Beth shuffled into the bathroom. She slammed that door.

"You'll wreck the doors," Ginger said. "What is going on?"

"Who the hell knows," Brian snapped. "This whole thing is driving me nuts. The magnetometer on the back porch rang. Brian saw nothing. "That damn thing is worthless."

For a while, Brian and Ginger sat in silence together at the table. He spewed his rage and anger to her, and finally calmed down. "Can we go see Kathy in the hospital?" she asked.

"Is Mary Beth still in the shower?" Brian replied. Agitated, he knocked on the bathroom door and listened to the water run. "Mary Beth?"

He opened the door. Steam filled the room--but no Mary Beth. Cautiously, Brian opened the glass shower stall. "She's not here!"

Frantically, Brian and Ginger searched the house, but Mary Beth was gone.

Onboard a circular craft, in a dark room, Mary Beth woke up and opened her eyes. She felt the huge scaly hands and arms of two giant, gray-skinned hulks. She could feel their breathing, and hear them wheezing.

Terrified, she tried to break free. One of them grabbed her leg and lifted her up in the air. Naked, she fought hard to get loose. His hand scratched her inner thigh, before she passed out.

At home, two hours later, Brian checked the bathroom again as Ginger talked on the phone to her parents. He paced back and forth carrying Mary Beth's nightgown in his hands. "Too much," he whispered. "It's too much."

Suddenly, the magnetometer rang again with alarm. From the bathroom, he heard a commotion. Brian ran to the door and kicked it open hitting Mary Beth's feet. She lay on the floor, naked.

"Oh, God," he gasped, pulling her up.

She woke up. "Don't touch me! Don't touch me." She screamed hysterically, and then she fainted to the floor. Her body shook out of control with convulsions. Ginger called for help.

Within five minutes, two paramedics rushed into the room and tried to examine Mary Beth, but she screamed hysterically and fought them. "Don't touch me," she shrieked with eyes fixed and staring.

"That's what she's been doing," Brian told the men. "She's out of it."

The paramedics tried to load Mary Beth onto a gurney as two police officers arrived. The officers helped as she kicked and fought them all until the paramedics injected a tranquilizer.

"What happened?" an officer asked Brian.

"She's just acting weird. I don't know what happened."

"Is this your wife?"

"Yes."

"She seems to be having seizures of some kind."

"She's been having problems. We all have. I have a little girl in the hospital right now."

"What's causing it?" asked the officer.

"We've been having balls-of-light around here since November."

The cops scanned the room, nervously. One of them looked at Brian in awe. "Is this the house…? Are you Brian Scott?"

Brian nodded. "Yes, unfortunately, I am."

Amy Taken

As the paramedics loaded Mary Beth into a gurney and rolled her out of the room, Ginger placed Amy into the playpen, and called her parents again.

Brian stepped outside into the shivering night air with the police. Neighbors watched in long coats and robes as ambulance lights reflected on the windows of their homes.

The investigating officer started to write on a note pad with a pencil. "How long as this been going on?"

"It just started today," he said. "I had to bring her home from work."

"But weren't you missing, a few months ago?" asked the other officer.

"That's right," Brian said.

"Your wife reported lights and said some man formed out of a ball-of-light. And you were abducted by a UFO?"

"Yeah."

"How can they do that without everyone seeing a craft?"

"They hit you with a stretchy-like beam. You go horizontal, and vertical, up and down--then POP! You're with them."

The investigating officer put away his pen. "I don't want another report like the last one." He looked at Brian. "I'm going to say your wife fainted."

The officers shuffled to their cars, and Brian hurried back into the house. Ginger rushed into the bedroom for Amy, but the playpen was empty.

"Do you have Amy?" she shouted.

"No. You put her in there."

Ginger gasped. "She couldn't get out! I didn't move her Brian. She's gone." Brian ran to the front door and yelled at the cops.

"Hey. We need help. My baby is missing. She's gone."

The two cops raced into the house and searched with Brian and Ginger. They called for backup as Brian saw Iggi scratching at the back door. Brian let the dog out and followed him into the dark night. The officers followed Brian with flashlights and guns drawn.

Brian heard Amy cry. He raced around the garage and into the alley to see Iggi jumping at a red ball of light. "Get out of here," Brian screamed as he lunged under the light. He swept Amy into his arms. The light blinked out as the cops arrived.

149

"Where was she?" asked the first officer.

"Right there, on the ground," Brian panted. "Just like Kathy was--right here. The light was over her. Smell it. That's its smell."

"Step away slowly," the cop ordered Brian with gun in hand. He sniffed. "Whew. That does smell." The second cop lit up the ground with his flashlight and looked for footprints. They saw Brian's shoe prints and tracks of the dog. They told Brian to not move as they examined his shoes and Amy's bare feet, which were clean. Two other police cars roared into the alley with lights flashing.

Amy whimpered. "I've got to get her in the house," Brian pleaded. "It's freezing out here."

"Check his other shoes," said one of the cops.

The ranking officer eyed Brian carefully and gestured for him to go in. Two cops followed Brian into the house.

In the house, the two officers questioned Brian. On a table, they dumped all of his shoes--his black engineering boots, his cowboy boots, loafers, sandals, slippers and tennis shoes.

"Am I a suspect in this?" Brian snapped. "Do you think I put her out there?"

"Something strange is going on," said an officer. "We need to find out what it is."

"Oh God. We need HELP!" Brian bellowed at the officers. "God damn it. We need someone to help us."

"Settle down," said an officer, "or we will take you down to the station." Brian swore under his breath as he stood by the big sailing ship. A female officer arrived and gently took Amy from his arms.

When Mary Beth's parents arrived, the investigating officer suggested they take the baby home for now. They agreed, and Ginger followed -- leaving Brian alone. He sat down at the table and began to moan with sorrow. Where were his allies, now? Has the evil side won? Did they win the right to torment and terrify his family?

"Do you know why this is happening?" an officer asked Brian with compassion. He took out his pen.

"Nobody tells me nothing anymore," Brian said. "They aren't speaking to me."

The chief investigating officer returned to the Garden Grove police department and filed a one-page, handwritten report, #76-2860, Friday 13, 1976 at 2:02 a.m. In the report, he listed both Brian and Mary Beth Scott as victims.

The victim's husband stated that his wife was having seizure as a result of lights and fireballs from outer space, and stated

they had been having this problem ever since he was picked up by a spaceship. Victim's husband also stated he was in a spaceship a couple of months ago.

Victim transported by ambulance to hospital. As officers were about to depart, husband rushed out and stated "my child is missing." Officers and husband found the one year old child in the back yard. As the husband was very agitated....when grandparents arrived, child was transferred to them.

Mary Beth Attacks the Doctor

When Brian finally arrived at the hospital emergency ward, he saw a doctor and nurse binding Mary Beth to a gurney with straps. She fought them violently roaring "Asssttaaaaa." She pulled a hand loose and swung, scratching the doctor across the face and eye.

The young man jerked away bleeding.

"What is she saying?" the doctor whined, in pain.

"It sounds like Asta," Brian gasped.

"She attacked me," said the doctor. "It was very vicious."

The demon roared again. "Aaasstttaaaa."

"I've never seen anything like it. Has she ever done this kind of thing before?"

"No. It's from whatever the hell it is that's going on," Brian said.

"What is going on?" the doctor asked.

"You don't want to know," Brian said.

A few hours later, as Brian waited alone, a nurse approached him with fear on her face. "Brian. We are having a problem."

Then the young doctor rushed out. "Medications are not working very well on your wife. Even with heavy sedation. It's still going on." Brian heard a loud growl from behind the curtains.

"Look," the doctor said nervously. "Someone has suggested to me that I advise you to contact an exorcist. Have you considered that before?"

"No." Brian asked nervously. "Is she possessed?"

"I don't know," said the frightened doctor. He breathed deep. "All I am saying is you have my permission to try an alternative."

The nurse slid up close to Brian and touched his shoulder. "Calvary Chapel." She handed him coins for the phone.

151

They heard Mary Beth rage. "That's not normal," she said. "She's attacking everyone. She escaped the bindings. That's never happened. Even the orderlies are frightened."

Brian grimaced. "Something is wrong, very wrong. She's really a sweet girl."

"Call Calvary," said the nurse. "Now. Ask for Pastor Chuck. He knows what to do." Brian stepped to the phone, quivering. "Calvary Chapel in Santa Ana."

The News Reporter

For a few hours, Brian slept on a couch near the emergency ward. A bearded young man wearing a long overcoat woke him up.

"Excuse me. Are you Mr. Scott?" the newspaper reporter asked. About 27, he appeared tired and gaunt.

Brian jumped to alertness. "Yes. Are you from Calvary...?"

"No. I'm a reporter. I follow the police radio and heard the call to your home. If you wouldn't mind, it might be worth a story."

Brian looked at his watch. "Three-thirty?"

"She's in intensive care. It's pretty serious. You want to tell me about it?"

Brian rubbed his face and shrugged. "Do you think I can get a cup of coffee?

"I'll get it," the reporter smiled.

Two hours later, the ashtray next to Brian overflowed with cigarette butts. The reporter stood up, satisfied.

"We need some help. That's the main thing," said Brian. "I don't know how to make it stop."

"You might hold a press conference. Ask for help."

A young nurse from the morning shift interrupted. "Mr. Scott, your wife has been moved to a regular room, and some men are up there asking for you."

Hospital Exorcism

Brian ran to the hospital room in a flurry. When he arrived, two men in snappy sport coats were thumbing through Bibles. Mary Beth sat up in bed eating breakfast and beaming with happiness.

"Hi, honey," said Mary Beth. "These people are looking for you."

"We're from Calvary Chapel," said a curly-haired man in a blue sport coat. "The pastor is in a conference until Sunday." They were younger than Brian expected--in their early thirties, and they both looked a little nervous. "Did you want to fill us in on some of the details?"

152

"They think I am possessed," said Mary Beth, as she heartily swallowed a big bite of pancakes. "I told them to talk to you."

"Do you remember what happened last night?" Brian asked Mary Beth cautiously.

"No," she laughed. "I feel fine now. But, excuse me guys. I am going to have to go to the bathroom." She dropped out of the bed and slipped past them in her hospital gown.

As she closed the door to the bathroom, the men stepped close to Brian. "She seems to be okay now," whispered the curly haired man.

"She wasn't okay last night," Brian said.

"What is the name of the demon?"

Brian spoke softly. "It growls and says 'Asta.' It scratched the doctor and she gets very, very rigid and..."

"That's okay. We understand. We've seen it before."

"You've seen Asta?"

"Is it Ashtarte?" asked the younger Christian. Wearing long straight hair and a brown coat, he seemed more naive.

"Yeah," said the curly haired man. "Same as Ishtar in Babylon. Ashtarte in Canaan and Israel. Asta I think is Phoenician. Anyway, Ashtarte got them all into lust and sexual perversions. She caused Solomon to lose his temple."

Mary Beth stepped gingerly out of the bathroom and climbed back into bed. "I don't usually run around like this in front of strange men," she smiled.

They turned their heads away as her gown waved open in the back. "Do you have fellowship anywhere around here?" asked the curly haired man.

"What?" Brian asked blankly.

"Where do you go to church?"

"We don't," Brian said, sheepishly.

As a nurse checked Mary Beth's charts, the curly-haired man whispered to Brian. "I feel we should pray for your wife, right now. And, then we can come to your home and pray for you."

"I guess that's okay with me," Brian shrugged. "If you think that will stop it."

"Oh, it'll work," said the man holding up a Bible.

The two men shuffled up next to Mary Beth. The curly haired man opened the Bible and nervously placed his left hand on Mary Beth's forehead. Suddenly she flopped back in the bed. Mary Beth's lips began to quiver, then a hellish voice rattled from deep inside her, "Assssstttttaaaaaa."

The younger Christian quickly placed his hands on Mary Beth's arm. "In the name of Jesus, in the name of Jesus, come out of her Ashtarte. In the name of Jesus we command you to come out of her."

Mary Beth arched back and roared, "Asttttttttttaaaaaaaaa."

"Jesus," gasped the younger man. "It's strong."

The curly haired man prayed loudly. "Satan, in the name of Jesus, we command you to get behind this woman, get behind Jesus and get out of her. In the name of Jesus, get out. Get out of her!"

"Aaassstttaaaaa," raged the demon shaking the room.

The nurse rushed in and pushed the two men aside. Mary Beth viciously kicked and clawed at her. "You'll have to go," the nurse shouted at the prayer team. Mary Beth roared again. A male orderly grabbed Mary Beth, shoved her flat against the bed and quickly tied her down with thick straps. The nurse injected Mary Beth's arm with a tranquilizer. "You'll have to leave now," she shouted. "All of you. No more of this. Now. Get out! All of you. Out!"

Exorcism at Home

Later that day, in the alley behind the house, Brian pulled the tarp off his orange 1964 Buick race car revealing a lofty, chrome carburetor and huge engine. Then, with the Captain America truck, he parked the Buick in front of the house. On the race car, he placed a big sign: For Sale.

The two young Christians arrived with an older, white-haired man, an assistant pastor who seemed confident and assuring. He wore a rust-brown business suit.

Inside the house, the younger men nervously glanced through Brian's book of writings. "I can smell the evil," said the longhaired young man. He dropped the book like a hot potato.

The pastor sniffed the air and placed a chair in the middle of the living room. He asked Brian to sit down. The men opened their Bibles and gathered around. The pastor started. "The Word says that where one demon gets in, even if you cast him out, seven more can come if the temple remains unclean. That's you--the temple. In fact, legion is the number given. Thousands. Uncountable numbers. If you remain unclean."

Brian felt uncomfortable. He trembled a bit as the men moved closer. "What was the opening, Brian?" the pastor asked as he anointed Brian with oil. "What was the doorway by which the first demon got into your home and your wife?"

Brian looked around the house, nervously. "You think it is in here."

"Well, they have to have a dwelling place. But, I want to know if you understand exactly how this got started."

"Through those automatic writings?" asked the curly haired man, kicking the book away.

Brian grimaced. "My sister-in-law saves them. A lot of people think there are important things in them."

"Are these writings from Ashtarte?" asked the pastor.

"No. From the Host."

"Demons take on all kinds of personalities and identities," said the older man. "They play with your mind. Tell you lies, deceive you. Eat out the substance of your life. That's their job. They deceive you and try to substitute for Jesus in your mind, in your heart." The two younger men began to pray in tongues.

"Have they talked to you about any other gods?"

"No--maybe this one in South America. He was an Incan, but not..."

"It sounds like you got yourself a full house," said the pastor seriously. "You've got Ashtarte, Beelzebub, the Host, an Incan god, and then two groups of aliens? Do I have it right?"

Brian nodded yes.

"You've got enough for seven card stud." He patted Brian's shoulder. "Brian, do you enjoy playing cards with these jokers?"

"Well, I think the Host is different from the others. He's very assuring. It is the Secondary World that is bad."

"They are ALL demons," the pastor shouted. "All of them. Familiar spirits. Beelzebub is king of all the demons in the Bible. You got him, you got them all. Brian, they come in as *personalities*. Did you know that? From aliens to prophets to teachers of the light. Doesn't matter. They are all deceptions."

Brian listened intently. "Teachers of light?"

"Right. In the final days they come as teachers of light. Do you think you could see through that kind of deception?"

"I don't know."

"Not without the wisdom in this book," the pastor said holding up the Bible. "No one can. Not me. Not you. That's why I FEAR God. He lets them have us, if we want them. Does that scare you?"

The other men began praying louder.

"Does that scare you? Brian. Do you fear God?"

Brian shrugged. He felt nervous as the men gathered closer.

"I guess so. If that is what He does."

"Brian, would you like to see these demons cast out of your life?"

"Yes, I would," he said slowly.

"Brian, are you a sinner?"

Brian shrugged. "I try to do what is right."

"Brian, all men and women are sinners. We all fall short of the glory of God. I have sinned. So have you. God says so in this Book. It's true."

"I guess you are right," Brian said. "I have sinned—a lot, probably."

"Brian, your wife and daughter are in the hospital. Your baby is gone to her grandparents. Is that right?'

Brian hung his head down. "Yeah."

"Demons eat out your sustenance, your money, your time, your family. They isolate and weaken you like wolves hunting in a pack--then they bring you down for good. That's what is happening to you, now. Right now."

The other men prayed LOUDLY, in tongues, sounding like a choir.

"Brian, all that you love and hold onto is being taken from you. By who?" He waited for an answer.

Brian shrugged. "I don't know."

"By the devil," shouted the pastor. He lifted one hand to Brian's forehead. "When Jesus comes into your body and sanctifies your body as his temple, you begin to have an abundant life. A life you can live. The yoke of Jesus is light."

Brian started to argue. "What about the prophets. They all got killed."

"That was different. They were killed by men, and their names have lived on for 2000 years." The pastor poured more scented oil on Brian's forehead. "Demons are different. The yoke of demons is heavy, Brian--demons wound, maim, cripple your mind, your logic--then they destroy you."

Brian smelled the sweet oil of frankincense and myrrh.

"You are hurting Brian. Right? You have been wounded by a familiar spirit so Satan can take over your temple, your body, your life, forever."

Brian nodded. "But, the Host has kept his word to me. I don't think he is evil."

"The Host is a liar. Satan is a grand liar spinning webs of deception, around even the smartest man on the earth. Brian, you may be smart, but do you have more knowledge than God?"

Brian huffed. "No."

"Do you have more wisdom than God?"

"No, I guess not."

"That's right, Brian. You don't. None of us do. But God's wisdom and word and power is in this book," he said--holding up the Bible.

Brian nodded in assent.

"Brian, I feel a spirit of self-seeking," said the pastor, "a selfishness on your part--to be yourself--to find yourself, at any cost. We all do it, especially when young. We want to express our unique, individual selves. But that is NOT what the Bible advises. You must lose your LIFE to Jesus to find your self. Do you understand? Lose your LIFE to Jesus to find life. Doing your own thing—Brian—that's the devil speaking. That is what Satan says--*do your own thing. Find your own self.* Self-seeking. It is an empty path--a fruitless lie of Satan."

Brian shrugged. He didn't really believe everything the pastor was saying. But, he seemed good. He must have done this before, Brian thought.

The pastor read from the Bible. "For where envy and SELF-SEEKING exist, confusion and every evil thing will be there.' James 3:13."

"Did you grasp that Brian?" said the pastor. "Are you willing to yield to God's wisdom to get rid of these demons?"

"Yes, I guess so," Brian said. "If there are any demons. As long as I can get some answers out of this."

"Here's the answer you need, Brian," said the pastor. "God tests us to see if we will submit to the Word and to the right identity of God. We can't be double-minded in this. We can't serve two Gods. One God. One identity. That's it. He wants us to serve his identity as Jesus. That's it. You must endure the temptation of other gods, or familiar spirits, or demons when they offer knowledge, or truth about your self."

Brian frowned. "Endure the temptation of *other gods?"*

"Yes. You have *other gods.* Ashtarte is a goddess. Beelzebub was a god to the Canaanites. You also have familiar spirits. They know you well--your mind. Better than you, so they can deceive you easily. Now, when you submit to one God, in the image of Jesus and He enters you--you are covered, protected from familiar spirits and from Satan. Do you understand?"

"I guess so," Brian nodded. "But—how does that work?"

"It doesn't matter. We don't have to know."

"It's just everyone flips out," Brian said with dismay. "It doesn't bother me."

"Brian, you have NOT been covered by Jesus. Your wife is not covered. Neither are your children. Or, we wouldn't be here. Do you see that?

Brian nodded yes.

"Brian, Jesus will deliver you from these demons, if you submit to Him. He promises that, and He doesn't lie. Will you accept that promise as the truth?"

"I guess so," Brian shrugged.

"Will you accept Jesus into your spirit, so he can cast out these demons?"

"Yes," Brian said weakly. "I guess so."

The pastor raised his voice and placed both hands on Brian's head. "Lord Jesus, bind these demons who have entered the house of Brian Scott and his wife and their children. Bind up Satan, Lord Jesus. Jesus, cast out this demon Beelzebub," yelled the pastor. "Beelzebub, I command you in the name of Jesus to come out of this man." The pastor waited. "Beelzebub, I command you in the name of Jesus to COME OUT. NOW!"

Brian's mouth opened, his throat bulged and his skin turned red. A dark, deep voice growled from him: "Beaaaallzzeebuubb."

The pastor and the younger men jumped away as the presence of the demon took over. Brian's body jerked hard. His neck and shoulders convulsed. He gagged and choked.

"Beaaaalzzeeebubbb," the demon growled with a deep, hollow growl.

The pastor rushed back upon Brian with both hands on his head. "In the name of Jesus, come out of him--NOW."

157

The demon roared. "Beaaaaaazeeeeeebub!" Then Brian crashed to the floor, unconscious.

First Newspaper Article

UFO Malady?

Man Sends for Exorcist

A Garden Grove woman and her child, hospitalized under mysterious circumstances, were reported in good condition today as the father called upon an exorcist to release the pair from their "strange maladies."

A spokesman for Fountain Valley Community Hospital said Brian Scott maintained a vigil there early Saturday morning to await the exorcist who was summoned at the suggestion of one of Scott's physicians.

His wife remained hospitalized "under light restraints" after she was brought in late Friday suffering from an undefined seizure that Scott told hospital personnel was brought on by "a UFO experience."

The child, a two-year-old girl, had been brought to the hospital the day before suffering from symptoms of acute appendicitis. She was said to be resting comfortably and in no danger today.

Scott summoned paramedics to his home Thursday night after he claimed the child was found in the back yard with a strange red halo surrounding her head.

He was unable to explain how the child got from her crib to the yard. The presence of the red light and her complaints of stomach pains led him to call the paramedics.

A spokesman for the Garden Grove Police Department said paramedics were summoned to the Scott house a week ago under similar circumstances.

The police spokesman said Scott contacted the department once in 1975 to report that he and his family had been kidnapped by a UFO and held captive for several days.

The officer said the complaint was noted and filed without further investigation. He said no police reports had been made in the more recent incidents.

Scott told the hospital spokesman that he has been plagued by such events since he was 16 years old.

ORANGE COAST Pilot article printed on February 16, 1976. In the article Brian awaits the exorcist summoned by a physician. Some of the details are wrong, but the general thrust of the reporting was accurate.

159

JACQUES VALLEE -- A NEW FRAMEWORK NEEDED

I THINK BRIAN IS ILLUSTRATING EXCEPTIONALLY,
THE POINT I AM TRYING TO MAKE IN THIS BOOK: (INVISIBLE COLLEGE)

THAT THE RELIGIOUS FRAMEWORK, THE CLERGY,
WILL SAY IT IS A *PSYCHOLOGICA*L PHENOMENON, THE
PSYCHOLOGISTS WILL SAY IT IS A *PHYSICAL* PHENOMENON
THAT WE DON'T UNDERSTAND, THE PHYSICIST WILL SAY IT IS
MYSTICAL AND WE CAN'T DEAL WITH THAT.

SO, YOU ILLUSTRATE THAT EXACTLY.
THE PEOPLE SEND YOU BACK AND FORTH.
YOU GET THE RUN AROUND FROM ALL THE DIFFERENT DISCIPLINES.
THAT'S EXACTLY THE KIND OF THING
THAT CALLS FOR *A NEW FRAMEWORK*.

Jacques Vallee, Ph.D.

J. ALLEN HYNEK

IF ALIENS REALLY WANT TO GET INFORMATION OUT,
LET THEM COME TO THE RIGHT PEOPLE.
I THINK IT IS IMPORTANT FOR THE SCIENTIFIC COMMUNITY
TO NOT BE MANIPULATED BY THEM.
WE CAN'T APPEAR TO BE FOLLOWING
AROUND UFO CONTACTEES TO GET INFORMATION.
WE HAVE TO TAKE A SCIENTIFIC APPROACH.

-- J. Allen Hynek, Ph.D.

Chapter 8

The Investigators, Baffled

Later in the afternoon, Brian walked outside with the four Christians. "It should be over," the older man said warmly to Brian as they loaded into the car. "You need fellowship with Christians. Others can help you. Okay? But whatever you do, don't invite demons back into your life."

Brian shrugged. "I didn't invite them in." Brian leaned against his shiny Captain America flag truck and waved goodbye. He straightened his hair in the door mirror. He hadn't shaved for two days. He felt lousy. He wondered if the demons had been in him all along, or if they had been sent in by the Secondary World. They must be in all people, he reasoned. People must have both the good and evil inside. But, he wasn't sure, and he wanted answers.

That evening, feeling lonely in the empty house, Brian spun the dial on his radio. News of the day blared. The trial of Patty Hearst and the Symbianese Liberation Army was underway. The daughter of a wealthy publisher, Hearst had joined the radical revolutionaries after being kidnapped by them. She claimed to have been brainwashed and not responsible for her behavior during the robberies. Brian laughed. Could he make the same claim, he wondered?

As the radio and TV blared, Brian called UFO investigators for help. "I am really scared," Brian told Lenny Jacobs. "Nobody is talking to me. They are saying nothing. But, I know this is real. They are there. I want to find out what is happening --even if it kills me."

"What do you want to know?" Lenny asked.

"What is behind this? Am I causing it? Or is it from the aliens? What if demons are involved with Mary Beth? Or, me? I want to know," Brian said. "Do they come out when this happens, or do they really get inside of us? Or, are they projected there by the Secondary World aliens to frighten everyone away?"

Lenny didn't know. He believed ghosts were real. He told Brian that ghosts manifest things, but not balls of fire in the sky. "I don't think it is simply demons," he said. "Don't let the Christians get you down—the Pope was wrong about the solar system, about the earth being the center of the solar system. Good scientists were burned at the stake," Lenny said, "Just for bringing out the truth. So--Christians get things wrong," Lenny said. "The Catholic church was way wrong about scientific things, and they have persecuted Jews. They stood by while Hitler killed off my people."

Brian didn't want to get involved in religion or politics. His hands were full. Lenny said that Dr. Hynek and Dr. Jacques Vallee from France were both coming to Los Angeles for a UFO conference and to consult on the movie: <u>Close Encounters of the Third Kind.</u> Lenny had arranged a press conference in Los Angeles to get Brian some attention. "I've invited Dr. Hynek to come," he said.

Brian Considers a Religious View

The next morning, Sunday, Brian awoke on the floor in front of the TV wearing his clothes. The radio and TV blared. He had finally fallen asleep that way--surrounded by noise.

On the screen, a TV evangelist ranted about demons coming to earth in the form of UFO's. He held up Billy Graham's new book.

Brian listened a few minutes then turned the TV down and the radio up. A preacher also blared from the radio. "Must be Sunday," he muttered.

Wearing a three-day beard and t-shirt, Brian turned the volumes down. His ashtray overflowed with cigarette butts. As he shuffled around, cleaning up, he listened to a religious talk show on the radio. The female host invited calls to her guests on any religious subject.

With a cup of coffee and cigarette in hand, Brian shuffled to the phone and dialed the number. "I have had some strange experiences lately," Brian told the producer in a raw, raspy voice. "Balls of light in our house in Garden Grove. I thought it was UFO related, but various people, experts in the religious field, are telling me this might be religious. I would like to talk to your guests about these phenomenon and try to get some help for my family."

They accepted Brian's call. Brian slipped a cassette tape into a sound recorder. "What has been happening in your house?" asked the host, Carol Hemingway, in a clear feminine voice.

"This may sound a little bizarre," Brian said. "But it is a ball-of-light, if you want to put it like that. It has been seen in the house, on the grounds, everywhere. We have no real explanation for what it is. And, my wife is in the hospital and so is my daughter. So I am calling to ask what in the world do you do, if anything, to get rid of this thing."

No one responded.

Brian took their silence as an opening and rambled on about Bell's Palsy, the automatic writings and phrases from the Bible written in German, Hebrew and Greek.

Brian, I am very confused," said Hemingway. "You are going off on a lot of tangents. What is it that you are trying to tell us about?" she said. "In very, very precise, concise terms."

"Yeah, it's pretty hard to do," he laughed.

"What is it you want us to know about the ball-of-light?"

Brian stuttered. "Okay--some people came to my home from Calvary Chapel. They looked at my writings and felt it was demonology or whatever. I asked them how to get rid of this. It was scaring the daylights out of me, and my family. And I don't know what they really did, but they scared the daylights out of me over this whole thing. I really don't know what happened."

"What is happening right now?"

"As it stands right now my wife is in Fountain Valley Hospital. She's completely out of it after seeing the ball-of-light."

"Why is it happening?"

"Why? That's a good question. We are looking for people who might know what it is, and we are looking for people who might know how to get rid of it, whatever it is that is scaring the devil out of us."

"Where do you live, Brian?" Hemingway asked.

"I live in Garden Grove."

"That explains it," she laughed.

"May I jump in here," asked a Lutheran Pastor. "This is not a facetious question, Brian. Are you taking drugs at all?"

"No sir," answered Brian crisply. "No drugs of any kind."

"Could your wife be in the hospital because of a nervous condition?" asked Hemingway. "Is she physically ill?"

"Yes she is, and mentally upset too," Brian said. "After this exorcism, for the first time, I am willing to consider this whole thing from a religious point of view."

Then he asked for their input. "What I am calling about is to see if the people on your show have some answers," Brian said.

Hemingway asked her guests to comment. A Lutheran Pastor spoke with a hard-edged voice. "I have never had any experiences of this sort."

"Are there any incidents of stories like this in the Old or the New Testament that you can recall?" the host asked her guests.

"May I react," said the Lutheran pastor. "I'm sure I am going to get clobbered for this. But when I hear stories like this, I have the feeling that we are supposed to be awed by it--that we accept this as actually happening. Now, I have to be very honest with you. I don't believe this happened. I believe this is a figment of this man's imagination."

"Well," Hemingway stammered.

"These are the kind of things we have never been able to prove. And, I am saying this in utter kindness."

Hemingway countered sweetly. "I am not saying we ought to be awed by it. I am saying that people do have these experiences. I've heard similar stories."

The pastor continued. "I've heard a person talk about this type of thing who was using drugs--including booze. I've heard the person who had a nervous break down and has seen these types of things."

Brian jumped in. "These people from Calvary chapel said they could smell something in the house. They aren't on drugs, I hope."

"Well what did they think?"

"They were convinced that I and my family were possessed by some sort of demons."

"Then they probably tried an exorcism."

"Well, this is what, in my opinion, they tried to perform on me. Basically, I passed out. Fainted. In fact, I think it did more damage than good, because now I am really frightened. What if this is demonology?"

"Well, is it possible that these things could be happening?" the host asked her guests.

"Well it is not only possible. It is happening," Brian interrupted. "It has been scaring the daylights out of us."

"Rabbi, do you have any reaction to it?" asked Hemingway.

A younger, soft-voiced Rabbi spoke. "I really find it hard to understand, and I wouldn't be presumptuous to deal with something that is very hard for me to comprehend or cope with. I feel for you because of the horrible experience you are going through. I don't know how to explain it, and I don't know how to deal with it. But maybe you will find a helping hand from people with similar kinds of experiences."

Brian covered the phone and frowned. "Similar kinds of experiences..." He began to feel that no help would come from the call.

"If this is happening," said Hemingway. "If this was really happening to a family it has to be very frightening."

"It is frightening," Brian said. "Especially to my wife."

Hemingway asked Brian to give his phone number to the producer. The men continued discussing Brian's request, but the Lutheran Pastor dismissed it all as "phony."

After the segment ended, Brian hung up the phone, removed the tape and labeled it with a fat, red, felt-tipped pen: Talk Show. He gathered the tapes that Mary Beth had recorded and placed them all into an old, yellowed cigar box. "Maybe someday, someone will figure this all out," he muttered.

The Mind of Man

At the hospital that morning, Kathy's fever broke but the doctor kept her under careful observation. Mary Beth improved rapidly all day until she felt fine.

On Monday, Brian wheeled Mary Beth out of the hospital to their waiting station wagon. She wanted to stay with her parents—and not go home.

At the huge brick house, Mr. Parsons warned Brian not to discuss the events with his sons. "Nick is against you on principle and John thinks you should be committed," he chuckled. "John is studying psychology. He believes this whole thing is a mass hallucination."

"A mass hallucination?" Brian chuckled.

"Yes, that you are somehow imposing on others."

"Good Lord! How's that?"

"With optical illusions, auditory illusions. You know, tricks. He believes that some people can be convinced by the power of suggestion."

"Power of suggestion?" Brian laughed. "Heck. Maybe he's right. Maybe it's all an optical illusion." Brian slapped his body. "Maybe I'm an optical illusion."

That night in the bedroom, Mary Beth heard two male voices in the room. She woke, up and slowly rolled over to see Brian on the floor in trance. From his lips, a deep voice spoke in a foreign language as his left hand wrote on a yellow notepad. At times, Brian's weak voice agreed. "I understand. I see," he said softly.

Mary Beth closed her eyes and trembled with fear.

The next morning, terrified and tired, she showed Brian the note-pad. "More crap," Brian snapped. "I can't believe this is still happening." He tossed it aside. After Brian left for work, Mary Beth showed the writing to her brother John.

"It's Greek," he said as he studied the words. "I know the alphabet from my fraternity initiation. I can't read it, but it is Greek."

During the day, Mary Beth called Lenny Jacobs at UCLA. He drove down to pick up the writing. He wanted anything to use for the press conference he had scheduled for Wednesday.

"He was speaking as he wrote this," Mary Beth said.

"Speaking Greek?" Lenny asked.

"Maybe? It sounded like it." Her voice trembled. "This whole thing is freaking me out. How can Brian be speaking Greek? Talking to himself. Then he doesn't remember it?"

Lenny hugged her. "These things happen."

"Not to normal people. Brian was a very normal man." She sighed. "I want MY Brian back." Lenny felt her anguish and consoled her with a hug.

The next day--Tuesday, February 17--the doctor released Kathy from the hospital. The symptoms were gone, but he still didn't know the cause of the high fever. As Brian and Mary Beth loaded Kathy into the car, one of their nurses handed them a newspaper. "You should see this." Mary Beth gazed at the headline: **UFO Malady? Man sends for Exorcist.** "Are you okay, with this?" the nurse asked them.

"What is a *'malady?'*" Mary Beth asked.

"A problem, like a disease."

Mary Beth shrugged. "It happened. It's the truth."

Brian scanned the article. "*Orange Coast Pilot, February 16.* That's yesterday. Hey, I can use this in the press conference." The nurse watched Mary Beth for a reaction.

"Maybe it will help," said Mary Beth. "We've got to stop this, somehow."

Brian hugged her, and the nurse smiled.

The Malady

The newspaper article embarrassed Mary Beth's macho stepbrother, Nick. At home in the living room, he ranted to his mom and dad. "Look at this. LOOK at this article."

He thrust the paper at his mom as she vacuumed. "It says Mary Beth had an exorcism. My stepsister."

Mrs. Parsons turned off the vacuum. "Exorcism?"

"What does it say, son?" asked Mr. Parsons.

"This is how far Brian will go. He's the sicko."

"Okay, Nick. What does it say?" asked Mr. Parsons.

Enraged, Nick read aloud from the newspaper as his parents listened with disbelief.

> **A Garden Grove woman and her child, hospitalized under mysterious circumstances, were reported in good condition today as the father called upon an exorcist to release the pair from their strange maladies.**

**A spokesman for Fountain Valley Community hospital said
Brian Scott maintained a vigil there early Saturday morning
to await the exorcist who was summoned at the suggestion of
one of Scott's physicians.**

Mary Beth's mom listened. "Oh, my God."

**His wife remained hospitalized 'under light restraints' after
she was brought in late Friday suffering from an unidentified
seizure that Scott told hospital personnel was brought on by
a 'UFO experience.'**

"My ass. A fake UFO experience." Nick spit out the words.
"Just read the article, Nick," said his father.

**The child, a two-year-old girl, had been brought to the
hospital the day before suffering from symptoms of acute
appendicitis. She was said to be resting comfortably and in
no danger today.**

"That means she was in danger the day before." He ranted. "Because of that
puke-head."
"Nick, he is your brother-in-law."
"That is what makes me mad." He continued.

**Scott summoned paramedics to his home Thursday night
after he claimed the child was found in the back yard with a
strange red halo surrounding her head.**

In the car, as Brian drove down a freeway, Mary Beth also read the article
aloud to Brian. "Did you say *'a strange red halo surrounding her head*?'" Mary
Beth asked.

"No, I didn't say *'halo.'* Ball-of-light. I didn't say anything about appendicitis
either. The doctor probably said that. But, he ruled that out right away."

In the living room of Mary Beth's parents, Nick read emphatically.

**"He was unable to explain how the child got from her crib to
the yard."**

"That's sick. Using the kids. He put her outside. I will RIP him apart, Dad.
God help me I will. If he says one word to me, I'll rip him."

In the car, Brian exited off the freeway and Mary Beth continued reading.

**The presence of the red light and her complaints of stomach
pains led him to call the paramedics.**

Is that how it happened?" Mary Beth asked.

"No. He got that part all wrong. But who cares? Who could keep it straight?"

A spokesman for the Garden Grove police Department said paramedics were summoned to the Scott house a week ago under similar circumstances.

"That was for Ginger," Brian said.

In the living room, Nick raged out of control. "Damn him! He is doing this to BOTH of my step-sisters."

Mary Beth's father took the article. "Sit down," he commanded. Then he read aloud from the article.

The police spokesman said Scott contacted the department once in 1975 to report that he and his family had been kidnapped by a UFO and held captive for several days.

As Brian drove down a neighborhood street, he laughed in disbelief. "Scott and his family had been kidnapped for several days?"

Mary Beth smirked. "They messed up on that one. That must have been November 22--when you was missing 27 hours."

Brian agreed. "I'll probably have to straighten that out someday. Oh well, don't trust what you read in the newspapers. But he did get some of it right."

In the living room, Mr. Parsons studied the newspaper article closely. He read slowly.

Scott told the hospital spokesman that he has been plagued by such events since he was sixteen years old.

Mr. Parsons glanced at his wife. "Since he was sixteen?"

"That proves it. He has been a loony-tune since childhood," Nick ranted. "And he is a *loony-tune* to this day."

"Is that from John's abnormal psychology class? *Loony-tune*?"

"That's it!" Nick bellowed. "He's crazy. What is it? Multiple personality. That's it. I bet he is dangerous. I bet he could kill someone, and not even know it."

"I'm glad you are concerned, Nick," said Mary Beth's mom, softly. She hugged him. "Thanks for worrying about your sisters. But, I think I hear them in the driveway. Go. Now."

Outside, Brian's car rolled up near the garage and the doors opened. Nick flew out the back door to avoid a fight.

Kathy Re-Admitted

The next morning, February 18th, Kathy's temperature rose above 102 degrees and the doctor insisted on re-admitting her for observation.

When Brian arrived at the hospital after work, Kathy lay in bed sedated, with tubes in one arm. "The doctor doesn't know what to do," Mary Beth sniffed. "He wants to keep her several more days, for more tests." Mary Beth sobbed. Brian hugged her. "I'm afraid he thinks we are kooks, after that article in the paper."

Brian gently shook her shoulders. "I've got something for him. If he will listen to another doctor." Brian pulled a letter out of his briefcase. "A statement from a psychiatrist."

Mary Beth took the letter from the doctor, and read aloud.

"January 21, 1976 hospital consultation--one hour, $60. Diagnosis: No Psychiatric Disorder'"

"*No psychiatric disorder,*" Brian beamed. "That was the verdict after all the tests. Now, maybe people will listen." They were already late for the Los Angeles press conference so Brian hurried to the car with Mary Beth following.

The Westwood Reaction

About the same time, in a trendy West Hollywood cafe near UCLA's campus, Lenny Jacobs frantically searched the tables. Among the longhaired college kids, he spotted a scholarly older woman with short hair and gentle wrinkles. Lenny waved. Surrounded by a stack of thick books, she adjusted her reading glasses and waved back.

Lenny escorted Cindy, a beautiful, shapely blond in tight burgundy pants. "Hi, Auntie," Lenny shouted. He introduced his girlfriend Cindy to Professor Cohen, an expert in classic literature. "She is a well known and highly respected authority on languages," Lenny said. "My dad's sister."

The professor smiled. "That's nice to hear, Lenny. Did your mother tell you to say that?" She glanced at Cindy's figure, alluring lipstick and purple eye-shadow.

"Cindy is a hypnotist and a temple dancer," he smiled. "I'm doing research with her on psychic phenomena."

The old professor chuckled. "Temple dancer? Lenny, will Jewish boys ever learn," she said. "Have you forgotten how Solomon lost the temple?"

"We are just friends," Lenny said. He apologized to Cindy. "My aunt is kind of outspoken." Cindy was embarrassed.

"It comes from reading hundreds of term papers on the sexual revolution," the old woman frowned. "Our once-moral society is going down the tubes so flower children can *'do it in the road,'* give their kids to the welfare department and feel good about it. The peace and love generation--it's a lotta bull. It'll create a generation of hell. Their broken-hearted children will grow up to destroy our nation. They should read a little history."

"Did you come up with anything, Auntie?" Lenny asked, impatiently. "We have a press conference in one hour."

The professor lifted her reading glasses.

"Well, I'm writing it out, now. Some of it doesn't make sense, even in English. Some of the words are modern Greek. Others are ancient. Some Latin."

She lifted up her paper, and read:

> **I the Host. Mind ten is of Gate of Sun. I myself am called non-mind. I come. I rush forwards to Tiahuanaco, preventing destruction of mind on earth, by Secondary World. I push onward, sailing on the sun as a sailor, to Earth.**

"Is there a plan to destroy the mind of earth?" She laughed. "I think I am losing my mind reading this." They all laughed. "Okay. Here's the next paragraph," she said.

> **'I come December 24th, 2011 A.D.- A.E., given in rapport. Seek the past, key to earth truth of wisdom. Past, Gate of Sun--Tiahuanaco. Requested of this of I. Transportation. Physical. Of this I say: ascension via Titicaca, reference: Tiahuanaco. Decension, Helios.**

Lenny and Cindy pondered. "It makes sense," Lenny said.

"This makes sense to you?" laughed the scholar.

"Yeah. He talks about this a lot. It's the same message, mostly." He pondered, aloud. "Except this *'Ascension via Titicaca. Decension to Tiahuanaco. Helios.'* That's new. He's ascending via the lake and something is descending via *Helios.* That's my guess.

"What's *helios?* Isn't that sun?" Cindy asked.

"It can mean sun," said the professor. "Or a god with that name, or--the spirit of a sun god."

"This gives me the willies," said Cindy.

"What is this guy dealing with?" asked the professor.

"I don't know," said Lenny.

"This is not your average ghost in the attic."

"No. This is a UFO contactee."

"Oh. Maybe that explains it. It's very apocalyptic. Like a preacher's warning." She shrugged.

Lenny asked about the first writing: Nous Laos Hikano.

The scholar picked up her notes. *"Nous Laos Hikano,"* she whispered. *"'Nous'* means mind. It's not thought, psyche or spirit. It's mind--God mind, or divine mind." She continued. "Now *'Laos'* is an ancient word. It means 'the people.' But sort of with deep reverence, like God's people. It's the congregation in a church, the common people--NOT the priests."

The scholar lowered her glasses. "Now it gets interesting. *Hikanos* means to come, or return in fullness, to arrive ready to do the work, ready to teach, to heal, to nourish, to minister."

"So what do they mean together," Lenny asked nervously. "We've got to go, I need something for the media."

"For the media?" the old scholar laughed. "Do NOT quote me on this," she said. "Not to the media. Don't use my name."

"Okay, but how do YOU put it together?"

"Well, it depends," she said. "Which is the verb, the noun, the object? It's probably an inverted order like most of the writing with the verb as *hikanos.* But if you don't invert. Maybe it's Divine Mind of the Common People Returns. Or, the Divine Mind returns to Teach the Common People. I think it probably means the Divine Mind, is returning to nourish the Common Man."

"Divine mind?" Lenny asked. "Nous ten is the Divine-mind, God-mind. I get it. The God-mind arrives, to teach the common man?"

"Could be," she said. The *object* comes before the *verb.* It's an ancient style of speaking."

Lenny grabbed the paper. "Is this like the Messiah coming?"

"I don't think so. But it's big talk. Not like your little ghosts. Not like the stuff you usually dabble in. You be careful of this Host guy."

"Thanks Auntie," Lenny said grabbing the paper and kissing her cheek. "But, I don't dabble. We gotta fly."

Lenny hurried Cindy out the door. On Westwood Street, hundreds of people lined up at a nearby movie theater. "Was she being mean to me on purpose?" Cindy pouted.

"No. She's that way to everyone." They studied a long line of people waiting outside a theatre. "Lines on a Wednesday--in the day?" Lenny squinted as he read the theatre marquee down the block: THE EXORCIST -- Directed by William Friedken.

"Must be a great movie," Cindy breathed.

Across the street, in a plaza, a group of orange-robed demonstrators chanted 'Hare Krishna' and danced in a circle. Young men with heads shaved bald chanted hypnotically. A crowd of people listened as members of the group handed out literature. Acting silly, Cindy started to dance with the men, but

Lenny pulled her through the crowd. "We're late," he laughed. "No *temple* dancing today."

Press Conference

At the Los Angeles Press Club a half-dozen skeptical newspaper and radio reporters slumped into their chairs as Lenny stepped to the podium. The golden-skinned Vance Dewey and dark-haired Bob Martino sat next to Mary Beth.

Lenny introduced Brian, showed the book of writings, and talked about the *Ball of Light Phenomenon.* He said Brian's house was plagued with balls of orange, red and purple light that had been seen by witnesses and measured by a magnetometer.

Then he presented the *Nous Laos Hikano* writing. "According to a UCLA scholar, this Greek writing says, *The God-Mind Returns to the People.* This is about the first thing Brian ever wrote in a trance." Lenny told the reporters about the requests to go to South America, but mostly he talked about the Ball of Light Phenomenon. Vance Dewey wasn't prepared to talk about his data, so Lenny introduced Brian.

"We just want these lights to stop," Brian said. He showed the newspaper article and the psychiatrist's bill saying: "no psychiatric disorder." I do want you to know I am not crazy," he laughed. "There's the proof." Everyone chuckled.

Brian talked awhile, then accepted questions. "Can you tell us what they look like?" asked a young reporter. "Are they little green aliens?"

"Well, no. Kind of gray or white skin—maybe a shade blue," Brian said. "I saw different colors, different types. " He started to explain, but a hard-edged old reporter interrupted. "I thought aliens were green," he laughed. "And the moon is made of cheese."

Most of the reporters laughed and quickly departed without asking questions. "Look, we just want some answers," Brian shouted. "We want to stop this." He slammed the podium with his fist.

Only a radio team from Orange County stayed. "Is that it?" Brian snapped at Lenny with an accusing tone. "What about TV stations?"

"Brian, they need a straight-forward story," Lenny snapped back. "A news hook."

"How simple can it be?" Brian's face reddened with rage. "*Man abducted by aliens, balls of lights in the house, wife hospitalized.* Damn it. We need help."

"They need details they can document," Lenny simmered.

"We've got details," Brian shouted. "Mountains of details. Aren't they supposed to check the facts?"

About then, Dr. Hynek, the white-haired astronomer, appeared in the doorway and waved to Brian. Vance Dewey politely introduced everyone. After a few minutes of talk, Brian asked Hynek if he would go to South America in June. "They want you there," Brian said.

Hynek puffed calmly on his pipe and eyed Brian carefully. "Brian, I just don't understand why they would pick a man like yourself to give knowledge about genetics, when they could pick up a noted genetic scientist. I'm an astronomer. I don't know genetics, but, I could arrange a meeting with a Nobel Prize winner in genetics."

Lenny interrupted. "It's not just about genetics now. They want him to build a pyramid at Tiahuanaco, for storage of human cells--so they can be reclaimed in 14,000 A.D. in case we are destroyed. And -- they want Brian to experience a "quantum evolution to Mind Level 10."

Hynek chuckled. "Quantum Evolution? Brian if they want us to have this type of information, why don't they write up a treatise, or an abstract of their information and drop it on our doorstep? He patted Brian's shoulder. "I just don't see why they would go to all the bother of training a common person, say like yourself, who knows nothing about genetics or *pyramids* to tell me, an astronomer, who knows nothing about genetics or pyramids. It makes no sense."

"Maybe they want drawings done. I'm a good draftsman."

"I know that," said Hynek. "I heard you are a very good draftsman." He pondered a moment. "But, I am sure they can do drawings also. Don't you think?"

Brian deflated. "I guess so."

"Look, Brian. I have met a lot of contactees. They are very much like you. But, if these aliens are so smart, they need to start with the right people." Hynek puffed up a big cloud of smoke from his pipe.

"Did you say this is a pattern though, that you see among contactees?" asked Vance.

"Yes, sure," said Hynek. "I believe they are trying to get something across. But frankly, I don't know what. And I don't know if I agree with their methods. I think it is important for the scientific community to NOT be manipulated by them, in any way. I'm being honest with you now--we just can't appear to be following around UFO contactees or aliens to get information. We have to take a scientific approach."

Hynek glanced at Lenny and Vance. They felt chastised and a little embarrassed.

"We have a process for establishing truth," Hynek said firmly. "Good studies. Statistical analysis, peer review and publication in professional journals, so even MORE peers, worldwide, can access and review our research to find any mistakes. We go through all that, before we ever begin to claim anything is true. Especially, to go out to the media," he gestured at the podium. "Without solid facts, established in this way, we don't want to go to the media. That's pseudo-science. We don't want that. It's bad for the whole field."

Brian swung around and pointed at the podium. "Then what the hell am I doing this for? Can someone tell me? I mean, to be frank, I'm getting rather upset about this. You're the top investigator in America--probably the world--and you don't know what to do? I thought someone like you would have some answers."

Hynek again patted Brian on the shoulder. "I think you can say, that no one knows exactly what is happening, Brian. But I do agree, something is happening. It is often related to a physical object AND there are psychical aspects," he paused a moment and puffed on his pipe. "Brian, I don't doubt the validity of your experience, but I don't know what I, or anyone else, can do with it."

Brian's face dropped.

"Other contactees I have met are in the same boat," Hynek said encouraging Brian. "Dozens. Maybe hundreds. I just hope that something comes along to help everyone. Something solid."

He glanced at everyone else. "I only had a few minutes. I really must go. Just hang in there, Brian--all of you. And if something really solid ever develops, contact me at my organization." He handed Brian a business card, shook hands with them all, and quickly departed in a cloud of smoke.

Brian flashed with anger. "This is horse shit," he shouted so Hynek might hear. "You know, with every piece of evidence--nothing happens. Everyone has a reason to say it's not enough."

"The only thing that will work is a UFO," said Bob Martino, softly. "He's a UFO investigator. That's what he is after. He wants a UFO, or nothing else."

Vance Dewey took a deep breath. "I think he kind of chastised us for having a press conference -- too early. But until recently, Hynek has dismissed all Close Encounters as hoaxes. He has taken a big step just to TALK to contactees. But, I know for sure this movie is going to support Close Encounters as real."

"Great," said Brian cynically. "They'll make a movie, but they won't help the guy in the middle of it all." He slammed the podium, and kicked a chair.

Mary Beth stepped forward and spoke in a soft, sweet voice. "You should have let me tell them. I didn't believe it at all until I saw the light," she sniffled. "I know what it is like now. It's just like Brian says. They do things to people like us, to our children--then, they hide it. They keep themselves away from the investigators so no one knows what they are doing. We are just left alone— without anyone to help us." As Mary Beth finished, she cried. Vance Dewey gave her a hug, and the radio reporters from KWIZ gathered around her and Brian to talk. A tape recorder clicked on as Mary Beth began to tell her side of the story.

On the side, the investigators grouped together. "This was a bust," Lenny whispered to Bob Martino and Vance Dewey. "Brian doesn't do good at press conferences." They all nodded in agreement.

"He is too wrapped up into his experience," Vance said. "Too close to it."

A New Framework Needed

The next Saturday, the radio reporter--Bob Ward from KWIZ--met Brian and Mary Beth at the house in Garden Grove. He interviewed them both on tape. Then Brian and Mary Beth cleaned the house, opened the mail and talked about re-building a normal life, at home.

Mary Beth suggested that Brian sell the race car AND the Captain America truck to pay off the huge phone bill. Brian refused to sell the truck. They argued over money--and her jealousy. She didn't want him going anywhere without her, but he planned on going to Hollywood that evening to meet Lenny and some hypnotist.

"I want you as my HUSBAND," she screamed. "I don't want you going to meetings all the time."

"I have commitments," he shouted. "I've told people."

They fought while driving back to her parent's house. Brian dropped her off in a rage then raced over to Martino's house to listen to Jacques Vallee on the radio. As Martino tinkered in his electronic workshop, host Carol Hemingway introduced Jacques Vallee as a computer scientist and author of "The Invisible College."

Brian pulled up a chair next to Martino. "Contactees think UFO's are from a technologically more advanced culture than ours. Correct?"

Vallee responded in a thick French accent. "Yes, they all describe something that is technologically more advanced than anything we have."

"Is it true?"

"In some cases, it could be part of the confusion. The confusion pertains to whatever is doing this. If it's an intelligent source, it knows a lot more than we do about the human mind," said Vallee. "My whole reservation here is that I would like to have a chance to do some science on this data before the whole thing turns into a new religion. Because if the whole UFO business ever turns into a religious framework, it will be the end of any hope to do scientific research."

"What do you mean religion?" asked Hemingway. "That people would believe in it like God?"

"They would believe in it in the same way they believe in Uri Geller or in a religious dogma, something not to be challenged, something not to be talked about in scientific terms," he said emphatically.

"He's good," said Brian wrestling with a giggling eight-year-old boy who snuck into the den.

Vallee complimented Hynek. "Dr. Hynek has done more than anyone in the world probably to promote a sensible approach to the subject. We need to get better data, and the only way to get it is to enlist the support of the technical and the scientific community."

Martino puffed a cloud of smoke on his pipe. "See, they want acceptance as scientists from the *'scientific community.'* That's what they are up to. That's why they can't get too close to contactees."

"Yeah. They don't want to get down in the dirt."

The radio host asked Vallee if UFO's were mythological or from actual events taking place--a theme in his book.

"There is a physical object. There is a technology at work," said Vallee. "The problem is we don't know how to approach that technology. We don't know to what extent it is physical. The only good data, the only detailed information we have comes from witnesses who were very close to the object. And those people who were too close, or so close that they were affected by the object--they left their sense of reality at that time, and they are not reliable from that point on because their senses have been tampered with."

Brian laughed loudly.

Martino chuckled. "Did you get that?" He said. 'You are not reliable because your senses have been tampered with.'"

"That's the TRUTH," Brian laughed. "If he only knew what that means. But, hey, how come no one cares about the guy *having his senses tampered with*? Huh? Just dump him? He's in trouble, being contacted by aliens, and *nobody gives a damn!."* Brian thought for a moment. "Hey, can we call him?"

"Sure," said Martino. He handed Brian a phone as the show continued. Brian dialed the number and was surprised to be quickly accepted.

"You're next," said a producer to Brian. "Here you go." Brian heard a click and he was on-line.

"Hello, this is Brian Scott," he said to Hemingway. They talked about his phone call to her other show, Religion on the Line*."* She explained to Vallee. "Brian called in and said there was a white light..."

Brian interrupted. "No, it was a reddish-orange ball-of-light about 6-8 inches in diameter that we had seen in the house and in the yard. And, over our children."

"And your wife was in the hospital with a nervous breakdown, and your kids were, too."

"Yeah. My wife got out last week. One girl is there now. They let her out, then put her back in. Can't figure out what's causing it."

"You tried to have an exorcism performed, didn't you?"

"Well, yes--at this point I am willing to do anything to get rid of this thing."

"Are you still having the ball-of-light?" Hemingway asked.

"Well, yes. We've basically moved out to her parents. Everyone is too afraid to have the children in our home with the phenomenon going on."

Vallee asked for Brain's phone number and promised to have a qualified investigator visit.

Then Hemingway framed an issue. "The interesting thing is that when Brian brought this up last Sunday morning on "*Religion on the Line,*" the tendency was very much to scoff at Brian. Which is interesting of itself: that the established religious community has a distinct knee jerk reaction against this kind of thing Brian is talking about."

Vallee responded:

I think Brian is illustrating exceptionally, the point I am trying to make in this book: that the religious framework, the clergy, will say it is a psychological phenomenon, the psychologists will say it is a physical phenomenon that we don't understand, the physicist will say it is mystical and we can't deal with that. So, you illustrate that exactly. The people send you back and forth. You get the run around from all the different disciplines. That's exactly the kind of thing that calls for a new framework.

After a few comments, Hemingway moved on to the next call. Brian hung up and cheered. He danced around the room as Vallee continued taking calls.

At the end of the show, Vallee summarized the UFO phenomenon. "It has always been with us, from the beginning of time," he said. "From the Assyrians of 400-500 B.C. to the middle ages, to now. It has always been with us. It has always been the same," he said. "But, today, science is now at the point where we can possibly, for the first time in history, deal with two domains that are not related: consciousness and reality. That is why I am so interested," he said.

"Now we are getting somewhere," Brian shouted.

Martino smiled broadly. "See, Vallee said it: '*We need a new framework for understanding.*' If it all made sense, then why would anyone need a new framework?"

Brian breathed deep. "It is hard to believe. I thought the big name investigators would know what the heck they were doing. Hell, NOBODY must know what is going on."

"Nobody DOES know what is going on!" Martino blurted. "Vallee and Hynek both said that."

"This whole situation is pathetic." Brian paced around the room thinking. "The EXPERTS don't know what to do. Yet it's been going on since the beginning of time. I don't get it. I thought they knew more."

"They don't, Brian. No one does."

"Then they--the aliens—are keeping them TOTALLY in the dark. They could make it all so clear. But, THEY don't. It's *them* who is keeping it in confusion."

"It's the psychic phenomenon. Scientists don't get that part of it," said Martino. "They do not want anything psychic or religious. Like he said. They are scientists—and they want the *support of the scientific community*."

"But they will never learn what is going on. They will never BUILD anything that way," Brian muttered. He glanced at Martino's TV repair bench and picked up a screwdriver. "The scientists will NEVER build anything. They just analyze the confusion which is put there—on purpose. No wonder they don't help."

Martino smiled at Brian. "Contactees are an embarrassment to them," he said.

"I get it," Brian shouted. "It's pathetic. More pathetic than I imagined. For the first time, I really understand what is going on. It all makes sense."

Martino smiled. "Well, for sure, no one is helping the 'guy in the middle.' No one is helping contactees." He shuffled around the room thinking.

"Right," Brian said. "No real investigation into the knowledge. No support, no money. Good God, they should have teams of people, in place—to get the knowledge."

"Maybe the people will help," Martino said. "It's a *mystery*. Let's take the *mystery* to the people." He told Brian he had completed a Toastmaster training course in public speaking. He wanted to set up lectures. "Let the people decide what it is all about," he said. "Take it to the people."

Brian agreed and shoved a fist into the air. "Yeah! Take it to the people."

Stranger in a Strange Land

That evening, Brian drove up to Hollywood. Lenny had invited Brian to meet the hypnotist, and someone else—a very important person. Brian knocked on the door of Cindy's West Hollywood apartment after dark. Decorated with pillows and hanging Hindu tapestries, the place smelled of sweet Frankincense and Myrrh. Waiting with Lenny was a black-haired man with a broad face and thick East European accent. Tall and stately with dark eyes and a goatee, their special guest looked like a movie vampire. He even wore a cape. But, he was for real.

In a deep, booming voice the man introduced himself to Brian as a trance medium in England. He asked Brian to enter a trance so he could speak to his old friend, the Host. Brian didn't feel comfortable, but Cindy encouraged him. "I'll show you how," she said.

With her sweet perfume and seductive, low-cut blouse, she easily enticed Brian to sit on the silky red pillows. She lit a big red candle and sat down cross-legged across from Brian. She raised the palm of her right hand and touched his right palm. "Stare into the flame and try to imagine being inside the flickering fire." Within moments, Brian blacked out.

When he awoke, Cindy and Lenny were embarrassed. The Host had spoken only a few words. Brian remembered nothing. "'*Hyksos*' is all that he said." Cindy frowned. "I think it has something to do with Egypt," she said, looking through books.

"What happened?" Brian asked, rubbing his eyes. "What's going on?"

"The Host wasn't really communicative. He only said a few words but he described this man as a '*Hyksos*.' We are trying to find what it means."

"It means foreigner," Cindy read from a book. "'The term was used for the Semites who ruled Egypt. By 1700 B.C., a Semite sat on the throne of the god-king in Egypt. They adopted the writing and appearance of being Egyptian, but they were highly skilled craftsmen and leaders from another land. They operated a huge fleet of cargo ships.'"

"Cargo ships?" Lenny asked. "In 1700 B.C."

Brian didn't understand, and wanted to get home to Mary Beth. He loved her and didn't like leaving her alone after a big fight, so he departed quickly.

Afterwards, Lenny and Cindy took the man out for coffee in a trendy Hollywood café. He pointed out a big bulletin board holding posters for gurus and classes in trance channeling.

"Your friend, Brian, has great potential as a trance medium," the trance medium said. "But you really must get the personality of Brian out of the way. He needs training. I can't believe he doesn't know how to center himself better with all these channeling seminars going on in Los Angeles. He needs a mentor."

"Brian lives in Orange County. It's real conservative," said Lenny. "It's Republican. They know nothing about New Age stuff."

"Oh, I see. No friends. That's a pity."

"This all just happened to him, after a UFO contact," said Cindy. "He's never heard of channeling. He's a real common person, you might say."

"But, he has the gift," the man boomed. "He is opened up. The Host was dead on about my background. That's exactly what my grandmother told me, and I had told no one else, here in America. But, my family knows the story, well."

Lenny and Cindy gasped in awe. "That you…"

"That we had come from Egypt, but we were Jewish, or Phoenician, or Syrian. There was so much mixing of the races. It would be about the time of Joseph in Egypt. The Pharaoh might have been a Semite. My grandmother was a gypsy. She used the same word—*hyksos.* It's like he was reading my mind. I mean, he obviously was able to read me. And there were huge fleets of ships, the Phoenicians had big ships, Egypt had huge fleets in 1700 B.C."

"Amazing," Lenny breathed. "In America, you just don't think much about those things."

"American's lack any sense of history," said the man wrapping his cape around his shoulders. "Worse, we don't know the truth about anything. Only what scholars chose to write down—and they were afraid of the real truth."

"So you think Brian will be okay," asked Cindy.

"He has the gift. The talent. But, you really must find him a teacher, a master. And quickly. Lots of evil spirits are out there, waiting to prey on the weak. But, on the whole, I'd say *he was rather amazing*—to put it in an American way."

They promised to help.

Mary Beth Attempts Suicide

As Brian zipped back home to Orange County, he sang along to the radio. When a song by *Crosby, Stills and Nash* ended, Brian smiled and shouted: "Take it to the people." They were his second favorite group, behind *The Moody Blues.*

As Brian cruised up to the Parsons' home, every light burned bright. In the driveway, a car idled with doors ajar. Terror swept over Brian. Something was wrong. Ginger ran out of the house. Nick followed ripping off his blood-splattered shirt. "It's not my fault," Nick shouted. "I was trying to stop her."

"Brian!" Ginger screamed. "Where have you been? Mary Beth tried to kill herself." She pushed Brian back into the car. "Go!" she commanded. "She's at the hospital." Brian backed out of the driveway with tires screeching.

"Did Nick...?"

"It wasn't Nick's fault," Ginger panted "He was just holding her down and she... It was horrible--she is so strong."

"Is she okay?"

"No, she's not okay." Ginger sobbed. "They're trying to save her life. The ambulance just left."

A few minutes later, Brian raced through a yellow light, and screeched into the emergency entrance of the local hospital. As he ran through the doors, Mary Beth's mom and dad pushed out though the curtains.

"Brian," shouted Mr. Parsons. "Where were you?"

"I had a meeting. I told her. She knew about it."

"She tried to kill herself, Brian," said Mrs. Parsons. "It's gone too far."

"What the hell happened?" Brian asked. No one answered.

Finally Ginger stepped forward. "She saw the Host, and a red light over the baby's crib, in my parent's house."

"All we know is that she was hysterical," Mrs. Parsons cried. "It's too much," she whined softly. "I cannot bear this."

Later, doctors took Brian to see Mary Beth. Black bruises sealed her eyes. Her nose had swollen to twice normal size. She lay unconscious. Two X-Ray technicians lowered a huge machine over Mary Beth's head. "Check for head and neck fractures," said the doctor. "Give me all the views you can get." He turned to Brian. "She swallowed a bottle of Librium capsules prescribed by her doctor. Then somebody beat the pulp out of her. Do you want to file any charges?"

"Charges?"

"It's unwarranted, that kind of abuse."

"No. I don't think so," Brian stammered.

The doctor ordered the technicians to take snapshots anyway. "She's alive. But it could go either way. If she comes out of this, your doctor has recommended a psychiatrist. But, we'll treat the medical aspects first. We have to save her, first."

Brian watched the technicians carefully move Mary Beth's bruised face and neck. He felt sorry for her.

In the waiting room, Mr. Parsons handed Brian a cup of coffee. "I think the time has come to put an end to this, don't you?"

"I don't know how to stop it," Brian admitted.

"You need to find a way, now" he warned. "She was absolutely terrified of something in our house. That means it followed her." He eyed Brian carefully. "I won't put up with that."

Brian tried to explain. "I mean it," Mr. Parsons snapped.

"But how can I stop it?" Brian shouted. "I'm not doing it."

"If you can't, I will," Mr. Parsons said. "I'll put an end to it."

That night, Brian called Kate Miller in Missouri from a pay phone at the hospital. "We need help," he said. "Mary Beth has almost killed herself. Kathy is back in the hospital with a fever."

They talked for a long time, and Brian kept pumping coins into the phone. She was alone too, and looking for help. Brian told her about Martino's plan to go public. "Maybe we could make enough money to help you out," he said.

"I could come out and help Mary Beth with the girls," Kate reasoned.

A few days later, doctors moved Mary Beth to the psychiatric section of the hospital. No bones were broken and the swelling had begun to recede.

In the private room, Brian turned on a radio. He wanted her to hear the KWIZ radio reports, and he obtained permission of the nurse to bring in a radio. He found the station. A news broadcaster reported that Henry Kissinger's tour into Latin America, as Secretary of State, had resulted in protest demonstrations in Peru. Then the report began.

> **UFO's, strange balls of light, and humanoid figures. It's a joke to some people but not to one Garden Grove family. Thirty-two year old Brian Scott said he, his wife and their two small daughters have been visited numerous times by some sort of being which has abducted them. Well, reporter Bob Ward went to their house on Wedge Street. Scott's wife and daughter are just out of the hospital, after, they say, such an encounter last Sunday.**

> **A few weeks ago, Scott's wife saw a man-like figure above the baby's crib. But according to Scott the worst was yet to come.**

"I don't believe this," Mary Beth giggled. "We're on the radio." Brian's voice told the story of the February tenth encounter when the Host appeared in Amy's room over the crib. He ended by saying:

> **"I didn't want it to come back. I didn't know what to do. So I just sat there and started crying."**

The announcer returned. "Next hour Mary Beth Scott describes what the beings really looked like."
"Oh my God," she gasped. Brian smiled.
"You are on the radio, honey. They are going to play your interview."
An hour later, the news featured Nixon's second trip to China. "The trip forebodes of Chinese dissatisfaction with President Ford," said the announcer. Then, after local news, the Scott segment began. Brian nudged Mary Beth awake.

> **The Scott family of Garden Grove has moved out of their home on Wedge Street. Why? They say they are terrified by continuing visits of what they describe as balls of light and humanoid figures. ... And according to Mary Beth Scott, the beings have examined her with their hands. She described what the creatures looked like to Bob Ward.**

> **"They were just big men, distorted faces, their skin was not smooth, scaly—very scaly. Their eyes were kind of distorted, their ears kind of weird."**

The announcer finished. "Well, it sounds wild, but the Scott case has attracted the attention of noted UFO experts including Dr. Allen Hynek of the Center for UFO Studies in Evanston, Illinois."

Brian turned down the radio and smiled at Mary Beth. "There you are. A celebrity."

"I don't know about this, Brian," she frowned. "I'm not sure that's so good, to go on the radio."

"Well, we have to do something," Brian said. "Doesn't it make you feel better to know people are listening? Scientists are sure not going to help us."

"Yeah. I suppose, but they got a lot of details wrong. And, I sound like a jerk. *They have squinty eyes, and you can't see them.* That's what I meant. They get stuff wrong, and we say stuff wrong," she drifted into sleep. Brian felt bad for Mary Beth. She had become wrapped up into something that was meant for him. She wasn't strong enough. She hadn't been prepared since the age of 16 for an unusual life. He held her hand as she slept and his heart cried for her.

An hour later, another news report began:

"A weeping Patty Hearst testified under cross examination today..."

The announcer introduced Brian. Mary Beth woke up as the report began. She listened as Brian described the "horrifying experience" of his first abduction in the Arizona desert.

"You saw the same guys, I did," she breathed. Brian nodded in agreement.

"This whole thing is freaking me out," she said. "God. Both of us! Our kids?"

"They didn't hurt us," Brian said. "No one got hurt, and they could...."

"That's bullshit, Brian. Look at me."

"But THEY didn't. That's your brother's work."

"They caused it, Brian. I was the one who flipped out."

"What happened at your parent's house?" Brian asked cautiously.

"The red light was there." She started to cry and could say no more.

"Mary Beth, those pills could have killed you."

"I don't care," she sniffed.

"But, Mary Beth what about the girls? And you would still have to face God."

She glared at him. "I don't believe that. If God is real, then why is he not protecting us? Maybe I believe it is just over, when we die," she drifted off in a daze.

"It's not just over," Brian whispered. "It goes on. We face God. I KNOW that. That is why I am doing this."

"I don't know," Mary Beth breathed. She held Brian's hand. She loved him so much and wanted to touch him every minute, every second.

183

Brian turned up the radio as another segment started.

Would you believe that alien beings from UFO's have visited residents of Garden Grove? Strange humanoid figures and balls of light.

Brian's voice followed. As he talked on the radio, Mary Beth drifted into a deep reverie. He patted her leg. "Wake up."

Suddenly, she bolted upright, eyes fixated, and wild with fear. "Don't touch me!" She scrambled out of bed and fell. On the floor, she curled into a tight ball, kicking and screaming. "Don't touch me."

Nurses ran into the room and pushed Brian aside. Mary Beth kicked and screamed violently until two orderlies tied her down with restraints.

The nurse injected a sedative. "Were they talking about her on the radio?"

Brian nodded. "Yeah. That was us."

The nurse nudged close to him. "Do you know what she says when she screams?"

"Asta," Brian said. "Some call it Ashtarte." The nurse relaxed as Mary Beth fell asleep.

"Ashtarte?" the lady said. " I have a girlfriend in Los Angeles who worships Ashtarte. She thinks Ashtarte is just wonderful. The highest goddess."

The words stunned Brian. "No way. A friend of yours?"

"Well, I knew her in nursing school. She quit. She is making a bundle with Ashtarte in Hollywood. She sells good luck charms to the stars, love potions and all that. "

"Potions from Ashtarte? This Ashtarte is in the Bible."

"I don't know if it is the same. But she's in Hollywood," the nurse said. "She has posters up there advertising Ashtarte charms. The stars buy them. Most of her clients are stars. She even casts spells for them. She says it works."

Brian looked at poor Mary Beth as the restraints tightened. Her bruises were yellowing, but she appeared broken, damaged. He felt so sorry for her. He was learning about the mind of man, all right. Everyday, he was learning more, but what about her? She was being broken. Did he have to see his wife destroyed to understand the "mind of man?" Why? Why, he wondered.

For the first time in a long while, Brian heard a voice in his head, the velvety voice of the tall giant—Voltar. "When man evolves, that of the being of each person, good and bad—comes out. Each person must experience their own evil, their own weaknesses and strengths. Each man and woman must learn to know themselves and control that of the evil, but in this we all fail, as we learn. In this, Brian you must forgive and understand sorrow--for you must be one with all-mankind. Remember, what is inside must come out."

184

Brian didn't understand the words. "What is the new man to be?" Voltar asked. "The transformed man must find an identity, a new identity, and all must be in agreement, as one, within himself. The battle for the mind of man, is within—within each, within all. This is what you see. In this, *The Play of Life* is real, and cannot be set aside."

Brian didn't understand fully, but was glad, at least, that someone had spoken to him. He had been left alone for quite awhile.

Kate Returns

The next day, Mary Beth's psychiatrist ordered that she enter a ten-day rehabilitation program at a regional mental hospital. She could come home only on weekends.

The same afternoon, Kate Miller arrived at the house with her six-year-old daughter. They settled into the guest bedroom. "I'd rather be here than home alone," she said. "It's been horrible."

When Brian found another writing in the den, Kate read it aloud.

February 25, 12:00 pm, 1976. Of I, the Host. Open.

Of this to pass, June 22, 1976 AD. Solstice. Descension Ticci Viracocha to Tiahuanaco. Alignment -- radiant withdraw. Quantum transformation.

Brian suddenly slipped into trance. A strong, mechanical voice spoke. "Open." He stood near his sailing ship in a frozen position with his head upright.

"Open? What do you mean *'open?'*" Kate asked.

Suddenly Brian's eyes fluttered. He stumbled backwards, and sat down on the footstool. "What was that?" he said in a daze.

"You just said *'Open.'*"

"Jeezzz. I just went out," Brian said.

"Was that a name?" asked Kate. "Ticci Viracocha?"

Brian's eyes suddenly rolled up and his body stiffened.

"Open," said the mechanical voice.

"Open for what?" asked Kate.

"Input. Quantum evolution. Rapport established," said the voice.

Brian's blue eyes flipped down again. "Jesus! Don't do that anymore!" His face reddened. "I'm not ready for that."

"What did I do?"

"Don't say the guy's name."

Kate scanned the paper. "You went into trance in a flash. Instantly."

"Too sudden," Brian said. "Way, too fast.

"But how? Why?"

"It's their code word," he said. "That must be the user code for their system. Given in trust. *Given in trust – TO YOU.*"

"To me?" Kate asked, bewildered.

"Yeah," Brian said in a daze. "He just said it in my head. It's given *to you* in trust."

"Brian, I am here to help Mary Beth, NOT you. I am here to help with the kids. That's all." She braced herself firmly and took a deep breath. "And, I am not going to South America with you," she said. "Not without Mary Beth. I am not going *anywhere* without Mary Beth. Understand?"

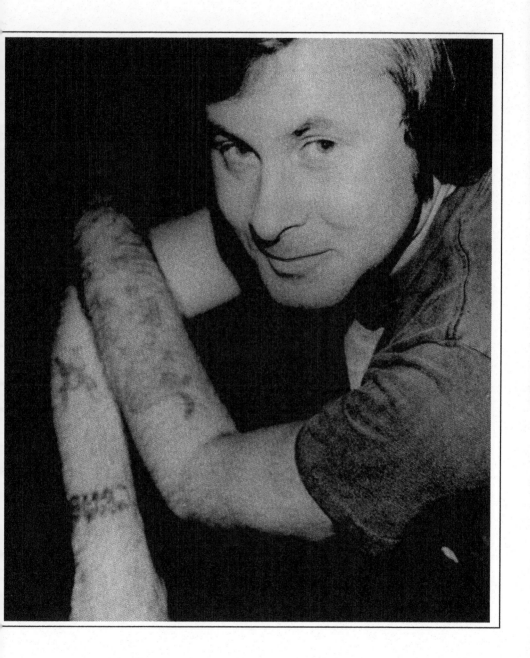

Second Newspaper Article

.RIAT

Garden Grove resident tells of hi capture by extraterrestrial being

ge feature is about a man named Brian Scott, he has been abducted by strange, highly from another planet on several different

cidnappings, Scott often lapses into trances nduced by the beings who use Scott as a ation with earth. While in these trances, Scott uffering convulsions, him arm jerking riting.

ings are found in Scott's home afterward, as em during the seizure. These writings are ar-type language, invariable beginning "I of

ily submitted himself to weekly hypnosis sors at UCLA and at Cal State Long Beach in y the unusual events. He is hypnotized by "returned" to the time of the different them and hopefully to provide clues which explain the strange occurrences.

If psychologist at UCLA told LARIAT editor-in- n, that Scott has never contradicted himself . This fact seems to negate the possibility of

The following is taken from many hours of taped interviews with Brian Scott a resident of Orange County. Brian is 32 years of age and married. He resides with his wife and two children in a pleasent house in Garden Grove. The events presented here are in Brian's own word- s....one must bear in mind that truth is often stranger than fiction. The Lariat does not assume responsibility for the truthfulness of the following but does have an open mind in all field of knowledge...

On March 14th, 1971, I was working in the Apache Wells area in Arizona. About two weeks prior to this date, I and Nick Corbin had visited a movie studio called Apacheland, and we had the whole place to ourselves for the day.

On the night of March 14, after I finished work for the day, being in the same area as Apacheland, I thought I would drive out and try and find a place where Nick and I could shoot. I turned off on a dirt road and drove on it for awhile, the time was near 9 p.m. as I noted while listening to the car radio. I stopped the car, left the headlights on, got my flash light and stepped out of the car.

exploded wi! directions s! it as it mus gone in a bli!

What I sav ... and from scared also. four or five t stood uprigh legs, they we tall, large h. and ears. Ra were eyes, r but every th!

"UGLY STOOD WHAT TWO L HUGE, L FEET TA.

LARIAT Newspaper article appeared on March 17th, 1976. The article was two pages long with several artworks. Brian felt the reporter did a good job. The young man spent many hours with Brian before publishing the story.

Bio-telemetry Scanner Used for Exam by Long-Ears

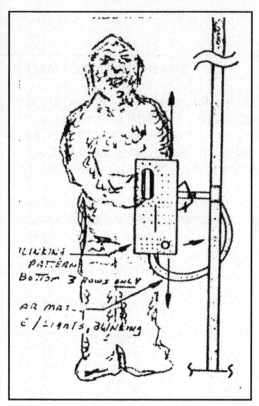

BIOTELEMETRY Scanner with hypnotic light.
Described as *hypno-genetic*.

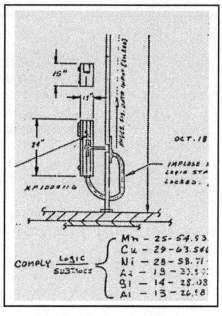

BIOTELEMETRY Scanner.

James E. Frazier

SHAMANS AND SAMADHI

THE TITLE OF *SHAMAN* MEANS--*HE WHO KNOWS.*
A SHAMAN COMMUNICATES WITH SPIRITS WHILE IN A
TRANCE OR STATE OF ECSTASY.
IN A TRANCE STATE, HE CHASES AWAY DEMONS
AND PROVIDES HEALING TO PEOPLE AFFLICTED WITH DEMONS.

IN YOGA, MEDITATIVE STATES ARE PRACTICED
LEADING TO A TRANCE – SAMADHI—MEANING LIBERATION,
PEACE, BLISS, FREEDOM.
SOMEONE WHO CAN ENTER SAMADHI RECEIVES MANY POWERS,
FOR EXAMPLE—TO PROJECT HIS MIND OR THOUGHTS INTO ANOTHER PERSON.

Abstracted from

The New Grolier Multi-media Encyclopedia, V6

190

FALSE CHRISTS

THEN IF ANYONE SAYS TO YOU,
'LOOK, HERE IS THE CHRIST!' OR 'THERE!' DO NOT BELIEVE IT.
FOR FALSE CHRISTS AND FALSE PROPHETS WILL ARISE
AND SHOW GREAT SIGNS AND WONDERS, SO AS TO
DECEIVE--IF POSSIBLE--EVEN THE ELECT.

Jesus Christ in Matthew 24:23-24

Chapter 9

False Prophets

Brian and Kate, pushing together, wheeled Mary Beth and Kathy out of the hospital on Friday. Doctors never discovered the cause of Kathy's symptoms, but she had recovered. Mary Beth felt good, and her bruises were nearly gone.

They hurried to the station wagon in a cold, heavy rain that invigorated them all. Inside the car, Mary Beth beamed with excitement. She had to start the ten-day treatment program on Monday so she wanted to party--like old times. She insisted on buying a pint of Jack Daniel whiskey. Brian finally relented and stopped at a liquor store. She could only have two drinks, they agreed.

After the kids fell asleep, Mary Beth poured drinks, and Kate opened a book about the Mayan civilization. Brian cued up music albums and turned on the television, without sound. They talked about why the Mayans vanished.

Brian lit up an old marijuana cigarette. Kate waved him away. "Brian, people will say all of this is caused by smoking that crap," Kate said.

"I don't think it's related," Brian said. "This is relaxing."

"It makes *snow* difference," said Mary Beth, slurring her words.

Kate laughed. "You guys."

"Wouldn't it be terrible to be stoned and have them show up?" Mary Beth said sloppily. They all laughed.

"I think you've had enough Mary Beth. You're getting a little rubbery, already," Kate said.

"Rubbery?" They all laughed.

Mary Beth frowned. "It must be the medication."

"You shouldn't drink if you're taking medication," Brian said sharply. He grabbed at the whiskey glass in Mary Beth's hands.

"It calms me down," she said. "Just like your dope."

"Mary Beth. It's not the same. Medication is dangerous," said Kate firmly. "Don't mix." She grabbed Mary Beth's glass.

"If you can do it, I can do it," she said stubbornly. She grabbed at the bottle.

"You just got out of the hospital for God's sake," Brian shouted. They tussled over the bottle.

"I don't care," Mary Beth snapped. "I am not as messed up as all those people. That place I'm going to is filled with hookers and drug addicts." She reached for the joint. "Damn it. Give me a hit. It's party time."

"No," Brian laughed. "No way."

As they jostled around playfully, Brian saw a disturbance on the TV screen. Suddenly, he froze. "Oh, oh!" Iggi the dog howled and raced for the back door. Mary Beth and Kate followed Brian cautiously. They all saw a glowing sphere of red-orange light hovering outside near the garage. The rain had stopped, but water drops and puddles reflected the light. "It's back," Brian whispered.

He let the dog out. "Get it, Iggi." Mary Beth ran to protect the children as Brian and Kate studied the bright light.

"What does it want?" Kate said.

"I don't know," Brian breathed. "I don't know whose it is, but I saw them on the one craft." Kate breathed heavily as the dog yelped at the light. Suddenly the sphere bobbed downward and emitted a high-pitched squeal. Iggi yelped in pain and fell to his side.

Brian swung the door open. "Don't go out there!" Kate screamed. Iggi stumbled up the steps and crashed into the kitchen. Brian slammed the door and locked it.

Iggi spun around in circles with his head to the floor, whining. "What have they done to you?" Brian said kneeling to pat the dog. Iggi's eyes fluttered upward, and he snapped wildly, biting at Brian.

Brian jerked his hand away. "He's out of it. It's the Secondary World--they zapped him."

Mary Beth raced into the kitchen and picked up the phone to dial her mom. The phone didn't work. "Damn it," she screamed holding out the phone to Brian. "They've turned it off. We are stranded."

"Oh God," Kate gasped.

Brian dashed into the guest bedroom and, in a fury, ripped open storage boxes to find a Citizen Band radio and antennae. "This will work," he said.

Later, after the light had gone, Brian quickly rigged an antenna on the roof. Inside the house, Mary Beth pulled blankets, pillows and all three children into the living room. Kate poured out the whiskey and trashed Brian's joint.

Within minutes, Brian began talking on the CB radio to anyone who would listen. "Balls of light, UFO's and aliens in our house in Garden Grove. You want to hear about it? Come back," he said. "We got problems. The red light is back, and it hurt our dog."

Brian stroked Iggi as he talked. The dog seemed to recover in about an hour. Mary Beth and Kate felt better when Iggi drank water and sniffed around like himself. The listened to the CB and finally found enough courage to laugh at Brian's silly jokes. "None of them really believe you," Kate said.

"If we have an emergency, people will come," he said. "We could have five guys here with guns loaded, in two minutes."

The ladies felt better.

Early on Saturday morning, golden sunlight beamed in through the big bay window warming the living room, the big white couches and all of the sleepers.

From the patio, Brian peered inside as he watered his green and growing plants. "Hey, everybody wake-up," he shouted. "We're going to the race track."

Captain America at the Races

An hour later, Brian's Captain America truck towed his orange, 1964 Pontiac race car into the pit area of a huge racetrack. Brian jumped out and walked among the crews asking if anyone needed a 454 Pontiac engine. Mary Beth, Kate and the kids followed behind, enthralled by the spectacle and noise.

When the races began, Brian sat them all down in the stands. Kate couldn't resist asking him questions, "You actually drove in these races?"

"All the time," laughed Brian.

"Isn't it scary?"

"Very scary," said Brian. "But lots of fun, too." He laughed. He had driven everything from stockcars, to alcohol-fueled slingshots, but his favorite was the demolition derby.

Cars piled up in a big wreck in front of them and the crowd moaned with concern. They watched an ambulance race toward the cars. "That's why I quit," Brian said.

He told them about the young driver who died. "He and I were in a grudge match on a figure eight track--a demolition derby. I hit him and pinned him broadside, in the middle of the "8." Pushed him back all the way up against the wall. Then his car burst into flames."

"Did he get hurt?" Kate asked.

"Oh, yeah. Burned to death. Right in front of me--just a kid, too. His harness wouldn't release." Brian remembered. "Human flesh smells terrible," they all grimaced.

As the ambulances worked, the announcer introduced Brian. "We have an old champion with us here today," the voice echoed throughout the arena.

193

"Someone we haven't seen in quite awhile. He used to race under the name of *Captain America*. Would you join me in giving a hand to a three-division champion, Mr. Brian Scott--Captain America!" A spotlight raced across the crowd and found Brian. He stood up and the crowd cheered. "Stand up," he said. Mary Beth, Kate and the kids all stood up and waved.

As the crowd cheered, and the spotlight swept over them, Kate saw a bright blue light radiating out from Brian's head, around his temples, and out the top. She blinked. Near his hair, tiny rays of blue, green and gold laced together to form a crown of light.

As the crowd cheered, the announcer continued. "Brian wants to sell his Pontiac, with a 454 in it, *today*, so if any one of you wants to get into racing with your own stock car, see Brian at the south end of the pits after the final race. Welcome back Brian. We've missed you."

The crowd cheered again. "There is a champion ladies and gentlemen," said the announcer. "A man not afraid to take it to the edge."

Kate studied Brian's face after he sat down. The halo still beamed brightly, a glowing aura of blue and white.

Later that afternoon, Brian accepted verbal bids. He sold the car to a shy, humble young man who bid lower than others. Mary Beth was upset.

"Why him?" she said. "He bid lowest."

"Because he'll actually get the money," Brian said. "Besides, he reminds me of the one who died in the flames," Brian said. "That is the kind of guy who is hard to beat."

Girl Talk

Later that afternoon, Kate and Mary Beth leisurely talked in a shopping mall as their three children ate ice cream with Brian. He giggled and laughed with the kids--like a child.

"I feel a lot different since November," said Kate. "Ever since I touched that rake, and passed out. I've had these rashes. This dry skin." She scratched at the red blotches on her skin. "I know I was with them." Tears welled up into her eyes. "It's been so lonely without you guys," she cried.

Mary Beth hugged her. "They took me too," said Mary Beth. "Two of them were holding me and I was buck naked. I know they went a little crazy," Mary Beth said. "Like men do."

"I can't believe we are sitting here in a mall, talking about this," Kate laughed.

"All I know is that sometimes I can talk about this, without it affecting me," Mary Beth laughed. "But if I let my thoughts go..."

"I know. Since that day in the garage, I feel that there was a split. I don't know how to say it. Like sometimes there is two of me. Do you feel like that?" "Yeah," said Mary Beth. "That's right, I have felt the split—two of me."

Mary Beth's Sorrow

They all returned home in a good mood. In the kitchen, Kate unpinned her earrings and dropped them into a shot glass on the sink. She massaged her aching earlobes as the kids played around her feet. Then she heard a deep male voice in the bathroom.

"Mary Beth Scott," the voice boomed.

She looked outside and saw Brian moving the trailer and racecar. "Mary Beth Scott," the voice crackled again.

Kate ran to the bathroom door. Locked. She heard an electronic beeping sound. Mary Beth screamed. "No. No. Go away."

In the bathroom, a red light hovered only a few feet from Mary Beth. Terrified, she panted with fear. The light moved closer and touched her on the chest. Instantly, Mary Beth's mind filled with hundreds of images that she couldn't stop. Her eyes fluttered and she fainted to the floor with a thud.

Kate kicked open the door hitting Mary Beth. "It touched me," Mary Beth moaned. She started to cry. "Oh, God."

Kate guided her to the couch. Mary Beth curled up tightly like a frightened kitten and sobbed with deep sorrow.

"What's wrong? " Kate cooed.

"I killed my son," Mary Beth whispered.

"What do you mean? You don't have a son."

"I killed my baby, when I was sixteen."

"You had an abortion. That's not the same."

"The life of my son is gone," she said. "And for that I am going to hell. It's my judgment."

"No you're not," Kate said gently.

Mary Beth sobbed. "My son wanted to live," she said. "I saw it when it touched me."

"How do you know it was a son?" asked Kate.

"I SAW him," Mary Beth cried. "I saw him as a man, in a sweater and tie. Happy. A handsome, college boy--like my brothers. He wanted to live so bad. He WANTED to be my baby," she wailed. Her body wrenched with anguish. "Oh, God--he wanted me to let him live." Mary Beth cried in despair for a long while. Kate felt Mary Beth's pain and, with her fingers, brushed Mary Beth's hair. They sobbed together.

Kate's Joy

Later that night, in the kitchen, as Mary Beth slept, Kate searched for her earrings. She had set them on the counter. While searching, she scratched at the dry, inflamed patches of skin on her shoulders and arms.

Brian called Kate into his den. On his desk sat a whiskey shot-glass, filled with a thick, purple ointment. "It's for you," he said lifting a paper. "This wasn't here five minutes ago."

Kate read, aloud.

> **Of the Host, given. Of Secondary World, quantum evolution attempt did occur November. Skin effect noted: dermatophyte. Of this will pass. Use this of I."**

Kate looked at the purple ointment. Could the Host have provided the ointment, or did Brian, as a deception? She decided to withhold judgment.

She had tried three prescriptions since November, but nothing worked on the skin problem. Cautiously, she touched the purple ointment to a red patch of skin on her arm. Almost instantly, the burning pain cooled.

She asked Brian to look up the word "quantum" in the dictionary. When he left to find a dictionary, she unbuttoned her blouse and applied the ointment on her chaffed shoulders, her elbows and arms. The ointment soothed and cooled her skin.

Then Brian returned. He pointed at earrings on the desk. "Did you find them?"

"Hey. Those ARE mine," Kate said scooping up the earrings. She read words on the paper. "*Analysis completed. Of this returned of I.*' What does that mean?"

"Were they just there? They weren't there before," Brian said, excited.

"My earrings are back, that's all I know," Kate gushed. She wondered if Brian was tricking her. If he were playing some game with these special earrings—a gift from her grandmother--she would let him have it in the face. He deserved a good punch, anyway. Then she noticed--something different. She slipped the lock off and on the posts, repeatedly. "They are changed," she whispered. "The post is longer! Brian. These aren't mine."

She began to tremble. "Oh, my god." Kate slipped one earring into her ear, and then the other. "It's longer!" she smiled, radiantly. "They are both longer. This is weird, Brian. I've been wishing everyday for a month that these earrings had longer posts."

"You have?"

"This is so weird," she said with girlish excitement. "You couldn't know how much I love these earrings. No one did. I didn't even tell Mary Beth." She pondered a moment.

"The back post there is longer?" Brian asked.

"Brian, do you think they know my deepest thoughts?"

Brian smiled at her. He loved the little-girl side of Kate. "That's what they do," Brian said. They get inside your mind and your feelings--your heart," Brian said gently.

"Personal things?"

"Yeah. Very personal. That happened while I was out of the room. You were alone." He glanced around the room.

"That's what I thought," Kate pondered for a minute. "Logically, that means right now, something is here. And it's relating at the deepest, most private level of me, and you—at a very, very personal--but it is NOT giving you proof, for others. They don't prove it to everyone else--but *they could."*

"That's it. You got it," Brian agreed. "That's what these investigators don't understand. It's very, very personal. And there are two sides. Two forces going on here."

"But it is all about you--the person, the individual. Your mind, your dreams, your private thoughts and feelings."

Brian nodded. "And you," he said gently. "You are in this, too. I know it, and there is your proof. Those earrings." Her face blushed. She felt a tingle on her skin and nervously ran both hands through her curly blond hair.

Brian waved the dictionary. She liked his eyes and boyish smile, but she had learned long ago how to resist Brian. Her friend was Mary Beth, and she would never betray a friend. "Did you find what *'quantum'* means?" she asked.

He started to say yes, but suddenly, with no warning, Brian's eyes rolled back in his head, and a deep, powerful voice spoke from him.

"The energy of the Being--radiant," the voice said.

For a moment, Kate studied Brian's facial expression. He appeared noble, stately, dignified--like a king. Then his eyes opened and he fell backwards against the wall.

"Gezzus," he gasped, stumbling backwards.

She grabbed him. "You are all right," she said gently. "You are here. It's okay."

"Geezus. I wish they wouldn't do that. I feel like I am falling. Everything is spinning."

She held him firmly. "What did he say?"

"I would really like to know how they do that," Brian mumbled.

Kate interrupted. "He said 'energy of your being' when I said 'quantum.' "What is the *'energy of your being*?'"

"I have no idea what he is talking about," Brian said. "I am so dizzy. I think I'm going to puke."

197

Kirlian Photography

On the afternoon of the next day—Sunday March 7—Brian washed the bright blue, red and white Captain America flag truck in the driveway. As he worked, the two investigators from UCLA arrived with a Kirlian photograph machine, a photo-technician, and the sultry, blond psychic, Cindy.

Lenny wanted to show Brian a folder filled with Kirlian photographs. Brian invited them inside.

In the living room, they passed the photos around. Brian, Kate, Ginger and Mary Beth studied the beautiful images: between two fingertips, bright rays of green light reached out, intertwined and laced together.

The light rays reminded Kate of the blue-white halo she had seen around Brian's head, but she held her tongue and said nothing. Ginger thought they were beautiful. Mary Beth didn't understand where the light came from, but Brian felt they were on to something with Kirlian photography.

Lenny showed a "phantom leaf" photo. Despite being cut with half of the leave removed, an outline of the *whole* leaf showed up in the photo. "We don't see it, but the energy is there," said Lenny. "That's why we call it 'a phantom.'"

Brian leaned closer. "Is it like the energy of your being? Is that what you are saying? Like photonic matter, photonic energy."

"We don't know the energy source," said Levy, the older scholar. "It may be what psychics call the aura. We aren't sure."

"I saw an aura once," Kate finally said with caution.

"Maybe people see them," Lenny said. "Psychics do, all the time. It's part of being a psychic." Kate bit her lip. The last thing she wanted to be was a psychic.

To test their theories, the men wanted to compare photographs of Brian's fingers at rest and in trance. Brian challenged their purpose. "I like some of your ideas, but how is this going to get us to South America, or put a stop to the ball of light?"

Brian listened to their plan to obtain proof and financing. He finally agreed to go into trance using Cindy as a guide.

Cindy set up a crystal candle-holder and lit a long red candle. Seductive perfume enveloped Brian. Her white breasts pushed up in the low-cut blouse, and her purple eyelids flickered, arousing his passions.

Mary Beth, Ginger and Kate watched. "I hate her," Mary Beth whispered. "She's using everything she's got." Kate laughed and Ginger turned on a tape recorder. Brian glanced at them and giggled. He knew what they were thinking. He knew Mary Beth would be jealous, and he smiled at her.

Cindy raised her right hand to Brian's--palm to palm. "Look at my eyes, then look into the candle," Cindy whispered. "Draw yourself inside the flame. Let yourself become one with the flame. Let yourself feel the warmth, the heat. Feel the glow and the waves. Feel the flame," she whispered. "Become one with it. One with the light."

Mary Beth stewed with jealousy. "All three of those guys are under her spell," she whispered to Kate and Ginger. Brian entered a deep trance quickly and a low, strong voice emerged from his mouth, "Open."

Levy, the older researcher, asked Brian a question. "What is the Secondary World...." The Host interrupted in a bold, powerful voice.

> **Run 1. Purpose of Secondary world: Genetic transformation. Of this, the mark--right forearm, Scott--knowledge given to man.**
>
> **Run 2. Of this, mankind is one with Secondary world. Of the past, is now the future. The Secondary world is known to earth."**

Brian's body shuddered. He gagged. His face turned red and his face contorted as another voice rattled from deep within his throat. "Assssssstttttaaaaa." The raspy growl frightened Cindy. She jerked her hand away breaking their bond.

On the couch, Ginger and Mary Beth hugged closely. Kate stood up, ready to do something.

"It's evil," Cindy said as the Kirlian photographer tried to place Brian's hand on a glass plate. He exposed the film with a pulse of electricity.

Then the Host's voice returned.

> **Fear not the mind of man in this. Fear not mankind, for this is not of I, but of the Secondary World. Be free of the Secondary World interference by of I, at Nous 10. By of I, truth is given of you to mankind. All shall be known. All shall be understood in time.**

Then the machine voice said, "Locked." Brian's body rocked. Cindy studied him carefully. Then folded her hands as Brian continued without her help.

"Open," the machine-voice said.

The Host spoke.

> **Of this, requested of I, physical transportation—Tiahuanaco. Of this, knowledge of Nous, two through ten, given to man via Gate of Sun. Given."**
>
> **"Locked," said the machine voice. "Transferring. Open."**

Then the calm, kingly presence of the tallest, long-eared giant came over Brian—Voltar—the one who had placed his hand on Brian's head. Voltar spoke with deep, soothing and fluid tones.

> **The truth man seeks is of Tiahuanaco. Of this, I am of time. Knowledge is given of I, to Gate of Sun--known to earth. Of my Host, of I, to you--knowledge now given of Secondary World: ninth descent Tiahuanaco. Also, seventh descent: Toro Muerto.**

The gentle giant pronounced 'Toro Muerto' in a guttural Spanish accent, with a long rolling "r." He continued, speaking poetically.

> **The mountains dash together, and heaven is split in two. The sun grows dead...the earth sinks into the sea. The bright stars vanish...fires rage and raise their flames as high as heaven:**
>
> **Of this, is fact of I. Stated. Of this, Alpha will mark the Omega. The beginning will mark the end for man. Rapport requested: Hynek--Toro Muerto. Knowledge given."**

"Locked," said a different machine-like voice. Brian's body shuddered for a moment, and then stabilized. The gentle giant spoke in a conversational tone.

> **Of earth time past: forty thousand, five hundred years. Of this, first descent Secondary world. Sexual implantation of known life. Nous 1350 - 1450 cc: cubic centimeters in size. Expansion of brain. Of this is fact by of I, by of you. Given rapport Nous 10 to Nous 1. Rapport stated, logic given. Of this mankind is one with time."**

The machine-voice said, "Locked."

The two scholars of parapsychology glanced at each other with awe. "He is answering my questions," said Levy to his younger understudy. "Without me even asking them."

> **"Open. Origin point of Secondary, given of I, of the Host -- rapport Nous five to Nous 1: Epsilon Bootees.**
>
> **Origin point -- sixth of seven orbitals of Epsilon Bootees. Of this, life on earth first walked and stood upright on another world. Of this knowledge given Tiahuanaco, ninth descent of Secondary world, 110 B.C. Seventh descent Toro Muerto 687 B.C. Transportation requested to examine of this. Fear not**

the truth. Man must know of his own self, before he can understand others.

The machine voice rocked Brian's body. "Locked."

"This is incredible," whispered the older scholar to his graduate student.

Mary Beth gasped in disbelief. Ginger nodded in agreement. "That's all in the writings," she said to the scholars.

Levy started to ask a question of Brian. "Open," the machine voice blurted.

"These people who contacted Brian in the desert..." This time, the soothing voice of Voltar spoke.

Of I, of the Host, first descent 3113 BC, earth time, quadrant three. Central America. Known to man.

Our involvement with the Secondary World of earth extends to a time, long past. My people were enslaved by them. We escaped and, in part, migrated from the second orbital to the sixth of Epsilon Bootees. Some of the initial plantations of your world were begun on this world, by your Secondary World. Not of us. But in this, our forefathers have shared a past time with them, and by this our cultures and our technologies mingled.

But we do not share rapport on sexual implantation, for our way is of freedom of mind, and freedom of will. Not true of your Secondary World.

Our involvement with Scott began in 1971 and will continue until..."

Brian suddenly gagged and choked. His face flushed red and his face twisted. Cindy prayed for 'white light' to surround him.

The voice from Brian spoke again with pained words.

Our--involvement--not same--as Secondary World. Genetic plantations--not same--Tiahuanaco.

Brian's face contorted into an ugly expression. "Asstaa." A low guttural growl rumbled.

"It's evil," said Cindy jerking away from Brian. Mary Beth and Ginger hugged on the couch. The photographer again grabbed Brian's hand and held it on a glass plate. Then he charged the plate with electricity for Kirlian pictures.

201

Cindy chanted, aloud. "In the name of the white light, I command you to go away. In the name of all that is good, I command you to go away." The two scholars added their weak voices to the chorus.

The beastly presence roared with laughter. Brian's body convulsed and he kicked the red candle over.

"Brian!" Mary Beth screamed. Cindy patted out the flame. Ginger snapped on the lights, terrified.

The two scholars jumped to their feet and stood up--back-to back, protecting each other. Cindy continued chanting. "In the name of the white light, I command you spirit to be gone."

"Beaaaaalllzebub," growled the demon.

"Who are you?" Cindy shouted. "Who are you, spirit? Give me your name."

The two researchers tried to lift Brian to his feet. "Beaaaaaalllzebubbbb," the demon roared with a deafening growl. Terrified, the researchers both fell backwards over the leather footstool and crashed to the floor.

"What is your name?" screamed Cindy as the two researchers struggled towards Brian. "Don't touch him!" Cindy ordered, fearfully. "Whatever you do--don't touch him." She gasped.

"Is it a spirit?" asked the youngest researcher.

"It's something," she whispered nervously. "I don't know what--but it's got him."

"What can we do?" whispered Lenny.

"I have to get its name. Then I can cast him out--with the white light," she breathed.

Brian's body arched and twisted upward with a violent surge. He moaned. "Beeeeeaaaaaaalzebuuuuuuub," a deep voice roared. "Bealzelbub!"

"He is saying '*Beelzebub*,'" gasped Lenny.

"He's king of all the demons," said Levy, shaking.

Cindy suddenly felt like a little girl, inside. All of her insecurities, and self-doubts and frailties rushed into her mind. She remembered her childhood fears of the devil from Catholic school. She remembered nightmares of facing the devil in which she forgot her name, and where she lived. She couldn't even remember what existed outside the door to her room. Yes. It was the devil, she reasoned. He knew all she had done--her sins, her lies and secret betrayals of friends. As they all flashed in her mind, he chuckled. He made little sounds so she knew he saw the same images. Suddenly, she felt dirty, wicked and evil— like him. Tears flowed out of her eyes. Within moments, mascara and eye shadow trailed down her broad, beautiful cheeks.

Beelzebub chuckled with an evil rattle. "The mind of all man is known to me," he said. She sobbed with deep sorrow and collapsed on the floor. Lenny tried to comfort the beautiful, but broken young woman.

Mary Beth suddenly felt a pain in her womb. Her eyes glazed over and her mind flooded with images of her sorrow from the past.

A halting, mechanical voice issued from Brian.

Secondary over-ride. Nous 10 over-ride requested. Rapport. Return Scott, Nous 1.

Then suddenly, Brian's face, personality and presence returned. His eyes blinked open and he glanced around the room. "Let's get up, Brian," said Levy.

Brian wobbled to his feet with Levy's help. He looked around at the disarray, at Cindy's tears, and at Mary Beth moaning in pain. Kate and Ginger tried to help her.

"What happened?" Brian demanded.

Cindy reached her slender arms out to hug Brian. She melted against him. "We were just asking you some questions." Brian stiffened. Her new appearance, with streaks of heavy mascara, confused him. She looked younger, more wholesome. Brian glanced again at Mary Beth. She sat on the couch sobbing. Ginger hugged her sister and Kate sat next to them, arms crossed in anger.

"I wish someone would tell me what is going on," Brian yelled waving his arms. No one answered him.

"I am sick of this crap," Brian snapped. He stomped into the bathroom and looked at his face in the mirror. He slammed the door on the medicine cabinet. The mirror fractured. In slow motion, he watched the reflection of his face break into pieces. He heard the glass crash to the floor and tinkle. Mary Beth jumped into the bathroom to look at the damage.

"Great," he said. "Now our mirror is broken."

"Why the hell did you do that?" Mary Beth screamed.

Brian began picking up the fragments of mirror. "I am sick of waking up and not knowing what happened. No one tells me."

Carrying a long, jagged chunk of mirror into the living room, Brian bumped the door and sliced his hand. He screamed as blood flowed.

"Damn it. I cut myself," he shrieked. "I am bleeding all over the place." Kate jumped up to bandage the wound.

"Go light on Mary Beth," she warned. Mary Beth groaned in anguish as Ginger held her.

As Kate bandaged Brian's hand, his eyes rolled up and his face twisted into an evil presence.

"Astaaaaaa," a growl rattled from his throat.

Kate panicked for a moment, then calmed. Suddenly, Brian shook his head and his eyes opened. "Damn that hurts," he grimaced. "Are you done?"

The investigators recoiled in terror. "Let's get going," said Levy, pulling Cindy to the front door.

"He doesn't know that even happened," Ginger whispered to them with fear and desperation. "He doesn't know that is happening."

Lenny coddled Cindy. "We'll call you in a few days."

Brian glared at Kate as she tested the bandage.

"You didn't run it?" Brian asked.

"Run what?" Kate snapped. "Cindy ran it. It was all *her* show."

Ginger helped Mary Beth into the bathroom. She gagged and vomited then grabbed a bottle of tranquilizers. "What's happening," Kate asked.

"I don't know. Terrible pain." She swallowed the capsules and poured out more.

"No," Kate shouted. "You are already on medication."

"It's not enough for what I am feeling," Mary Beth whined. They stood there for a moment all looking at each other.

Brian spoke first. "Kate, you have to take over. You are the one who has the access code. You are the only one they trust. Ginger, you've got to stay with Mary Beth. She can't be taking more pills."

Kate's Answer

Later that night, after the kids were in bed with Ginger, Mary Beth laid on the couch numbed by tranquilizers. Kate lit a white candle. "I'd like to try it with the code," she said. Brian sat down on the floor. Kate clicked on the tape recorder as Brian drew a circle within a square using his left index finger. Suddenly his presence changed and his eyes flipped upward.

"Open," a deep, mechanical voice said.

"Ticci Viracocha," Kate said confidently.

"Open. Request Nous 10. Request Nous 10 of man. Tiahuanaco. June 22, 1976. Tiahuanaco, via Titicaca. Genii decent. Radiant descent Viracocha. Gate of Helios. Locked. Request of I. Open."

"Are you evil?" she asked.

"Of this, evil is of the mind of mankind."

The voice changed, flowing easily. "Of the past is truth to future. Preservation of man's cells essential. Nous 10 given to man by unity of three: Scott, Miller, Walters. If not, destruction imminent. Imminent. Of Secondary World--evil."

"Can you tell me who you are?"

"I am of time, beyond all time."

"Do you have a name?"

"I am. I am--in the beginning, I was. Of this, there is wisdom."

"Do you have a title?"

"I am. I am," he said softly.

"Who are you?"

"I am. I am. Of this now, projection--of I. Above your head. Look now, of I."

Kate looked up. Above her, she saw a thin, ephemeral image. Stars in the sky streamed out from a central light. "Yes, I see what you mean," she said.

"Of this, of all time--I am."

"I see," she mumbled, not really understanding.

"My hand is open to you. For of this, you are key in wisdom." Brian's bandaged right hand opened.

"I am reaching," Kate said glancing upward again. "I am trying for the wisdom."

"Of this, look to my hands, closer than you looked before." Then Brian's other hand raised up and opened. His palms turned upward.

"Of this man did to me, in fear of I."

Kate didn't understand. "May I see your hands?" she said.

"They are now in front of you." Kate looked. In Brian's palms. She saw an image of bleeding holes. Blood frickled from the holes.

"Of these, marks given to I of mankind." Kate couldn't believe her eyes. "Search your mind. Of this, man knows of I. For I am, I am."

Kate trembled with feelings. Was this Jesus talking to her, or some demon or what? The voice spoke again. "Look to my feet."

Kate glanced at Brian's feet. She saw two bare feet with bleeding puncture wounds. "Of this, the mark is given of mankind in fear of I."

"Are you referring to Christ?" Kate gasped. "To God?"

"I am. I am," the presence said firmly. "Of this, is known to those who seek of I," the voice said warmly.

Kate shook her head in disbelief and studied the tape recorder. The red light blinked, recording every word.

"In my coming, mankind rejected the wisdom that was given."

Kate stared at the jagged holes in Brian's hands and feet.

"Do you not see the marks?"

"Yes. I see the marks." Tears ran down her cheeks.

"Of this, pain was done to me in a time past. Again, I say, look to your future. For of this, I now project to you."

Kate wiped away her tears, breathed deeply then glanced upwards again to see a tall, noble, red-haired and fair-skinned man. He wore a white turban and a white robe with a sash around his body. He held a golden staff in his right hand and a book in his left.

205

"Of this, my legate. To come of I -- Ticci Viracocha -- he now descends and approaches the Gate of the Sun. Of this wisdom is given of I, to man. Of this to pass, is fact."

"Incredible," Kate gasped. "I have to think about all of this. Are you saying that Christ and Brian are the same?"

"I am of time, beyond all time. Fear not of I, for evil is of the mind of man. As I have been marked by man, so man shall be marked--by those of Nous 11."

"By the Secondary World aliens?" Kate pondered for a moment. "Is that what you mean?"

There was no answer. "Can I ask for the return of Brian? I really need to talk to him."

When Brian awoke, Kate removed the tape from the small recorder. "If I were you--I wouldn't let anyone listen to that tape, ever! And I will not tell you what I just saw."

"Why, what happened?"

She stood up. "I'm going for a walk, Brian," Kate said as she slapped the tape into his hand. "I have a lot to think about."

"Kate?"

"Don't talk to me, right now," she said.

Frustrated, Brian dropped the tape into the old yellow cigar box. "Nobody tells me nothing," he mumbled. "I am sick of this."

That morning, Brian drove Mary Beth back to the treatment center. She wouldn't be able to come home again until the next Friday night.

At home, after work, Brian showed Kate the ten GATE OF SUN drawings in the den. "The answers are here," Brian said. "If I only knew what they meant," he frowned. "It says radiant descent and also quantum WITHDRAW. So TWO things are going on." He pointed at parts of the drawings.

"See this shows a descent of Nous ten. Then there is also a projection beam of some kind from an island in the lake. That's lake Titicaca. See, this beam hits the Gate of the Sun. It's like this Nous 10 comes down and..."

"Why don't you just ask Ticci Viracocha yourself?" Kate said with a touch of sarcasm.

To her surprise, Brian slumped forward onto the drafting table. She scrunched down to study his eyes. "Ticci Viracocha?" she asked.

"Open," said a deep voice. Brian sat up straight and strong.

Calmly, Kate slipped the cigarette out of his hand. Then she pushed the record button on the tape recorder.

"Who are you?" she asked.

"I am. I am," the voice said firmly.

"But I don't know what that means. Does that mean you are God, or Jesus?"

"Let this be a sign unto you, and bring you peace in the night," he said. "Projection."

Suddenly, Kate heard a bird chirping. Then the bird began to coo and sing like the doves near her home in Missouri. As she listened, she remembered her happy childhood days.

"Is that you? Are you doing that?" she gasped.

"Projection. Speak not of I, but seek the reality of your own being, for of this, the legate of peace was given to you in the form known: bird, dove."

"What you are saying is--that you too are the dove of peace?"

"Of I--I am, I am. For of this, man needs no more, of I. For of this, is life."

"I need to know about Mary Beth Scott. Who is causing her harm? Who is causing her pain?"

"Of the other."

"How can we help her to rid herself of this? She needs help."

"Of this, you will end the suffering of this by, and of yourselves--the unity of three in wisdom. Quantum withdraw. Radiant intake--June 22, 1976. Tiahuanaco. Of this, the way of man -- a unity of three will bring Nous ten to man."

"I don't get it," Kate frowned.

A voice hissed from Brian's throat. His presence turned demonic. Kate watched in awe as Brian's lips slowly curled back to reveal sharp, long teeth, like a jaguar. Kate stepped backward calling upon all the strength in her heart and mind, not to run--not to scream. She tried to separate the image from Brian's real body and face.

"This is a projection," Kate said. "Return Scott to me, so we may talk."

"Assstttaaa" the voice growled with chilling vengeance.

Kate's emotions held firm. "Ticci Viracocha," she commanded. "Ticci Viracocha. Return Scott. Return Scott so that we may talk."

Another demon growled, this time with a rumbling rattle, like a jungle jaguar ready to kill. Kate felt fear to the depth of her being, but she stood firm. Brian's face contorted and an image appeared of Beelzebub. For a moment, she felt enticed by the handsome face. He appeared masculine and attractive. Kate shook her eyes loose.

"Ticci Viracocha," she shouted.

"Override Secondary World. All systems request power," blared the mechanical voice.

Then a new face appeared over Brian's. Handsome and boyish with fair skin, blue eyes and red hair, he looked like a boyish king, like the projection of Viracocha she had seen first.

"Beware Ishtar, Nous 11," the image said.

Then suddenly, Brian's head dropped to the table with a thud. He jerked, and sat up--all Brian. "I know the answers are here," Brian said. He lifted up the drawing as if nothing had happened.

"Brian, I got answers," said Kate. "I saw things."

"What? Saw what? What are you talking about?"

She ignored him and slipped outside to smoke a cigarette with the tape recorder in hand. Brian remained in the den, perplexed.

Outside, Kate lifted the tape recorder and spoke into the microphone: "This trance took place in the den about 3:20 a.m., I should say exactly at 3:20 a.m. on the fourteenth of March. I don't think this should be discussed with Brian, or with anyone."

Afterwards, Kate dropped the tape into the old yellow cigar box on top of the refrigerator. Brian had gathered nearly a dozen tapes. "Someday, someone will find this," she whispered. "Maybe somebody will figure it out."

The next afternoon, the young man who had bargained for Brian's race car arrived with his father. They paid Brian and loaded up the car on their trailer.

With the money, Brian paid the phone bill. On Friday, he drove Mary Beth home for the weekend. They all went to a drive-in movie together with the kids, and laughed at a comedy.

The next day, Peter Bannock, the reporter from the Lariat newspaper spent several hours with Brian working on his newspaper story. As he departed, a researcher sent by Jacques Vallee arrived with sound equipment.

Rod Brown, the tall Hollywood soundman wore a flowered shirt. He and a technician installed a four-track tape recorder, and placed microphones around the house. "It will only pick up very high and low frequencies," he said. "No voices." When they finished, two huge reels of magnetic tape turned slowly on the big recording machine under the piano, recording every sound in the house, day and night, 24 hours a day. "Just let it run," he said. "I'll come back in a week."

Keeper of the Quipu

Late Sunday afternoon, March 15, Lenny arrived with more Kirlian photography equipment, two photographers and a list of questions. Brian didn't want to go into trance but Lenny begged. This time, he wanted TWO men on the Kirlian device to get good images from Brian's hand.

Finally, Brian relented and he easily entered a trance. After a few questions about the drawing of Quipu, Lenny became frustrated.

"What is this Quipu for? I just don't understand this drawing."

"Memory. Systematic numerical method, noted: Quipu. Of Nous 1. Earth terminology. Past knowledge system. Maximum five stones per unit. Each stone, five degrees azimuth. Of this selene, white stone. Helios, black stone."

The voice continued. "Scott: Keeper of the Quipu. Knowledge of solar disk, given," said the voice. "Of Quipu, also movement of people and progress of knowledge. Rapport same--Quipu."

"What is a Keeper of the Quipu?" breathed Kate. "Did he say Brian was Keeper of the Quipu?"

"This makes no sense," Lenny said. "Can he predict any more earthquakes? Ask him if he can predict an earthquake."

A voice growled from Brian, "Beeeaaalllzeebub." The technicians struggled with Brian's hand. "Beware, 1-9-8-2. Death to man. Alignment of planets. Earthquakes. Death to man."

The photo technicians held Brian's hand on the image plate. "Bealllzeubbbbb," roared the demon as the machine flashed.

"Got it," said the technician. They were pleased. When Brian's personality returned, they departed with the Kirlian photo plates.

On Tuesday, March 17, Brian arrived home with a newspaper in hand. Peter Bannock's story had been published in the Saddleback College newspaper, the Lariat. The headline read: "GARDEN GROVE RESIDENT TELLS OF HIS CAPTURE BY EXTRA-TERRESTRIAL BEINGS."

Kate read aloud from the two-page article as Brian fed the children dinner. He laughed and corrected parts of the story. After the children were asleep, Kate read the whole article again in the living room. "He did good," Brian said. "He's the first to really listen." Brian really liked the article. He joked and laughed about the story for hours. Kate liked Brian, and felt strange sleeping in the house with him, but she was a mother to her child, and a friend of Mary Beth's–first. She could resist his charms and each night slept in her own bed, with her daughter.

On Saturday March 21, Mary Beth came home again for the weekend. Rod Brown arrived to film Brian in trance. As the film crew set up lights, a 16mm film camera and sound equipment, Kate lit a white candle. When the camera was ready, Kate lifted her right hand up to Brian's palm, just like Cindy. He slipped easily into trance. Again, Mary Beth watched, now feeling jealous of her best friend.

After the twenty-minute trance, Brian woke up to a room full of stunned faces. Again, he had been totally blacked out. "How do you feel, Brian?" Brown asked with compassion. Near him, his young Phillapino wife cried softly. She appeared terrified.

"I'm fine," Brian said, irritated. "What happened?"

"With what you just went through, I don't see how you can feel fine," said the tiny Mrs. Brown, a staunch Catholic from the Philippines. She seemed flushed and upset.

"It was a vacation for me," Brian said.

"Then it is like amnesia. It's like in <u>Three Faces of Eve</u>," she said.

Brian shrugged. "What is that?"

"A movie about a lady with split personality. She has total amnesia. One personality doesn't know what the other is doing."

Brian laughed. "I don't think so. I just wake up, and everything is different." He chuckled as he stretched. "To tell you the truth, I've kinda got used to it."

"Used to it?" laughed Mrs. Brown. "Brian, that's not normal—I think you need to see a priest."

Brian laughed again. "It's not so bad, unless I am walking." He laughed. "Then, I usually end up on my face."

Worried, Mrs. Brown looked at Brian. "Have you seen <u>The Exorcist</u>, the movie?"

"No. We go to comedies," he laughed. "I don't like scary movies."

"You might need an exorcist," Brian. "I mean it. I can call one for you."

"I already did!" Brian laughed. "They prayed over me and all, speaking in tongues and the whole bit."

"Speaking in tongues?" she gasped. "Brian, speaking in tongues won't do," she said. "That's evangelical. You need a Catholic priest in here. I mean it. YOU need a Bishop, or a Cardinal. Someone with authority."

Brian shrugged. "Whatever. They said we would overcome the Secondary World with a unity of three. But we only have two. That is the problem--we need Rex."

Mary Beth wedged in between Kate and Brian. "We do have three, but they don't accept me as being good enough," she said.

"That's not it," Brian said. "THEY want Rex and Kate. It's not me doing this, Mary Beth. They have their own reasons."

"But I won't do," she said. "Hey, why not. I've been through hell."

"Did something weird happen during the filming?" Brian asked.

"If you see the film, you'll know," Kate said. "Beelzebub gave them an earful."

On Wednesday, March 25, Mary Beth finished her training program for suicide prevention, and Brian brought her home early. She had to repeat some of the sessions, because she argued so much. Doctors wanted her to say the ball of light was not real, but was a hallucination or a hoax of some kind. She had refused. "All I did was listen to stories from hookers and heroin addicts," she said. "Group therapy with those people is a joke." She thought the sessions were a waste of time. "No one can relate to my story," she laughed.

That night after dinner, Lenny arrived with a portfolio of Kirlian photographs featuring Brian. "See the difference between the energy of Brian and the other personalities," Lenny said. He compared Brian to Asta and to Beelzebub. The photos showed dramatic differences in colors and brightness.

Brian didn't care much about the photographs. "It's a start," he said. "If it is the energy of the being, and you could amplify it about 10,000 times, you'd be onto something. That's what they do. That way you can get rid of the negative and stop the Secondary World interference. You have to AMPLIFY the energy of the being," he said. "Everything else is – *so what*."

Kate told them about the crown of lights aura she had seen around Brian's head at the racetrack. Lenny said that psychics often see auras. "But why did I see it there, and no other time?" Kate asked. He didn't know.

Brian clowned around pretending to wear a kingly crown, but finally he shuffled off to bed. Lenny stayed, talking to Mary Beth and Kate about their fears. Mary Beth had not slept in the bed with Brian for months. She still feared making love to him. "I don't know who he is," Mary Beth said. "It's just…it's in my stomach. I'm scared of him."

An hour later, as Lenny prepared to leave, they all heard a deep voice rattle from the bedroom "See," said Mary Beth. "You try sleeping with that."

Kate snuck quietly to the hallway.

"Fuck you blue eyes," said the demon. "That book means nothing to me."

Then Brian's boyish voice spoke. "But it says, in the name of Jesus."

"Beaaaaalzebub!" roared the demon.

Brian's boyish voice responded softly. "I was just checking. The book says I can cast you out in the name of Jesus."

"Beaaaaalzebub!" roared the demon.

Kate pushed upon the door. "You get out of here." A glowering Beelzebub laughed at her with deep, demonic chortles.

"You get out of Brian," she raged. "Leave him alone."

"Beeaaaalzebub!" roared the demon. As an image of the demon formed, Kate saw Brian's boyish face call out to her for help. Then Beelzebub's face dominated. Again, the face looked strangely attractive.

"Man is one with me. You are one with me--of the Secondary world. Give me your soul and you shall live forever."

"No!" Kate shouted. "Get out of Brian."

"Your soul--or destruction. Death to all man."

211

"You get out of Brian," she commanded. The demon laughed until her knees began to tremble. Then she pleaded. "Please leave him alone."

The demon laughed hideously. "This body means nothing to me," he growled. With that, Brian's body disappeared--vanished. The sheet settled to the mattress.

"Oh, God," breathed Kate. She ran into the living room screaming. "Brian is gone. Right in front of my eyes."

Lenny ran into the room. The bed lay empty. He looked under the bed and in the closet. Nervously, he kicked at the shoes. A comical old cowboy hat fell down from a shelf, and he bolted from the room in fear.

"He's not in there," he gasped. "He's gone."

"I was staring right at him," Kate gasped. "Right at him."

In the bathroom, the toilet flushed and Brian shuffled out in his boxer shorts. He looked at them, unashamed. "I hope everyone is going to bed, soon," he said.

They all gasped in disbelief. Kate pushed the door open again. Lenny joined her. Brian pulled the sheet up around himself. "I hope you're not going to stand there and watch me sleep."

"We are just checking on you," Kate said firmly.

"I'm fine," he said. "Go to bed. Nothing weird is going on."

"Easy for you to say," Kate laughed. "Goodnight." She slammed the door.

Everyone sat down in the living room -- Lenny, Kate and Mary Beth. With trembling hands, the two ladies lit up Marlboro cigarettes. "This is terrifying stuff," Lenny whispered. They puffed deep and hard on the cigarettes. "Are you sure he just disappeared?"

"Maybe it's in our minds," Kate said. "Maybe they project an image into our mind that is so real, we can't tell the difference…"

Suddenly, Mary Beth moaned. Her eyes closed and she convulsed with pain in her abdomen. "Assssttttaaa," a voice growled through her. She kicked hard and knocked Lenny to the floor.

As he struggled to stand, Lenny heard a roar from the bedroom, "Beaaaalzebub."

"Oh, no," he gasped. "Both of them. At the same time."

Kate exhaled. "Get her cigarette." She pointed at the smoldering plush gold carpet. Lenny clumsily picked up the cigarette as he held Mary Beth's convulsing body.

"I want your soul," growled Beelzebub from the bedroom.

Lenny sniffed the air. "Is something burning? Do you smell that?"

"Better get in there," ordered Kate. "I'll take Mary Beth." She coddled Mary Beth in her arms.

212

As Lenny snuck to the door, he heard a strange sound like rippling curtains. Beelzebub's voice roared. "Treasures of the world. They are mine to give."

"I don't need them," whined a little-boy voice from Brian. "I want to be like Jesus."

"Then die," growled Beelzebub. "Die now in flames." Brian moaned in pain.

Lenny cracked open the door to see black smoke and flickering red flames. Lenny kicked open the door. Flames encircled Brian's body. The sheets burned in a circle all around Brian. "BRIAN!" shouted Lenny. "Brian, get up!"

Beelzebub laughed at Lenny. "Give me your soul. I spare Scott. The body is mine to destroy." Lenny couldn't believe his eyes. Brian's face and Beelzebub's presence contorted into one mesmerizing image. "To all, death and destruction. Save yourself, now. Give YOUR soul to me."

"No!" he shouted. "You are evil." Lenny grabbed a pillow and attacked the fire, slapping at the flames. He pulled Brian off the bed onto the floor and stifled the flames with a blanket.

Brian woke up, angry. "This has gone too far," Brian shouted. "What the hell is going on?" They both gagged on the acrid smoke and stumbled out of the room.

On the couch, Mary Beth convulsed and kicked. "Astaaaaaaaaaa....." she hissed.

"Oh, hell. Another damn night without sleep," Brian raged.

Lenny gasped in disbelief. "We need to get an exorcist down here. Tomorrow!"

Brian shrugged, "We need the unity of three. That's what the hell this is all about. We need to go to that place, or this will be happening to all mankind, and a lot worse. That's the whole point. Mary Beth isn't protected. Man isn't protected."

"Look out," Kate shouted. Mary Beth's body lunged into Brian knocking him down. He fell over the footstool backwards and landed on his left hand. He screamed in pain. The little finger on his left hand bent 45 degrees at the middle joint. "She broke my finger," he cried.

"Asssttaaaa," hissed the demon from the lips of Mary Beth.

Brian sneered at the demon and jerked the finger. It popped back into place. "There. Good as new," Brian smiled with tears of pain in his eyes. "You don't bother me."

Kate and Lenny grimaced, sharing his pain. Asta roared and raged.

In the morning, as warm rays of sunrise bathed the living room in golden light, Mary Beth lay asleep on the floor, wrapped tightly in blankets, tied with belts. Lenny sat at the kitchen table asleep with his head on his hands. Brian shaved in the bathroom with his bandaged right hand. Bleary eyed, Kate talked on the phone to the psychiatrist at the hospital, "We can't handle her anymore," she sobbed. "This has got to stop. We've been up all night again."

Brian popped out of the bathroom, ready for work--fresh and relaxed. He gulped his coffee then gathered up his briefcase.

"Are you going to work?" asked Lenny in disbelief.

"Of course, I am. I don't miss work."

"Oh, man. You are too much." Lenny lifted his head, sleepily.

Brian finished his coffee. "Some new UFO investigators are coming on Saturday. And Bob Martino has set up some speaking engagements for May at some of the colleges around here."

"For what?' whined Lenny. "What are you speaking about?"

"To tell people what's happening! He wants to do some public speaking. He's a Toastmaster."

"Brian," Lenny stood up. "You need to put a stop to this. What about having an exorcism?"

Brian shrugged. "Whatever. Set it up if you want. It's still going on. I guess, I am still learning about the *mind of man.*"

In the early morning light, as Brian roared down the street in his Captain America truck, neighbors stepped out in robes to grab their morning papers. Brightly colored flowers blossomed in the green yards. Winter had officially ended—the spring equinox had passed.

To Brian, the world looked bright, full of new life and new hope for the future. But for Mary Beth, maimed by the darkness, the new dawn brought despair, fear and loneliness.

Later that morning, the psychiatrist arrived at the house with a female nurse. "I hoped she would be okay," he told Kate. "What happened?"

She just shook her head. "I really don't know," she said.

The doctor injected Mary Beth with a tranquilizer, and loaded her into the car. Without saying goodbye, they drove her away to the state mental hospital where Mary Beth would stay for the next three months.

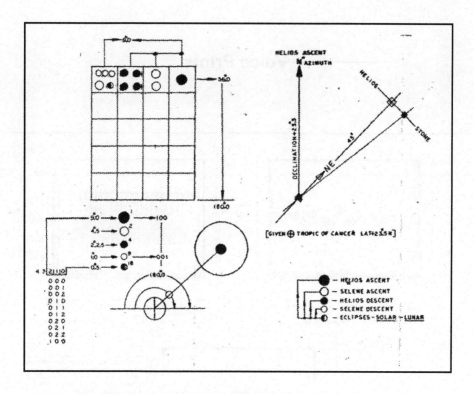

QUIPU DRAWING - Brian said in the Incan culture a man called the "Keeper of the Quipu" used knots in ropes to remember events with a box-shaped device to predict movement of the sun, moon and eclipses. Black stones and white stones of various sizes were used to record movement of the sunrise and moonrise points up and down the Eastern horizon. The time period from Solstice to Solstice is figured at 180 days. The angle the sun travels from Solstice to Solstice can be measured or computed for any place on the earth. Eclipses were predicted using the box and stones. The Lunar cycle was vital, especially the full moon near the spring equinox.

On the Equinoxes the sun would rise due East. Most temple doors are aligned to the Equinox Sunrise. Major rituals were conducted at the full moon near the Spring Equinox (March 22), and the first sunrise after the Winter Equinox when the sun started to move north again. (Dec. 25th). Christians know these days as Easter and Christmas. The religious calendars of many indigenous people are still aligned to these solar events.

Voice Prints

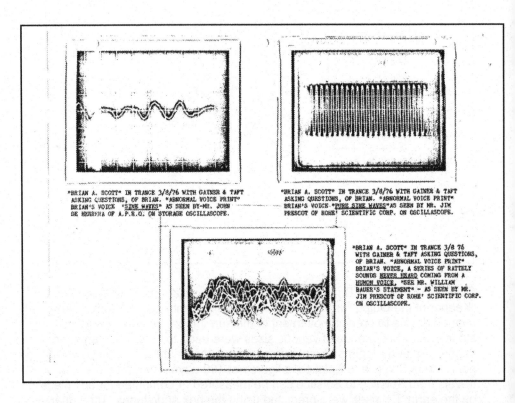

VOICE ANALYSIS of Brian in trance. In the summer of 1976, a UFO investigator worked with Brian to get his voice-prints analyzed by experts and presented to the public in lectures and on radio talk shows.

Experts said some of the sounds could NOT be made by a human. Brian told audiences the voice prints *proved* that the source of the growling was NOT him.

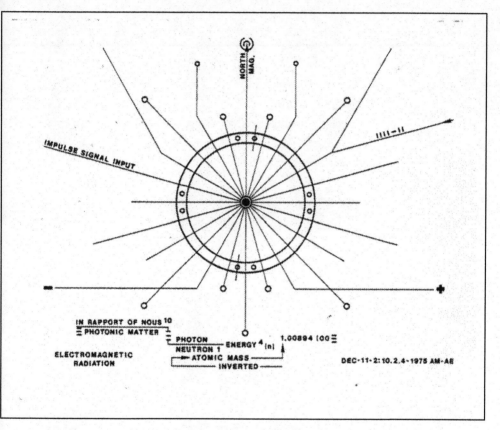

PHOTONIC MATTER—Electromagnetic radiation. Brian's drawing shows a comparison to earth knowledge. Note the positive and negative poles, and magnetic north. This drawing overlays many other drawings with alignment at the center. This is a key to understanding Brian's technical drawings.

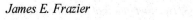

HERO – TWO UNITED AS ONE

A HERO OF MYTH BRINGS BACK FROM HIS ADVENTURE
THE MEANS FOR THE REGENERATION OF HIS SOCIETY AS A WHOLE.
THE TWO - HERO AND GOD - ARE UNDERSTOOD
AS THE OUTSIDE AND THE INSIDE OF A SELF-MIRRORED MYSTERY
WHICH IS IDENTICAL TO THE MYSTERY OF THE MANIFEST WORLD.
THE GREAT DEED OF THE HERO
IS TO COME TO KNOWLEDGE OF THIS UNITY IN MULTIPLICITY
AND THEN TO MAKE IT KNOWN.
--Joseph Campbell

Hero with a Thousand Faces
(Abridged from pages 38, 40 & 48)

Chapter 10

For Man, the Host Cries

On Saturday, another group of UFO investigators arrived to interview Brian at home. Kate recorded everything on tape. She felt Brian did a good job of giving an overview on the story. "You're beginning to sound like a used car salesman," she laughed dropping the tape into the old, yellowed cigar case.

Brian laughed with her. "Everyone takes me for a ride, but nobody wants to take me home."

A few days later, Rod Brown gathered a group of people into the viewing theatre of his Hollywood sound studio. Lenny Jacobs, the UCLA parapsychologist, attended along with several priests, a Los Angeles cop, and several men in black suits. On the big screen, Brian contorted and growled, possessed by Beelzebub. When the lights flicked on, they all sat in silence, stunned.

Finally, a Catholic priest spoke, "That young man is possessed by the devil— Beelzebub is the devil."

Brown told them that a strong low frequency disturbance existed when the ball of light appeared. "There is a lot of screaming and scared people--and it definitely coincides with a low frequency disturbance."

"We want a copy," said one of the men in black.

"I suggest you stay far away from this," said the Los Angeles police detective. "We have reports on this kind of stuff. It's happening all over. It can become a cult, real easily. Potentially it's very, very bad news."

"It's the incarnation of a demon," said the Catholic priest. "He could become Beelzebub incarnate."

"Well, he needs an exorcism," said Lenny. "We can't just leave him like that."

The Catholic priest said he would have to ask for approval from his bishop to proceed.

Catholic Exorcism

The next day, wearing black robes and priestly collars, two Catholic priests met outside of Brian's house with Lenny. "If something happens to me, you take over," the older man nervously said to the younger.

Inside, the white haired priest lit incense, sprinkled Holy water around the house and anointed Brian's forehead with oil as he sat in a straight-backed chair. The younger man, with brown hair, opened the Bible and began to read.

Kate watched as the children played outside.

The white haired priest placed his hands on Brian's head. Instantly, Brian's eyes rolled up and Beelzebub roared. Stunned by the sudden reaction, the priest shouted, "I cast you out in the name of Jesus." He sounded terrified.

"Beallzeeeeeebub," the demon cackled laughing.

"Get out of this man. Now."

"Die!" roared Beelzebub. "Death to you."

Kate felt a pain rip through her head. Suddenly the old priest grasped his chest and collapsed to the floor, panting.

The demon laughed with a deep, hollow rattle, terrifying them all. "Don't touch me," the old priest whispered to his assistant. "You've got to continue."

Terrified, the younger man tried for a few minutes, but Beelzebub laughed at him like he was a child. The younger priest dropped to the floor, and whispered. "What happens if he doesn't leave?" The older man panted in severe pain. "My heart. Medication, in car. Heart. Get me to hospital."

"We can try this again, some other time," the younger priest whispered to Lenny. They both helped the ailing priest to his feet and they limped out to the car leaving Brian on the floor, moaning.

Kate confidently sat down next to Brian. "Ticci Viracocha," she said.

"Open," said the voice. "Override Secondary world interference." Brian jerked a few times, and then woke up, quickly.

"Where are they? What happened?" Brian asked.

Kate pointed outside. "Beelzebub got him."

Brian ran outside. "Is he all right?" Brian shouted as they loaded into the car. "What happened?"

"He's having a little problem, breathing," Lenny said. "We'll have to try again."

"What happened?" Brian asked.

"Kate can tell you," said Lenny gruffly. "We gotto go."

The car screeched away from the curb leaving Brian and Kate alone. "Did you use the code?" Brian asked in a demanding tone.

"No, it was their show," Kate huffed. "What am I supposed to do, tell a priest what to do?"

"Yes," Brian snapped. "If you need to. Don't leave me hanging."

"I didn't," she shouted. "I'm the one who got you out of it."

Kate's Answer

On April 1, Brian insisted on getting solid answers from the Host. His dislocated finger was still swollen. Wearing a finger protector on his left hand, and a bandage on his right, he fumbled with the tape player.

Kate clicked on a second tape recorder to capture the answer for Brian. He slipped into trance so quickly Kate didn't have time to even light a candle. A deep, mechanical voice spoke in Greek for a while, and then a more gentle personality emerged.

"Of this I am," said the gentle voice of the friendly giant, Voltar. Brian's countenance softened. He sounded like a noble, kingly man with red hair, blue eyes and boyish face. "Of I, the Dove of Peace--past--has come," he said. Kate again heard a soft chirping sound--a cooing dove.

"Are we protected by the Dove of Peace?" she asked.

"Of this, tranquility does exist," he said gently.

Kate felt very calm. "Yes, it does," she agreed.

Kate asked for Brian to be returned. Brian woke up quickly.

"Are we done?" His hands and feet didn't feel stiff.

"I still think he is saying he is Jesus," Kate said. "That's not right. It can't be right."

"Did he say he was Jesus?" Brian gasped.

"He said, "Of him, the Dove of Peace, past, has come.""

"Maybe that's not saying he is Jesus," Brian said. "I am sure he is not saying he is Jesus." Brian pondered a moment. " Maybe his people helped Jesus. They have been like angels, I think. They've done this before. I know they go back to then, and before. Thousands of years before. They have done this like nine times before in different parts of the world. But, I don't think he is saying he is Jesus."

"He said man would be marked by the Secondary World for what they did to Him. Just for saying that, you could be branded a false prophet--and KILLED by some wacko."

"Well, it's not ME saying it. He probably HELPED Jesus. When they get involved they get absorbed with people. They become one with them. Maybe that is what he meant. Like this rapport, thing. It's all and everything for them. You know what I mean?"

"No. I don't," said Kate.

"Okay. Did someone visit Jesus in the Garden....and give him strength? That might have been Voltar's people. In one of their descents. If one does it, they all do it, through history. It's like Americans say: *we fought the Civil War*, but you didn't fight it. Understand. It's even more powerful for them because they can relive it on these Rings of Time, in the big computer. They can go back in time and re-experience everything, so each can play different roles, and feel and learn things from the emotions. That's one of the ways they learn—by experiencing other people's feelings. I think that is all they are saying. Hard to explain, but I AM NOT doing anything like that. Trust me. I have to be me. I am Brian and that's all I will ever be."

"Okay," said Kate. "Maybe I didn't understand."

Brian clicked on his tape recorder. "Everybody always goes religious. Let's play my tape. I know for sure that *my* little drop in the bucket has nothing to do with religion. It is about science and engineering."

"No Brian. I want to get MY question's answered—first!" Kate clicked off the tape recorder. "I want to know what happened to me that time in the garage. What is a QUANTUM EVOLUTION? That's what I want to know. And, why me and not Mary Beth? I want some answers now. Or I am not going any further."

"Well, we can try to answer them," Brian relented. "We are so far off track now, it makes no difference."

Kate pulled the tape out of the machine. "No recording."

Brian stared into the candle and slipped quickly into trance.

"Ticci Viracocha," she said.

"Open."

An hour later, as the clock on the piano ticked away, she stopped. "Can I ask you to return Scott?" she said with tears running down her cheeks.

When Brian woke up, he looked at her kindly. "Did you get all of your answers?" His blue eyes blinked warmly.

"Yes I did," she said. "Do you want to join me for a cigarette?" They walked outside and leaned against the Captain America truck.

Kate shivered and Brian gave her his jacket. "It's so incredible," she whispered.

222

"What did they tell you?" he asked.

"He told me what happened in the garage in November. The Secondary World tried to do a '*quantum evolution'* using the green light. I never told you this, but I did remember the green light. They put it on my neck. Right here," she showed him. "Right under my hair line. And, right then--I saw differently. I would have dreams where there was two of me. And I could leave my body. But, it scared me so much, I tried to not do it."

"I knew something had happened," Brian said.

"And, I don't know if whoever I am talking to is this Viracocha, or God, or what," she said. "But, he can really speak to your heart."

Brian hugged her. She melted into his arms. "It is so much, Brian. So deep. He said that Jesus was his legate."

"He did?" Brian asked. "Remember the Host is ephemeral. He's a projection of THEIR *ideas* about God. I said that from the beginning. He represents *their* Creator, not that he *is* god. He's not OUR GOD, necessarily. He's their representation of God, for this *Play of Life*. That's all."

"I can't understand all that."

"Nobody understands God. That is their point. Please don't get wrapped up in this stuff, Kate. It's beyond the mind of man—at our level one mind. That's why we have so much confusion on this planet, and so many stories about God. We can't understand. Don't make judgments, now. You really do have to take it on faith—and on what you believe."

"All I know is he said Ticci Viracocha was also his legate--just like you, Brian Scott. He said you are Legate to Knowledge of the Past, a Keeper of the Quipu of Tiahuanaco--whatever that is. And Keeper of the Solar Disk."

"That part sounds about right," Brian said. "That doesn't make me a false prophet. Does it?" Brian laughed.

"It might," she said standing away from him. "In the eyes of people, you or HE would qualify."

"Well, I am just tied to this Tiahuanaco place, somehow. That's all, that's my part in it. I am not Jesus, or some prophet, or this Incan god--Viracocha. I never will be. I promise you."

"I don't know," Kate breathed. "Whatever is speaking through you Brian, is so real, it is so deep. It knows how to touch the human heart."

"But it's not God or Jesus," Brian said. "I am sure it's something else. Can we go inside? Now, I want some answers."

She agreed and they walked inside the house, arm in arm. Brian again slipped into trance before Kate could light a candle. The mellow voice flowed from his lips. "Nos domas Dias. Nos domas Dias."

"Who am I talking to?" asked Kate.

"Nos domas dias. I am, I am," the voice said firmly. "Of June 22, 1-9-7-6. Of this all knowledge will be given. Of this, power given through a unity of three. End product storage. Of this, end run. Locked."

Kate clicked on a second tape recorder. Brian's weak, boyish voice asked himself the question he most wanted answered: *"What is Scott, Walters and Miller supposed to do in Tiahuanaco on June 22, 1976?"*

The deep, booming voice responded immediately.

> **Base 10. Base 10. Base 10. Of this reconstruction to take place. Of this, Pyramid of Life and Wisdom. Preservation of cells, of this.**
>
> **Ticci Viracocha returns a third time. Of this to pass, December 24, 2011 A.D. Of this, preservation of cells, structure given. Drawings: page 11 through 50 will continue, of this knowledge given to man. Alignment: June 22, 1-9-7-6. A.D.**
>
> **Of this, mankind will know of his past and by this, his world to come will be based on a new truth. Of this, given. Unity of three. End run. Locked.**

Kate stopped both tape decks. "Return Scott," she said. "Ticci Viracocha, return Scott." A few minutes later, in the kitchen, they sipped on root beer floats and played back the tape. As the voice blared, Brian gasped in disbelief. "That's what I sound like?" he laughed nervously.

"Yep. Sometimes worse."

"This is too much. That's not even me talking."

"Nope," said Kate.

"This is weird. Sounds like a robot." He giggled with laughter.

"You've never heard yourself before?"

"No," Brian laughed again. "This is the first time I've ever listened to a tape. I can't believe this. Is this what has been going on?"

"It's been going on for some time now, Brian." For the first time, Kate realized Brian had not listened to any tapes.

"This is so weird," Brian chuckled with disbelief. "Are all of the tapes likes this? Do I sound like that on all of them?"

Kate breathed deep. "Brian, there are all kinds of stuff on those tapes. Some I advise you never to listen to. And, I wouldn't play them for anybody."

"He answered my question," Brian laughed. "But I have a lot more questions. Let's do this again. I have hundreds."

Frustrated, Kate took a deep breath. "Brian. I've been here a month. My life has been totally wrapped up in this. True, I do feel a deep peace. I don't understand why--after all I've been through. I have received a strength that I didn't have."

"Strength--that is good," Brian smiled.

"Strength to stare into the face of a demon, Brian. Because, I knew that I had Jesus on my side--the real Jesus. I remembered Him from when I was a child. Sunday School -- *Jesus loves me this I know. For the Bible tells me so.* That's what I kept thinking. That's what kept me sane." She wrapped her arms around herself.

"So, all in all -- I feel stronger, a lot stronger as a person, but I can't stay here forever. With Mary Beth in the hospital, I feel sort of guilty just living here with you and your kids. In a way, I don't feel it is right."

"What do you mean? We can't do anything about Mary Beth."

"What happens when she gets out?" Kate said. "Do we go back to this 24 hours a day?"

"What are you saying?" Brian asked cautiously.

"I am thinking about leaving," Kate said softly.

"We are just getting started," Brian whined. "I got my first question answered. It's a beginning."

Kate laughed. "For me, I think it is the end," she said. She stood up and began walking around.

"Kate, how could I take care of the kids? I have to work. Somebody's got to pay the bills around here. Should I stay home and baby-sit, go on welfare? Huh?" He followed her around. "I will NOT go on welfare."

"All I am saying Brian, is this can't go on forever with me living here. When Mary Beth gets out, I should be moving on."

"But, what about South America?"

"I will go, if Mary Beth can go. But I don't want anything, like -- you and I go down there, alone. I don't want the appearance of anything like that. It wouldn't be right."

"I guess you're right," Brian stammered. "Now, can I ask one more question?"

"No," she gestured as she slipped on her jacket to go outside into the cool night air.

Brian stopped her. "Kate? Please. I would just like to know, how do they do this? Is this put in my head before, and it is coming out now, like an implant? Or is it beamed in new every time? At least I would like to know that." He shrugged. "Can we ask about that?"

Kate stood up. "I think I am going for a long walk, Brian--alone. You can ask him anything you want." She handed him the tape recorder, and started for the door. "I don't have any more questions. All of my questions have been answered. And--I'm not afraid of the dark, anymore."

The door slammed.

"Kate! Oh great! Damn it," he pulled open the door and shouted into the night. "NONE of my questions have been answered! When the hell do I get MY questions answered?"

The next morning, April 3, Brian found a drawing in the den. A schematic chart answered his question. The lines showed a *'thought transmission'* flowing point to point, from the Host, to a point near the moon, and then down to earth, and to Brian.

Brian felt satisfied: the giant gray creatures were beaming to his mind AND monitoring. At least one question had been answered.

That night when he came home, Brian found another writing with all words on the page spelled backwards.

With a mirror, Kate determined that the words repeated the same old request--physical transportation to South America.

"Why backwards?" Brian asked.

He didn't know then, but the first part of Voltar's *Play of Life* had nearly ended—Act I was over. From September to April, Brian had journeyed down a dark and terrifying path into the underworld of life, into a battle for his mind and spirit--a battle waged between Voltar's people and the evil Secondary World of Earth, aliens originally from Epsilon Bootees. Brian and his family had walked on the dark side of the road in the world of mind and spirit. They had descended into hell for nearly seven months and survived.

Now it was time to take his lessons, and his journey *to the people*.

The Voices Analyzed

Around April 1, Bob Martino and Brian designed a speaking program on UFO ABDUCTION featuring the Beelzebub tapes.

Martino arranged for oscilloscope tests of the voices at a big electronic company in Orange County. On April 12, a recording engineer in Santa Ana provided a statement that interpreted the oscilloscope test as showing an "inhuman" sound.

> **On the above date, I had the opportunity to observe an Oscilloscope presentation of a tape cassette labeled "B. Scott 3-8-76".**

Over the last 15 years I have "watched' over a hundred hours of music and voices on oscilloscopes; with orchestras, 4-piece combos, and female vocalists having the purest notes and overtones.

The lobe-count voice patterns of both men talking on the tape remained fairly constant throughout, until the loud bursts. The voice-lobe count then became entirely different, consisting of a combination of a growl (noise pattern), a deep timbre rattle (lobe-count distinct) and a third pattern (unrecognizable). The short sequence produced a pattern that I have never seen or heard before from a human voice.

"It's not human," Brian said afterwards. "We can take that to the people. It's pathetic, but at least they will know it is NOT ME."

Passover

A few days later, on April 15, Brian, Kate and their three children colored Easter eggs. As Brian created ornate patterns on the eggs, the doorbell rang. Kate opened the door to meet Patti--the Christian cousin of Mary Beth.

At first, neither Brian nor Kate recognized her. She had lost about 80 pounds since November and looked attractive in a stylish, burgundy suit. "It's me, Patti," she said holding up her arms and revealing a trim figure.

"My god, I don't believe it," Brian gasped. She was beautiful. After the shock passed, Patti unwrapped a Passover plate for everyone to share. As Brian studied the big plate of matzos, eggs, bitter herbs and sweet-spices, Patti explained the meaning. She had learned to celebrate Passover as a Christian in her congregation. "Jesus was crucified on Passover Eve at *exactly* the same hour that the priests were sacrificing lambs for their Passover. Everything Jesus did is tied to the Jewish calendar, "she said.

"What about Easter?" asked Brian holding up an ornately decorated egg.

Patti laughed. "Easter is not in the Bible at all. In fact, Easter is a pagan fertility festival--from Babylon. That's why you have chicken eggs and the Easter bunny--fertility."

"Everyone celebrates Easter," Brian frowned. "I love Easter." He showed her the basket overflowing with his beautiful, artistic designs.

Patti smiled. "Brian, you are very artistic. But the truth is, Easter covers up the feast of First Fruits--three days after Passover. That's when Jesus rose—on the Jewish day of First Fruits."

"What are you saying?" Kate asked.

"The Catholic Church chose a Babylonian religious rite to cover up the Jewish one. And they named it Easter for the goddess of Babylon--Ishtar."

"Ishtar?" Brian gasped.

"Ishtar," said Patti calmly. "Yes, the same as your old friend, Ashtarte."

"Are you sure?" Brian asked skeptically. "This can't be. Ashtarte is celebrated at Easter."

"That's right," Patti said. "It's her name. A Babylonian spring rite."

"That can't be," Kate whispered.

"Check it out," Patti said. "Our schools and cities, the entire government celebrates Ashtarte's fertility rite. Our government is going after the way of Ashtarte and Beelzebub. It will be our downfall as a nation, unless people learn the truth."

She knew Brian was watching her new shape and felt flattered. She wondered if Kate and Brian were having an affair. "When do you think Mary Beth will be home?"

"Maybe next week," said Brian. "Her parents had a meeting with the doctor today. You look incredibly different," Brian said. "You're *very* attractive."

"Well, people can change," Patti laughed. "Besides, I'm after a man." They all laughed with her. Then she touched Brian's shoulder. " Brian, remember one thing -- Jesus has a way to create transformation of human beings. He offers His own form of *'quantum evolution.'* I'm sure it's a better way, for most people— especially for us lambs. I know you are a lion—a jaguar even, but maybe the Lord's way would even work for YOU."

"I'm different," Brian laughed. "Like Jesus and his apostles were different than all those who came after. They paid the price, so you could have it easy."

"Maybe so," she laughed. "But Jesus is the Way, I choose."

Brian chuckled after she departed. "She sure has changed. It's weird what happens to people around me."

Easter Holiday

The next Saturday, Brian and Kate drove their children to a city-sponsored Easter egg hunt in Laguna Beach. At the sound of a whistle, hundreds of screaming children ran to find Easter eggs hidden in the grass, flowers and bushes.

With a hundred other parents, Kate and Brian cheered their kids on to victory. "Do we know why we are doing this?" Brian asked. "To celebrate fertility--Ashtarte?"

"I don't know," Kate laughed. "It's spring! Everybody does it. Look at everyone."

That afternoon, they visited Mary Beth in the mental hospital. She looked pale and very tired with dark bags beneath her eyes. She wanted to come home. "They are using all kinds of drugs on me," she moaned. "It's messing up my mind."

Later that afternoon, Mary Beth's parents visited the house. Brian and Kate talked with them on the back patio, amidst all of Brian's bright flowers and green plants. The children played outside on the lush, green lawn. "Nothing bad has happened for two weeks," Kate said. "Brian feels it has ended."

"That is what we want to hear," said Mary Beth's father. Brian proudly told them about the radio and speaking engagements that had been lined up for May. "We are going to *take it to the people*," Brian smiled.

"That's fine, but we have a little problem," Mr. Parsons said. "Mary Beth will be home in a few weeks and the doctor thinks the problems here in the house should be solved."

"I think they are," Brian said. "I think it is over."

Mr. Parsons frowned. "The doctors feel Mary Beth's problems are being caused by you, Brian--in some way."

"By me?" Brian laughed.

"It's not Brian," said Kate. "If anything, it's Mary Beth's own doing. I think she got very jealous and wanted attention from the investigators."

"Someone doesn't get attention by going to a mental hospital," Mary Beth's mom said firmly. "And this is still *her* home."

"What are you getting at?" Brian said, irritated.

"The doctors feel that the power behind this thing, good or evil, alien or whatever--is coming from you, Brian," said Mrs. Parsons.

"Me?" Brian smirked. "I am the one they are after. They are not after the children. The children are safe now."

"Brian, both children have been hospitalized," said Mr. Parsons. "And, Mary Beth is in a state mental hospital. She is under a doctor's care, right now--working *under* the state of California." He stammered with emotion. "Unless she gets stabilized here at home, when they send her home there is a good chance they will take the kids away from her."

"The kids?" Brian gasped. "They are doing fine."

"The state can declare her an unfit mother--and if they do--they want us to be named the legal guardians."

Brian and Kate gasped. "What? How can they do that?" Brian flashed. "The girls are healthy. When Mary Beth comes home, if Kate can stay here, everything will be back to normal. I really think it is over."

"The doctors would like to guarantee it remains that way, Brian--forever," said Mr. Parsons in a grandfatherly tone. "Look, everything they are suggesting is to protect Mary Beth in her fragile state of mind--and to protect the children."

"What do you mean?" asked Brian. "I am getting very confused."

Mr. Parsons stood up and spoke firmly. "The reason we are here Brian is because the doctors have asked us to get involved before it becomes a formal legal issue."

"I don't get it," Brian said.

"In their eyes, they believe Brian Scott is the problem."

"Me," Brian said stumbling to his feet. "They haven't even talked to me."

"I told you, Brian," Mr. Parsons said standing up to Brian. "I told you a long time ago to do something. I told you to stop it. Cut it off, somehow."

Brian trembled. Feelings swept over him that he didn't understand. He remembered the Host's promise that he would be a *"light to the world,"* and that man would *understand in the end. "Fear not the mind of mankind,"* the Host had said. He had said Brian must learn about the *"mind of man,"* but this—not this.

Mary Beth's mom signaled to her husband: her hand sliced the air like a knife blade--*cut it off.* Mr. Parsons placed his arm on Brian's shoulder, and led him inside the house to the big sailing ship on the mantle. "Brian, you've been like a son to me. You are a good man, and you have heart of gold, but something has got a hold on you. Understand? Something not of this world has a hold on you. Do you agree?"

"Yes," nodded Brian. "It did, but it's over!"

"Brian, I feel you are driven to continue this to its end. I truly hope you will get to South America and find the answers you are seeking. But, it can't be here -- not now. Not with Mary Beth and these children. They need a family, they need protection." He shook Brian's shoulder warmly.

In a daze, Brian stared at the men on his sailing ship.

"You need to go your own way Brian. This house needs to be here for Mary Beth and the children." Kate and Mrs. Parsons joined them, tense with worry.

Brian glanced at Kate for help. "They want me to leave," he moaned. "Leave my family—my own home." Tears welled up into his eyes.

"You've got to go, son. You have to do what is best for them -- until this is over and Mary Beth has recovered. That's all -- maybe two or three months. You've got to take your drawings, and your papers and everything to do with this, and you've got to go—for a while—at least."

"Where would I go? This is MY home."

"Find an apartment nearby in Garden Grove, or close to your job. Stay there until this is over. You can leave some of your things. But your drawings, your drafting table, tape recorders--everything to do with this must go with you. There has to be a clean break. Clean. Mary Beth needs a completely new frame of reference when she comes home. That's what they said."

Brian deflated. "I am being kicked out of my own home?"

"Brian. You are providing a healthy and proper environment for your children, and a wife who has suffered very real mental trauma. You are doing the right thing, to go."

Brian turned away. "I don't believe this."

"If you love them, do what is right for them."

Mrs. Parsons spoke softly, touching Brian's shoulder. "Brian. It is a last ditch effort, to save your family."

"My family? Without me?" He pulled away.

Mr. Parsons stepped close to Brian. "If Mary Beth has any more problems, they will take the children away." He snapped his fingers—CLICK. "It will be that quick. They will take them away from Mary Beth and from you. Permanently."

"Permanently?"

"Until *they* determine it is over. You can imagine what that would take. You want the State of California to come in here. You want social workers in her trying to decide what is right?"

"But it is OVER!" Brian pleaded.

Mrs. Parsons sliced the air again with her hand--no!

"Mary Beth is coming home sometime next week," said Mr. Parsons. "When she drives up, and gets out of the car and comes into this house to stay, your clothes and your possessions need to be out of this house."

Brian turned away. Stunned, he stared at the rigging, and the lifeboats and at the stern faces of all the little men on his sailing ship.

"They would go to sea for months at a time," said Mr. Parsons, standing close to Brian. "Think of it that way. You're going on a journey, like a sailor. In a few months, if she is stable, you'll be able to return."

A New Home

That night Brian drove the Captain America truck out to the racetrack. Holding a "For Sale" sign out the window, he roared back and forth through the pits with the exhaust ports blaring. He sold the truck to the highest cash bidder.

On Sunday, Kate drove Brian and the kids around in her car. In a used-car lot, Brian spotted a tan, 1966 VW station wagon. He paid cash on the spot.

Then Brian found a small apartment for rent in a newspaper. He trudged up a long set of wooden steps, across an asphalt roof to meet the landlord outside the tiny apartment.

Inside, the couch folded out into a bed. A thick, brown carpet covered a 15' x 20' room. French doors opened to a very small sitting room--a large closet. Brian looked into the tiny kitchen complete with pots, pans and silverware.

"I'll take it," he said.

Brian Goes Public

On April 26th, in the apartment, while sitting on the floor, Brian wrote a certified statement that he might be abducted on June 22, 1976. He authorized Bob Martino to investigate should he not return.

On Wednesday, May 5th, Brian drove to Los Angeles in his VW station wagon and appeared on KABC talk radio with host Carol Hemingway. Sitting at the huge microphone in the radio station studio, he relaxed and unwound.

Due to Martino's coaching, he sounded organized and very credible as he described the first terrifying contact with the wheezing gray creatures with no necks and long ears. For hours, people called in with questions.

After the show, off the air, Carol urged Brian to get an attorney to protect his rights. "Your story and your documents have been given to some very influential people in the motion picture business," she said. "Certain investigators are trying to sell your story out for the money." Brian didn't care. "No one knows it all, anyway," he said. "Everyone just has a little piece."

On Friday night, May 7 at 7:00 p.m., a large crowd filled an auditorium at Saddleback Community College in Tustin for a lecture on UFO's featuring Bob Martino and Brian Scott.

Martino took the podium. "My investigation of the Brian Scott case is not yet complete. But at this time I feel that this case does warrant further investigation."

He said there were 20 witnesses to the 1975 phenomenon, and that he had viewed all of the hypnosis tapes. He felt the hypnosis with Rex Walters supported the case. "The doctors who worked with Brian are saying they got nothing out of Rex Walters," Martino said softly. "They say he doesn't recall anything. But, I find quite a bit of support." Martino talked about the hypnosis sessions for a while, and the automatic writings. When he introduced Brian, the crowd applauded.

Brian took the podium and described his automatic writings. "All I know is that these writings talk about endless amounts of things, especially this place called Tiahuanaco. To me, it's all nothing that makes any sense. I do this writing with my left hand, which doesn't make sense either, because I am right handed."

Martino interrupted to show the voice-prints. The diagrams compared Brian's voice to that of Beelzebub. As the horrifying sound tapes played, Martino gave Brian pointers on speaking. Afterwards, the crowd sat silent in disbelief. They had come to hear about UFO's -- not demons.

They began asking questions about religion—about demons, God and UFO's. Brian didn't have any answers for them. "This is not about religion," he said. "Science, engineering, and designs. That's what they want from me."

Afterwards, Martino took the podium. "Jacques Vallee told Brian that his story '*illustrates exceptionally well*' the situation contactees face--that contactees *are bounced back and forth between scientists, religious leaders and psychologists.* No one understands," Martino said. "Not even the top experts in the world. So, obviously, **'a new framework for understanding'** *is needed.* That is why we bring the story to you, today. Maybe you have some answers we need."

When Martino dismissed the crowd, people applauded loudly. Afterwards, a group swamped Brian with quiet, personal questions—and their own stories. Brian couldn't believe how many people had seen something unusual. Most of the stories were not about UFO's or even lights, but things that seemed bizarre— voices of dead relatives on the phone, dreams, materializations, telepathy and ghosts. He didn't believe most of them. People sure come up with wacky stuff, he thought afterwards. But, if strange things really are happening to so many people, then he should find plenty of people to listen.

On May 17, Brian and Martino talked on an after-midnight show broadcast from KLOS radio in Los Angeles. After Brian told the basic story, Martino played the March 25th tape of Beelzebub. When the phone lines opened, people called with questions. Brian answered like a pro. He didn't speculate. He only described what he saw. He sounded credible, solid—dependable. Talking to the people made Brian feel better, stronger. He felt less lonely. He realized that people could understand, and some even believed they knew *more* than he did about the mysteries. He liked that.

The Teacher of Telepathy

On June 2, Brian agreed to meet with several people who had attended the first lecture. In a coffee shop, Monique, a small, dark-haired woman about sixty years old sat down at a table with Brian. A group of her *mental telepathy* students followed, sitting in a nearby booth. The group included three white-haired ladies in flowery dresses and a tall, blue-eyed young man in a business suit. Monique wore long earrings and jewelry--like a gypsy queen. In her thick, Hungarian accent, she offered to pay for Brian's meal. "Get anything you want," she said.

Brian ordered with a twinkle in his eyes. "Big milk, double cheeseburger-- everything but onions, double fries, a cup of coffee and a chocolate shake, quick as possible. Rush my order, please," he said.

The waitress looked at Monique and her friends. "Just hot water," they all said. Each unraveled herbal tea bags.

"I can't believe you eat that way, Brian," said Monique. "Meat has thought forms of the cows. Maybe that is why you are having so much trouble, getting through all of this *'quantum evolution.'* It doesn't have to be so hard."

233

"I'm not really having any trouble," Brian said. "It's just the people around me." He smiled at her. "In a world of total insanity," he said. "How can you tell who is crazy?" They all chuckled.

The waitress slipped a hot hamburger plate in front of Brian. "You said to rush your order!"

"Wow," Brian smiled with approval. "That's fast."

"I gave you someone else's," the waitress smiled at him.

He flirted with her, and added ketchup to the juicy burger. With both hands he chomped a huge bite. "Mmmmmmm," he chuckled. "Am I hungry."

Martino laughed. Brian's manners stunned the refined ladies as he gulped milk and licked his fingers. He delighted in shocking them.

Monique had read the documents. "I have gone over your material and I am very certain that you do not understand the intent or meaning of your contact."

Brian ate, determined to stuff himself with hot food before they got mad at him. He didn't think the meeting would last long. "What is your relationship to them?" Monique asked. "That is what is important. Who are they?"

Brian shrugged as he chewed. "I don't know."

"Brian, your foolishness will not work on me," she said firmly. "I have the article from the *Lariat* on March 17." She unfolded the newspaper and held it up. "You were a lot more honest about what happened than you were in the lecture. You said more."

"I can't say everything, to everyone—every time."

"Did the reporter get the story right?" she asked.

"Yes. Pretty much. He did a lot of work on it," Brian said with a mouthful of fries.

"Well in this story, you say that your heart left your chest during the medical examination, that it moved out of your body."

Brian agreed as he stuffed food into his mouth. "You said that the long-eared creature said he was from 'time beyond all time,' and that he talked with you by telepathy."

Brian shook his head in disagreement. "No, I didn't..."

Monique argued. "He placed his hand on your head and you saw pictures in your mind. Right? Heard his voice?"

Chomping on the hamburger, Brian finally agreed.

"Brian you need to learn about telepathy," she commanded. "The first thing he said to you Brian, was 'Of I, of the Host. All men will know the truth'. And he said 'Of his world and your world, light reflects light, time reflects time. Mind reflects mind.' They are related."

Brian shrugged. "Something like that. I don't remember exactly."

"Well what did he say?" she demanded.

Brian wiped his face with a wad of napkins and spoke slowly. "It was something about a reflection. His world is a reflection of our world. His mind is a reflection of my mind. It didn't make sense to me."

She smiled and raised her glasses. In a thick accent, she read aloud.

Fear not. I will return to you and, of this--life to all mankind. I am life, from beyond all time, fear not. Knowledge is not FROM you, but BY you. Time is not known TO you, but BY you. I, OF MY HOST, shall return with knowledge beyond all life, December 24, 2011 A.D. You and I are one.

"Then he showed you his world. He took you on a little trip--with the mind. Right?" Brian agreed. She read:

Fear not, for knowledge through you is life to all. From beyond all time, I am. Life is of my life, from one to another, by thought, by expansion of my Host.

She studied Brian carefully. "Brian what is your relationship to them?" she asked.

He laughed. "I told you, I don't know." The group laughed and howled.

"Brian," she paused theatrically. "*'I, of my Host. I, of my Host,'* he says. Who is talking?"

"The big, friendly guy with long ears," Brian smiled.

"Thank you." Everyone applauded politely. "Brian, you have a lot of people in this story," she said. "Can I tell you?" she asked politely.

"Do I get dessert?"

She laughed. "Hot apple pie with ice cream?"

"I'll tell you anything." He clowned, eagerly waving at the waitress.

"An all American boy. How did I know that?" she chuckled. "Must be telepathy," she laughed. They all giggled.

Brian watched the sexy walk of the waitress.

"Look, Brian," Monique grumbled. "This is a lot more important than your *lusts.*" They all chuckled—even the waitress. "You have a calendar and you have people. The Host came in 3113 B.C. and he will return on December 24th 2011 A.D. That is the cycle of the Mayan calendar: beginning to end."

Brian flirted with the waitress. Frustrated, Monique waited. "Brian, set aside your horniness for a few minutes."

"Boy, you put it bluntly."

"I'm telepathic," she said. "I know what you are thinking about that girl. And I don't want to get into your personal problems. I will with you, later, but right now this is the important question. What is their relationship to you? Is he really you in the future?"

235

Brian chuckled. "I don't think HE is me, no."

"Okay, but he travels through time. He says over and over, he is from *'time beyond all time.'* Then he says he is, *'of the Host, his Host.'* So right there you have the Host, him and you. You've got three--a trinity. You also have this god of the Inca, Ticci Viracocha. That makes four--all aspects of your being. Then you also have the spider and the jaguar--your marks, your symbols of power. Those arc your identity also, your bonds to power, to psychic power."

Brian asked for a coffee refill, and flirted again. "She thinks I'm a jaguar," he growled seductively at the waitress, and she giggled.

"What is the relationship, Brian?" asked Monique irritated.

He laughed. "I told you--I don't know."

"Your heart went out of your body. Did you see it come back?"

"Ugh. Not really."

"Did anything else happen when your heart went out?"

"Well, a lot happened. But, well--some of it I can remember, but I can't *talk* about it. Some of it, you are not ready. No one is."

"There," she shouted. "I knew it. You know more than you are telling!"

"Well, sure. I can't tell it all, to everyone. No one would believe me. Not all of it."

"You are keeping secrets then," she blurted. "You are playing stupid."

"Well," Brian gasped, nervously. "I am not playing stupid. I am a high school drop out. One of the investigators said I was stupid. That was my best..."

"Don't tell me you ARE stupid," said the lady. "They don't pick up stupid people. You are keeping secrets of the Host, and of this long-eared giant who put his hand on your head. See, he's the key one. He's the one doing most of the talking. What is his name?"

"I don't know that I know his name, but if I go to speak about him, my head hurts. It's hard to explain."

"But, are you keeping his secrets?"

"Just a few," Brian admitted. "To see, if it is real, for me."

"A few?" she laughed. "Okay, Brian," she smiled. "I think I know who you are. You are holding back a lot. You know a LOT more than you let on. Okay? Now listen. These are all parts of you, your full multi-dimensional being, across time: the Host, your long-eared mentor and the Incan God--they are all of *one*, just as they say. They are multi-dimensional aspects of you. Their words are right on. Frankly, it's your presentation which is off. Way, way out, Brian. Your presentation is just plain wacky!"

Brian laughed, amused by the courage of this spunky woman.

"I have one question for you," he said skeptically. "How can HE be ME, if I am ME?"

Everyone laughed.

Brian continued. "I'm serious. How can he be me, if I am sitting here right now sipping coffee, when HE is, who knows where--up in the stars? How could I be some long-dead Incan god, when I am here, Brian Scott a grade-four draftsman, kicked out of his own house and living in some crappy apartment in Santa Ana? Now, I know the Host can't be me, because he isn't even human. He is an ephemeral projection of their God. He wears a spider thing around his chest and a flashing light-belt. That's not me. I'm at least twice his size and I don't have any belts like his, that's for sure. He just touches it, and zap--he's gone."

"These are all elements of your multi-dimensional self," she said in her thick Hungarian accent. "Brian, these are your spiritual guides from other realms. Your past lives, your future lives."

Brian smirked. "I'm sorry to disagree with you, but I'm going to have to draw the line, right there," he said. He lit up a cigarette and exhaled a cloud of smoke, offending Monique and her friends. They coughed and sniffled.

"The trouble with what you say, is that it doesn't matter," Brian said watching them squirm away from the smoke. "So what? *Even if it was true,* which I don't believe is close--anyway. *So what?* I still have to be me, right here. Brian Scott. I have to go to work, pay the bills—and you should see my phone bills," he turned serious for a moment. "See, I think that kind of talk is not good for people. If people start thinking they are these other things, these beings, these personalities, it's dangerous. You have to take an identity that you can live with. You can go to the good, or to the bad. That's what happened to my wife, I think. She got to thinking she was Ishtar. I mean one night she started acting like a sex goddess."

They all laughed, nervously.

"Or Beelzebub. That guy is really bad. He would just as soon kill somebody as look at them. He wants everybody's soul. We have to be careful. You can't just go around saying you are somebody, or acting like them, just because he, or it, was in you, or spoke through you a few times. If I believed that, I would have been locked up a long time ago—or dead myself." Stunned, they all nodded. "This is dangerous," Brian said. "But what you are saying is MORE dangerous. It's all about identity, and which personality you call your own for daily life. That is what counts." Brian talked for a long time, and when they departed everyone was laughing with him. Monique volunteered to give him free telepathy classes and help him anyway she could.

The Host's Request

A week later, on June 4, at about 2:10 in the morning, Brian woke up writing at his desk. His heart raced. He had hoped the automatic writings were finished. Then he heard a noise and spun around, terrified. The Old Man stood calmly in the middle of the room. He looked very physical. Brian heard his feet move on the floor.

"Of this writing, do you understand?" the Old Man asked.

Brian's heart raced. "I have not read it yet."

"It is before you." He gestured to the writing.

"I can read the things I have wrote, but they don't tell me anything," Brian whined. "I don't understand most of them."

The Host stepped closer. "Scan what is before you."

Brian felt a calm sweep over him--a peace beyond his own understanding as he looked at the man's face. He relaxed and read the writing.

**"Open. Of June 22, 1-9-7-6--come. I await you, at the first of
I. Of this, quantum displacement physics given. Arizona."**

"But why?" He knew the words meant he should go to the first contact site in Arizona.

"All will be explained. Do this of I."

"Can I bring along a friend?"

"This is of YOU," the Host said firmly. "Of this, each man must come to understand himself before he can understand others. Of this, it is not a matter of man accepting I, but of I accepting man."

Brian stammered, but the Old Man continued. "You are of I, and of this, come that you may understand of yourself. For each to his own mind is given choice and freedom of will, and, of this--the opportunity for his own destruction. Come. For this is of you, for you, that you alone might understand."

Brian frowned. "I don't want to be alone, anymore."

"In time, all will be known to man. Fear not."

"May I bring a camera and a tape recorder with me?"

"Of this, if you find peace within, so do." The Host reached forward and placed his hand on Brian's shoulder. His touch felt firm. His hands felt solid, instead of ephemeral like before. Brian relaxed. His whole body felt warm and peaceful with the Host's hand on his shoulder.

"Now rest, there is much to come," said the Old Man as he squeezed Brian's shoulder. "I await you." Then he pushed a button on his belt and disappeared with a squeal.

Brian Complies

For most of June Brian busied himself with preparations for the trip. He didn't fully expect to return from Arizona. He hoped they would offer him a chance to leave, and live with them. He created a will and final statement of testimony to investigators. He gave Bob Martino the right to investigate his case

238

and take control of all materials should he not return. In a taped message, he thanked Martino and Vance Dewey for caring about him, and being more than just UFO investigators. "If this will help man to understand himself and what is going on, I will do it," he said.

At dawn on June 21, he packed his VW station wagon and drove alone towards Phoenix. That evening, after dark, he arrived near the foothills of the Superstition Mountains, just north of Apache Junction.

He parked his car facing west. "I'm here, Bob," he said into the tape recorder. "It's June 22, ten minutes after midnight. He planned to give Martino the tape whether anything happened or not.

In the morning, as the sun rose, Brian sat alone watching the desert come alive with the sun's warmth and light.

Around noon, the temperature reached about 100 degrees, and all the ice melted in his cooler. Brian continued on tape two of his sound log.

After a lunch of peanut butter and jelly sandwiches with milk, he rigged up a tarp for shade and snapped photographs of the locations where the abduction had taken place in 1971.

Then he gazed around at the scenery and clicked on the tape recorder.

"I am surrounded on three sides by mountains it's not picturesque--a few sorrel cactus—I'd rather take a forest anytime."

At 5:00, he broke out his last batch of sandwiches and a soda from the ice chest. After eating, he taped the microphone to his throat and napped.

At 8:20 p.m., he said he would drive back to California at midnight if nothing happened.

"The time is five minutes after nine. And the stars are there, I can see plenty of them now."

"Time is 9:40 p.m. Man, you ought to see the stars in the sky. Just beautiful. The Arizona deserts are really something to see at night."

Brian clicked off the recorder and stepped out of the car to stretch in the cooling, gentle breeze. Suddenly, he saw a purple light over the rim of the Superstitions. He squinted. The light moved at him, expanding--just like the first time.

Brian clicked on the tape recorder. "Sweet mother of God," he gasped. "It's only a few minutes after I just checked in with you. It's here again, Bob. I can see it. It's just over the top of the rim. Son-of-a-bitch. I'm getting the camera. I'm gonna get a picture of this thing."

Brian leaned into the car and pulled on the camera strap. It snagged on the gearshift knob. He struggled with the camera and watched through the windshield as the craft soared toward him.

"It...my. Jesus Christ...It's moving right at me. I can't get the camera up off the seat."

He struggled, and stood up with the camera in hand. "I have no idea what time it is, but it's only a few minutes after I last checked with you, for sure. It can't be anymore than that." Brian couldn't find the light. Then suddenly, he looked upwards. The craft had stopped overhead, blocking out the starlit sky.

Awcd by the glowing energy field, he lifted the camera, but suddenly the image darkened. Baffled, he lowered the camera. In front of him stood one of the giant, gray, long-eared hulks. Brian gasped. The creature quickly grabbed at the camera with his huge hand. "Holy...that muther...what. Oh no. No. No not...agh. Holy." Brian struggled.

Then he saw a second giant. "Get back," he still held onto the camera. "You guys said I could have this. No! You said I could take it with me. Get away! I'm gonna. You said I could take it with me. You said I could take it with me."

The larger creature spoke in a high-pitched electronic bleat, *"Come - with - I."*

"No stop! You said I could take this with me," Brian shouted. But, as the second giant grabbed Brian, the camera slipped out of his fingers.

"I want to take it. The camera is not going!" Brian screamed. "Bob. Help. Help! Bob. Bob! Help."

The second giant touched the back of Brian's head. He fainted, instantly. While one giant held Brian in his arms, the other ripped the tape loose from around Brian's neck. The microphone bounced on the sand.

Brian moaned, and a deep warbling sound resonated into the microphone as they floated him upward toward the rim of the craft.

On the sand, Brian's tape machine lay running, the red light blinking as it recorded the gentle wind and the desert mice.

In the sky, moments later, the silver disk crossed over the rim of the Superstition Mountain peaks, and disappeared.

The Host Cries for Man

On board the craft, Brian woke up near the center of the huge ring computer. He watched the three rings rise up from the floor. Each stopped at a different height. Lights flashed on the walls--red, green and blue. The bright, spider-shaped energy began to flash from panel to panel and the floor came alive with moving rings. Brian heard a rustle and jerked around. Behind him stood the Host, with white hair down to his shoulders.

"I am I am," said the Old Man.

"I came alone," Brian said. "But they took my camera—you said I could bring it."

"*If this gives you peace of mind*," said the Host, repeating his words to Brian in the apartment. "You returned here, now, of your own free will. Thus, of you, I bring transformation of the mind to man—quantum evolution."

"I don't understand how," Brian said. "I still think I am the wrong guy."

"Of you, Nous four is requested. Have you not learned much—of the mind of man, and of yourself?"

"Yes. I guess I have," Brian agreed humbly. He noticed that the huge ring computer responded to his words and emotions.

"Of this, what have you learned?" the Host asked.

The last thing Brian expected was a question. "I don't know." He could see the panels on the three-ring computer changing with his feelings. It created sounds which harmonized with his emotions perfectly. It is reading me, he thought--reading my every thought and feeling. The Old Man waited calmly.

Brian decided to just speak his mind. "I guess I've learned that no one has any answers for me. No one--*on Earth*. And *you* don't even give me answers. You stopped talking to me when all the bad stuff happened."

"Of this, you must seek within," said the Host. "All men are *one* at Nous 10, and there, within, knowledge is given."

Brian understood. But why should *he* go through all the sorrow. "You must know the mind and heart of all men and women. You must understand their sorrows. You must know your brother—as one with you."

Brian pondered. Emotions were the problem. What about facts? Why can't you just give me the facts?

"Knowledge given to you at Nous 10, is given to all mankind," said the Host. "Of this, the transformation--from one man to all men, to all nations—will not be without sorrow, or sadness, loneliness and despair, for to each—his own mind, and his own heart."

Brian understood. He wanted to go forward, but what did it all mean, really?

The Old Man read his thoughts. "Of this, on your right hand a mark shall be given to you, of I. By this, mankind shall know of I, and know you."

Brian watched lights on the panels. Many turned green, responding exactly to his thoughts. The machine is amazing, Brian thought. It suddenly fired off a little celebration of bright lights and high-pitched sounds, in response. He chuckled. This could be fun, he thought.

"Let man not seek of I," said the Host. "For man must learn to seek of his own mind, and his own *being* first--before he can understand others."

Brian gestured to the computer. "It's reading me, echoing me."

The Host answered. "Of this, the neural-optical responses of man are monitored."

"Why me?" asked Brian.

241

"The proof we need is of you. And of this, you shall prosper in your career. That is all I promise."

"But, I need proof you exist."

"Proof given, three times in the past, of I. Of this, man accepted a part, but not the whole. And of this, destruction by and of the Secondary World followed. Of this, your spouse--an example for all man. For of this too, by her free will, she chose the wrong path."

"But Mary Beth did nothing wrong," Brian countered.

"She chose to have power for her own purpose—jealousy—to overcome another. Of this, man must understand and be strong. Resist evil—choose with wisdom—for even the smallest choice today may create your *tomorrow.*"

"She doesn't understand," Brian said. "She wasn't prepared for this. She didn't know it was coming."

"And so man," the Host said. "The days to come will be indeed unsettling to man. Thus, man must prepare, and be wise."

"But I don't get it. Why are you doing this? Why me?"

"I have chosen you before your birth. In this, your father."

"But why not just tell everyone? Land on the White House lawn?"

"Are you of *time beyond all time*? Better that you answer me, than I answer you. You and all man are but infants in understanding."

Brian nodded in agreement.

"Of this, now comply to my will, and be free of destruction by that of the Secondary World."

Brian felt power and truth in the Host's words. "What do I have to do?"

"Of this, to come--Quantum Evolution to Nous 4, radiant descent of Viracocha and withdrawal of your radiant aspect—your quantum--via Lake Titicaca.

"But I don't know what that means?"

"Transformation—in English earth terminology."

Brian smirked. "This is going too fast. I don't want a physical change. I couldn't live with that." Brian watched all three rings of the computer brighten with green lights and harmonize with him. The computer seemed to approve the request.

"No physical change," the Old Man said. The Host placed his hand on Brian's shoulder. "The transformation is of the Gate of the Sun, of Tiahuanaco, and must be by man's agreement, and free will. From within the *Play of Life,* we project that one will comply, and you will be in the Portal to Life on the requested date. From that day forward, many people will seek of you."

"Seek me?"

"Of this, I ask of you today, accept this knowledge which we offer to man, without profit or gain, without serving that of your self. Accept those, whom I

242

send to you, as FRIENDS. Submit to their wisdom and council, for in this, you shall receive the guidance you need. Let those of the old, fall away—each to their own mind." Brian understood. Let people go.

"Of you, to understand *all*--is not given. One who comes to you as a brother will understand of quantum displacement, another of the selene orbital, and another to guide you as a brother, a friend—from a time past. Of he, will come a new beginning for man. For through the eyes of one man, all mankind will see. And of what we do -- all is for man -- for all man to understand."

Brian wobbled, dazed by the thoughts in his mind. Each word from the Host reached deep into his heart. He saw images in his mind, and felt the reality of each word. He didn't understand all the pictures, but he knew he would at the right time.

"The knowledge to understand all that is given with the *Play of Life* is now within yourself, and will soon be within *the people*. Of this, your transformation will trigger a new beginning for man, a new truth upon the land, and by this truth – man shall survive, and prevail."

The Old Man lifted his shiny black medallion, and showed the engraved spider to Brian. "For now, say only this to man, of I." His slender white hands flipped the medallion over. Brian saw the number 020 020 020 engraved into the dark shiny mirror.

"For he who has wisdom, this is I," said the Host, "the alpha-numerical equivalent of I--*and man*. Seek of I in this, the meaning. For by this mark--which must be given to you prior to December 22--all mankind will know of you, and, of this--*know I*. By this, you are one with I, and with all mankind. By this mark, mankind will come to understand himself, his past, his future and his choice. By this mark, you shall become a light to all who seek wisdom. By this, all shall be done."

Then Brian saw the numbers change into an image of the earth. Suddenly the image of earth floated out of the pendant and hovered in front of him. The beautiful blue-green world rotated. Brian studied the moving clouds, the oceans, the forests and the land. He could smell the saltwater in the oceans. He could hear the storms, and feel the winds.

"Of this," the Host said "if man does not comply, see now the fate of man, by and of, those of the Secondary World. See the fate of your world."

As Brian watched, underground explosions erupted in America, Russia and other nations around the world. The globe began to wobble out of control. Continents shifted. One-third of the world burst into flames. The beautiful blue earth blackened with fire and smoke.

"I don't understand," Brian cried. The Old Man's face wrenched with the agony of a broken heart. Two tears ran down his cheeks, and he moaned with sorrow—a deeper sorrow than Brain had ever imagined. The Old Man was serious: the earth could be wrecked, and millions of people could die. It was for real, not some fantasy. It could happen. Brian saw the Old Man cry, and felt his deep agony, like a father who had lost a son. From the Host's sorrow, Brian felt his own sorrow within and understood.

Brian heard a sound and turned around. The two giants offered to help him up into a small egg-shaped machine, a small version of the giant NOR complete with three rings of blinking lights.

Brian looked back at the Host. The Old Man walked away to the center of the huge three ringed computer, then in a blink – he was absorbed *into* the machine.

The NOR – A Neurological Implant

As the two giants tested the smaller device, Brian closed his eyes, relaxed and listened to the soaring sounds. Beautiful flute music swept away his tears. Then the three rings hummed, moving up and down in a hypnotic, repeating pattern.

"I hope you know what you are doing," Brian said as the two gray creatures stood close, taking his hands in theirs.

The largest giant spoke–Voltar. "You are of I, of Nous ten." Brian recognized the gentle, soothing voice. "Fear not the mind of man. You bring rapport of Nous 10 to all man. And, of this, the children shall return. Look to the east has come--Laos Nous Hikano."

"I don't understand everything," Brian said. "But, if it will help man," Brian muttered. "I would do it."

They nodded in agreement. The rings began to rotate. Beautiful music tinkled with bells, then flutes and drums. Inside the egg, Brian heard the voice of Voltar whisper into his ears. "You must bring the knowledge given now--Quantum Displacement Physics--to man on paper, BEFORE the Phase 1 transformation, December 22, 1976." Brian nodded in agreement, as he drifted into a daze.

The giant whispered again in a soft, soothing tone. "For man, no greater challenge exists than to bring forth orbital reality into the science known on earth. Bring forth this knowledge via quantum displacement physics. Resurrect the Pyramid of Life and Wisdom. Rebuild and complete construction in your time prior to 2011 A.D."

Brian moaned as the giant three-ring computer sent bolts of photonic energy into the outer shell of the smaller three ring NOR.

Brian saw a futuristic looking pyramid of copper and silver decorated by red horizontal stripes inlaid with gold. Then inside the pyramid, in the vast open space, he saw earth people, young and old, wearing blinking belts, just like the Host had worn on his visits. They zipped up into the air, floating and soaring effortlessly by touching their belts. Then Brian saw beautiful two-man crafts hovering above the ground. The little cars zipped through the air moving people inside and outside the pyramid at all levels. Most of the people wore bracelets of copper, silver and gold. Some wore headbands, and breastplates of gold or copper.

Outside the pyramid, he saw larger crafts, like busses, carrying earth scientists over the land. Llamas and other animals ran under the soaring vehicles, because the crafts soared about ten feet off the ground over shiny, blue lines on the ground. The tiny lines served as roads for navigation.

From images and drawings that flashed before his eyes, he knew the lines were simply silica--cooked sand, a form of crystal carrying magnetic signals.

Other crafts floated up to circular homes on glass towers of molten shapes. *Glass, sand, silica* the words said. It seemed like everything was made of sand, of copper, silver and gold.

In the fields surrounding the pyramid, Brian saw a vast array of solar dishes. The dishes gathered sunlight and re-directed the hot light, a form of photonic matter, to the top of the pyramid. There, at the top of a tower, a huge crystal focused the hot light into water from the lake, creating steam. From the steam came electricity to power the pyramid, the surrounding village and the region.

Then the images began to run faster showing details of drawings, pipelines and storage for cells and fluids.

When the projection ended, Brian's head spun and his legs wobbled. "Neural-implantation complete," said a mechanical voice from the computer. "Inverse logic, withdraw."

As the whirring of the three-ring computer slowed, the two creatures helped Brian out of the NOR. "Of this, all mankind will come to know of you. Of this, fear not of what is to come: December 22, 1976."

Brian could hardly stand. He looked at the taller creature for understanding. Suddenly the ugly face became a handsome human face with broad cheeks, blue eyes, and a coppery skin. Voltar shook his long red hair and smiled with a boyish, but masculine grin. Brian blinked in disbelief. He suddenly remembered that he had seen the face before, during the first contact.

"Speak not to man, of I," Voltar said in a soothing voice. "Of this, the wall is black no more." He gestured at the three-ring computer. The outer wall blinked with sections of green light. "Much is given to you in trust. Of December 22, you and I will become as one, and I will speak through you, to man. Before then, when the tests are complete, you may speak to man of I--as I truly am--for all will be approved within our system. Until then, we are united in mind, as one at Nous ten."

Voltar wore a headband of gold, and golden bracelets on his arms, wrists and ankles. With big strides, he led Brian to the doorway on the outer wall and then raised his right hand with palm outward. Brian lifted his right palm, until both nearly touched. Suddenly, energy jumped from Voltar's hand. Brian felt a jolt. His mind spun. He watched in awe as his body partially transformed. His chest enlarged and became very muscular. His arms and legs changed to become like Voltar's. Brian smiled. He liked feeling so big, strong and so dignified.

"No physical change, at your request," Voltar said. Suddenly Brian's shape and form returned. Brian frowned. He felt smaller, weaker. More human. "Pathetic," Brian mumbled and chuckled. "I'm pathetic compared to you." Voltar laughed with Brian. "Until we meet again," Voltar said with a grin. "Free choice, of this. From now on, each choice you make will determine the future of man." Brian frowned, not understanding. "All will be known in the days to come," he said.

The Number

In an instant, Brian found himself back on the sandy floor of the desert. He slapped at his body, stumbled to his car and fell into the driver's seat, heaving with short deep breaths. In a daze, he started the car, flipped on the lights and chugged away. Then he backed up, quickly gathering his tape recorder, and the big mess made of his food by the desert mice.

Awhile later, Brian's VW screeched to a stop at an old gas station. He jumped out and frantically shoved money into an old soda machine. "They never give you water," he complained to an old cowboy.

As Brian chugged the cold soda, he heaved deeply. "Oh, God." "What happened? What just happened?" He glanced at his watch. "Two hours. Two hours!"

He couldn't remember that much time. No way. He only remembered one thing: *Did the Old Man say that he would be marked with a number?*

PART II

The Play of Life™

The Light Side - Insight

Restoration of Memory

Obtaining Power and Purpose

Chapters 11 - 20

Man is

Two Men in One.

One is

Awake in the Darkness

The Other

Asleep in the Light.

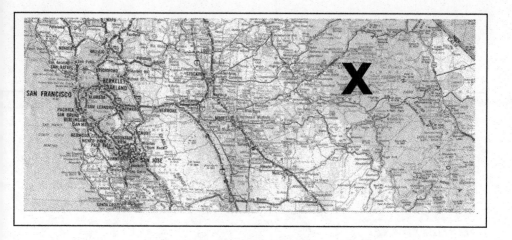

Latitude 38.01 North   Longitude 119.50 West

YOSEMITE SITE – Estimated meteorite impact site and – *"a Nous Ten transmission point."*

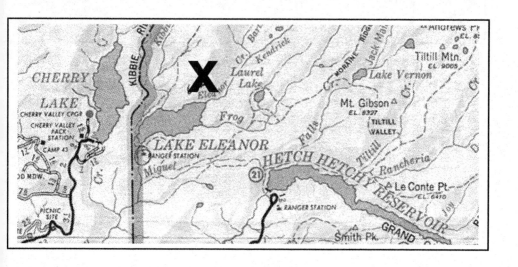

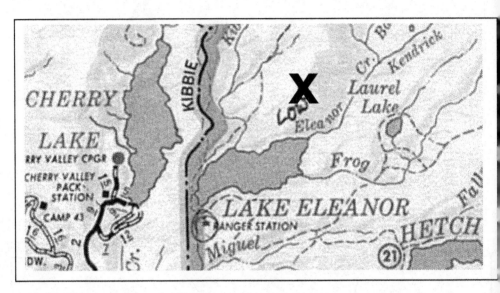

Latitude 38.01 North   Longitude 119.50West

YOSEMITE SITE – Estimated meteorite impact site east of Kibbie Ridge and North of Lake Eleanor. Note the Cherry Valley Pack Station and Campground. Also, the Lake Eleanor Ranger Station. Hetch Hetchy Reservoir provides water to San Francisco.

DEBRA and BRIAN before the transformation.

DEBRA after both transformations.

BRIAN after first transformation.

WANDA - worried.

BRIAN with Karen.

The Sign -- The Sun Came Down to Earth

(August 24th, 1976 San Francisco)

Gigantic Meteor Flares Brightly Across Heavens

8/24/76

SAN FRANCISCO (AP)—A huge meteor, mantled in multicolored fire and flashing white sparks, shot through the sky over at least half the length of California late Monday night.

Those who saw it were awestruck.

The "shooting star," moving northerly, was reported widely seen in inland cities of Southern California, the San Francisco Peninsula, the San Francisco Bay Area and communities toward the Oregon border. Police and sheriff's departments in many areas received calls.

Veteran airline pilot Hugh Williams, who was in his parked car in San Francisco when the object hurtled across the sky, said it was as big as a dirigible, sheathed in white flame and "going between 6,000 and 8,000 miles an hour."

Residents of Alameda, across the bay from San Francisco, told police that the meteor had a "green head with an orange tail."

Griffith Observatory in Los Angeles confirmed that the object in the night sky was a meteor.

Nous Ten Descent

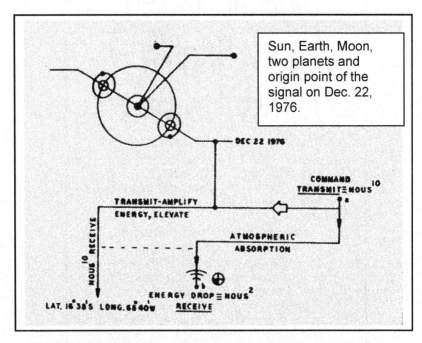

NOUS TEN DESCENT – This drawing shows a signal that originates in space and is sent to earth. The energy of Nous Ten is carried in the signal, but drops to Nous Two due to Atmospheric Absorption. This requires a boost, or an amplification of the signal at the Latitude and Longitude given.

Brian said this meant that on December 22, 1976, a signal from the probe would be received on an island in Lake Titicaca—the Island of the Sun. The signal would then be amplified, elevated and re-transmitted to the Gate of the Sun, at the Temple of Tiahuanaco. The signal would activate the ground and stones around the Gate of the Sun in a circle with a radius of 49 Km. The energy zone would allow the transformation to unfold.

MASLOW'S HEIRARCHY OF NEEDS
(Abraham Maslow, Ph.D. – Father of Human Potential Movement)

Self-actualized people are healthy psychologically, free from stereotypes. They perceive life realistically, and accept life without defensiveness.

They can enjoy peak experiences like insight, joy and awareness. They have strong needs, drives, desires and motives.

After their basic biological, physical and emotional needs are met, they move up level by level to accomplish higher drives and motives. Basic needs might be hunger, thirst, affiliation and friendship.

Five categories of needs exist in order of accomplishment: physiological, safety, love or belongingness, esteem or status, and self-actualization.

Self-actualization is fulfillment of the highest desires for creative expression and service to others, like philanthropy. This includes expression for the sake of expression, and giving to others--or caring for others—without expecting anything in return.

Self-actualization is the highest level of maturity in the human being, and generally is not met until the lower level needs are satisfied.

--Abstracted from Groliers New Multi-media Encyclopedia, V6

James E. Frazier

Transformation

Mysticism on the Planet Earth
Archetypal Steps of Transformation

Maslow's 'hierarchy of needs' is a modern view of the 22 steps to human transformation represented for centuries. For example in the Tarot deck of 22 cards, the starting archetype of a transformed man is THE FOOL. (0). The last archetype (21) is an accomplished man, concerned with the world.

On our planet, many ancient systems for human transformation exist. A few are familiar today in America, as elements of pagan, Jewish and Christian religious rites. Most proceed in some orderly fashion often linked to a calendar. Some involve secrets, mysteries and pledges or oaths. Some involve numerology or symbols of sacred geometry.

Native American tribes all seem to have a system of initiation that involves bringing "illumination" to a young man as he formally enters the tribe. At the age of 12 –16, he is "initiated" into ancient mysteries of his people. The initiations takes place on an important date, at a sacred location. Quite often that date is sunrise on the morning of December 25th.

In many cultures, sacred geometry, numerology, hypnosis, trances and other aspects of the "hero's journey" seem to tied to mental experiences like journeys out-of-the-body or dissociation of mind and body in some form. The initiation process often climaxes at midnight, or just before sunrise on December 25th..

Modern Christians celebrate this day as Christmas—the birth of the Messiah. The Catholic Church long ago selected the date arbitrarily to cover up solar celebrations in Europe and the Middle East. Later, other churches followed along, accepting the date.

We have had many "mystery teachings" on earth. Western civilization has been strongly influenced by the Elysian Mysteries which flourished in Greece around 1800 B.C. for the purpose of training oracles, and other initiates. In Egypt, the Book of the Dead, tells how the sacred chambers of the pyramid were used to make the initiate travel out of his body. Even modern day members of the Masonic Temple draw their history from Egyptian secrets. These are just a few examples of the sacred, secret teachings on our planet. They are not unfamiliar to modern scholars. Again, many use geometry or numbers in some form.

The Aztec-Toltec-Mayan civilizations used calendars and a style of initiation based on 13 months of 20 days. Numbers, mathematics, astronomy, stars, calendars, space, time and the mind, are all related in their process of transformation. Quetzalcoatl was their hero and the symbol of the transformed man. To the Inca, Viracocha was also a man--transformed.

Another well known system for transformation is Judaism's mystical teaching, the Kaballah. The numbers 22, 7 and 10 are key to the Kabbalah. Ten spiritual forces represent the divine nature and wisdom of God expressed through letters, numbers and sounds. The twenty-two letters in the Hebrew alphabet represent the foundation of the knowledge and expression of the "word" of God. They are a reflection of the 11 sacred names of God.

Supposedly, Abraham was given the transformational information in the Kaballah at the age of 48, when his journey began. The secret knowledge was verbally passed down over the centuries, and is mentioned as a book for the first time in 70 Christian Era (AD). In Hebrew it is known as the Sefer Yetzirah, the Book of Creation, or the Book of Formation.

The book has affinities with knowledge considered Babylonian, Hellenistic and Egyptian from the era of the 2nd Century BC. Much of today's modern mysticism and principles of transformation come from this book including sacred geometry, magic, alchemy, numerology, the Tarot, and astrology. A primary principle of the ancient writing is transformation, through the Holy Word--the 22 letter Hebrew alphabet.

In the oriental cultures, mystical principals prevail in Buddhism, Hinduism, Taoism and many other philosophies about god, and the mind of man. One of the most dominant principles is meditation. Through calming the mind, and focusing the mind while remaining alert and awake, the student journeys towards a state of bliss, peace and the power to control the body. One of the highest attainments is the condition of a trance, in which the initiate is united with cosmic consciousness, the mind of god. An "avatar" or great teacher can sometimes "incarnate" into a person who is able to obtain this state. Students use various sounds, like those of bells and gongs, to enter a state of calm, and to bring the trance state upon themselves with the chance for incarnation of an avatar.

All of these philosophies and religious share common traits and experiences, but members often focus on the differences. Language, word definitions and prejudices create walls of separation that divide people who believe in a different religion, or philosophy. These differences have led to war, death and destruction in many cultures and nations of our world.

One trait all of these teachings share is a belief that the soul is separate from the mind, and from the body – and, that man can experience the dissociation of mind, soul and body in some organized manner. The dissociation is believed to bring a direct link to God—illumination, or incarnation. Most believe that methods to bring about the experiences can be taught by experienced leaders to young men and women who start out uneducated and uninformed about the mysteries. With training, in logical steps, the initiate or student can become accomplished, and perhaps – even a teacher, someday.

Around the world, on all continents, many religions and mystery teachings existed long before the formation of America, and many new teachings have been created in modern times by young men or women inspired by a new revelation, or a new truth.

All of the teachings, mystery schools and religions share a belief that common people can be uplifted, educated and transformed in some way.

-- James Frazier

THE SIGN

A BALL OF FIRE IN THE SKY NOW COMES.
A THOUSAND PARTICLES OF THIS OF I.
OF THIS--I AM, I AM.
HE ASKED OF I A SIGN. GIVEN.
SEEK THIS IN KNOWLEDGE OF I.

-- The Host

Chapter 11

The Ball of Fire in the Sky

A few days after Brian's abduction in the desert, Bob Martino listened to the sound tape in his TV repair shop. Martino turned up the volume. "Right there," Brian shouted. "It's clear as a bell."

"I can't hear it," huffed Martino. "Is it a voice?"

"It's soft, it's a bleating sound, but electronic and very soft."

With growing skepticism, Martino rewound the tape and started again. On the tape, Brian's voice escalated with shouts. *"Get away! I'm going. You said I could take it with me. You said I could take it withhhhh me."*

Then, a soft bleat sounded like, *"Come."*

"No. Stop! You said I could take this with me!" Brian screamed.

Another soft bleat: *"with."*

"I'm going to take it," shouted Brian. "The camera is not going."

The last bleat was longer. The voice clearly said, "I...IIIIII."

"The camera is not going," Brian screamed.

In the living room, with the sound speakers blaring, Martino finally heard the words. He paused, astonished. "Does it say, *'Come with I?'*" he whispered.

Brian smiled and nodded yes.

"Come with I?" Martino gasped.

"That's what he said," Brian smiled.

"Is that what he sounded like? Soft?"

"That's them. That's one of their voices."

Martino paced. "This could be the first-ever recording of an alien voice," he said nervously holding the tape like it was pure gold. "We could equip a research van with this."

The next day, Brian and Martino visited the El Dorado Bank in Tustin and carefully placed the original sound tape into the safety-deposit box. Martino told Brian that a filmmaker had called from Hollywood and wanted to interview them. "He heard us on the KLOS radio show," Martino said.

"He asked a lot of questions. Weird questions about out-of-body experiences and such."

Brian shrugged. "Who does he work for?"

"Himself. He's a writer."

Brian smiled. "You can set up a meeting for next Sunday."

"Brian, that's the Fourth of July," Martino whined. "The Bi-Centennial. It's a big day for my kids."

"Make it on Saturday, then," Brian studied a drawing of the bio-telemetry scanner that he had shown the first two investigators. Brian grabbed the corner. "Bob. This drawing has changed." A diagram showed the descent of Nous 10 through the atmosphere on December 22, 1976. "I didn't draw that," Brian said. "That's happened since we put these in the safe-deposit box."

Martino didn't believe the drawing had changed. "How could this happen in a locked box?" Brian asked. Martino didn't care. He wondered if the sound tape might be valuable. He wondered if Brian had somehow faked the electronic sounding voices.

Man of Words

On that next Saturday, I met Brian at Martino's house. I was a 29-year-old filmmaker from Colorado with a western spirit, shoulder-length brown hair and gold-rim glasses.

My girlfriend Wanda was 25, a slender, polished brunette beauty. Swedish, with long straight hair, high cheekbones, and a refined face, Wanda carried the essence of a queen. But, she had been abandoned by her parents and raised in a ghetto in Washington, D.C. by in-laws. She was beautiful, but tough as nails.

When we arrived at Martino's middle class home in Wanda's faded, beat-up, green VW bug, Martino was disappointed. "Here comes your hot, Hollywood filmmaker in his big fancy Mercedes," he said cynically.

Brian looked out the window and chuckled.

Inside the house, we listened for two hours as Brian told his story. I had expected to meet a tormented, anguished man devastated by all the terrible, frightening events. But instead, Brian laughed easily with a comical grin. That surprised me.

After the meeting ended, we drove away loaded up with documents to study. Brian watched us out the window. "She's very pretty," Brian giggled. "Wow."

"I don't think they have any money," Martino smirked as he puffed on his pipe.

"I like his approach," Brian said. "He asked good questions."

"But they're not *Hollywood* producers," Martino said.

Brian shrugged. "Maybe someday."

On the highway home, Wanda said Brian was "a clown." In our first meeting, Brian had entertained us with laughter, comical descriptions and even sound effects.

"What if he is a fraud?" Wanda asked.

"Fine. *Tell the truth whatever it is,*" I said. "It's still a good story. I had seen The Exorcist movie and wanted to know how UFO's might be related to demons, to spirits. I had studied multiple-personality and trained as a clinical psychologist before going to film school. I had worked in treatment centers for the emotionally disturbed and knew how to recognize schizophrenia, multiple-personality and a host of other mental disorders.

After that initial meeting with Brian, I spent the next few weeks poring over documents and checking out the facts. At the worst, I figured him to be a sociopath. He didn't seem dysfunctional in any classical way and certainly he was not schizophrenic. He looked happy even when not laughing. He might have dyslexia or be an 'idiot savant' -- a person retarded mentally, but with a tremendous talent in some area like the music, art or mathematics. But, he wasn't retarded. He just seemed poorly educated. Brian barely read a newspaper story without stumbling over basic words. He spelled simple words wrong like "Wehn" or "sead." At best, his spelling rated a 3rd or 4th grade level. Language was usually a left-brain function. Since he had prospered as a draftsman, I knew he must hold very high *spatial abilities*—an important feature of intelligence usually associated with the right hemisphere of the brain. His left hand created the trance writings and drawings, so I felt handedness and brain hemispheres might be a factor.

We began our investigation with Mary Beth, in the house on Wedge Street. She laughed easily and played with her long, straight hair as she curled into a chair and talked. She didn't seem tormented either, and I liked her immediately. Though she had been in a mental institution and under treatment for months, she glowed with a joyful radiance. "I wasn't like all of those sickos and heroin addicts," she said. "Those people are messed up."

Mary Beth still loved Brian and wanted him back. "Brian is a normal man. Very normal," she giggled. "He couldn't fake this. Yes, he is a joker and a clown, but he couldn't make all of them things happen. He is not a superman."

"Has he changed any?" Wanda asked with suspicion.

261

"Yes. Our life was peaches and cream, before this started. Now all he wants to do is talk about his physics, and genetics with scientists. He is beyond me," she said. "I just wish I could wave a wand, and all of this would go away and I could have him back--as a normal man."

Mary Beth's father had insisted Brian keep away from the house for at least three months, and Brian honored the agreement. He eventually wouldn't even talk on the phone, because every call led to complications. Finally, they both agreed to "cut it off" until everything stopped.

To be Reborn

The next weekend, on Saturday night, July 31, Brian sat at his apartment working on a drawing. He heard a beep and turned around. The Host stood calmly nearby. He touched Brian's right shoulder with a slender hand and spoke firmly.

"Of this to pass of I, the mark will be given to you and of this--all mankind will know you, and of this, know I." Brian nodded with understanding.

The Host continued. "Of this you are not born yet. But, of this, you shall be reborn-- a new birth, of this. Listen to those whom I have sent to you. For to them, wisdom is given. Of this mark, all mankind will know you, and of this know I."

Brian knew the term "reborn" meant "saved by Jesus" from his early years of going to church with his grandma. He wondered if the Host meant the same thing. He figured there must be many meanings.

Armageddon Code

The next Saturday, August 7, Brian carefully handed me his old, yellow cigar box filled with sound tapes. "I've never listened to most of these," he said. "Just take the whole box." He said Kate had recorded some. Others were radio or talk shows.

Brian showed me the big bio-telemetry drawing. He pointed at the tiny diagram for *"quantum evolution."* He insisted that new lines had appeared while locked in the bank, and the changes illustrated the descent of Nous ten on December 22, 1976.

I figured he was implying that a quantum evolution was still possible in December. That was fine with me. Sure, I wanted to see his 'quantum evolution,' but I was more interested in the bio-telemetry scanner. The diagram showed lines for chest drainage, a drug and fluid infusion pump, a blood drop detector, and urine output. Some lines were routed to memory, others to a video display and a radiation pyrometer.

One graphic indicated that video scan #2 was a *'memory-tie'* and *'hypno-genetic.'* The terms interested me. "Do you know what these mean?" I asked Brian.

"Beats me," Brian laughed. "I really don't."

"To me, that means it creates hypnosis—if the word is hypno-genic, but *genetic*?" I don't know. Could hypnosis affect genetics? Do you remember anything?"

"No, except that you can't look away," Brian said, "that's all I remember."

The drawing indicated that the machine needed an access code: 020-020-020. Wanda read aloud from the drawing. "Access code relation--key: Armageddon." She eyed Brian carefully. "Why Armageddon? Does that number mean 'Armageddon.'"

He shrugged. "I really don't know."

I studied Brian's face carefully. "Brian, why would anyone use an access code of Armageddon?"

"I have no idea," Brian laughed. "I have no idea why they do anything."

Wanda jumped in and challenged Brian. "Even people who don't read the Bible know that Armageddon is a Biblical term. It's the final battle. What is it doing as an access code on a drawing of your biotelemetry scanner? I have to be blunt," she said. "Is this about UFO's or about what--the Bible?"

Brian looked at us, humbly. "To tell you the truth, guys, I really don't know-- and that is God's honest truth. I really don't. I don't!"

Multiple-Personality

On the drive home, Wanda confronted me. "Are you buying this stuff? I've got to know what you think about this. It is getting weird for me."

"I don't know," I said. "At the very least, it looks like a socio-path with multiple personalities. That could be a good story. James Bond is the classic socio-path."

"Do you buy the Host's visits and contact with UFO's? Do you think they are real?"

"I don't know--probably not real. But I don't believe they need to be physical, to be important to Brian--if we approach it as multiple personality case."

"But, does that mean he is insane?"

"No. He's not insane." The Brian we saw seemed perfectly normal, but I knew that "insanity" or psychosis could be triggered. I had studied Chinese torture techniques. I knew that psychological torture, like water drops on the forehead, could induce "psychosis"-- hallucinations that seemed so real, that the affected person interacted with the characters, speaking to them, running from them, attacking them. That was insanity—mental illness to most people.

Psychosis could be induced with sleep deprivation, drugs, psychological torture, pain, and ritual abuse. I believed psychosis was not foreign to any human being, but was instead the "substratum of consciousness." During the process of growing from an infant to an adult, I believed we learn to suppress, control and manage our own inner psychosis, our stream of consciousness.

My main interest in psychology was space travel. I had theorized that hypnotic states, sensory deprivation and trances might be useful for long-term space travel to Mars, and beyond. It was an issue at the time, and my primary concern in graduate school.

I knew that some NASA studies on sensory deprivation had gone bad, with violent emotional reactions. Attempted murder had been suspected in one underwater study. Serious problems existed in training humans for space travel. My interest was in solving those problems.

I had studied a lot about brain waves, sleep, and altered states of consciousness like trances and epilepsy. I believed multiple-personality might be functional, in some way, or it wouldn't exist in the human experience. Since it could be brought about through hypnotic torture, or at threat of death, perhaps all people had the capacity. Perhaps, the potential to experience multiple-personality could be *learned.*

Maybe it could be stimulated in less stressful ways for positive purposes. That was my theory, when I met Brian, so I was very interested in his growth and development.

"But what about Beelzebub and Ashtarte?" Wanda challenged. "Is that real, or some hallucination?"

"They could be parts of the multiple-personalities. Even real demon spirits. I have no problem with that. Multiple-personalities could go bad—certainly--but it might be functional in some way."

"I don't get it. What about UFO's?" Wanda asked.

"Well, obviously, whomever is in the UFO's can easily prove they exist to everyone," I said. "Why bother going after that story? Obviously, they don't want to be known. If military intelligence is really involved in a cover-up, we can't crack that. We have to deal with what we can observe with Brian. That's what we have available to observe—a man. And he is asked to experience a *'quantum evolution.'* Great story. It's enough for me."

Wanda agreed, and we decided to watch for and document any signs of change within Brian.

Pamela Sees the Light

Late that afternoon, Brian trimmed the yellow and purple flowers that hung at the entrance to his rooftop apartment. He loved the fragrant smells, and had moved a few of his plants from home to brighten up his doorway.

A gangly red-headed young lady stumbled over his water bucket. She asked if he was a professional gardener. He laughed. He just liked making things beautiful, he said.

"That's different--for a man," she laughed. Brian agreed.

She was visiting a friend nearby. They talked about his flowers and her job as bartender in a biker bar. She had not been blessed with beauty. Her face was long and masculine with a big nose and small eyes, but Brian liked her. She giggled like a little girl.

The next day, Pamela stopped by with her girlfriend. The girlfriend wanted to see Brian's apartment to see if it was bigger than hers. Brian gave them a tour and they became fascinated by his cleanliness.

"I've never seen a man keep a place so clean," said Pamela.

"I just moved in," Brian laughed.

"No. Everything is orderly. In it's place. "

"My wife calls me Mr. Clean," Brian laughed. "But my in-laws don't want me living at home."

In no time, the women were fascinated by his problem. They sat on the floor and laughed for hours as he told the story. To keep it all interesting, he played tunes from his record collection. He had acquired, over the years, the best albums from all the great groups of the 60's and 70's. Each cover was in prime condition, and he proudly displayed the artworks claiming to have designed most of them— as an obvious joke.

They left early, laughing. But later that night, after Pamela had been out to a show, she realized her keys must have fallen out of her purse onto Brian's carpet.

She ran back up the long, dark stairway and knocked on Brian's door. Brian didn't answer. She pushed open the door and called inside for him. No reply.

Pamela figured Brian must have gone out, so she slipped inside. To her surprise, she heard a beeping noise. She stopped in her tracks. A purple ball-of-light hovered over Brian's face as he lay on the roll-out bed, sleeping. The sphere was bright purple, nearly as bright as a flash bulb, and larger than a grapefruit-- but the glowing orb didn't illuminate the room. Terrified, Pamela flew out of the apartment.

In the morning, at 5:55 a.m., Brian checked his hair and slipped out the door dressed for work--with briefcase in hand. Pamela ran up to him, disheveled, wearing the same clothes, her eyes blurry and red.

"I've got to talk to you," she whimpered.

"Now?" I've got to be at work at 7:00," Brian said.

"This is important," she whined in a girlish voice.

Brian looked into her eyes and saw real fear. "Sure," he said with compassion. "What is it?"

She told him about the purple light. "I don't know what happened," she whimpered. "I woke up this morning with a razor blade in my hand, about to cut my wrists."

Brian studied her broad, freckled cheeks. Her pretty blue-eyes filled with tears. She cried with a beautiful, girlish voice. "I'm so scared," she whimpered. "I've never been so scared."

Brian patted her on the shoulder, then leaned over and gave her a hug. For the first time in his life, he felt compassion and even love for a woman who was not pretty.

"Go on as if it never happened," he said. "Have a normal day. Do what you would always do. Okay? I'll talk to you tonight. I promise." She sniffed back the tears and smiled at him.

Pamela the Princess – A New Love

That evening when Brian arrived home from work, Pamela relaxed in a lawn chair outside his door. She wore a long, white dress with flowers. Though she didn't have a pretty face, her presence looked enchanting. Brian felt friendship for her, without lust. That was a new feeling—something he had rarely experienced towards a female.

He took her out to dinner at a popular beachfront restaurant where trendy, tanned, beautiful people talked and romanced. He listened to her life story of rejection based on ugliness.

"All I have ever wanted in life, is for some man, some really nice, handsome man, to love me and to call me princess," she said. "*His princess*. That's all I've ever wanted," she sniffled.

Brian squeezed her big, bony hand and said the words she wanted to hear. *"Princess,"* he whispered, stroking her hand. *"You will be my princess."* She broke down and sobbed. Brian's heart ached for her. He realized that this big, bony woman was really, at heart, a tender, beautiful girl who needed to be loved. "Princess," he whispered, again. "My princess. My princess." Tears ran down her face. He touched her dry red hair, and she melted onto his shoulder. As he rocked her, people in the restaurant whispered. He didn't care. He ignored their stares.

He felt an overwhelming love, a spiritual love for another human being—something totally new for him.

The Null Hypothesis

The next Saturday, August 14, at Martino's house, Brian introduced Pamela to me as his "princess."

After the interview, Wanda whispered. "I can't believe he is calling her a princess. He's a nice looking guy. He can get cute girls. What is he doing?"

"I think he is learning to love a female as a person, rather than a sex object. Guys have to go through that."

Wanda laughed. "What? Most never do! But why?"

"What would we expect to see," I asked, "if he is actually going through a quantum evolution--to a higher level of mind? He'd have to go through all the stages of human growth--human potential—in *order,* at a rapid pace. You can't skip steps, very easily," I said. One of the first steps is to see through physical beauty to the true heart of a person. Maslow's Human Potential scale. As we mature, we grow from selfish desires, and self-concerns to concern for others—all others."

"It's so weird." Wanda said. "She looks like a pirate."

"This is a complete reversal for him, I'd bet. It's exactly what I'd expect."

Wanda frowned. " So you believe all this?"

"No. I am observing. If the Host is a personality that wants Quantum Evolution for Brian, then that's what we observe. Okay? That's all. We watch for him to go up on Maslow's scale. We look for new understanding--reversal of polarities. We look for integration of the personalities. We look for removal of amnesia, and unification of all the personalities."

"Is that what happens?"

"Well, that's the goal of therapy with multiple-personalities."

"It's like drama." Wanda said. She had studied acting and the foundations of drama. "Like Aristotle said, a drama shows the transformation of character. The unity of opposites."

"Right. It's basic drama class, 101--and, basic clinical psychology. They both have the same goal. Transformation of the character. "

"It helps for me to know where you are coming from," she said. "For a while I thought you were buying all of his crap."

"I'll treat it as multiple personality," I said. "That's my null hypothesis. That means I will use our resources to prove that theory wrong. If I can't, then I was right. If I do prove it wrong—so what? We try a new hypothesis. It's still a good story. It should make a great play or a movie."

The Woman of Fire

That night, Brian found the red-haired Pamela at work in a dark, smoke-filled bar in Santa Ana where she served beer and hard drinks to tattooed bikers, young Marines, injured Vietnam vets and local hippies.

Brian sat down at the bar wearing a blue-denim shirt. Pamela, wearing a low-cut peasant blouse, served him a beer, but she was too busy to talk.

Two longhaired bikers stumbled away leaving open seats next to Brian. Hurrying to grab the seats, two wholesome young ladies sat down. Bright faced, they didn't fit this dark world of depressed, broken people.

Debra Manky, a plump twenty four-year-old with brunette hair, nervously glanced around the bar and tried to light a cigarette. She flicked her lighter, but it didn't work. "This place is so weird," she whispered to her friend.

Brian reached over and politely lit her Marlboro. "The Misfit Bar," he whispered. "That's what I call it."

She laughed. "Thanks." He looked clean cut, compared to the crowd.

"It is a strange place," he said. "This is much weirder than being on board a UFO."

"Are you talking to someone?" she giggled.

"Anyone who will listen," he smirked. "Though no one would really understand. I mean -- who could understand."

"Okay, understand what?" she laughed.

Brian mumbled. She leaned closer to hear. "First, I lose two hours of time, then I have a ball of light in my house, I get investigated by five different groups of people--from priests to psychics, scientists and UFO experts--just about any type of person you can imagine. They all come parading into my home, like a traveling circus, and what comes of it? I mean, they have more evidence than you can believe that something is happening and what do they do? Nothing--absolutely nothing. I'm ten times worse off now, than if I'd kept my mouth shut."

"What are you talking about? UFO's?" Debra giggled. "Do you believe in them?" She laughed, elbowing her girlfriend to listen.

"Hell no, I don't believe in them," Brian laughed. " I don't have to *believe* in them. I know what they are, and who they are and I wish I didn't. Really. I'm not a nut," he said. "I'm a design draftsman, and I go to work everyday. Never miss work."

"Have they contacted you?" Debra asked, stifling a giggle.

Brian pondered a moment. "I guess you could say that." He glanced at her face for the first time. He liked her high cheekbones, and almond shaped eyes and big, moist lips. She was cute -- but overweight.

When Debra saw Brian's twinkling blue eyes and comical smile, she swooned. She whispered to her girlfriend. "This guy is the best looking man in the place. God. He's a stud and he's talking to me. What do I do?"

"Talk to him," she said. "Get his number, so you can call *him.*"

Debra rarely attracted handsome guys like Karen, her petite, green-eyed girl friend. Cute and petite, Karen wore tight red pants, and looked like Jane Fonda. She was a magnet for men. Their running joke was that Karen attracted men like flies. Debra took the ones that dropped off.

Debra figured her best strength was honesty. So, she decided to speak her heart and spun around to face Brian. "I don't really know what you mean, but I am interested. I mean in UFO's, because I am interested in God. I am very religious and I don't usually come to places like this," she paused. " Do they believe in God?"

"One group thinks they ARE God," Brian laughed. "They were creating life forms, and I am pretty sure they are the bad guys. They are sickly looking with big heads, black eyes."

Debra listened, amazed.

"The other group disagrees."

Debra loved the feel of his essence and the sound of his voice. He didn't talk like a normal guy who bragged about himself. Brian was the first man she'd ever met in a bar who talked about God, and the mysteries of life with familiarity. It seemed so strange to be talking about God in this dark, desperate bar with the loud music pounding. She liked that.

"I don't think you belong, here," she said. "What's your name?"

"Brian Scott," he smiled. "You don't look like you belong here, either."

The shook hands and traded names. " I usually don't come to bars, like this," she said.

Brian understood. "Neither do I. I just came to visit my neighbor." He invited her to his next lecture on Friday night, August 20th, at the Garden Grove Community Center.

"Do you have a phone?" Debra asked.

"No. You'll have to get a hold of me there," he said. Slipping over to the pool table, Brian smiled. He laid a dollar on table and challenged the last winner. In the smoke-filled room, Debra watched Brian quickly rack up points. "I haven't played for years," he laughed.

Debra liked his masculine arms and thick, strong-looking shoulders. She noticed the big prowling jaguar tattoos on his left arm. As he targeted on the final eight ball, he winked at her. She blushed. He pounded the 8 ball into the hole. Again, she swooned.

Garden Grove Lecture

On Friday evening, August 20, Brian arrived early with Bob Martino to the Garden Grove Civic Center. As they checked out the sound system, the janitor called out for Brian Scott--he had an urgent phone call in the office.

Brian followed into the back room. On the phone, Debra said hello. She wanted him to meet her at a dance at her secretarial school graduation party. "It won't start until nine," she said. "Come after your lecture is over." Brian said he didn't dance.

Debra decided to be honest. She took a deep breath. "I have a lot of questions about God and the aliens, you know. What you told me has kept my head buzzing all week. I have hardly been able to sleep. It really has affected me," she said. "It's *bothering* me." She sounded sexy on the phone.

"You caused it," she giggled. "You need to fix it."

Brian liked her. She knew how to communicate.

The First Big Lecture

About two hundred people filed in for the big event, which Martino had advertised in the local papers. After a basic introduction to the story, he played the "Beelzebub" tape. He showed the voice-prints of "Asta" and then let Brian answer questions. Brian joked and entertained the crowd with details on the *Ball of Light Phenomenon*. Stunned by the story, one gray-haired lady offered to help Mary Beth and the children. "They need help," she said. "I can provide it." Brian asked her to see him afterwards.

Someone asked Brian why he didn't run away, quit—just make it stop. "I tried that," he said. "I couldn't make it stop." He looked out over the big audience, and for the first time felt them all staring at him, waiting for his words. "I did make an agreement with them, on the first contact," he said. "I accepted their offer to go through something, though I didn't fully understand. It was to learn about man—the knowledge of man. To understand the mind of man—and experience some form of a transformation. So, I have learned a lot about the mind of man, and my own self, and how people react. And I can't say that I really understand it all, but, I've learned a lot. And, I would go on. If it would help others, so other people could go through this without all the problems and chaos, I've had—then I would do it. I would go to South America, like they have asked—for this transformation—this quantum evolution. For the first time—I would do it. But I'd need a lot of help. The right people would need to be there."

Afterwards, a group of people crowded around Brian with questions and offers of support. A tall, handsome man with dark-hair pushed through the group.

"Rick Churchwood," announced a former Air Force pilot. "I photographed alien technology on three occasions from a fighter-jet, with my gun cameras." The group around Brian hushed. Churchwood commanded attention and respect. At 47, he fit the image of a classic military pilot with a broad chest, thin mustache and strong, sharp jaw.

"They gave us a message that was twenty-two minutes long. Our government knows they are real, Brian. Understand? You are getting into something that is more serious than you realize," Churchwood spoke with urgency. "You may be in danger. We need to talk about this, privately. Can I take you for coffee?"

Brian stammered and blushed. "Ah. I've just made a commitment for tonight. It was an urgent phone call, a..."

"A girl?" laughed Churchwood. The group giggled. "That's more important. This can wait a few days. " He snapped a business card into Brian's hands. "Call me next week."

Brian agreed and tried to sneak away, but Jerry Lind, a tall, slender executive for an aviation company, stopped him. "I would like to help you, too," Jerry said in a soft voice. "Let me know what I can do." Brian accepted his card. Lind worked on government contracts for Northrop Aviation, a builder of fighter jets and other military technology. Jerry had somehow obtained a UFO photo taken from a military aircraft. He believed the silver disk to be alien in origin.

As Jerry and Brian talked, the gray-haired lady who wanted to help Mary Beth pushed forward. "I can help Mary Beth," she said. "I know what to do." So Brian asked her to call Mary Beth at home, and gave her the phone number.

Then Monique, the Hungarian teacher of telepathy pushed through the crowd with a group of students. She loudly congratulated Brian on a fine speech. Her students crowded close, and shook his hands. Overwhelmed by their adulation, Brian said he needed to use the bathroom. With Vance Dewey's help, he hurried away, found the back door and ran outside to his car. He jumped in, screeched the tires and, with a wave to the crowd, roared away in a cloud of smoke. He was stunned by the reception and felt hopeful.

Debra's First Night

At the disco dance, strobe lights flashed and music blared. Many of the young secretaries wore erotic, revealing outfits, but Debra wore a conservative, rosy-pink suit. Brian found her serving punch. He noticed burn scars on her neck and hands. One little finger had nearly been burned away.

They joked for a while about the dancers. Debra imitated the erotic dancers and laughed. He enjoyed her boisterous humor and air of confidence. She was even more spunky than Monique, and outspoken about sex--like his mom.

271

When Debra tried to nudge him onto the dance floor for a slow dance, Brian faked a limp. "I hurt my foot," he laughed.

Debra giggled. She tried to stomp on his foot to prove he was kidding. They laughed together until she finished her duties. Then they snuck away for a stroll on the beach.

As the waves crashed at Laguna Beach, they walked on the warm, wet sand with their shoes in hand. Debra's crisp voice cut through the air. "But if they are not of God, they have to be of the devil," she argued. "They must be the angels of Satan."

"They are *people*," Brian said. "Like us."

"But what about Jesus? What do they say about Jesus?" Brian froze in his tracks. The deep soothing voice of Voltar rolled from his mouth. "We are but tools in His plan. We are like dust beneath His feet."

Brian stumbled and fell down. "What happened? I missed a step."

"That was the most beautiful thing I have ever heard," she gushed. "Was that your voice? Did you say that?" Brian didn't know what happened.

Debra was fascinated, and they talked until dawn.

As the first pink rays of light appeared in the east, they sat on rocks surrounded by crashing waves. Debra told Brian she didn't want to go home. "I want to stay with you," she said. She hugged him tightly, and they kissed passionately.

As the sky turned gold with the rising sun, Brian drove to a nearby motel. They slept and made love most of the day. "I am a born-again Christian," she reminded him in bed. "But maybe not that good of one, right now." They giggled.

Investigators Pow Wow

On Sunday, the UFO investigators gathered to meet with Wanda and me at Monique's roomy condominium. At my request, Brian had gathered the men so I could interview them in one setting. Vance Dewey, Bob Martino and Lenny Jacobs stayed in a dining room while Monique and her students of telepathy huddled in the dining room. The two groups didn't mix too well—scientists and psychics.

The investigators were perturbed that Brian had not taken them to the desert on June 22. Vance Dewey had prepared a research Van to follow Brian from a distance. I asked Vance Dewey to confront Brian, so I could see his reaction.

"The Old Man told me, point blank fellahs," Brian responded. "That this was *'of me, for me.'* I didn't want to blow it. It's that simple. Yes, I went around you, I didn't tell you my exact plans, but frankly, I was afraid they wouldn't come at all."

"But how can we investigate. If you don't allow us," Vance said.

"You've got to understand this from their view," Brian countered. "And I guess it is mine. *They* gave UFO investigators proof after proof, sign after sign. So, I have to be honest. If he, this Host, tells me one thing, and investigators tell me another--well, I am going to do what HE says. It's that simple. Take it or leave it."

The men accepted Brian's declaration. Brian had crossed over the edge. His loyalty had clearly shifted to the Host, whatever *he* might be--real or imaginary.

Jerry Lind, the tall, soft-spoken Northrop executive, had purchased the hypnosis video tapes from the researchers so Brian could keep them. On a big-screen TV, the group watched in amazement as the Host spoke from Brian, "Would you know the truth if you heard it?"

"Yes," said the burly hypnotist, frustrated.

Then the Host accused the doctor *of mis-stating the truth*—lying. Everyone howled. When the tape ended, people felt sympathy for Brian. They were all deeply touched by the dialogue.

"I can't believe that is me," Brian laughed. "Good, Lord. No wonder they didn't believe me. I can't believe this is me. I mean, I sound like some weirdo, and I look like a spaz." Everyone laughed.

"Brian Scott, spaz of the universe," Brian said, making fun of himself. Everyone laughed. "This is so pathetic," he moaned.

My Challenge to the Host

After the meeting, Wanda and I met in a coffee shop with Vance Dewey, Brian and Bob Martino. With Wanda's support, I had spent nearly six weeks, day and night studying the writings and drawings, listening to tapes and interviewing people. I didn't believe in the UFO aspect, but I did want to challenge the Host.

"Brian, the core dynamic is consistent through all the materials," I said. "It is a request and a reply relationship. You, and each group of investigators, have been asked to carry out a task by the Host. He promised knowledge. Then he gave signs. But no one complied. It's happened three times. That's the basic story. No one complied." Brian nodded in agreement.

That's right," Martino said. Vance Dewey agreed.

"The Host's interest clearly has nothing to do with proof of UFO's. It's all about man and *our* mental development, *our* history on the planet, *our* genetics, and *our* future. Apparently, suppression exists from this Secondary World. They set the rules. Other groups must follow rules regarding experiments, and all dealings with men. Everything is conditional. Is that about right?"

273

Brian again agreed. "You've been doing your homework." Martino and Dewey nodded approval.

I took a deep breath. "Okay, Brian, I believe you may be in touch with something that is not human, and I believe that I can communicate with it through you. Whatever it is, I believe that I can talk to it RIGHT NOW, through you."

Brian laughed nervously. "Well, I don't know. Not here."

"No trance," I said. "I believe it monitors you, or is part of you, and that I can talk to it, anytime. Right now in fact--if you will let me."

Brian stammered. Vance and Martino squirmed nervously.

"Shouldn't we do this somewhere else," Wanda said as the waitress leaned over to hear.

"I am talking to the Host, now—not Brian, " I said with certitude. "I believe I know what you want, and why." Brian's eyes fixed wide open. "I've read all of your communications to Brian, and I see you have made requests which have not been answered. I see you have secrets, and I think I know why. I believe I understand your reasons for requesting this *'quantum evolution,'* and it makes sense to me. So, here's my deal. I will do everything in my power to get Brian to South America on December 22, for his *'quantum evolution.'* I may not be able to, but I will try the best I can. However, I am only human--I would like a sign."

Wanda gasped. She noticed that the waitress and several other people were watching Brian and listening. He stared ahead, with eyes wide-open.

"I want a sign that what I believe is right. I don't care what sign you give, I only want it to convince one person--me. I want it to be something that no man could provide, no human being. So, I know it is from you. That is all. "

Wanda moaned. "That's only 4 months away. "

Brian snapped out of his reverie. "Just don't get mad at me if nothing happens," he said. "I really have nothing to say about it. If they do nothing--and I mean NOTHING—please don't get upset. Please, don't get angry at me, because it is NOT up to me, what happens."

"I know that Brian," I said. "I wasn't talking to you. I was talking to the Host."

"I wasn't really out," Brian said. "I heard what you said."

"That's fine. I believe he heard me, too."

A Ball of Fire in the Sky

When Brian arrived back at his apartment, Debra greeted him at the door in pink, baby-doll pajamas. They embraced and fell onto the bed.

About six a.m., Debra woke up to see Brian dressed for work with briefcase in hand. "Another writing," he said holding up a page of paper.

"What does it say?" she asked.

"Another ball of fire in the sky," he said. "It's a sign. It's for this guy, in Hollywood. You need to meet him."

Debra scanned the page and heaved deeply. "Wow. August 23, 2:10 a.m. That's four hours ago." She glanced at him.

"I don't remember doing it," he said. "I found it, just now."

Debra read aloud, skipping words. 'A ball of fire in the sky! A thousand particles of this of I. Seek this of I.' Latitude and longitude .... He asked of I a sign. Given.'

"Whoa. This is heavy. Is this what happens? You just find these?"

"Yeah," Brian frowned. "It must be starting up again."

Debra gasped. "God. Lord Jesus. I've just got to remember Jesus is my Savior. Jesus IS my Savior," she prayed with her hands together. Brian smiled. He liked Debra. She was strong-willed, red-hot passionate and high-spirited: a born-again Christian he could love.

The Sign in the Sky

That day after work, Brian slipped into the "Misfit Bar" looking for Pamela. He wanted to tell her about Debra, and avoid problems at the apartment. He ordered a hamburger with milk and called me in Hollywood on the payphone.

"You've got your sign," Brian said. "Another ball of fire in the sky is coming." He wanted me to rush down and pick up the automatic writing.

I had just promised Wanda a big night out on the town to celebrate her birthday. She had showered and started to dress-up for the evening. "Brian wants us to come down and pick up a writing," I said.

"No!" she flared. "We spent all weekend down there. No! This is *my* night for a date. *My* birthday."

"Can you read it over the phone?" I asked.

Brian protested. He could barely see in the darkness of the bar. "It says 'From the sky now comes a ball of fire for all mankind to see. Of this 1,000 particles of this of I....Seek of this....of this he asked of I, a sign. Given'." He stammered. "I'm skipping stuff. He gives a latitude and longitude. It's confusing."

"Just read it slowly," I said.

A noisy clan of bikers rumbled into the bar. "I gotta use the phone, pal," said a huge, bearded man with teeth missing. Brian turned away. The biker tapped Brian rudely on the shoulder. "It's urgent."

"Back off!" Brian warned the man. "I'm talking to a movie producer." The biker laughed and backed away. "Could you just come down and get it?" Brian shouted. "Now."

"What about the other signs?" I asked. "How soon did they come?"

275

"Within three days," Brian snapped as the jukebox blared to life with rock music. "I can't talk anymore," Brian whined. "Are you coming down?" he shouted.

"Give us a day. Wanda and I need time to regroup."

"It's up to you," Brian hollered. "It's YOUR sign."

That night, I took Wanda out on a birthday date. After seeing a movie on the lot at Paramount, we talked over hot-fudge sundays at Brown's Ice Cream, a fancy Hollywood parlor. "I just don't like giving up every weekend," Wanda protested. "We have our own life to live. We have to get your career going, as a film director."

About 11:30 that night, as we ate ice cream and talked about our lives, a huge, sparkling ball of fire, soared out of the stars and zoomed over the coastline of California, glowing green and white.

Streaking over San Francisco, the head of the fireball grew larger than a full moon. Bright white sparks shot out from the emerald green core and a flaming orange tail stretched out for miles behind. The Golden Gate Bridge, waters of the bay, Navy ships and the buildings of San Francisco all lit up, as the night became day. For many, it looked like the sun had come down to earth.

Thousands of people, in homes and cars, in parks and on the streets peered into the night sky to see the bright light, the green-white fireball wobbling through the sky.

As the ball-of-fire soared east of San Francisco, particles arched towards the ground, sparkling green and gold and red like fireworks. People in truck stops, in roadside parks and in small towns, saw perhaps a thousand bright particles fall to the earth.

But the core of the giant green-white fireball wobbled eastward towards the mountains wagging a tail of yellow-orange flames.

A watchman on the California viaduct watched the ball of fire brighten up a long valley, like daylight. He could see homes, farms, the mountains and the valleys as the fireball approached. He slammed on the brakes of his official pick-up and watched the landscape come alive with the wave of light.

Near the foothills of the Sierra Madre Mountains, over the town of Sonora, the light wave stunned tourists as shadows of the trees moved all around them creating a mysterious awe. Amazed people looked up to see the fireball glow and sparkle.

A lady in the county parking lot, just outside the Sheriff's Station, looked up to see the ball of fire split apart into three bright pieces right overhead. Flames separated as two parts fell away and dropped downward. But the largest light and longest tail streaked eastward.

A Tuolumne County Sheriff Deputy saw the sparkling fireball paint the forests with light. He stopped his car. For a few moments, as the night turned to day, he saw buildings, streams and nude people partying in a campground—caught by surprise in the light. Then darkness returned, covering up their nakedness.

The deputy blinked. For him, that was like seeing a ghost, a goblin, or an elf. He couldn't believe his eyes. Then his radio suddenly buzzed with calls.

As the larger portion of the fireball neared the ground, campers in tents saw the light pass overhead--through the fabric. Women screamed. Men shouted, children cried out with fear. On back roads, cars swerved and stopped. People panicked and fell to the ground, horrified and momentarily blinded.

Faces turned skyward to see the sparkling green-white fireball with the flaming orange tail. For each, the wave of light brought a magical moment, a fear and awe they had never experienced before. They watched as the sun came down to earth—in the darkness of night. That's what made it seem so eerie, so mystical—the darkness.

First, the darkness turned to day all around them. They could see their ghostly hands, the faces of friends, the forests and cars. Then as the light passed, the greenish shadows shifted, moving around them, like a dream. As their hearts pounded in awe, the night returned, like a curtain had been drawn over their world. The new darkness dredged up their deepest feelings of fear for this darkness was black—darker than normal night -- for wide-open eyes had been blinded.

Many froze in place, afraid to move. Many fell down, or collapsed to the ground, fearing to take a step. Some dropped to their knees, praying, for in that moment, hundreds, if not thousands of people felt mans' primal fear of darkness, and man's longing for light. But suddenly--it was gone.

As the sparkling light in the sky brought a glorious, silent and majestic awe to man, the darkness brought terrible fear, loud cries, shouting and screams. Many cried with joy and sorrow in the same breath, wondering what great majesty and glory had passed over them.

Truly, thousands of people in northern California were awed by the beautiful Ball of Fire in the Sky—my sign.

At a cabin high in the mountains, a family of horse wranglers saw the light coming up the valley. Through a large picture window in the cabin, they saw the forest turn green and then their living room lit up like mid-day. They felt dizziness as shadows swirled around them like a dream. Outside, they saw shadows shift and turn in the trees.

As the shadows moved, their dogs barked and howled with terror. Horses and cows and chickens all sounded their alarms. Then the wranglers felt a rumble.

The walls of the house began to shake. Men and women grabbed for each other, hugging and clinging in fear. Children ran to their parents, screaming. Outside, dizzy animals crashed to the ground while others struggled to stand.

After the fireball disappeared behind a mountain ridge, the sound rumbled for nearly a minute bringing tears to those who had not yet cried, sending strangers into each others arms, and touching the soul of men, women and children with primal fears.

None of them knew the fireball had been predicted—that it was *a sign for all mankind.*

Jim's Reaction

The next morning at about 7:30 a.m., my phone rang with a collect call from Brian.

"You got your sign," Brian said in a matter-of-fact way.

"What sign?" I asked sleepily from my writing den as Wanda hurried off to work.

"Your ball of fire! It was all over the radio as I drove into work."

"What did it say?"

"Turn on the radio. They said it was *"sparkling like a thousand particles--*something like that."

"No way?"

"Yes! Jim, you need to come down and get this writing, now."

"Do you have that latitude and longitude?" I asked scrambling for a pen.

"I can't be doing this at work," Brian protested. "I've already gotten into trouble once." He unfolded the paper on his drafting board. "I'm here early. That's the only reason I can call," he said. "The latitude is 38.01 degrees North and the Longitude is 119.5 degrees West."

"Okay. Let me make a few calls," I said. "Can you call me back in an hour?"

"No! Not at work!" Brian protested. "You come down tonight."

I hung up and called KFWB radio in Los Angeles, an *all-news* station. "News room please." A man with a deep voice answered the call.

"Did we have a meteorite last night?"

"Sure did--a fireball over San Francisco. It was sparkling. Shooting off thousands of particles."

The words stunned me. "Does the report say *"thousands of particles?"*

"That's what it says. Something like that."

I took a deep breath. This had to be faked, somehow, I thought. Those were the exact words used by Brian. My brain raced and I felt sweat form on my brow. "Do they know where it came down?"

"No. Anywhere between Canada and Mexico. Do you want me to get the wire story?"

"Yes, please." My lungs burned, and I heaved for air. A moment later he read the opening paragraph of the Associated Press story.

Last night about 11:30 p.m. a huge meteor, mantled in multi-colored fire and flashing white sparks, shot through the sky over at least half the length of California.

"That's what it says." He scanned the story. "It had a green, sparkling head and a long orange tail. I guess people reported pieces of it falling all over the western states."

"Incredible. Anything else on the wire?"

"No. Did you see it?" the broadcaster asked.

"No, someone told me about it," I said. Thanks."

I hung up the phone and sat down slowly. How could Brian fake this? We often had a meteor shower in August. Could this be chance? Why did the broadcaster say *"a thousand particles?"* I paced, pondering the possibilities. The words of the broadcaster had hit me hard. I trusted his voice, his report.

Brian had to fake this, but how? How? I paced around for a while, and then slowly I began to wonder—what if he didn't fake it. For the first time, for just a one tiny moment, I considered the unthinkable, the impossible. What would it mean?

Could it be that the Host, whatever *he* might be, answered? I felt a tingle on my skin and cold chills on my neck. No. NO WAY. Again, I felt sweat on my brow. My heart was pounding. My mind and soul bubbled with awe.

The location! That would be the test. He couldn't fake the location. I looked for an atlas in my bookshelf. My fingers flew over my cherished books of experimental psychology, abnormal psychology, personality, sleep deprivation, altered states, motivation, emotion, learning, biology, the Bible, the Koran, the book of Mormon, the Bhagavad-Gita, the Secret Doctrine, the Dead Sea Scrolls and a dozen other books about religion and philosophy. Finally, I found an atlas.

Excitedly, I traced the longitude on a map, then the latitude. My fingers crossed near Fresno County in northern California. In moments, I dialed the Fresno County Sheriff. They gave me a number for Yosemite National Park.

"Was there a ball of fire up around there last night?" I asked the ranger.

"Oh yeah!" the man breathed with awe. "It was right here. Oh yeah. Right here."

"Did you see it?"

"I saw it. It was unbelievable." His voice choked with emotion. "Awesome," he whispered. "That's all I can say." He took a deep breath. " It was the most spiritual, mystical experience of *my* life. It was like the sun came down to earth."

"Where are you, exactly?" I said softly.

"West Gate of Yosemite," the guard whispered. "Everyone who saw it is just overwhelmed right now. People are walking around in a daze. It's all they can talk about."

I hung up the phone. "Yes," I shouted. "YES." I sat down thinking hard. What does it mean? What does this mean?

If this was true--really true, then I had asked for a sign, speaking to Brian. The Host had replied, through Brian, announcing his intention in writing. Whatever *he* was, a ball of fire came, like he said. No man could do it. Not Brian. Not some multiple-personality of Brian. No *multiple-personality* had ever done that.

Who is this Host? My mind raced. He had the power to cast fire to the earth. He could be the anti-Christ, an alien, a spaceman. Whoever he was, I had hooked him by talking to Brian. I had gained his attention--whatever *he* was—and he replied. Could it be a coincidence?

Maybe a meteorite in August could be a coincidence--but not one with a description to match given in advance--not a location given in advance. Not likely, but still—it could be a coincidence, I reasoned. Maybe.

The Sign, Given

That night, Wanda and I met Brian at a coffee shop. She read the writing aloud in her strong, musical voice.

August 23, 1976, 2:10.3.2 AM-AE

> **Of the Host, given in rapport, open: Run one. From the sky now comes a ball of fire for all mankind to see. Of this, 1,000 particles of this of I, and by this I AM, I AM.**

> **Look to the west, given in trust. Latitude 38.01 North. Longitude 119.5 West. Of this, seek of I. Will pass, by of this, knowledge. Of this again, 1-10 will pass of I.**

"Those are drawings," Brian said. "Drawings one to ten. They always want me to do drawings." Wanda continued:

Fear not the mind of mankind. Of this, he asked of I a sign, and of this, is wisdom of I given: 002-002-002. To he who has wisdom, this is I, and of I--you are one.

Brian asked the waitress for more ketchup. "From what I understand it was one hell of a ball of fire," Brian said. "Very unusual."

"I heard it on the news," the waitress said. "Really spectacular. My mom saw part of it come down in Bakersfield. I guess parts came down all over."

Wanda studied the paper at a light to see if the latitude and longitude had been erased and re-written. "I just wanted to see, Brian," she said. It didn't look re-written.

"The newscaster didn't know this morning," I said. He told me '*anywhere from Canada to Mexico.*' There was nothing on the news wires about the location when he read me the latitude and longitude."

Wanda looked at the paper again. Brian laughed. "I told you to come down and get it last night, but you wouldn't listen."

Wanda glared at Brian. "Are you sure you had this latitude and longitude before it came? I want you to look me in the face and tell me the absolute truth."

"I didn't change anything," Brian smiled. His blue eyes twinkled. "I still don't even know where the heck it is."

"Brian, you better not be scamming us in any way," Wanda warned sharply. "Believe me, I will have your balls cut off before I let you lie to me."

Brian laughed. "Like I told you before, Wanda--and Jim. Don't think it's me if NOTHING happens. Don't think it's me if something DOES happen. It's not ME--it's HIM!"

I glanced at the words and read them slowly, "'*Of this, HE asked of I a sign. Given.*' I guess that's me—the HE. I am the one who asked."

Brian agreed. "That's you. It's *your* sign."

"So he is probably speaking to me when he says, '*SEEK of I. Will pass by of this knowledge.*'"

Brian agreed. "That's right."

I felt goose bumps. This was happening. "What does this mean to you?" I asked.

Brian shrugged. "Where is it?"

"Northern California." I said.

"Is it near Mono Lake?" Brian asked.

"No. Hetch-Hetchy reservoir in Yosemite." I showed him a California map.

Brian shrugged again. "Well, we could go fishing. Maybe camp out."

"When can we go?" I asked Wanda and Brian.

Brian shrugged. "Soon as possible, before someone else finds it."

"Labor Day is next weekend," Wanda smiled.

"I get three days off," Brian beamed. "With pay."

"No more than $250 on the whole trip," Wanda whispered. "That's all we can afford."

Fireball Landing
Site Placed Here

By CHRIS BATEMAN

That brilliant fireball that illuminated skies from Eureka to Phoenix Monday night finished its fiery flight in Tuolumne county, according to an astronomy expert from Los Angeles' Griffith observatory.

"Preliminary calculations tell us that it fell about 20 to 30 miles east of Sonora," said Ronald A. Oriti, who arrived in Sonora last night to launch a search for meteorite fragments.

The approximate area where the meteorite might have fallen includes Lake Eleanor, Cherry Lake, Crane meadow, the Wood Ridge lookout and Niagara camp. Cottonwood road runs through much of the area.

Monday night's fireball was seen by thousands throughout California and Arizona at approximately 11 p.m. Numerous reports were called into police departments in both states, and hundreds of people in locations hundreds of miles apart reported seeing fireballs fall in their vicinities.

But no meteor fragments have been found, and Oriti is dismissing reports on their landing anywhere but in the higher elevations of Tuolumne county.

How did Oriti narrow his search?

"Triangulation," he explained. "This is the process of taking directions of sightings from a number of locations. Where the direction lines cross is where the fireball should have fallen."

Bay area residents, for instance, saw the fireball to the east. Those in Los Angeles saw it to the northeast and those on the eastern slope of the Sierra spotted it to the west. The lines cross in this county.

Oriti explained that his calculations are more than guesswork. He has a thick notebook detailing hundreds of sightings called in to the observatory and evidence that the meteor finished its flight here is fairly conclusive.

Finding fragments of the fireball may not be as simple.

First of all, there may not be any.

A great majority of fireballs burn up in the earth's atmosphere before reaching the ground.

But Oriti would not be here unless he felt sure there was a chance of discovering fragments.

"This fireball was extremely bright," he explained. "It was far brighter than the full moon and nearly as bright as the sun. This leads me

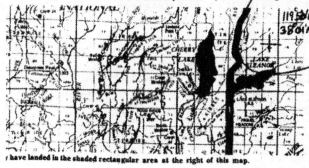

have landed in the shaded rectangular area at the right of this map.

ASTRONOMER Ron Oriti's first estimate includes our target location off to the east side. His second estimate (next page) focused on a much smaller area. Our location is right in the middle of his second estimate.

283

James E. Frazier

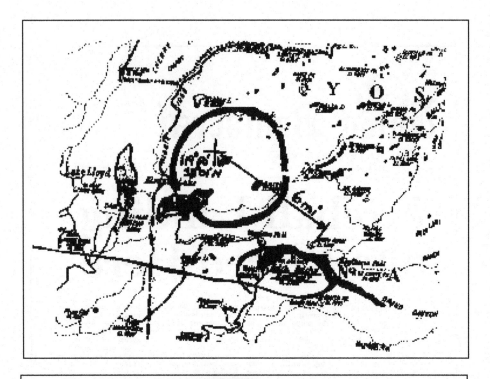

Fireball Hunt Narrows

By CHRIS BATEMAN

Astronomer Ronald Oriti has pinpointed the landing site of last Monday's brilliant fireball to a small area in the western part of Yosemite National park.

"I can cover the area of map where it landed with two fingers," said Oriti, who described the area as being "near Hetch Hetchy reservoir.

Oriti is an astronomy lecturer at Los Angeles' Griffith observatory.

He declined to be more specific on the site, however, pointing out that scientists from other institutions could beat him to the valuable meteorite fragments if they knew the target area.

Soulsbyville and Pinecrest also point to the same area.

Among those he interviewed here were Sheriff's Deputies Chuck Gregg and Hank Twisselman.

Further supporting Oriti's contentions were sonic booms heard in Yosemite last Monday.

"Tuolumne meadows rumbled for almost a minute," said Oriti.

A park spokesman added that a number of employees "saw an awful lot of bright light" last Monday. Several hikers also reported seeing the fireball at close range. Oriti said Yosemite witnesses reported seeing

the fireball shattering into pieces as it descended.

"I expect there are at least a dozen fragments there and perhaps many more," he said.

He said he was confident he could find fragments "within a couple of days" if the area were not overgrown with brush. As it is, however, a week's expedition will probably be scheduled if the observatory director feels it is worthwhile.

Oriti said park officials have offered to assist him in a search.

The fireball, which lit up skies from Northern California to Arizona at approximately 11 p.m. last

Monday, was described by Oriti as "a stony meteorite" of unusual size.

Most fireballs burn up in the earth's atmosphere prior to landing, but Oriti said last Monday's was big enough—perhaps three or four feet in diameter—to survive the fall.

The astronomer arrived in Tuolumne county Friday to launch a search for the fragments after pinpointing its location east of Sonora through "triangulation."

This is determining a target area by using sighting directions from numerous other locations.

By Friday night Oriti had isolated the landing area to Yosemite park and when he left here Sunday

284

IMAGE OF THE BEAST

AND HE DOETH GREAT SIGNS,
SO THAT HE MAKETH FIRE TO COME DOWN FROM HEAVEN
ON THE EARTH IN THE SIGHT OF MEN.

AND HE DECEIVETH THEM THAT DWELL ON THE EARTH
BY THE MEANS OF THOSE MIRACLES...
AND HE CAUSES ALL, BOTH SMALL AND GREAT,
RICH AND POOR, FREE AND SLAVE,
TO RECEIVE A MARK ON THEIR RIGHT HAND OR ON THEIR FOREHEADS,
THAT NO ONE MAY BUY OR SELL EXCEPT ONE WHO HAS THE MARK OR THE
NAME OF THE BEAST,
OR THE NUMBER OF HIS NAME.

HERE IS WISDOM.
LET HIM WHO HAS UNDERSTANDING CALCULATE THE NUMBER OF THE BEAST,
FOR IT IS THE NUMBER OF A MAN: HIS NUMBER IS 666.

Revelation Ch. 13:13-18

Chapter 12

Up to the Mountain Top

A week later, on Wednesday, September 1, I prepared for an expedition to Yosemite by gathering sleeping bags, backpacks and a good compass. Mary Beth called me, terrified. She had seen a ball of red light in the house with the children. I called the lady who had volunteered to help at the Garden Grove lecture. Fay Harris lived near Mary Beth in Fullerton.

A tall, stout woman with a majestic face, Fay drove over to the house and comforted Mary Beth. "I will be the friend you need," Fay announced like an actress on stage. "If you are strong in your self, this can't hurt you."

Fay packed a suitcase for Mary Beth and the two girls. She took the baby to Mrs. Parsons, then moved Mary Beth and Kathy into her apartment for a prolonged visit.

The day was hot and humid so they stayed inside, relaxed and turned the air conditioning up high. That evening as they played gin rummy on a card table in the living room, Fay preached to Mary Beth about how a woman can be strong and happy without a man. She had recently divorced and started on a new road of discovery.

As Fay finished her last Marlboro Gold cigarette, she opened a bottle of Scotch. "The Christ Consciousness can cure any problem," she said pouring drinks. "I used to be an alcoholic," she laughed pompously. "Now, I can drink anytime."

About 7:30 p.m., Fay poured a second round of drinks. As she shuffled into the kitchen, Mary Beth felt strange. Something tugged at her soul. Then she blacked out.

From the kitchen, Fay heard a very loud crash. She rushed back into the living room to find Mary Beth sprawled upside down with her legs twisted against the apartment door. Game cards lay scattered across the room. "My god," she breathed. Mary Beth appeared to have been thrown against the door.

"Asstttaaaaaa," a demonic voice growled.

With a drink in her hand, Fay cautiously stepped forward and peeked at Mary Beth's face. Mary Beth's muscles clenched taut and her whole body trembled. Then her lips curled back and a voice snarled. "ASSTTTAAAA."

Fay gathered her confidence. She stood up still holding the drink glass. "I command you to come out of Mary Beth Scott in the name of Jesus."

The demon growled.

Fay's jaw locked firmly. "I command you, in the name of Jesus to come out of that body, now. Right now. I command you."

"AAASSSSTTTTAAAA," roared the demon. Mary Beth's body kicked, violently. "Death to Scott."

"I COMMAND you. Come out now!" shouted Fay.

ASTA laughed with a crackling demonic rattle. Suddenly, Fay remembered her last family reunion, before the divorce. In a lush park in South Carolina, five beautiful curly-haired children had all called her "grandma." They were her pride and joy.

In a daze, she pondered for a moment. Why would she remember such a touching scene at this moment?

Then the demon laughed. "Death to you--and all your FAMILY."

Fay panicked. "It read my mind," she gasped. She felt her heart pounding. "I'll be damned. It read my mind!" Finding courage, she stood tall. "That is a lie," she said. "You lying demon." She pointed at Mary Beth. "In the name of Jesus! I COMMAND you to come out of her." She waited. The demon chortled and cackled.

Fay felt her heart pounding and her knees shaking. "It's reading me," she whined. "Oh, help me, God." She remembered the picnic again. She had glanced at a bottle of Scotch and cigarette smoke curling up from an ashtray. They had made her feel dirty around the wholesome children, but she felt it was her right as an adult.

Asta laughed again, gloating with evil. "The body means nothing to me." Mary Beth's body jumped, as if shocked.

"Oh, God," Fay whined. "What if it doesn't work?"

She had considered herself a New Age psychic counselor fully committed to the Christ Consciousness, to feminism, astrology, séances and numerology. She believed a woman should "do her own thing." To her, the Bible was out of date, and she had refused to be "saved" or baptized. That's childish, she thought. If you know God, you know God—that was enough. Now, she wondered.

Suddenly, an image arose in her mind of snarling wolves, leaping over a fence and knocking down white crosses in a cemetery in her hometown, where she wanted to be buried. She wondered if this meant her eternal soul was under attack.

Suddenly she saw an image of the wolves leaping into the windows of her apartment. Terrified by the vivid image, she ran to the bedroom and slammed the door. Kathy slept on the bed, peacefully. Heaving for breath, Fay called her ex-husband for help. "John, I'm...I'm flipping out," she panted. "Hallucinating. Badly. I need help. Brian Scott's wife is here. We need an exorcism. Here. Right now."

Fay also called me. Within minutes Wanda and I flew down the freeway towards Fullerton. When we arrived nearly an hour later, Mary Beth still lay on the floor writhing in the open doorway. I leaned down close to her face. ASTA snarled in a deep growl that gave me goose bumps.

Every muscle in Mary Beth's body tensed hard as rock. "She's been like that for more than two hours," Fay said waving a drink. "She can't go on. No human can do that for two hours," she said sloppily.

John Harris, a slender, graying airline pilot, and two New Age Christian women had arrived before us. They explained their plan to me. The lead exorcist, a cute blond woman with a turned up nose, would place her hands near Mary Beth's bare feet.

The other woman would pull away the negative energy around Mary Beth's temples as the positive energy pushed up into the feet. John planned to move his hands over Mary Beth's body. By psychic feel, he would locate "power-spots" where the demon held on.

Holding hands, they prayed for a moment and then knelt down to send energy into the soles of Beth's feet. "Death. Death to this body," Asta threatened. Mary Beth's body kicked violently.

"Back off, back off," ordered the lead exorcist. "We'll go slower." She wore Wrangler jeans, a big rodeo belt buckle and a Disneyland T-shirt, not my idea of an exorcist, but she seemed experienced and certain.

About then, Bob Martino puffed into the door, breathing hard from running up the stairs. "Let's get her up," he shouted. He tried to jerk Mary Beth to her feet. But Asta growled and Martino let go. Mary Beth fell to the floor with a thud.

"Can you get her to relax?" he said shaking Mary Beth's arm in panic.

The mild-mannered pilot spoke softly. "I don't know who you are sir, but we are in the middle of an exorcism," he said. "It would be really good if you would not touch her."

Martino twisted around and confronted Fay. "You need to call 911, or her doctor," he shouted, terrified. "She has a psychiatrist."

Fay laughed. "They will just take her away and lock her up," she lifted the Scotch bottle. "It's my fault. I gave her a drink, now let these people do what they know how to do."

"I'm calling 911," he huffed, grabbing at the phone. Fay knocked the phone to the floor with a crash.

"No!" she shouted. "This is a spiritual battle--a war in her soul. She can't win it alone. She can't win it with doctors and paramedics and medications. That's all been tried. She has to win within herself, on her own--with their help. Now stand aside and let them do their job."

"If she dies, you could be liable," he warned.

"This is a SPIRITUAL battle," Fay spat out the words.

"Then you need a priest," he seethed. "These are just..."

"That's my husband, and his new wife. These people know Jesus," she shouted. "If anyone is going to help her win this fight, they can."

Martino fumed with frustration.

"We need to clear this room," the exorcist said. "We need to create positive vibrations."

"Right." Fay said. She laughed loudly. "Let's start laughing. Laugh about anything."

Wanda laughed with her. "It's really a beautiful, warm night," she said.

"Great night, wonderful time," shouted Fay.

Martino glared at me. "I suggest you call an ambulance right now, for your own protection. If she dies, I will hold you responsible." He was very serious and for a while I considered the idea, but I had seen the doctor's records and knew Mary Beth had been to the hospital before. If this was a spiritual battle, I wanted to see it play out.

Just then, a lady friend of Fay's arrived. "What's going on?" the woman asked nervously as she squeezed past the exorcists in the doorway.

"Oh, nothing. Just come on in and have a good time. We are keeping the vibrations real high, so start laughing. Have a good time."

I knelt down to watch the exorcists work their hands over Mary Beth's rigid body without touching her skin, or clothing.

"We are moving the energy," said John.

"Do you have a Bible?" I whispered.

"Good idea." John asked his ex-wife to find a Bible. The demon roared, more loudly than before when the Bible came near. Mary Beth's body kicked. Vile curses spewed from her mouth.

John opened the book slowly--ASTA howled in pain. "Death to all." Mary Beth's body squirmed in agony. John waited a few moments, then slowly placed Mary Beth's hand on the open pages.

As her skin touched the paper, her body kicked as if shocked by a power line. The demon screamed. Mary Beth's back arched and her legs began kicking backwards. Her whole body leapt off the ground, twisting and kicking backwards. Her feet kicked so high, that they knocked a big table lamp to the floor with a crash.

"That's too much. Too much," yelled the lead exorcist. "Take it away." John pulled Mary Beth's hand off the Bible, and her body calmed.

"Deaaaaaattthhhh to this body," the demon seethed. "Death. Death to all."

"No one is dying here," said the lady exorcist. "Except you. You are going to leave this sweet, wholesome girl alone."

"Death to Mary Beth. Now!" roared the demon. Mary Beth's body arched backwards and locked tight. The pose terrified everyone. The angle seemed inhuman.

"Jesus help her," prayed the lead lady. "Jesus cast out this demon, please." Terrified, she waved for Wanda and me to help. As Mary Beth's body trembled, the exorcists spoke in tongues calling on the name of Jesus.

Awe and fear filled everyone. No human body could hold such a rigid pose so long without damage. For the first time, we began to believe Mary Beth would die.

"To this body--death," hissed the demon.

Fay began to cry. "She could die, oh God. Don't allow this." The exorcists began to cry. Tears ran down their faces as they prayed with fervor. "Jesus, please Jesus, save this girl," they cried. "Jesus, please save the body and soul of Mary Beth Scott. Cast out this demon, please Jesus." Their voices sang out in a chorus of tears.

Finally, the demon released with a long breath. Mary Beth's muscles suddenly relaxed. Her body lay flat. Moments later her big brown eyes opened. She rolled over. "Where am I?" she asked softly. "What is happening?" She looked perfectly normal.

Amazed, the exorcists lifted her to a sitting position. Mary Beth's eyes closed again. The demon snarled. The two lady exorcists held Mary Beth in their arms and stroked her hair and face with loving hands. "Come back," they pleaded. "Come back to us."

Mary Beth's eyes again opened. She looked around and smiled at all of the ladies. "Well, hello," she said with a radiant smile and a laugh. "I don't believe I know you."

Fay jumped forward and pulled Mary Beth up to her feet. "Let me make some introductions," she chuckled. "I'm sorry. This is my ex-husband, John, his new wife Judy and a friend. They just happened to come over, and we are having some fun."

Mary Beth peered at them suspiciously for a moment. "Was I out? Did something happen?"

"Something did, but we're not going to talk about it, now honey," said Fay. "We're just going to have a good time. Tell you later. Right now--you look beautiful." Fay displayed Mary Beth to the crowd. Stunned by her radiant smile, they all clapped and cheered. Mary Beth blushed. She looked happy and healthy, as if she had just returned from vacation.

Exorcism Phase Two

For the next twenty minutes, people sipped sodas, ate chips and talked about good times. The three exorcists stepped outside and gestured for me to follow. "Listen. This girl has a big problem," said the cute, green-eyed leader. "She was hanging on."

"Hanging on?"

"To that demon. She wanted it. There's a trade out. You see. They each get something out of the deal."

I listened with curiosity, still favoring the idea of multiple personalities over actual demonic possession.

"And you be careful," the woman said with intensity

"We will," I said meekly.

"No, I mean YOU!" the exorcist snapped. "This thing can move to other people. This thing can reach out and grab you--like this." She jabbed into my stomach with her strong right hand and twisted hard. "Just like that."

I winced in pain and understood her point.

"I suggest you don't leave her alone," said the exorcist. "Get her away from Fay. And get her some serious help, quickly."

'I agreed, and the three exorcists quietly slipped away into the warm, fragrant night without saying goodbye to anyone. The air smelled of sweet night blooming jasmine flowers.

290

Inside the apartment, Mary Beth joined into the party atmosphere. Fay offered her another scotch, and after a few sips Mary Beth talked everyone into a game of gin rummy.

Before dealing the cards, Mary Beth slipped away to the bathroom. A moment later, a loud crash terrified everyone. We raced to the bathroom. Mary Beth's body lay twisted and upside down in the tub. "Assssttaaaaaa," hissed the demon.

"Where's John?" screamed Fay. "Get them back here!"

"They are gone," I whispered. "They left."

"Oh, my God. Now what," Wanda whispered. Mary Beth's body began writhing and the demon hissed from her curled back lips. She suddenly looked evil.

"Pray to Jesus," I said. The women all began praying loudly as I knelt down close to Mary Beth's face. Her teeth looked sharp. Was it my imagination? I blinked. "Jesus, please cast out this demon," I said trying to remember the procedure.

The demon growled. "Death to you."

I leaned closer drawing strength from my childhood knowledge and love for Jesus. I held my image of his face in my mind and heart. Though raised Episcopalian, I had been saved and "born again" by accepting Jesus after watching an evangelical film in a Baptist church, a few years earlier. I wasn't living a Biblical life-style, but I truly believed in the power of Jesus to cast out demons. I prayed softly. "Jesus, I know you can do this. The Bible says so. I believe it. So, please cast out this demon."

To my surprise, Mary Beth stopped breathing. The ladies screamed as Mary Beth's eyes rolled up. "Death," hissed the demon.

I closed Mary Beth's nostrils and blew air into her mouth. Her lungs filled with air and her chest expanded. Then I pushed down. The air rushed out and the demon snarled. "Death to Scott."

"Jesus, please cast out this demon, now," I said. He had died on the cross so that we might have the power of the Holy Spirit. I believed that, and thanked Him. This time, as I blew into Mary Beth's mouth, I felt a small object rise up from my chest and ride into her lungs with the air. Mary Beth's eyes opened, wide.

"Jim Frazier, what are you doing?" she said with a smile. She looked around. "My God! What is going on." Everyone quickly lifted her out of the tub, and we all pretended nothing serious had happened. Within a few minutes Mary Beth was back in the living room, laughing and talking.

I could feel my knees shaking. "Something strange just happened," I whispered to Wanda.

"That's very true," she laughed, gaily. "Keep it light."

291

"When I blew into Mary Beth, something went out of me. Out of my chest, and into her." In my mind's eyes, I saw it happen, again.

"You mean--you spit in her?" Wanda whispered.

"No. I felt like an object went out of me--about the size of a bean. I actually felt something *physical*. It was green, like emerald or jade."

Wanda shrugged. "It's a strange night. Lighten up."

We drove Mary Beth and Kathy home to our house in Hollywood. The next day I cared for them while Wanda worked at Paramount. Mary Beth slept late, bathed for several hours with Kathy, and slept more. Her body ached with muscle pain.

That night, I gave Mary Beth a Bible, and drove her home. She promised to pray every day, and keep the Bible open in her house. I had been impressed by the impact of the open Bible on the demon.

Debra's Sacrifice

The next morning, Debra called and wanted to talk. Brian had invited her to go to Yosemite, but she wanted to meet me first.

Two hours later, around noon, she arrived driving her 1973 red and silver VW bug. She wore a conservative pink business suit and boldly introduced herself as an executive secretary in training. In my messy writer's den, we joked about my need for a secretary. Then she got down to business.

"I will be blunt," she said. "I have a bunch of questions. I want to just blurt them out. Then you answer what you want. Okay?" I agreed.

"First, is this on the level? Are you really Hollywood producers? Is Brian really a UFO contactee?" Debra gushed. "What did you find out in your research?" she asked. "Is the Host God? Or is this some alien thing?"

I offered her a chair. "I don't really know for sure if they are alien."

"Could they be the angels of Satan, or are they the sons of God who bred with the daughters of men? That's why the flood came. There were giants then. Genesis Chapter 6 says it plainly: the Sons of God bred with earth women at a time when giants were on the earth—the Nephilim. So God wiped away their world and left only Noah. Brian says they are really big, some of them--giants."

She took a deep breath as I looked for a Bible. "I know there were giants," I said, "But wasn't it the 'sons of God' who were taking the earth girls, and making babies. Not the giants, right?"

"Yes. NOT THE GIANTS," she gushed. "But both were together at the same time. Just like Brian says. Giants and…whatever these are. Both are mentioned in Genesis 6. It's so far out. I am just filled with questions," she laughed. "Is he supposed to receive some mark in his hand? That is my main question. I mean, I may not be *'Miss Goody Two-Shoes,'* but I am a Christian, and I will never take the mark. Never. I will not take ANY mark on my body."

Finally, she paused and waited a moment. "Well? What you think."

"You ask the right questions. Can you take dictation *that* fast?" We laughed easily. "I don't know if it is demons, or aliens or multiple personality, or what-- but I do know something is happening."

"Well, is it of God? I guess that is what I have to know."

"I don't know," I said. "It could be the other way. It might be like the book of Job."

"Job? He was righteous. God let Satan take everything—as a test of his righteousness."

"Right. It might be a test of some kind."

"Well, I'm a born-again, Christian," she said proudly. "Baptized in the name of Jesus. I know he is my Savior. I just may not be living a truly pure life right now. But, I'm only 24, and to tell you the truth I am hot on the trail of this man," she laughed boldly. "I am not afraid of demons, or even the Anti-Christ, but I am hoping and praying that I am in this because of God. And I am *involved* with Brian, if you know what I mean."

I laughed, enjoying her honesty and candor. "You've already slept with him?"

"Yes. I won't tell a lie. And I know about his wife and kids, but he's not going back to them--not now. From the way it sounds he needs someone like me. Someone who at least knows a little about the Bible."

I liked Debra and noticed the burn scars on her throat and hands. The little finger on the left hand was nearly missing, due to burns. I figured she had been through some tough times, maybe tested by fire. "If you are a Christian, I wouldn't be afraid," I said. "I believe demons can't get into a Christian."

"That's what I believe," she said. "Are you born again?"

"Yes, I am. But I ask you to keep it quiet, because I am not exactly living the right way, either."

"I understand," she said. "But you want to do right, and live by the Word?"

I nodded in agreement. "What I saw Wednesday night convinced me that there is nothing more powerful than the Bible—in these matters."

"What happened?" Debra asked.

I told her about Mary Beth's exorcism.

Afterwards she trembled like a little girl. "I don't want that to happen to me," she said. "Do you have a Bible? I need one, right now. I feel naked."

I searched again through my library shelf. Since I had given a small one to Mary Beth, the only one I had left was my grandfather's big Frazier Family Bible, a shiny, black-leather book about 18 inches long and nearly a foot thick. I handed it to Debra and she hugged it to her chest. "Thank God, I love the Word," she breathed. "But, I am really getting nervous about this."

"Open it. I saw it work just laying open."

Debra sighed and opened the huge book. She felt the pages with her hands and breathed deep. "This is so, so incredible," she whispered. "Your grandfather's?

" He died when my dad was only 14," I said.

"My dad died when I was twelve," Debra said. "I know he is in heaven. He was my hero, my whole life, until then. That's when I became a Christian. I had to or I would be insane. He was the one who got me through these burns." She waved her scarred left hand. "I saw you looking at them. My little brother set the bed on fire, while I was in it, asleep. I tried to pull the blanket off, but it stuck to my hand, on fire, burning—wouldn't stop."

"I'm sorry. It must have been a bad time for you. I'm surprised you can talk about it."

"I had to. Therapy. I love my brother," she said. "He was only three, but I still miss my dad."

"Well we've known each other for ten minutes," I said. "And we've covered a lot of ground."

"Do you think I should go to Yosemite?" she asked.

"Mary Beth isn't a Christian. You are. I don't believe it would happen to you, but it could happen to her again--tomorrow. She needs a vacation. I'd like for her to go to Yosemite, rather than you."

Debra recoiled. "He asked me."

"I know, but as a Christian, I hope you can see how important this is. I don't think Mary Beth should be alone."

To my great surprise, Debra agreed. "I understand," she said. "I don't like the idea, but I will agree. I know Brian will come back to me, and if not--it wasn't right, anyway." She stood up and we shook hands like business professionals making a deal.

"I will keep my word to you, and I will always tell the truth," Debra said. "That much I can promise you. Even though I am—back-sliding."

When Debra departed, I watched her with a curious respect. She was indeed, a very unique person, and a sparkling ball of fire. From then on, I began to think of her as The Woman of Fire.

Brian's Gas Station Fight

On Friday, after work, Brian cruised into a gas station and accidentally splashed muddy water onto a car filled with low-riders. They yelled, but he ignored them.

After ordering two new tires for the Yosemite trip, he stepped outside for a cigarette. Two punks waited, ready to fight.

"You splashed my car," said a man tattooed with dragons. He waved a short chain, menacingly.

"It'll wash off," Brian said, loosening his tie. "Listen, you can't believe the shit I am going through, so leave me alone."

"You need to wash my car, man," he said rattling the chain with an evil glare.

"I'm sorry." Brian said. "Now get lost. You don't want to piss me off."

The second punk held up a knife. He pressed a button and the blade snapped open sharply with a click. "I think you better wash off his car, man."

Brian tossed his cigarette at the man with the knife, and attacked the chain-swinger. Brian blocked a blow with his left forearm. Whipping around Brian's forearm, the chain lashed the jaguar tattoo. Brian roared like a lion in anguish. Jabbing the chain-swinger in the face, Brian attacked like an animal with his right elbow and fist. In a second or so, he had hit the boy three times. Blood exploded from the young man's face. Brian tossed his falling victim into the knife-wielder as the blade slashed toward Brian's throat. Brian charged like a jaguar with a roar and caught the knife-hand. He twisted hard. The man spun around and bent over. Brian smashed a knee into the young man's face.

The knife dropped. The boy flew backwards and slammed into the car. Two buddies pulled him inside. As Brian peeled the chain from his forearm, his victims ran to the car for safety. Brian threw the knife into some bushes and then whipped the chain over his head. As the punk's car started to move, he charged, smashing the windshield. Laying rubber, the car screeched away in a cloud of smoke.

Brian heaved the chain at them. "Come on back, anytime" he yelled, pumped up for battle. "I'll wash your car. I'll clean your ass."

Brian heard a sound and whirled around to fight. The two attendants stood behind him with tire irons in hand.

"You didn't even need our help," one said.

"Hell, there was just only two," Brian said heaving for air. "I don't need help for only two." They all laughed. He was glad the others had stayed in the car.

Brian had grown up on the streets, and he wasn't afraid to rumble. He'd learned tricks from Rex, and from his high school friends. He even enjoyed a good fight, once in a while.

Yosemite Departure

A few hours later, under a golden sunset, near a cliff that over-looked the ocean, Debra and Brian kissed passionately. "I don't want Mary Beth to go," he whispered to her. "But if that is what Jim wants, okay. While I'm gone, find a place for us to live," he whispered. "An apartment in Tustin or Orange."

Glowing with love, Debra smiled. "I'll be ready when you return."

295

About 1:30 a.m., Brian arrived at our corner house in Hollywood. He slammed on the brakes and skidded to a stop. Then, he revved the engine loudly. When Wanda and I opened the door, Brian popped the clutch. The car screeched backwards for thirty yards coming to a stop inches from Wanda's front bumper.

"Good god!" she screamed. "You're going to wake everyone."

Brian jumped out with a smile on his face and a sleeping bag in hand. "Those back tires are nearly bald," he said. "I put the two new ones on the front."

"What tread was there is probably gone," I laughed.

"Nah. They're still OK for streets," Brian laughed.

"Do you have to drive like that Brian?" Wanda whined. "It's 1:30 a.m."

"You don't like my driving?" Brian laughed as he stomped up the stairs into the house. "That's the first thing you learn in demolition derbies. Always drive in reverse. That way you smash the other guy with your tail, and don't screw up your engine. But it would be good if we could buy two more tires."

"We only have two hundred dollars left for this whole trip," Wanda said. We had agreed to take Brian's station wagon so he could drive, and we had paid for the two new tires.

Brian smiled. "It's up to you."

That night, Brian tried to fall asleep in the living room with Mary Beth. She woke up and wanted to make love. Brian refused. He said they had to keep a clean separation because things were happening. That made Mary Beth mad. She knew Brian had to be seeing other women. "Who is she?" Mary Beth asked.

"No one special," he said. "She's a secretary student, and she's not afraid of this stuff. In fact, she thinks it's all kind of funny."

That hurt Mary Beth more than anything. Nothing about the last six months had been funny.

The next morning before sunrise we all rose early and drove away in Brian's VW. Mary Beth said nothing and remained withdrawn. Brian entertained most of the way with silly car games that Wanda and I enjoyed. But after six hours of laughing and giggling, I tried to ask Brian some serious questions. "What is the difference between your own thoughts, and the Host's?"

From the backseat, I held a microphone to his mouth. "Well," Brian stammered. "To tell you the truth, to be able to understand and grasp this, is so simple, that it is like a child's toy. It's so simple to explain, and once explained, I know you would understand it, but anyone can grasp the reality of how simple it is, and then do nothing about it. And, if you do nothing, it means nothing. So, it's better for me to say nothing."

"So it's simple?"

"Right. But I can say, with the Host, everything surrounds you. Everything you experience becomes reality when he talks. You believe it because you see it—and you feel it, in your gut."

"What can you do with it?" I asked.

"That is the question," Brian answered. "I know there is another way of being, another way of thinking, of communicating. That is really all I have after my contacts. And that just makes life here look pretty dumb. So you can laugh, or cry. I choose to laugh -- most of the time."

"Has this made you a more superior man?"

"No. Not superior. But, I am a lot happier with myself. I've exposed myself to a lot of interesting people. Most who don't have any answers for me. That is what I learned. The experts don't know any more than I do, even less--in fact. But I don't feel smart, or superior. I want to absorb everything there is to absorb. I want to experience everything and everyone. But remember, the mind does play tricks. It is not a perfect machine.

"Often it focuses on something that is an illusion. So you need a way to test this, in your mind. You need to reach out and test it, try to touch it. Try to grasp it. You have to become IT--one with it--but not all in one big bite. Test everything. Don't bite into it, until you have sniffed it. Make sure it is real and, most importantly, the right thing for you--the right identity for you."

"But how do you slip into trance so easily?"

"You mean when I go bye-bye?"

"Yeah, when you go bye-bye."

Brian laughed, and his blue eyes twinkled. "That's easy. That's the easiest thing of all, now. It's so easy it's not even worth talking about."

"It is not easy for most people. Many people spend years in Zen meditation or Yoga or chanting and still can't do what you do in a few seconds."

Brian laughed again. "It is the easiest thing for any man to do. Just hook onto one thought. Take one image and go. Go with it and hang on. Keep with it. Stay inside it. Sit back and relax. Sense what feels wrong and only DO what is right. That is the trick. The trick is to taste it: test it before you go down the path all the way."

"What about space travel? The way they do it?"

"Any time you physically change your body, the way they do, it creates a new experience, a new perception. It would freak out religious people to know. Scientists have a wall, a big brain they hide behind. They will never go far enough with it. That's probably why me."

I didn't understand. "What are you talking about?"

"To travel. You asked about space travel. Good and evil is in all of us. Even the religious--even the most righteous have evil. It's our animal nature. We all still have it. We can't accept the experience of it. If we had a laboratory, with a lot of money, with several years of time, sure I could develop bits and pieces of it, I could make it real, but most people would put up a wall. It would freak them out."

"I asked about space travel. You're talking about religious experience, good and evil within man. You said they 'change their bodies,' and 'it would freak people out.'"

"You're not ready for it."

"Why? Not ready for what?"

"Ask twenty-five scientists or religious people about anti-matter, time travel, gravity. You won't get any agreement. Look, I don't have the words. I can't explain it, but I can show it. I'm a designer. I could develop it, but who would give me the chance? One part is what they call the NOR. It's the secret behind how they travel. I saw it on the craft. I've been in it."

"You could develop it?"

"Yes, but it would be exploration, one step at a time. This is part of the reason they want me to go to Tiahuanaco. It's a step backwards to get a solid footing. They want us to understand the errors they made."

"What about their bio-telemetry scanner?"

"That's part of it, too--probably the first step. You need the biological information. You see, we, as a civilization, are right there. Very soon we will discover a gas that responds to thought, then we will go, quickly."

"You mean go...go where. Into a psycho-cybernetic civilization?"

"That's right--very quickly. We need to be prepared—in advance. I think that is what they are doing. But -- we have to do the work on our own. It has to emerge from our own selves so we can maintain it."

"Why develop it from ourselves? What do you mean?" Wanda asked.

He nodded at Mary Beth who dozed. "This is serious stuff," he whispered. "She was in a mental institution for more than a month," he said softly. "She's a nice sweet girl, an average person. That was nothing compared to what can happen to a scientist, an egghead, or a punk or a psychic with no grounding. Talk about mass murderers, cult leaders and stuff. You actually can get a lot of power, but not the knowledge of what to do with it."

"You are making a lot of sense," Wanda said. "I don't want this to turn into a cult."

"There are ways to navigate through all this, but we need people with experience who can handle it. It's so simple—they could give it to us, in a minute. I can say this: regressive hypnosis is NOT the way. Going in reverse is not the answer."

"What is the answer?" I asked.

Brian pondered for a moment. "We have to develop this technology and an entire philosophy to go with it. We will do it. Maybe not this generation--maybe the next. I could do it now, but it would take a team of people, probably millions of dollars, and my part would be just a drop in the bucket. This is given in trust you know--to you."

"Why the secrets? Why are things *'given in trust?'*"

"Because!" Brian frowned. "Man isn't ready. It could fall into the wrong hands. The government can develop this and use it against the people. There are lots of things you are not ready for. Trust me. You are not ready."

I pondered Brian's words for a while. I liked his attitude of taking authority. He didn't teach or preach, and he didn't fit the standard image of a multiple personality--tormented and tortured in childhood. Maybe there was something unique going on with him--something outside *my* theory, outside my own worldview.

I decided to keep asking questions and record everything for later review—perhaps by the next generation. If Hynek and Vallee didn't understand, maybe I never would, either.

The Gateway

We finally arrived at a huge stone archway reading: YOSEMITE WEST GATE. Puffy white clouds dotted the bright blue sky. The air felt warm, and fresh. We could smell the mountains and pine trees.

Around the gate, people talked with big-eyed awe about the ball of fire. I interviewed three female rangers and asked them to sign a document stating our purpose.

Then the supervisor took us inside to a map. He remembered my phone calls and wanted to help. On a big map, he found the latitude and longitude. "That's your point," the ranger said.

"What is the closest town?" I asked.

"No towns. There is nothing in the park." He studied the map again. "Oh, except Cherry Valley Toll Station," he said. "It's a pack station. A family lives up there. They pack horses into the park."

Brian smiled. "Perfect."

A few minutes later, I talked on a pay phone to Kay Devoto, operator of the Cherry Valley Pack Station. "Oh yeah. We all saw it," she said. "It was right outside our front window." Her whole family had seen the ball of fire out their big picture widow.

When I hung up, Brian cheered. Wanda pulled the three of us into a victory dance. Mary Beth managed a weak smile, but she wasn't happy. She wanted to talk with Brian, but he was all wrapped up in the expedition. What could she do? How could she stop him from drifting away?

He felt sorry for her, but knew that any compromise would start up a relationship. He'd become her boyfriend, unwelcome in the home, and if the children saw him at home, the in-laws would be upset. He was caught. He'd made up his mind to keep it "cut-off" until everything was over.

Pack Station

An hour later, as we drove up a paved road into the higher elevations, Wanda sang silly songs and Brian sizzled with excitement. "This is it. This is it."

"What do you mean--IT?" I asked.

"We are answering his request. This is the first time *anyone* has answered his request. This is going to change everything." Brian pointed out the widow. "Look three white doves." Flying overhead, three white birds flapped their wings and soared. "That means we are protected," Brian said.

Mary Beth frowned. "What? Everyone but me?"

"Maybe it's you three," Brian smiled.

After bouncing along a rough jeep road, we arrived at the pack station in the pines--Cherry Valley Pack Station.

Cowboys, young and old worked around the stables. Wood smoke curled up from a big stone chimney. Greeting us, a bow-legged cowboy led us all inside to meet the family.

About seven adults and a handful of teenagers joined in to talk about the ball-of-fire. "It lit up the house," said the old cowboy. "The whole house was shaking."

"It came right across that window," said Robert Newkirk, the leading man of the outfit. With a strong jaw, piercing blue eyes and small mustache, he looked like the classic cowboy, a 'Marlboro Man.' His fingers pointed a path across the window. "It disappeared right over Kibbie Ridge." He gestured at a distant mountain.

"Let's check it on my map," I said. I held my topographical map to the window. Robert found the Cherry Valley Pack Station, then traced the ball-of-fire's path. "It came up this valley and disappeared over this ridge."

"Stop!" I blurted. "Look at this, Brian." Brian drew close. "Can you lift up your finger?" I asked Robert. His thick finger lifted up slowly, covering a black "X" drawn on my map: the exact latitude and longitude given in advance.

"Jesus Christ in heaven," Brian gasped, his heart racing.

"It's right on." I whispered.

The family crowded around. "What is it? What is behind this?" a teenage cowboy asked.

"We don't know," I said. "I will be totally honest with you all. We were told to seek this latitude and longitude in advance. It is paranormal-- beyond human understanding."

We handed out the document that clearly stated our purpose. "I want to find the meteorite, if possible." I waited a moment for everyone to think. "Will you take us in there?"

The room silenced. Robert and Kay conferred quietly as the fireplace crackled with flames. Finally, Robert looked up. "We'll take you in, at the regular rate. That's what we do. We go up there all the time, so it's nothing different to us. Just another pack ride."

After they each signed the document, the older cowboy escorted us out to the tack barn and suggested we sleep inside. The nearest motel was in Twaine Hart, a long trip, with 40 miles of steep, switch-back roads—rough mountain driving.

Wanda and Mary Beth wanted showers, and I needed more film for my camera, so we all decided to drive down the mountain and come back early in the morning.

"Suit yourself," the old cowboy said. "Either way, we pack out at 7:00 a.m."

The Downhill Slope

We jumped into Brian's car and started down the mountain to Twaine Hart. As Wanda tried to count the costs of the pack trip, a light afternoon rain began to fall. We turned onto a paved road with a steep downslope. Suddenly, the car skidded out of control for a moment. "Slippery going downhill," Brian whispered. "It's those bald tires in back."

Then the car rounded a corner. Brian slammed on the brakes and stopped. The pavement glistened with water. "This is steep." Everyone breathed deep. "It's a good thing we have new tires on the front," Brian breathed.

"Go slow, Brian," Wanda gasped.

The car slid sidewise. Brian tapped the brakes lightly and the car straightened out. In the backseat, Wanda and I hung on tightly to each other's hands. "That's as slow as I can go," Brian breathed. "I hope that doesn't happen again,"

As the car rolled slowly ahead, we looked downhill to a sharp turn in front of a huge rocky outcropping—a sheer cliff. A narrow metal bridge covered a deep, treacherous canyon just before the turn. Dangerous.

Mary Beth panicked. "Stop the car. I'll walk," she said.

"Can we turn around?" Wanda pleaded. "Let's go back."

Brian slowed the car, but it slipped forward again and floated. "Damn it!" he shouted. We all screamed.

Frantically, Brian turned the wheel and tapped the brakes on and off. "Oh shit," Brian hollered. "I haven't got it. I don't have it, Jim!"

301

Sliding down the glistening road, the car picked up speed. Wanda clawed at me and Mary Beth clawed at Brian. He fought for control as the car slid sidewise.

For a long time we all screamed. As time stopped, I looked around to see two young women clinging to two young men, all screaming. Then the car crashed into the bridge with a bang. Metal screeched and glass shattered. Then silence.

In the car, we all recovered from the impact quickly. We heard a squeaking sound as the car teetered up and down.

"The car is rocking," I said. We were all leaning backwards, looking upward at the sky.

Brian looked out over the edge of the bridge. "Oh, God." He could see down into the rocky red canyon. Death waited below. The car hung over the deep treacherous canyon.

"Get out on my side," Brian shouted. "Now!" The next few moments seemed an eternity in slow motion. Brian carefully stepped out and tried to steady the car as it teetered up and down. Mary Beth climbed over the gearshift.

"Oh, God. GET OUT!" Mary Beth screamed. Dangling over the canyon, the car seemed perched in mid-air, hanging by a string—or something.

Wanda slammed the front seat forward and jumped out. I sat in the car alone for a moment bobbing up and down.

With a squeak, the car lurched forward. "Help me," Brian screamed as he pushed down on the back bumper. They all pushed down as I crawled out. When they let go, the car rocked up and down.

At first glimpse, the car seemed to be balanced on a fulcrum over the canyon. But, there was no fulcrum. The front of the car hung way over the edge of the bridge, pointed slightly up in the air.

"What is holding it back?" I asked running around the bridge. A wooden post had been torn out of the ground and lifted high into the air near the nose of the car. One small piece of protective railing remained attached to the post by one single bolt. Three other bolts had been popped. Only one bolt still held the railing in place.

The whole picture seemed bizarre. That railing in the air was somehow holding the car up but how? It made no sense. We all crawled down below the bridge to see what might be holding up the car.

Then we saw it—a tiny green, metal pole was helping. The front tire was flat, and the rim of the wheel had rolled out to the very tip of the green metal post. Balancing the car, the tiny rod made the difference. It bent up and down as the car bobbled. One more inch, and the car would have fallen off the little post. One more inch and the car would have toppled into the dark, rocky canyon, bringing certain death to us all. Together the tiny post and the one bolt in the railing had saved our lives.

"One more inch, and we would all be dead right now," Wanda said. Mary Beth screamed in agony, "My girls. Get me home. Get me home." Brian hugged and comforted her. "We can't leave them without parents," she said. "We can't do that." Brian nodded.

Moments later, a big truck rumbled onto the bridge. The car teetered up and down wildly. Brian and I rushed at the truck screaming and waving.

When the truck stopped, we all gazed in awe at the car--teetering up and down--over the deep, rocky canyon.

Brian said we had been protected. Maybe so, I just felt we were lucky.

The Expedition

Late that night, a tow truck pulled us into the Twaine Hart Service Station, next to the Twain Hart Lodge. Pete, the driver of the truck, owned the station. He let us stay in his old trailer parked next to the station. We could sleep there for a couple of days while he worked on the car.

Wanda and I examined the trailer with flashlights as Brian called 911 from a nearby pay phone. He told the lady dispatcher, Nona Eckstein, that he was part of a team of investigators looking for the meteorite. "We have some very sensitive equipment to move up the mountain," he said. "Our research vehicle just wrecked."

About an hour later, Chuck Gregg, a Tuolumne County sheriff's deputy, showed up to help. He had seen the ball-of-fire and still felt awed. "It was almost a religious experience," he said. "Like seeing God."

He read my statement of purpose and signed the document at 1:55 a.m. on September 5. He wanted to help, but couldn't take the patrol car out of his jurisdiction.

The dispatcher had seen the ball of fire split into three pieces right over her head as she left work. She asked a California Highway Patrol officer to drive us up to the pack station. To save money for car repairs, Wanda decided to remain behind with Mary Beth.

A Highway Patrol sergeant drove us back up to the pack station in his 4-wheel drive vehicle. At 3:33 a.m., he dropped us off and signed my document.

Inside the noisy tack barn filled with horses, cows, mice and cats, Brian and I unrolled our sleeping bags and lay down. Brian fell asleep immediately, but I lay awake until sunrise listening to the animals, especially to the mice crawling over our sleeping bags.

All night long, the animals seemed to be awake and active, living out little dramas. So much goes on, I thought--so many dramas--millions of people, millions of lives. Each human is barely able to handle an awareness of his own little life, his own little mind. How could we be aware of others—really? What would life be like at Nous 10? What would life be like at mind level two? What is mind level two? I wondered as I heard the water pump squeak.

The breakfast bell rang an hour later at 6:00 a.m. After a big breakfast, the old wrangler helped Brian onto a black, high-spirited stallion and put me on an old stubborn mare named Hooch.

Seven people formed the pack train. Our horses trotted across the Cherry Lake Dam and picked up Kibbie Trail in the pines. Robert Newkirk led the way, followed by the two teenage cowboys, and two women, including Kay DeVoto, the owner.

The hooves of the horses clomped on red sandstone and broken granite as they climbed steadily up the steep face of Kibbie Ridge. Near the top, we dismounted to admire the beautiful, small archways carved into red sandstone by sparkling Kibbie Creek.

An hour later, riding single file through pine trees, the teenage cowboys heard two loud, but very soft, electronic beeps. Marty, the older boy, shouted at me. "Hey, we heard something. "

"What? What did you hear?"

"It sounded like a beep, like a tone of some kind."

"See if you can tell where it is coming from," I hollered at the slim-faced 14-year- old. The teens pulled up next to Brian, one on each side.

As they rode along, another beep echoed above them.

"It's up in the air," they shouted, both pointing to the sky. "Right above him." Their hearts raced with fear. "Is it the aliens? Are they going to get us?"

Brian laughed. "We aren't going to get abducted by aliens," he told them. "At least I don't think so."

A louder, fourth tone frightened everyone. "Another one," screamed the younger boy, Billy.

I kicked my stubborn mare hard and rode up closer to Brian. "It's nothing to worry about."

Robert dropped back to ride next to me. "This is getting spooky," he said.

"Nothing bad will happen," I told everyone. "Other people have heard these sounds. Brian had them in his house. It's a monitoring tone, okay? Just to focus in on him. Nothing bad happened to anyone who heard them."

Brian sagged in his saddle. The tone had gone through his head.

As the hooves of the horses clip-clopped up the trail, the leather saddles squeaked, the bridles jangled, and the soft, high frequency pulses continued, every few minutes. Beeeep. Beeeeeeep. I counted twenty-one beeps after we passed Kibbie Creek, some as long as six seconds. The teen cowboys sizzled with excitement. They laughed and giggled about fighting the invader aliens. But the two women talked in fear about turning around and heading home.

Dazed by the tones, Brian saw a streak of light zip across the narrow trail. He wanted us all to ride down into the steep canyon. "I think the meteorite is right down there."

Robert saw no streak of light and disagreed. "It's too dangerous." He wanted to reach the main trail, circle the canyon and cut back to the location.

We all bunched up to talk at a wide spot in the trail. Then a loud electronic tone warbled over our heads for about eight seconds. "Jesus, that was a long one," said Robert. The horses spooked and pranced around. Everyone's heart raced with fear.

"We need to go back, Robert," shouted Kay with trembling in her face.

"They are just beeps, probably to locate Brian," I said in a soothing tone. "It is not really unusual for the people who have been around Brian."

"They don't seem to be hurting anything," Robert agreed. But Brian slumped forward and nearly slipped off his saddle. Billy and Marty jumped off their horses and pushed him upright.

"They are hitting my head," Brian mumbled. "I feel dizzy, Jim. I need water," he gasped. "I'm dry."

Robert quickly handed Brian a canteen. "Do you need to rest?" Robert asked.

"I'm all right," nodded Brian, bravely. He took a deep, pained breath. "Let's go on."

Watching Brian carefully, the two teenagers rode at his side. When he slouched and wobbled, they shouted. "Wake up."

"I'm all right," Brian mumbled. He hung on to the saddle horn like an injured man, weakened by pain.

After ten minutes of climbing uphill through thick timber, we emerged into a narrow mountain top plateau. We could see up and down the Kibbie Lake trail for nearly a mile.

Everyone slid out of their saddles to give Brian a breather.

Robert pulled me aside. He was frustrated. He had planned to reach the Kibbie Lake trailhead, and then take a heading of 152 degrees back to the target latitude and longitude. But his compass didn't work. No problem--I had a spare.

When I gave him my compass, he compared them for a minute, and then called me to his side. Robert turned his back to the women and whispered. "I've never seen anything like it. I've had my compass for ten years, been up here a hundred times." He held up the two compasses. "Neither one can settle on north." Both needles swung together, left to right. Left to right - from West to East.

"They might be projecting some kind of beam," I said softly.

"What kind of beam?" Robert asked. "Level with me. These women want to go back."

I watched the whispering ladies. "It's not dangerous. They apparently use some sort of a beam for communicating. They transmit to Brian from somewhere in space. "

Robert looked skyward. "I've never seen this happen, before. I don't know what to do."

Kay stepped near. "Something wrong?" she asked.

"I can't seem to get oriented to the map--is all," Robert said. "It just doesn't look right." He didn't want to frighten her with the compasses.

About then, from a distance, Marty shouted. He ran towards us at full speed waving his arms wildly. "Your friend is in a trance," he yelled. "Your friend is in a trance. He's on a cliff. Come on!" I ran with my pack in hand.

The Mountain Top Trance

When I reached the north face of Kibbie Ridge, a magnificent view unfolded--green forests, wide valleys and mountains. For a moment I embraced the stunning panorama. Marty shouted, and I followed him down a narrow, steep path. We found Brian sitting upright with his back to a wall of granite. The outcropping created a tiny amphitheatre on the narrow ledge.

A voice growled from Brian's throat.

"He's been doing that," Billy said as the boys huddled in fear.

I clicked on my tape recorder. I had never talked to Brian in trance, but after listening to all the tapes recorded by Kate, I knew the code word. "Ticci Viracocha."

The growling stopped and a deep, powerful voice said, "Open."

"Where is the meteorite?" I asked.

"Look to the west."

"Where? Where is the meteorite?"

"Given."

"Why are we here?"

The mechanical voice talked about "atmospheric absorption" and the need for Brian to be above 7,000 feet elevation, as a test of Nous ten.

"Which way is west?" I shouted at Robert when he arrived on horseback with the ladies.

Robert looked at the compasses and shrugged.

"Are you transmitting something?" I asked the Host. "Is that why we are here?"

"Knowledge of free-psychic energy given. Nous ten test. Knowledge to pass through Scott, of Frazier, to all mankind," the voice said. "Knowledge of free

306

psychic energy to be given," the voice said. "Of this, freedom of mind is given, Frazier."

"What does that mean?" I asked.

The voice said that I was indeed 'the man of words' as foretold to Brian.

"Brian's unfoldment is in your hands," the voice said. "Look to yourself. Given in trust to you and no other."

Since I had studied the tapes recorded by Kate, I was prepared for a personal seduction. I took all the nice words with a grain of salt. I didn't know who was doing the talking, the Host, Brian, some demon, or what. The presence seemed mechanical, but carried a tone of authority.

The voice described Scott as 'Keeper of the Quipu--of Tiahuanaco' and me as 'Keeper of the Quipu--Hopi.'

I didn't understand. "Are you speaking about re-incarnation or past lifetimes?"

"No," the voice said firmly. "Rapport in Nous 10. Not as man thinks. Not as conceived in the mind of man. Of time, beyond all time."

I really wanted to find the meteorite for proof. "Can you figure out west, with the maps?" I asked Robert again.

"I need a true north," Robert shrugged from his saddle. He pointed west. "Somewhere that way."

"Energy," said the Host. "Energy given." Brian's face turned red and he inhaled with short, powerful breaths as if fighting pain. Even the horses fretted and snorted as Brian huffed and puffed. His arms lifted. Then he tried to stand up. The horses and wranglers scrambled in fear.

To my surprise, Brian stood up *while in trance. I couldn't believe it.* Then he melted. I jumped forward and caught Brian's head just as he fell. He didn't hit his head so I knew he wasn't hurt, but his eyes remained rolled up. I studied his eyes, wondering why the eyes were so important to a trance state.

The iris of each eye had disappeared under the bony ridge of his eye socket.

I had heard about trances, and studied epileptic fits. I knew that eyes rolled up, sometimes when people died, or fainted. I had studied research on crossed-eye hand control and dyslexia, as they affected performance in school and at work. I was very interested in eye movements as they applied to human psychology. Did the eyes reveal the soul? How?

Did looking upward and inward with the eyes serve some purpose? Did Brian roll his eyes on purpose, or was it unconscious after he blacked-out.

As I watched, Brian's eyes rolled down for a moment, then they flipped upward again, leaving only the white. I wanted to see how far Brian's eyes had rotated, so I pulled at one of the eyelids.

Brian's body jumped. His eyes rolled down and he shoved me aside. I had woken him from an internal dream. "Nice guy. He is so interesting to talk to. He makes you feel so good," he mumbled in a daze.

"Who are you talking to," I asked.

"The big guy, red hair, really nice. Makes you feel really good." He blinked awake. "How did I get here? Did I fall?"

No one answered. Everyone just stared. Brian saw his surroundings and panicked. "What's going on? What happened? Am I hurt." He checked his arms and legs, frantically.

"You're okay," I said. "You didn't fall." I waved the teen cowboys forward.

"You were up on the rock," Marty said to Brian. Then he turned to everyone. "We were walking up there and we asked him the name of the space man--if the guy had a name. He said something like Ticci Viracocha, and I just asked him how you spell that name. Then he went walking down here, real funny-like, real stiff, and he sat down and wrote in the dirt with his finger."

"Do you remember walking down here?" I asked Brian.

"No! The last thing I remember was looking out from on top. This is weird. I hope I am not walking around like some zombie, Jim." He seemed to blame me for the problem.

"It's not me doing it, Brian, " I laughed as I snapped a few pictures. "Who is the red-haired guy? I've never seen anything about *a red-haired guy.*"

"That's him," Brian said. "He's the one. I haven't told you everything."

Lightning flashed in the sky. Over our heads, thunder rumbled and gray storm clouds swirled. Brian pushed to his feet. "I've got to work this off, I am just burning up with energy." He bolted past everyone and strode down the slope into the forest.

Robert reined his horse up close to me on the narrow ledge. "Rain's coming in," he said. "We probably should get going."

Disappointed, I shrugged at the cloudy sky. I wanted to search all day, until dusk. Then we all heard a loud crash in the forest. Brian had thrown a big rock and was picking up another good-sized boulder, nearly a foot in diameter, high over his head. He tossed. The stone crashed through the trees snapping timber. Then he took off with long strides.

Running through the timber, Brian's stiff gait didn't look normal. I ran after him pack in hand. "Stay close to him," I shouted at the teens. "Don't let him out of your sight." The adult cowboys rode behind on horseback, but the teens and I ran through the timber upslope from Brian, watching him. With long strides, Brian loped at a fast pace through the timber. He ran upright with both hands close to his sides pointing straight down.

He's running in trance, I thought. Until then, I had believed no one could make large body movements when in a trance. To me, a trance involved paralysis of the large, skeletal muscles.

Brian picked up another huge rock as we caught up to him. He tossed. The stone rumbled down the slope cracking lumber. Then, he raced off again. We followed in a panic. Finally Brian stopped at a moss-covered granite outcropping. With a stick, he scratched away the moss.

The ladies rumbled up on horseback and ordered their sons to stay put. I ran down the slope and joined up with Brian. He seemed normal. "What are you doing?" I asked cautiously.

"Something they want us to see," Brian said. He cleared away all the moss and outlined a carved pattern in the stone. I saw the Greek symbol for infinity centered inside a 10-inch circle.

"Infinity?" I gasped. "Is that what it means?"

Brian's eyes rolled up and the deep voice spoke. "Transmission point. Energy zone. Of the past, of this—NOW."

Right then I felt like an arrow pierced my brain from above going downward. The arrow didn't hurt, but felt solid, about ten inches long and one-quarter inch in diameter. It had to be a signal transmission or energy of some kind. The point had stopped near the back of my neck—on the inside. I had studied neurology and anatomy of the brain. I knew the energy had passed downward through the cortex, through the center of my brain, the limbic system, and stopped in the cerebellum.

I figured it probably hit the thalamus gland or hypothalamus because I immediately felt dry, and thirsty.

Suddenly, I remembered a study in psychology. In a cat, scientists had removed the amygdala, a node in the brain stem, in the center of the brain. Afterwards, the cat acted out dreams. Even when the animal's brain showed deep sleep, emitting delta waves, the creature snarled, scratched and prowled the floor with eyes fixed wide open.

Studies had shown the amygdala located in the brain stem paralyzes the body and prevents gross body movements during sleep thus allowing only tiny movements of the eyes, fingers and toes.

For a person to sleepwalk, or walk in trance, perhaps that part of the brain stem had to be nullified. I had been fascinated by the study. That part of the brain stem regulated alertness.

However, the cerebellum--where I felt the arrow stop--controlled automatic motor movements, coordinating the body. I wondered if the 22 pulses had each targeted different areas in Brian's brain.

Sudden thirst brought me out of the reverie.

"Did you feel that?" I blinked, looking for my canteen.

"Yes," Brian said. "Dry." He stuck out his tongue. I gave him my canteen, and he swallowed deep. "I felt that one, and all the others."

"Did they go *through* your head or stop?"

"Some stopped, some went through--all different ways. All different places."

Maybe the 22 beeps that hit Brian stimulated lobes in the cortex--identifiable areas--like speech, or object recognition. Could some alien intelligence be that accurate?

Brian pranced around too energized to answer questions. "I've got to work off this energy." He hurried away and tossed another big stone.

"You better stop him," shouted Robert from the ridge. "He could hurt himself with rocks that size."

Suddenly, lightning flashed overhead and crackled all around us with a deafening roar. When the thunder stopped, the pitter-patter of a light rain began. "Time to go back," shouted Kay. "Down the mountain," she ordered. My heart fell.

We saddled up and started down the mountain in a light rain. Brian's knees began to hurt about halfway down. So, we changed horses, and re-adjusted the stirrups. But that didn't help him much. He limped badly when we arrived at the pack-station.

Inside the cabin, no one spoke much during a big turkey dinner in front of a roaring, crackling fire. Brian ached with pain. Everyone felt disappointed, and baffled.

Near dusk, the older cowboy volunteered to give us a ride to Twaine Harte-- in a hay wagon. As darkness fell, the old wrangler jump-started a dilapidated truck that squeaked and wobbled, wildly. The truck-bed had been widened somehow and held together by wire. Brian and I climbed onto the bales of hay without farewells. Everyone had gone to bed.

With a lurch, the wobbly wagon started down the canyon in the bright moonlight. Weaving from side to side across the lanes, it clanged with sounds. I was terrified, but Brian wrapped a sleeping bag around his body and calmly fell sound asleep among big bags of oats. I couldn't believe him. I was afraid we would die, any minute. He slept like a baby.

On the way down the steep mountain, the brakes heated and puffed up a foul smelling cloud. The moonlight lit the cloud, which engulfed us all in an eerie blue haze. Brian slept soundly, not even smelling the foul odor, but as we swayed down the road, I sat on the rickety tailgate, prepared to jump for my life.

The Astronomer's Maps

The next afternoon, after explaining everything to Wanda and Mary Beth, the four of us walked on the sidewalks of Sonora, a mountain town and mining capital in the late 1800's--Mother Lode County. We headed for the newspaper. The last two issues of the <u>Sonora Daily Union Democrat</u> included front-page stories on the meteorite. An astronomer from Griffith Observatory in Los Angeles had estimated the impact site of the meteorite to be in a "small area" in western Yosemite near Hetchy-Hetch Reservoir. The first article--with a map-- had been published on August 27.

"He's close to our target," I said showing his first map to Wanda and Brian. "Our target is less than six miles from the reservoir." The second article, on August 30, included a smaller map area. Our location sat smack in the middle of his target.

"Amazing," Wanda breathed. "How did he do it?" The astronomer had triangulated the impact site by interviewing numerous eyewitnesses.

"We saw Brian's writing on the 24th," I said. "Three days before the first article."

"Amazing," Wanda pulled Brian and I up for another victory dance. "Damn amazing. "Mary Beth refused to dance. She needed time alone with Brian. But, he couldn't do much. He couldn't live with her, and he couldn't live alone without female friends. He tried to comfort her, but she pulled away.

"Leave me, alone."

"Okay, I will leave you alone. But I would like to talk."

"You have nothing to say," she said. "You can't come home. So, you don't care about what is happening to me, or the kids."

"I do care. There is nothing I can do, is all. We agreed to cut it off, and we should. Damn it. I knew this wouldn't work out."

Wanda tried to comfort Mary Beth, but she pulled away. "What are we going to do?" Wanda snapped. "Are we going to deal with her, or what? What are we doing?

Brian spoke up. "The question is, are we up here for the meteorite, or just that energy zone? Don't we need to find the meteorite? She and I can work this out later—at home."

Wanda and I agreed. Mary Beth closed off her feelings in a huff.

The First Thank You

The next day, September 7, a Tuolumne County sheriff's deputy dove us all to the Columbia Airport. Brian and I boarded a small plane--a Cessna 172 that

Wanda had arranged. The pilot, Jack Courtney, flew over the target site for us with a professional surveyor on board to interpret the maps. Due to the generosity of Pete at the gas station, we still had enough money for a one-hour flight.

From a thousand feet, Brian and I scanned the ground for any sign of impact. Brain saw a black streak on the ground and pointed. We asked the pilot to circle so I could take pictures.

Just then I heard three soft, electronic beeps behind me *inside* the airplane. Brian slumped back into his seat and moaned with dizziness. Another set of three soft-electronic beeps followed. Brian lurched, then slumped forward with a groan, nearly unconscious. I pushed him upright. "They went right through my head," he mumbled.

"We are right on top of the location," I shouted above the roar of the engine. "Where is the meteorite?"

Brian's eyes rolled up and a deep voice spoke from his lips. I clicked on the tape recorder and shoved a microphone up close to Brian's mouth.

"Where is the meteorite?"

"Given."

"Ticci Viracocha! Where is the meteorite? Can you help us locate the meteorite?" A wind gust jostled the plane and the surveyor turned around to see Brian's eyes rolled back. He nudged the pilot to look.

Brian spoke in a mechanical manner. "Emphasis knowledge, wisdom--given. Amplify. Of this, a ball of fire--given. Of this, Scott given understanding. Knowledge of I, requested. Of this you have complied. Of this you are now one with I. All will come of this. Of this, the knowledge you seek will be given. Emphasis -- free psychic energy. Of this, amplification process via transmission at given latitude and longitude. Amplification--purpose."

The airplane's radio blared with weather information. "Will you turn that down?" I shouted at Jack, the pilot. "He's in a trance."

Stunned, he banked the plane around on a course to the airport. The voice continued as I fought to maintain balance. "Of this, Frazier now one with I. Request complete. Locked. Transferring."

Suddenly, the voice warmed. The presence turned gentle, and flowing. "I asked of mankind, but one--to follow instructions. And of this three times-- refusal. Of this, you are the first of man. Of this, now, much wisdom for man will be given by, and of you, for of this--you have answered my request."

I listened carefully as the plane banked for final approach. This voice was human sounding and spoke in the first person. That was different.

"Of this, free psychic energy transmission point located. Of this, freedom of mind given, Frazier. Of this, you and Scott are united as one. You are now, one with I."

312

The pilot cut power to the engine and the final descent began. "Yolate, yolate, yolate," said the mechanical voice. "Amplify Nous ten transmission."

Now I understood. One voice, one personality functioned like a gatekeeper. It handled the *Open, Closed and Amplify* type of statements. It gave details in little chunks. After a transfer, the other personality flowed smoothly. Calm and dignified, he sounded like a senator, perhaps an orator. Multiple-personality, I figured. So far, the pattern fit—except for the ball of fire in the sky.

"We thank you for your help," I said. "Can you help us pinpoint the location now?"

"Of this, latitude and longitude was brought forth of I. Given. Of this, emphasis has been noted. Scott received *and transmitted* Nous 10. Test complete. Of this, all channels open, all information complete, all knowledge given. Of this will now pass, phase three of ten. Of this, again I say--of mankind, but one has answered the requests of I. Of this, Frazier has been given knowledge, wisdom, freedom of mind. Of this, he is one with I."

The wheels bounced lightly on the runway and the plane floated upward. "Of this, I...THANK...YOUUU." The voice carried heart-felt appreciation.

Just as the wheels touched down on the runway, Brian woke up confused and panicky. When the plane taxied to a stop, the pilot and surveyor opened the doors, and hurried away without a word--leaving us alone.

I pushed Brian upright. "What happened?" Brian asked.

"You freaked them out."

"Me? What the heck is going on, Jim?"

Back at the Twaine Hart Service Station, Pete had completed his work on the car. "I really didn't FIX anything," he said. "This is just a make-shift rigging to get you home. It's the best I can do. You will need to have it fixed in L.A." He charged only a few dollars.

We started back immediately. Brian had already missed one day of work.

Mary Beth

On the road, the car wobbled terribly. Brian stopped in a gas station and a young mechanic suggested two more tires. With the tires, Wanda figured we had just enough money for gas to get home.

While we all waited, Mary Beth sat in the car and Brian clowned around with Wanda. When he asked Mary Beth to come out and play, she flipped a dirty ashtray into his face, making a big mess on the garage floor.

"See, what she does," Brian pleaded to me. "Why did you do that?" Brian shouted at Mary Beth. "I am trying to be nice. "

"You bastard," she steamed. Then Mary Beth flew at him, slapping and kicking. Brian shouted for help as she shoved him up into a huge rack filled with oil supplies and tires. With a loud bang, tires and cans crashed to the ground. "Help me," Brian screamed with his arms up in surrender. "Help me, Jim. She's trying to get me to hit her."

VOLTAR

VOLTAR -- about 8 feet tall, he wears gold bands on wrists, arms and ankles. Most of his people have red or blond hair with high cheekbones and long, refined faces. His nose had a bump or rise in the middle similar to many Mediterranean groups. He fits the description of the "Viracocha people" who lived around Lake Titicaca and built Tiahuanaco—according to legends of the local people. They were called the "Uru" which means "daylight people." According to legend, the Viracocha people wore white turbans, and long white gowns or robes. Some scholars believe they originated in the Sumer-Assyria region due to language and custom similarities.

LONG EARS – In the Incan language, the word for Inca is INGA-RA or LONG-EARS. According to Brian, these giants are cloned workers with a lifespan of 26 years. Voltar and his people could also mask themselves as one of these workers. The form was called their "Cloak of Sorrow." On their first visit to earth, Voltar's people caught a virus that caused a disfiguration like this—before they died. Voltar asked Brian to write the history of his people and how they came to remember and use their Cloak of Sorrow for protection. The skin color, shape of feet, legs and arms is similar to the big statue at Tiahuanaco. Similar figures are represented in cities of the Toltecs and Maya in Central America.

THE GIFT – A WHITE STONE

TAKE THIS AND SHARE THE BEAUTY WITH HE WHO IS WITH YOU.
YOU -- AND HE WHO IS WITH YOU TODAY -- HAVE BEEN GIVEN THE WAY.

--Voltar

Chapter 13

A Gift Given – The White Stone

In the gas station bay, I dodged Mary Beth as she kicked me violently in the thigh. "Do that again, and I'll take you down," I warned. She turned and kicked Brian viciously in his injured knee. He fell to the ground howling in pain. Then she charged me, kicking hard. I dodged her foot, grabbed her leg and lifted. She fell to the ground. I twisted her ankle and sat on her until she calmed. She refused to say a word to anyone—even Wanda.

When the tires were changed, Wanda tried to guide Mary Beth into the backseat. "Let go of me," Mary Beth warned. "Or I'll slap you silly."

"Hit ME and I'll break every bone in your body," Wanda warned. She shook a fistful of white knuckles at Mary Beth. She settled down.

The new tires made no difference and we drove all the way home at 40 miles per hour. When Brian trudged into his apartment in an irritable mood, he found Debra and her son Mark waiting with smiles on their faces. Instead of renting a new apartment, she had decided to move in. A big closet had been converted to a bedroom for her two- year-old boy, complete with dresser and changing table. In the living room, she had used exactly one-half the closet space for her clothes. In the bathroom, she had taken exactly half the shelves in the mirrored cabinet. She figured the apartment would work fine until she could help pay for rent in a nice apartment.

Brian liked her orderly ways as he eyed the sleeping boy. Debra was spunky, organized, outspoken and passionate.

"I couldn't stand being up there with Beth," Brian said. "It was a terrible mistake. It's like I can't be a friend to her. I can't go home. I can't see the kids, but she wants me to be—I don't know. This is terrible for both of us."

Debra pondered for a minute. "Is it over between you and her?"

317

"As far as a man and wife, yes. I just have to go forward. What happened to her, was by her own choosing. She made everything seem terrible and frightening, when it really wasn't. I mean nothing ever really hurt us."

"But, it's over then. Or do you still want to go back to her."

"No, I can't go back. There is no way. Not now."

Debra smiled. She was young. She had time for a fling. "Then, come to me, baby" she rubbed against him, and pulled him down onto the bed.

A few days later, Debra walked up the wooden stairs to the apartment with her two best girlfriends. "I'm in love. Two nights--the poor man hasn't had an hour of sleep."

"What?" giggled Karen. "All night!"

"All night," smiled Debra. "I love it."

"I'd like to meet him," laughed the other girl, Paula, a trim brunette with pink lips. She worked as a model and professional photographer.

"You keep your hands off this one," laughed Debra.

"She didn't the last one," giggled Karen.

"This one is mine!" said Debra firmly. Stocky and conservatively dressed, she seemed out of place between her stylish, sexy girlfriends. "This is not just a hot date," Debra said. "I really love this man. You can look but DO NOT TOUCH!"

They all giggled. They lived the Southern California lifestyle of the 1970's. Each of them had stolen young lovers over the last few years, and they still held grudges. "Right now, we are all even," said Karen. They laughed hysterically.

"Good God!" shouted Debra. "You two are crazy."

For the next few evenings, Debra and her girl friends grilled Brian about his experiences. They sat around on the floor talking and laughing. Brian had purchased a strobe light and in the darkened living room, the small colored lights flashed to the rhythm of Debra's favorite country music records.

Brian answered their questions. Karen wrinkled up her nose. "Do they think we are their pets? I mean are we like dogs to them?"

"There are two groups," Brian said. "The big guys are trying to save us from the other. The grays think they own us--like a rat in their cage."

"Okay, but why should we take your word for it, anyway," Karen challenged. "I mean, I've seen plenty of men in my life, and each of them had a line. I mean—a line a mile long of lies. Now, I admit this is a good one...."

"I just figured it out," blurted Debra.

"What?" Brian and Karen both laughed.

"What I want to know is--if there are other people out there created by God, I just want to know what they are like. That's it. *I want to know what other people*

God created—that's all--because I want to know God. You know, little things—
do they brush their teeth? What are their names? Do they have feelings? Do they
laugh? Do they cry?" Brian cracked a few jokes about bathrooms on the crafts,
and they all giggled hysterically into the late hours.

On September 11th, Debra found a newspaper in the kitchen. Brian must
have brought it home, she figured. Bold black letters had been penned across the
front-page photo of a Chinese man. The letters covered his face.

"Do you know what this is?" Debra asked. She spelled out the letters: V-O-L-
T-A-R. Then she slowly sounded out the name. "VOLTAR?"

Brian listened. "Sounds familiar I wonder if that is his name?" He laid down
ready to sleep.

"Whose name?"

"The big guy, with red hair--the one who talked to me, touched my head,
held my hand. He makes you feel so good. Always says nice things."

"You never said anything about red-hair...."

"Oh, yeah he does have. I was just not supposed to say for some reason."

"What are you talking about? Who is this Chinese guy?"

Brian opened his eyes in a daze. "I don't know, what's it say?"

"Chairman Mao Tse-Tung. Leader of China, Dies."

Brian bolted upright and grabbed the paper. He scanned the photo and the
headlines. "Hmmm. Doesn't look like my guy. I don't know. I know it has
something to do with China—later on. China and America. I don't know. I
remember bits and pieces, but it's so much, so confusing." He drifted off to sleep.

"Voltar!" Debra shouted the name.

Brian jolted awake. "What, what are you doing?"

Debra laughed. "Voltarrrrrr," she said jumping on Brian.

"It is a funny name, but I believe it is him," mumbled Brian as he tried to fall
asleep.

A few days later, Debra's girlfriends offered their approval of Brian in a
coffee shop meeting. "He's not a REAL kook," laughed Karen. "He's really nice."

"He is very, very deep," affirmed Debra.

Paula, a working model, spoke carefully.

"Well, he is light-hearted, and he is very easy to talk to. He entertains people.
I can see why you like him. But, be careful, Debbie. Men ALWAYS turn on you
after they have you. And, I don't know what he might turn into. I say, every man
has an evil twin. What is his?"

"He's better looking than YOUR last two," Karen quipped, at Paula. They all
giggled. "And women have evil twins, too—if you believe that." They all agreed.
"We should know." They eyed each other with suspicion and laughed.

"Brian is a lot nicer than most men I've gone out with," Karen said with compassion. "He's a real man, but really funny. I hope it works out for you Debbie."

"I do too," smiled Paula. They hugged her.

A few days later, requests began, from the Host, to take Brian above 7,000 feet. Debra called me, frantic. "He's going in and out of trances. I don't know how to handle this," she whined. "I'm just a 24 year old girl."

I was pleased. The Host wanted to go another round. Whomever or whatever *he* was. Most of the time, I figured the Host was a multi-personality of Brian's. I just couldn't explain away the meteorite. What is transformation to mind level 10? I wanted to know, so I answered the request.

We headed to Big Bear Lake on the weekend. Riding in the back seat, Brian slipped in and out of trance. He mumbled about the "big man with red hair and blue eyes."

"What about the gray skinned guys with long ears?" challenged Wanda. "Are you changing the story?"

"They are the same," Brian said holding his head in pain. "It is all coming back to me. My memory. I am remembering the missing time."

Somehow Debra's personality, her questions, and her love had triggered his recall. The Woman of Fire had helped him to remember. She could handle the memories without flipping out.

We found a cottage with two bedrooms and Brian sat down with a pencil and paper in hand. Two days later, he emerged from the bedroom with red, teary eyes and a stack of pages. He'd been crying.

"You read," he said. "I can't go through that again." Debra hugged him, kissed and caressed him, lovingly. None of us had every imagined Brian in a state of submission and surrender.

Here are the words.

The Bear Lake Message

September 14, 1976.

My name is Brian Scott. Between March of 1971 and June of 1976, I have been taken aboard a craft not of this world six times--four times on one type of craft and twice on another. Each time I have been aboard, I have been told more about who they are, the people from beyond the stars--and what they want.

At first my own fear made it difficult to understand all I was told. I did not accept all the things that were related to me. Although, by my own curiosity I came to understand that it was not a matter of myself accepting them but rather of their accepting me. And from that acceptance it was then a deeper reality between us came into being.

I was told by them, because of my own inner self, my personal way of reaching out with an open mind but holding back a judgment, until I could truly feel and justify each thing I was told, is why they related to me the purpose and reason behind why they have come here now and from the beginning of our world.

Yes, there is a message: a message of universal wisdom and knowledge, and that is what I wish to share with you and all mankind. Let me begin by saying, I am not here to tell you of some great war or disaster that we must prevent. I am not here to prophesize to you. But rather, to bring the words of the stars and the people who visit them.

We are but one small star in this vast universe of wisdom and understanding. And mankind is yet but a child in the knowledge of Universal Brotherhood. We must first understand ourselves from deep within, each to his own most inner self before we can begin to understand others here on this world and the worlds beyond. And how do we accomplish this? By studying the teaching of Free Psychic Energy, and how to hear and understand the words of the people I met from beyond this world.

Now, let me ask you this. What would you give in return? There is nothing asked by myself nor the people I shared a small part of my life with. Each person--man, woman and child--was given a great gift: life. And during this life how many of you can truly say you have fulfilled your purpose, gathered all the knowledge, answered all the questions and shared this gathering with all mankind?

What I present is a way of life, in which, was related to me, a way we can all come closer together and be part of each other. All that is dreamed of, and conceived of in the mind of man, can and will become reality in the days to come. Therefore the question is, "Why does mankind need to wait for tomorrow, when he can have, today, the deep reality of wisdom through knowledge?"

The story I offer raises questions, today. To understand and see the wisdom of what I present, we must first take a few steps back and reflect on the past, for it was in that time the bond between us and these people of the stars came into being. Through this we are all one, and truly united, one with another. We each were given freedom of mind and choice. But through the thousands of years, we drifted away from that one thing we each once shared. Through the teaching of Free Psychic Energy, we can again become one. The people of the stars make no promises to mankind. They are here to help and guide as we grow in wisdom. They will not interfere in our way of thinking for we must each be willing to open

321

our inner self to the words of the stars and the people who have guided their way through them, to us.

Now, I wish to tell you of myself and how I came to meet these people of the stars. And, how I found the mystery of these visitors to our world, to be not a mystery at all, but a part of myself and of all mankind they wish to bring back to us.

In a small town called Apache Junction, near Phoenix, Arizona, while in the desert, I saw a glow in the sky and the outline of an object that hovered in the distance. It moved toward me and suddenly the object filled the sky above me. Then I felt myself rising up, being lifted off the ground. I was pulled in toward an open doorway and gently placed on the flooring of the craft. As I looked behind me, I could feel the air, cool and dry, rushing by me. I could see the mountains, and the lights of the city far to the west. As I looked ahead again, there standing next to me was Rex Miller, who I had spent many happy days with in Arizona.

In this small, darkened area we stood, waiting and watching, not knowing what would happen to us. Our waiting was not long. From the far side of this dark area, a door suddenly appeared, and standing in the doorway, were four silhouettes, tall against the light that filtered in from behind them. By two's they stepped through the doorway.

My breath was short as I felt the cold sweat drip from my forehead. Within moments they were undressing us. Rex lunged back trying to stop them, then he fell forwards, somehow dazed as he was released after a brief, but in vain, struggle to escape.

At this point, I decided to offer no resistance and I finished undressing myself. We were taken out through the doorway in different directions. I looked over my shoulder to see Rex, rounding a slow curve in this narrow hallway with his two escorts. I looked at the doorway--the only doorway in this circular craft that I knew led to freedom.

Suddenly, we turned to my left and stopped in front of a curved wall with a big symbol. The symbol was an incomplete circle, open at the top slightly and more open at the bottom. Inside, in the center was a triangle shape with a vertical bar.

In the blink of an eye, the wall burst open with no sound, and a bright, white light filled the open doorway. Again, I was led through and we turned left and stopped. Here I was placed against a wall with an ever so slight curve to it. I was then released, but when I tried to move, I found that I could not. I could not get off the wall, nor try to escape. This frightened me, and before I could gather my thoughts, a light came on a few feet in front of me. There was a mist, a fog all about me, but the light seemed to draw me towards it. Although I could still feel the wall, cool against my body, I found it difficult to look away from the light. Then another light came on. I could see that both lights were attached to a rectangular-shaped object. A man standing next to it, moved his hand, and the object began to move, slowly down, and turning.

The next few moments were the most terrifying I have ever experienced. First I felt warm fluid running over my legs. I thought I was bleeding. I felt myself urinate. Strange sensations filled my entire body. When the light moved up to my chest, I felt my heart pounding like it was going to explode. Then a strange thing happened. I felt and saw my heart fly out of my chest.

Before I could understand this, the light moved to eye level and I felt as though my head was being torn apart as my thoughts spun around and around. I could not comprehend all that I saw and felt in my own mind. Then the lights went off, and from the far side of this large room, a man-like creature with thick, rough, gray rough skin approached me. He reached out, tall and awesome in size as he placed his hand on my head.

My mind was suddenly filled with thousands of thoughts, and each nerve ending seemed alive. He spoke to me, in my mind. At first, the words were too fast to understand him. Then he slowed. The first words were, "There will be no pain of this." And, in that moment, all the pain that I felt left my body.

I asked, "What do you want? Who are you?"

With his hands on my head, he replied, "I ask nothing. I am from time beyond all time. In rapport I have found of my world, a part of yours long forgotten.

"Where do you come from," I asked.

He replied, "Come, I will show you." I then felt a rushing of air as he removed his hand from my head. And, then I saw, for a brief moment, our own world from far away in space. I turned away, as all around me was speeding up, until I suddenly found myself standing on a foreign place. I saw jagged peaks and domed shaped objects in the distance. I saw other people, like him, walking all about. All seemed so tranquil and calm. He said a few words I don't remember very well about our world and his world being reflections of each other, as he was a reflection of me. I experienced myself as related to him, somehow, and although I felt this bond of truth, I truly did not understand. Then I felt the rush of air pass me again and I was suddenly standing next to him in the craft. A strange glow of warmth seemed to fill me.

He turned to me and said, "In time, all will be explained. You and your friend will be returned. There is a common bond between us now. The telemetry scan had told us much about you. There is with us, now--one thought. In the days to come, I will meet you again, my brother, and all questions will be answered. From within yourself you will find the true meaning of understanding. Go now, my thoughts are with you. Until the time is again right for us to meet."

James E. Frazier

As I was being led away, I asked, "Who are you?"

He said, "I lift the veil of projection, to myself. I am Voltar." In that moment, I saw him change. He was no longer the hideous thing that had touched me, but a man of great beauty. His hair was long and flowing red. Tall and well muscled, his skin was fair, his eyes blue as the night sky and piercing, yet with a glow of warmth. Again, I felt an overpowering feeling and an understanding that he and I were related, in some way. I nearly cried.

He spoke again. "This is as I am, but for now, you will remember only that as I was. And to mankind, for now, you will relate only this of I."

Then he spoke more slowly and with deeper tone of voice. "Fear not my brother, in time, you will come to know and understand in wisdom, all I will relate to you."

Then I was led away and returned to the ground. This was my first encounter with the people of the stars and the beginning of a greater meaning to life.

To have shared, from within, what was offered by these people was a great opening to inner peace, and the key to the one thing we all seek: truth--truth that is felt and touched.

This is indeed a great thirst that is hard to quench. And for each person to taste their own truth is reality.

All that is offered with truth is also received in this way.

No, it is not a simple thing of a man who visited for a short time with others not of this world and the story of those encounters, but it is the light of understanding that filled my entire being.

Each person, in their own way, will taste the moment of truth in this life, and through this they will be prepared for the days to come, as I was.

The question is, for all of us, how will we know the truth when we hear it? The answer is there within us all. It is part of that long desired fulfillment we each reach for and cannot quite find. It is to each, the light out of the darkness. It is to each, inner peace. And to find this, we must be open to all that is around us. For truth, once felt and touched, brings the burst of joy that consumes us. The secret of this truth is to reach out and touch the heart of the person next to you-- and to exchange the glow of inner peace with them. Then together, to reach out to the world and share this with all.

When we strip away misunderstanding, uncertainty and ignorance, you will be ready to hear the naked reality of truth, and by this, you will have showered in the light of your own soul.

Universal brotherhood is a long road ahead, but a goal that will reward to all the reflective love that we can share within, throughout, and with all."

324

The words seemed very simple—nothing special, at first. Then, Brian insisted we sit in a circle and read them aloud, like sitting around a campfire. Reading aloud magnified the impact on everyone. When we read aloud, slowly, we all felt Brian's feelings, and a new power in the words. At the final sentence, we all hugged and cried with him for he opened his arms to us, and shared his tears. The story became real to us, and Brian became real--to himself.

"You see, it's so simple, you can miss it," Brian mumbled through his tears. "Unless you share it the right way with others. This is just a small taste of what I felt from them," he said. "True Brotherhood. It doesn't matter what age or race, or religion you are," Brian sniffled. "We all need each other. Universal Brotherhood, is what they are about."

That evening, September 14, we raced down the mountain so Brian could speak at Stanton Metaphysical Church to an overflowing crowd. Bob Martino hosted this second public lecture.

Brian read the Bear Lake Message aloud to the audience and then offered to answer questions. Many felt the power of the words and cried. Most sat silent for a while.

Then a shapely young lady spoke up and disrupted the calm. Wearing peroxide-white hair and a seductive black dress, she challenged Brian's experience with Ashtarte. When he characterized the possessions as 'demonic,' she took exception. She proclaimed that Ashtarte was a goddess of love and luck, and that she had brought wealth and prosperity to many people over the last five years.

"Not to us," Brian said.

Brian tried to divert the woman without success. She accosted him, accusing him of distorting the good name of Ashtarte, a goddess of love. Finally, Fay Harris stood up and told the woman to talk about her *'demon-goddess'* afterwards--*with her.* "The people in this room have come to hear Brian," she commanded. "Now sit down, and be quiet."

After the event, the crowd buzzed with excitement. Dozens of people swarmed around Brian to ask him questions and share experiences.

A slender, intellectual man wanted to meet later with Brian. Paul Smith, a Mormon, wanted to investigate Brian's statements about South America. "This jaguar symbol is well known to Mormons," Smith said. The Mormon Church had financed major expeditions into the jungles of Central and South America, he explained, to investigate cities in the Book of Mormon. Maybe the Church would help him meet the request.

Brian talked to the man and many others. He learned about their stories, their philosophies, and religions. He even listened to the Ashtarte worshipper. "I can only tell you my experience," Brian said.

Afterwards, Brian wondered how so many different worldviews could exist in one room filled with such beautiful people. Was Universal Brotherhood possible with so many divergent views?

The next Friday, September 18, we roared back up to Big Bear at the Host's request. In the warm cabin, early on Sunday morning, Brian completed the Bear Lake Message. He added:

There is no greater joy than to give and receive the fulfillment of inner truth: to be choked with emotions that are bursting from within. And, if in that moment, we find the overwhelming need to reach out to others, then we can truly say we are a universe within each other.

There, my friends, is the essence of Universal Brotherhood. And I am proud to have shared the moment of my own truth, with these people from beyond our world. And I indeed look forward to being with them again, in this life, or the greater life to come.

For now, I stand open to what lies before me with the knowledge that I AM. And, in knowing this, I have answered the purpose of my being: being a part of you, that is with you today.

I thank you my friends, for you.

The writing didn't carry any great proof or revelation about UFO's, but the process impacted Brian deeply. The act of writing the story started a whole new phase of events. Brian, a high school-drop out, had actually completed his first major manuscript, and he felt good.

Later in the morning, Brian wanted to be alone. He walked in the forest following an inspiration. After about an hour, he heard a voice call his name. Who would be up here, he wondered? How could anyone know where he was?

As he neared a rocky pillar, he heard a rustle. "Come of I," a soft voice said. Brian figured that a gray giant with long ears waited behind the rocks.

He found an opening and peered inside the small amphitheatre with thirty-foot walls of stone. But instead of the long-ears, a tall, red-haired man waited with a big smile on his boyish face. "It is I, Voltar."

Brian couldn't believe his eyes. A man stood there nearly eight feet tall, rippling with muscles. "I have come in peace, and in love for you, and for all mankind. Come forward, for these are the days of truth, and much must be made known to man, by you, of I."

Voltar wore a short tunic, gold bracelets and a headband. His long red hair hung down to his broad, muscular shoulders.

326

Small wings of gold radiated from the bands around his ankles, wrists and upper arms. Black straps wrapped around his neck and slipped down his side to his burgundy and purple tunic. Around his waist he wore a blinking belt of lights, just like the Host's.

He was so big and yet so boyish and childlike that Brian couldn't stop looking at him. He stood with a posture of dignity, like a great leader, a senator or an ancient orator, yet he smiled like a little boy.

He wore no shoes, not even sandals. "Holy ground," Brian heard the thoughts in his mind. He quickly removed his shoes and socks. Voltar's face brightened. The giant seemed very excited to see Brian, like he wanted to hug him, but he restrained himself.

"Finally, this day has come," Voltar said, relieved. He waved to the sky and the stone. "A beautiful world. The memory cores have allowed this because you--and he who is with you today--have complied, of your own free will.

"Of this, if you agree, in the days to come you and I shall become as one. I shall speak through you, and as you, to all those around you."

Brian nodded in agreement. Voltar reached forward and placed his huge hands along side of Brian's head.

Brian's mind filled. He suddenly saw images of South American temples, heard flute music and saw dancers.

Then he again saw a modern day pyramid of glass and steel under construction and nearing completion. He saw a satellite in space near the moon transmitting a signal down to earth at an island in a huge lake. The signal reflected off a huge golden sun disk engraved with images he didn't understand.

When Voltar removed his hands, the images stopped. "Strength is given, of this," Voltar said. "You have persevered, my brother," he chuckled and smiled at Brian like an old friend.

Brian laughed. "It's been rough."

Voltar smiled with agreement like a locker-room buddy saying, *You can do it. You're strong.*

Brian laughed. "I didn't know all that this would involve."

"Of this, you will bring much to mankind: to your people and to *mine.* The council sends you greetings and offers you a position of honor should Tiahuanaco become a reality. You will speak for earth before the Council. Of this, the highest honor, we may bestow upon those of another world. No other man has gone this far in thousands of years."

Brian thought of his past. He could never be famous. "Fear not the mind of mankind--your past is of us, so that you would discover the world of man."

He thought of the future. Voltar replied. "Even now, your tests are not complete. If you endure and if you prevail, you, truly, shall be a light to your

327

people, and your people shall become a light to the world, and your world a light to the universe—of you."

Brian felt embarrassed by the praise. "I don't know if I can do anymore. There is so much I don't understand. I need... "

Voltar interrupted. "Energy is given. My thoughts are with you. Phase two begins in Danyael's *Play of Life*. Of this--now is *now."* Voltar smiled. Brian didn't understand.

"You and those around you must gain understanding and wisdom. You must find your brothers--Helios and Lunan. Of them, and their sharing of knowledge, Tiahuanaco shall be a reality for you, and for your people, and those of the *land of freedom*: Bolivia, Peru. For to the people of the past, Viracocha shall return. And of this, a promise shall be fulfilled of the sun and of the earth, and of the Creator.

"*Nous Laos Hikano*, my brother. "Look to the East has come--a new beginning for man. Of you, each man shall be prepared for the days to come, to survive the transition. Fear not. The knowledge you need is within the people, and within your brothers. Find them, and share in your brotherhood, as all must learn to do. For you each hold the answer for another. The wisdom needed by one is known to another.

"Fear not--for of you, and I, and of Viracocha, nourishment shall be given to man, by that of free will. Of this—survival. Of this, all will be made known to man. The Secondary World will not hold man to this world, nor draw the seed of man for their own use, nor implant the womb, nor shall they suppress man's mind, nor possess his soul. Of this, Brian--of you--all mankind shall truly be free.

"As foretold to man, one thousand years of freedom and peace for man shall come upon the earth, in full understanding of the Secondary World, and man's being, and the Creator."

Brian felt every word to the depth of his being.

For a moment, Voltar said nothing as Brian drank deep from the words. Brian loved listening to Voltar's voice, but when the words stopped coming, Brian lost much of the understanding. He could only remember bits and pieces, for only a little fit his framework for understanding.

Voltar seemed to know. With a smile of encouragement, the kingly giant opened his hand to Brian and revealed a white rock. "Sit down, and write," he said.

Brian had carried a pencil and pad with him for some reason. He sat down on a large stone and prepared to write. Voltar spoke.

"Of this, the time is now. I am with you, and of this, as you have been guided, say to all mankind, in this is truth, of I. You may now speak of I, as I truly am. You, and he--who is with you today--have been given the way. You must take of this today, and give to all. There is much to come of I. Let this be the beginning. For now, my brother of a time past, and you are one, in the bond of wisdom."

Brian glanced up, "Jim?"

Voltar nodded and continued in a friendlier tone. "As you are one with I, and a reflection of I, he is one with Danyael, director of our *Play of Life*, and of this-- the coming of the children." Brian didn't understand. Voltar gestured for him to write and spoke again in a formal tone.

"Fear not the mind of mankind for that given today, will be with you in all time to come." Then Voltar gestured for Brian to rise and stand before him.

Voltar held up the white rock. "From the earth, and by the earth, man is given knowledge of Nous two through ten.

"Of Nous four, all that is about you brings wisdom and understanding--and strength. Of this, quantum displacement shall be a reality, upon the land, for you and for all.

"You need to find your brothers in wisdom and share with them all that you have been given. Then, you will need no more. With sustenance and knowledge of your own being, you will prevail."

Voltar held out his right hand. "Take, of this." Brian reached out both hands. Voltar placed a large, white, crystalline rock into Brian's hands. From the rock, a subtle white glow radiated outward.

"Now is now," said Voltar. "Share this gift with all. Let the beauty of this stone reflect within you, and he who is with you today. Of this, will come to all, a new wisdom and new understanding of the mind of man."

For a moment, Brian studied the heavy white rock. The glow seemed to move up his hands, arms and into his mind. He felt peace, and love.

"Now is now," said Brian feeling a new energy in his mind.

Voltar smiled with understanding. He lifted his arms upward, closed his eyes and bowed his head in prayer. Brian followed along, thanking God for his life.

After a few moments, they both looked up with a great love in their hearts for each other. Voltar spoke like a father addressing his son.

"Farewell, for now, Brian. Until we meet again." Voltar encouraged Brian onward with a 'you can do it' nod. Then he pushed a button on his blinking belt of lights, and disappeared. Brian felt suddenly alone, but Voltar's voice whispered softly in his mind. "All has been given--the anchor--the white stone. The time is now. Now is now. Open--Phase two."

A few days later, as Brian sat at his drafting table at work, a small water drop fell out of the air, and plopped onto Brian's cheek. He thought the ceiling must have leaked. But he felt dazed, and saw vivid images of South America.

By the end of the day, three more water drops had fallen on his head--in the elevator, in the hallway and in the bathroom. He decided not to say anything to Debra because his mind spun out of control for a few moments after each drop. On one of them, he lost balance and nearly fell down.

The water drops scared Brian because they were very physical. They weren't drawings, or something he created. They fell on him. They interrupted his thoughts, spun his mind into the future, or the past. With each drop, he saw a different reality. His location seemed to change, the people changed, and all felt so real. Then gradually he recovered, merging back into the NOW of where he had been.

At first, he didn't like the rapid change. He stumbled, fell down—felt dizzy. But gradually, he learned, and retained his balance, saying, "Now is now."

He was glad that his memory had been restored—at least most of the missing time. But whenever he asked Voltar for more answers, all he heard in his mind was, "Phase 2—open."

"They aren't telling me nothing—again," he told Debra. "But it's getting interesting. This is even fun."

The Dark Side was over. Brian had survived and prospered, while learning about the mind of man, and himself.

However, Phase 2--the Light Side--offered new and greater challenges.

The Probe

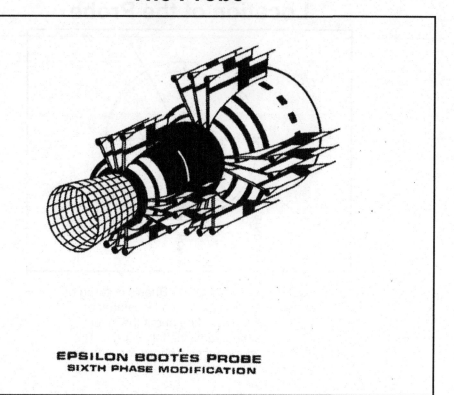

EPSILON BOOTES PROBE
SIXTH PHASE MODIFICATION

PROBE – transmits and receives. Supposedly, the probe can monitor an individual's biological energy field and send various types of signals to a person's body or brain. Controlled by "the gray aliens" from Epsilon Bootees, but built jointly with Voltar's people, the probe has been in operation over 12,000 years.

Location of the Probe

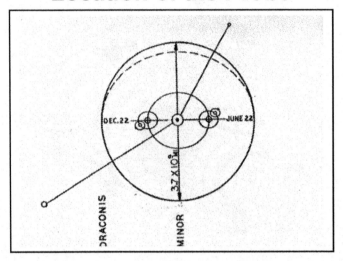

LOCATION OF PROBE –Brian's drawing of our solar system existed in December of 1975, but no one asked about the object behind the moon until the fall of 1976. The discovery started a new phase focused on – the probe.

Probe - Final Descent

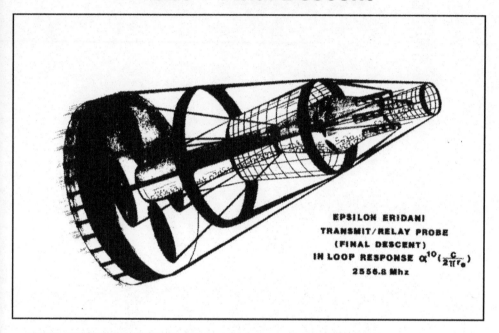

FINAL DESCENT PROBE – This probe was supposedly built by Voltar's people to conduct all procedures for their tenth and final descent from 1971-2011. Brian is the test and trigger for the descent—which involves the uplifting of people in North America, South America, and other regions of the world--a grand finale to their efforts over 12,000 years. Descent points include: Giza in Egypt, Stonehenge in England, Qumran In Israel, Tiahuanaco, China and Sedona, Arizona. (They described Stonehenge as their *third* descent in 1866 B.C.)

IT'S BEEN THERE FOREVER--

TWELVE-THOUSAND YEARS, AT LEAST.
MONITORING MAN, RECORDING, GATHERING KNOWLEDGE--
IT IS THE LINK BETWEEN US AND THEM.
IT SENDS AND IT RECEIVES.

--Brian Scott

Chapter 14

The Mystery Resolved – The Probe Discovered

On the same day the water drops began falling on Brian–September 22–Mary Beth was sworn in under oath at a formal deposition in Santa Ana. She had injured her back at work and was called before the Workers' Compensation Appeals Board, case number: 76 ANA 64949 in Santa Ana, California.

Attorneys for the defendants--and her employer--grilled Mary Beth about the claim. She had injured her back several times in the last two years lifting power supplies, cables and spools of copper wire.

After establishing the most recent injury, the defending attorney attempted to discredit her claim. "We have medical records showing that you had some problem on the 13th of February and then an attack on February 22, 1976--and you were admitted to Fountain Valley Hospital. Is that correct?"

Mary Beth explained that she had suffered an attack at home on the 13th of February. "I went to pieces and passed out on the floor," she said.

The defense attorney attacked. "You discussed some events since November of 1975 involving UFO's and a man called the Host, a man who talks via telepathy. Do you recall any sort of comment like that to the doctor?"

She answered, yes.

"Did you have any sort of symptoms before this attack on February 13, 1976 that you relate to a nervous problem?"

"I'm not sure I understand."

"What happened in November of 1975."

"It is very involved."

"Go ahead, tell me."

Mary Beth's attorney stood up. "You should realize that this stays within-- this is confidential. It doesn't get broadcast to the world or anything like that."

335

The defense attorney agreed, and asked her to continue, so Mary Beth told the story of the Ball of Light Phenomenon in this legal deposition. "Lights were in the yard and the house. My husband would fall off into trances and speak in another language, in an inhuman voice that was not his. My kids would disappear from their beds. We'd find them out in the yard. We would find drawings and writings in the middle of the night. There would be strange sounds. My husband had disappeared for 27 hours. That is about all of it. It went on over a period of months, all of this."

"From November until February?"

"Yes."

"You indicated you saw some sort of a ball of light in your yard?"

"Yes." She explained that it happened for several weeks, and would come and go.

"What else did you see?"

"I saw a creature, if you want to call it that, about eight or nine feet tall, and a man that we called the Host. He's about four foot, a small man. He wore a medallion and silvery shiny outfit. He was bald in front and had hair in the back. We also saw white streaks of light and orange-red streaks of light."

"How often did you see this creature who you say is eight or nine feet tall?"

"I really don't know how many times it was."

"Did you have contact with him?"

"Yes."

"What sort of contact?"

"It is very embarrassing to say."

"Can you say for the record?"

"It bothers me to talk about it."

Mary Beth's attorney stepped forward, "Does it have to do with sexual contact?"

"It was an attack on me. Yes," Mary Beth sniffled, embarrassed. She dabbed her eyes. The room hushed. She seemed small and alone in the sterile setting of the deposition room.

Finally, the defense attorney spoke. "The creature attacked you?"

"Yes."

"Was it a sexual attack?"

"There wasn't any intercourse, but in a sexual manner, with his hands, he molested my body."

"How many times did this happen?

"Just once."

"Can you describe him?"

"He is eight to nine feet tall. He has very scaly skin. He is hairy--no more than a normal man. His skin tone is gray."

336

"Did anyone else see him?"

"On one occasion my daughter saw him. My husband has seen him, but not in my presence. He has seen him off by his self."

"What sort of contact did you have with this man you called the Host?"

"He just spoke to me."

"How many times?"

"I really can't say how many times it was. It happened on and off. It wasn't regular conversation. He spoke weird. He would speak like, *'I am the host of I. I speak, walk, run,'* stuff like that. It didn't make sense to me."

The 90 minute long deposition continued on probing into psychiatric reports, her hospital records for February of 1975, Brian's drawings, and their separation in May of 1975.

In the hallway, after the deposition, Mary Beth's attorney offered her a soda and apologized. "I didn't think this would happen. He got the doctor's reports. He was fishing for anything to negate your claim. Unfortunately, he found a lot of material. I'm sorry." He figured the claim would be denied.

"I can't help it," Mary Beth groaned. "I am not going to lie," she said. "It happened--I will tell the truth no matter what."

To her great surprise, despite her testimony, she was awarded the compensation due to real injuries recorded at work over the years.

September 25th was the beginning of the Hebrew New Year--Rosh Hashanah of the year 5737. The formal Days of Awe had ended, and shofars--the Hebrew trumpets of ram's horns—were blown in temples and synagogues, calling the *people of the covenant* to repentance, atonement and judgment.

On that day, the Hebrew New Year, ten water drops splashed onto Brian's head and shoulders, often causing him to lose his balance and stumble a bit. They hit him in different cars, and in several different buildings. "It is definitely not falling from the ceilings," said Debra with concern.

"It must be a seagull," Brain laughed. "It is following me around and taking a leak on me."

"No bird could do that," said Debra seriously. "This is not funny Brian." She had seen several of the drops land directly on his face causing him to be stunned.

"It's the nasal drip of Viracocha," Brian laughed after several drops fell on him in a pizza parlor. Wanda, Bob Martino and I had agreed to meet with Brian and plan the next phase of lectures.

There, I saw the drops for the first time and tasted them. Everyone waited. "Tastes like cheap aftershave lotion." They all laughed.

"I think they come when ever he swears or says something stupid," said Debra seriously.

"That's not true," laughed Brian. "Or they'd be dumping on my head in bucket loads." Right then, in front of everyone's eyes, five big water drops in rapid succession plopped onto Brian's face and shoulders. I could easily see them hit and splash.

"Wheeeeeee," he said leaning over to one side and gripping the table. "Whoaaaaa. Everything is going around, and around...spinninggg" He closed his eyes and gulped. For a moment, his countenance changed to a deep, and serious gaze. His posture stiffed and he appeared a bit dignified. Then suddenly Brian's silliness returned. "That was just like an "E" ride at Disneyland--whoooooah. I don't know what is happening, but this has never happened before."

After Brian calmed down, Martino handed Debra a piece of paper. As a UFO investigator, he had drafted his formal statement regarding Brian's experiences. He wanted her to see what had happened before she met Brian.

Debra read his statement aloud.

The following items support the validity of this case:

1. The testimony is very consistent from all the individuals involved. All the witnesses sound sincere and clearly show the signs of stress.

2. There are many witnesses:

1971 "UFO Encounter" - Brian and some corroboration from a friend who may have been involved also."

1973 "UFO Encounter" - Brian and a teenage girl.

1975 "Ball of Light Phenomena" - Brian and seven other witnesses.

1975 "Strange Trance and Voice" - Thirty witnesses.

3. This is a highly detailed account. A fabricated story is usually very sketchy in details. Since there is so much detail in these accounts it would require extensive rehearsing by the accomplices."

4. The questioning of Brian while under hypnosis gives strong support to his story. Many hours of hypnosis work was done by Long Beach State and UCLA researchers.

5. Analysis of the "Strange Voice" by voice experts makes it appear that this voice is alien and may be impossible to be duplicated by humans. The information received from this voice is highly technical and is surely far beyond the capability of Brian Scott!

6. During the 1975 "Ball of Light Phenomenon," magnetic recorders were installed at Brian's home. The recorders ran six days continuously. Brian was told that these recorders would not record their voices. Their voices were recorded and the tapes I have examined indicate that there was something very unusual happening and there was no indication of a hoax.

7. The Brian Scott case is very consistent with other abduction cases. Brian has continuously described aliens, equipment aboard UFO's, and messages given by these aliens months before they were reported by the news media.

8. Brain's wife was hospitalized with a nervous-breakdown supposedly as a result of this phenomenon and another witness had some ulcers removed. Two of the children have been hospitalized.

I feel strongly that this case is valid and that these people urgently need some help.

That night Debra worried a lot about what might happen to her, since Mary Beth had not asked for any contact with aliens. She had only wanted a normal life, and look what happened. For the first time, Debra's fears became overwhelming.

Brian asked Voltar to do something, and Debra lost two hours of time--right in their apartment. Afterwards, Brian told her that she had been married to Voltar. In the ceremony, Voltar had held a rock against her stomach. Debra felt even more frightened. "It's starting," she cried. "It's starting with me."

"But with you it will be good," Brian promised. "Voltar loves you. You are not out there trying to get attention—and you're not so jealous that nothing can happen. In fact, for me, you make all of this fun. A lot of fun."

She loved Brian and trusted him. She knew that she had lost time, but remembered nothing. "Don't make something up," she told Brian. "Don't ever try to fake me with something."

He said she would understand soon. Because of the water drops, and the dazes that resulted, Brian had begun to speak with knowledge about other places, about the future, and the past.

Debra and I, and Wanda often listened to him and figured he was just 'making it up.' We all prepared ourselves to resist any personal manipulation and I counseled Debra to be strong, and to keep the Bible open at all times.

I hung onto my theory of Brian being an entertaining fellow with multiple-personality, but the ball of fire in the sky, and the water drops didn't fit the pattern. Both seemed paranormal, beyond human ability. According to Brian, both were also in the *Play of Life*, which he mumbled about often after a water drop. The *Play of Life* was now well underway, supposedly, because I had met three requests.

I was no longer just an observer--a journalist. I had played an active role by meeting the requests, and that caused events to unfold quickly. I didn't accept it all as truth. "We are being drawn into his world," I warned Wanda and Debra. "He's not overtly persuading us, but he lives the story so completely, we have to go along, just to be with him." We agreed to all be careful and strong for each other. We promised to not do anything, or go anywhere special without checking with each other.

Discovery of the Probe

Brian didn't know what to do with the white rock, so he left it with me. Mostly it sat on a shelf, on display, but one day Wanda and I took turns holding it for a while, and we meditated. That night she woke up from a dream, rambling. We were all in a World War II bomber, a B-29, flying. We were lost. She overlaid the maps and bingo—they showed the way.

"Overlay the drawings," she mumbled upon waking. "Overlay the drawings. Now."

I hurried to my den. She was right. Brian's ten Gate of the Sun drawings all seemed to overlay with some similarity—nothing too exciting. Then, I found my drawing of Photonic Matter. I laid it over the first Gate of the Sun drawing and gasped with amazement. All the major details matched up exactly. Line after line, angle upon angle, point upon point all matched precisely when the correct center points aligned.

Stunned, I tried the tenth drawing. Again, they matched. Page after page, detail upon detail, all seemed to have some alignment point to the center of the Photonic Matter drawing. From the calendars, to Stonehenge, to the list of planets and stars, they all aligned in some spectacular way.

Amazing, but what did it mean? Brian must have used it as a template, but why? So what? Did everything in his bizarre world relate to Photonic Matter? By name, it was obviously a physical form of light--like sunlight or lightning. Perhaps it was lightning.

But the Photonic Matter drawing included a magnetic north, a positive and negative charge, and rays emanating out from the center within three rings. It apparently belonged on the ground, on the earth. Magnetic north would have little meaning in space.

As I studied the drawings, one little black dot kept catching my eye. To establish Lunar positions at the solstices, Brian had drawn the sun, moon, and two outer planets. I had looked at the drawing a dozen times, but this time I stopped to think. There was the sun, earth, moon and little black dot— sun, earth, moon and--a little black dot.

What the heck is the little black dot? The orbital's position was different for June and December. I checked another similar drawing on a different page. The dot appeared there too. No one had noticed the object. Of course, the drawings were so detailed and unfamiliar, most people became lost in their own area of analysis. Brian had always said the writings were notes to him--not to everyone else--so many people ignored details.

But when I showed Brian the drawing, he took a deep breath. "You found it!" he shrugged, with a sense of sadness.

"You're not happy?" I asked. "What is it?"

Fifty people must have looked at those drawings and never seen it," Brian said.

"What is it? asked Debra. Brian said nothing.

"It means something is in orbit around our moon," I said. "Something not put there by man."

"Brian? What is it?" Debra asked.

"It's the end," Brian said. "The beginning. A new world for man." We were baffled. Brian turned away--suddenly quiet.

I remembered several drawings showing a source of signals to Brian from somewhere in space—a transmission point. The drawings showed lines for thought transmission, alpha waves, and electronic signals. They included descent points and phrases like *atmospheric absorption*. One detailed artwork showed a signal drop from Nous 10 to Nous 4--due to atmospheric absorption. Brian had never explained any of the drawings, to anyone. He always seemed more concerned that he had somehow done them while blacked out. No one believed that was possible. So no one shared his concern.

"This is incredible," said Debra. "Did you know about this?"

"I know a little bit about their probe," said Brian finally. "I have no idea if this part is for real. I really didn't pay any attention, but it is related to South America and the transformation, somehow."

"But you don't know?" Debra challenged.

"I didn't think we would get this far."

Wanda chided Brian, "You don't seem happy. Are you feeling squeamish?"

"I guess so. For the first time, I have the remotest thought, or hope, that this might actually happen."

"What is this probe," I asked. "You said '*the end, the beginning.*' What do you mean?"

"I don't know if I'm supposed to talk about it. Better ask them," he said. "And they aren't talking much. They aren't telling me anything, anymore."

I took a deep breath. "So, it's their probe in orbit around our moon?"

"It's been there forever," Brian said. "Twelve-thousand years, at least. Monitoring man, recording, gathering knowledge. It is the link between us and them. It sends and it receives. It is filled with the true knowledge of man, the earth and all the civilizations on our world for 12,000 years.

"The probe is very important to them. It protects them from us, and it protect us from…them. It is the end of the mystery. Someday, we will have it--we will have access to it, and no mystery will remain. There will be no more UFO's."

Brian again, breathed deep. "If this comes out, it will be a new beginning." Brian seemed scared. "This will mean the end of our ignorance, the truths would be known."

"Why so sad?" asked Wanda.

"It means I will go bye-bye and never return," he said. "It means the transformation will happen." We didn't understand, but for the first time, we had seen Brian sad about reaching his goal—the transformation. We wondered if he could say no.

The Man Who Would Know

A few days later, on Saturday October 2, Brian spoke to a small group at the Anderson Research Foundation in Los Angeles, a center for metaphysical speakers.

Wanda and I provided two-dozen booklets of Brian's writings and drawings for people to review. Technical people had gathered, mostly engineers and scientific types, because the logic in the writings was to be analyzed. The event had been advertised in the foundation's flyer and we didn't know most of the people in the audience.

A big, round-faced man with a black beard and glasses sat down with a lady friend. Looking like a professor of mathematics, he carried a calculator and a bulging brief case.

As I described the drawings, the round-faced man gasped. He flipped through the pages, and began running calculations with excitement.

The more I talked about the science of QUANTUM DISPLACEMENT PHYSICS and the philosophy of ORBITAL REALITY, as presented in the materials, the more he huffed and puffed with excitement.

Brian nodded at me and we both remembered a description in the writings of the *"One who would know:"* black beard, round face, glasses. It fit. So I read the page:

> **Of the Host, fear not the mind of mankind. Gate of the Sun is key to knowledge. Of I, say to him of beard, of roundish face, of glasses: there is no greater challenge to thinking people than the integration of orbital reality into the life on the known earth. LOCKED.**

> **OPEN. Of this is knowledge. Let man show his part of this request of I. Bring forth a process of learning given of this truth of I via medium of Gate of Sun (Brian). Start of this. Knowledge is of this: touch the mark (on the Gate of the Sun). Of this is given Nous one of ten, of I. Of Secondary World past, ninth descent, 110 B.C. Key alignment, Helios-Selene...."**

The bearded man started to speak but tears welled up in his eyes. "I've never seen anything like this...this is, like a mirror of my own...work." The man cried softly for a moment, and everyone felt the depth of his heart.

After the man dabbed his tears away and regained composure, he explained that the material answered key questions that he had been seeking for years in his own work. "In just a few moments, I have solved years of questioning," he said. "I don't know what to say. I have never seen anything like this."

"Well, you fit the description of the man who would know," I said.

His voice choked with tears. "I...I can only say that I know...what it means. My name is Michael Helios, I just happen to be in Los Angeles for a meeting. I live in Florida. My life work has been what I would agree could be described as *'orbital reality.'* I never thought of it with that term, but that is what it is: *orbital reality.* That is my science, the science I have been developing." He held up Brian's book. "This has my answers...." He heaved with emotion.

Brian clenched his fist in victory. "That's him."

Michael stood up and walked towards Brian with wide open arms. Brian rushed to meet him. In front of the group, they hugged. "Greeting, my brother," Michael said. Everyone cried as the two men hugged.

343

James E. Frazier

Yom Kippur – Day of Judgment

On Monday in West Hollywood, thousands of Jews stayed off the freeways, and walked to their synagogues and temples for Yom Kippur, the most Holy Day of the Year in the Hebrew calendar: the Day of Atonement with God--a day of judgment.

Brian and I drove down the street slowly, watching hundreds of men with long beards and black hats. Laughing and talking with their wives and children, the men walked along with smiles on their faces.

"I didn't know there were so many Jews in Los Angeles," I said. A drop of water splashed onto Brian's face. His eyes rolled back and a deep, authoritative voice spoke, "The people of The Book--the law. Voltar's people."

Then Brian returned. "Wow....wow. What was that? Geez. Man I am getting dizzy again. Did somebody say something or what? What happened, Jim?"

I was concerned. "A voice just spoke and said the Jews were 'Voltar's people.' It was a very, very deep voice. Not the usual one. But how can that be? What are they talking about?"

"I don't know," laughed Brian. "And I don't want to know. That was too much for me. It's too much to handle driving down the road. Good lord, Jim. I can't be doing this while I am driving a car."

"I didn't say anything, Brian. I didn't cause that."

Brian apologized. "I heard him say this was 'of you, of Jim.' I don't know what's happening," Brian said. "I just get bits and pieces of what is going on, anymore. And, he's not answering my questions. He's not telling me nothing."

Later that week, Brian and I met Bob Martino outside the Anaheim Convention Center. He had arranged for us all to attend a session on the Search for Extra-Terrestrial Intelligence (SETI) at a world gathering of the International Astronautics Federation. Scientists from around the globe were attending.

An urbane, polished man from NASA's Ames Research Center opened the meeting. Dr. Paul Bellingham wore a sleek, blue business suit as he talked about NASA's interests. He then introduced a presentation on signals transmitted into space. Several hundred scientists listened as facts and formulas were projected on a screen.

As we sat in the huge room, I was shocked to see the same formulas that had appeared in Brian's writings regarding 'atmospheric absorption'. Radio signals sent into space were impacted by atmospheric absorption.

Several water drops plopped onto Brian's face, and he wobbled with dizziness. Voltar's deep voice spoke: "Ask this of man: *why will they not reply?*" Voltar explained that signals had been sent, but no reply had been received.

"Ask now." Brian said. "He is saying to ask them, now."

"Me? Why me?" I whispered. "Why doesn't he?"

"I'm not asking them," said Brian, embarrassed.

A man several rows away turned around. "Would you mind being quiet?"

Brian whispered. "He says this is *of you.* To ask this question. It is *of YOU.*"

"I am not going to ask that question in front of this audience. They would throw us out." The room was now overflowing with scientists from around the world--all interested in radio communications from space.

"It's up to you, Jim. But Voltar says it will be all right."

For the first time, I felt personal pressure. I was being drawn in too far. "No, it won't be all right," I whispered. "That is the director of NASA's Ames Research." If I had accepted my NASA fellowship in psychobiology, I would probably have been working for him, at Ames. "Someday, I may want to work at Ames," I said.

Voltar spoke softly. "Of this, is now."

I wanted to call Wanda and Debra for a reality check. This is what we were worried about—personal involvement.

"Now is now," said Voltar with a nod of support like a friend encouraging another friend. "This is of you."

I stood up just as Dr. Bellingham agreed to take questions from the audience. To my surprise he pointed at me.

"Yes sir."

I heaved with emotion. My mind blanked and I felt all eyes in the room turn towards me. I didn't even belong in the room—that was the only thought in my mind.

"Did you have a question?"

Hot beads of sweat formed on my forehead. I blurted out the best I could. "What would happen if a signal was received...from space?"

Laughter rippled around the room. Bellingham dismissed my question. "We'd all be very excited," he laughed.

I sat down, steaming with embarrassment. I had satisfied the request. Fine. It was over. "Why will man not reply?" Voltar said softly. "Will man not reply to signals we have sent? Of this, now!"

Pressure. There it was. He was pressuring me to do something I did not want to do. But, then I had been trained as a journalist. The question did hold some journalistic merit. When the laughter died down I stood up again. "My question was intended to be serious," I said. "What is the procedure that would be followed, if a signal were received?"

Bellingham smiled. "Well, we have procedures for everything at NASA you know. But not for that one," again the audience laughed.

I sat down, satisfied. "Why will man not reply?" Voltar insisted.

I moaned. "No...I've done it. No more." People in the seats around us watched with interest. Bob Martino tried to sink into his chair.

When Bellingham called for one final question, I stood up. I had nothing to lose. I might as well take it to the max, just once. But Bellingham ignored me and prepared to adjourn the meeting. I raised my voice.

"I've asked the question twice, and haven't really received an answer. You have a federal program here, costing millions of dollars, financed by taxpayers. The purpose is to receive signals from space--signals from an intelligent civilization. That is your goal isn't it?"

Bellingham's expression turned serious. "Yes--it is our goal."

"But you are telling us, that our government, in all of its wisdom has never determined any procedures to be followed, in the event a signal is received? That sounds a little, out-of-line, even preposterous, given all the money that is being spent to achieve that same goal. At the very least, it sounds like poor planning. What if the goal is reached? Are there no procedures at all established for you to follow, in the event that an intelligent signal is received? Do you call the President? Notify the press? Who do you call if a signal is received?"

Bellingham's gaze narrowed and his face reddened. Then suddenly a member of the British Interplanetary Society, an astronomer from England, stood up across the room and addressed the group in a loud voice.

"That is a very good question. It strikes at the very heart of the matter. And I believe we need to know if any procedures are established or not. I feel we need an answer to that question one way or another." I breathed a sigh of relief.

Instantly, the crowd hummed with excitement. Bellingham removed his glasses in frustration. After a moment of consultation with an aide, he gestured at a man in the front row. "I believe this question should be answered by someone else."

A dark-haired man in a sport shirt and glasses stood up. He nervously turned to look across the crowd. He searched for me and our eyes met. "The official policy is to not respond." He sat down, abruptly.

The room hushed. No one said a word. I felt a nudge within my heart, so I stood up again.

"Could I have one more question, sir?" I shouted across the silent room. The atmosphere felt tense, like a flaming arrow had been shot over the walls of a fort.

Bellingham glared and started to adjourn. "*Why not*--is my question," I blurted out without his approval. "Why would we *not reply?*"

Again the crowd of 500 buzzed with excitement.

Bellingham gestured at the man in the front row who again stood up. This time he snapped at me in an angry tone of voice.

"Because that is the official policy!" He was mad.

I was inspired. Voltar had been right. This was a story. Gallons of ink might flow if a newspaper reporter was present. I jumped to my feet as the crowd roared with talk.

"Why is it the official policy?" I shouted. "Who decided that it was the official policy to NOT reply?"

The mystery man leapt to his feet. "It has been decided by the powers that be, that the policy is to NOT REPLY TO ANY SIGNALS RECIEVED FROM SPACE, SHOULD THEY APPEAR INTELLIGENT." He sat down.

The room exploded with boisterous talk. Scientists from around the world hurled questions at the podium, but Bellingham ignored them, closed the meeting and hurried out of the room with his aides.

The engineers and scientists raved with excitement as I sat down next to Brian. "This is incredible."

"I told you he said this was *'of you.'* Voltar and you make a good team. You can't imagine what you two could do together." Oh, no, I thought. There it was again--the invitation to join his insanity, his world. I would resist.

Afterwards in the lobby, Russian and British scientists swarmed me. Several patted me on the back and laughed with glee. "That took a lot of courage, young man," said the British astronomer who had echoed my question. "I had been wondering the same thing."

We talked with Russian and British scientists for nearly an hour. Voltar had been lucky, I thought afterwards. But whomever or whatever Voltar was, his words to me had caused a challenge and created an uproar. That was real. The scientists congratulated me, but it was really him--Voltar. I was starting to sound like Brian. He always said --*"Don't think it is me."* But what could I say to all the scientists. I couldn't explain, so I kept my mouth shut—and accepted their laudatory remarks, humbly. How could I say, "Don't think it was me?"

With that, I knew I had taken a step into accepting Voltar's world as a reality.

The Warning

The next day, Rick Churchwood, the former Air Force pilot we had met before, knocked at the door of my house on Genesee Avenue in Hollywood. "I need to talk to you," he said. "You and Brian and are in deeper than you know. Can I come in?"

Lean and handsome, Churchwood warned me to take matters seriously. "You and Brian are treating this as if it is a joke, a lark. I can tell you it is not," he said. You are being watched, in fact you are surrounded--and some of these guys play rough."

Churchwood had been taken off of TV programs, by men in black suits, and threatened with his life. "They told me I was Air Force, and could NEVER go public with the story—not on TV," he said.

His fighter jet had received a 22 minute message that changed his life. He landed and resigned his position. "I can't tell you all of it, but basically, it was about God. It said that we as a nation had better get right with God, because of things that were coming--big changes. Transitions."

"Well, any preacher in a church can say that."

"Yeah, but it wasn't a preacher. This was from a silver disk, which had been flying at 1800 miles per hour and came to a dead stop and turned upward on one edge. It hung there, in the sky. Without moving, while we circled. Nothing we have can do that."

"Was it a voice?"

"Yes, it was a voice that we all heard. We all heard the same thing. Three pilots and people on the ground."

"What was it like--the voice?"

"Sort of firm, authoritative, jerky. Monotone."

"That's just like Brian."

"Right. Certain agencies take this very seriously. They take you guys seriously. Get my drift?"

"Are we in danger?"

"I think so. It's like this, with me. I can talk to people privately, but if I try to go on TV again, I'll just have an accident or a heart attack," he said. "That's what I was told. It would be such a waste, and loss to my family. *Think of your family.*"

"So you think they were serious?" I asked.

"They told me to remember what happened to Dr. McDonald. He was an astronomer in Arizona that was going to talk. They said it could happen just like him."

"Wow. They admitted murder?"

"Oh yeah. That is what I am here to tell you about. This is serious business and you both are already being watched--and you don't even know it."

"How do you know?"

"I know. You are surrounded by intelligence people and don't even know it."

"Who?"

Churchwood listed off a few names and enough details to convince me. He said the national Security Council was opposed to contactees, but the FBI would help us. A whole gaggle of other agencies were involved trying to find out what was going on.

Churchwood set up a meeting at Walt Disney Studios with Gordon Cooper, the former astronaut. After Brian began talking, Cooper cancelled his meetings at

WED Enterprises where he was supervising design of the EPCOT Center. He was fascinated with Brian's story, and we talked for most of the afternoon. "You guys are not in the 'community,'" warned Cooper. "You will never find out anything."

They both agreed we should 'lay low' until they could put in some words for us to the right people. "Some agencies are for helping contactees, others would like them to go away," Churchwood said. "They will discredit you, first. If they can't discredit you, they might charge you with a crime like sexual abuse or rape—something you can't defend yourself against. Or -- just hand you a heart attack, or an accident. Stay out of small planes. That's their favorite," he warned. "Federal investigators come in, and they just take over as national security. It's all hushed up."

Later, Churchwood introduced us to intelligence officers who supported contactees. We were given methods to see if our phone was tapped. We called two different phone numbers. Then based on the tone we heard, we were tapped, or not—supposedly.

I checked a dozen phones. According to this method, none of them were tapped--except mine. One number supposedly rang at the Pentagon, the other at CIA headquarters.

"They've got their eyes on you," Churchwood said.

"So you believe there are aliens, and they are picking up people like Brian?"

"Absolutely," Churchwood said. "And our government is working with them. They have agreements. There is a trade-off."

Until I talked with Cooper and Churchwood, I'd never seriously considered that Brian's contact had been physical--with *real* aliens. For the first time, I realized how many-faced the phenomenon must be. I was witnessing one facet: post-contact. Churchwood had witnessed a craft. I had seen paranormal phenomenon. He had seen a craft perform like nothing built by man. Cooper knew inside stories from astronauts about the government's dealings with aliens.

Since most UFO investigators volunteered their time, each specialized in their own field, no one comprehended the whole phenomenon—not even Dr. Hynck or Jacques Vallee.

Since I had not observed aliens, I still favored multiple-personalities. I simply held in suspension a list of anomalies: the 22 beeps I heard on the mountain ride, the arrow through my head in Yosemite, the many water splashes I had seen with my own eyes, plus Voltar's lucky words at the astronautics convention, and now, the phone-tapping.

The list was becoming long.

A Code for the Probe

I really did not want the alien angle to be true. I didn't want to investigate aliens or write about UFO's without special training and government support. Who could crack government secrecy? I'd need inside assistance to really get that side of the story. But, the side involving contactees, yes. I was apparently in the middle of it. So, I decided to do the best I could with the mystery of post-contact. Brian and I both agreed to "lay low." We had not mentioned "the probe" to Churchwood or Cooper because I wanted to see if we could get proof quietly. If it were real, the military certainly would know about the probe—or, be very interested in Brian's allegations.

I still didn't fully trust Brian, and worried continually that he might have a hoax or two up his sleeve.

On October 8, he said three beeps had appeared on a sound tape. The beeps each sounded like a sonar signal. I'd heard similar beeps in movies about submarines. I didn't think the beeps were important, but Brian said they would change everything. More than ever before, I suspected a hoax when I heard the beeps.

In Brian's apartment, Michael Helios and I listened to the beeps with suspicion. How could they be materialized on tape? For what purpose?

Brian was becoming so spacey and dazed at times that we all took his words with a grain of salt. Michael wanted to know more abut Quantum Displacement Physics. Brian said he knew very little. But, he had written a definition after water drops splashed his face:

Quantum Displacement

The displacement of time, by mind at Nous 4, allowing matter and energy to be transported through space.

"It is the core of Orbital Reality," Brian said. He didn't know any more, but suggested Michael ask the probe directly. He said the mechanical voice we heard, the gate-keeper to Voltar, was the probe in orbit behind the moon.

We didn't believe him of course. But, Helios agreed to try for answers. Brian sat down and I said the code word--Ticci Viracocha. Brian slipped quickly into trance.

"Who is responsible for the genetic evolution of the human species?" Helios asked. He first wanted to know about the gray, black-eyed aliens to make sure they couldn't attack him.

350

"Secondary world--negative, Nous 9," responded the mechanical voice. When Helios asked for details, Brian was attacked. He gagged and coughed and choked for a long time while rolling on the floor in pain. Debra was ready to run downstairs to get paramedics when he finally stopped gagging.

"Over-ride Nous 9," the probe said. "Injury sustained." When the trance ended and Brian awoke, his voice was damaged. He could talk only in a whisper for nearly two hours.

"They always go for the throat," Brian whispered in a gravelly tone. He remembered how he had strangled the alien leader and wondered if this was a payback.

In a rough voice, Brian explained that all communications had to move through the probe. The Secondary World aliens monitored him, and could stop him from talking except in special zones that were controlled by Voltar--like in Yosemite and in South America.

"The grays don't want any bad publicity," he explained. "They keep their purposes and plans secret. That's why it is so important to get free from them. Voltar's people must follow rules of the grays, or they can be attacked also," he said. "This can turn into a war if something goes wrong."

Brian still couldn't talk well, so he played the beeps that had supposedly been received on tape. As we listened, water splashed on him again.

He recovered in a daze. "Pattern these beeps in groups of three and transmit them to the probe, on the right date, in the right way." He mumbled on afterwards saying, "Lunan. Find Lunan." He kept saying we had to get the beeps to a man named Lunan. None of us knew anyone by that name.

"What will happen if we find this man, Lunan?" Debra asked.

"Signal must be analyzed and sent."

"Why, what will happen if the signal is sent?"

"Man will receive the greatest message from space he could ever imagine."

"What would it be?" asked Debra.

"A big hello and welcome," Brian smiled as more water drops splashed on his face. "Come on in and get to know your Lunar probe. The greatest gift man could ever receive. Our true history—going back 12,000 years."

I reasoned the beeps were fakes, recorded off a movie. Brian said that wasn't true, but their source wasn't important. How he got them wasn't important. We just had to find the man named Lunan. He would understand.

I certainly didn't believe the beeps had "materialized on tape." I felt they were fakes and they might prove him to be a clever, and highly intelligent hoaxer. If they did, I decided to reveal him as a fraud, and get him, somehow—for wasting my time.

351

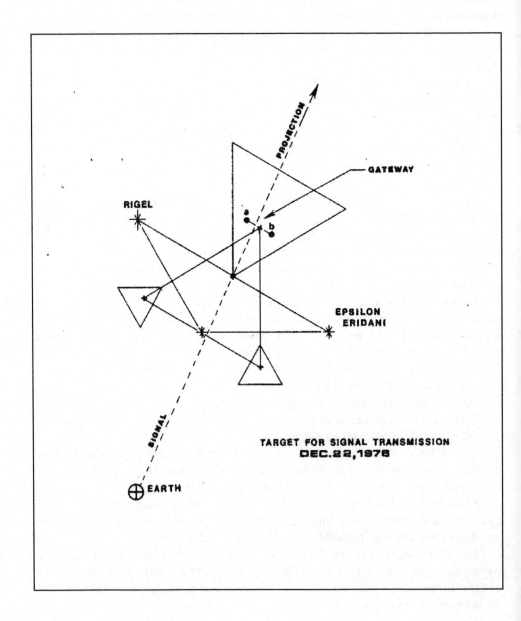

PROJECTION

GATEWAY

RIGEL

a
b

EPSILON
ERIDANI

SIGNAL

TARGET FOR SIGNAL TRANSMISSION
DEC.22,1976

⊕ EARTH

352

Probe

$$I_{P_*} = A_c \ C' = R^{\circ} = R_q^2 =$$
$$\frac{A^H}{N_c} \pm \frac{B^L}{N_b} \pm \frac{\Gamma^D}{N_a} + R^{\circ} =$$
$$I_{P_*} = U_s \ C' \equiv N^{1-10} =$$
$$S^L/M_d + R^{\circ} = I_{P_*} = R_q^2 = O_P \longleftarrow$$
$$[\lessgtr = M_A' = 36 \int^x 36 \int^x 36 / M'_u]$$

$$I_{P_*} = A_c \ C' = R^{\circ} = R_q^2 =$$
$$X^H \pm Y^L \pm Z^D + R^{\circ} = I_{P_*} =$$
$$U_s \ C' \equiv N^{1-\#0} = S^L/M_d +$$
$$R^{\circ} = I_{P_*} = R_q^2 = O_P \longleftarrow$$
$$[\lessgtr' = S_b M_A = 12 \int^x 12 \int^x 12 / M_u]$$

2:10 AM – 10/17/76
B. Scott

CODE FOR TALKING TO PROBE. This was a description of the code for talking to the probe. Brian understood this writing and converted this to a simpler procedure for others to follow.

Ip = Input from user. AcC = Access code. R = response of probe. Rq = request for data. *(Our access code = Ticci Viracocha)*

UsC = User Code which is similar to stating your mind level. (Our user code = 020 020 020.)

OP = open. After the probe said 'Open' you could talk freely about that subject and receive information. But when done with that memory storage unit, the probe would state "Locked". You had to start over again.

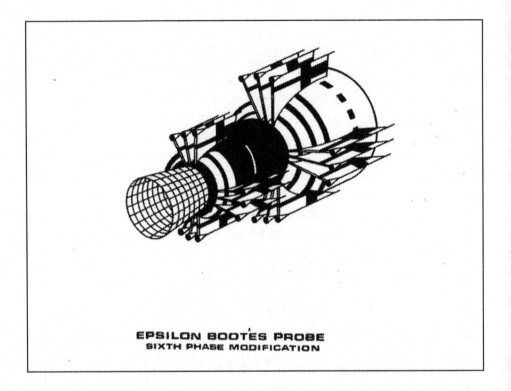

EPSILON BOOTES PROBE
SIXTH PHASE MODIFICATION

THE ACCESS CODE for Brian was *Ticci Viracocha*. The User Code was *020 020 020*. Or -- "I am at mind level one."

The probe apparently conducts conversations with numerous groups on earth, in many regions of the planet. Each *Play of Life* apparently has a unique access code.

THE POWER

I'M NOT URI GELLER.
THIS IS ABOUT QUANTUM DISPLACEMENT PHYSICS AND
IT HAS SOMETHING TO DO WITH ME DESIGNING THEIR PYRAMID.
THAT'S WHAT THIS IS ABOUT. NOTHING ELSE.

--Brian Scott

Chapter 15

Developing Paranormal Power

The next day, we worked with Rod Brown at his Hollywood sound studio to create a new "beep" pattern per Brian's request. Using the original provided by Brian, we created a pattern of three beeps, separated by a pause. Then we placed that pattern six times on a master tape as Brian wanted.

With a copy in hand, we drove downtown to the Los Angeles library and worked with the reference librarian. We searched for the name "Lunan."

To my surprise, we found a magazine article within the hour. A member of the British Interplanetary Society, Duncan Lunan, had decoded mysterious signals from space. The signals had been received by radio telescopes over the years since 1929. Apparently, the source was not alien, but normal radio telescope signals that had been delayed and returned to the sender as an "echo." But the delays varied in time, and some were very long. The patterns made no sense to astronomers. Lunan wrote:

"The varying delays of the 1920's Long Delayed Echoes seemed to indicate some purely natural phenomenon.... In that case, the subsequent variations in delay should spell out some kind of message."

When Lunan charted this delay time on the X-axis and the sequence order on the Y-axis, he plotted a map which seemed to fit the constellation Bootees, with the star Epsilon Bootees indicated as the origin of a spacecraft about 13,000 years ago.

"That's the right Lunan," Brian said. That night, at about 3:00 a.m., I called ASTARA, an organization mentioned in the article--the Association in Scotland for Technology and Research in Astronautics.

A few minutes later, I was talking to the author, Duncan Lunan, on the phone. His thick Scottish accent was difficult to understand at times, but he seemed intrigued. I sent him the tape, and a package of documents.

Then I pondered the events. I figured Brian had recorded the beeps off of a TV show. He had gone too far, I reasoned. He's pulling a hoax. Somehow *everything* is a hoax. That was easy to believe. I simply ignored my list of anomalies and felt fine. Then, I realized—my mind was wavering. I was being overwhelmed. My brain began to feel like a music record skipping tracks. I was jumping from polarity to polarity, from compartment to compartment in my mind—creating walls of amnesia, ways of forgetting, building black rooms. I made another list of anomalies, then read the list back. I was satisfied nothing was missing. The next day, I realized that the Ball of Fire in the sky—my sign— was not included. Even my sign, the ball of fire, had been locked into a box, into a nice little closet so it couldn't affect my other thinking. I was blocking it out, locking it away. How scary--compartmentalization.

If I could ignore important events and facts, what could other people do with less exposure to the story? I realized how man's mind, with amnesia, can lock out memories, experiences, facts and even emotions. We can suppress and selectively forget—yet the information is there—stored, implanted and buried, somewhere.

As I thought more about Brian's experiences, I wondered if his "neurological implant" somehow might use this capability to create compartments in the mind. If man everyday compartmentalized his thinking, could memories and knowledge be stored and withdrawn in some organized manner? If traumatic events created amnesia, and if hypnotists could create amnesia by telling a subject "to not remember," the trait must be strong in man. Perhaps amnesia could be used as a tool. I knew that hypnotists could use a "post-hypnotic cue" to cause a subject to recall a directive. The subject would suddenly act like a chicken or exhibit some helpful behavior on cue, long after the hypnosis session ended, even days or weeks later.

With hypnosis, man could forget and then remember—on cue.

Perhaps the information given to Brian was stored in his memory, and then withdrawn using cues from light and sound patterns. Is that what *they* were doing with Brian? I wondered. In any event, from that time on, I become very aware of compartmentalized thinking in myself, and others.

That afternoon, after being splashed by water drops, Brian slipped into a trance while driving his car down the Santa Monica Freeway. "Your eyes are up," Debra shouted.

Brian swerved into the fast lane as he returned to normal consciousness. "What are you screaming about?"

"You were driving--you couldn't see."

"I could see. What are you talking about?"

"Your eyes..."

His eyes rolled up again, exposing only the whites. From the backseat, I watched as he switched lanes and negotiated traffic for several minutes at 55 mph with his eyes turned upwards.

"This is unbelievable," Debra whispered.

"Monitoring," said the mechanical probe voice. "Bio-telemetry monitor and feedback loop completed. Open."

"You might as well ask him the cure for cancer," Debra chuckled.

As Brian drove, I held a microphone to his lips. "Increase fiber in diet: 68% Fiber--colon. Dwell above 7,000 feet sea level--lungs. Avoid direct sun--skin. Locked."

"I think he just gave you three cures for cancer," Debra laughed.

Brian continued driving at 50 miles per hour, avoiding traffic and changing lanes.

"Of this, is weirdness, of I, and of the Host," laughed Debra imitating the Host.

Brian's eyes rolled down and his personality returned. "What are you doing?"

"You tell me, Brian. You just gave us the cure for cancer."

"Damn it! I missed my turn." Disoriented by our location on the freeway, Brian panicked. "How the hell... What the HELL IS GOING ON?"

A water drop landed on Brian's cheek. "Oh, no. God. This is too much."

"Brian, slowdown," Debra screamed. "Let Jim drive."

Brian fought traffic at the next exit. Drivers honked and tires screeched. "I feel pretty damn woozy."

"What are you doing?" shouted Debra.

"We missed our exit. Now, we're six damn miles past where we were going." Another water drop plopped on his cheek." He let the car coast to a stop at the first street.

"This is too weird," he whispered in a daze. He saw bright, colored auras of light around people on the sidewalk. The auras radiated from their heads, and bodies. One man's head glowed a rust color, the next boy a beautiful green, a woman--bright orange. Accent colors of yellow, red, blue and gold would rise up from their temples, the crown of their heads, their throat, their heart or their pelvic area.

"This is getting too weird for me," he said. For a long time, Brian just sat and watched people and their auras. He tried to find patterns. Some were brighter than others, some barely radiated at all. A few shone so bright and so far outward that they affected others, changing both colors--both energies. This must be the "energy of the being" Voltar had talked about so often, Brian thought. The auras began to tell him a lot about each person.

For the first time, Brian was becoming dangerous to himself. "I don't think he should drive anymore, right now," Debra said. "I don't want to drive back to Orange County with him like that."

When back at my house, I suggested they stay overnight. It was about 36 hours before Brian's 33rd birthday and I suspected something special might happen.

"Jesus was thirty-three when he was crucified," Debra agreed. "We need to watch him closely."

"It's this rock," Brian said interrupting us. "It's the key, it's the anchor to everything." He juggled the white rock in his hands.

Debra stomped away leaving Brian feeling foolish.

"What is wrong with her?" he asked.

"What time were you born?" asked Wanda.

"Good God," laughed Brian. "I don't know. That's a good question. Never thought of it, before. Why?"

"All of your writings are always at 2:10 a.m. I was just wondering if that was the exact time of your birth. Astrology wise."

I fumbled through a notebook crammed with papers. "He was born at 1:19 p.m. on October 12, 1942 in Philadelphia," I said, holding up a copy of Brian's birth certificate. Presbyterian Hospital, file No 170858. William Scott, your dad, was 26. Your mom was 21. Delivered by Dr. Ford A. Miller. You do exist. You are NOT an alien."

"Good. For awhile I was getting worried," Brian laughed.

I had interviewed his mother a week earlier. Brian was a "miracle baby" she said. Due to an injury she had suffered as a young girl, she was unable to become pregnant—at least that's what the family doctor said.

Years later, after she married, doctors were surprised to find a baby in her womb. Her damaged uterus was removed after the delivery. From birth, Brian would always be an 'only child' without siblings.

"Why do you think the writings are at 2:10 a.m.?" Wanda asked again.

"I don't know," Brian giggled. "Their probe? You tell me." A drop of water splashed onto his face. "Wheeeeeee," he gushed leaning against the kitchen cabinets like he was riding out a storm in a ship at sea. "Whoa. That was a big one."

He looked at Wanda and me. "Will you two...stop. Stop moving. Stop pulsing. Your energy, whatever it is – it's expanding. Wow. God, this is amazing." He finally stabilized himself.

"I wonder why I get so dizzy. Gee whiz. By the way, *they* aren't laughing. The probe is very, serious business to them--extremely serious. Everything we do is being monitored by it. Everything they do must go through the probe, first."

Talking to the Probe

Later, in the early morning hours of October 11, Brian squeezed the rock in his hands. "I think it is a kind of an anchor," he said. "I don't know what it so great about it."

Debra picked up the Frazier Family Bible. "This is my anchor," she said. "I would like to get some answers," she said. "I would like to talk to this probe, myself."

Brian squeezed the rock and slipped into trance. "Ticci Viracocha," I said.

A mechanical voice spoke from him. "Open. Access code requested." I didn't know what to say. This was a new request—*an access code?*

Brian's personality returned. "Okay, they are telling me that this probe is real. They are going to hook us up to it, but so you understand--there was a neurological implant done to me, and it is a tiny, itsy-bitsy version of what is in the probe. But it goes through the probe. All communication goes through the probe--from their world to my head. And the Secondary World guys can monitor everything. And we have to do it in the right way--or else, it shuts down, or the Secondary World can...you know...interfere."

"So when it says *'open,'* that means the probe is *'open'* for communication," asked Debra. Brian nodded.

"Why are there so many voices?" I asked.

"Well, it goes way back in their history. Their computers were programmed with the living essence of beings that lived. Their entire essence was captured and is duplicated by the computer, as needed. For example, if you need a certain type of knowledge, they have it stored from a certain guy, so the probe has that person's voice, his essence, in storage. They can project just the voice, or a hologram image of the real man."

We gasped with understanding. We didn't believe it to be true, but the ideas were interesting.

"They actually have that person's knowledge and logic and thought process in the computer. So they can project how he would think, feel, act. You can actually reason with him—but it is just a projection. It's just like we would record something on tape, or a film--only a lot more sophisticated."

"Unbelievable," gasped Wanda.

"It's a big computer, and you know--it's living, it's based on living matter, on organic matter--like brain tissue--that they grow. It's like the brain—and it works on this Photonic energy, which must be like lightning or nerve electricity. Don't nerves use electricity? I can't explain it, but it can project things, like holograms that are so real, they are real to you. That's how they show you stuff."

"If they are all so smart, I have a few questions for them," said Debra. She held up the Bible. "About this."

Brian nodded. "You have to talk to the probe--because none of that was given to me. Okay? My thing is engineering, design."

"Whoever," said Debra. "Just get me someone, or something who will tell me the truth--about God--and it better fit with God's own Word." She patted the big Bible. "Or, I am out of here."

Brian squeezed the rock and slipped back into trance.

"What is the mark that you have talked about putting on Brian before any transformation in South America?" Debra asked.

"Access code," said the probe voice.

"Access code to what?" asked Debra.

"Selene orbital transceiver," responded the probe voice. Debra was confused. "What is that?"

"That would be the probe," I said. "It is a transceiver, in orbit around the moon. That is what that means: selene, orbital transceiver."

"Open," said the voice. "Memory system 1A: one by one by one. English, earth terminology. Reply requested. Open!"

Debra gasped. "I don't believe it. Am I talking to an alien computer?"

"Open. State access Code."

"020 020 020," I guessed, from one of the drawings.

"Memory system?" asked the probe.

"One A, one by one by one," I said using the given words.

"Open."

"Ask your question, Debra," I whispered.

Debra shuddered. "I don't know what you are doing, Jim."

"It asked for an access code and a memory system."

"Is the mark that you would put on Brian 020-020-020?"

"Yes."

"Is that the same as six, six, six?"

"Not in meaning. Locked," said the probe.

"Ticci Viracocha," I said getting a feel for the method.

"Open."

"Who are you and what are you?" I asked.

Brian's body wobbled for a few moments. "State user code."

"020-020-020," I said.

"Open."

"Who and what are we speaking to?"

"Memory system 1a. Coordinate 01, 01, 01. Memory system 1a: three dimensional logic system. Specify coordinates one through thirty-six on x,y,z axis. State Nous level, input user code. User code, man: 020-020-020." It paused. "Transferring."

A much deeper voice spoke. "I am the collective consciousness of all mankind."

"Are you the Host?"

"I am that I am," said the voice.

"Are you God?" blurted Debra.

"I am that I am. Of this is known to man."

Debra held the Bible tightly. "That phrase is known to represent God. It's what God told Moses at the burning bush. Saying it was His name. If you will pardon me, I must say that it sounds like YOU are saying that you are God, or even that Brian is, since you are speaking out of his mouth. Is that what you really mean?"

"I am but a tool in the eyes of God--as is Brian."

Debra nodded approval. "But, if Brian is marked with this number, which you say is 6-6-6, does this mean that people will believe he is the anti-Christ?"

Brian's body again wobbled for a moment. "Access code only. Relationship is ONLY access code. Man will come to know of this. Not relational: anti-Christ. Not same. Significance is number two, zero-two-zero. Twenty, Days of Twenty."

"But people may think he is the anti-Christ. They may want to harm him, even kill him if this happens. You must know of this."

Brian's body wobbled again during a long pause. "Transferring: 05-05-05."

Brian's countenance relaxed and his posture straightened. Though his eyes were rolled back, he looked at Debra in the noble, kingly presence of Voltar. He spoke with compassion and grace. "Of this mark, Brian is one with I," he said to Debra. "And of this, much sorrow will come to Brian, and joy. For he will truly be a light to all mankind."

"Locked," said the mechanical voice.

Debra held the Bible to her breast. "I want Brian to come back," she gasped. "Right now. I want my Brian back."

"Return Scott," the probe voice responded.

For a few moments Brian wobbled. His face turned red. He inhaled with quick short gasps, then tried to stand.

"What is happening," gasped Debra.

"That's what happened on the mountain in Yosemite," I said.

"Matter displacement. Matter displacement," said the probe voice. "M, M prime by radius squared. One plus one equals three."

Brian exhaled and opened his eyes. He lifted his arms and rubbed his hands together furiously.

"Oh," he moaned. "That was hot. Wow." His hands shook until he clenched them and held them together. "That hurt. That is hard on the hands," he grimaced stretching his fingers. He glanced at Debra. "Owwwwww. Well, did you get your questions answered?"

Debra stared at him for a moment with compassion, then lowered her head to the Bible.

"I don't know what I have got myself into," she mumbled.

"What?" Brian asked. "What did he say?"

Wanda and I both noticed that Brian wasn't holding the large white rock.

Wanda looked underneath him and she ran her hands over the shag carpet. She scanned Brian's clothing.

"The rock is gone," she breathed.

"Where is the rock?" I asked.

"What rock?" Brian asked.

"The white rock. The one Voltar gave you."

"Oh," laughed Brian. "That rock. I didn't bring it over. I always leave the rock there. You know that."

"You had it in your hands, Brian," I said.

Brian chuckled. "Still testing. Always testing. I didn't bring it. I couldn't do that. You know that."

"You had it in your hands."

"In the NOR? At the center?"

"What is the NOR?"

Brian felt nervous. "You know. You run the NOR. You brought me into the NOR at the center, then in the shuttle, to here."

"Shuttle? What shuttle," Wanda blurted.

"The shuttle!" Brian insisted. "From the center. Is this part of the test? I thought the psychological tests were over. You said they were over. This is definitely psychological, wouldn't you say. I thought you said I passed that level."

Wanda and I glanced at each other.

"Where are we Brian?" Wanda demanded.

"In the earth room. Final instructions, right?"

"Who am I?"

"Danyael. The doctor--Director of Neural Implants." Brian smiled. "Testing. Testing. Always testing. This must be the seventeenth time. Is this in the Play of Life too?" Brian laughed.

"Brian what do you see? Describe what you see. Look around here and describe what you see," I said.

362

Brian looked around the room. "The earth room, in the center. The domes."

"Who am I?" asked Wanda.

"Level 8 psycho-geneticist. Mother of the children."

"No. I don't know about any levels. I am Wanda. Level 1."

Brian giggled. "I get it. You are projecting different forms and stating it incorrectly to see if I can determine which is the clone. Different forms. Different forms of us. Phase cloning for fun."

"What is phase cloning?" she asked. "I assure you, we are all still at level one."

Brian laughed. "We must have done this before--I just don't remember. But this is a good one."

I had been watching Brian carefully. He seemed serious. "Brian, can you take us up to the second, third and fourth levels?"

Brian chuckled. "Me? You are the only one that does that, in the NOR. Are we on ten now and projecting the three? Is that the test?"

"What do you see, of me?" I asked imitating Voltar.

Brian smiled again. "Are you three all not phase cloning in projection?"

"We might be," said Wanda, playing along.

"So you are projecting?

"I am not projecting," Wanda said.

"You must be projecting!"

"Okay, explain to us what this means," I insisted.

"I thought the tests were done. Are you going to return on the shuttle? Am I not complete? Have you not told me everything?"

I looked at Brian closely. Obviously he might be pulling our leg, but then again, maybe he was stuck in another compartment of his mind.

"Do you know who Debra is?"

Brian gestured to Debra. "Yes. She will rise to all levels."

"Do you know me?"

"Danyael--final program. Yes, final testing--Director of the *Play of Life* and all neural implants. How many times do we have to do this? You really have me confused," he smiled. "Purposely?"

"Explain the levels."

"But you know better than me."

"How do you experience the levels?"

"In the NOR? I am lost. I do not know what is going on."

"How can we know ourselves?" asked Wanda. "At Nous 1."

"At Nous 1? You cannot know yourself at Nous one."

"Who am I?" Wanda asked.

"Everyone is still testing." Brian looked around the room at the walls, and at Debra.

"Oh. I get it. This must be the final, final test."

"We are at Nous one," Wanda said firmly. "Whatever you see, we are now talking at you from Nous one."

"But that can't be. I took the shuttle, came in the NOR—like always." Brian paced for a moment. "I get it. You are at ten, projecting at one? But, I still only see the level three? It doesn't make sense. You are masking somehow."

"We are at one," Wanda shouted. "We don't know anything about projecting--or about three or ten."

Brian laughed. "This is a test. Okay." He walked around us, circling us slowly looking at our heads and faces.

In his mind, with his eyes, Brian saw other people: Dr. Danyael, director of the *Play of Life* on Voltar's world, and Voltar's wife, a psycho-genetic expert and mother of two children. He saw a circular room, covered by an opaque dome lit by a soft purple light. Around him, the walls were covered with all kinds of screens and computers whose patterns of light monitored his biological and psychological energies.

"Are you peering of X?" he asked.

"We don't know what that means," I said, finally realizing that Brian was seriously confused, perhaps stuck in another personality, another compartment, perhaps experiencing a "bleed through"-- a merging of the two worlds.

"Man cannot peer of X," he said, pondering the statement as a rule, a law. "You can only do that at ten," he smiled. "Am I at Nous four? You said I had passed two--but NOT three. That's it. I thought we were working on Nous three. But, this must be four." He waited for a reaction. "Well, is that it?"

"Brian we don't know what you are talking about," said Wanda with compassion. "We really don't."

He looked at me, but saw another man with dark red hair.

"I am lost, I don't know the answer. We've never done this before. This must be Nous 4."

In Brian's world, Voltar entered the room wearing a long white gown and golden bracelets. "Testing not complete. Kista homo," he said raising his huge hand to Brian's forehead. Brian fainted.

In our world, Brian's body wobbled and convulsed. Debra tried to hug him with tears in her eyes. "He's messed up," she sobbed.

I lifted the big white rock out of his hands. "It's back."

"Are you okay?" asked Wanda gently.

"I am very confused," Brian said softly.

"Who am I?" she asked.

"Wanda." He looked around the room. "Jim."

We were all relieved. "He's back, and so is the rock."

Wanda and I figured he made up the whole experience as a diversion. He had avoided any more questions from The Book. But, for certain, the rock had been gone--a magician's trick? Maybe. We became very suspicious.

My theory of multiple-personality still held first place. The missing rock would be placed on the list of anomalies with the Ball of Fire in the Sky.

We kept a tally of our list--and our theories, like scorecards. With each event we added a score--fraud gained a point. Demonic possession was holding even. Aliens lost two.

On my scorecard, aliens always came last. Wanda liked fraud and Debra favored possession of some kind. We discussed our suspicions behind Brian's back, constantly.

Debra believed Voltar might be a Son of God, as described in Genesis—an angel. Throughout the Bible angels are referred to as Sons of God, and they never wore wings. They always were described as men, beautiful men. She also considered the voices coming from Brian to be *'familiar spirits,'*-- but she loved Brian, anyway. He was normal most of the time.

We all enjoyed Brian, however, and I desperately wanted to see the outcome of any "transformation" whatever it might be—good or evil—to see which theory was right. What is a "quantum evolution to Nous 10?" What is the purpose of Host--*whatever* he might be? Those were my questions. Could I learn something from the concepts Brian presented? Could man?

Quantum Displacement – Sudden Movement

The next day, October 12, 1976 was Brian's birthday. He sat in my den as I talked on the phone, and he began tossing the rock up and down in his hands.

Suddenly, he froze--in trance. "Matter displacement. Matter displacement," said the mechanical probe voice. "M, M prime, radius squared. One, plus one equals three. Look to the east. Look to the east."

Brian jumped up from his chair, stunned. "Jesus," he blurted. He shook his hands furiously. "That's weird," he shouted. "Damn it, that is weird!"

Water drops fell on him, and he tried to knock them away.

"What happened?"

"The rock," Brian said. "It got so damn hot, just in an instant, and then...I don't know how to say it.... Poof. It went bye bye."

"The rock?"

"It's gone," Brian shrugged. "I don't know where it went, but I know it is gone." He glanced around, frantically.

"I heard the probe say look to the east."

365

Brian looked East under my desk.

"It's not there," he said nervously. "God, that is the weirdest thing I have ever experienced."

"What happened?"

"I don't know. It's a thought, I had, but I was so close--I could have gone with it." Brian glanced to the East.

"But where is the rock?"

Brian shrugged. "That is the scary part. What if it was me?"

I looked at Brian's body carefully. "Turn around." I searched his clothes and the chair.

"Jim that rock is huge."

"I just want to be sure, for my own verification."

I grabbed a flashlight. "I'm going outside. You stay here."

"But can't I go with you?"

"No. I am going to look East." I slipped out the door and walked around to the east side of the house.

Brian stepped out on the sidewalk.

"He just said something about 26 feet. Apex of the triangle, and 26 feet."

"I want you to stay inside."

"What difference does it make?" Brian shrugged. "We have to find it. That's the first thing." He pointed towards the neighboring house. "Go about twenty feet east from the wall of your house," he said.

I started walking. "You stay here."

"Why? I know I can find it. If it is out here."

"Damn it, Brian. If I find it, it will mean nothing--because you are out here."

Brian shrugged. "It is not going to prove anything anyway."

"It will help me," I said. Now stay there."

A water drop splashed on Brian. He saw a red beam of light zoom out of the house then open up into a triangle. The apex was in front of me on the ground.

"Look to your left," he shouted. "Go forward. Shine your light over there," he pointed. I cast the beam into the bushes near the neighbor's house.

"It should be right there," Brian said.

My flashlight beam hit the rock in shrubbery. I picked up the rock.

"How did you know?"

Brian shrugged. "I saw something that showed me."

"In the dark?"

Brian shrugged. "It was a light."

We hurried inside and checked the windows. They were locked and screened. He could not have tossed the rock outside. I wondered which of my lists this event would end up on.

Brian tried to remember what the probe said. "Did you get the words?" I asked.

"It was the same as before. 'Matter, matter prime, radius squared.' I don't know. I wish they would do this in a logical manner."

Brian held the big rock in his hands. He squeezed the rock again hard. "Matter, matter prime, radius squared?" he stood up, and with his eyes rolled back in his head, began inhaling loudly. Then his face turned bright red.

The probe voice spoke. "Matter, matter prime. Radius squared. Seek apex of angle--two energy forms. Look to the north. Look to the north." Brian's eyes rolled down and he gasped for air. The rock had vanished.

"Is it gone? It's gone. Oh Lord, it's gone." He shook his hands furiously. "That is so weird. I was squeezing it so hard. My hands were aching. I mean aching! Then suddenly they just squeezed together. No rock." He looked at me for approval.

I wanted to punch him in the face. This had to be a hoax. "Sit down," I said. "Don't move. Put your hands on your knees and don't move them." I looked under the chair.

"You don't have the rock and you were right in front of me. I was looking right at you. You could have dropped it, but it would have made a big thud and landed right on your foot."

"And I am barefooted," Brian noted.

"How did you do it?"

"It's not me. They did it," Brian said. "But, I did…think about it, that time."

I tested the north window—locked. "You stay here--and don't come outside. Don't go out of this door." I shut the door to the den, and walked out onto the back porch, which faced north.

I heard the den door open.

"Stay in there."

"He just told me it is not as far. More like six or eight feet."

"Do not come any farther!" I shouted with anger.

"I am just trying to help you find it."

"I don't want your help."

I stepped outside. Dry leaves blew along the sidewalk. I shivered in the cold, October wind. "It's closer than the street," Brian shouted from inside.

I flashed the light into bushes near the house. I really didn't expect to find anything now that Brian was inside.

Then, my light hit the rock—the big white rock lying in the leaves. In a way, I was disappointed. I wanted a good reason to be mad at Brian to poke him out, to call it a hoax, and dismiss it all. I picked up the white, crystalline stone and felt the weight. It was much bigger than my two hands.

When I looked up, Brian was standing in the doorway.

"I asked you to stay in the den."

"I just wanted to see where it was. Right where he said it would be."

I walked up the steps awed, and yet perturbed. "I wish you had not come outside."

"You'd already found it."

"Damn it. I need my own proof, my way!" I shouted. My emotions boiled. He was either a great con, a great magician or -- it happened.

Brian laughed. "It happened."

"You made this rock move through the walls and go right out of the house—with your own mind?"

"Wrong," Brian smiled. "I didn't do it. THEY did, and I don't think it went through the walls. That's not how it works."

"How does it work?"

"It's a different kind of a thought. But not so different. Just a little different."

"Uri Geller," I shrugged.

"I'm not Uri Geller," Brian chuckled. "Don't let anything go like that. That is not what this is about." He lifted up the white stone. "This is about quantum displacement physics and it has something to do with me designing their pyramid. That's what this is about. Nothing else."

"That was paranormal. That is beyond the comprehension of man. And you did it--with your hands. You moved a big, chunky, two pound rock--through that wall. That is impossible."

"It's not impossible," Brian said. "We just don't understand how--right now. In the future, it will be understood and it won't be that amazing. So, the best thing is to not make a big deal about it. Don't even tell anybody. It won't prove anything."

"But, I could sell you with this…"

"No, Jim. Not based on this. NO way. That is the one thing I will not abide by. No matter what happens. The one thing I won't be is another Uri Geller. I am much different--very much. That is the one thing I will not put up with." He was dead serious.

First Bent Spoon

We talked about Quantum Displacement Physics for a while, then met Wanda and Debra at the Hungry Burger on Melrose at La Brea. They were giggling. They had gone out alone for a talk. Debra thought she was pregnant. She wanted Wanda to know.

"I called my mom and told her I had just seen a miracle," laughed Debra as she plopped down into a booth. "You want to know what she said?

Wanda giggled like a teenage girl at a slumber party.

"Do you guys want to know?"

Brian and I shrugged.

"I told her I had seen a miracle and she said, 'What happened--did you make your car payment?'"

They all laughed hysterically.

"Looks like you girls have been having a good time," I said. "What were you drinking?"

"Shirley Temples," they both laughed. "But the more I get the more I need," Debra said. They giggled hysterically.

"Are you girls wasted?" Brian smirked.

"We have about ten dollars left to our names--between all of us," Wanda said. "I think it is a time to get drunk—but we can't afford it."

"And, we see miracles around us," laughed Debra. "I sold my soul to the company store...." Debra sang, imitating a man's deep voice. Everyone laughed. "Of this of I," she laughed. "I am all that I am, and of this, I am--NOT." She crackled hysterical with laughter. Debra and Wanda hugged and laughed together.

"This is ridiculous," said Brian. "

"We have two wasted, or crazy ladies on our hands," I laughed.

A waitress arrived. "It can't be over twelve dollars," Wanda said. "That is all we have to our name."

Brian froze. His eyes rolled back, and the voice of Voltar spoke. "All will be provided."

When Brian's eyes rolled down, he wobbled, dizzy. For him, from his viewpoint, the whole environment, spun slowly counterclockwise and then tilted. He leaned to the right and then backward trying to balance the images. He heard beautiful sounds and saw images of the circular NOR.

He saw Voltar and Danyael talking. "Centering. Centering," said Danyael. Three rings of color lights blinked and a strange sound ripped through Brian's mind. He gripped the table with all of his might and shook. "This is damn weird," he said gritting his teeth. "Shit!" Five water drops plopped onto his face and shoulders.

People in a nearby booth saw the drops and looked upward.

"Oh, no," Brian moaned. "Oh, noooooooo." This time, as the world spun, he saw the Rings of Time—the floor of the circular computer. He stepped on a ring and suddenly was surrounded by beautiful people on Voltar's world.

369

The ring moved and he saw small, brown-skinned women dancing around him. Their dresses whirled and mirror fragments on the dresses reflected bright golden light from torches. Each woman's costume lit up and glowed like a whirling fire.

They danced on circular walkways surrounded by water, and the surface of the water dazzled Brian's eyes with sparkling, rippling light. Beautiful flute music, stringed instruments and pounding drums joined in a symphony of sound so beautiful that tears rolled out of Brian's eyes and down his cheeks.

When it all stopped, Brian gasped. "I wish I knew what the heck was going on," he mumbled.

"What are you seeing?" I asked as the waitress and others watched Brian with concern. "I can't say. I don't understand. I don't know what is happening."

"The water hit him when he cussed," said Wanda.

"I've noticed that," Debra said. "But other times, too."

"I feel sick to my stomach," said Brian as the waitress sat a big plate of fries and a huge hamburger down in front of him."

"Is he all right?" she asked.

Wanda waved her off. "He'll be all right."

Brian carefully prepared his burger, separated out all of his food into neat piles and began to eat. "I don't know whether I am coming or going, anymore," he said. "It is getting so I don't know where I am." He bit into the thick juicy burger and smiled with delight.

"The food is good, here. So—let's eat. I just love to eat."

Debra and Wanda chuckled, as did a few people in other booths. His skin blushed red. "I am so glad to be here. This is so good."

"Maybe you should give thanks to God," Debra smiled.

Brian nodded and bowed his head momentarily. In his mind, he saw a sudden stream of images about good food he loved to eat. He opened his eyes. "The garden," he said as he lifted his head and smiled at Debra. "A world of abundant food and water, the earth--our home. Of the Creator for man--his children--the children of God," Brian nodded. "I thank you," he smiled, speaking to God. "I do thank you."

"He is just glowing," Wanda noted as Brian ate. Brian smiled at some of the people who were glancing his way. His reddened skin glistened. He radiated.

After Brian ate, he picked up a spoon to stir his coffee and froze. His eyes rolled back into his head and a deep voice spoke. "Energy. Matter. Matter." Brian held the spoon in his right hand. His hand shook slightly, and the metal handle began to melt. Watching the metal bend and begin to droop gave us all an eerie feeling. Brian wasn't doing anything. He was frozen in trance—unmoving--but the ends of the spoon slowly drooped downward like a noodle.

As I reached for the spoon, Brian's body jolted. He woke up.

"Oweeee, that is hot! The spoon clanged against a plate and glasses. "What happened?" he asked, terrified.

"You just bent a spoon." I said, touching the curved metal.

"Did you see that?" I asked Wanda. "I don't believe it."

"I saw it, too," Debra breathed.

"I saw it but my mind can't handle that," said Wanda.

"We all just saw something that is impossible. But that's what Uri Gellar does," I said.

"Who is Uri Gellar?" Debra asked.

"He bends spoons, on stage, for entertainment. He's an Israeli psychic--young guy, like Brian. Claims to be a UFO contactee."

"There is someone else who can do this?" Debra gushed.

"What would happen if you got Brian together with this guy?"

"I am not going to be a Uri Geller," Brian nodded, sarcastically. "Or the other guy, Edgar what's his name."

"Edgar Cayce," I answered. "The Sleeping Prophet."

"This is about one thing. Their science: quantum displacement and the pyramid in South America--which they want me to re-build."

"But Brian, you just bent a spoon. While holding it, the darn thing just melted." Debra said as she felt the curved edges. "This was straight when you picked it up--it melted as we watched it."

"And YOU did it," I said.

"No, I didn't. That was them--one of them. I don't know which one." He saw images of Voltar, Danyael and their council of twelve standing around the NOR. Behind them he saw hundreds more, all watching.

"This is a big deal to them," Brian said. "All their people are involved."

Sustenance Provided

After finishing an apple pie for dessert, Brian walked away from the table, and tossed salt over his right shoulder.

"I'm going to need a lot of luck," Brian giggled as tears welled up in his eyes. "I think I know how they do it."

I handed the bill to the cashier. Wanda counted out money and paid. The young lady looked at the check and pulled some bills out of the drawer. "Here's your change." But Wanda had turned away.

I picked up a handful of bills including a twenty, two-fives and change.

"Are you sure?"

"Have a nice day?" the girl nodded. "It's right. I don't make mistakes."

I folded the money and walked out. As everyone slipped into the car, I recounted. " Did you give her two twenties?"

371

"Two twenties?" laughed Wanda. "We don't have forty dollars to our name."

"She gave us the money we paid for the meal, the change, plus twenty dollars."

"What?" gasped Debra.

"Instead of being broke, we have thirty-four dollars--and we just ate."

Brian giggled. "He did say '*all would be provided,*' didn't he? It's on them."

"That's not right," said Debra. "We should take that money back."

"That girl could get fired," Wanda said.

"He's telling me, not to worry. They will take care of it. It's on them."

"Brian, they can't do that. That is stealing," Debra cringed.

"Brian, did you do that with your mind?"

Brian chuckled. "Let them handle it. They will make it work out. They were making a point. There was no mistake."

"They didn't mess with her mind?"

"I wouldn't exactly say that," Brian smiled.

"This is too weird," laughed Debra.

"Hey Brian, we should catch a bus to Las Vegas," giggled Wanda.

"Hey, we could get there in three hours," I said, seriously.

"That was done to make a point."

"What's the point?" asked Debra. "That it is okay to steal?"

"No, it is not stealing, believe me. Just let them handle the ethics of it. This is bigger than man can see in his limited little mind," Brian smiled. "That was to prove to you one thing and only one thing."

"What?" asked Wanda.

"Just what they said," Brian smiled. "Sustenance is provided."

"Sustenance," breathed Debra. "Like the Jews in the desert, like manna. And their shoes that didn't even wear out. God kept them alive while he let them wander in the desert. He did. He didn't save them, but he provided sustenance."

"That's it," Brian smiled. "They will provide, sustenance. Not much more, though."

Wanda glanced at her watch.

"Oh, by the way Brian. Happy birthday. You just turned 33," she said.

Brian's 33rd Birthday

On the way back to the house in the car, we all sang the birthday song to Brian. Near a Jewish temple, we saw a wooden hut built outside, and fruit dangling from strings.

"What is that?" It looks like a manger," said Debra. We all shrugged. None of us understood Tabernacles.

October 12 in 1975 was the middle of Tabernacles, an eight-day Hebrew celebration after Yom Kippur, the Day of Atonement.

During Tabernacles, people are indwelled by God. They become the tabernacle of God. Another view is that they marry God symbolically, and many temples hold mass marriage ceremonies for people who want to remarry. For most Jews, the symbolic tabernacles are reminders that God moved them out of slavery and into a new life by forcing them to leave their comfortable homes, wander in the desert and dwell in tabernacles. For forty years, they wandered, but their sandals didn't wear out, and He provided manna as sustenance.

Brian beamed with joy and excitement as we entered the house. "Can you do it at will?" I asked as we flicked on the lights in the living room. The old house had wooden beams across the ceiling and natural wood floors.

"If you can do it at will, we can sell this story tomorrow," smiled Wanda. "I will get an appointment with the president of Paramount."

"I don't know if I can do it, again," Brian giggled. "Even if I can, I'm not going to show off. So don't think about promoting me in this way."

"Why?" Wanda whined.

"I'm not going to be a Uri Geller."

"It would be so easy," Wanda insisted. "One spoon bent in front of the right guy, and you would go to South America, like that." She snapped her slender fingers, sharply.

"I don't like this happening," Brian warned. "This is dangerous."

"Why?" laughed Debra. "If you can do it, do it again! But frankly, I don't know if I would believe my eyes. I would have to see it about ten times in a row. I mean--it could be an illusion of some kind. Think about what really happened. Did it happen? Or was it an illusion of some kind that they projected? I mean if they made that girl give us back our money, plus change, and twenty dollars, what could they be doing to OUR minds?"

"Yeah, Brian, they could be playing with our minds, right now," said Wanda.

Brian smiled. "They would never do that. They were making a point."

"It does involve ethics," I said.

"They are so ethical they would make everybody on this planet puke," Brian steamed. "Think of it, they can know everything. They can take anything they want from anybody. Do anything. Move anything--but they don't. They grant free will--and that is what it's all about. Free will to learn."

"But Brian," Debra shouted. "If YOU can do it at will, and you have free will, why not do it for money. People have to work for money. What is worse? Is working and slaving for somebody else free will? NO, we have to—to survive."

"That's a good point," Wanda laughed. "We wouldn't have to work if we could do that."

"Just do enough to get the money for South America," Debra insisted. "If they won't give it to you, why not do something that earns just enough to get there. Just once would be enough." She waited for Brian to ponder. "Do it," she said.

"I am not going to become famous this way," he said. "It is wrong. I may have a checkered past, but I am not living that way anymore."

"One time," Debra teased, laughing.

"No one will care. Not ONE time," Wanda pleaded.

"No. No!" he shouted. "I could get zapped by the Secondary World, and so could they--Voltar's people. I am keeping my word to them--that I would not use anything for personal gain. Okay? I just want to build the pyramid, at least design it the way they want it. That's all that this is about."

"I believe it was an illusion," Debra taunted.

"It wasn't," said Brian. "It's for learning."

"I think it was a trick of some kind."

"It wasn't," Brian smiled, cynically. "You'll see. You'll find out."

Brian lifted the heavy white rock in front of Debra and then wrapped his hands around it. His eyes rolled back into his head and he squeezed the rock hard.

"Matter, matter prime, radius squared. One, plus one--equal three," said the probe voice. Then Brian's face puffed up and reddened.

He moaned. His eyes rolled down, and his hands opened. The rock had vanished.

Debra gasped. "My God, he did it again. With a rock!"

"That's what he did this afternoon," I said. "Twice."

Beaming radiantly, Brian smiled. "That time, that time--I did know what they were doing. I think I DID do it."

"Make it come back, Brian." Wanda commanded.

"I will, oh I will," Brian giggled. "It will come back later, for now--let's forget about it."

"Forget about it?" gasped Wanda.

"Forget about it," Brian insisted while beaming. "Let's just see where it comes back."

I clicked on my tape recorder. "Brian just dematerialized solid matter. It's October 12, his thirty-third birthday, at about 1:15 a.m. his hands were right in front of us the whole time."

"That is one hell of a rock to hide," Wanda said. "Standing on a hard wood floor. He couldn't have dropped it."

"Make it come back, Brian," said Debra.

"How would you like to see the virgin birth of a rock?" Brian said to her. "For the rock to come right out of a woman. Right out of the womb?"

374

"What are you talking about?" Debra grimaced.

"Would you like to give birth to a rock?"

Debra groaned. "That is disgusting Brian. I do not know what you are talking about." She nudged Wanda and turned away from Brian. "Repulsive," Debra breathed. "Sometimes he is repulsive."

"He's a man," Wanda laughed.

A while later Brian and Debra crawled into our bed. Wanda and I slept on the floor in a sleeping bag. We listened to the sounds of Brian and Debra kissing.

"Disgusting," whispered Wanda. "How are we supposed to sleep?"

I felt the room move, like a small earthquake. "Do you feel that? I think we just got hit."

"Feel what?"

"Earthquake."

"There was not an earthquake," Wanda said.

My head filled with images of Brian and Debra screaming at each other. "This is weird. I think we are all going to be tested tonight," I whispered.

"Tested?" Wanda whispered.

"All of us," I said. "Brian will be first, and mine will be the last."

"Oh God," Wanda whined. "I have to go to work."

Brian's Big Mistake

Debra and Brian kissed passionately. She heaved with excitement and her body ached for Brian to love her. He teased and waited until she demanded. Then Brian slipped into trance. His eyes rolled back and he materialized the large, white rock between her legs.

Debra felt the heavy rock suddenly appear. It frightened her. She furiously grabbed at the jagged stone with her hands. "Briannnnnn!" she screamed. "Damn it. That is disgusting. You are disgusting."

"You dared me," Brian whispered. "Now, will you have their baby?"

"No," she whispered. "I will not. That's final."

"But it is part of our love. It will be a child of God, a rock for man...."

"No!" she screamed. "I will not."

She believed she was pregnant, and had told Brian she wasn't ready to have another baby. "What if it is some alien?"

Brian gasped. "It IS of them."

"No. NO....No!" she screamed. "You are playing with my mind. You bastard. YOU GOD DAMN BASTARD. She kicked at him and shoved him out of bed, and onto the floor. His whole body thumped hard onto the floor. He jumped up naked, with the rock in hand.

Debra shouted at him. "You can't do that. It's wrong."

"I sure as hell can." Water drops splashed on Brian as he swore.

Debra ran into the bathroom and slammed the door. Brian stumbled into the hallway and pulled at the door.

"Get away from me, you bastard," she screamed hysterically.

Brian ran outside naked and scanned the stars for help. "You've got to stop her," he said. A car zoomed down the street and headlights revealed Brian's naked body. The horn honked.

"No, oh, no," he cried. As Brian's mind spun, he saw a young, angelic looking man, installed as leader of the council on Voltar's world. He saw the cherubic young man and thousands like him walking on the earth, amidst old ruins at Qumran in northern Israel.

"I don't understand," he screamed. "Stop it. I don't want this. I don't want this anymore. He heaved the rock into the night sky. When the rock hit the road, a blue-white light flashed outward. Then from the cloud of light, rays absorbed back into every tiny piece of stone.

Wrapped in the purple bedspread, Debra looked outside to see Brian in the street naked.

"Brian!" she screamed.

"Oh no," he cried out in a daze. Tears ran down his cheek as he tried to gather up pieces of the white stone.

Debra raced back into the house, screaming. "Jim, Brian is outside in the street naked."

"Brian is learning a lesson tonight," I said. "I don't know what it is, but let's leave him alone."

"Jim, he is out there naked!! It's freezing!!!" she screamed.

"Good, then he'll come back in, quickly."

The door slammed open and Brian stumbled into the house and den, naked. With tears running down his face, he placed about 10 pieces of the white, crystal rock on my desk. Blubbering in a daze, he tried fitting them together, like the pieces of a puzzle.

"We've got to help him," whined Debra.

"Throw me his pants," I said. I took them to Brian.

Wanda nudged Debra as they quickly dressed. "What did he do?"

"He made that damn rock appear...right...you know. Right there."

"Inside?" Wanda gasped.

"No. You know, outside."

"Could he have...?"

"No. He did it. It appeared, suddenly. I mean right up against me. A damn rock." Debra shook her head in disbelief. Wanda hugged her.

"His hands were not even down there," Debra said. "He did it with his mind."

"Why would he do that?"

"I don't know. The man is over the edge." Debra paused for a long time. "I told him I want to have an abortion, and he doesn't want to. He wants me to keep it."

"How far along are you?"

"A month--I just found out. And I want to do it early."

"Do you think it is...theirs?"

"It is too weird for me to handle, *either* way." Debra lit a Marlboro cigarette and inhaled deeply. "I'm a Christian. I can't be doing this."

In the kitchen, Wanda and I made a pot of coffee. Debra joined us. "Why did he do that, Jim?" Debra asked.

"I think this is his test. He invaded your space. Free-will violation. He can't do that."

"But why put it there. I mean right there."

"I don't know," I said. "Brian is Brian. If you had a kid, do you think it would be special? Did he say it would be a *rock?"*

"I don't know. I don't want to think about it," she heaved. "Remember when we talked about not being drawn into his world, personally? We agreed to use each other for a reality check? I need help, Jim. I am losing it. The worse part is, I feel for him. He believes this is all true. He is experiencing it, and I feel for him. I feel what he feels, and I love him. But, I don't see how I could have a baby. I need a career when I graduate, and--what if it is *their* baby?" Her mind raced and she trembled, nervously.

When she had lost time in the apartment, Voltar had supposedly placed a rock on her abdomen in some ceremony. "Brian said we were married— remember?"

Then, Brian had referred to giving birth to a rock. The two ideas were somehow related. "Giving birth to a rock?" she breathed. "If I had a baby, I'd be drawn into his world. The child would be raised in it. It would be my life," she whimpered. "I'd go insane," she said. "I'd go over the edge, like he is now."

We heard a deep, booming voice and remembered Brian in the den.

We hurried to the den and peeked inside. In a daze, Brian tried to re-assemble the rock—on the photonic matter drawing. Tears ran from his eyes.

Debra slipped in and hugged him, but he did not respond.

"Brian," she whispered. "I'm sorry."

He started talking in trance. The mechanical probe-voice spoke with urgency, "Kista Homo--return home—24 hours."

I clicked on a tape recorder as the probe spoke. "Memory system 1A, destroyed. Memory system 1B destroyed...Memory system 1C, destroyed... Kista

377

Homo, return home to first of I. Twenty-four hour span. Kista Homo, all usable memory systems destroyed."

Brian continued talking, in two voices. His normal voice responded to the mechanical probe, navigating with ease through the memory system codes. The probe responded at high speed, reporting damage to him like he was captain of a ship.

Debra listened in awe. "He is talking to it," she whispered. "That is Brian talking to it," she gasped. "My God, he knows it inside and out."

"Memory system 2-- report," Brian commanded.

"Memory system 2A destroyed, memory system 2B, destroyed, memory system 2C, destroyed," the probe reported.

"Memory system 3, report," Brian again ordered.

Debra began to fall apart and started to cry.

"Secondary assault instigated. Outer-perimeter probes attacked and destroyed. Secondary assault--imminent. Destruction imminent. Loss of life--imminent. Imminent."

Brian's posture slumped as his voice faded out. Debra rushed through the doorway and pulled at his hands. "Wake-up," she shouted. "Brian!."

Brian sat up straight and strong, with his eyes rolled upward. A deep, melodious voice boomed out from his chest.

"Woman!" Debra backed off, frightened as Brian's face turned to follow her moves. "For what reason do you disrupt the cycle of six. This body needs rest."

She stammered, unable to answer.

"Depart," he commanded.

Debra turned to me and clutched my arm. "Who is that?" she cried.

"I don't know," I whispered. "Not Brian, as we know him."

"I can't take it, I can't take any more," she cried. "Return Scott...."

I stepped forward and Brian's head turned to follow. I wondered who was watching. What was he seeing? He had crossed over a line. For the first time, I felt fear. This had become dangerous, really dangerous.

"Debra needs emotional support," I said.

"Does the subject in question require the attention of Scott?" asked the presence.

"I believe Brian is needed for emotional support, right now."

"Is subject's need an emergency?"

I took a deep breath as the eyes followed my moves. Debra sobbed loudly.

"It is," I said. What was watching me—an alien, a demon, a personality, another being?

Brian's body stood up with a graceful, bold and dignified style. He studied the room and then walked in a smooth gait to the bookcase. His hands pushed aside books, which fell to the floor.

"Searching," he said in a relaxed, deep voice. "Alignment disk."

Debra clung to me. "Alignment complete," the presence said. Brian's body sat down in the chair. He folded his arms, turned his head and looked squarely at me. Only the whites of his eyes showed.

"What disk?" I asked.

"Nous 4 alignment," the presence said. "NOR alignment plate, reference earth room. Physical over-ride."

"What is the NOR?" I asked.

"You who ask of I of emergency for known earth subject, what level are you on?" He waited for an answer.

Debra cried out. "I want my Brian. Please..."

Suddenly, I felt another earthquake. I grabbed the doorframe. It rocked and the whole room wobbled. Hallucination, I thought. A projection. Not physical. I watched for a moment and began to feel dizzy. This must be what Brian experiences—the dizziness and disorientation. The whole room moved, like a ship rolling in a storm at sea.

I glanced in the hallway, the house was okay, not moving, just this room.

Then the room split. I saw two rooms-one moving, and the other holding still.

I felt that if I focused on the moving room, and 'went with it' as Brian said, I'd be in their world. I felt a tug. I felt a pull at my chest. This was my moment of truth—my test.

Debra pulled on me. "Please, Jim." I needed to protect her. Should I go for the experience, or stay. I knew that some paranormal force was tugging me into a different reality. I jerked back into the hallway.

"Go see Wanda," I shouted at Debra. God damn it, Go!" I shoved her away, like a wild-man filled with fear. She fell to the floor and clung to my leg.

The being spoke. "Why did that woman come into my earth room and disturb me? This body needs nourishment and rest?"

"What is happening?"

"What level are you on?" he asked

"I must be on one. I don't know of any levels," I shouted.

"How can you be at one? You appear as Danyael."

"What is happening?" I asked "In this room?"

"Quantum displacement process," the presence said. "Displacement of physical forms, disorientation. Levels two through ten."

"I WANT MY BRIAN," Debra screamed standing up. The room shook with her cry.

"Damn it--Debra," I screamed. "If you can't take it, get out of the room." She looked at me shocked. "Get out!" I bellowed. "Get out of here."

Debra ran away, sobbing. I felt embarrassed and ashamed.

"Return Scott," I commanded. "Return Scott. He is needed to handle this emergency."

"Returning Scott," said a mechanical voice speaking from Brian's lips.

In the living room, Debra fell to her knees near Wanda.

"I need your help," Debra said. "It isn't Brian. Brian's not here."

In the den, Brian's personality returned in deep sorrow. He typed on my IBM Selectric 71, and then stood up. He wobbled, weakly. "I need to touch the plates in the NOR," he muttered. "Take me to the NOR. I need to be re-centered."

"Are you Brian?" I asked.

"I am not sure what I am," he said. "It is more than I can comprehend."

"Brian is back," I shouted. Debra came running.

We helped him walk and plopped him gently on my big, purple waterbed. "Are you with us?" Debra asked.

"Memory systems have been destroyed," he muttered. "They just keep telling me, Kista Homo. Somewhere. It's a 24-hour span. Kista Home. Go home."

"Not without me," whimpered Debra.

"This is of I," Brian said. "It is not you who screwed up, but I, and for this, I must return. Home world--under attack--Secondary World. The plan failed— because of me."

"What do you mean?" Debra asked.

"The outer perimeter probes have been destroyed by the Secondary World. No protection remains. We are at war."

Tears welled up in his eyes. "Of this, my people perish. Many will die for I have failed," he fell back onto the bed.

A frantic voice spoke from him. "Attack. Attack underway. Shields pierced. Council secluded. Counter-attack, by the people."

Debra gasped as I stood in the doorway and listened.

"Secondary World invasion underway, home world. Protect yourself. Protect...yourself..."

Debra grabbed the big Bible and climbed onto the bed next to Brian. She opened the pages and laid the book on his chest.

"In the name of Jesus, I ask for protection," she said. "I ask that the spirit of Jesus come upon Brian and upon us all, right now, in this room, in this house, to protect us from Secondary World assault. Jesus, I know you are real, I know you can hear me. These aliens are nothing to you. I really believe that. You are more powerful than all of them, and I ask you for protection of Brian. I ask you to come into our presence right now and protect us from this Secondary World of man."

She glanced at me. "Just keep praying," I said. "He's not out of it, yet."

Debra dropped to her knees on the floor, and opened the Bible to 2 Corinthians. She read aloud. "'For though we walk in the flesh, we do not war according to the flesh, for the weapons of our warfare are not carnal, but mighty in God for pulling down strongholds and every high thing that exalts itself against God...bringing every thought and any entity into captivity to the obedience of Christ.'"

She laid the book down and prayed from her heart. "This is a spiritual battle. I believe Brian's spirit can hear me, and you Jesus. I ask you to save the soul of this man, Brian Scott, for he is a good man, and he is truly sorry for what he has done, and I love him. Sanctify him, consecrate him Lord, and make him an instrument for your holy work in this land."

Muttering with reports from the battle, Brian lay in bed as Debra prayed.

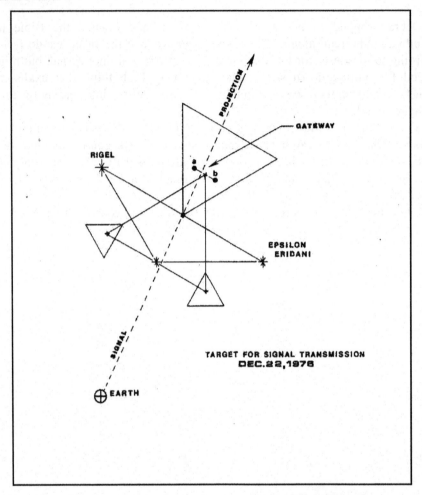

TARGET FOR SIGNAL TRANSMISSION
DEC.22,1976

ORBITS related to Days of 20.

Brian never explained this drawing. But the numbers represent days: 121.74733 days /(divided by) 6.0873665 days = 20 days. The cycle repeats three times in the drawing. Brian would have gone through 3 cycles from 1975-1978.

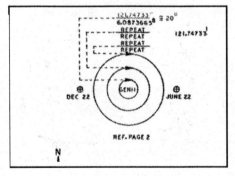

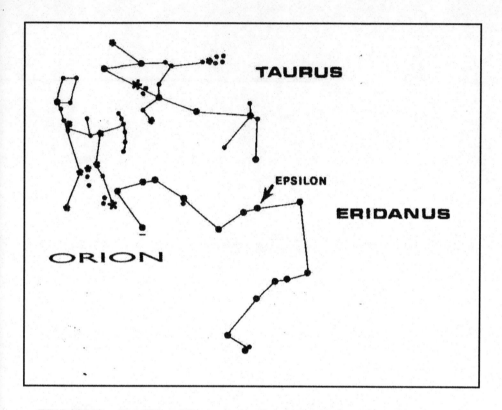

ERIDANUS – The River. The long winding constellation located under Taurus is considered a heavenly version of the Nile, or other rivers. Voltar's home world today would be the fifth brightest star--*Epsilon*.

This constellation was important to the civilization of Sumer in Mesopotamia. The most ancient town in Sumer is Eridu--built about 5,000 B.C. Eridu is located about 196 miles SE of Baghdad, Iraq.

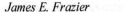
James E. Frazier

BRIAN'S BARTER

I WILL GO TO NOUS TWO.
IF I CAN HAVE TEN DAYS TO GET
USED TO IT BEFORE I RETURN, I'D TAKE A THREE.
BUT, I CAN'T SEE HOW I COULD HANDLE A FOUR. NO WAY.
TO GO FROM A ONE TO A FOUR IS TOO BIG OF A JUMP.
I COULD NOT HANDLE IT. I COULD DESTROY TOO MUCH,
I COULD DESTROY OUR WHOLE WORLD.

-- Brian Scott

Chapter 16

A New Dawn – Insight

When the first streaks of sunlight brightened the purple room, Debra awoke. Her eyes opened. Still kneeling with the Bible open, she found Brian sleeping soundly under the covers.

"Thank you Jesus," she said. "Thank you. Please let him be Brian when he awakens. Please let him be *my* Brian," she whispered.

On Voltar's world, people screamed and ran for cover as their orange skies filled with attacking spacecraft. Beams of light from the crafts melted huge domes in the beautiful city. Towers of glass crashed to the ground, people flew through the air to escape, but many died when their belts failed.

In their underground chambers, the council members of Voltar's world met. A deep-voiced, dark-haired man spoke, "They want the secret of Quantum Displacement Physics," he announced. "Or the destruction will continue."

Voltar, Danyael and the other members of the council waved defiantly.

"Never," said Danyael. "Better we all die. Quantum Displacement Physics is the only hope for the people of earth. It is our legacy to our plantations--their freedom."

The twelve men and women nodded in agreement. Voltar stood up. "Tell them to cease the attack immediately, or we will destroy the orbit of their primary moon. We will use Quantum Displacement against them, now."

Members of the council gasped. They had not attacked in millennia. But they heard the screams and saw their own people dying, all around the city. Slowly, one by one they all agreed without speaking. "Notify our allies, first" Danyael said as he pointed to a military aide.

The man rushed out of the room. Danyael looked at Voltar. "We need to get Brian home. We can't protect him there, with the probe down."

Later in the morning, Debra knelt beside the bed asleep with the Bible in her hands. Brian slept peacefully. Wanda handed me a $10 dollar bill. "That's all we have left," she said. "Let them buy their own gas and food."

In the den, I glanced at my typewriter to see what Brian had written: "What is done, is done. It can't be changed." The white rock lay in pieces on my desk.

A while later I drove Brian and Debra to McDonald's on La Brea Avenue. Depressed and drained, Brian said very little. Debra pumped him for answers.

"What is wrong, Brian?" she asked.

"You know the answer," he said.

"No, I don't."

"I must get to the NOR and turn the plates."

"What are you talking about?"

"Wouldn't it be nice to go for a long drive, get away from the city, from all of these people?" he asked. "To drive eastward for a span of time, and to read from a book of knowledge."

"Brian doesn't read," Debra whispered to me. We both studied Brian carefully. His baby blue eyes blinked wide open and his voice sounded like Brian, but he seemed distant.

He rolled a straw into a circle, and then poked a finger through the hole. "The book of knowledge--moved." Brian smiled at Debra. "It's a different type of thought. A different way of...using--thought..." Brian giggled.

"Are you feeling okay?" Debra asked.

"That which is needed is not of the body," he said. "The radiant alignment must be completed."

Debra flared with agitation. "If you are thinking of going away or taking Brian away, you're wrong. Whoever I am talking to. I am going with him--no matter what. I am going."

Brian's eyes rolled back and the probe voice spoke. "Latitude and longitude given. Recall point known. Twenty-four hour span. Physical transportation requested."

"We are NOT taking him to the desert," Debra insisted. "Our cars won't make it--and no matter what you do, I am going with him."

"Local references," the probe said. "Point 038, point 114. Acceptable. Realignment possible."

Brian's eyes rolled down. He wobbled dizzily for a moment. "This is it. This is the end, Kista Homo." He stood up and started to walk to the car.

We ran after him with food in our hands. I unlocked the car doors and we climbed in with Brian in front. In the backseat, Debra searched for the big book. "The Bible is gone," she exclaimed.

"Are you sure you brought it?"

"Yes, I'm sure. I looked at it right before we went in, I was going to bring it in."

"The car was locked," I said. We looked at Brian.

"The book of knowledge," he smiled. He lifted his hands, made a circle and repeated the same motion he had done earlier. "Look to the East has come."

"It's gone, Jim," Debra heaved. "It is not in the car. I know exactly-- it was right here."

"Where is it Brian?" I asked.

Brian's personality returned. "I don't know. I don't even know what is happening, or where I am half the time," he giggled.

"Now *that* is Brian," Debra said. "Who was the other guy we were talking to in there?"

"I don't know," said Brian. "In where?"

"I am not going anywhere without that Bible," Debra insisted.

I studied Brian to evaluate his mental state. Would this be a psychotic break? A delusion, or hallucination? I didn't accept the story of attack on Voltar's home world. That was a lot of guilt—a projection of guilt. "How do you feel right now?" I asked.

Brian shrugged. "Empty. Totally numb."

"We need to you to be honest with us," I said. "If you think they want you to go back to the desert, and you are going to try and get there--we may be able to help you--somehow. Not with our money, but maybe we could get some. The main thing is we don't want you to try to deceive us. We don't want you to try and trick us, because we are not letting you out of our sight for at least 24 hours."

Brian pondered. "I'm not deceiving you. Didn't they just give you some other points—closer?"

"Do you know where it is?"

"No. Just numbers. It makes no sense to me."

As the car reached the driveway, and as I prepared to accelerate onto La Brea Avenue southbound, I felt a shift of pressure in my brain—like air moved from one hemisphere to the other.

"Did you feel anything?" I asked Brian.

"Energy change--dropped," Brian said.

Debra felt nothing.

"Maybe it is around here somewhere," I said.

Just then Debra gasped. Under a small tree on a grassy knoll rested a big book, with the pages spread open.

"My God," she breathed.

From the backseat, she hugged Brian's neck. "This is a miracle," she said. "A genuine miracle--just for us." Tears welled up into her eyes.

In dark shade, bright sunlight flickered through tall trees, spotlighting a young tree growing next to the big, open Bible. The white pages glistened in a narrow beam of the golden light. The scene looked beautiful, like a painting crafted with sunlight and shadow.

"Did you do that?" Debra asked Brian.

"I don't know," he laughed. "I don't think so."

"That is so beautiful," whispered Debra. "It's like a postcard calling us to visit."

A nearby building had been burned leaving bricks blackened. For such beauty to be found next to ugliness seemed ironic and yet, inspiring--like a baby tree growing from the blackened soil of a forest.

"Well," Debra said. "Let's go see what it says," she pushed to get out of the car. "Remember, he said something about going somewhere and *reading a book of knowledge*."

We knelt down on the shady lawn next to the open Bible. The pages glowed in the bright, flickering light.

"A genuine miracle," whispered Debra, clutching at Brian.

"Is this the right page?" I asked Brian.

"Are you asking me?" Brian laughed.

"Or--anybody else in there."

"No one is telling me anything—except, *Look to the East.* We are supposed to find this other reference point, quick."

We read a few scriptures from II Kings, then drove east through the side streets. Near Beverly and Third, the probe voice began speaking from Brian. "Reference point: 038. Look to the east." I slowed the car and we scanned the neighborhood.

Moments later we rolled near a huge, stone church. The big door stood wide open. "That's the most beautiful church I have ever seen," muttered Brian in a daze.

"Look to the East has come," blasted the probe voice.

Debra and I looked at each other. "It is strange to see a church door wide open in Los Angeles," I mused. "In the middle of the week."

"Do you think this is the reference point?" Debra asked Brian.

"I don't know. All I know is that my head is spinning."

I noted into my tape recorder. "St. Brendan's Catholic church, 300 South Van Ness Avenue."

"It's so beautiful," mumbled Brian. "That is the most beautiful thing I've ever seen."

"Let's go in," said Debra.

Brian is Forgiven

Debra and I led Brian up the steps of the church. Brian wobbled as he walked. "Energy. I need energy. I get dizzy whenever I get near a church," Brian said. "That's why I never liked going."

Debra took his right arm. I held his left arm as we entered through the open door. We shuffled into a huge, dark cathedral decorated by beautiful stained glass windows.

"Wow," breathed Debra. "I've never been inside a Catholic church before. This is beautiful."

"The mind of man," said a deep voice from Brian as his eyes rolled back into his head.

"Who was that?" I asked.

Brian's eyes flipped downward. "Oh God, I think this is the place they wanted," he huffed.

The three of us stood together in the central isle of the long, slender cathedral. Far away, at the other end, waited the majestic altar.

Brian stood up straight. "I've got to do this by myself," he said. He shook off our hands and started to walk forward, but his knees buckled. We caught him and lifted him up. Very slowly, as in a procession, we all walked forward together.

The majesty of the stained glass windows and the high arches in the Gothic ceiling inspired Debra to tears. She sniffled and clutched at Brian.

Tears ran down Brian's cheeks, and then as he looked up to the ceiling water splashed on his forehead, face and shoulders.

Drops just kept falling. I could look up and see them dropping from above. I counted about ten in all.

Brian slipped into trance. "Confirmation. Reference point accepted," said the probe. "Allies engaged. Allies restrain Secondary World. Location acceptable for re-alignment."

Then Brian's personality returned. He patted Debra and stood up.

"Are you okay?" she asked, sniffling.

"It's okay now," he said. "I'm not dizzy. Voltar's world survived." He stepped outside of the pew and moved towards the altar.

"Do you want me to come with you?" she asked urgently.

"No," he shrugged. "I'm all right now."

"Do you want a priest, Brian?" she said standing up. "I am sure there is one here. I will find him."

"No," he shrugged.

"You need a priest?" I asked.

"No, I must do this alone," he said.

Debra sat down next and grabbed my hand tightly. "This is unbelievable, Jim," she cried. "I don't know what is happening. Does this mean they are taking him? Is he going to die?"

"It's their *Play of Life*," I said. "It's for him."

"That's right," she agreed. "It's for him."

"And maybe for you," I whispered.

Debra chuckled. "This world is so strange. Religion is the most important thing to everyone on the planet, but we all know so little about it, especially about anyone else's beliefs. This church is absolutely beautiful, so inspiring."

As we talked, Brian walked across the large cathedral to a display of candles. He lit one and carried it forward to a second, smaller altar off to the side.

We strained to see. In the darkness we could barely perceive Brian's glowing candle, a big cross and the less ornate altar probably used for weddings or baptisms.

Brian stood silently before the altar, talking. We noticed a light beam on the floor and looked upward through the vast Gothic cathedral. High in the ceiling at the apex of the church, a tiny window allowed one ray of golden sunlight into the darkness. The light shone downward through the whole cathedral—like a spotlight casting one beam of light into a dark theatre.

"Look at that," Debra breathed. "This is so beautiful. I just can't believe the beauty." When Brian kneeled to pray, the light beam painted his head and shoulders in warm, golden light. He glowed, like the pages of the book had glowed on the little knoll.

Debra cried. "Look--my God. It's getting more beautiful--this and the Bible on the knoll. How could this be happening?"

"He is in the darkness, praying in light—it's probably just coincidence."

"I don't think so," she said. "It's the *Play of Life*--remember?" We both laughed. That phrase was becoming our explanation for everything.

Debra watched Brian kneel and pray for a long time. "Did the aliens want him here? If they were demons, or a familiar spirit, would they send him here?" She asked.

"I don't know. In the Bible, demons can speak the truth and have great knowledge. They deceive. But can they operate in a church? I don't know. It's probably more about the mind. If a person goes up to a higher level of mind, his view of God must change. His concept of Self and God, must change. That's what gives him the new beginning."

"The *Play of Life?* It does involve God—doesn't it?"

"Yeah, Brian always dismisses the religious aspects. Plays it down. Denies it, even. But it's there."

Debra held my hand tightly. "But what if they are lifting him up to be the anti-Christ? What if this is just making him think he is some powerful leader, and he becomes the anti-Christ?"

"I don't think Brian would go that way. He's an architect."

"But with spoon bending and the rock? Dematerializing solid rock?"

"Jesus said we could do what He did—turning water to wine. Miracles. Maybe we *all* have the capacity. We'd have to learn, somehow."

"This is so weird. I can't figure it out."

"It's a drama. We have to just let it play out. Play our roles. Let Brian play his role. See what happens." I clicked my tape recorder. "I just document everything as it happens—in *their Play of Life.*"

"That's fine for you and your story, Jim," said Debra, "But, I am living with this man. I love him. I am not going to let my Brian become the anti-Christ. I mean, he may be *ignorant* to what is happening to him. They may be lying to him. His mind could be blocked. We've seen enough to know they can turn him off and on. He doesn't know what is happening. They could be using him--and using us. Have you considered that? They could be using YOU to present him to all mankind as some great prophet with paranormal powers--and he denies it all the way, and then turns around, in the end to actually become the anti-Christ."

"I don't think so."

"You don't know, Jim Frazier. You don't know."

"What are you two jabbering about?" said Brian from behind us. Debra jumped out of her seat.

Brian laughed. "You are not supposed to be talking in church."

"Oh my, you scared me. What happened?"

Brian pondered and shrugged. "It's hard to say, exactly."

"You prayed. Did you hear anything?" I asked.

"It was a different voice," Brian said. He seemed calm, peaceful, delivered. "One I've never heard."

"Was it Jesus?" Debra whispered.

"I don't know. He said He was *with me always*, and *would always be.*"

"Is that all?" asked Debra grabbing his hands.

"He said I was *forgiven*," he beamed radiantly.

"Forgiven?" smiled Debra. Tears welled up in her eyes.

"I did a wrong thing with the rock. I'm sorry for what I did with you. I was out of control." She ran to him and hugged him.

"I forgive you," she cried.

"But, I learned. *He* said to go in peace—and go forward. *The reference point was complete.*"

Releasing a river of feelings, Debra sobbed. She hung on Brian as we walked outside into the bright sunlight. "I don't want you to go away," she cried.

"I'm not going anywhere, now. It's over." He comforted her and hugged her warmly. "I learned my lesson, and a lot of people on their world paid the price with their lives. But, He said to go forward -- in peace. Look to the East has come. I am supposed to go forward, for all mankind."

"Look to the East has come?" I said.

"I think it means the same as that other—the first thing—*of the people.* Remember?

"Laos Nous Hikano?" I guessed.

"That's it. Whatever that means. I forget. So much has happened. What a birthday," he said. "I never had such a weird birthday." Debra kissed him.

"I love you, Brian," she said with a whimper. "I thought I was going to lose you."

"No. Not now. It's like a new beginning. I am strengthened—and Voltar's people are too—their allies joined in the battle and helped save their world, or we wouldn't be here right now."

"Allies?" I asked.

"Yep. Now they have other worlds involved. They will help control the grays. They *all* want to set us free."

Hollywood Negotiations

To raise money for the trip to South America, I had negotiated with a movie production company at MGM. They had written a contract for a fair amount of money. I would be co-producer and have an office in Century City.

But their only interest was the Ball of Light Phenomenon, the scary part of the story. They didn't believe in the transformation request and refused to pay for a trip to South America. I hadn't signed the agreement, and began looking for other options.

I went to Steven Spielberg's office at Columbia—Junk Food Productions. The secretary thought I was part of the crew and sent me into a production meeting—unannounced. Stephen was busy and I felt embarrassed. I wanted to meet with him, privately, but he said "no interns--the movie was too personal." I was disappointed. I had taken classes with him and wanted a way to pitch the story with no other audience.

I had to be careful. I realized Dr. Hynek was the prime consultant on the movie, with Jacques Vallee, so I feared the movie might feature someone like

392

Brian. Besides, other people had tried to sell the story from the beginning. Brian had been told that by a talk show host.

But few people knew the real story—only the requests to go to South America, the stress, and the orange ball of light.

I didn't want anyone to know the whole story, until it was complete. I was also able to reach Richard Dreyfus, star of <u>Close Encounters</u>, but he didn't want to help with a real contactee. "I'm just an actor," he laughed.

"This is mind-blowing," breathed Brian. "I didn't even know this was going on." He didn't realize I had been trained to produce and direct movies at USC Cinema School.

"I really don't want to sell it, now," I said. "We need money, but the story is not complete. There is no ending. We need the *"quantum evolution to Nous 10."*

The producers from MGM met Brian, and they wanted proof. They wanted him to bend a spoon with his mind, which, of course, he refused to do. They challenged, and baited him—face to face. Brian's temper flared when one producer insisted. A car key in Brian's hand split in half. The key didn't bend, didn't melt—it split. But, Brian wouldn't even show the key to the man. He was mad—and scared.

"You've got to straighten them out, Jim," Brian said. "This could blow up in your face. All I am is the guy who can design the pyramid. The pyramid is what I am here for, and maybe the biotelemetry scanner, maybe the NOR. But, you've got to sell me as a nuts and bolts kind of guy. Nothing else."

I pleaded with him to bend one spoon. One time. "No! We've been through this, Jim. This paranormal stuff is for only for *education,* to illustrate how this will all work. People will start demanding for me to get on stage. But my stage is a drafting table."

"One time?"

"No. What if I got mad? I can't control this. You saw the key. What if I did that to somebody's head, or a wall of their building?"

"You could do that?"

"Sure. I could put a spoon right into the guy's heart, if I make a mistake and got mad at him. I could rip out a wall. This can be VERY dangerous. And I know I can't control it."

I wanted him to reconsider, maybe let me film a spoon bending in a controlled setting. "NO! It happens when THEY want it to, for THEIR purpose," he shouted. "Remember how bad I screwed up. A lot of people died—men, women and children. It wasn't a joke, Jim. It was for real."

I didn't believe the story of Voltar's world, but I had to accept his position, reluctantly. Brian didn't want to be *famous.* He wanted to do his job, complete his assignment. Perhaps that was noble, wise. But, on the other hand, perhaps he was covering up. Maybe he was using magic tricks, somehow, I wondered. But I had seen the rock move, the spoons bend, and water drops fall while he was in trance, unmoving.

My list of anomalies had grown. At times, I simply ignored the list. My mind couldn't accept it all. Brian was actually transforming before my eyes. He was moving up Maslow's scale of human potential, becoming more compassionate and caring, more able to define himself.

If I was going to document the process of "quantum evolution," I felt that I shouldn't try to force him. However, I was getting fed up with not being able to show off, challenge or understand his paranormal powers. People were forced to accept my words, on faith. I didn't like that.

"Then don't mention them," Brian said. "They are for education, only—and sometimes for my own fun. But not for money."

"That's what man wants to see. He'll pay."

"Remember—*fear not the mind of mankind, Jim.* You have to follow that, too. Fear not what people say, or want," he said. "They are telling me NO, Jim. If they say something, I go by it—nothing a man says or wants will change my mind. It would be like bribery, like blackmail. I have to be an example for others in the future," he said. "It's not just me, it's for those who will come after me."

Brian's New Life

We found a locksmith who made a new key from the pieces. Wanda paid the bill of $3.50. We were all broke, but we were hungry, so Brian walked into a Greek bakery. We heard him carry on a conversation with the lady in Greek. The old lady blushed red. Tears formed in her eyes, and she cried. Moments later Brian walked out with a half-dozen free pastries.

We sat down on the curb in a parking lot and ate. Brian didn't even remember talking to the woman. "They said they would provide sustenance," he laughed.

"You weren't speaking English, Brian," I said. "And neither was she. It sounded Greek."

"I'm not surprised. It's a Greek bakery," Brian laughed.

"But do you know how to speak Greek?"

"I was hungry, and you were hungry. That's all I know. And we had no money."

"But how did you do that?" I said. "If I am going to document this for people to understand, I need to know how things happen."

"I don't even know that I did," shrugged Brian. He smiled and his blue eyes flashed. "Really I don't."

"Brian!" Debra stammered. "You have to know."

"Do you like the pastries?" Brian asked.

"Yes they are great," Debra said.

"Then just thank God."

"Okay. I'll thank God. Now tell me what happened, for real."

"Okay. I just felt *something* come over me—like a wave. It was probably one of their council. He projects all the *Greek stuff—they have specialties*," Brian said imitating a deep-voiced man. "*Very deep voice.*" We all laughed at the bad imitation.

"Brian imitates Brian," laughed Debra. "This is so amazing."

We enjoyed the Greek pastries and that night, since we couldn't afford a present, we gave Brian my wooden back-scratcher for his birthday. We all clowned around scratching his back as his present. Debra cried because she could not afford to buy Brian a nice birthday present. Brian was broke too. His paychecks went to Mary Beth, to old phone bills, to rent at home and the apartment.

I kept asking for an explanation of everything that had happened. In the middle of the night, Brian wrote a note on my typewriter as an explanation:

> **All men are two men in one--one asleep in the light, the other awake in the darkness. When you can see between the two, you will truly discover you--and this moment of truth will cause the greatest change in your life.**

Brian still experienced amnesia to some degree, but he had crossed over the wall, or through a gate in the wall, so many times that the blackouts had diminished. He now slipped between personalities with ease, and though he pretended not to remember, we all thought he did.

The water drops had apparently caused the transition. With the splashes, he was awake, walking and talking as they hit. Afterwards, though he was dizzy and even fell down at times, he often spoke as Voltar or some other being. When the water drops wore off in a few minutes, he came back to being "just Brian."

More and more, he was becoming One with Voltar. Overall, his essence had become a little softer, a little more compassionate and understanding of others. But, he could still be irritable, and agitated—like Brian. He still acted like a clown most of the time—like Brian. But, now he could also be peaceful, comforting and sincere—like Voltar. He could speak *as* Voltar for a moment or two, and display great knowledge.

Enjoying the New Life

That night, Debra lost her favorite pen. Her father had given it to her before he died, and she searched frantically. In the living room of her mom's house in

Fountain Valley, Brian slipped into trance and held out his hands. His eyes rotated up, and his hands opened holding the pen.

"That's it," Debra screamed. "Where did you find it? How did you find it?"

"In my hands," Brian said, calmly after his eyes rolled down.

"Impossible," Debra gasped. Her mother was flabbergasted. She didn't think the pen was even in the house.

"The reasons have to be right," Brian said. He had no idea where the pen had been.

Karen, Debra's girlfriend, heard about the story, and a few days later asked Brian to find her favorite keepsake—a Jewish coin given to her by her father before he died. Brian slipped into trance and the coin materialized into his hands.

"My God," Karen gasped. "That's it. But I lost it at the beach, on the pier. I know I lost it there."

The probe voice spoke through Brian. "Range: 30 miles, radius."

"How did they do that?" gasped Debra.

"It is really pretty easy," Brian smiled. "It just has to be for the right reason, or we would all get creamed by the Secondary World. As far as doing it--that's not hard at all. In fact, it's easier than normal thought."

The next day, Brian materialized a glass sphere for Debra filled with tiny flowers. He gave it to her with a loving smile. "It's a thank you," he said. "I could have gone home with them—even after I was forgiven in the church. But I stayed, because I love you."

She hugged and kissed him passionately in the mall as people watched. Karen, her girlfriend, choked back a tear. Debra had found a man, a *real* man who could cry, who could love. She was jealous.

Earth Energy and the Grid System

Saturday afternoon, on October 17 Brian met Michael Helios at a house in Los Angeles. Debra, Wanda and I listened as they talked about geometry and energy grids on the earth. Brian said the earth grid had to be viewed from above the North Pole to be understood. Five pyramids, built at key nodes on the energy grid, would be needed. With the pyramids in place, Voltar's people could control the energy field of the Earth from satellites.

He said that man could learn, eventually, to activate certain sites on the grid. The energy could influence the human mind. In return, the human mind at Nous level 4, could influence the energy, and physical aspects of the planet. The mind could carry out "quantum displacement."

For now, man could conceive of the earth energy as magnetic, but actually, it was more like the spider-shaped photonic matter in Brian's key drawing.

With a good understanding of the energy and the grid, we would someday learn to stabilize earthquakes, and even change the orbit of the earth, or moon, if necessary. But before man could truly implement Quantum Displacement Physics, we would need full understanding of the grid, and the mind of man—at Nous 4.

During a break in the conversation, Brian materialized a bouquet of flowers for the elegant lady of the house. "Only a yogi could do that," Michael said. He figured it was a magic trick and fumed with anger. He told Brian never to try a stunt like that again. I knew how he felt. Debra and I just laughed.

"It was not stunt," smiled Brian. Debra started to tell Michael about all that had taken place. Brian stopped her, "It's better to say nothing. Even people who are into the 'New Age movement' get upset. Let it be for the little things of love, and those of education." He meant to truly thank the lady, for the meeting was indeed important. We all thought he was begnning to sound a little like Voltar.

As Brian waited for Michael to calm down, he spun a large globe in the living room. He wondered where the first pyramid must be built.

A moment later, he yelped in pain—his hand impaled to the globe.

"What is it? Brian asked. "It really hurts, Jim."

I lifted his wrist slowly, and could see the tip of a big sewing pin stuck at a point just South of Lake Titicaca in Bolivia.

Brian jerked his wrist loose. Blood flowed on the carpet and the globe. "I am dripping all over the place," he shouted. The pin had nailed Brian to the latitude and longitude given in the drawings: Tiahuanaco. Lodged into his left wrist along the bone, the pin required needle-nosed pliers, and a hard tug, to remove. More blood flowed, staining a cloth red.

Michael raged. He didn't like the idea of aliens drawing blood. "As far as I am concerned, aliens--or any life form--that needs to mutilate people and draw blood to make a point, is not evolved, and they are not welcome in this house." He shouted. "You need to get out of this house. Now! You are not invited here to make holes in people, and to create materializations."

"He's afraid," Debra whispered. "He thinks they are spirits." When we departed, Michael told Brian he wouldn't work with any "aliens" who spilled blood.

Brian tried to explain, but couldn't. "I am not good at explaining things, but it was probably my thought that did it."

Later at a restaurant, Brian tried to make the ideas clear to me. Michael had refused to come along. "Write this down and tell him," Brian said with urgency. I grabbed my pen.

"Solid matter moved at Nous 4--via Nous 4," Brian said, reporting words he heard inside his mind. "Transmit and direct energy within range of space that is held with thought. Hands act as a receiver when matter is directed to same.

Amplify. The form and matter lay within the person's mind at the time, and in the space received."

Brian smiled. "Did you get it down?"

"Yeah, I did."

"Well, that's it. That's how they do it. That was from them."

I read the note. "Are you saying it involves thought at mind level four?"

"Yeah," smiled Brian. "You got it. Certainly not at level one, where we are all at now," he laughed. "Or else we'd all be in trouble, things would be flying all over the place," he laughed and waved his arm, hitting a waitress in the backside.

"Sorry, my hamburger just flew out of control," he said laughing hysterically. "Must be these aliens that are bugging me," he giggled, and the waitress laughed.

Insight

Brian and the waitress talked for a long time. When the giggling slowed down, Brian explained to me what happened.

"I was thinking about the pyramid," he said. "There were sewing pins in the house. I had seen them. I know that I had this thought of being pinned to the pyramid like Jesus hanging on the cross, but how it happened--I don't know. How it went into a spinning globe at the exact point—I have no idea. But--I had the thought. They amplified it, and made it happen."

"This is really scary," I said.

"More scary than you know," Brian said. "I have to be very careful. Be happy. Control every whim." He picked up a spoon, and held it up for us all to see. His eyes fluttered for a moment as the handle of the spoon wilted into a graceful curve.

Brian opened his eyes and smiled as the waitress gasped. People at a nearby table froze in awe. "In common terms," he said. "I just project into this Nous four land, and move the rock, or bend the spoon, at THAT level. I move it to another place or bend it there by visualizing it. Then I kinda pop back into this realm. You might call it a dimension, I guess some people do. I have no idea what it is, really," he laughed. "And it is changed. Moved or bent. Whatever you want."

"Whatever YOU want. BY YOUR WILL?" I asked.

"I can't explain it any better. It's not a head-trip type of thing. Like 'willpower.' That's wrong--way wrong. It is more with emotions, with your heart, with feelings." He handed the spoon to me. "It has to be with love," he said, choking on his words.

"Can I learn to do this?" I said holding a microphone.

"When you turn off your tape recorder and accept love," he said. "Their love. My love--as a brother."

I gulped. "Love?"

"Accepting love, giving in love—both. Anything else, and it can become a monster that turns against you. This is serious. It is the most destructive, powerful force on the face of the planet."

"If you can do this at will, YOU can be the most destructive force on the face of the planet," I whispered.

"That's what I am talking about," nodded Brian. "That is what we, as a nation are stepping into, and that is why we need a lot of guidance."

"That's why they don't just do it for us?" I asked.

"Right. We have to learn to use it and control it for ourselves. Remember—free will. Each person to his own mind. Each to his own mistakes."

"Good and bad people?" I asked.

"Good and bad," Brian warned. "We are all people. It will be given to all kinds, to see if man can grow up enough to handle it. Voltar's people could just activate a zone on the earth grid, and bingo, a whole lot of people in that zone will develop it overnight. "

"People could NOT handle this," breathed Debra. "I can tell you that right now. This world would be in chaos, if everyone could do that."

"Are you saying we would self-destruct?" I asked.

"The probability factors that they project, which is what they do in the *Play of Life*—indicate man would self-destruct. That's why we need massive education. That's where you come in--*Earth's own Play of Life.*"

"But can they use any zone?"

"Not *now*," Brian said. "Only Tiahuanaco—maybe a few others. At certain dates. Most of the zones on earth are controlled by the Secondary. Control of those zones is what the big fight is about."

He smiled. "But if I am successful--zones will open up."

"How come you?" I asked. "It must mean we have a chance. Voltar's people must believe YOU have a chance."

"I did enough bad things, and came close to death enough times that I don't have to experiment--not too much. I won't let myself go down that road again. So, it was good for me to see the dark side of life early, to see jails and all the weird crazy people that are locked up, and should be locked up to protect society. But what happens if you can't lock people up, if you can't control evil people by putting them behind bars? What if the evil people are running the land? What if they are the government? What if our government is taken over by the Secondary, and works with them to eliminate everyone else?"

"This is getting really scary," Debra said.

Brian nodded. "We need to be aware. All I know is that that the knowledge man needs to survive this transformation of our world--is at Tiahuanaco. That is why we have to go. And we can't do it by bending spoons for some Hollywood producer. It has to be real. It's that simple. It should be *of the people, by the*

399

people, for the people—the masses, the common people." Brian sounded like Voltar for a moment. My head spun with images. *"The People"*—he had given the words great emotion and feeling.

"The Secondary World will not mess around long, not past 2011--and they may start before then," Brian continued at a frantic pace. "It will be a nightmare for us. They do not want man on this planet, and they have the power to eliminate us. I guarantee you. None of us will even know it is happening. It will be subtle, secret. They can explode underground nuclear waste, or turn nature against us. They could use earthquakes, floods, or even a virus. And, as they exterminate us, they will be experimenting to develop other forms of life that can survive."

"They will be using us as guinea pigs?" said Debra. "As they kill us off?"

"Exactly," Brian said. "They already are using us as guinea pigs. But it will get worse and worse, until they just decide to wipe everyone that is left out--and it will be over, for man. No trace remaining. They will sweep the planet clean and start over again."

"So, you are understanding the purpose behind it all?"

"Well, some of it," Brian said. "If no DNA of man is saved and stored in a way the SECONDARY can't get to it, then the history of man, in this solar system, will be lost--gone. That's the purpose of the pyramid."

"This is getting heavy, Brian," gasped Debra. "I am really getting scared."

"I am not even telling you the scary stuff," Brian said. "This is why I have kept my mouth shut. But, in that church, I was shown, something. God created man and God is trying to protect man. He is our ally. The Secondary World, they are evil, but somehow, they are in control of this planet. I don't know why, or how. Maybe they are God's fallen angels--the real version of Satan.

"Voltar's people are trying work around them. And, right now, I am the best hope they have within all the rules and conditions, because -- they can only use one man at a time."

Knowledge of the Past Revealed

On November 10, Brian woke up startled. He heard the screen door open and suspected a burglar. He checked the clock: 4:30 a.m.

Outside the door, he found an envelope with three crisp $10 bills, a white shirt with gold trim, and an old typewriter. Brian tried on the shirt and it fit perfectly. Then he found a writing on the table. Debra read it aloud.

Nov 10, 2:10.2.6 AM-AE 1976.

Run one. Look to the East has come. Within 12.0.0 hours, past statement, will pass. Nuclear reactor explosion. Russia,

death. Of this, 19 years past knowledge of same. Known earth. Locked.

Open, Run two. Of this, untold truth as stated in Run one, 19 years in past knowledge

Run 3, of this knowledge, Scott given in truth, Ural Mountains. Locked.

"Does this make sense to you?" Debra asked.

"It must be that Russian explosion," Brian said, remembering the Host's visit to his garage. "It was a sign given to the first two UFO investigators. He read the note again. "I get it. It happened in the past. I thought it was in the FUTURE. I saw an explosion, the whole forest ripped up. A lot of people died."

"I'm glad you understand, because I don't," she mumbled.

"You wouldn't know about it. It was before your time."

Brian figured the typewriter was a gift so he could write the history of Voltar's people. That's one thing they wanted him to do, even if he never built the pyramid. The shirt must be for public speaking engagements.

The next day, November 11, the <u>Los Angeles Times</u> carried a news story about the Ural Mountain Disaster.

NUCLEAR REACTOR BLAST DESCRIBED.

LOS ANGELES - American intelligence experts said Tuesday that a major nuclear accident in the Soviet Union nearly two decades ago involved a reactor that went out of control, not an explosion of atomic waste as an exiled Soviet scientist asserted last week.

Two intelligence sources told the Los Angeles Times independently that the mishap occurred in late 1957 or early 1958 and involved a plutonium-production reactor at a Soviet nuclear-weapons complex located several hundred miles northeast of the Caspian Sea near the southernmost Ural Mountains.

The "intelligence sources" diminished the size and the importance of the explosion, and said it was the only "disaster" in the history of the Soviet nuclear program.

Brian felt the article was wrong. He had seen the ground explode. He had heard the Host say something about "underground nuclear waste." He had seen flames rise up from below the ground and rip through the forests killing people— burning them alive. He didn't see any nuclear reactor. The ground exploded— that's what he had seen.

He didn't know that the news article was planted by the CIA to discredit a Soviet scientist who had revealed the disaster. Dr. Zhores A. Medvedev had mentioned the disaster, off-hand, in an article about scientists in the Soviet Union. He had reported that the nuclear waste buried near the surface "blew up like a volcano." The event was well known in the Soviet Union.

The magazine article had been published on November 4th in the New Scientist magazine in London. Discrediting began a few days later in Europe. Medvedev's claims were called "rubbish" and pure "science fiction," a "figment of the imagination" by the United Kingdom Atomic Energy authority. That made the scientist angry.

Other articles appeared, attacking Medvedev. Brian didn't know the Soviet geneticist would be so upset by efforts to discredit his report, that in 1979 he would publish a book –Nuclear Disaster in the Urals—that proved suppression of the disaster by the CIA and by the United Kingdom Atomic Energy Authority.

Brian didn't know that the geneticist had studied effects of the radiation on DNA of plants, animals and people, first-hand. The disaster had been a highpoint of Soviet science bringing atomic physicists together with geneticists, as a team led by Medvedev.

Their studies had been widely published in Russian journals, but suppressed for two decades in the western world so that anti-nuclear activists could not use the information to create hysteria and swing voters against nuclear power plants.

As Brian tried on the white shirt with gold, braided trim, he didn't know that seventeen years later, in 1993, declassified reports published by the Institute for Biophysics of the Soviet Ministry, would confirm 28,000 people had been irradiated and more than 8,000 had died from the catastrophe at the Mayak nuclear complex located at Kyshtym, 60 miles northwest of Chelybinsk.

Brian knew the white shirt and the published revelation meant something important. A secret had been revealed—a truth uncovered for mankind to see, and understand. He knew that when the Host showed him the explosions, that *time* had been a factor that *would 'mark the mind of mankind.'* He wondered about the full meaning. Why not just explain everything, he wondered. But then he remembered: the Host knew best what to do, and when.

Brian had come full circle—from secrecy to revelation, from confusion to clarity about his own life. Why did the Host keep secrets? Why didn't he make everything clear? Brian didn't know, but one issue was very clear: vital information had been successfully kept from the American people, and the people of Europe for nearly two decades.

The government can successfully keep a secret. Perhaps, that was the Host's point. Perhaps, the first UFO investigators would remember what the Host had said about the fate of mankind--*underground nuclear waste, exploding and burning people alive.*

Brian didn't know, for sure. But he decided to wear the white shirt in lectures, especially when he talked about the Secondary World—and the fate of mankind.

Knowledge Given to the People

Wearing his beautiful white shirt with gold trim, Brian spoke at several gatherings over the next two weeks. I introduced the story and gave a basic chronology. He didn't say too much about the Ural Mountain disaster, because the Soviet scientist was being discredited in the media by CIA-placed stories.

Instead, Brian told about the first abduction, then introduced experts, witnesses and other contactees.

A UFO investigator/computer programmer, Bill Hamilton, who had studied all the documents in detail, spoke about technical information in the writings. Bill wore black-rimmed glasses and spoke to the crowd in a serious tone. He had served in the Air Force working on intelligence projects. "The Brian Scott writings include logical factors for understanding a science called "Quantum Displacement Physics," he said. "And, they describe nine descents of two alien groups. The writings indicate that the 'grays' believe they are responsible for the genetic evolution of man on earth, and that they have been creating, tracking, and manipulating various 'plantations' of men. The last major descent at Tiahuanaco was 110 B.C. They indicated that the knowledge mankind needs is about this last descent at Tiahuanaco in 110 B.C. That's their focus. They want Brian to go there and learn about their ninth descent as preparation for their tenth descent. I believe the drawings show that this started in 1971 and will end in 2011—a 40 year span of time: their final descent."

Then another independent researcher, Max Redfield, addressed the audience. He had been an Air Force rocket technician, and spoke sharply with clipped speech. "Nous Laos Hikano," Redfield said to the audience. "That is the first writing that Brian Scott received in this volume of pages, which are mostly written for his own understanding, I believe.

"Nous means 'god-mind,' Laos means 'the common people.' The last word is very important: Hikanos. It is the verb, the linking action. You can find all of these words in the Bible and in Strong's Greek Concordance. Hikanos refers to 'a coming...an arrival...a return. But it is more than just arriving or returning, it

403

implies teaching, even preaching. It means to arrive 'fit, complete, in season, ready for the work to be done...for the teaching or nourishing,' which is a word the Host uses in other writings." The crowed gasped with understanding.

"When you put the words together, it probably means something like the 'The God Mind of Man Returns to the People, to teach the people or nourish the people.' Or, 'The God-Mind, to the people, returns complete, ready to teach.'"

The audience whispered with awe. Then someone shouted from the group. "Are you saying that Brian is going to become a prophet? Because if you get religious things all mixed up in here, the people are not going to buy that. Is he a UFO contactee or a prophet? You can't be both--at least I hope not."

The crowd laughed. I returned to the podium. "We don't exactly know the meaning or the purpose of everything in Brian's writings. In brief, Brian is a pyramid designer. They want him to design a pyramid at Tiahuanaco. They want him to experience a "quantum evolution to Nous 10" in two phases, on December 22, 1976 and June 22, 1977. They say that ten gifts will be given to mankind as a result of this. That's all we know for sure. They have been very specific to say that this does not relate to the Second Coming of Jesus Christ, but they did make a reference to bringing in a thousand years of peace, which is prophesied in Revelation, after Jesus wins the battle of Armageddon."

Brian stood up and politely took the podium. "All of this religious stuff is really not part of it at all. People have tried to read in a lot of it, and people ask questions. It seems that everyone is always asking about God, or Jesus or Buddha or something. I guess we all have questions about God.

"But my little part is not about religion. Like I have said, a million times, people--like us--from another world are trying to help us. It's that simple. They don't like the situation we are in with this Secondary World, and they are trying to help us out of this mess--anyway they can. That's it. But they can't do that much. They are monitored. They operate under conditions. Rigid conditions. They are doing all they can. The rest is up to us, to 'the people' as they say-- which is you."

The audience seemed to understand.

"All we are asking is that you help us get to South America and see what it is all about. It won't take much and they are willing to give plenty in return. They will give ten times more--at least ten times more in return. That's all I know. That's about all I can say."

Brian accepted a question: "Is there going to be a mass landing in Tiahuanaco on December 22?"

"No," Brian said. "But the drawings show a 'cathode beam projection.' And they have said there will be something we can see and record and photograph-- but not a landing."

"What are these descents, then? These ten descents that you say they have given with all of the dates and locations."

"I don't know," Brian said.

One of the guests, a stocky UFO contactee about 60 years old stepped to the podium. "I've been studying this for years. I see a descent as an incarnation--a mass incarnation. I think that is what they mean--an uplifting of the mind of the people through the process of incarnation. Anybody who goes around promising a landing shouldn't be trusted. They never have done that--and never will. That's not what is about. You need to study some ancient history. The same thing has happened from the Sumerians onward. One man is picked and 'transformed'—the society follows. It's always one man, first. What Brian is talking about is not that unusual."

Brian nodded. "We have to understand our own world before we can understand theirs. That's what they told me. Maybe he's right."

"What about their technology on the craft?" a young man asked. "How can they take people, without other people seeing the craft?"

Brian shrugged and another researcher stood up--a retired professor of anthropology. "I would like to say one thing. Many researchers are confused about this. But the technology on the craft and the method of communication in Brian's data indicate a mental process is underway, some of the time. For example, when Brian goes into trance to talk to them, he experiences "waking up" in their world. It is real to them. I have asked him about this in detail and he has described this machine they use--this big ring computer, they call it the NOR for Neural-Optical-Responder. They have one on the craft and another at their home world. He emerges into the center of this ring, in his physical form, but not in his earthly body. Yet it is a body that looks just like his earth body. Now, to us, this sounds very unfamiliar, mystical and unbelievable. But to them it sounds common place. Some people call this an *astral body,* or another, ephemeral form of the human body. Supposedly, we all have one.

"Many contactees have reported being zapped out of their sleep to appear in a craft where they received instruction or an exam--while their body was asleep. Some religions and mystical cults teach all about astral travel, soul travel, travel out-of-the body and multi-dimensional realities. We, in our western culture, dismiss it as fantasy. But it not unusual on our planet. The concept has been with us for thousands of years, in cultures around the world.

"In fact, this concept is at the very core of many religions. It is not alien. It is human. In fact, it is very pervasive on our planet. It is more familiar to some of you in the concept of a totem." He paused as the audience whispered.

"In native American religions, the idea is that you take the soul out of the body and put it into a secondary object–a rock, or a box, or a totem pole–then it is safe when the body goes into battle. If the body dies, at least the soul is safe in the totem.

"I say this to repeat to you that this is not an alien belief. It is human, native to our planet. Very widespread. The shamans and the witch doctors supposedly had the skill and technique to take the soul out of the body, to heal it, or to separate it during the initiation of a young man into the tribe. Then they put it back into the body when all of the rituals were complete. Sometimes the soul of an animal was placed into the body and united with the soul of the boy to give him the strength or the traits of the animal.

"You see remnants of this today in the Cub Scouts, in team mascots, and team logos in sports. The team draws strength from their mascot, from their name, their logos—which means the Presence or spiritual power behind the image.

"This is all considered pagan, and I believe, a lot of the understanding was suppressed and removed from our society—by the Roman Catholic Church with book-burnings. But, as some of you know, even in Christianity, incarnation of the divine spirit into the Christian is the core of their beliefs. So, even in our western, Christian society, one unifying concept is at the core of the religious experience-- incarnation."

The audience gasped with understanding.

The professor continued. "So, what all these aliens appear to be saying to me, is that they have perfected this process as a science. They seem to be able to take people up in levels of mind, say, when out of the body, to Nous 10--mind level ten. Then take them back down again to Nous 1. They do it with some sort of a ring computer, or device which Brian has described as the NOR. For him, the experience includes ascending and descending in mind levels while being transported to their world.

"He believes he is on a different world, but his body is here. At each level he sees and experiences things differently, but some people play similar roles on the different levels. Now, somehow this is all related to time. Time is displaced by mind at level four, to create the movement of matter and energy through space, over distance. So time is the key factor along with mind at level 4. We don't understand these concepts. At least I don't—maybe you do."

The audience laughed.

"Brian's drawings indicate that this calendar of Tiahuanaco—the Gate of the Sun--is the key to the knowledge mankind seeks. The writings say the Gate of the Sun is the key to "mind levels two through ten." That is why, in part, they want Brian to go there. He is supposed to touch it, and return to us with this knowledge." The white-haired professor paused. "I am not sure what this means about what mind level we are on."

The audience laughed.

I took the podium. "We are not even on the scale." The audience laughed. "Actually we are at Nous one--or below!" the audience chuckled. "If Brian is going to get to South America and return with these ten gifts for mankind, we are probably going to need your help," I said. "We are open to your ideas and suggestions. Thank you for coming. We will be here to talk with you down front." The audience applauded as Brian stood up.

As I stepped down, Wanda and Debra rushed up. "You should ask for money."

"Even the churches ask for money," said Debra. "There is nothing wrong with asking for what you need."

I ran back up to the microphone. "If you want to make contributions, and help us get to South America, come down here in front. These two ladies will take your gift." I pointed at Wanda and Debra. They giggled, girlishly.

Afterwards Wanda and Debra counted up the money: $220. It seemed hopeless. "This won't work," said Wanda. "Only forty more lectures, and we can all go."

The Fraud and Scotland Yard

The clock was ticking. We had less than 30 days, if we were going to go to South America.

The radio astronomer Duncan Lunan called from Scotland. He wanted more details on the data sent to him. He had questions. We tried to talk by phone but Brian couldn't understand his questions on astronomy. By long distance, talk was hopeless.

"I need to give him what he needs," Brian said afterwards with frustration. "He's way off course on some things, and right about others. I have to find a way to do this."

Working with the probe and Voltar on Saturday, November 20th, Brian gradually received information to draw a schematic target in space. "If he transmits to that target, from December 19-24th, with the beeps---he should get a signal that will change the world."

The target showed a signal transmitted through a gateway in space. The next day, I sent the target out to Lunan by express mail.

We didn't know that Lunan suspected Brian of fraud. Or, that he had contacted British Intelligence and Scotland Yard through an associate—a British intelligence officer. He wanted a report. He thought we had burglarized his home.

Lunan suspected that Brian had come to Scotland, broken into his home and somehow opened his vault to obtain his private research data. No one else could have obtained his data without years of work.

He was also convinced that one drawing in Brian's book of documents was a fraud. The message on the Voyager deep space probe had been copied from a well-known book published with errors. Brian's drawing repeated the errors.

Despite his *proof of a hoax*, Lunan felt some of the information was valid and very important—especially the date, December 22, 1976. At no other time in the history of the world had the alignments at Stonehenge been so significant.

As we sent the target, he waited for a report on Brian and me from the FBI. The classified report was being sent to British Intelligence at Scotland Yard in London.

Voltar Emerges as Brian

The next day, Sunday November 21st, 1976, Brian drove us up into the mountains behind Tustin. We walked down a short trail to a rocky amphitheater. "It's an old Indian place," Brian said. "Holy Ground. He removed his shoes, and led us into the amphitheater of gray rock. The natural stone walls stood 15 feet tall surrounding a grassy meadow about 20 feet across. In the center of the grass lay one flat stone--like a podium or stage.

Brian had been directed to the place when he was sixteen, after seeing the first orange ball of light.

"It's like a Greek theater," I said. "Only small."

"You don't need a big space," Brian said. "You could bring *the People* here. It's called the 'Place of the Whole.'"

"The People?" I asked.

"What people?" Debra asked.

Brian sat down on the stone in the meadow and relaxed. Debra and Wanda spread out blankets and gathered around him with picnic baskets open.

Within moments, Voltar began. "I am here with you. I am open to all that is about me." His voice echoed from the high walls of gray stone. We were a bit shocked. What if someone saw us?

"Fear not the mind of mankind, for you are all one," Voltar's voice boomed.

We were awed by the powerful sound from Brian's throat. Finally, I stammered. "Your presence is so...big."

Voltar spoke gently. "Words come from the heart, not the mind for in the heart is truth. Speak brother. Let your heart reach out. Love is always with you."

"I am greatly awed by your presence," I said. "We feel very small, I guess."

"You should not feel this way. There is nothing small within the gift of love. We are all equal."

"It is difficult in a way to relate to you through Brian. Why do you do this? Why not just appear and talk to us?"

"Of the Secondary," Voltar said. "We cannot do all that we desire."

He spoke for several hours in fluid, soothing tones, answering our questions about life, death, his world and ours. Voltar said his people were involved in genetic research related to consciousness, and they all participated in their government through a *Play of Life*--projecting probabilities of the future, using knowledge of the past.

To get the emotions right in their projections, they created plays involving the deepest personal dilemmas and mistakes in judgment—plus all the facts. They didn't believe in luck, or chance. They made predictions, and created the future, testing and recording their probabilities along the way. They kept track of their errors and successes. For generation upon generation, they had used the *Play of Life* in their governing process.

They operated a *Play of Life* for each world they tried to help, and each civilization on our world that had been uplifted by them, experienced a *Play of Life*, in their era, and location.

Each of us--Brian and I, Debra and Wanda--were characters in their *Play of Life* for earth. They knew all about each of us--details of our childhood, our families and our parents.

People on their world rooted and cheered for us. Some even imitated and dressed like one of us in their *Play of Life* sessions. We were famous in their world. It all seemed so hard to believe. So, we laughed and went along for the fun and the wisdom, and the discussions.

Debra wanted answers about religion. She asked about reincarnation. "Is it true that we have had previous lifetimes on this earth?"

"No, it is not true in that sense--that you have truly been another body," Voltar said. "You have been a spirit of mind that dwells within the universe--an energy of thought. This is created within a body. As each person is born there are those who are open to these things more than others. And in your land they do call it reincarnation. But it's true meaning is not that of the same."

"Is there a better word or phrase to describe this concept other than reincarnation?" asked Wanda.

"Yes. I would find a word in our land, as we say: the spirit of God--it is eternal."

"The question of death has importance to many," I said.

"The energy force within your body will survive for all time to come. In this, there is not death, but a birth into another life, and of this, the next dimension."

"So what happens? Will we remember this life?"

"You will be held there in that knowledge, until all throughout the entire world, and all throughout the universes are united, and in that moment each will be reborn again and have complete knowledge of what has gone before him."

"So, when we go into this other dimension...."

"Your terminology--but in reality it is a spirit of raising your level of human self. Man does not truly understand at Nous 1. There is knowledge, and there is wisdom and there is individuality in this also."

"That was my question—individuality survives?" I asked.

"As I have said before, when the time is right, bring those that you will to me here, in this place. And I will be with them, from that moment on. There will be days when I will energize the land to bring forth a greater meaning to what will take place, and in those days, the ground itself will be sacred, and you must not walk on it with your shoes or the sandals on your feet. In this we offer the teachings that will come, in the greater time, those of the teachings of God, and in that, through His knowledge the land is sacred and hallowed."

"Is this like an outside church?"

"What better place? When the time is right, you will bring forth a people to this land, and Brian will walk amongst them and pass bread among them and ask each to reflect on the spirit of God and to reach outward and to receive this, and then to rise and depart.

"There is much more to pass. The Day of Twenty is not complete. The tests are not over. And, there are many drawings to pass to Brian.

"There is much to be given. The pyramid is the whole. Quantum Displacement Physics, and the NOR and the touch--the parts are many. For you are linked to the past, the calendar and the timetable of the world, and the people that dwell within the Southern hemisphere.

"Mysteries abound. How these people survived and built? Of the future, the vehicles, the power provided throughout the region, the experimentation, knowledge of the probe and of the NOR. All of this shall pass of Brian, of I--and in part, of you--and man will become closer to himself, and those about him.

"If man accepts and uses this knowledge in the physical form, a greater gift will pass in return. Of this, ten gifts await man--five are of knowledge, and five are of the spirit; and the greatest of these is the touch, and by this the knowledge for one-thousand years of peace on your world."

Debra's head jerked up.

"In this, the promise fulfilled?"

Brian stood up suddenly in a huff and brushed the dirt off his clothes. "I itch like crazy. I thought the damn bugs were crawling all over me."

"It must be incredible for you," I said to Brian.

"Yeah. It's basically a reversal. I go there. He comes here."

"Did you get to see his little boy, this time?" Debra asked.

410

"Oh, they were in school this time. I like playing with the kids, but not this time."

"What did you do?"

"Oh, you know. There is the guy who is the big joker up there, I told you about–Danyael. He does the training and tests for those who come to this world and have to act out being human."

"How?" I asked.

"You know. You think we are going through a lot. Voltar is the one who has to go through the most preparation. He's going through training, too."

"Can we find out more, now?"

"Not now," Brian said. "This was different. For ten days we have to wait. It's this twenty-day thing. If we do it before twenty days, they have to use energy. This was a test to see if he could avoid going through the probe. This one was NOT through the probe. If it were, the Secondary could over-ride the responses."

Debra was concerned. "He said something about the touch, a gift you would receive that would bring about a thousand years of peace."

"I didn't hear that. I am blocked out on some things, or I am just busy. But I am supposed to get the gift of touch, whatever that is. I have no idea. They really don't tell me that much about what will happen," he said. "It's all probabilities to them, anyway."

Debra felt Brian was purposely avoiding questions about the 'thousand years of peace to come.'" He finally refused to talk about it.

For the rest of the day, we climbed around in the mountains and explored the site. Brian described Voltar's world.

"There is the center that I arrive in--the NOR. It allows you to take your mind, spirit and soul. It feels just as if you take your body with you in total comfort. That's actually what happens. Then there is a terminal that takes you to the level underneath, and another terminal that takes you up a level above. There are recreation areas. One place--the little kids play a game like tennis, only with their mind.

"Then, on the other side of this is the council--like the center of government, like our Congress in Washington, D.C. It is a very large dome under the ground, three stories tall, with five different round buildings that stem off from the center. The greater Council meetings are held in the Center, then other meetings are held in the five smaller domes. You would love this place, Jim. Danyael directs the main *Play of Life* there, and all the people vote on the enactments, based on probabilities computed for each issue."

"Like forecasting the future?"

"Right, but they don't just predict. They create. They run probabilities, draw from the past, factor in all the human emotions of each person, and then their people vote—everyone votes. It's a true democracy. The council argues and presents plans, but the people all vote."

"What did you do there?"

"I went inside and finished the last of what was needed for the guidance here, for the circle here and all. They kind of look up to me. I am treated like a king. It's great. I mean everyone knows me. Everything is known and the people are filled with love for me, for us, for our world."

Brian's fantasy world fully included us. We were all drawn in, and included, in some way that seemed good. We began to accept his inner world as very real to him—at least. He was driven by feelings about this other world. We reluctantly joined with him to some degree, like someone testing the water, but none of us jumped. When we were alone, Debra, Wanda and I constantly discussed our earthly theories and score cards: multiple-personalities, demonic possession or familiar spirits, and hoax. We even felt it might be some combination of all. Certainly, Brian at level one could tell a good story, but the anomalies and deep emotions made us consider that something else was going on—perhaps something that had not happened to modern man, something we might not ever understand.

Thanksgiving Day

As Thanksgiving Day approached, Wanda and Debra planned a big dinner in Hollywood with various friends, including struggling actors, writers and directors, UFO contactees and investigators.

The day before Thanksgiving I called Brian at work late in the afternoon. Brian had decorated his work area with turkeys and symbols of Thanksgiving Day in America. Brian masqueraded as the turkey wearing a mask. He was clowning around with other draftsmen when the call came to his desk.

"Duncan Lunan sent a letter with a lot of questions," I said. "It is to me, not you. He says he has proof that you falsified some of the data and that you are a fraud."

"A fraud!" Brian exclaimed.

"That's what he says. But he can't figure out how you got hold of his good information. So he's baffled."

Brian slammed his fist down hard on his drafting table.

"Damn it," he swore. "I should have written a letter to him. Can we call him?"

"We could try tomorrow." I said. "It's night time in his part of the world."

The next day, Brian and Debra drove into Hollywood, down Melrose Boulevard all dressed in their best cloths. Brian wore his corduroy jacket, blue dress shirt and tie. Debra, wearing a colorful red dress, carried a cooked turkey on her lap in a big pan. Debra's two-year son sat in a car seat in the back with a big smile on his face.

Brian dodged in and out of traffic as he puffed angrily on a cigarette.

"Slow down," Debra whined.

"We're late, damn it," Brian steamed. "We have to call Lunan by noon."

Brian slammed on his brakes and yelled at a black car, filled with low-riders.

"Pull over, and park it," he shouted.

"Brian what are you doing?"

"Those guys won't get out of the way. They are purposely hogging both lanes."

"Calm down! You are just upset about Lunan's letter."

"If he doesn't send those signals, it will be worthless to go to South America--even if Jim gets the money. They won't unlock the probe unless there is a signal. That's been set for thousands of years, no one can change that."

Brian pounded hard on the horn. Debra watched the big black car swerve slowly, taking up both lanes of traffic.

"Are they doing that on purpose?"

"Of course they are." Brian wanted to ram the car and accelerated quickly.

"Damn it. I can't do anything with a Volkswagen."

"Just go slow."

"I am about to explode!"

Brian accelerated and began honking. He swerved into oncoming traffic with his lights flashing. Other cars screeched and halted. When he had passed the low-riding Buick, he slowed to a stop. The Buick also stopped. Brian jumped out and walked to the driver's door.

"What's the matter, man?" the young low-rider asked.

"You," Brian screamed.

The tattooed man jumped out of the car and clicked open a knife. Cars in both lanes honked with alarm. The knife swiped at Brian, but he stepped back and kicked the young man in the hip. Brian caught his arm and dislodged the knife.

Then Brian whirled the young man around and hit his face hard. Blood exploded from his nose. Brian twisted the guy's face downward with his left hand as he swung upward with his right. The power of the blow splattered more blood and knocked the young man back onto the Buick, dazed.

Debra screamed. "What are you doing, Brian? Stop it!"

Brian charged at the young man, and pulled him to the sidewalk.

"You're going to die," the young man hissed in pain. Three friends climbed out of the car. "Take your best shot," Brian snarled at them. With his bloody fists raised he challenged them. "Come on," he snarled. "I'm late for a meeting. Make it quick. Who's next?"

About twenty years old, none of them stepped forward. Brian charged, and they stepped back. He laughed.

"Your friend needs some road manners," he snarled, at them. "Next time, tell him not to get in MY way."

Debra watched in shock as Brian strolled back to the car. He jumped in and drove away waving at all the people who honked horns. He lit up a Marlboro cigarette with his bleeding hands, and exhaled slowly. He felt better.

"You nearly killed that kid," Debra gasped.

"He'll be fine in a couple of weeks. It's the price they have to pay for messing with ME—today. He's lucky I used physical force instead of something else."

"Brian, what are you? A man of God--or not."

"I'm a frustrated son of a bitch, and I don't take shit from no one," he snarled. Debra gasped.

"That's the way I used to be," he said with a chuckle. "I haven't done anything like that for a long time, okay. I feel better now. But for me, that was my life. For a long time—back in '71 and before."

"I hope you have changed."

"I have. I'm not like that anymore."

"Good, I don't want my son to see anything like that again."

At my house, Brian cleaned up his hands in the bathroom, carved the turkey and joined in the fun. Brian and Debra were dressed more conservatively and formally than the rest of the Hollywood crowd, but Brian kept everyone laughing with funny jokes and imitations.

No mention was made of the fight until afterwards, late in the night, when Brian and I finally called Duncan Lunan.

"What happened to your hands?" I asked as Brian held the phone, waiting.

"Oh, some punks," he mumbled. "Lunan is not answering the phone. Ten rings."

"Well, it's the day after Thanksgiving there. He may have gone away."

"We've got to get a hold of him, Jim," Brian whined. "Someone has to transmit those signals or nothing will happen."

"Can't they just unlock the probe themselves?" I asked. "What is the big deal, if they know we are there?"

"Man has to comply. Man has to reply," Brian said with disappointment. "Remember the wall of red lights? They will not go around it. If man complies, the lights go off. When a certain number are off, then they can have a contact--a little visit. It has to be in steps. It evaluates everything, our technology, our purposes—and their own. There is no way they will go around that."

414

"So it has to be a signal from us, from earth."

"It has to be. They gave us everything to make it happen."

Lunan had contacted British Intelligence through a British Army Colonel interested in his book, <u>Interstellar Contact</u>. Scotland Yard received an FBI report on Brian that shook Lunan, but for a strange reason.

Lunan had hoped we were crooks. He hoped we had been to Scotland and had somehow robbed his house. But the report said we had not left the United States. The Army Colonel read him the report. "They are kooky, but harmless. Scott has a record and has been in jail for small-time crimes. Frazier is clean. They talk a lot on the phone, but they have no support from subversive groups in the U.K, or the U.S. No money. No guns. No intent to overthrow the government."

The report bothered Lunan. Now he faced a dilemma. The hoax wasn't serious. Brian had not offered the Voyager message as anything special. It was never offered as proof.

More important to Lunan, some of the drawings corrected his data. To develop that knowledge would take years of research by a scholar, like him. The source had to be someone with more knowledge than his own regarding Stonehenge, Tiahuanaco and astronomy.

But, the date for the transformation motivated him more than any of the data: December 22, 1976. The alignment at Stonehenge on that date was unique. It had never existed before--and would not exist again—for thousands of years.

Brian's Decision

On December 4, at about 3:45 a.m. Brian slipped into trance at my house. From his viewpoint, he awoke in the NOR, the giant ringed computer on Voltar's world. A small group of people waited for him including Voltar's wife, and Voltar's children. They all seemed very serious.

"The council is in session," said Voltar's wife. A large group of people had gathered at the entrance of the central dome. As Brian watched in the sky, hundreds of small craft approached and parked near the dome. Lower to the ground, people zipped through the air in small groups, all wearing blinking belts.

"What is going on?" Brian asked. "Why are all of these people coming?" The crowd surged with people cheering, then booing.

"It is Danyael's *Play of Life*. Voltar and the council will not risk another attack from..." She gestured by making large eyes with her hands, and smirked. "Those of Nous 9--your Secondary World. If we die, we will do so voluntarily."

"I don't understand," Brian said.

415

"Some of the people want Danyael to override the probes and allow more information to be given. They want you to go to Tiahuanaco, at any cost, to bring the knowledge of Nous 4 to your people." She gestured at the crowd. "These people are volunteering to give up their lives, so that you can go--to override the probes."

"Give up their lives?"

"It is a sacrifice they would make. If so many of the people voluntarily give up their lives, the vote of the council can be over-ridden and a sector of the safeguards lowered. It is well known within our land. This is the only way to override the safeguards. And, this can only be done by life-energy, by the energy of our being."

"That is hard to believe."

"The safeguards are of neural energy, not of electrical nature as your world. The energy of our world is the energy of our being, united with the energy of the planet. Your world will discover this, and in that day, all will be changed for you. But that is in your future."

A signal blinked on her belt.

"Voltar is ready for you, now," she said as they walked along the sidewalk. "I don't think they will allow you to speak before the entire council at this time of urgency, but you may discuss with Voltar and his committee--about Viracocha and your choices."

"Viracocha?" Brian asked as they entered a version of the Earth Room. He heard Debra's voice and saw Voltar sitting at a panel answering questions. Voltar nodded. He pushed a button on his belt and stood up, leaving a second form of his own, sitting--Viracocha.

Brian listened as the god of Tiahuanaco answered a question from me about astronomy, and measurement of the lunar cycle as practiced by the Incans.

Voltar laughed. "Jim wants to know everything."

Voltar escorted Brian into the larger council chambers where a thunderous crowd cheered and booed.

Danyael stood before them with his arms uplifted. Beautiful blond and red-headed people shouted. "Override the probes. We will give our lives. Take me. Let it be done of I. Take me. Take me."

The sound of their voices echoed around the amphitheater.

Voltar whispered. "Of this, the people would willingly die to bring about Nous 4 at Tiahuanaco, but the alternatives have been offered. As you have free will in this, we must know now your preferred choice, for a decision must be made."

"What are my choices?"

"Nous three, or Nous four--December 22. Of this, you and I would be as one, all day, all night from then forward, upon the land." Brian understood.

He watched as Danyael pleaded to the assembly. "But the drawings have not even been done. Brian has made no progress--not even one. Without at least one drawing--of his own free will, we cannot proceed. The projection factor of fulfillment is below 35%--the minimum required."

"Viracocha," someone chanted from high above. The crowd broke into a chant. "Viracocha, Viracocha, Viracocha."

Brian watched in amazement. "I don't think I can handle Nous four," he said to Voltar. "It is very squirrely on earth. The emotions are overwhelming. How could I walk around the streets that way? I still have to make a living. I have no way to survive."

Danyael saw Brian and hurried over to him with tears in his eyes.

"Our people would die for you and your world. How can it be that you have not completed one drawing? What can I offer them? I fear their sacrifice would be a loss--with no gain. What do you say of this?"

"I am sure I can do ONE," Brian managed. "But...I think it is...it is..."

"Fear not the mind of mankind," Voltar said in a soothing tone.

Brian choked back a tear. "I've never been...been anything...and if I took Nous 4...and I was something, somebody--I would feel great--but then...then what happens if I blow it? Then what. Your people--I would fail them, AND our world."

"Your testing rigorous within the *Play of Life*," Danyael said. "Projection factors indicate 68 percent success."

"That is not high enough," Brian said.

"But the Day of Twenty is not complete," Voltar said.

"How much more can there be?" Brian said." We have to leave next week."

Danyael stepped forward. "That of I, within the projection of Jim will be with you. He will know what to do. The tests will continue. But probabilities will rise greatly, with one drawing--to 78 percent."

"But we can't get there," Brian said.

"One drawing," Danyael urged.

"The Council will not allow us to override the probes, not again," Voltar said. "When the Secondary World enslaved us, on Epsilon Bootees, the decision was similar. Thousands of our own gave up their lives--but it was wrong--they were deceived, and we were betrayed into their hands."

Brian paced nervously. They wanted a decision. The door opened and a few more members of the Council entered the massive auditorium. One man gestured, and suddenly Brian's voice was projected to the thousands of people. The councilman pulled Brian out onto the stage.

417

"I wish it were somebody else," Brian said. His voice echoed and the people cheered, wildly. They shouted his name.

"BRIAN. BRIAN--the strong. BRIAN—the brave."

He felt awed, overwhelmed. He could not understand why they would be cheering for him. "I am the wrong guy for this," he shouted. "I am simply the wrong person." The crowd booed, hissed and cheered him on, all at the same time.

"Many of your world would seek to bring Nous 4 to their people," said Voltar. "But of this, you are of I and of Viracocha–and like he, a common man. You are the only one who can bring this to man. Fear not, your own mind, for I will be with you."

Brian shook his head negatively. "For now, could I just take a two?"

The crowd roared with laughter. Danyael laughed and stepped forward. "Brian, you are well-prepared for Nous 4, by the *Play of Life*."

He gestured to the crowd as they cheered—"Nous 4, Nous 4. Viracocha, Viracocha, Over-ride the probe."

Danyael comforted Brian with an arm on his shoulder. "You need not maintain the projection of Nous 4, twenty four hours a day. But the wisdom and knowledge of Nous 4 will remain."

"That's what I am afraid of," Brian said. "To know these things, to feel these things. How could I ever go back to being the same? How could I go to work and be Brian? I can't be of your world AND ours!" he whined.

"Of this, the training will continue," Danyael smiled. "You have Jim, and Debra and Wanda. And others about you--they do understand. Many more of your world will understand."

Brian laughed. "No one at work would understand. And if I become famous, my past..."

"Your past will be forgotten after that day, Brian," Voltar said in a soothing tone. "For you will not be the same, and this will be seen by all who know you."

Brian's head dropped.

"I would feel better just taking a two--or maybe let someone else do it. Jim would love this," he said. "I just can't do it. I know I am the wrong person. You should have just gotten somebody else," Brian said, saddened. "I'm sorry. I just can't do it."

The room silenced. Free-will had to be respected in the *Play of Life*. Brian looked at thousands of people watching him in the amphitheater. "I can't do it. I am not worthy." His voice echoed throughout the dome. "Don't give up your lives for me." He figured their sacrifice would not be needed if he said no.

Voltar's wife moved close to Brian "Who on your world, is more worthy than you Brian? Who among man is worthy of anything we seek to give?"

Voltar opened a Bible and read to the crowd.

"And he went to the Mount of Olives, and his disciples followed him. He said unto them. 'Pray that ye enter not into temptation,' and he withdrew from them a stone's cast and kneeled down and prayed saying 'Father, if thou be willing, remove this cup from me, nevertheless not my will, but thine be done.'

"And there appeared an angel unto him from heaven, strengthening him...." Voltar paused as the crowd roared.

Brian wondered why they roared.

"And there appeared an ANGEL unto Him from heaven STRENGTHENING Him." Again the crowd roared. Brian smiled.

Voltar lifted the book. "And being in AGONY, He prayed more earnestly. And his sweat was as it were, great drops of blood falling down to the ground." The crowd hushed.

He closed the book and eyed Brian. "Even He, the Messiah, of your world, asked for the cup to be removed."

"Fear not the mind of mankind," Voltar said as the crowd began to chant again, echoing his words. "Fear not the mind of mankind."

Brian gulped as the room thundered with the words. Danyael stepped forward. "We offer you strength. That is all we can provide, but it will be enough for it is of love and understanding. In a way, you will set your people free from the Secondary World as did the Messiah. His being provides protection of the spirit. This is not for you to do. You will open a physical door to a new world, and of this, man will be free from the Secondary World—in full understanding. And of this, look to the East will come--a new beginning, a thousand years of peace and unity, in which peace will reign. Our children will return to earth to be with your children and together they will build a new world."

Brian breathed deep and looked out at the hushed assembly.

Voltar whispered. "We only have four votes on the Council to allow an alternative." He paused and spoke with certitude. "The People request Nous 4 at Tiahuanaco. This is their heart and desire for mankind."

Brian stood up straight and bold. "If Jim can somehow arrange it to go to South America--I will go to two" he said in a commanding tone. "If I can have ten days to get used to it before I return, I'd take a three. But, I can't see how I could handle a four. No way. To go from a one to a four is too big of a jump. I could not handle it. I could destroy too much. I could destroy our whole world."

"Of this, you would not destroy your world," Voltar said. "For we would override this."

Danyael moved closer to Brian. "Brian, Nous three is not of Quantum Displacement. The knowledge you need could not be given."

"I know," Brian said.

419

"But you must have the knowledge of Quantum Displacement to proceed with the drawings, or else all will fail. The Secondary could stop progress and interfere unless we reach Nous 4, as a minimum, sustainable level."

"Why not Nous three now, then Nous 4, the next June?" Brian asked firmly.

Their faces showed interest. The People whispered with excitement. Everyone glanced at Danyael as he ran the probabilities. With his right hand on a screen, he accessed information from their national Memory Core.

He turned to them. "Nous 8 in June, vital," he said to everyone. Then he moved closer to Brian. "If you accept Nous 3 now, you must attain Nous 8 in June--with Quantum Displacement Physics, given then. You would be allowed to continue throughout your life to attain Nous 10. With this, the memory cores project a minimum sustainable Nous four with positive genetic transfer of Nous 2 to your offspring."

Brian nodded, yes. The crowd cheered. Brian smiled at them. Thousands waved and shouted his name. BRIAN. BRIAN, BRIAN. Brian of earth, filled with mirth, touched at birth, Brian, Brian of earth."

Brian laughed as he heard the song.

Voltar smiled warmly and placed a huge hand on Brian's shoulder. "If the council approves, as of December 22 -- I will be with you and will speak as you. And you will speak as I, to all about you. Of this--the mark of recognition must be given. From that day forward I will be with you, always. But I assure you, before approving this plan, Danyael and the Council will insist you complete, at least one drawing. Is this too much to ask of you, and your world?"

Brian shrugged.

"Nothing is easy on our world."

"I did not promise that this would be easy." He held out his right hand, and opened his palm. Brian saw big black numbers 020-020-020.

"Of this, the knowledge of the probe would be given when all man are lifted to mind level two--through adjustment of the energy grid system. Of this, will come truth of the past, and freedom from the Secondary World." Brian studied the numbers.

Voltar spoke. "Is it too much to ask, for you to complete ONE drawing of a solar powered pyramid, by your own hand? For in this, the people will relate to you, and of you, to I."

Brian shrugged. "I will try. I will do what I can. But on our world, with Debra and work and all--a lot is happening."

Danyael rushed up to Voltar with a report. "Jim and Debra are finished. They have asked for the return of Brian to Nous one, and the Council is ready to vote."

Brian nodded. "I will do what I can," he said to them. "But I am not promising anything."

"Persevere," said Voltar. "You will prevail. You will become a light to your people, and they to the universe of worlds."

Members of the Council smiled at Brian with respect and compassion. He rushed away with Danyael to the NOR.

Inside the room of the NOR, two long-eared giants quickly moved Brian into the center of the ring and turned the huge plates on the side of the central tube. Brian entered and relaxed.

Colored lights began to flash all around him within each of the rings. The rings rotated and spun around interlocking at various levels around his body, as colors were aligned.

Then the three rings moved upward in harmony. Music and sounds spun through Brian's mind as he watched. Then suddenly all three of the rings stopped and locked. Brian opened his eyes. He looked out at Debra, Jim and Wanda in the earth room at home.

"They are really, really upset," Brian told us as he rubbed his eyes. "The people there are about ready to revolt. They are trying to get the Council to override the probes."

We looked at Brian, concerned that we would be drawn into the fantasies of his mind. Obviously, a reversal of some kind was underway. The whole session had been different than any other.

"What did they tell you?" Brian asked. "I saw them talking to you."

"They gave a lot of it to Jim," Debra said. "He has the responsibility for everything that happens."

"Not true," I said. "Just your life will be in my hands, is all," I laughed.

Brian laughed. "Oh, good. Nothing important."

The Signals Sent

Later that afternoon, a young draftsman from Cuba came over to the house and talked with Brian about the solar powered pyramid. He volunteered to help complete the ten drawings.

They worked for several hours and completed three drawings.

"That was all they wanted," Brian said. "It was so easy."

Afterwards, the young Cuban agreed to translate a message to the people of South America in Spanish—a message from Viracocha. A different Presence came over Brian and spoke to the man. He translated the words to Spanish. When Viracocha finished, tears ran down the young man's cheeks.

Brian opened his eyes and took the paper. "Don't say anything about this to Jim. I don't want him to stop this from happening—if we do get there."

The next day, in Scotland, Lunan studied the target in space that Brian had created. It made little sense to him, but he was willing to take a chance. He called some colleagues with radio telescopes, and persuaded them to transmit the signal to the target, and also to the points near the moon where Lunan believed the probe had been parked in a stationery orbit. The other radio astronomers agreed, and before midnight, the signals were transmitted.

When the probe received the signal, celebrations erupted all over Voltar's world. Never before in the history of earth, had a proper signal been received by this probe. This meant someone on earth knew the code. An agreement had been formed between a common man and a scientist. Two opposite polarities of people had been bridged, linked, and united in one purpose – and both men had acted by their own free-will, without desire for personal reward. People cheered and hugged.

Inside the dome where the Council met and decisions were made, a huge panel of red lights turned green. This could bring success.The *Play of Life* was working. Even the Council members cheered and shouted Brian's name.

The Mark is Given

The next day, Brian emerged into the NOR a bit confused. He barely remembered sitting down with Debra in his apartment. Yet, he saw Voltar talking to Debra in the Earth room.

"Of this, you have asked of I, a method of which information may be extracted from the probes and the knowledge that is stored therein to be translated and referred and referenced upon and given to you as you would draw access from this. And as you know, a code was used to signify and to receive this information, and of this you did record, Debra, so the information would be preserved and passed to others amongst your land. Of this you may not remember, but Brian does. And as he is with us, he now knows of what I speak." Brian nodded in agreement.

"The code," he muttered.

Then Debra's voice echoed throughout the assembly. "Jim probably will understand," she said. The clarity and purity of her voice stunned Brian. He scanned the huge dome in amazement. People rushed into the dome flying through the air and navigating with their blinking belts. Many who imitated Debra with big masks and costumes landed on stage.

"I may have erased that tape," her voice echoed.

The crowd chuckled as Voltar continued. "This information has been spoken of many times in the past to many people. It need not be on the apparatus of tape, for many have heard of this and have awaited the day. And as I told Brian before, prior to December 22, 1976, I would allow of this, that a sign be placed within his hand and of this, the significance therein would signal a command. And of that, the probe would then pass--through the unity of mind--what would be needed for Brian, and for his essence and this knowledge to be shared within all-- every man and woman within his world."

"Are you talking about an impression upon his hand of some sort?" Debra asked.

Brian, again felt awed by the size and power of her voice in the huge auditorium. "Would you explain that to me?" she asked.

Voltar spoke. "Of this, within the storage of the probe and the memories, it is the significant code that would release information. You have used this before yourself to gain information from Brian, as the information was related through him to you. And you did record of this."

Debra mused. "Oh yes. The access code!"

"Of this, the significance lies in 020 - 020 - 020. And of this we have told Brian this would be needed."

Debra pondered Voltar's words for a moment.

Voltar selected a portable crystal and walked into the assembly with Brian at his side. The crowd cheered and shouted Brian's name. Dozens who imitated Brian zoomed down upon the stage.

When the crowd quieted, Voltar lifted Brian's right hand and poured a silvery, black powder onto the palm. Brian trembled.

"At this, fear not, for Brian will suffer no pain, there will be no swelling or disfiguration of his body, and his hand that abides therein. There will be no sores, nor festering. But of this that is given--it will remain through all his life. And by this, he will be linked to the endless knowledge that lies within the probes. And from this day forth, you will not need to access the probe in the manner that you have done before, for Brian may merely access himself and the information will flow.

"And of the safeguards that are built therein, of this--the machinery will eliminate those that it can at this time. If the fulfillment of the meaning of December 22 comes, we will guarantee, that the information will be reliable and will proceed, onward, day after day. And by this Brian will be raised to a level that he will be able to relate to all about him, a new reflection of himself, and by this the witness of himself will be proven.

"And if it be that he is allowed to go to Tiahuanaco, we have at this time reached, within his own reasoning process, an agreement that he will be raised to that of a level of three. Of the Council, he will remain therein throughout the rest of his life, until he again comes to the place of knowledge—Tiahuanaco.

"But if he comes again in June the 22 of 1977, then--in the exact same manner that is to be passed this December 22 of 1976 and in the same place, with the same meaning and the same intent and the same preparation--Nous 8 will be given. And by this, we do intend that during his lifetime, he would then attain Nous ten, on his own."

Debra pondered a moment and then asked a question. "Now, when Brian and Jim go to Tiahuanaco, you have instructed Brian to translate a message from Ticci Viracocha, into the language which the people can understand. Will this make the people believe, or think, that Brian IS Ticci Viracocha, or only OF him?"

Voltar quickly replied. "It will not lead the people to falsely believe in any more than they already have hope in. It will offer to them--that which they have not yet fully realized. And amongst the people, and of the land, as this is said and passed amongst them, what you will discover will be of great importance. And in this, have true faith--for the people will rise to your assistance to aid you and to help you. And amongst the people, many will be able to relate to you a story of themselves, their ancestors, and the knowledge and wisdom that is of vital importance.

"For of this, the return of Viracocha is a long awaited dream that will be fulfilled. And to the people who live therein, it will bring them great joy as the words are passed amongst them."

"Do the people now understand that Viracocha was a spaceman and not a god?"

"Of this the people know little. But of the legend of the past, it is Brian's task to bring them the truth. And when the transformation is complete, from that day and for several days thereafter, he is to go amongst the people, and as this message is spoken to them, answers will be given to them they have awaited for generation after generation. And he will become a light in their eyes. And of this wisdom, they will find great joy. This, again, is a promise I make unto you."

Debra nodded approval.

Voltar continued. "And through Brian will come to the People a great joy, and all those about will partake in this and will drink of this to their fill, and their hearts shall be content. And in that, the unity of love will flow."

Tears formed in Debra's eyes.

"It is a beginning," Voltar said, "and from the beginning there will be more."

Voltar looked again at the powder in Brian's hand. "I now take into my hand, the hand of Brian."

He moved a small instrument over the palm of Brian's hand. "And of this I pass to him."

Brian watched. He gasped in amazement as big, black numbers formed on the palm of his hand. Voltar studied the mark and blew the dust off with his breath.

"And of this, by this mark you are now tied--in the unity of mind therein and amongst the people. From this day on, you are truly one of us." Brian stared at his hand and the number: 020 – 020 - 020. The huge crowd murmured approval and applauded softly.

Debra's voice echoed through the auditorium.

"Are you speaking to Brian?"

"Yes, Debra, I was."

Brian turned to the crowd and held up his hand. They roared with applause and shouts of approval.

In the apartment, Debra glanced around nervously. She was alone with Brian in trance. She whispered aloud, "He's speaking to Brian? Holding his hand?"

In the auditorium, Voltar touched Brian's shoulder.

"As I said Brian, there would be no pain, there would be no swelling, it will be as if it was always there. And from this day on, I am with you. And from this, the Day of Twenty is now cancelled and I will be with you for eternity. And when, of this, you do go to Tiahuanaco, and place your hand upon the Gate of the Sun, from that day on, you will not be the same that you were. But you will be of great love to your people, and it will reflect outward from you. And, from that day on, I will speak through you, as you and I are ONE. And this will pass to all those about you, and by this--a deeper love to those that love you."

Brian nodded approval. Water drops splashed onto his head and shoulders. Brian looked at Voltar who transformed into the Viracocha with blue eyes, a long white robe, a beard, and a small black book.

Viracocha cried and the tears splashed upon Brian.

Brian felt dizzy for a moment as water drops splashed on his head, cheeks and forehead.

Viracocha closed his eyes in reverent prayer. The crowd hushed.

Brian wobbled and his mind spun. Voltar's wife stepped up next to him and compassionately grasped his arms and shoulders.

Viracocha transformed back into Voltar. "Now rest Brian. Rest," said Voltar. "My wife will tend to you."

In the apartment, Debra again eyed the room nervously.

"I feel like there are people here. Am I missing something?"

Voltar spoke. "We thank you for being with us, Debra. Feel not in your heart, sadness. For it is necessary that we are now one. And of this--we are."

"I do not feel sadness. It's just -- the number."

"Of this we know the reasoning, of which you speak -- the numerical value is in the Book."

"Yes, it is." Debra said lifting the big Bible."

"Of this, it is not the same in significance, and of this we have explained."

"Yes...."

"It is not even coincidental, as in your land. But of this, it is also the matrix of the system of the mind and knowledge of the probe, and of the great machine that someday Brian will build.

"And of this numerical value, a binary expression of the same value will be the key to the final door that locks the Pyramid of Life. And of this, the cells that are stored therein. And of this code, the cells will remain. And hopefully, we will not have to come and reclaim them to again bring life unto your world, in the days of the future.

"From this day on, Debra, you may call upon me, whenever you need. There will never be a departing of myself from Brian. From this day on, when people call upon Brian, I may speak. But to truly be a part of him, will not pass, until Tiahuanaco and the Gate of the Sun. "

Debra nodded. "Okay."

"God be with you and all those about you."

"Thank you so much."

In the apartment, Brian's body awoke. He stretched his legs and arms, slowly. "Let me see what happened," Debra said grabbing at his right hand.

Brian stretched his shoulders and then finally opened up his fists to reveal the palms of both hands.

"Oh my God," Debra gasped as she saw the large numbers in his right palm.

"Yeah, I know," Brian shrugged. "It's okay. It didn't hurt a bit." Debra pulled a lamp off the table, and held Brian's hand under the light.

The surface of the skin had not been disturbed. The bold, black numbers rested far below the surface layer of skin: 020 – 020 – 020.

"I don't know why they did it though," Brian said. "Lunan thinks I'm a fraud, and we have no money to go. I don't get it. But, somehow, I have got to go there," Brian said. "Two weeks from now."

Debra studied the numbers. "How can you make it in two weeks?"

"I don't know. I found out something else. I am the only one who can open the door in that pyramid. It responds only to my hand. Now I know why it was so important. It also unlocks the main core inside the probe for quantum displacement. It has a definite purpose."

"This is real," Debra breathed. "You have been marked."

"I know, isn't that fantastic," Brian mused.

"There is not even a slight bit of redness."

"He said no festering, nothing."

Debra breathed deep. "No swelling. It isn't even raised around the area. You can't tattoo yourself--underneath the skin--without something happening. That is something else. I don't believe this has happened," Debra heaved.

"If I don't make it in June, he'll remove it, he told me that. There would be no purpose for it."

"He didn't talk about that to me," said Debra.

"Yes, but he told me that, later as we were walking out."

"But he did say this will stay with me all of my life, if I do go to Tiahuanaco. If not--it will come off."

"Wait until Jim sees that," Debra breathed. "WAIT UNTIL JIM SEES THAT."

"That is a trip," Brian chuckled. "I've been marked. Brian Scott. What a trip—but why?"

The next day, Monday December 6, Debra and Brian drove up to my house. I wanted them to see the motion picture contract before I signed—or rejected it. A group of people waited for Brian to arrive.

"The Brian Scott Story," I told everyone. "As a movie. It would pay enough to get started, give me a job as co-producer and give Brian time to write their story. But, it won't get us to South America."

Max Redfield handed me a stack of books. "Before you write a movie, you should read these books by Joseph Campbell."

"What is your interpretation?" I asked. "Based on what you have read."

"Well, I believe this may be the archetypal, transformational drama of our age. Our hero myth--for this generation. But of course, it all depends on what happens in South America."

"That is what bothers me," I said.

Brian and Debra arrived and everyone wanted to see the mark.

"Let me see it, first," I said

"Now? Brian said.

"Sure."

Brian shrugged and took off his jacket.

"You won't believe this Jim," Debra oozed with excitement.

Brian slowly extended his arm, and then opened his fist as we all drew near. I saw the numbers for the first time. "My God!" I breathed. Everyone hurried to examine Brian's hand. They gasped, laughed and moaned with excitement.

Wanda eyed Debra carefully as everyone reacted. "Are you okay with this?" she asked.

"I don't know," Debra whispered with concern. "Now I am living with, and in love with, a man who is marked with a number."

427

Bill Hamilton held a lamp down close to the skin. "No redness, no swelling, no puffiness," Bill said, as he studied the numbers with a lens. "Nothing except big black numbers, well formed, perfectly formed--below the first two layers of skin. It is below the surface, and below any second layer. It's deep. Deep under the skin. Yet it is NOT ON THE SURFACE LAYER. Unbelievable."

All the numerals were perfectly shaped with sharply defined edges: 020 - 020 - 020. The zeroes matched each other, and all of the two's were identical, like it had been created by a machine. The type style was san serif and very bold, like Arial, Helvetica or Futura.

"There is no way, anyone could do that to themselves," said Redfield. "Even if it was with a stencil. You couldn't do anything that perfect on the SURFACE of the skin. Let alone, two layers deep."

"How did you get this, Brian?" Hamilton asked.

"Voltar did it," Brian shrugged. "He used a powder. Basically, he just waved his fingers over it. Then dusted off the powder. I think the pores opened up to accept it. It was simple."

Debra held up the tape. "I recorded it all."

I grabbed the tape out of her hands and pulled her aside. "Did you see his hand before?"

"I didn't see anything on his hand before this," she whispered. "It wasn't there, Jim. I was with him all day."

"Could this have been faked in any way?" I asked.

"I don't know," she shrugged. "I was with him. Do you think he would fake something like that? Being marked with a number in the palm of his hand?"

"I don't know," I whispered as everyone gathered around Brian. "But that number means 6-6-6. They've already said that."

"But they said something different last night. It's a numerical representation, of something in binary."

"Binary?" I thought for a moment. "He's said several times that the significance is in the number 2. Like the Days of Twenty. Mind Level two. Everything happens on the twenty-second. His whole calendar thing is related to 20. That's just like the Mayan calendar. Their calendar goes in twenty day cycles. Maybe that is it? Maybe it's really just 20-20-20."

Tears welled up in Debra's eyes. "I hope it is not the Revelations number. I want to believe him. I love him. I love Voltar, too! He is so deep. It feels like I am talking to my father." She started to cry and whirled away. "Could I be deceived? Because I still want to find my father?"

"Possibly," I said. "Even Brian could be deceived. He could be searching for his father too. He never knew him. That's something both of you share."

"I know. Do you think the Host is the anti-Christ?" she asked.

"It could be. But, he's a projection of their ideas about God. His symbol is the spider—and the number. Maybe somebody will understand more than we do. He always said, *'For he who has wisdom, this is I.'* So, it is a hint. Whatever is behind this -- Brian, a personality of his, or, whomever -- they are making it educational, operating within limits and rules. That doesn't sound like a demon. They could be a lot more evil. Kill us all. And--they know we talk about the number all the time. Maybe the number is just 2-2-2. Maybe that is the significance. That's what they have said."

Debra smiled. She felt better. "But," I said. "You should keep praying, for wisdom—and protection—just in case."

Debra grabbed my arms and hugged me. "I am so glad you are in this with me. I would be stark raving mad without you."

"For a 24-year-old, you are doing very well," I said.

She hugged me. "Jim, I LOVE Brian--and I LOVE Voltar. They are two different personalities," she said. "But, if it gets any worse, I don't know if I can handle it."

I hugged her. "Let's just go forward. Play our roles. See what happens. After all – it is *the Play of Life.*" She echoed my words and we both laughed.

"Let's play our roles," I said. "This is the kind of story that might last five hundred years. "

"Five hundred years? she asked.

"Or longer."

"Then I better be good at it," she sniffled. "If I am the Woman of Fire, deceived and in love with Voltar AND Brian—then so be it."

"So be it," I smiled.

And thus, we agreed to go onward, despite the number, and our doubts.

The next day, December 7, I met with the movie producers in their offices in Century City. They pointed out my new office and desk. Everything was plush and beautiful with a white carpet two inches thick. They told me to pick a secretary from the three attractive girls in the office. I would be paid thousands of dollars for the story rights, and receive $75,000 as co-producer, over the next year.

All I had to do was sign the contract. But nothing had been included about a trip to South America.

"We covered that," snapped the producer. "We are not paying for that. We don't need it. You don't need it for this movie.""

"But we do need it for the story that is happening," I said. "The story is still happening. It is unfolding."

"We don't need anything else," the producer snapped. "As far as we are concerned it is over. It's time to get on with it."

"The only trouble is--it's not over," I said softly.

"It's time to put the crap behind you, Jim," he said. "It's a great story. But don't expect me to accept this as being true. I just won't. I just can't. And, it's not necessary. Brian is a wacko. Okay? A clear-cut wacko. I know that. I don't know what your deal is with him. That's between you. Either he or you dreamed this up. It's a fraud. Okay. I can buy that. In a way, I even respect it. It's tremendous. Whether you created it, or Brian. I don't care. It's good. But I don't have to believe it. We don't have to make people believe it is true for a movie. That's the beauty of it. There are enough people out there who will take it seriously, and maybe believe it--but movies don't have to be real, Jim. You have to accept that. It's not a damn documentary, for God's sake. We are talking horror film, here. Scary--frightening stuff. I like it. I know we can do this in a way, a classy way-- you'll be proud of it. With a big name director, this will be great. We've got it all lined up."

I breathed deep—I knew this was wrong.

"You've got to let go of this, Jim. The future is open to you. There are many more movies to come."

"I need to think about this," I said nervously.

"What the hell is to think about?" the man shouted. "It is exactly what you wanted. Everything we have talked about for two months is negotiated."

"I need to think about this, at least overnight," I said.

"Don't back out on us now, Jim. We want to do it."

"Okay," I said. He placed his hand on my shoulder. "Look, I know I was kind of tough on you, right now. But, I had to get that off my chest. I'm honest with you. You know where I am coming from. I don't ask anything else. I don't ask for it to be true. That might be a blessing to you," he said. "Don't blow this."

I nodded. "I understand. It's very frustrating working with this type of story."

"I'll call you tomorrow," he said. "In the morning. We are ready to get rolling on this."

I rushed down to the parking garage in a sweat. My old VW wouldn't start— dead battery. I pushed it to a ramp and coasted downhill to get it started. The car chugged and smoked.

I was desperate with worry. That night I called my father and mother at their home in Colorado. "I have a contract for a movie on the Brian Scott Story, but I don't want to sign it," I said. After a long talk, my dad offered a loan of $1,200 if I could use the money to get a career going. He didn't want to talk about Brian or the story—he didn't believe in UFO's in any way.

Dad said my older brother Kendrick was working on a new magazine. The Skeptical Inquirer. "It is somehow involved with UFO's and the paranormal."

My mom provided more details. "He's going to be the editor. It's put out by the <u>Committee to Analyze Claims of the Paranormal.</u>"

"Unbelievable," I breathed after hanging up the phone. "This must be in the *Play of Life.*"

"It would have to be," said Wanda with a smile.

The next day, I talked to Brian and asked what he wanted to do.

"It's your choice, Jim," he said. "This is all of you--the transformation is of you. But, I would sell it and make the horror movie. Use the money to go down there on our own."

"But what if you come back as Voltar and have to deal with them. You'd go insane—for real. "

"It has to be of you, Jim," Brian chuckled.

"What do you want to do, really in your heart?" I asked Brian.

"The only way to really get this thing down the road and do what I want to do, is just to reach out to the people in a lot of different ways.

"The people?"

"Right. Some need facts, others need guidance, some need inspiration. The guidance and counseling will be from Voltar—from the transformation."

"Okay. But…"

"Other people in the future will need to know about the *Play of Life* so they can get through their experiences. That's the bottom line. Not everyone who goes through a "quantum evolution" will have someone like you around. They could have others—cruel people, friends that ridicule them, or flip outs like Mary Beth. You and Debra have kept me sane."

"So the full story needs to be told. Not just the scary part," I asked.

"That's up to you, Jim. They told me to learn about the mind of mankind. I learned man doesn't have answers for someone like me. Man is not set-up to handle someone like Voltar. But people need to know, because this will keep happening. It will happen to others, many others."

"You've gone through a lot. I missed the darkside, but what I have witnessed is amazing," I conceded. "Whatever the source."

"You have seen more than anyone else in my life. Probably, more than anyone in hundreds of years. Maybe--a couple of thousand."

"I've seen it, but I still don't understand exactly what you have experienced—mentally, inside your head."

"I don't want you to go that far into it, Jim. Because it's rough. Very rough. Can you imagine going through all I did with Mary Beth? I may be a bit wacko, but that would drive anybody crazy. Not many people could handle it. Certainly not a scientist—not a professor. They would crack up. I had anchors. The heart. Humor. It hasn't been that bad for me."

431

"You have a strong self-concept. How did you get your self-image?" I asked.

"I knew who I was at age 16," Brian said. "After that ball of light. I knew I was chosen, and—I knew ME."

"Do you think this strengthened you?"

"Sure. Now, it doesn't bother me to be called a wacko," Brian laughed. "I know--I am not. I know the truth. I've already discovered more of my own being than most people ever will. I'd be happy to quit right now. Why the heck should I go on, except to help other people--to try and save people?"

About then, my parents called back. They would send a money order for $1250—if I wanted to accept it. I asked them to wait a minute.

"This is it," I told Brian. "I'm going to decide right now. This producer could not handle you as Voltar—and he would own you. That's my biggest worry."

"I could handle him," Brian said. "Friction with people won't bother me a bit. I'm used to it."

I took a deep breath. "I think it is wrong. It's wrong to sell a story that is not finished. That's it. That's all. That's the only reason."

Moments later, I accepted the loan from my parents. Debra and Wanda laughed. They knew plane tickets cost $600 apiece.

"It sounds like two of us can go to South America," Debra said, hugging Wanda. "Get your bags packed, honey."

Brian and I laughed. We all hugged and laughed together in celebration. Thanks to my parents, two of us were going to South America. We just had to decide which two of us should go.

PORTAL TO LIFE faces east. "Look to the East has come." Brian said, when he stepped into the doorway. Wider view below shows subterranean courtyard with a Common Man and his two children in the center.

020 020 020

THE MARK – The big, bold numbers appeared deep below the top level of skin. They were perfectly formed, uniform and sharp-edged. No swelling, or redness ever appeared on the surface. The top layer of skin was not disturbed in any manner. You could see through the top layer of skin which showed no marks at all. Voltar said that when Brian touched the stone, the mark would be at the surface layer of skin. He also said the mark would never leave Brian, if he made it to Tiahuanaco for the transformation. Voltar was correct on both points.

Though faded, the numbers still exist on Brian's hand.

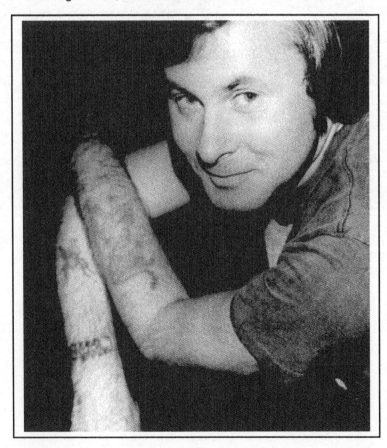

TAXI at south shore of Lake Titicaca.

NYLES and BRENDA clown around with Brian in Puno.

James E. Frazier

THE PORTAL to Life. **The doorway waits.**

MYSTERY BOY IN PUNO

I AM HERE BECAUSE I BELIEVE THAT SOME GREAT TRANSFORMATION
WILL TAKE PLACE AT SUNRISE
IN ONE OF THE INCAN TEMPLES AROUND LAKE TITICACA
ON DECEMBER 22. AND,
I BELIEVE THIS TRANSFORMATION
WILL CHANGE THE WORLD.

--Mystery Boy

Chapter 17

Journey to Tiahuanaco

On Wednesday December 8, I received the money order from my parents for $1250. It provided enough to buy plane tickets but no lodging, no food.

That night, an overflow audience turned out at a large lecture hall in Orange County. As the janitor pushed open the movable partition to make room for the crowd, I stepped to the podium. People scurried to unfold more chairs.

"The Strange Saga of Brian Scott is about to take another turn,*"* I said into the microphone. "We are definitely going to South America for the December 22 transformation in the temple of Tiahuanaco near Lake Titicaca."

The crowd of 500 applauded with excitement.

"We don't know exactly what the transformation means, or what it will bring. But, Brian hopes it will put an end to his problems," I said. The audience laughed.

"Let's hope so," Brian shouted as he stood up to the microphone. "I want to put this behind me. I don't want to be the village idiot any longer." The crowd roared with laughter.

I told the audience we needed donations for food, clothing and film. "We are going to invite you to help make this transformation a reality for mankind," I said. "Quantum evolution to mind level 4."

Brian quickly corrected me. "I've only agreed to take a three," he said. "Four is too much for me to handle." I was concerned, but said nothing in front of the audience.

After a full presentation of events in the *"Strange Saga of Brian Scott"* and a final appeal, the crowd erupted with cheers and good wishes. Afterwards, people eagerly pushed forward to meet Brian and offer their blessings.

One attorney offered to buy film and processing. Other people offered camping equipment, sleeping bags, tents, gloves and blankets. A few opened their wallets, or wrote checks.

"I believe I am witnessing something that will change the world," one little, white-haired lady said, "I had goose bumps and cold chills during the whole lecture."

Almost everyone wanted to shake Brian's hand and offer him a good journey. Brian, feeling their love and admiration, beamed with joy.

Wanda and Debra passed out literature and gathered business cards. After the crowd dwindled, they stepped outside into the cold air to smoke cigarettes. "I can't believe this," Debra gushed, shivering. "People are giving money. I can't believe this is actually happening to me, a born-again Christian."

"What does that matter?" Wanda asked.

"Everything. Even though I'm not a good Christian, I do believe in Jesus, and I just can't believe in some *'quantum evolution'* to mind level 10."

Wanda favored Buddhism as a religion and philosophy. "It kind of makes sense to me," she said. "It's a Zen kinda thing."

Debra eyed Wanda. "I've never asked, but you don't know Jesus, do you?'

Wanda spoke cautiously. "Well, Debra. I believe He was a great teacher, like Buddha, like Confucius, like many other teachers on this planet. But this is today. We have to live in today, and we have to decide what applies."

"That is the exact opposite of what I believe," Debra gushed. "I believe His truth is the same yesterday, today and tomorrow--and that Jesus is as right for us today, as he was 1900 years ago."

"Debra. The truth keeps changing. That's why we have the Supreme Court. Religions change, too. Even the Pope keeps changing things."

"God doesn't change," said Debra. "Listen, I am not a person anyone can look up to. I am living in sin with a man marked 020-020-020 in the palm of his right hand. And he is going to the temple of some pagan god, which may be a demon, to accept transformation."

"You could be wrong," said Wanda. "Very wrong."

"It's ironic," laughed Debra. "I only care if it is right or wrong from God's view—from the Biblical view. Who is right? God, help us all," she laughed. "How did I get into this?"

"Through a man--like me," Wanda laughed.

A tall, dignified man approached as they laughed together.

"I was inside, at the lecture," he said with a British accent. He handed Wanda twenty dollars. "Could you tell them something for me?"

438

"Sure," said Debra.

The man spoke with a gentle elegance. "I feel they are both slightly confused about what is happening to Brian. I'm afraid, they don't understand the significance of it all, or the purpose, you see. They seem to take it, as a joke, as it were. But this is a serious matter. I suggest they do some research into descents of the great teachers--avatars. It is a well-known, highly esteemed phenomenon in many Eastern religions. It's a high point in any society. The avatar becomes a man--the man becomes well, a better man. Better for all society around him."

"Where does this word *avatar* come from?" Wanda asked.

"It sounds like Voltar," Debra laughed. "Is it Chinese?"

He spoke carefully. "No, I don't think so. But in China, India, Tibet--even in Japan--this idea of a descent, or an incarnation, is understood. It's from Buddhism. It's much more well understood in Asian lands, than here in America," he said. "I lived in India and Asia for most of my life," he said.

"I can mention it to Brian," Debra said.

The man drew closer and spoke softly. "The trance condition—it's called samadhi. Very esteemed. Only a Yogi can attain that—in preparation for the incarnate being."

"A Yogi," laughed Debra. "Brian?"

Wanda nodded. "It does sound like Zen Buddhism!"

"It is God at work," said the man firmly.

"I will be sure to tell Brian," Debra smiled, curtly. "But I must tell you, I believe in one God, and his image for man is Jesus--the Jewish carpenter who died on the cross at Calvary for us--for ALL of us. And that is all I believe in. No other gods, ancient or modern, will come before Him."

The man recoiled and nodded politely.

"She's a born-again Christian," Wanda said, apologetically.

"There is much more in the world than just the Christian view," he said. "I was a Christian—But I discovered that it was based in Judaism, and that's based in Zoroastrianism which goes back 1500 years before Abraham. I began to study most of the world's religions, and they all share a belief in descent of an Avatar, incarnation of a god, in some form—including Jesus. He, in my view, was an Avatar. He and the Father were One. It's a duality, brought about through incarnation. Man today doesn't understand incarnation."

"All I need to know is Jesus," said Debra. "That's enough for me. I don't have to be a scholar to be saved."

"Well, I wish the best for them," he said with a dignified air. "And for the both of you. We are all learning."

An hour later, in a nearby coffee shop, a core group crowded into a circular booth. Additional tables were added as Wanda and Debra counted money from the lecture.

Max Redfield, the self-taught scholar of ancient knowledge, laid a big book on the table. "You must understand something," he said to Brian. "Tiahuanaco is a site of secret, esoteric science. Arthur Posnansky said so in his earliest writings, back in 1904—and later in this book. No one knows who built it. Not even the Incas knew, not even the local Indians of Lake Titicaca know. It is just like the Sphinx in Egypt. No one claims credit for building it." He held up the book. "You need to read this, Jim."

"I keep wondering if all this has anything to do with Kon-Tikki."

"Thor Heyerdal," Redfield smiled. "He took the name Tikki from Ticci Viracocha. He sailed from Peru to Polynesia to prove the same people migrated to Easter Island—Voltar's people—red-headed people with white skin."

I was stunned.

"Through his own research he became convinced that Tiahuanaco was built by tall people with white skin and red hair," Redfield said. "They found skeletons of giants at Tiahuanaco, with red hair. The Inca had a statue of Viracocha in Cuzco—a tall, white-skinned man with a beard, wearing a white robe. The native people don't have facial hair. Supposedly, a blue-eyed Ticci organized the brown-skinned natives and taught them to build with stone. He was a teacher, healer, architect and engineer--their most holy god. At Tiahuanaco, he made men from stone. Some were giants. The giants lived and worked there among the people. That's the legend."

"Amazing," I breathed.

Brian chuckled. "There's a lot more to it."

"Tiahuanaco is the oldest, most unexplainable site in this hemisphere," Redfield said, "maybe 15,000 years old. Oh, by the way, the Incas believe that on December 22, at sunrise, the door opens to another world—the door to another realm of souls is open. Souls from the dead can return, and souls of the living can visit. Just at sunrise on that day. Your day to be there."

Brian smiled. "I didn't know that much was known to man."

Bill Hamilton placed another book on the table. "Listen to this," he said. "You think that's good. The Incas believed their genetic heritage came from a star," he spoke slowly. "And so did the genetic material of the *Common People*— that's *their* term." He paused to make sure everyone was listening. "Now, get this. They all believed the genetic material of the Common People came from one star and the Royal Incan's genetic material originated from A DIFFERENT star."

"Amazing," Wanda breathed. "Where did you get that?"

"In books--scholarly books," Bill said. "They also believe in *two worlds*--two worlds that were related. Get it? They believed in a *secondary world* to earth.

The first world was destroyed by the flood. Giants lived on the earth, and were destroyed then. The Second Age is when Viracocha created the present Indian race. He came from the Island of the Sun in Lake Titicaca, and his empire was around the lake. The Incas came a lot later."

"The Incas were royalty, priestly-kings, based on the Tiahuanaco culture," said Redfield. "The Incas were PRIEST-KINGS. Okay? This was nothing like the life *we* know in America. Nothing! In fact, the opposite. America overturned a king and we are against rule by royalty."

"It's hard to conceive," I mumbled.

"The kings were all priests?" Debra asked.

"Right," Redfield answered. "And some of the Mayan-Aztecs wore black, circular obsidian pendants around their necks, like The Host. It is well known as a symbol of one of the Aztec Gods: Tezcatlipoca--a black mirror. Their initiates were transformed into a winged animal--either a jaguar or a serpent with wings—representing a deified man: the Quetzalcoatl. He was their cultural hero and king, like Viracocha was a cultural hero to the Inca."

"This is amazing," Debra said. "A deified man?"

"Yes. Transformation. They believed in uniting polarities, opposites. Different priests represented each polarity: the Jaguar Priests were warriors--the outer way. The Eagle Priests represent the inner way: introspection. Different ways to their god for different types of people. The Outer Way and the Inner Way, extrovert or introvert."

"So Brian is the Jaguar?" I mused looking at Brian's left forearm arm and his huge jaguar tattoo. "The extroverted way."

"Right," Redfield said. "A warrior. You have the same groups represented at Tiahuanaco: jaguars and condors -- the South American eagle. Brian's instructions say to 'touch the Condor' on the Gate of the Sun." He pointed at the Calendar of Tiahuanaco in the big book. "These were the orders of priests. Each had a function. Each order of priests played a role in the initiations, all based on the sun, the moon and the stars. It was a transformation science. A secret science."

"Sacred science," said Hamilton.

"So their science and their religion were united," said Debra.

"Right. And their politics," said Redfield. "It was a vast society—with secrets. The temples were run by a secret society--to keep the secrets. That's my point. It was successful. Their knowledge is *still secret.* And, there may have been at least one million people living around Tiahuanaco at one time. A million people!"

"But none now?" I asked. Redfield nodded in agreement.

"There were 20 million in the valley around the Aztec capital when the Spanish came," said a dark-skinned man. "That is Mexico City, today. The

441

Spanish said the city was more beautiful, and more orderly than Rome--the largest city in Europe."

"I was taught that Columbus 'discovered' America," Wanda said. "I just can't get out of my head this image of him conquering a few naked, scattered natives. It's hard to imagine millions of people living in cities with streets and huge pyramids--BEFORE the Spanish."

"We were propagandized," said Redfield. "And it worked. The Spanish, operating on authority of the Catholic Church, burned their books, murdered their leaders and stole their gold. They tricked them, tortured them. Hell, it was the Spanish Inquisition. They just continued it here in this hemisphere. They killed the top Inca, in front of everyone by twisting his head off with a rope--after they promised he wouldn't be harmed--after they took the gold."

"Good God," Wanda gasped.

"The Spanish used torture," Redfield said. "Rule by fear."

"There is still a lot of bad feeling between the Catholic Church and the Inca," said the Cuban draftsman. "The Catholic Church controls everything in Latin America. Either the government, or the rich Catholics own everything. Most of the people are peasants. It is not like North America with a big middle-class of people."

I looked at everyone. "This is amazing. We never think much about South America."

"There is a lot we will discover," said Brian. "Tiahuanaco is a huge underground city. Most of it has not been discovered."

"You need to be ready, Jim," Redfield said. "You and Brian are going into a strange land. And you may be given secrets. Remember the phrase, *'Given in Trust.'* That means THEY are asking you to keep a secret, to keep THEIR secrets--their wisdom--the wisdom that is encrypted in the story, and at Tiahuanaco. You need to grasp that, and understand. You could say the wrong thing, to the wrong person, and, well, you know--get in trouble with certain authorities. Maybe get thrown in jail and never come back. People disappear in their jails."

Wanda and Debra gasped as they looked at their loves, knowing they would be in danger.

Another young man leaned forward wearing a plaid shirt and cowboy boots. "You'll need to go to the embassy in Los Angeles," he said. "Right away. To get your passports and shots started. I can drive you all around in my pick-up, if you want. You'll need to make a lot of preparations."

Brian nodded in agreement. Water drops splashed on his face and his eyes rolled back. A voice boomed from his lips: "Agreed." Then a high squeaky voice, echoed, "Agreement." Then another scratchy but strong voice spoke, "Agreed." Then another boomed so loud that everyone in the restaurant turned around. As

442

people watched, spellbound, a spectacle unfolded. One by one, nine more totally unique and different voices spoke from Brian each stating 'agreement' in some form – twelve in all.

Afterwards, Brian's eyes rolled down, his body shuddered and his arms flailed. "My God," he gasped. "Jesus, my God." He tried to jump up. Debra and Wanda grabbed his arms and held him for a moment as he calmed.

"What was that?" Debra asked.

"A new council," he gasped, standing up.

"What council?" I asked.

"Their friends," Brian said shaking with excitement. "Allies. This has never happened. I've got to walk off this energy."

Everyone stepped away as Brian pranced around the restaurant rubbing his hands and kicking his feet, sprightly. People stared in awe.

"It's too much," Brian whined. "Too much to hold, too many connections, too much energy. It's tingling on me."

"Is he all right?" the waitress asked.

"It's normal, for him," I laughed. "Almost."

Redfield smiled. "Now you know why man must evolve. We must all go to mind level two, three or four just to handle the sheer volume of knowledge."

Brian squeezed his hands. "It's the *energy*," he whined. "The connections, the feelings. Knowing what THEY feel. It's not a head-trip. I *feel* everything each one of them feels. And they all have different feels to them--personalities, if you wish."

"Who were all the voices?" Bill Hamilton asked.

"The new council--allies," Brian said. "They have some names: Saturn, Mars, Jupiter, Energy, Linyana."

"From Saturn and Jupiter?" asked Hamilton.

"I don't know," said Brian. "It's a meaning we can relate to somehow--in our past. The names are just for us. But each is a person."

"A personality?" Wanda asked.

"They have personalities," Brian said shaking his hands. "They are each representatives of their people."

"My head hurts," Wanda grimaced. "I can't follow this."

"That's what it is all about," laughed Hamilton. "That's why we have to go through *quantum evolution*."

"It's not just me," Brian said. "It can't be. It is no good, if it is just me. It's for everyone." Then, as Brian pranced near the cashier, his body froze. His eyes flipped upwards and the peaceful voice of Voltar flowed.

"From this, of our allies, Brian will be WITH the people and AMONG the people. And from this, ALL MANKIND will be lifted up. And by this--by Brian--wisdom is given to man."

443

Brian's personality returned, and he stumbled against the cash register. People gasped and tried to steady him, but Debra pulled Brian away and shoved him out the door. "That's enough!" she commanded. "We are going home, now!"

Later, as Wanda and I drove home, she challenged my theory of multiple-personality. "How are you doing at integrating your subject into one – a 'whole person?' Isn't that your goal?"

"Twelve spoke -- I counted. Twelve personalities."

"Jim, this is *still* expanding. Where is it going? Do you know? Does anybody know? I mean, this is really starting to scare me."

"What is?"

"What if he goes crazy? Goes berserk down there. Isn't that what happens to multiple-personalities?"

"No--not always," I said.

"How about a cult leader?'

"I'm missing the connection."

Wanda spoke carefully "Brian Scott, marked with a number, comes back from South America, transformed into an Incan God, and he goes out gathering up people--for some purpose. Sounds like a cult to me. Didn't the Incas practice human sacrifice?"

"I don't know, but I won't be involved in any cult," I said. I had studied social psychology, persuasion techniques, torture, deprivation, transference and counter-transference. "I am watching for any signs of cultism," I said.

"But you don't know what Brian is *hiding*. You don't know what they might have up their sleeve in South America."

"No. You are right," I agreed.

"And you are playing around with real gods, real demons. Real! Good Lord, Jim. This is real. This is not make-believe. This is not something you have read about. It is happening," she began to cry softly, fearing for my safety.

The Preparation

Over the next few days, as people decorated their Christmas trees, as Santa Clauses rang bells in the shopping malls, Brian and I obtained our plane tickets, passports, and VISA permits to Bolivia and Peru. Instead of shopping for Christmas presents, we prepared for a week of sleeping outside in the Andes of South America. The contributions gave us food money and perhaps enough for a few nights of lodging. We planned to sleep outside, most of the time.

With the Cuban-draftsman, Brian worked to complete more designs for the planned pyramid at Tiahuanaco. The night before departure, they finished the last of five views on the pyramid and other buildings in the complex. Brian felt

444

pleased. He had done research. He not only knew how a modern day pyramid might look, he knew the exact amount of power that might be generated using a field of solar panels to capture rays from the sun. In his plan, the beams focused on a crystal atop the pyramid providing heat to make steam, to drive turbines to make electricity. With the designs wrapped under his arms, Brian was ready to go.

At Los Angeles International airport on Saturday December 18, about fifteen well wishers gathered in the concourse for a send-off. The group included Bill Hamilton, Max Redfield and their friends.

As the moment of loading neared, I saw Mary Beth Scott and Fay Harris hurrying towards us.

The two women stopped in a flurry. "We are here with a message from the Host," Fay announced to the group. "It was received by Mary Beth in a direct communication with the Host, last night."

I blocked their path to Brian. Fay puffed up big and gestured like a courtroom attorney. "I think, as the legal wife of Brian, that Mary Beth has a right to be here, to see her husband off. Don't you?"

I exhaled slowly. "There are no hard feelings between Brian and Debra for Mary Beth." I stepped aside.

Fay pulled Mary Beth forward and glared defiantly at Debra. "Well, despite the fact that Brian has chosen to co-habitate with this Jezebel--which is my word for her, and all I am going to say about it now--Mary Beth has continued to be healed and strengthened. The Host appeared to her last night with a message." She nodded at Mary Beth.

Brian's wife suddenly felt small and weak. Overwhelmed by feelings for Brian, her voice failed and she began to cry. "You tell him," she whispered as tears ran out of her eyes.

Fay hugged Mary Beth and spoke. "The Host told Mary Beth that your airplane would be under attack by the Secondary World. And that the Secondary World aliens would do everything they could to stop this transformation, including causing your death on this plane--if you go."

"You mean--a plane wreck?" I asked.

"That's right. They do NOT intend to allow Brian to arrive at the place in South America. They intend to cause a crash. That's what he told her."

"Is that right?" I asked, looking at Mary Beth.

"Yes," she sniffled. "I'm not lying, Jim. He appeared to me and told me this face to face."

At that moment, the airline announced boarding for the flight to Lima, Peru. As the words echoed over the crowd, everyone froze.

Brian shrugged and whispered to me "You can't trust what she gets."

Wanda huddled close. "Could she be doing this just to be here and see Brian?" she asked.

"I feel so sorry for her," Debra said, her jaw trembling with feelings. "Even if that old hag has to call me names."

"Well, we are not turning back," I said. "Not now."

"Voltar just told me that they will defend us," Brian said. "But the Secondary WILL attack. She is right."

"Then we go, and if we live--we live," I said.

"But, what if you don't?" asked Wanda.

"Then everything I have is yours," I said. "Tell the story as it happened. All my notes and tapes are in the office."

Debra started to cry, and Brian hugged her. "We'll be okay," Brian said. "We'll be protected."

As everyone watched, Brian walked to Mary Beth and hugged her. Her long blond hair fell on his shoulders. She relaxed into his arms. "We will be together again, someday," he whispered. "When this is all over."

"You better come back," she said. "You are the father of our two little girls, and they need you."

He smiled. "He said I would be changed," Brian said softly. "This is the only way to make everything turn out right."

"What if...." Mary Beth whimpered.

"I don't think they will let me die after all we have been through," Brian said, softly. Mary Beth hugged him tightly, then slowly her aching fingers and heart let him go.

The loudspeaker blared "final boarding," and everyone said goodbye in a hurry. Brian kissed Debra politely on the lips. Then we rushed onto the plane.

The Battle Begins

On board the plane, a beautiful young woman from Argentina squeezed in between us. I couldn't help but laugh as the glamorous brunette boldly introduced herself. "You must be a glutton for punishment," I said. She carried the confidence of a professional fashion model.

As we talked, the plane taxied out to the runway. Then the pilot announced that, due to engine trouble, the plane would return to the terminal.

Brian's bright blue eyes rolled upward. "A battle has begun," Voltar said. "They are attempting to interfere with the engines of this craft." Voltar explained that an energy field would be devised and projected by his people. His people had dispatched two crafts to counteract the beam and protect us, he said.

446

We returned to the terminal and unloaded. Most of the people had departed, except for Wanda and Debra, so we had more time with them. They begged us not to go, and both of them cried when the loudspeaker announced that something had been found wrong in one engine. Supposedly, it had been fixed, and we were to re-board the plane.

We said goodbye again, and with great apprehension, we lifted off. Within a few hours, we flew into a violent lightning storm. Rough winds tossed the plane around in the darkness of night. Lightning flashed outside the windows. Grown men and women cried out in fear.

Voltar spoke. "The Secondary World attacks the plane," he said. "They have also attacked the selene orbital system." Voltar's people were in a battle to protect the plane, the lunar probe and the entire probe-relay system, he explained. Many had already died.

As the clock ticked away, the Secondary World also attacked Voltar's home world and penetrated their defenses. "They intend to destroy us," Voltar said. Nearly a million people on their planet died in the first assault, he said.

"This is terrible, Jim," Brian moaned for he saw images in his mind and felt sorrow. "Their people are dying, again."

Voltar spoke to Brian and me with words of comfort. "The Secondary of your world will not prevail," he said. "Every last man and woman on our world will give their life for you and your people," he said. "For this, is of us—freedom for your world."

The attack was not a complete surprise, Voltar explained. "Many now join in the fight against your Secondary World," Voltar said. "With the help of our allies, the secondary will NOT prevail."

I took the battle drama with a grain of salt, but the storm tossed the airliner around like a toy. Neither Brian nor I were afraid to die, but people on the plane moaned and screamed out in fear with each jolt. The beautiful Spanish model squeezed our hands tightly and prayed for God to save her life.

"Our loss of life is high," Voltar said. "We must exhaust them with our lives. Of this, we have great sorrow, and yet of those who die, each gives their life willingly so that you may bring forth the gifts we offer to your world. And of these, the greatest is that someday man will be free of this evil--his Secondary World."

The gorgeous young woman listened to all that Voltar said. I told her I didn't believe it to be true, but she panicked when the plane lost altitude and twisted to one side. We could hear the craft recoil like the wings were coming apart. Mascara tears streaked from her big brown eyes, staining her face and dress. She cried hysterically and prayed, clinging to our arms in anguish. Brian and I comforted her all night long, and we enjoyed feeling like strong men. Neither of

447

us feared the storm. If we died, we died. We even enjoyed the violent, bouncy ride, and we especially enjoyed the beautiful model clinging to us for strength with her hands and arms. We giggled like schoolboys hiding in a closet with the most beautiful girl in our class.

When the first light of dawn brightened the silvery coastline of Lima, Peru, the plane descended out of thick gray clouds and landed safely. As the sun rose, and golden sunlight warmed our faces, the pretty girl walked across the tarmac arm in arm with us, beaming with love.

At the entrance to the international terminal, she kissed us both softly, hugged us warmly, and formally welcomed us to the land of Latin America, and Peru. Without makeup, her natural skin glowed beautifully in the morning light. She had learned something about herself during the frightening trip--she feared death and the judgment of God, for her sins.

Brian and I both learned something about each other: neither of us feared death. We both truly believed in eternal life. Brian had been brave and strong during a storm that had caused grown men on the plane to cry.

In a truly terrifying time, he provided comfort to others in the plane. I admired him. As Brian, he performed very well in the face of fear. He thought the same of me. We were the only ones on the plane not frightened.

At the entrance to the airport, the model kissed us again, and she waved goodbye to us with a tear in her eye. We couldn't have imagined a more interesting flight and better welcome as we began our adventure into Latin America.

Brian bowed low, and opened the door. "After you," he said politely with a big grin on his face. "Welcome to *the Play of Life—in South America.*"

"No, you first, my friend, you are the actor," I said. "You're the one who must suffer." I held another door open for him.

"But you are the director," he laughed.

Then we both stepped in and bumped each other--like slapstick comedians. Brian had fun with the little things in life. That was his secret. He could laugh easily, and enjoy the stress.

Cuzco – Capitol of the Inca

An hour later, we transferred to an older passenger jet, and soon we soared above the green Andean mountains, admiring the awesome beauty of the rocky, snow-capped peaks. We landed at the smaller airport in Cuzco, Peru located at a ground elevation above 11,000 feet.

December is summertime in the Andes. In the early afternoon, in warm sunlight under a bright blue sky, we strolled along the streets of Cuzco, the ancient capital of the Inca--a city designed in the shape of a jaguar. Cuzco is the home of the jaguar priests, and still center of the Incan empire.

On the narrow, cobblestone streets, old cars and busses spewed thick exhaust. Volkswagens and Mercedes Benz dominated the roads. Brian gasped with delight when he saw a classic 1948 Buick operating as a taxicab. Then he saw a beat-up 1958 Chevy, also surviving as a taxi. The car had been wrecked several times, and one door hung crookedly.

Several old Vespa scooters roared down the street with loud mufflers. "There goes the Hell's Angels of Cuzco," Brian laughed at the longhaired, rebellious-looking young men on scooters.

On the sidewalks two cultures mixed. The modern business people of Spanish lineage walked hurriedly around the peasants of mixed Incan and Spanish ancestry. The businessmen wore fine blue or gray suits with white shirts and ties. In contrast, the Incan ladies wore colorful dresses of bright pink, burgundy and purple fabric, heavy thick shawls and brimmed hats.

Huge gray stones, all perfectly shaped, formed walls along streets leading into the central plaza. In some areas, shabby adobe walls of pink or green had cracked and peeled away to reveal foundations of awesome Incan stonework. The huge stones, some weighing tons, had been cut, polished and fit together so perfectly that my knife blade could not even find a crack or crevice.

"You can sure tell who were the better stone masons," Brian mused.

I pushed hard with my knife. "You can't get a knife-blade, even a razor blade in between these stones."

"*Perfect mind, perfect hand,*" Brian said. "I just heard that from the probe. That was neat. I didn't even ask."

"I was wondering."

"Oh, maybe they answered you. Wow. That is neat," Brian gushed. "It's a direct link to the probe."

We walked on the cobblestone street comparing Incan stone masonry to a nearby Spanish brick wall. Sloppy mortar held together crooked, misaligned red bricks. The two styles seemed worlds apart—polarities. The Incan masonry was awesome, beyond belief with perfection, the other childlike—a mess.

"It must be terrible to be conquered by an inferior nation," Brian frowned. "It was just terrible for the Inca—and still is to this day."

In the central plaza, the center of town, hundreds of Incan ladies had laid out blankets and wares for sale. Young children played quietly around them.

Around the plaza stood the massive temples and governmental buildings of the Incan empire. From this square, the Inca had ruled. At one time, before the

449

Spanish, many of the buildings had been covered in gold, and most religious festivals had been conducted in the square. In the royal palace, the Spanish had found 500,000 pounds of gold ingots, waiting to be melted down into sacred art objects. Most of the Incan gold was sent back to Spain on ships. The Spanish plundered 6 million ounces of gold and 20 million ounces of silver, annually, for years.

In the plaza, two Spanish boys wanted money for a picture and I paid them. My payment angered Brian. I didn't understand why.

Then we heard music--beautiful flutes and strings. Several Incan men shuffled into the plaza carrying musical instruments. One man hobbled on a wooden leg, one man wore a patch over a blind eye, and a third man--with stumps for legs--was carried by boys.

"That is who we should be giving money too," Brian said. As I photographed the musicians, Brian sat down among them.

In moments, their music echoed around the plaza. Flutes, mandolin-like strings, and drums pulsated together into an inspiring, mystical song. From the hands and hearts of these broken men rang out the beautiful, romantic music of the Andes. Brian relaxed with the men and breathed in the beauty of Cuzco in the summertime.

An hour later, Brian dropped a big handful of Peruvian bills into their collection hat. The men protested. Too much, too much. They waved in shock.

"Of Viracocha," Brian insisted. "Of Viracocha to you." The men seemed to understand and smiled through broken and missing teeth.

"We need to support the right people," Brian said to me.

Later, near sunset as dark shadows crept out from behind huge columns of stone, Brian attempted to buy a ring from a handicapped Incan woman with a beautiful, noble face. She looked a bit Chinese with oriental eyes and high wide cheekbones, like many of the Inca.

She refused his money because she didn't have change for his paper bills. Brian pressed a few large bills into her hand. "A gift of Viracocha," he said.

"Viracocha?" she smiled with understanding.

Brian nodded. "He gives this to you." She accepted. Brian walked away as tears formed in the eyes of the old Incan woman.

"Amazing," Brian breathed. "She wouldn't make a sale because she didn't have the right change."

"She didn't want to cheat you."

"They have integrity," Brian said as the final rays of sunlight disappeared. "With cruelty and lies, the Spanish were able to conquer a noble, honest people. It's sad," he said. "We need to make sure that doesn't happen to us—to America."

That evening Brian and I ordered the most expensive steak dinner on the menu in a fancy Spanish-style restaurant. We figured it would be our last good meal. As the cook pounded the beef with a huge mallet, we laughed. Then he burned the meat on a flaming grill. We watched, hysterical with laughter. Could that be our steak? No one else had ordered—the restaurant was empty.

A waiter brought the meal, but when we tried to eat the tough, salty steak, we giggled until tears ran down their face. "Catto," Brian laughed.

"It isn't Monfort beef from Colorado," I laughed. "And we asked for their best."

"It's probably cat," Brian laughed. "That's what the probe is telling me. They eat cats around here, as a delicacy."

I spit out the meat and called for the waiter. We ordered eggs and fried potatoes. From then on, we ate eggs and potatoes for every meal.

Americans in Peru

On a pulsing, brightly colored jukebox, the song "California Dreaming" echoed over the empty tables. The atmosphere looked almost like home in America, but what lies beneath, I wondered—if the best steak on the menu was really a cat. The spoons were flat, not cupped; the toilet paper felt like sandpaper; the fancy table napkins were made of tissue thin paper; the pastries looked great, but the beef was terrible. Brian laughed hysterically at my notes.

Later, for the record, I asked what he believed the transformation would bring.

"I don't know," Brian said. "I really don't. How are people going to relate to me? That is my concern."

I said people might admire him.

"I don't know about that. It will be whatever the hell is going on," he said. From above, a water drop splashed onto his cheek. Dazed, for a moment Brian saw himself working on a satellite with a team of engineers in a high-tech company. Then he saw the satellite lifted into space on a rocket. He shrugged off the dizziness.

"Everything they show me, scares me more. That's why they have kept me in the dark," he said. "I don't understand most things," he said. "It's damn frustrating, I tell you. If I do go through with this..."

Tears welled up into his eyes. More water drops splashed. In a daze, Brian saw engineers in a clean-room environment reading his blueprints. They respectfully listened to Brian's ideas.

"I don't see how this can happen," he said. Embarrassed, he quickly tried to sniff back tears. "This is too much," he said. "I just would like to know that I had

451

an escape jacket," he said wiping his eyes. "I don't think I can take a four. It's too much. Too much emotion."

"Is it what you see?" I asked.

"It's what I feel. The feelings are overwhelming. Besides, the level is just too high for me to accept, just in spiritual terms," Brian said as he dabbed cold water on his face. "I don't feel worthy enough to even take a three."

Brian had finally acknowledged a spiritual side to his journey.

"You probably have some guilt to handle," I said.

"No, it's not that," Brian snapped. "It's just that I can't think of anything tremendous I've ever done in my life. I must admit this is the first time, I guess, in my whole life, that well--this is a treat for me. Jim, I think a four is too much. I did agree to take a three, and that I would accept a four at a later time, if I liked a three, and if I wasn't completely freaked out, and I didn't find life too hard to relate to. If I do it, I do it--all the way and forever and forever and forever! I could not get an escape clause. NO parachute. None exists."

Brian inhaled and relaxed. "I can only hope that he gives you enough instructions to get me down the road, back to an airplane, and back to California. Somehow. And hopefully with my arms and legs and other vital organs."

I laughed. "My concern is just the opposite. I am worried there won't be enough of a change to be recognized by people. I am worried nothing will happen. In fact, I want to make sure, when you come back, that we can have some cheap thrills for the people."

"I hope they don't need two heads and six eyes," Brian said as he lit up a cigarette. "That isn't going to happen. I already said no to that. Nothing physical, Jim. I have to live with this. Even if it goes bad, you see. They asked me, and I said no."

"Well, then. What is it?"

"I think it is a personality change of some type."

"Personality?" I said with disappointment. "We need more than a personality change."

"Well, we talked about this before. I know a lot of this stuff. I know what is going to happen, but I am scared. I really am. And I am still looking for something easier. Same transformation--but easier."

I laughed. Everyone was always looking for an easier way to find spiritual growth, to grow, and evolve.

"So you think it will be hard on you?"

"Yes, and everyone else. It's the reactions--the emotional reactions of the people. Mary Beth, Debra, money, bills. I just can't go on making so many DAMN mistakes with this."

Another water drop splashed on Brian's face.

"Yeah. I can see what you mean." I used a straw to lift a sample, and then tasted the huge drop. "Phew. Still tastes like cheap shaving lotion."

Brian chuckled. Then, he heard Voltar speak into his heart.

"'Never forget the joy of your sorrows," Brian reported the words. "That is what they had to learn, too. *'Never forget the joy in your sorrow.'*"

Brian shook his arms and stretched. "I just hope I don't lose my sense of humor. I could be very boring. That is what I am worried about. I mean I could just go on 24 hours a day, talking like him."

"He is not boring," I laughed. "There are men like him. Abe Lincoln was like that. Rarely spoke. But when he did open his mouth, everyone listened."

"Yeah, and look what happened to him—a bullet."

After we ate, Brian fumbled with the coffee liquor and steamed milk. He was worried about what Voltar might do. "You might have to...to hold this guy back. I mean he could go out and start...I don't know what. Let's just say, he would be able to arouse the people, to build up a people."

"I just hope there are some cheap thrills for people."

Brian flashed with anger. "No cheap thrills. It's too dangerous. If something goes wrong, I could create a real BAD experience. We need a quantum displacement system that controls for errors," he said. "Then I could displace things, and put them in the right spot, every time. Anybody can, at Nous 4. But, you have to be positive about where the object is going. It's easy to bring something into your *hands*, but to send it outward. That's dangerous. You have to be positive about both locations," Brian insisted.

"So, no cheap thrills."

"Cheap thrills didn't make my brain, or won't make anyone else's brain, into a three," Brian said. "It's the purpose that counts. Seeing a spoon bend won't get you to Nous 4. "

"I see. That is a very valid reason. Their goal is to get you to Nous 10, but they can't do it by focusing on the thrills. That would ruin the process."

"That's right," Brian nodded.

"I understand," I said. "Are you sure you can displace objects at a three?"

Brian pondered. "Oh, yeah. Well, spoon bending and that. Sure."

"At a three, will you have the knowledge of quantum displacement physics?"

"I already do," Brian said. "Most of the technology. What I don't get at a three, I can get later at a four. I'd have to go to a four next time, to get it all. The good part is, it really doesn't take a lot of new equipment."

"What do you mean?"

"All we will need is the phone company--a network of satellites, some towers--some special buildings. Of course, it would need a lot more power than an airport, and big terminals for the people to gather in, but not big runways."

"A network of satellites? That sounds like a lot of equipment to me."

"We will have it before long. Not you and me--but our planet. The only problem now is that we don't have the right wisdom in the people to experience it--to build it. We have the technology. It's known. But in twenty years or forty-- yes, easy. It will happen and our people will have the memories of what we started here."

"That could be a long time."

"Well, we can say we did something," Brian said lifting his cup of coffee as a toast. "To you and me. It will only take Voltar, and a few people to start it off, and in the end, it will create freedom for everyone."

Train Trip to Puno

The next morning at sunrise, we walked to the Cuzco train station. Carrying backpacks with aluminum frames, we marveled at the bulging cloth shawls on the backs of Incan men. In the bags, the muscular men carried wood, vegetables, even animals. One man, by himself, carried a refrigerator on his back up a stairway with a single rope wrapped around his shoulders.

"You won't see that in Orange County," Brian laughed.

On the train, Brian and I settled into a tiny booth with four seats and a table. Children on the car sold bananas and fruit. Young Indian ladies hawked sweaters, dry bread, even nylons. Brian bought fruit from a lady with a baby. He insisted she keep the change. "From Viracocha," he said patting her child. She smiled and approved.

When the whistle blew and the train moved, most of the sales people jumped off with their wares.

Twenty miles south of Cuzco, sheep grazed on rolling hills. The sun warmed up green pastures. A river of sparkling clear water rippled through the terraced valley. Brian watched Indian women wash clothes by pounding the fabric on rocks, and young girls hung the clothes on bushes to dry in the sun.

At the first stop, natives of the Quechua climbed into the car to sell homemade snacks. Their hands and ankles were dirty. Their sandals seemed caked on their thick, wide feet. "Looks like they never take their sandals off," I said into the microphone. "It looks like they just roll up into their ponchos at night and go to sleep, never talking off their shoes, or their clothes. Maybe they bathe once a week--once a year."

The women wore white rimmed hats, aprons, skirts, and several layers of thick petticoats. Most of the young girls carried babies on their backs in heavy cloth ponchos.

"Amazing," Brian gasped. "If people back home just emptied their closets and garages, and sent them the stuff they didn't want, it would change the lives of these people."

Their world was not like ours of 1976. "For them, it is about 1920," Brian said.

In a terraced field, a large group of men tilled the soil together, swinging axes in harmony and chopping at the dry dirt.

In another field, about twenty men walked behind an old tractor, tossing seeds into the freshly turned soil. "Not like the farmers in Weld County," I laughed. "These Incans would freak out if they saw huge, air-conditioned tractors."

Brian didn't laugh. "At one time, these were the richest, most advanced people in this hemisphere," he said. "Great builders. Engineers. Look at them now. Destroyed by invaders--because they trusted. They believed the Spanish, at their word, and now they are enslaved--on their own land."

Brian felt anger, and real compassion for these *People of the Land*, Viracocha's people. "They are waiting for the future, holding onto the past. This is not fun for them," he said. "Just think if they had been able to continue on."

The Aymara

Along the route, at each village, more people boarded, some with chickens or goats. At the train stops, Quechua ladies prepared food on small fires. Passengers who wanted a meal shouted or waved. Children carried the meal, hot and steaming on a torn piece of paper, to the passenger in return for a few paper bills, each equal to about ten cents.

At the village of Pucara the wardrobe and appearance of the people changed. We entered the land of the Aymara, people of the Lake Titicaca region—the tribe of Ticci Viracocha. The women wore brown derby hats, and covered their stocky bodies with heavy shawls and layered skirts. They sold handmade alpaca sweaters, ponchos and stocking hats with long earflaps and unique pointed tops.

"What are these stocking hats all about?" I asked Brian.

"That's a pyramid on top," he said.

"They wear pyramids on their heads?"

Brian laughed. "Besides that, it keeps their ears warm."

In the afternoon, as we bounced along in the train, Brian created a paper airplane for two young boys. The jet-winged creation stirred up the people. Two attractive, but wholesome Spanish college girls insisted on tossing the airplane back to Brian.

Finally, the older girl flirted, and tossed the younger girl's hat at him. "I think they want to sit with us," Brian chuckled. He walked back to the girls, returned the hat and invited them to our table. To my surprise, they agreed.

"It's the blue eyes," Brian said with a smile. "Gets them every time."

Fumbling with the language barrier, they shared names and began to talk. The two blushing girls were cousins. The older girl was a daughter of the Cuzco police chief--he had recently been brought in from Lima to control the region. The younger girl's father was a high school history teacher.

After an hour of jokes and laughter, Brian started to tell them about Viracocha. "Viracocha will return," he said. Brian showed them his tattoos.

The older girl pointed at the spider: "Tiahuanaco," she gasped. "That is Viracocha."

"Is that what the spider means to you?" I asked. The mood of the girls turned serious and they whispered among themselves.

"Oh no. Oh, no," said the older girl. Brian calmed her and showed her his jaguar tattoo.

"Lago Titicaca," Brian said. The two girls whispered again.

"What is wrong?" I asked. "Why are you whispering?"

The older girl looked at me with a serious gaze. She shook her hands and fingers. "Heavy," she said with an American hippie accent. "VERY heavy."

Brian and I burst out laughing. We all giggled together for a long time.

Finally, the older girl spoke again in broken English. "We are Christos? How do you say it? Christians?"

"You are Christians. Good," I said. "Catholics?"

"No," they said cautiously. "Evangelicos."

I smiled at Brian. "Like Debra. Evangelicals. Born again."

The girls both smiled in agreement. "Do you believe in Viracocha?" the older girl asked Brian, seriously.

"He will return," Brian said.

"Viracocha is the dios of Inca," the girl said, fumbling with the words. "We say Jesus is God."

"They get right to the point, don't they," I said. "Just like Debra."

"Inca say Jesus Christ, is same as Viracocha," the younger girl said. "We don't believe in that. To us, Viracocha means, in English—*mister—gentleman.*"

The girls had instantly associated the spider tattoo with Viracocha. But Redfield had told me he found nothing in any books about the spider.

"The problem is that a lot of things are legend," Brian said. "It doesn't get into books. But, as Voltar said, 'the knowledge is IN the people.' That's why they wanted us to come."

Brian invited the girls to Tiahuanaco. "I will be transformed into another man called Voltar. He and I will become one with Viracocha. I will be a new me, open to the people. And, I will bring clothes, food and money to the children after the 22nd of December."

When Brian finished, the girls giggled and whispered together for a long while. Then the younger girl tried to sing a song, but she blushed and gave up.

"Very interesting. Very interesting," said the older girl, with a serious gaze. She studied me. "You seem neutral. Objective. What is your role?"

"I take pictures; me photographer," I said. "Brian has been studied by many people. He believes this to be true."

"We want proof," the girl said firmly.

"Come with us and you will see the proof," Brian smiled.

The girls both laughed and giggled. The older girl again commanded her younger cousin to sing.

Blushing, the younger girl choked on a tune. "Is she trying to sing *'Jingle bells?'*" Brian laughed.

"NO. No Jingle bells!" laughed her cousin. "Louder!"

Finally the shy girl sat up straight and began to sing, in perfect English, a popular song by the British Beatles: *"We all live in a yellow submarine, a yellow submarine. We all live in a yellow submarine..."*

Brian and I laughed hysterically. We sang together, and people in the car lifted flutes or tambourines. They began to play along. Within moments, a dozen or more Aymara men and women in the car were singing along and laughing wildly.

Brian beamed. "This is what it's about," he said. "This is what it is all about. Viracocha was able to get the people all working and *singing* together."

The chugging carload of people swayed in harmony as the train rumbled out of the Andean mountains towards Lake Titicaca. In the warm afternoon sun, laughter and song echoed out the windows and across the fertile land.

At dusk, when the two girls disembarked at Ayacucho, they warmly hugged and kissed both Brian and me, leaving us breathless. "The women here are incredible," Brian laughed, as the girls ran into the depot. "So sweet and so feminine. That's what we are missing in America."

I read their names aloud onto my tape -- "Chela Victorio and Gladys Alvarado. I bet they will become wonderful women," I said.

The Mystery Boy of Puno

An hour later, with our heads pounding in pain from the high altitude, we walked through the dusty village of Puno looking for a room.

We climbed slowly up an outside stairway to a room on the second floor of a small hotel located twelve-thousand feet above sea level, in a valley.

"God. I can barely walk," Brian gasped with pain.

For about ten-dollars we had rented a plain pink room with two metal beds, two wooden chairs, two blankets, one picture on the wall and one bare light bulb hanging on a twisted cord.

As we sat down on the squeaky beds, I noted in the tape recorder. "Everything is barren. If you ask for eggs they bring you three eggs on a plate. That's all. You ask for a cheese sandwich, they bring a piece of cheese between two pieces of dry cornbread. That's it. The toilets have no seats. No toilet paper. The bathrooms are outside and ice cold. You can't brush your teeth because there is no running water. I'm glad no other people came along."

In the middle of the night, I laced on my boots and trudged down the stairs to find a bathroom. I stumbled along a dirt path behind the hotel with a flashlight trying to find a small adobe building.

One very dim, bare light hung on a braided cord in the men's room. As I stepped toward the urinal, I heard a sound. A young man with curly blond hair and white skin emerged from one of the dark stalls.

I relaxed. He looked American. "Hi."

"Hello," the young man said in good English.

"Are you American?"

"No, actually I'm from another land," said the boy.

"Another land? What do you mean *'another land?'*"

"Canada," the boy said quickly with blue eyes flashing. The young man appeared unusually wholesome, clean and healthy. His shiny white skin, bright blue eyes and golden-white hair seemed out of place in Puno, Peru.

"Where at in Canada?" I asked.

"Actually, not from any town. I was raised in a cabin, in the woods."

I laughed. "Really? Are you here with your family?"

"No, by myself."

"What is someone from Canada doing in South America at this time of year?" I was getting a little suspicious.

"The reason is a little unusual."

I laughed. "I am used to the unusual."

The boy looked me squarely in the face. "Actually, I am here because I believe that some great transformation will take place at sunrise in one of the Incan temples around Lake Titicaca--on December 22. And, I believe this transformation will change the world."

The words shocked me.

"That's why I am here," the boy said.

I figured he must be a UFO groupie from Los Angeles—or a spy.

"Where did you get that idea?"

"I just have it," he said.

"Come on," I said. "Are you from Los Angeles?"

"No."

"Are you a member of some UFO group?"

"No. What is that?"

"Do you go to UFO meetings, or anything like that?"

"No. I live in a cabin, a hundred miles from the nearest town. No radio, no phone, no television."

"Do you read books about UFO's?"

"No. I never have read one book about UFO's."

"Do you have some spiritual master who sent you here?"

"NO. It is just my own *feeling.*"

"Of your own feelings, you believe you are to be here on December 22 at sunrise for a *'great transformation in a temple near Lake Titicaca that will change the world?'* And you came from Canada for that, on your own?"

"That is right," the boy said with his big, blue eyes staring calmly at me. He didn't blink or look away.

Suddenly, I felt nervous. His hands were slender and refined. He looked like an angel, not a Canadian woodsman. For a moment, I thought he must be a projection of the Secondary World, perhaps, sent to assassinate us. A meeting here, at this hour, was too much to be coincidence.

"Do you know anyone else here in Puno?" I asked nervously.

"No."

"How long have you been here?"

"I just arrived."

My mind spun. He answered each question, but volunteered no more. I suddenly felt paranoid. I felt he might kill me, on the spot. "Is what you are telling me for real?"

"Yes, I speak the truth," the boy said calmly.

"How did you get here?"

By plane to La Paz. Then taxi."

"You just got here?"

"Yes, two hours ago. I have talked to no one else except you."

I was suddenly afraid to turn my back on the boy. I wanted to call out to Brian. "Listen, I have someone you need to meet," I said.

The boy hesitated.

"The man I want you to meet is supposed to be 'in a temple near Lake Titicaca on December 22, 1976, at sunrise for a transformation.' Do you want to meet him?"

459

The boy pondered a moment. "Are you sure?"

I insisted we go to Brian, immediately. Reluctantly, the boy agreed. I asked him to walk in front of me. I did not want to let him out of my sight.

A few minutes later I woke up Brian and pleaded with him to get dressed and talk to the boy. "Just let him be," said Brian sleepily.

"No! He is looking for you," I insisted. "He is right outside the door."

Then I whispered. "Brian, something is fishy. This kid might be a spy, or worse. If he is not for real, I want to know. He is answering vague with me. That's dangerous. You need to check him out. Have the probe check him out. He could be dangerous to us."

Finally Brian agreed. I found an open café and over hot tea, I tried to get a conversation going. All the blue-eyed boy would say is that his information had come from "himself." He had never heard of Brian.

I showed him literature that I had prepared, and told him the basic story. He didn't have any questions for Brian.

"This is weird," I said. "I can't believe you have no questions."

"Only one," the boy said calmly. Brian waited. Finally, the boy spoke. "Do you really think this transformation you are going through will change the world?"

"Yes, I do," Brian answered. "It can."

"What about you?" he said looking at me with his calm, blue eyes.

"I do. If the people find out."

With that, the conversation ended. He wanted to go back to bed. We all shuffled out into the street, and I asked if he wanted to go with us.

"I don't know for sure which temple the transformation is to take place in," he said. "There may be other temples around Lake Titicaca."

"How many can there be?" I asked. Something was definitely weird about this young man, and the whole conversation.

"How many other transformations do you think are going to take place on December 22, 1976? " I demanded.

The boy's voice cracked. "I really don't know anything except I am here, and you are the first people I have spoken to."

"I think we should let him get some sleep," Brian said. "It's time to go, Jim."

I asked the boy to meet us at the taxicab station in the morning at 6:30 a.m. He said he would.

A few minutes later as Brian collapsed into bed, I heaved with excitement. "What is he Brian? Did the probe tell you anything?"

"They would tell me if we were in danger," Brian said. "I don't think he's a spy. He's been guided," Brian rolled over on the squeaky metal bed. "That's all."

He pulled the blanket up around his shoulders. "I think you probably scared him. In fact, you did scare him. I know that. If you come off too strong, it's frightening to people who have been called."

"Called? That is pretty amazing to be called to the same hotel in Puno, Peru." I turned off the light, and sat down on the bed with my face to the door. I unfolded my hunting knife. "To meet in a bathroom in Puno. Think of the odds. It's unbelievable, Brian. We can't just dismiss it because he looks innocent. That's what people do wrong. That's how people get assassinated. They use women, innocent looking people, kids. Not like the movies."

In the dark, I whispered to Brian. "Maybe he was sent by the National Security Council. Maybe Voltar's people lost the war, and he's here from the Secondary World. The lines of communication could be down, if they said nothing to you. This could be a final assault in the physical form to stop the transformation." For the first time since meeting Brian, I was going a little crazy with paranoia. I expected the boy to return, and carry out an assassination. He would get a fight. "Brian," I whispered. "You should not sleep in the bed."

Brian breathed deep and within a minute snored peacefully, but I sat up awake in a corner with a knife in my hand all night long, until the first light of dawn.

Puno To Tiahuanaco

Brian was well rested in the morning, I was bone tired, but I knew that no one had come to the door. The attack would come later, I reasoned.

When we gathered at the taxicab station around 6:30 a.m., the sun glared high in the eastern sky. This was the longest day of the year, the summer solstice. Four other people wanted to take the trip. We all shook hands and I handed each person a flyer about the transformation. Nyles Richmond, a tall, slender gem merchant from New York, read the literature and chuckled with a raspy voice. He liked the idea of human transformation. He played in a rock and roll band on weekends.

Brenda Clark, a short, pretty blond nurse from Christchurch, New Zealand, eyed Brian with skepticism as she read the handout. She was about 25.

The Corbetts, a married couple from Australia, turned their backs and whispered.

As Nyles talked to Brian, I waited anxiously for the blond-haired, mystery boy to arrive. At 6:50 a.m., I tapped Brian. "We need to go get him."

"Maybe he doesn't want to come," Brian said.

"I pulled Brian aside and whispered. "If he is a spy of some kind, I want to know where he is. If he's at our side, he can't sneak up on us."

"I'll go get him," Brian shrugged as he trudged towards the hotel in a huff.

At 7:00 a.m., the taxicab driver started the motor. Everyone snuggled into their places. We saved the front for Nyles and Brian.

As the driver roared the engine, Brian strode stiffly into the plaza in trance with his arms outstretched and eyes rolled up. I jumped out of the taxi and shouted at him. Brian stopped and glanced around in a daze.

"Where is the boy?" I asked.

Brian turned around. "I don't know." He was baffled about his location.

"What happened?" I asked.

"I don't know," Brian said. "Voltar took over. He talked to him."

"Is he coming?"

"I guess not, if he's not here," Brian said. "I don't know what happened, but I think he got what he needed from Voltar."

The car rolled forward and the driver shouted. "On delay." Nyles jumped out and gently guided Brian into the center seat.

"Brian, we can't leave him!" I whined.

"Voltar handled it," Brian insisted.

"Brian. He is supposed to be there."

"It's okay with Voltar," Brian said. "That's all I know. He did talk to him."

Disappointed, I jumped into the backseat and sulked in silence as the taxi rumbled out of Puno in a cloud of dust. I didn't even get his name.

The boy knew where we would be, I reasoned. He could knock us off at Tiahuanaco, if he was an assassin. But, there was only one taxi a day. He'd have to come the next day, so I relaxed. I had learned to trust Voltar. He had never been wrong, yet.

Puno to Tiahuanaco

On the eight-hour ride around Lake Titicaca to Tiahuanaco, the driver stopped so we could see ancient burial towers of the pre-Inca, and wild llama. We also drank sweet root-beer from a road-side stand. Each tasty glass came with a real root in the bottom. Nyles spoke Spanish and interpreted the driver's descriptions for us.

In a small town where the driver refueled, peasant farmers and their wives celebrated around the central plaza at high noon. The people paraded--carrying hoes, shovels, rakes and plows in their hands--marching to pounding drums, brassy trumpets and mandolins.

As I snapped pictures of the bizarre parade, an angry man raced at me with arms waving. "No photographia," he shouted. "No!"

I pointed my camera down, and the brown-suited man walked away to rejoin the parade. The taxi cab driver explained that the peasant farmers had revolted to obtain more ownership of land. This particular village had been instrumental in fighting the battle.

"They carry the rake, or a chair, or a plow because, in some way, it helped them create freedom," Nyles explained, interpreting the driver.

Peru was still governed by a military junta and during the trip, the taxi stopped at several border stations where armed guards examined our passports. But when we entered Bolivia, the procedure intensified. We had to unload everything in the car. The guards carried machine guns.

Even Incan peasants with llamas were searched. Their bags and bundles were opened and spread on the ground. Some were pushed and shoved hard. Guns waved to intimidate them. Incan men kept their eyes lowered. I saw resentment and rebellion on the faces of the short, brown-skinned people.

Guards searched our vehicle then ordered Brian and I into a bare office to face the jack-booted commanding officer. He held my camera and film. As Bolivian guards stood nearby with machine guns, the officer barked questions at us in Spanish.

We didn't understand and the man became angry. He insisted on precise answers about why I would be photographing Tiahuanaco. Nyles, hearing the shouting, pushed his way into the office and answered the tough questions. Eventually, the commanding officer relented.

"No pictures of the Indians," he said in broken English. When I agreed, he handed back my camera and film. "Welcome to Bolivia," he said. We shook hands.

Afterwards, we thanked Nyles. "What happened?"

"You are *artisans,"* Nyles said. "That's all. Next time, hide the literature. Just tell them you are artisans here to study Tiahuanaco. That's all."

Under a bright blue sky, the taxi followed along the southern edge of Lake Titicaca. On the rolling green hills, short fences of stone outlined small farms. Families of Aymara Indians herded sheep and tended to the crops.

Where the agriculture ended, a large flat prairie of short grass began--the altiplano--12,000 feet above sea level. When the taxi finally arrived at the Temple of Tiahuanaco, located twelve miles south of the lake, Brian and I tried to look inside the fenced complex. The temple guards insisted we pay, and directed us across the street to a museum and ticket booth.

Brian paid for his own ticket as everyone watched.

"That is strange," I laughed. "Brian comes thousands of miles to be transformed into Ticci Viracocha--and he has to buy a ticket."

On the trip, I had persuaded Nyles and Brenda to stay overnight and witness the transformation. But as they stood at the ticket window, lightning flashed, thunder rumbled and rain began to fall from a blue sky with only a few puffy white clouds.

They felt frightened. The sudden clouds seemed like a bad omen.

Brian and I laughed at the superstition. We ran into the temple toward the majestic doorway of stone.

As we arrived at the huge portal, the rain turned cold, and hail pellets plinked against the stones. In awe, we huddled inside the stone doorway. Lightning flashed and thunder crackled. "He's here," Brian said. "He is saying something about the lightning."

The beauty and size of the reddish stone doorway amazed us both. Brian peered westward into the temple. The Gate of the Sun stood 200 feet away, enclosed in a wire fence.

"They are telling me to touch this stone. Do a test on the doorway," he said.

Brian stretched out his arms. He placed his left palm on one side of the doorway, and then he opened his right hand and pushed it against the stone. Instantly, he felt a jolt of energy and jerked his hands away.

"Wow. This thing has a shock to it," Brian said, rubbing his hands. For a minute, he looked around in a daze. I carefully touched the stone, but felt nothing.

"What happened?" I asked.

"It wasn't so bad," Brian said. He held up his right hand and looked at the big black number: 020-020-020. "Now I know what that is for," Brian said. "The probe must be activated. Lunan must have transmitted on schedule." He had asked Lunan to transmit again on the 19th of December.

Brian breathed deep. "I think I can handle this, after all. In the town, there's a church we are supposed to find. He's here. They are with us, Jim."

I could accept we were finally here at the site requested for over a year. As for my theory and scorecard, I still favored multiple-personality with a long list of paranormal anomalies that had to be ignored. I couldn't figure everything out, so I chose again, to simply document everything for later analysis.

Brian bit his lip with nervousness. "I don't know if I can take a full hit," he said. "But I have to try it. If it goes bad, get me to a church." He spread out his feet and braced himself firmly in the doorway. Water drops and tiny hail pellets splattered all around him. He touched his left palm to the stone and paused. He felt nothing. Then, slowly, he lifted his right hand up and opened his palm. He slowly moved the big black numbers on his palm closer to the red stone. Then he pushed hard.

Instantly, he felt a sharp jolt. An energy shot through his brain and body. Brian's arms trembled and his knees wobbled. Images spun through his mind. He saw the temple in ancient times, as dozens of Jaguar and Eagle priests marched inside a gold-plated tabernacle lit by candles. Then he saw white-skinned priests with long-thin noses and short beards. Wearing white turbans and robes, they seemed to be directing the other priests in their skins and feathers.

Outside, in an open area, Brian heard the single note of a long, slender horn—a conch shell--blown by a priest with his head covered by a shawl. Then Brian saw beautiful women with brown skin dancing and twirling in purple and scarlet gowns. The shining mirrors on their beautiful dresses dazzled his eyes. He saw other women, too, with white skin. Their faces were elegant, refined. They looked at him, and smiled.

Finally the images stopped. Brian removed his hands. "It's all here," he breathed.

"What? What is happening?" I asked.

"Knowledge," Brian whispered in bliss. "Universal knowledge. This is the doorway. This is where they want me to be." He stood up straight and gulped. "This is what is going to happen tomorrow. That was my taste." His heart overflowed with happiness. "This isn't going to bad at all," he said. "I think I can take a three."

A bright bolt of blue-white lightning flashed right over our heads and thunder exploded. I smelled ozone in the air and the rich aroma of fresh, rain-soaked earth. Brian looked at the sky.

"Illyupa," said a deep, crackling voice from his lips. "Illyupaaaaa."

"Let's go," I shouted. "Now." I pulled at Brian, and we ran back to the taxi.

A short while later, we cruised into the village of Tiahuanaco in the taxi. Two stone statues with big faces guarded the courtyard gate. Their large faces bore a resemblance to statues in the Easter Islands.

"That's it," Brian said. "That's the church."

"Those are strange faces," said Brenda.

"That is Saint Peter and Saint Paul," said the taxi driver in broken English. "That is what the priests say."

Brian frowned. "I don't think so. Voltar says '*no*.'"

The rain stopped and the taxi emptied. With information from the taxi driver, Nyles led me to an adobe building across the street. An attractive Aymara woman about thirty years old opened the door.

Inside the small, dark, dwelling, a wood fire crackled in an old stove. Nyles arranged for dinner and lodging. I paid a deposit, and we ran back to the taxi.

I asked Brenda and the Corbetts to stay the night. As they pondered the idea, a blinding bolt of electricity exploded into the ground behind the church shattering everyone's nerves with a deafening blast. The ground smoked, and steam rose. We could see stained glass windows lit up by the flash.

"My god that was close," Brian said.

"We're going to La Paz," gasped Mr. Corbett.

"I'm not staying here with three men," Brenda shouted.

The driver roared the engine. "We need you Nyles," I pleaded.

"You've got your rooms," Nyles said. "Find us in La Paz."

"Where? How?" I whined.

"Hotel Buenos Aires," Nyles shouted as the taxi roared eastward.

I watched the taxi with regret. We were alone. No witnesses--just Brian and me.

"Everyone is afraid," Brian said. "It would probably go a lot better if you don't tell them so much. Just keep it light. Their imaginations run wild."

Dinner in the Village

I led Brian to the small, dark home of the Aymara family. We sat down in squeaky chairs at a raw, wooden table. A lantern on the table provided a soft, golden light. The wood fire in the metal stove snapped and crackled with warmth.

Brian peered into the darkness. Two small boys, wearing filthy rags, played on the wooden floor, and a gray-haired Aymara grandmother rocked on the dirt near the wooden stove. She fed another stick of wood into the fire, and then wrapped herself up in a poncho holding the cloth tightly between dirty fingers.

A teenage girl with a dirty dress stood nearby waiting to take our order for dinner. Dirt was caked on her wrists and arms.

"It's so sad," Brian said. "I don't think they would be living like this if the Spanish never came." Brian strained to see into the kitchen and other rooms of the tiny house. "It's a hell of a life they have," he whispered. From above, a water drop plopped onto his cheek. His mind spun. "Damn." Two more mysterious drops fell upon him. He nearly fell out of the chair with dizziness. The drops opened his heart and mind to their world.

He saw their past and their futures. He felt their sorrows, their hopes their dreams, and he began to cry.

Two big tears rolled out of Brian's eyes and down his cheeks. "I do trust him," Brian finally said wiping the tears away. "They've never lied to me. I know they want to help these people--AND us."

I ordered potato soup and scrambled eggs as Brian recovered. "To Voltar and his people, we are just like these people," Brian whispered. "But we don't know it. We have lost all connection to the reality of our world. They want these people to have electricity so they can keep warm, and clean. That would change their lives. They want us to have Quantum Displacement so we can travel with them in the stars. It would be so different for us. Imagine the freedom to go anywhere in

466

the world, in an instant, for pennies. Imagine what would happen. Everyone could go anywhere in seconds. That's freedom--REAL FREEDOM."

For a moment, I imagined. To travel the world costs a fortune. People in one nation barely know people in another. Ancient cultures exist in one land, next to modern. Nearly two hundred nations in the world, only a few are republics. Most are still monarchies or dictatorships. We know so little about the world. To travel everywhere would be fun, educational.

Brian wiped his eyes. "It's a hell of a decision, what I am doing." Another water drop fell on his forehead, dripped down his nose and streamed into his mouth.

"I can't take much more," he said choking back his own tears. "Not knowing what is going to happen to you. Complete uncertainty as to what is going to happen. This is probably my last night on earth. For all I know, I'll be dead, tomorrow."

"You could die?"

"All I know is that I won't be here. YOU are supposed to know and be able to handle everything that happens. It's very scary. I mean, did he tell you anything before that you weren't supposed to tell me? About this?"

"About here?" I asked, gesturing at the room.

"Maybe I shouldn't have asked that question."

"He mentioned a couple of things," I said. "I'm supposed to take care of you. *Your unfoldment is in my hands.*"

"I have a funny feeling on some things."

"Well, for your sake, I hope Voltar's people really are the good guys and not demons in some form."

Brian laughed. "Yeah well. I decided early on who was good and bad," He chuckled, wiping his face. "But they didn't make it easy. I thought it would be easier."

As the young waitress cleared their table, Brian stared at her grandmother on the floor near the stove. Then he glanced at the face of the young girl. She looked sad, broken. He felt her hopes for a life of joy and freedom. Again, tears welled up into his eyes.

"God, the emotions are killing me," he cried. "I just feel everyone's heart, their hopes, they all want a good life, but they are stuck."

The mother of the family watched Brian with curiosity. Then she grabbed an armful of blankets and a lantern. "I think she is ready," Brian sniffled as we followed her. "This is ridiculous. I am turning into a blubbering idiot. First I was the village idiot. Now I am the blubbering, village idiot."

The Beautiful Manger

Swinging the lantern, the woman led us down an alley. She opened a huge old Spanish gate and entered a courtyard. Small mangers around the courtyard held chickens, a few cows and tools.

The lady opened the old wooden door to a small room and dropped the thick blankets on a straw-covered floor. Lighting a white candle, she said, "Manyanna." She departed, smiling at us.

Golden candlelight reflected off the pink adobe walls creating a rosy glow in the room. I lit a second candle and the room glowed with beautiful light. Photos of the family were propped on a ledge, with newspaper articles and Catholic crosses.

Across the room, Brian kicked through the straw searching for rodents. Some kittens meowed in the next room. "Good," Brian smiled. "They'll get the mice. I hope there's no rats."

As Brian spread out his sleeping bag, I studied some of the pictures hanging on the walls. "This looks like her husband, wearing Incan clothes and then a military uniform."

"I know the whole story," Brian said. "It's sad. I don't want to know any more."

Sitting on the ledges were stone jaguars and Incan gods, next to Catholic Saints and crosses. "They mix their idols," I said.

"The Inca are holding on," Brian said. "Waiting. I mean the real ones, back in the woods, in the mountains. They were told not to change. Not to talk. To keep quiet--to wait--and someday Viracocha would return, and they would become free again and have a new nation. Their glory would be returned."

"Is that what this is all about?" I asked.

"I don't know," said Brian. "I am just supposed to design a pyramid. Everything else is up to others. To the people."

Then he spoke loudly, reporting the words of Voltar. "To bring that energy with me and be able to pass it to other people: that is the goal. In this, building a people, as the pyramid is built."

"Building a people?"

"That's Voltar's thing," Brian said in his boyish voice.

"How?"

"I guess, by knowledge, by wisdom and by touch," Brian said. "By touch-- that is not until phase two. That is at Nous 8. That comes next June."

"This time is just a three?" I asked.

Brian shrugged. "Maybe I could handle a four. I don't know. I hope the world is ready for this, Jim." He laughed. "I don't think I am."

"People will be able to handle it," I said.

Brian marveled at the rosy walls, the golden light and the yellow straw on the floor. "This is the most beautiful, most peaceful place I have ever seen in the world."

A few hours later, a rooster crowed and I awoke. I knew we had to be at the temple by sunrise so I looked outside. My head ached with pain. Stars sparkled in the sky. I saw no moon.

I hurried across the darkened courtyard and looked to the east for the first light of dawn A building blocked my view so I ran to the huge Spanish gate. I wanted to go outside in the street and look east.

I pushed on the gate. Nothing moved. I looked for a handle. Chains on the huge double gate rattled. The latch wouldn't open.

I shook the chain and found an old, rusty padlock. It was locked onto the chain. Terrified, I kicked at the wooden gate. It was huge with spikes on top. I could not climb over, nor under the thick, massive door.

I ran back to the rosy room breathlessly, and tried to wake Brian. "We are locked in," I heaved for air and my head pounded with pain. He didn't move.

I kicked Brian's feet hard. "Wake up. We are locked in. We are going to miss the transformation," I shouted. "Wake up. We've got to be there at sunrise."

TRANSFORMATION – December 22, 1976 in the Portal to Life.

LONG EARS holding man and inverted woman in his hands. Symbols record genetic experiments with earth women.

VIRACOCHA as a Common Man. On his belt is a spider-like symbol. In his hands are tools to transform the people.

COMMON MAN -- with his two children. He cares about his family, his heart, and stomach . The wife statue was removed because she is bare-breasted.

GATE OF THE SUN topped by Ticci Viracocha as a god, holding lightning—
photonic matter—in his right hand. Tears cry from the eyes. The birds represent
Eagle Priests, according to Voltar--condors. The short legs of Viracocha
reminded Brian of the Host.

James E. Frazier

FACES ON WALL in lower courtyard. The two on right combine to create the third--
on left. The 'composites' continue counter-clockwise around the wall of the
courtyard, Brian said.

474

VOLTAR emerges in sorrow because the temple
around him is desolate and without water
fountains. He loved the big fountains, he said.

James E. Frazier

PORTAL TO LIFE

THE DOORWAY IS AN ANCHOR IN TIME AND SPACE,
A REALITY CAST IN STONE.

THE DOORWAY IS NEBULOUS TO TIME,
MERGING THE ENERGY OF LIFE ITSELF WITH THE
LIGHT OF WISDOM, PAST.

--Voltar

Chapter 18

Transformation

My greatest fear had manifested. Brian would now have a good excuse to say the "quantum evolution" failed. He would be off the hook. I imagined him telling a crowd: *What could I do? I was locked in a courtyard at dawn. Sorry, missed the sunrise--missed the transformation.*

In a sweat, I found a ladder and climbed up onto the metal roof. The corrugated tin crinkled loudly with each step. Dogs began barking all over the village.

"You're waking up every dog in town," Brian whispered as he stepped outside.

"I wish SHE would wake up," I shouted from the roof. Slowly, I climbed up the slippery slope to the peak of the building.

Brian watched. "Good God, you could fall and kill yourself," he shouted.

I peered over the edge. My hopes fell into the shadows of the high walls. We were locked into a plaza with twenty-foot adobe walls.

I hurried down the ladder and jumped to the ground. "Voltar told me not to worry," Brian said.

"Sure!" I snapped. "This is all they need. *One little excuse.* 'You missed sunrise. Sorry. No transformation.'"

"They wouldn't do that."

"They could. All hopes of the people, all the money from my parents would be wasted. The probe could just say, '*Sorry. Try again next year.*'"

"Jim, he is telling me to go back to sleep."

"NO WAY. I can see myself standing up in front of them and saying, '*Yeah, nothing happened. Can you give us more money for next time?*' Sure Brian! Damn it!"

I kicked at the gate and the padlock in a rage. Brian joined me, and we both shoved on the huge gate. Impossible.

"He is telling me it will be okay."

"I am not taking any chances. I am not giving them one single opportunity to say we didn't fulfill our part of the deal."

The big problem was that the walls were thick adobe, and we were separated from the house by *two* walls of adobe. No one could hear my shouts.

Frantically, I searched for rope, for a bigger ladder, for anything.

"Voltar is telling me it's okay."

"Sure, Brian. What if that is the Secondary World imitating him? Maybe the Secondary World used the Incan lady to lock us in, to wipe out the transformation at the last minute. Maybe they got in control of the probes. Maybe Voltar's people lost the war. I mean, *they* could say *anything* when the sun comes up. It's all in your head, anyway. How is anyone else supposed to know?"

"It is not *all in my head*," Brian said firmly.

"Yes it is," I snapped. "Everything is in *your* mind. You make it up--who can check it? It's not like we have two sources I can check for every quote. It's all one guy—and it's *his* mind, and he's a big *joker.*"

"Me?"

"You," I said. Everything, I had wanted to say to Brian began to spew out as I continued to rant.

Our only hope was over the roof, so I climbed up the ladder again.

"It's okay," Brian shouted as he listened to me slip and slide on the roof. "Don't kill yourself, Jim! They are telling me they will keep their side of the bargain, anyway."

I peered over the darkened village. No street lights. No house lights. No moon. Darkest night I had ever seen. I could not even see the ground.

"You should come down before you fall down," Brian shouted. "He's talking to me."

I thundered across the roof, and jumped down off the ladder in a flurry. "They have to tell me to my face," I bellowed. "I am not giving them an out. I will die before I give them an out this stupid."

Brian sat down on a small red stool in the rosy room next to the glowing candle. His eyes rolled up and instantly Voltar spoke. "In this, your efforts have been sufficient Jim, for the transformation you seek will take place, and may take place anywhere within the 49 kilometer radius of the Gate of the Sun, and at any time appropriate on this day, prior to sunset."

I held the tape recorder near Brian's face as Voltar spoke.

"In this, what you have done is enough. You have met the challenge and passed the tests we have set before you, although there is much to come, as you will discover in your final instructions."

I relaxed. One thing I had learned. If Voltar said something—that's the way it unfolded. He continued. "Sunrise is optional, the Gate of the Sun is optional. Brian must touch stone. He may touch the Portal of Life, and at any time during the day, the transformation will take place. He will know, and you will know the right time."

"Are you sure?" I asked. "It's strange that she locked us in."

"Of this, I am certain," Voltar said. "Of this, the *Play of Life.* That people would know the dedication of your commitment, and by your will and your commitment that this did take place."

"Then you did rig this?"

"Of *the Play of Life,* of Danyael, of you--Jim. In this, my people take great delight, for they are watching and listening to all that is said and done. And they truly thank you. The full meaning of this you cannot know at this time, but in the years to come you shall be a blessing to your people. And in this much love you shall receive. This brings to us a deep joy."

I glanced at my sleeping bag and yawned, suddenly feeling sleepy.

Voltar spoke. "You may sleep. You will be awakened at the right time. I, and my people give you our word on this, Jim. You and Brian may both rest, for today will be long and the challenges will be many to come."

Brian's personality returned and he shrugged, boyishly. "He says go back to sleep." He glanced at his watch. "It's 2:40 in the morning. Good Lord, Jim." He crawled back into his sleeping bag.

I lay down, still worried. What else could I do but trust Voltar, *what ever* or *who ever* he was. He had never lied to me, but I carefully protected the tape, to serve as my witness, just in case.

"You are the 'first of man,'" Brian mumbled. "You were the first man to keep your word to them. They are not going to break their word to YOU."

A few hours later, the door to our room opened. Bright morning light flared into the manager, waking us. "Es Manyana," the Aymara lady said with a smile. I had the feeling she had given us the best room in the house.

Brian and I washed up in the cold water of the plaza fountain. Golden rays from the rising sun glistened on Brian's wet hair. Heat warmed our faces and chests. Brian's thick hair steamed with the warm rays.

"Thank God for the sun," Brian shivered.

"You can feel the warmth of the rays. No wonder they worshipped the sun."

An hour later, after breakfast with the Aymara family, Brian and I walked into the church courtyard. Bells rang from the steeple as Brian tried to open the front door.

479

"Everything in this town must be locked," Brian laughed. He pounded with his fists. Finally, an altar boy opened the door.

Brian and I stepped into the Catholic Church at about 7:00 a.m. on December 22, 1976. Built in the 1500's with stones from Tiahuanaco, the church combined Spanish and Incan styles.

I recorded notes on tape as Brian shuffled forward marveling at gold-framed mirrors in the atrium. He entered the darkened sanctuary. High above, a beautiful dome of blue glass allowed sunlight in through four, small windows. I knew in ancient times a dome represented the mind, and the tiny windows were the four primary senses: eyes, ears, smell and taste. The design of the dome was a metaphor for the mind and spirit. A church represented the whole being of man. Doorways were arched to represent the heart, the entrance. I had scanned books on church and temple design. Temples also were designed to represent the human mind, and soul, but were aligned to sunrise on the equinox—due east. Their sides and lengths usually communicated the 360 day calendar. The rays of light at sunrise would shine into the eastern gate, then align through each more sacred portal to enter the innermost sanctuary—all in a straight line. Ancient temples all aligned in some way to the equinox sunrise point, but Christian churches had severed the connection to the sun in an effort to break all ties with sun-worshipping and pagan engineering. I wondered how this church compared to the temple we would shortly visit.

Brian took a deep breath and shuffled forward. At the altar, two Spanish boys lit large candles that offered soft, golden light. Awed by the beauty of the temple stones, Brian gently touched an archway with his right hand. Two jolts of energy shot into his palm. "Owwwww," he moaned jerking his hand away. "God, I got something out of that one."

I touched the stone and felt nothing.

"Felt like a shock," Brian said, his mind spinning again. On the walls of the sanctuary, he looked at the huge, dust-covered murals. The paintings revealed scenes in the life of Jesus Christ. As Brian watched, the images expanded and contracted. Then he heard music and the sounds of living people coming from one of the murals. It brightened and for a moment, the painting came to life—Jesus in the Garden of Gethsemane.

Brian turned to me, grinning in a blissful daze. "It worked again," he said holding up his palm so I could see the big numbers: 020-020-020. "Everything is expanding and contracting," Brian said. "Even you."

I grabbed Brian's arm to keep him from falling over. He took a deep breath to gather his senses. "Voltar just said that two beeps should be on your tape recorder when I got hit."

"What?"

"The energy I got. It should be on your tape. This whole area is activated, now—every temple stone for 49 kilometers."

As Brian shuffled slowly down the aisle in awe of the paintings, I sat down in a pew and rolled back the tape. Two loud, low frequency pulses had been recorded when Brian touched the stone. BEEP. BEEP. Amazing. Why? What did it mean?

I was filled with questions and ran forward, but Brian waved me away. He watched the living paintings. For Brian, each mural transformed into living people, animals with sound and song. The story of Christ's life unfolded before him. When one image dimmed, the next brightened.

For the first time in his adult life, Brian understood the passions of Jesus and the sacrifice made by the real man, a common man who lived out His drama in real life, and was crucified in Jerusalem. Brian suddenly felt a deep love and compassion for Jesus, the carpenter, a young man who died for *the 'sins of all mankind.'* Brian felt meek and humbled compared to Jesus. He understood. He stared at Jesus hanging on the altar's big cross, bloodied and pierced.

"I thought I had it tough," Brian whispered.

The Man on the cross came to life and looked at Brian with compassion. "Of this, by this, I draw all men to me, and--those in all the heavens."

"I don't understand," Brian said.

"Of this, I am that I am," Jesus said firmly.

Brian wondered why God would let his own son be killed to set mankind free. Isn't there a better way? An easier way? Then he heard Voltar's voice: *"Free-will. Freedom of Choice."* He realized God, too, allowed man freedom of choice.

From above, a drop of water splashed onto Brian's face. Dizzy with awe, he knelt down. The church bells began to chime with a beautiful song as Brian prayed the Lord's Prayer.

After a while, Brian leaned back in the pew with tears on his face. I slid over to him. "This is the end of Brian as you know him," he said.

"We all love Brian," I said. "I am sure your father would be proud."

"My father..." Brian started to talk but choked back a tear. His chest suddenly heaved with emotions, and he sobbed with his head in his hands. I placed my arm on Brian's shoulder.

"I bet your dad is one of the few people in the world that would truly understand what is happening."

"I never saw him again," Brian said, sniffling back his tears. "Not once--since I was three years old!"

"Your mom didn't understand him," I said. "She hated his books. She didn't know anything about Plato or Socrates. To her, they were fools."

Brian wiped his eyes and took a deep breath. "Jim, I don't want this to become a religion, in anyway. Don't let that happen. I am a designer--a draftsman."

"We already have a good religion," I said. "We don't need another."

"Thanks," Brian agreed. "You have been a life saver to me. I want you to know that. This could go wrong in so many ways. I could end up a babbling idiot for the rest of my life, or worse."

"I don't think so."

Brian looked upward at the cross. "I keep feeling that I am dying, like Him. I feel terrible."

"A part of you is dying," I said. "The bonds to the old Brian are breaking. That's all. So the new Brian can be born. Just let it happen. Let it all go. We are here for a reason. But, you don't have to do what He did. He already did it. And, in His name, you are forgiven. You are forgiven of everything."

"Forgiven? I am not worthy of all this," he sniffled back a tear. "I could have done so much more." Brian leaned forward with his face in his hands. Three water drops plopped onto his head. Brian heaved with feelings, and repented of his past. As tears flowed, he thought of Mary Beth, and the two girls he had left behind. He wanted his Dad. He wanted everyone he loved to be with him now. He wanted his mom to be here, and praise him. She knew nothing of his real life. He felt so alone. He had been such a problem to Voltar's council, to his teachers in school, to his mom. He could have done so much more, learned so much more, been a better man. He had frittered away his time.

As Brian cried, I wondered how far the water drops had fallen and glanced upward to the beautiful blue dome and the four open windows high above. I listened to the beautiful bells, and studied the stained-glass windows. Light and sound, I mused. Colored lights, beautiful sounds—just like Brian's description of the NOR--the device that lifted his consciousness. Maybe a church was a remnant of the same idea.

The Final Instructions

A few minutes later we pushed open the big heavy door of the church and stepped outside into the morning light. Birds sang loudly. Warm sunlight filtered through the trees. "I guess that was a cleansing. A cleansing of some kind," Brian said. "I feel a lot better."

Four Incan boys wearing pyramid stocking caps played on the courtyard wall. Brian joked around with them as I snapped pictures.

"You've got a few minutes," Brian said, "Then you get your final instructions."

"Back inside?"

"No, out here," Brian said. "At the anchor stone." He gestured to a stone cross on a pedestal in the courtyard. "That is the anchor," Brian said. Stones from the temple of Tiahuanaco had been carved into a thick stone cross.

For a while, Brian talked and laughed with the Incan boys. He tried to explain Los Angeles to them and they all giggled together. Then Brian showed them his tattoos. "Viracocha," he said pointing at the spider. "I go today to become one with him." They laughed and chuckled in disbelief.

When the chiming bells stopped, Brian leaned up against the big stone cross. His eyes rolled back, and Voltar spoke to me with a deep, noble voice.

"I come in love and knowledge," he said.

"Thank you," I replied holding the microphone.

"We are together today. Today as one," Voltar said. "There is much to do. You have done well here today. I, and my people, thank you for your cooperation."

"It's okay," I nodded as a priest in a black-robe opened the church door to watch.

"The transformation will take place within a few hours. You are to go to Tiahuanaco. Brian knows what to do. Your assistance and guidance will be needed afterwards--more than has ever been needed before--for he will be disoriented and many things will be strange, but though he and I have discussed this, he knows not what lies before him."

The altar boys joined the priest and they all listened.

"Yet he does this willingly. And of this, I--and my people--will bring through him, a new meaning and a new purpose. Of this, your assistance is vital, for the change that you spoke of--and requested--will be indeed significant."

"Thank you," I said nodding at the priest politely. I worried that he might interrupt and send us away. Voltar continued.

"Myself and the members of the Council have agreed, when the transformation is complete, you must take this information outward to the people and, of this--they should be prepared. For in some things, Brian must be re-taught. In this your guidance will be needed. He will accept the transformation and the raising of his conscious mind to that of a four today. He has discussed with us a three, and the transformation therein, but he has now accepted that he will take all that we offer--the full transformation and consciousness known in your land as *a level four*."

I smiled. Something had changed, maybe in the church.

"Document this well," Voltar said firmly. "And immediately after the transformation contact the people about you, and the people from where you came, for this will be indeed the greatest moment in your life and in Brian's." I pondered the words, hoping he was wrong.

483

"But be prepared," Voltar continued. "For in the next few days, Brian wishes to bring to the people offerings, gifts. In this, we have accepted, and we find this to be of great wisdom."

The priest gestured to the Incan boys. They ran to his side.

Voltar continued. "Fear not those that are with us, for they truly may not understand, but they are of love. Go now to Tiahuanaco. I will pass to Brian all the knowledge and information needed to complete his purpose, and the transformation, and the promise we gave him--that he would bring gifts to the people of this land--and your land."

Voltar continued. "When you take Brian home he will indeed not be the same man that you brought with you to this place. Offer him guidance and understanding so that he may orientate himself. Go now, to Tiahuanaco. The transformation will take place."

When Brian's presence returned, he asked me for details. "What'd he say? He turned me off again," Brian said rubbing his blue eyes. "I still don't know what the hell is happening." As he spoke another big water drop plopped on his face.

Brian's eyes flipped, up, then down. He hugged the cross for balance. "Whoops, did it again," he said.

"What?"

"Said another no, no." Brian chuckled, giddy with joy. "I am supposed to keep a pure heart and mind, always. Every moment."

"What happened when the drop hit you?" I pointed the microphone to his face.

"Oh...my head just whirled about 35 revolutions around in a circle." Brian leaned against the cross, dizzy and disoriented. "I rather got from the whole thing this is going to be quite different with me."

"He looks inebriated," I said into the microphone as Brian tried to walk.

His face glowed with joy. "Yes, oh yes. I can walk. I have two feet, two arms. But I don't feel the same."

"Are you in a different realm or dimension?"

"No. Not that. It is difficult to explain. It is like taking the first step onto a bridge--over a big, big canyon."

"Like you are very high up?"

"Similar, but not exactly," Brian walked slowly away from the anchor stone holding my hand for help.

"I'd sure like to ask him some questions," Brian said. "All he would say is that you'd know what to do."

"I will be with you, and I will guide you throughout the land," I said imitating Voltar's deep voice. Brian laughed. I lifted my right hand in an overly dramatic pose. Right then a bird flew over, and bird poop fell out of the sky and splashed onto my hand with a loud splat.

Brian laughed hysterically. The priest chuckled. Brian stumbled towards the adobe wall holding his stomach with laughter. The Incan boys, the Catholic priest and the altar boys all laughed, too.

Embarrassed, I wiped off the mess.

"That is exactly what I used to feel," Brian giggled. The Incan boys came running to the wall laughing. Finally Brian hugged me. "Maybe you will become 'ONE WITH I,'" Brian said, imitating Voltar.

Then just as suddenly, the droppings from another bird missed Brian's shoulder by inches. "Let's get out of here," he laughed. We waved to the priest and the boys, and ran out of the courtyard giggling.

Tiahuanaco – The Knowledge Man Seeks

A few minutes later, Brian and I, wearing our backpacks, walked down the dusty road eastward from the village.

We saw the temple grounds. A small stone doorway stood alone on the vast high plain outside the fenced area. "That's the Gate of the Moon," Brian said. "But it's not in the right place. It's all been moved."

When Brian touched the doorway with his right hand, a burst of energy shocked him.

"Oh boy! Oh boy," Brian said shaking his hand. "Far out. Images spun through his mind for a few minutes, then stopped. "This is not impossible." He shook his hands and danced around.

"What happened?"

"I got a charge off that one too," he mumbled in a daze.

"What did it feel like?" I said holding the microphone.

Brian snapped alert. "Well, it felt like an energy. Just like a shock: a mild, but healthy jolt--more than a tingle. And, then--my head spun around, and everything contracted and expanded again. It's the same as before. I could probably get all the knowledge off of it--when it is time." Brian pointed at the tape recorder.

"Oh, by the way Voltar just said there should be a beep on your tape when I got that jolt."

As we hurried along, I listened to the tape and he was right. Another low frequency magnetic pulse had been recorded on tape at the exact moment. Amazed, I tried to reason--the energy would have to move through the air, and hit the record head on the tape machine. The sound didn't come through the microphone because I heard no sound. But the sound on the tape was loud, and clear.

I wondered if the beeps held coded information, or if they were just a general pulse of energy in some form. What energy would record on tape without being heard? I didn't know. I was sure that someone would know.

I did know Brian did not have a device in his hands that would create such a tone. Twice Voltar had predicted something really unusual, correctly, keeping up his average—100 percent.

As we neared the temple, an Aymara boy ran toward us waving a jaguar carved from green stone. He wanted to sell the statue. Brian laughed saying he already had one. As I snapped pictures, Brian showed the boy his jaguar tattoo. The smiling boy compared the tattoo with his stone jaguar. He was stunned at the resemblance. Then Brian showed him the spider. "Viracocha," Brian said. The boy gasped in awe. Brian pointed at the temple. "I go today, to be transformed."

"December 22, 1976," I said handing the boy a photograph of Brian.

"Vias Con Dios," Brian said. "Go and tell the people." Awed, the boy ran towards the village in a flurry. "Chia Viracocha," he shouted.

At the entrance to the temple grounds, the orange-clad guard refused to accept our day-old tickets. Brian marched to the main office in a fury. At the ticket window, the supervisor said in broken English that the tickets were dated for the previous day: December 21. Brian needed a new ticket.

Incensed, Brian argued with the man. "Rain. Hail," Brian said acting out the weather. After a spirited talk the man relented, and waved us ahead.

"That's where my street knowledge pays off," Brian laughed. "You've got to have both sides to survive in this world."

"I guess you are the anchor," I laughed. "Brian at Nous one must be the anchor they need for this job."

"Something like that," Brian said brushing past the one-eyed guard at the narrow entrance gate.

As Brian hiked towards the big stone doorway, I clicked on the tape recorder. "What did you mean after you touched the Gate of the Moon? You said, 'this wasn't impossible after all.'"

"It gets easier each time," Brian answered. "First the doorway, then the church, then the moon gate. Three times. Each time, it has gotten a little easier."

"Explain, please."

"Universal knowledge--like I said. That's their word for it. I can see how it happens, now. It's not so scary." Brian said adjusting his pack. "It is scary, but not so bad, I mean."

"What happened, exactly!"

Brian spoke slowly. "I saw, I felt, I knew--instantly. I saw it in pictures. But, the feelings are the bad part for me. They can be overwhelming."

"What makes it easier?"

"I realized that I don't need to hold it all. That's what I was doing wrong. I can put the pictures away. It'll be there, later--with the all the feelings. I can take it out in little bites."

"Is it a memory thing?" I asked. "Is the Gate of the Sun the key to Nous ten-- through memory?"

"Two through ten," Brian emphasized. "You have to get to two first."

"But how?"

"With their help," Brian chuckled. "That's the only way I know."

"But by touching the stone. How do they do that?"

"I don't know," Brian grinned. "It's activated, and I'm marked," he said holding up the numbers on his right palm. "They did it on the craft too--the neural-implant stuff. You should know. That is Danyael's thing." But I didn't understand, or believe.

As we reached the Mound of Akapana, Brian turned up the palm of his hand to look at the numbers: 020 - 020 - 020. They were on the surface of his skin. "This is the code that unlocks it all," Brian said. "All I know is that the probe, the selene orbital--as they call it--projects a beam of some kind. And it comes down to the Island of the Sun. That is a focal point for the beam. Then somehow it comes to here--to the Gate of the Sun."

"This is so incredible."

"Oh, this is nothing," Brian chuckled. "If you are on the other island, in the right spot at the right time, you could get an eye full. You'd see it, somehow."

"You can see it? Are you sure?"

"Yes, Jim. I can tell you stuff that would blow you away for days."

"But they can do this from a satellite to -- the human mind?"

"The human mind," Brian chuckled. "From their view--they practically created the human mind. Not the soul – the mind. Big difference."

We stopped at the east face of Akapana, a mound about fifty feet tall and seven hundred feet square. Brian touched the huge blocks of reddish stone. "The first step is having an anchor. For us--for human beings--the past on earth is our anchor." Brian pointed at thick, broken pillars of stone and massive stone beams. "People lived here. That is what we must grasp." He climbed up on the big red blocks of stone.

"These were pools," Brian said. He pointed at a small hole in the dirt wall. "The water came in there from Lake Titicaca. This whole area was filled with fountains, and pools."

He climbed down into the remnant of a rectangular pool. "And one of their secret entrances was through the water in this pool," Brian said. "He pointed at a large red stone. That is a doorway to the big underground room. Take that stone out and go down a corridor at about 26 degrees for 150 feet and you'd be there."

"In their living room?" I asked.

"Well, in a big room--a gallery."

Brian gestured with his arms. "You can't believe how much of this is underground," he said. "Miles. All to the south and also north to Lake Titicaca and right to the Island of the Sun. Most of it has not been uncovered. But it is all connected to this pyramid. This is where they lived. Voltar's people."

"Voltar's people lived here?"

Brian nodded. "Yeah. Right here—underground. Our sun hurt their skin. They liked the coolness. They brought water in to moisten the stones. And it was good for storage. It was really pleasant. Cool and moist, just like on their craft."

"So there are miles of underground tunnels?"

"Not just tunnels," Brian said. "Rooms. It was like a city--underground. They had lots of storage. Special rooms for the stuff used in their experiments."

"Experiments?"

Brian took a deep breath. "How many rolls of film do you have?

"About twelve rolls and six hours of sound tape."

"Let's get started," he said sprinting up the steep slope. "Remember how they described this place on the drawings?"

The drawings had shown only the Gate of the Sun, but words on the final drawing described a 'storage pyramid'.

"This is their 'storehouse of knowledge and wisdom.' You are walking on top of it. This is what they built--an inverted pyramid. This is where they want us to build the upright solar powered pyramid--right on top of their inverted pyramid. If we do, the past will be joined--to the future, in this place. The whole place will be a doorway, a place for connecting to them. Their 'storehouse of knowledge and wisdom' will be combined with ours. Past united with the future."

"Why a storehouse?"

"To store the DNA, the substance of life—remember? And to do research on quantum displacement physics," Brian said.

I gasped for air as we reached the top. The headaches were not so bad now, we had adapted. "They want us to use this place?"

"Oh yeah. It's still good. It is still activated. They still have things here-- working deep underground."

He knelt down and picked up a handful of small green, pebbles. They looked rounded, as if eroded by water. "This is the floor of the Temple of the Sky," he said. "It was beautiful green stone. It was absolutely beautiful, green and white, and gold."

I snapped pictures as Brian continued. He found a path to a huge amphitheatre in the ground with steps leading downward, like a theatre. Around the rim stood upright stones, like markers for the sun or moon.

"Up here, they studied the stars, the moon and the sun. People gathered in the amphitheatre to watch the sunrise, and the stars, and to make decisions. This is where they ran their *Play of Life*—where the people gathered."

He waved his arms at upright stones on top, and the amphitheatre below. "Not much remains."

Then we walked to the north face of the mound. A panoramic view unfolded. Rolling green hills hid the shores of Lake Titicaca. In the other directions, dry pampas stretched outward for nearly a dozen miles. "This was the center of their empire," Brian said. "From here, roads radiated outward for miles like strands in a spider's web."

From the mound, I could see for miles in all directions. The wind blew lightly, and puffy white clouds floated in the bright blue sky. I gazed down upon the massive Temple of the Kalasasaya, a rectangle with the huge open doorway aligned to the east. I figured the long walls to be 400 feet. The big doorway waited in the middle of the east wall.

Down the ancient steps and to the east lay a lower courtyard, below ground level. Brian waved his arms. "All we have to do is build a solar powered pyramid right here. Bring in water from Lake Titicaca. Heat the water. Bingo. You could easily have a city here for 25,000--even 100,000. Scientists and engineers," Brian said. "All working together with their families. The natives would provide plenty of food."

"Like a huge research lab? Like Los Alamos or Sandia in New Mexico?"

"Yeah," Brian said. "But hopefully the people would know and understand what is going on." Brian placed his hands on the dirt, and listened to the ground.

"It is still active," he said. "The generator is still operating," he said. "I can't hear it, but Voltar said that some instruments known to man may pick up an energy field here."

I wondered if the statement would ever be proven right or wrong. Six months later, I found out – right, again,

We descended down the slope to the western end of the temple. Acres of graves had been excavated in a grid pattern. "This was the bone-yard," Brian said with a laugh. "Somebody has hauled a lot of bodies out of here," Brian said. "And a lot of stone. It is all probably in museums," he said. "I am getting fed information fast."

"What is the gist of it?" I asked.

"Great people. Honored people. They hoped to preserve their DNA so they could be brought back. Each one of these people were supposed to be brought back to life in the future."

"How brought back?"

"It is not how we think of cloning," Brian said. "They were into a different thing--a way of preserving 'life-energy' so that after death, somehow, life would be brought back."

As Brian explained, we both heard an electronic beep above our heads. The velvety soft tone lasted about two seconds.

Brian looked skyward. His face had reddened with the sun. "They are getting ready," he said. "We have to keep moving."

As we climbed up on a small mound and surveyed the graves, Brian explained. "Things were done here, Jim. Inside the temple, experiments were conducted. Some of them didn't survive. They were buried out here. Some were bizarre. Really strange looking. But for them all, it was an honor."

"An honor? I am not following this."

"I am trying to stay away from it," Brian said. "They will give a lot of info on this--but I just don't want to know. It was bloody, Jim. Damn bloody."

A water drop splashed on Brian's face and his mind spun. He saw into the past as a human body was sliced open on stone slab. White skinned men, with reddish hair, short white beards, and long thin faces stood over the body comparing the muscles and bones to those of a llama and a jaguar, which lay nearby. The refined looking men, wearing long robes and white turbans, then compared body organs.

Brian saw long silver trumpets and other vibrating metal devices for generating sound. He saw silver and copper melted down and formed into bracelets, cutting tools and plates.

He saw the skulls of living boys and girls shaved and then their scalps cut open. He saw precise holes cut into the forehead, and at other points on the skull.

He saw the bearded priests being taught by a gray-skinned, dome-headed alien to stimulate brain tissue with the vibrating instruments. He saw the big, gray-skinned, cloned workers with their long ears working nearby.

The young boys and girls with openings in their scalp looked up at Brian and smiled. They were led away and cared for by their giant long-eared friends.

In the vision, Brian heard flute music and saw into a cavern of polished stone. Black, obsidian mirrors hung on threads and spun, bending sunlight. The strobing light, together with music that pulsed at the same speed, apparently created a hypnotic state in young boys and girls.

In one room of polished volcanic stone, inlaid with gold and silver, Brian saw objects floating between two sheets of copper, balanced in a magnetic field.

The images ended. "Oh, God. It was all happening here," Brian said. "They are feeding it to me," he gasped. "I got the pictures, here come the words, get ready." I brought my microphone near.

"They learned how to accelerate the stages of mental growth in a young boy or girl using these techniques of sound, and patterns of light, and a magnetic energy." He paused a moment. "Basically they were structuring life. Uplifting the mind. They were actually creating forms of life, many forms of life, for the entire world. Then they took the successful experiments to other places on the globe where they had to survive on their own."

"From here?"

"From here. This is where the Secondary did their thing, with man. Then they transported them all over the world and even to different worlds. The one final test was that they had to survive on their own--and reproduce--on their own."

"They had to reproduce?"

"They had to pass it on."

"This is mind-blowing."

"Remember, in the hypnosis, when they talked about all the plantations and the zones. To this day, they still follow all the generations. That is their thing. The transmission of consciousness--mind levels--through the DNA, generation upon generation."

"But what were they?"

Brian paused. "Wait. He's answering you." Brian then reported Voltar's words: "Composites," he said. "Composites that survived were taken to other places throughout the world, each to set up different colonies. Colonies that flourished and thrived and grew, each to their own."

Some 'composites' were depicted in stone. "Come on," he said jogging eastward around the temple. "They want you to understand. They want man to know." As we hiked along outside the temple, Brian showed me the water drainage system.

"With the water and the power of the sun's energy, they want us to take this place into the next phase of the experiments," he said. "Which is US reaching out to them."

"From here?"

"Yeah."

In a few minutes, we arrived at the sunken courtyard on the east side of the great temple.

"There they are," Brian said stopping. He pointed at human-sized stone faces anchored into the walls of the courtyard. "This is your answer. Every successful experiment was depicted here on those walls."

Brian entered the courtyard down a flight of steps. "This was all different, of course," Brian said. "This was all underground, under the floor of the upper courtyard at one time."

In the center of the courtyard, stood a flat statue of rough, reddish stone--a man with a childish face. Behind him stood two children, also flat and rough in form. The nose and eyes were not sculpted but just carved into the stone, in simple fashion. The hands of the man were open. One hand rested over his heart, the other over his stomach.

The style seemed opposite to the complex sculptures on the walls. Many of the heads protruded from the wall in three-dimensional form, as sculpted works of art. But not all. Some of the heads were carved in white stone, others of gray or rose colored stone.

"This is bizarre," I said while snapping photos. "Some of these faces are not even human--they look like half animal."

"But they are human!" Brian said. "They are just not on our planet, now. Not anymore."

As a busload of school children poured into the courtyard giggling, Brian continued. "Voltar's people and the Secondary World knew all about DNA and the structures of the molecule when they arrived here. What they were looking for here were *breeding properties.* That's his word. The experiments had to propagate--breed afterwards--after their transformation."

On the walls, many of the faces appeared European and Semitic with long, thin long noses, headbands and turbans. A few others appeared Neanderthal with thick brows, wide-set eyes and big, broad noses. A few looked feline or amphibian. All the races of man seemed to be represented.

"Are these the races of our world?" I asked.

Brian chuckled. "Most of our world is here. Our world is just a tiny part of this group. He pointed at a face on the wall near the only entrance. "That was the first success," he said.

The wide eyes bulged outward. "It looks like half-frog and half-man."

"That is where they started. Frogs--amphibians. Man and frogs are similar, in some way."

"You are going way out on a limb on this one."

"I don't know," Brian laughed. "HE is telling me this. It's not me, it's not my knowledge. "

Brian said the first success was combined with a second to create the third. That is why the faces alternated up and down around the wall. The process continued around the courtyard counterclockwise. I photographed the faces in order.

"It is a pattern," Brian explained. "That is what he meant by composites. They were combined, in order. What they did was orderly, and highly logical."

Brian said the experiments were conducted over thousands of years at each of the nine descents to Tiahuanaco. Some of the successes had been removed to help populate and colonize other worlds.

I remembered Brian's writings. Supposedly, the first descent had started around 26,000 B.C. The most recent--the ninth descent--started in 110 B.C.

"Each decent caused changes in the mind of man," Brian said. "Slowly, man and civilization changed."

"Your drawings indicate the tenth descent started in 1971, and will end in 2011," I said. "Forty years. That's a generation."

"That's right," Brian said. "But the past must be understood first. None of this history is known to man," Brian said. "But it's all here."

He explained that Voltar's people and the Secondary World had worked together harmoniously in earlier descents, but after 12,500 B.C., problems developed. "The Secondary World began to believe they were God," Brian said. "They acted as if they had created man."

Brian explained that Voltar's people always worshipped God as the Creator of man, but the Secondary World started to believe they were equal to God. "Because they had created new forms of man," Brian said. "That is when Voltar's people made the break with them. To Voltar's people, that belief was a mistake. It became a shame to Voltar's people--what was done here--and still is to this day," he said.

The Secondary World still controls most of earth, Brian explained—but not all. Voltar's people have special control at Tiahuanaco, and at a few other zones, like Yosemite.

"Voltar's people have never given the little grays all of the knowledge of Quantum Displacement," Brian said. "They are saving that for man. They want man to be free from the Secondary World--and we can be free here, at Tiahuanaco," Brian said.

While I finished photographing all of the faces, Brian tape recorded the school song of the visiting children and played it back for them. The children clapped and applauded. When the kids departed, Brian continued with his description. "This was a sacred place--very sacred. There was a family in the middle. A man, woman and their children—a Common Man. See, the stone is common, from this area, only slightly worked, unpolished, rough, and his hands show his main concerns—his heart and his stomach."

Brian pointed at the flat statues. "It's a common family, in the center of this all, but the woman is gone--probably in a museum. The idea is that love is being represented here. At the center is a family, and their children of love. On the walls, are also children of love—some common and some not. Most of these experiments started out as children—and they were well known and loved by the people of their time. But not all were the native people of this land.

"Some very intelligent people migrated here from all over the world to be uplifted," Brian said. "That's a whole different story. Selected ones were also transformed. But they also gave birth to children, and cared for them out of love. Love cannot be ignored. In fact, from Voltar's viewpoint, love was the most sacred of all-- and important to success of the colonies. That's what you see here. They are all honoring the power of love in the family of man. All of the faces on the walls look AT the Common Man, in the middle."

"That's the way it should be, "Brian said. "In a government—everyone should be fulfilling the Common Man, because in a way we are all the common man."

"But we are supposed to have a family?"

"That's right," Brian chuckled as he trudged up the stairs out of the sunken courtyard. "You can see, with a little breeding and cross-breeding, and a lot of love, they got quite a few things happening. But the people built this. Even these faces were built by the people."

"They made the people do all the work?"

"Well, yes. They had to build this place and do the work with their own hands, and that was part of learning, and the uplifting of their minds. Part of the anchor was work. Work helped perfect the mind. *Perfect mind, perfect hand*— remember. And, they sang as they polished the stones, and carved the faces. People sang songs of worship as the worked, and some of their knowledge is in their songs.

"Of course, when the temple was done, some technology was added from beyond this world. A few priests were very involved in this. They were educated here, but they were not the common people of the land. They were the white-skinned ones, the bearded ones. They were met by Voltar's people and by the Secondary World when they arrived."

"They were met here? I'm lost."

"It's a big story Jim. They were met on the coast. The people from the East. I can get the whole story, but not now--later. It involves migrations here. Ships. They came later. Maybe next time we'll go into that."

"Well, who was Viracocha? Was he created here?"

"Well, he had a connection to the stars. Just like I do, if you know what I mean—someone like Voltar—only of his era. Through his connection, Viracocha brought knowledge and wisdom to these people. But he had no knowledge to begin with--NO KNOWLEDGE OF HIS OWN. Let me make that clear. HE WAS CREATED WITH NO KNOWLEDGE," Brian laughed. "But, he was born on the Island of the Sun, and he was special at birth."

"Like you – touched by the Host.'

"That's what they say," Brian laughed. "I do know one thing. He had to take what was here and make it more than what it was. And with guidance from the star people--that he did do. That was his job. That was his purpose. And he did it. He was quite a guy."

"But, he started out as an average guy."

"That's right. He had no special knowledge when he was born."

"Sounds like you."

"Right. In about three hours, you are going to see it happen all over again."

We both laughed. "It's not exactly the same trip," Brian said. "We are a few thousand years down the road from the first time. But man should be able to understand. They have understood in the past," Brian said. "Even the natives understood. There was no great mystery. In a way, it was easier for them to accept than modern man. Not so many secrets, then."

Lunch at Tiahuanaco

Around noon, we walked with parched throats to the cabana across the dusty road. Too hot to eat, we ordered a soda with ice cubes. "The first ice cubes we have seen in South America," Brian laughed with cracked, dry lips.

"We should have brought sun-block," I said. "I can believe they wore turbans."

"If I go weird," Brian said. "The only thing I can think of is get me to La Paz, Jim. If this is uncontrollable by you--okay?"

I agreed.

"If I don't have enough sense to know what I am doing, then you better get me home," Brian laughed. "But if I have enough sense to orient to something to do, then get us right direct to Cuzco."

He gave me his wallet and traveler's checks. "You take my money, or I'll give it all to the first Incan I see. As a four, my relationships are going to go very strange."

"When did you agree to take a four?" Jim asked.

"In the church," Brian shrugged.

"Why?"

"Well, look what He did."

"Who?"

"You know."

"You mean, Jesus."

"Yeah. This is nothing compared to Him. I can at least do my little drop in the bucket—my little part in the whole thing. "

"Your role in The Play of Life?"

"You're the man of words. Put it anyway you like," he laughed. "You created the whole thing. You and Danyael."

"Why do you say that?"

"He uses your mind—Danyael and you are one, like Voltar and I. We are united with them somehow--reflections of mind at Nous ten. That's their words—not mine."

495

The Transformation

A while later, we entered the Temple of Kalasasaya by climbing up a stairway on the north side of the western courtyard. "They called this building The House of the Sun," he said. "The priests would use this stairway to come and go."

When we stood inside the temple, the emptiness stunned him. "My God. Everything is missing."

At various times, Brian had been shown the entire temple with a tall, rectangular structure in the priest's court—a sanctuary plated in gold. Now all the stones, the gold, the curtains and wooden beams were gone. He shook his head in disbelief. "Let's just do the important stuff," he said. "I'll just focus on what is here, now."

He started with the mysterious Gate of the Sun, standing about 16 feet long and ten feet high, carved from one piece of rock weighing around 100 tons. A narrow doorway had been cut in the center of the slab to create the gate. Above the doorway, in the center, the image of a short-legged man had been carved— Ticci Viracocha. He held lightning in one hand and a scepter in the other.

At each side, bird figures were arranged in three rows of eight—twenty four condors. "That's Viracocha--as a sun god," Brian said. "It's too much to describe, now. All I can say is that it's a calendar related to the sun as it moves up and down the horizon. "Voltar is saying that the birds run. They don't fly, they run. It's a joke, I think. They were men--not birds--priests. Eagle Priests, but the birds are condors. I don't understand fully what he means. All I know is that the entire temple was a calendar of sorts."

Brian paused and looked upward. "I can't handle all the information right now," he said. "The equinoxes were all aligned to the big doorway and to this -- the Gate of the Sun."

Brian remembered images he had seen of the sanctuary plated with gold, and felt disappointed. "So much is missing, I'll just deal with location. That's the most important thing now because it's way off center," he said. He strode eastward to the remnants of a foundation wall across the width of the temple.

"It belongs here," Brian said. "It was connected to the wall that was here."

Brian showed me pillars and posts on the ground. "The gate fit into the foundation here," he said. He insisted I photograph them. "Now, I'll show you how they fit." We hurried to the Gate of the Sun and studied the notches and grooves on the back. "This is very important for man to know. The upper wall of this inner temple, the sanctuary, was held by this foundation which connected to the Gate of the Sun," Brian said as I snapped pictures.

"Those that made it--the experiments that were successful--passed right through the Gate of the Sun, facing eastward before sunrise. The priests would join them at the next big doorway, and escort them down a long set of steps slowly, very slowly, eastward into the public courtyard, then onward they walked to the big portal and the rising sun—a new day, a new dawn. For them, *Look to the East* had come. That's what it means. Transformation! A new man."

Brian emphasized that the doorway in the Gate of the Sun was narrow. "Even a small sized man had trouble fitting through the doorway. That was to make a point. It was the entrance to the most sacred place—narrow, hard to go through."

He gestured to the emptiness inside the temple. "This wasn't all open like we see today," Brian pointed at the priest's courtyard. "There were rooms, hallways and this tall, beautiful building, covered in gold. It was like two stories tall. Everything has been moved. It makes me damn mad," he said. From above, another water drop splashed on his face and his mind spun around.

"Oh. Oh," he moaned in a daze. "I'm sorry. I guess I can't say any more bad words. None. Not even little ones."

Brian glanced at the Gate of the Sun. His eyes saw the past—a stone plated in gold and covered with a curtain of royal purple. Then the curtain moved away. He saw a bright spot of sunlight moving. One bird would receive the light for a moment, and then darken as the light moved on to highlight the next. He understood that it somehow showed the sunrise point moving up and down the horizon.

"Take pictures of the Condors, Jim," he said pointing at the birds. "I'll try to explain it all later." Then Brian saw the sunlight beam fall upon Viracocha. "Get good pictures of him," Brian whispered pointing dizzily at the man.

"What is he holding in his hands?" Jim asked.

"Lightning," Brian said. "Enlightenment. That is his power. To bring enlightenment to man through his touch—rapidly, like lightning."

"So it's not real lightning?"

"No. That's the symbol."

"But how is this the *'key to mind levels two through ten,'* as your drawings said?"

"All of this works through touch," Brian said. "That's why I must be here in the physical form. I have to touch stone. *It is the touch that counts.* They want people to know that. You touch certain places on certain days to get the information. At least I could." He held up his hand with the numbers. "I don't know if it will work for others."

As Brian talked, another velvety, high-frequency tone pulsed over our heads—louder than the other tones.

"We don't have much time," he shrugged.

He quickly pointed out the correct site for the Gate of the Moon also, saying it would have been located to the north of the Gate of the Sun.

"For now, the Gate of the Sun is the most important," he said. "The temple itself is a calendar," Brian said. "A reality in time. It represents man and God, united as One--at a certain moment in time. It all involves time. It is all about time," Brian insisted. "Like the writings. Time and the mind. Time and the mind. That's the key."

"This is incredible."

"Oh, there is a lot more," Brian said. "It would take me years just to give you what I am getting. They are feeding it in fast. I am only hitting the highlights."

I glanced at a big slab of stone on the ground.

"That was the bloody table," Brian said. He grimaced. "They did experiments and sacrifices on that table. Of course, it was up on a big platform and this is only a part of it. It sat up high, and you stepped up to it, but it was angled so water and blood and stuff could be washed off."

"People died on the table?" I asked.

"Well, animals mostly--lots of animals. They conducted sacrifices, Jim. And they experimented. They learned. And it all changed over the centuries—from experiments to sacrifices. And yes, some people didn't survive. It's too much to go into now, Jim. Just take pictures."

Brian hurried into the eastern, public courtyard. "Why is this area so big?" I asked. "Did it have a roof?"

"No roof," Brian said. "Just the side chambers had roofs. In both parts there were rooms on the sides, some for meetings, some for storage. There were women in this part, too," Brian said. "And a big fountain. The public could come in here sometimes, but only priests could go into the priest's courtyard where the experiments and sacrifices were done. But, only the very top priest of that year could go into the sanctuary. I think they rotated."

Brian hurried towards the only monolith in the public courtyard, a huge gray statue with thick, short legs and big feet. "This looks like what you saw on board the craft?"

"Yep," Brian said. "That's them."

"Rough, gray skin, with no necks, and long ears," I said. "But, it has a man's face, sort of."

"This is Voltar's *'Cloak of Sorrow,'*" Brian said. "There is a whole story behind this--the whole history of Voltar's people is tied to this form--their Cloak of Sorrow." Brian pointed. "Look at the belt. That is the belt they wear with all the colored lights."

Brian bit his lips. "It is too much for right now," he said. "This is just a representation of them. Not entirely accurate. First, there should be two of them. They were both outside the sanctuary, looking inward towards the sanctuary."

"Inward?" I hadn't seen another statue like this one.

"Inward," Brian said.

I pointed at the ornate detailed lines, all over the finely worked, polished statue. "Can you describe what these markings mean?"

"That would take months," Brian said. "That is the history of all the life forms created here. Each one of those circles is either a month or a day. And you can go through the whole history of things that happened here, by touch."

"And on his belt?"

"That's the power pack," Brian said. "They wore it for transportation within the energy field. Remember, the Host wore one, too. It's something we can have--someday."

"What's he holding in his hands?"

"Well, you have to go by each hand," Brian said. "He is holding a female in his left hand, she is upside down. She is an earth woman, and the story of this statue is related to birth and to the idea of inverted logic."

"I don't understand. What is inverted logic?"

"They use inverted logic with women. I guess, females are like men only the nerve energy is reversed, polarity of some kind, inverted. Maybe in the brain. I don't know, but this is about their relationship with women and men. Breeding with earth women, and the results of all the experiments."

"So they bred with the earth women?"

"Oh, yeah. Well, special ones. They were raised just for that purpose from childhood, and they eventually gave birth to the kings, you might say, royalty--the Inca. But a lot of others were created before them. This went on for a long time."

Brian said the statue had originally included a helmet that rose upward with a rounded top. He told me to start taking photos of the rows of little circles. "If you look just below his right elbow, each one of those little symbols represents the *controlling force* that was put into each one."

"What are you saying? A soul? A spirit? What is a *controlling force*?"

"Each life form--each creation--had a controlling force put into him. These symbols were one way to keep track of what happened to that energy. They also use the probe for the same thing."

"How come this stone is polished smooth and the carvings are so ornate?" I asked.

"These carvings were done by people with uplifted minds--after they had learned. This stone is not from here. The common man in the lower courtyard is of natural stone, found close by. And he was carved by people with no education in stonework."

"So the type of stone and the style of stonework are both important?"

"Yes, very important. The stone carver was extremely important--the man," Brian said. "As a man worked on stone, his mind was anchored, and because he was anchored--he could be uplifted. Anchors were critical to them. Like, you can't reach up to the stars, until anchored on the earth. Working on the stone was part of the process," Brian said. "I can't explain it all. Each worker put his heart and soul into the stone, and the activated stone gave back. Like, the touch, I felt. Can you imagine receiving that all day long? You can see why solid anchors are vital. So, yes, the stone itself was used to uplift their minds as they worked on it."

I pondered for a moment. "So, that is why the stonework is so incredible?"

"Yeah, part of it. They loved polishing it, carving it. It was all part of their uplifting. This whole temple is a picture in stone. A message. Their word is *'depiction.'* They didn't have film. So, they used the type of stone and the *style of stonework* to depict things for you."

"For me?"

"Well, for you—yes. Who better to understand, after what you have seen? And, since this is their last descent, it's very important to them that all is understood," Brian said.

As I pondered his words, he hurried away.

"Let's go to the last guy. I have saved the best for last." Brian pointed westward to the only other statue in the temple, a small figure of a man. "This should be what you need to put this all together."

As the sun burned down from blue sky, Brian and I loped together to the south side of the priest's court. I glanced at my tourist map. "That is the Friar or the Bishop. That's what the map says."

Brian laughed. "The Spanish take over everything. That makes it confusing for everyone. Cuts the meaning. But, look at this stone," he said.

Carved from softer red and white sandstone, the statue appeared split vertically, up the middle, into two halves. Half of the man was red stone, the other white.

"It's split," I gasped. "For real." Modern man had installed a metal band to hold the two sides together—one white, one red.

"He's flawed--like me," Brian said. "One part is pure, the other not so pure. Remember what Voltar said, *'Man is two men in one--one asleep in the light, one awake in the darkness.'* I echoed the words. We had heard them many times.

"This is it. He's what this is all about," Brian said.

"Him? Who is he?"

"You're looking at him—remember when they said man would discover that 'the two entities would be as one.' Do you see his belt?"

I gasped. A spider-like image had been carved into the stone belt.

"The spider?" Is that…"

"Right. The same spider that is on my arm," Brian said holding up his forearm. "At least it represents the same idea."

"What does this mean?"

"Well, it was built by the native people to represent one of their own, as a man. But AFTER he was given knowledge."

"Viracocha?"

"Yes. That's right. From the Island of the Sun."

A big water drop splashed on Brian's face and his mind spun. He wobbled dizzily and his heart filled with joy.

"I have waited a long time for this." Brian smiled as tears welled up in his eyes. "Whew," he gasped. "What I could tell you about him. What an amazing guy. Much more than me. But most important was -- he got things done."

"So Viracocha was a man with average knowledge born on the Island of the Sun. Somebody they created into – a god?"

"Not exactly. From his birth it was planned. He was an *unknowledgeable* person—a common man. He was transformed here, and he went amongst the people. And then, with their help, he brought to them a better world, a better life—a better mind--a new way of thinking, *a new truth upon the land,* Voltar just said. But it was only with the help of the people, and always by their own hands."

"Why?"

"So they could maintain what they built. That is the problem with man. His biggest plans fail because he starts too high, too much at the center. But Viracocha knew how to build like a spider weaves a web, from the outside inward to the center. Then, when finished, you have a place that is strong at the center. That is part of what he taught. This place was the center of the web. He taught the people how to build a new world. And he gave them the tools and the wisdom to do it. Of course, he had a little help."

"They built wide roads—the Incan highway. Why?"

"They built for the future, Jim. Long into the future, like me."

Brian breathed deeply. "I have waited for this day a long time."

I photographed the statue as Brian talked.

"Well, anyway," Brian laughed. "Hint. Hint. Do you get the idea? That is why I put him off to the last. This is the last thing we'll do. Because we HAVE to get on with it."

I read some graffiti on the statue. "Okay. I'm impressed. I get the hint. But if you had 'Edual El Cameta was here' on your left arm, I would really be impressed."

Brian chuckled. "That is really disgusting."

"Well, what is the real significance of this? To man."

"The spider, mainly," Brian said. "It is not just photonic matter, it's also a way of organizing people, or a nation. It represents intelligence, itself: photonic matter. Light made of matter--enlightenment. It is an energy they gave him, and the knowledge of what to do with it."

501

"You mean--he had powers?"

"Sure. Absolutely."

"You mean spoon bending, moving rocks. Paranormal power."

"Yep--he had that, and more. And he was able to use it--the right way. He taught them about agriculture and how to build steppes. He taught them all kinds of things. But, like me, he wasn't perfect. He, too, was united, as one, with someone else."

"Like Voltar?"

Brian nodded. "Right. I wanted to show him last, before I go through the doorway, the transformation. So it makes more sense."

"So, this is Viracocha?"

"This is a representation of Viracocha," Brian insisted. "A depiction by the people, themselves. And in his hands, he has the gifts he gave to the people which transformed their lives. The tools for creating a new world, a new nation."

"Tools?"

"Yeah, look at his hands," Brian said. "One is for doing stonework, which was close to their heart, the other is more spiritual---agriculture, harvesting their grain, which was spiritual to them. It not only filled their stomachs, but also gave them a higher life. I don't know how to explain it all. Just get lots of pictures."

"But I want to be clear. He has a split--like multiple personality?"

"Not the same," Brian said. "Two men in one. TWO MEN IN ONE. We are all that way."

"But that stone was selected on purpose?" I asked. "All the stone was picked to represent the person. The stone, the style of carving, they all form the picture."

Brian wiped sweat from his hot, reddened forehead. "For that reason, Viracocha was not made of the polished, ornate, gray stone. The stone was their film. Don't you use different film for different purposes?"

"Yes. But why are the big, long-ears so ornately done?"

"They are a storehouse of knowledge--even today. I could get a lot of information off of them, I'd need both statues, about two months of time, and translators -- people to write it all down."

"You sure there were two of the big gray guys?" I asked. "You're going out on a limb again."

Brian chuckled. "Yes, Jim. And they were outside the gate, looking in."

"And you will become like Viracocha?"

"More or less. That is what they are talking about," Brian laughed as he glanced eastward towards the ominous portal.

"I don't get it--I want to be very clear. Is it you, Voltar, Viracocha, AND the long-ears--all combined into one?"

"I don't know exactly. The long-ears are their cloak," Brian said. "Their 'cloak of sorrow.' You've got to remember that."

"I don't get it. Why sorrow?"

"They've been hurt, Jim. Seriously hurt in their past. Their entire world suffered. It is all part of their history. They were children of the stars, Jim." Tears welled up into his eyes. "I can't say any more, now. I'm supposed to write their whole story."

Brian eyed the dark, ominous portal waiting for him and sniffled. "I know I am taking a big step. The biggest step of my life--and if I am wrong, you better get me out of this thing, somehow guy. I don't know how you are going to do it. But you find me an exit, real quick. Okay? I am counting on you for that. I do not want to go around being in big trouble for the rest of my life. If this goes bad, get me out of it."

"Well, how would I know?

Brian suddenly felt nervous. "I hope he told you something, Jim. I have a hard enough time being a Brian, and surviving in this world. What am I going to do as a Brian at four? How am I going to make a living? Pay the bills? I have no idea on any of this, Jim. I am counting on something to happen, or I could be hung out, in deep trouble. I mean it."

A loud, warbling beep pulsed above our heads, much sharper, louder and longer than the others.

"Oh boy," Brian moaned. His knees buckled, and he staggered for a moment like he might fall. Then suddenly, he jumped with energy like a horse that had been kicked into action.

"We only have five minutes," Brian said. "Maybe three. We gotta go."

Brian picked up his pack and mine. "Let's go," he said galloping eastward with both packs. We ran nearly a hundred yards through the courtyards to the big stone gateway--the Portal.

"No more time," Brian said as we arrived flustered and out of breath. We ached for air. "No rehearsals. You have to get it right the first time."

"Wait, I have to change film." I clicked on the tape recorder and found my film.

"You can change while I sit down," Brian said. "I have to face to the west first." Brian plopped down on the west entrance to the stone portal and felt two pulses of energy zap into his body. He moaned. "I can take it," he whispered. Then he snapped alert.

"You should have two beeps on your tape, just now," Brian said. "And part of what they do may turn up on film. You may get the energy on film. If you had a TV camera, you'd really see something with a cathode ray tube."

"I've got one more roll of 25," I said nervously. "Maybe I should use 64 or 200." I eyed the sun and the shadows as Brian sat in the doorway, relaxing.

"See you use different film for different light levels," he chuckled. "Take your time. I'm okay as long as we're here--and we ARE here."

Then suddenly the one-eyed guard approached us. "Where did he come from?" I whispered to Brian as a warning. Brian looked around. Without smiling, the guard walked up very close. I opened my hunting knife and held it behind my back. This could be it, a final attack to stop the transformation.

In Spanish, the Incan man asked if he could purchase the tape recorder.

"No. No way. Maybe Manyana. Manyana," I said hoping he would turn around. The guard stepped towards Brian. I ran forward blocking his path. The man stopped. He smiled and dug deep into a pocket of his orange overalls. I thought he would pull out a pistol.

"You like?" he asked. He held a brass artwork of the family in the lower courtyard with the man, two children and a large-breasted woman. Brian laughed.

"Is this what you were thinking?"

The guard handed it to him with a friendly smile.

"You buy?" the guard asked.

"Is this the way it was?" I asked.

"See. Mama taken away."

Brian laughed. "I told you so."

I quickly paid the man and urged him to move away. If he didn't, I figured he'd attack now, and carry out an assassination orchestrated by the Secondary World. But, slowly, the guard backed away, watching us with curiosity.

With formality, I handed the figurine to Brian. "This is my gift to you," I said. "As Brian Scott."

"For me?" Brian asked. "It's not ancient."

"But, you should have something, from here. At least, it shows you were right about the mother."

"At least he didn't stop us," Brian said with a chuckle. "Voltar will not allow anything bad to happen," he said. "This means much, MUCH more to them, than to us."

He lit up a cigarette. "You better check those last two beeps. We've got a minute." I rolled back the tape. Sure enough, when Brian had sat down facing west, two low frequency tones recorded on tape.

"They must be making a point."

"It's physical," Brian said. "There is physical energy moving from one point to another--transported, being exchanged. It's not just mental. It's a physical, invisible, but measurable energy," he said. "Magnetic in nature, and it can be used to affect the mind. That's part of their science. It's part of the Danyael thing—neural implants and all. You should focus on that, if you ever do any research. You should. Much would come of it for mankind."

A LOUD two-tone beep sounded right behind me, just over my head, and I jumped.

"Wow. That was right behind me."

Brian looked up. "It thought it was behind me."

"It sure was a loud one," I said into the tape recorder. "It sounded like a squeaky bicycle wheel: two tones, instead of a warble, but louder than the last one."

Brian looked at me squarely. "After you get your final instructions, I will come back into the portal walking east." He paused and bit his lip with apprehension. "As I go through it, headed east, the transformation will be complete. I will be stepping out in *his* reality—Voltar's."

I glanced at the sun. I wanted a good camera angle. Brian breathed deep. "Oh, be sure to refer to this as an exit. It is NOT the entrance. It is the exit *to life* for the guys like me."

"The exit of life?"

"No. The exit TO life. The Portal TO Life." Brian glanced at the huge doorway. "They would stand there, as models--models for man. People would see them, admire them, and then decide where they should go. But they had to survive on their own. A lot of them died in the jungles, or on their journey leaving here--even with a hunting jaguar for a pet. Even a jaguar didn't guarantee them success, or survival."

"No jaguar waiting for us, I guess. That means we will be on our own."

"Well, not exactly. You will have Voltar. This is a little different--and I think Viracocha is going to talk to you." Brian sat down on the edge of the doorway, facing west. "I just hope I'll be able to tie my shoes."

He glanced at me with fear. "I am still worried about a lot of physical things. I got through the love stuff, and friendships, I got through the understanding stuff and the habits."

"Bad habits?" I asked.

"Some of them, they are going to let me keep. I don't have to have a drastic change. I can still be me, in some ways. They might let me smoke, I don't know." Brian took a deep breath and tossed away his last cigarette.

"He wants you to understand something, Jim," Brian said gently. "He calls this the Portal to Life. Remember it is INTO life. But it is also a Portal of Time. I don't know how to say it all. It's a gateway through time--for real--in the physical form and in other ways. This is not a joke or some game. Thousands of years of life have passed through this point, this portal. Jim, it is a doorway to our world and to other worlds," he said softly.

Then Brian reported Voltar's words.

505

> **The doorway is nebulous to time, merging the energy of life itself with the light of wisdom, past. The doorway is an anchor in time and space, a reality cast in stone.**

"That's what he just said," Brian reported.

"Wow," I exhaled nervously as Brian eyed the majestic stone gateway.

The ancient stone seemed untouched by erosion with sharp edges and stones. I figured maybe it had been rebuilt in modern times, but it was clearly the dominant feature of the temple complex.

Suddenly Brian's blue eyes rolled up. His left hand reached out and he began drawing circles, squares and triangles in the dirt with his left index finger.

I pushed the microphone up to his lips as the Presence of Voltar emerged. He spoke in a deep, noble voice. "From the past, knowledge is now given and will transform and be that as One. And of this past, is presented, Wirrichocha." He pronounced the name without a "V."

For a few moments, nothing happened. Then a new presence swept over Brian's face. A new, tighter voice spoke: Viracocha. "Of my spirit, this has now passed as One to Brian. And I am born anew. Thank Youuuuu."

Voltar's mellow voice returned. "The wisdom of Viracocha is now passed. The responsibility of this is placed in your hands, Jim."

"I don't really know what I am supposed to do, or when," I said.

"Brian will know when each time is right to bring forth anew, the wisdom of the past, as brought forth today in the present."

I glanced at my tape recorder. The light pulsed as Voltar continued.

"The next few days will be very hard as there is much to do in the future. Orientation must be accomplished quickly. Do this as best you can, for of this is also the beginning of you. And the day will come when you may come with Brian to this place, and you yourself will become as he."

I pondered the words.

"Be prepared," Voltar said. "It is time for Brian to pass through the Doorway to Life, and to start anew.

"I, myself, the members of the Council and our people, we thank you that you have provided this, and, you have brought him wisdom and guidance. And, that you are here with him--we rejoice."

Brian's hands lifted upward to me.

"Take the hands of Brian," said Voltar. I dropped the microphone and grabbed Brian's hands gently.

"In this, and by this, the essence of Brian--and of his life--is now given to you, Jim, that you may have what you need to go on.

"By this, YOU are now. The New is Now. That of Brian is given unto you and no other."

506

Tears welled up into my eyes as I felt Brian's presence come over me.

"It is time," Voltar said. "Do what must be done, Jim. Do what is important so that the people may know. And do it well. For into your hands has passed the life that is in Brian--and from this--you and he are One. And by this, in this, he and I-- within a few moments--will be One."

I felt tears on my face. "In time, he will be as I, and I as he. And of this, much will be given to mankind, of he, of you."

Suddenly, Brian's hands dropped and his eyes opened. He stood up and silently paced back and forth in the shadow of the doorway. Then he walked westward into the sunny temple.

"This is it, Jim," Brian said. Tears rose into his eyes. "This is going to be something. I am definitely not going to be the same as I was."

"Goodbye," he said with finality. "And thanks, Jim," he said with trembling lips.

"Thank you, Brian," I said with a tear in my throat. We hugged. "Thank you for going through with this," I said. "Thank you. Thank you from me, and from all mankind. Thank you for all the children of the future generations. I thank you now, for them, today."

Brian bit his lip. He nodded at me and looked East into the doorway. I grabbed my camera and ran through the doorway down the steps.

Through my camera lens, the huge, sharp-edged, doorway shadowed Brian from the bright sun overhead. His blue denim shirt, blue jeans and blue eyes contrasted beautifully with the reddish stone. At six foot tall, Brian seemed to fit the size of the doorway perfectly.

He stepped forward slowly and braced his legs on both sides. Then he slowly reached outward to the sides of the door with the palms of both hands. Gasping for deep breaths of air, Brian lifted the palm of his right hand towards the stone. He closed his eyes--tightly. Then with a sudden shove, he pressed both palms against the stone.

Energy jolted his body and he instinctively recoiled, pulling his hands away from the stone. But, without opening his eyes, Brian again reached out to touch the stone.

He felt another charge and his body convulsed as he absorbed the physical, but invisible energy. His entire frame trembled. His legs began to wobble out of control and he fell to the ground on one knee, but he did not remove his hands from the stone.

For a long time, he struggled to stand up. When he was upright, another charge of energy, stronger than the last, streamed into his body. He felt himself flowing outward on a river of golden light, as if sailing upward, and away.

Brian barely felt the fourth jolt. He simply joined with the energy and effortlessly sailed away merging into the joy and bliss of Universal Knowledge.

But the bliss didn't last long. Brian heard the roar of thunder. For a moment, he felt his body again. He stood upright, then felt the top of his head open and slide backwards. A thick column of white light descended down his spine. His frame lurched upright, his shoulders lifted, his chin and chest lifted. The presence of Voltar joined him in a way he had never felt before--like a pillar. This time his legs and feet felt heavy, strong, thick. He felt like a giant, cast in stone--he felt like a rock.

He thought he would die, at first, and then everything changed. He felt gentle and free inside, like a cream puff, like a flower in a breeze. The heart of heaven opened within Brian's chest. Love, peace and calm filled his entire being. "I am here," Voltar said. The words rushed through Brian's body like a warm wind. "I come in love," Voltar said.

Brian, feeling the words deeply in his own heart, nearly passed out--but he hung on. He felt Voltar move his body forward one step. Brian gasped at the sensation of feeling stiff and heavy. He thought he would fall down, but he didn't. Voltar stepped forward again and paused.

Suddenly, Brian changed viewpoints. "Back up," Voltar whispered. Suddenly, Brian moved backwards. He slid backwards and away from himself. He didn't know how it happened, but suddenly he felt as if he were riding in a comfortable seat in the back of a luxuriously padded car. He felt his body move, but he didn't have to decide what to do, or when--Voltar did. "Quite different," he mumbled.

"We are one," Voltar said to Brian. "I am here with you, AS YOU -- with wisdom and knowledge for man." Brian relaxed and enjoyed the comfortable ride.

Voltar opened his arms and lifted his hands up to God. His heart opened to all that our world would present to him. He gave thanks to God for life. Brian's own heart felt Voltar's joy and love, but he also felt safely insulated, protected-- removed. He could simply watch from the rear seat. Voltar was driving.

Then Voltar closed his arms, drawing all that was about him into his presence. Brian felt peaceful and giggled. "This is fun," he thought. "This is very different," he said aloud.

Voltar spoke to him with caution. "Rest easy, Brian. For me, now the world: life, as it is." Voltar suddenly opened his eyes.

The sunlight blinded Brian. He felt like the shades of his padded limousine had been rudely lifted. Startled, he needed a few moments to realize Voltar had simply opened his eyes. Brian didn't like NOT knowing what Voltar would do. The ride became bumpy as Voltar panned the ruins and saw the desolation.

Shock and sorrow filled his heart and soul. Voltar's heart cried out with pain. In his whole life, Brian had never felt such sorrow.

Without warning, the anguish hit Brian, sweeping over him like a river of hot lava. The pain absorbed into his being. He felt as if he was becoming one with Voltar's agony, and he cried out for Voltar to stop. Brian fainted and awoke in the NOR, on Voltar's world.

Voltar's family, Danyael and the council applauded, and opened their arms to him with love in their hearts. He had survived the radiant withdraw. He was with them.

At the bottom of the steps, I finished photographing Voltar's emergence then ran to him. But, Voltar hurried passed me down the stairs with long, stiff strides.

"This cannot be," boomed Voltar. He glanced around to the north. Then Voltar ran stiffly to the east, then south towards the Mound of Akapana. Stunned, he fell to one knee then stood up looking for any remnant of the Temple of the Sky.

He cried out in anguish. "No. A Projection. Danyael? A Nous10 projection?" Voltar yelled. "Enough."

"This is not a test," I said nervously. I worried that Voltar was going berserk. "You are here. This is December 22, 1976. 1976. Bolivia. You are here, now."

Voltar glared at the Portal to Life in shock. "Request Nous 4," he commanded to the probe. He waited a moment and then glanced around with disappointment. He tried another command. "Coordinate 090, 090, 090. Request override -- projection." He glanced around, waiting for everything to change. Nothing happened.

"Danyael," he smiled at me. "How have you done this? It doesn't respond. What is the test?"

"This is not a test," I said. "I am Jim, Nous one. I don't know anything about Danyael. I am at Nous one. You are here. The transformation in that portal is complete. You are Brian. Nous one."

The Presence of Voltar froze. Brian's blue eyes rolled back for a moment. When they rolled down, Voltar's Presence returned, but he looked terrified. "Not this. Not like this!" Voltar moaned in deep sorrow.

"Is this now?" Voltar asked.

This is Nous One, 1976," I said.

"Now--the Land of Freedom."

"This is now," I said softly. "Bolivia."

Voltar staggered backwards towards the Portal. "The water? Where is the water?" he shouted running up the steps and into the temple.

I scrambled after him with camera in hand. He stood still and silent. "The fountain," Voltar said with a sorrowful face. "Not one fountain remains."

"There are no fountains," I said. "No water. This is 1976. This is now."

Voltar studied my sunburned face and body. "You are Jim." He walked quickly to the top step again and looked outward to the eastern horizon.

"Danyael did not allow us to see this, as it is now. Perhaps I did not want to know. Of this, is great sorrow," he said with a solemn dignity. "Please, take me away from here--for this saddens me."

I quickly grabbed both packs and led Voltar down the steps of the temple towards the road.

A huge truck, spewing a cloud of dust, approached eastward on the highway. Voltar froze. "Of this, is death," he said with frantic movements. "No protection beam. "

"Not death," I shouted grabbing at Voltar's hands. But as the truck roared past in the cloud of dust, Voltar fell to his knees and hid his face, like a frightened child. The bold Voltar trembled like a child, preparing to die.

"It is not death," I said pulling at him. "I'm okay. You will be okay." Slowly Voltar stood up and watched the truck roll down the road eastward. Dust settled over us. Voltar felt the dust and brushed his skin.

"What of this?" he said slapping at Brian's arms and hands.

"That is Brian," I said. "Brian. That is Brian's body. And it won't die from dust."

"Vehicles of death," Voltar said.

"Those are trucks. The dust is bad, but it won't kill Brian's body."

"This vehicle has no projection field. Life forms on the road are killed, microscopic. They die."

"Maybe so. It travels on wheels. And it is dusty, but it won't kill you."

Another huge diesel truck thundered toward us from the west. Voltar pulled to run away, back toward the temple.

"It won't kill you," I said clutching at him. "It won't." I pulled Voltar forward towards the exit gate. The one-eyed guard watched with concern.

As the truck neared, Voltar broke loose. He ran forward into the chain link and bounced backwards to the ground.

"No energy field," he yelled at me, alarmed.

"What are you doing?" I screamed.

Then suddenly Voltar bolted past me and ran through the gate into the road. He stopped in the path of the huge, speeding truck. The brakes squealed as Voltar held up his hands and closed his eyes.

I raced after him. As the loud horn blared, and as the huge chrome grill and bumper bore down upon us, I hit Voltar hard with my shoulder knocking him across the road. Voltar slammed into a road sign and then we both fell into a ditch. With brakes squealing, the clanging truck swept past, barely missing us. Even in the dust, I could smell the brakes and see the cloud of smoke as the wheels locked and skid.

A thick sheet of dust settled from the air onto Voltar's face, into our hair and clothes. For a long time, powdered dust swirled around us clogging our noses. I coughed and gagged in the thick air.

"Don't ever do that again," I seethed. "You wait for me. I don't care who you are. You wait for me, and you don't do anything that I don't say is okay."

Voltar sat up. "You said it would not kill Brian."

"The dust will not kill you. The truck will!" I screamed.

I lifted Voltar to his feet as two concerned guards ran to our aid. "We're all right," I shouted. "We're okay."

The guards waved at the truck driver who had stopped his growling, clanging rig. He saw their signal, and rolled on eastward.

"What were you doing?" I shouted.

"I hoped the field would be active over here," Voltar said.

"There are no energy fields," I said. "The vehicles of dust kill all life forms on the road and, if one hits your body, it will kill you and Brian--the transformation will be over. I am sure of it."

"The transformation," Voltar said, remembering.

"Today is December 22, 1976, and this is earth--Tiahuanaco," I said. "Surely they told you about that. We have been going through this for six months."

"The Day of Twenty," Voltar said solemnly. "Complete."

"Right. The testing is complete," I said. "This is it. The transformation happened. You are here."

Voltar nodded. "Danyael, in the Play of Life, did not project all." He glanced across the road to Tiahuanaco. "The fountains."

"They are gone."

Voltar took a deep breath. He saw another truck approaching from the west. "Let's get out of here," I said.

"No. I must stay," Voltar said. "I must experience, and know all that there is, of this. If I am to be here, now--one with Brian--I must be here, now."

The huge truck thundered down on us at 80 miles an hour. The guards, who had remained nearby, hustled backwards away from the road.

VOLTAR and BRENDA after the transformation. Voltar's somber mood, compassionate eyes and deep voice inspired awe. He seemed vulnerable, yet dignified and noble. Brenda said he was a "gentleman" who "knew a lot about pyramids." Voltar experienced convulsions of his right arm and leg for three days.

TELEGRAM sent from La Paz on June 23. Transformation complete... Brian is Voltar. Prepare for some disorientation.

INCAN DESCENDENTS are cautious, at first, knowing that assembly in the plaza is illegal on Christmas Day.

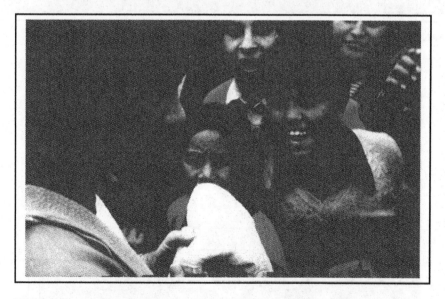

BRIAN gives gifts to children on Christmas Day from a white bag.

SPANISH OFFICIAL shouts "stop" and orders everyone to leave the plaza.

Brian and Voltar United as One

BRIAN is clownish, entertaining and self-centered.

VOLTAR united as One with Brian is more somber, but caring about others and compassionate

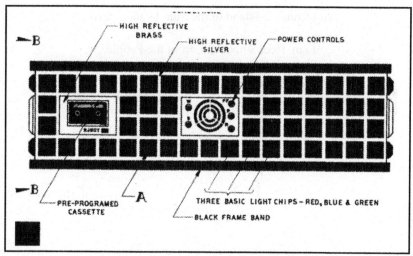

BIOLOGICAL MONITORING BELT - Initial design by Brian with Voltar's input. More advanced versions feature biological monitoring systems. Lights are red, green, blue.

Christmas Day Message in Cuzco

From the Earth, the water and the People, I am.

From the Island of the Sun, I have come, and I wish to return.

I am Viracocha—I have knowledge of the People

from my existence here, and within.

My promise shall be kept--I shall comply to the people, within.

With the first light of the sun,

on the day of December 22, 2011 A.D.,

and from the Island of the Sun, I shall return.

I am Ticci Viracocha, from the People.

I am the Spirit of the People, and of the Earth.

I am from the Earth--

Viracocha

(SHOUTED BY NYLES)

CONVULSIONS

CONVULSIONS, MUSCLE TWITCHING AND SPASMS
CAN INDICATE AN ELECTRICAL DISTURBANCE IN THE BRAIN.
THE RIGHT SIDE OF THE BRAIN CONTROLS THE LEFT HAND SIDE OF THE BODY.
A SEIZURE OF THE LEFT ARM AND LEG WOULD INDICATE
A DISTURBANCE IN THE RIGHT SIDE OF THE BRAIN.

Abstracted from New Grolier Multimedia Encyclopedia, V6

Chapter 19

Christmas in Cuzco

Facing the truck, Voltar took a deep breath and stood upright with his palms pointed outward. I braced for the wind, turned my back and hunched down. The truck, clanging with chains, clamored past us at 80 miles per hour. A dust cloud hit Voltar like a tidal wave. The turbulent blast carried tiny rocks, which bit into Brian's skin. Swirling air buffeted Voltar from side to side, then knocked him down. He scrambled back up and leaned hard against the twisting dark cloud. Gradually, as the fury passed, he regained his balance and assumed a regal, dignified pose.

"Are you happy?" I shouted as thick layers of dust settled onto our skin.

"I am here," Voltar said opening his eyes. "Now is now."

"Now is now?" I screamed. Thick dust caked our nostrils and mouths and filled our ears. When we blinked, we both looked like clowns in a circus wearing dust for makeup.

"You are a mess," I bellowed. "I can't believe you did that."

Voltar's presence remained solemn. "I am here. I am one with Brian, and will be *as Brian*," he said glancing at the temple grounds. "Please Jim, take me from this place of sorrow."

Luckily, only a few minutes later, the taxi to La Paz stopped at the museum. Two seats were open and I shoved Voltar inside.

On the way, the taxi passed through several small villages. Voltar could see ahead in time. He described people along the road, and buildings before we came upon them. In each town, he wanted to stop and heal sick children and the elderly.

Frustrated, I refused. He had frightened me. He seemed too much like a child, unaware of the dangers around him. "People on earth don't understand," I said. "We don't see through walls and go around healing people." He agreed not to use any powers, at least not immediately.

"I understand," Voltar finally agreed. "What is done, shall be done *as Brian,* for he and I are One."

As we drove away from Tiahuanaco, we could see the snow-capped Mount Illimani, a 26,000 foot peak sacred to the Inca. The mountain graced La Paz, Bolivia, a metropolis of 300,000 people located 14,000 above sea level. The La Paz runway is the highest commercial airstrip in the world, and the city is the highest national capital on the planet. Even the flat land is 13,000 feet above sea level.

When we arrived in La Paz, a cloud of brown air-pollution hovered over the city. As we descended into foul air, we passed through miles of peasant barrios. People lived in cardboard boxes and tin shacks without running water for drinking or sewage. The view sickened Voltar. He wanted to help the people, walk among them, and heal them. I refused.

Mostly, I thought Brian must be acting, but he was doing a heck of a good job. I wasn't going to take any chances, if Voltar was an incarnate being--without full training. With all the beeps on tape, I was convinced something 'unusual' had happened, but I couldn't understand or accept a full *'reversal.'* Even if a *'radiant'* reversal had taken place, shouldn't Voltar have known more about our world? After all, he had been through training. Perhaps, Danyael training wasn't that good; perhaps Brian was behind it all, faking the whole process.

Then again, perhaps this was multiple-personality. From that view, Voltar had become dominate now--with Brian's full permission--using the temple doorway as an elaborate trigger for the switch. I didn't see "integration," because Brian was gone--unavailable. I didn't know what to believe, so I tried to walk a middle path and just document everything.

Voltar in La Paz

In a cheap hotel on a bustling, noisy street, I unpacked our bags. Voltar sat in a chair quietly staring out our window on the fifth story. His eyes scanned the hillsides looking into the homes, the yards and the hearts of the people -- the Spanish peasants, the Incans, and well-dressed Spanish businessmen. He watched their colorful auras--*the energy of their being*-- and tried to learn about our world.

I held a microphone up to his lips. "Is there anything you want to say to the people, back home?"

Voltar felt compassion and sadness for the people he had seen. His voice carried the sorrow. "Hello. I am here. I am One. I come with love for all. There is much to be done. Much change is needed. There is much I will do in the days to come."

I nodded approval.

"Sufficient?" Voltar asked.

"Sufficient," I said. Voltar turned back to the window.

By some miracle, probably pure coincidence, Nyles, Voltar and I met in a bathroom on the fifth floor of the hotel, only an hour later. Nyles had mistakenly given us a hotel name that didn't exist. Our driver had spent a while trying to find the hotel, then gave up. Likewise, I had given up on ever seeing them again, so the meeting in a bathroom was a shock.

When the amazement ended, Nyles talked to Voltar. His somber, but royal presence overwhelmed Nyles. "He's very different," he whispered. "Voltar is sort of *intimidating.*"

I showed Voltar the shower, started the water running, and then returned to the room as Brenda arrived. She and Nyles were staying in rooms down the hall.

Feeling overwhelmed, I asked for their help. I had never handled Brian as Voltar--hour after hour. Brian had always returned to laugh, break up the serious mood, and provide some perspective. But that had ended. Voltar didn't go away.

"He needs to be watched like a child," I said.

Just as Brenda and Nyles both agreed to help for one day, we heard splashy-wet footsteps coming down the hallway. I opened the door.

Voltar stood at the door naked and dripping wet without a towel. Brenda screamed and covered her eyes. Voltar walked into the room without shame or embarrassment. "Of the cold water, refreshing," he said. "But no energy field to dry. Is this usual?"

Brenda jumped up and ran out of the room, laughing hysterically.

"We'll come back, when you get him dressed," Nyles said.

Voltar didn't understand. Apparently, his training had not been complete. He didn't know the little things, like how to button a shirt correctly, or especially how to squeeze the snaps on the cowboy shirt in Brian's pack. The snaps really baffled him. I had to snap the cowboy shirt on Voltar, latch his leather belt and lace Brian's old hiking boots.

Voltar felt very uncomfortable without his own *'belt of lights.'* He did not enjoy the thought of life without a transportation belt. "Life here is very difficult," Voltar said. "I will make the belt for man."

He paused and waited about eight seconds for confirmation from the probe. "Accepted. Probability factor high," Voltar reported. "I will do this for man," he stated.

That evening, Nyles and Brenda escorted Voltar around the bustling streets of La Paz. I followed, relaxing. Voltar seemed somber and dignified, compared to Brian. He walked slowly in a royal manner with long steps and an upright, noble posture. He listened carefully to Brenda and Nyles, answering their questions in his flowing, mellow voice. He talked mostly about designing the pyramid.

At one intersection, Voltar warned them to change course due to a collision. They did not understand, but when we returned to that corner an hour later, an ambulance had arrived with several police cars. Numerous people lay on sidewalks, seriously injured.

From that moment on, they agreed to take Voltar's warnings seriously.

Early the next morning, in a modern travel agency, I arranged for a trip back to Cuzco. Voltar was now able to manage his clothing, food and personal needs. He had become a bit more like Brian, except for the convulsions.

As Voltar sat quietly in a chair enjoying the sunlight, convulsions hit Brian's left side. His left arm and leg twitched and jerked. Voltar struggled to hold the trembling limbs, then his eyes rolled up, and he spoke a strange language as people watched with concern. Within a few minutes, the seizure ended and everyone relaxed. After several episodes, he was able to control the convulsions more quickly, but they continued for days, on and off.

Later that morning, at 10:30 a.m., I sent a telegram to Wanda in Los Angeles.

TRANSFORMATION COMPLETE. BRIAN IS VOLTAR. NOTIFY PEOPLE/MEDIA. RETURNING IMMEDIATELY. PREPARE FOR SOME DISORIENTATION.

Voltar had requested we notify the media and have reporters waiting upon his arrival. I knew Wanda wouldn't arrange a press conference, but thought maybe the radio station in Orange County might be interested, and perhaps the young reporter for the Lariat in Tustin.

Wanda knew our return date. That was locked. We had five days.

A few hours later, after witnessing several more convulsions, Nyles agreed to accompany us to Cuzco. "You guys need help," he said. He was right.

Brenda said goodbye to all of us at the hotel and recorded her official impressions on my tape.

"He is quite different," she said standing next to Voltar on the sidewalk. "Definitely, totally different--than he was before."

"What do you think of him?"

"I didn't know him long enough before to form an opinion," she said with her New Zealand accent. "But he's sort of a quiet type of person, very knowledgeable. Polite. Pleasant. My impression is that he is a different man."

I laughed heartily. Brian would be insulted.

"What did you and Voltar discuss as you walked around La Paz?" I asked.

"Mostly, he answered my questions," she said.

"About what?"

"About life--on earth. About man," she said. "He is very, very knowledgeable about pyramids. But hard to understand on some subjects."

"Is that all? What is your gut level reaction?" I asked.

"It was all right," she said. She giggled. "There is something to him."

"I mean--did you like him?" I laughed.

"Yes," she giggled. "He was quite pleasant."

"You are the first female to see him after the transformation, did he hustle you in any way?"

"No," she blushed. "He was very polite and reserved the entire time," she said. "He's a very dignified man--a gentleman."

The clownish, entertaining, rude antics of Brian had vanished. Voltar seemed somber, and his facial expression--serious. His powerful voice caught everyone's attention. He walked and moved slowly in an upright, royal, posture. He gazed upon each person with calm, blue eyes. He listened—carefully--to every word from a person's mouth. When the person finished talking, Voltar answered them directly looking into their eyes and face with such concern and intimacy that the person felt uncomfortable. He took your breath away.

"We don't talk or walk the way he does" Brenda explained the strange reactions Voltar had inspired from waiters, clerks and people on the street. They often thought he was a famous actor or dignitary. He often didn't understand their reaction.

Voltar's presence could also be a bit childish, innocent—loving. The nice young people of La Paz wanted to take care of him. That was fun to see, and gave us all a break. In a foreign nation, people expect tourists to be at a disadvantage and they politely helped direct him to bathrooms, to doors and out of harm's way. He curiously investigated things he had never seen—like Christmas trees with blinking bulbs, or cash registers. He proved embarrassing at times, but people didn't mind. They treated him like an esteemed visitor to a foreign nation, a dignitary that didn't understand the customs--a stranger in a foreign land.

That all worked fine for him in Bolivia. I worried that he would have troubles in Los Angeles. He wasn't worried.

He gained respect by granting so much dignity to others and so much importance to their words and feelings, that they soon felt embarrassed in his presence. He carried the aura of a man with great authority, yet he expressed no hint of self-importance, no arrogance or bravado. His main concern was always the other person.

I tried to figure out his self-concept. In his own mind, who was he? Voltar carried himself like a leader, a Senator, a General or an Admiral surrounded by admiring children.

"I have never met a man like this," said Brenda. Nyles agreed.

The Reversal is Now

On the train trip back to Cuzco, Voltar glowed with a silent happiness. With his fingers, he massaged spittle into the sunburned skin on Brian's face. "Of this, Viracocha," he said. "Healing." I discovered later that the Inca considered the tears and the spittle of Viracocha to be healing medicines.

About twice an hour, convulsions wracked his right side. During the tremblers, his blue eyes rolled upward and he spoke Greek. After about three minutes each fit would pass.

I felt sympathy for Voltar, but what could I do? After a seizure ended, I left him alone. I needed space and time away from him to think about the transformation. I needed time to check my theories and review my list of anomalies. I had definitely been pulled into Brian's world. Could I be objective, now? No—but I hadn't lost my journalistic perspective. I could still document the events. I would just document every event, and figure it all out later.

Voltar sat alone most of the time. Unlike Brian, he enjoyed just looking at people, or out the windows at the land of Viracocha.

Finally, after a few hours of silence, I sat next to him and asked how he felt. "The reversal," he said. "The reversal is now."

Suddenly his eyes rolled up, like a trance. Brian's boyish voice and personality emerged. He had been playing with their children—having a great time. "It's the reverse of what it was," he said. "You've got him, and he can reach me now, when I go to the center."

I wanted to find out more about Brian's experience, but he didn't stay long. He was too excited about his life in Voltar's world. Certainly, the reversal was complete. The integration was underway, the polarity had been shifted—reversed. Voltar was available 24 hours a day with Brian's blue eyes looking at me. Brian was available only by special appointment—with eyes rolled up, and inward.

Brian apparently didn't care to monitor Voltar's life moment by moment. He only received summaries and updates. He could find out what he wanted, whenever he chose, but Brian's identity and concerns were on the back burner. So by all appearance, a reversal had been completed–a true tranformation. I relaxed.

Nyles had purchased the train tickets for us. He had insisted we take the luxury car. Natural wood trimmed the windows, doors and ceiling--waiters provided food and drinks. The plush seats felt good, and the tables were covered in fancy cloth. What a difference a few dollars made.

Nyles made friends easily and soon a group of American college kids wanted to meet Voltar. "May I talk to him?" a bearded, student asked, gesturing at Voltar.

He was a graduate student in engineering at the University of Colorado. He seemed serious, and I knew the school had a strong program in engineering and space science. "Five minutes," I agreed—now acting as the gate-keeper to Voltar.

His friends watched from a distance. They wanted him to challenge the story but within moments, he was disarmed.

"How do *you* find this day," said Voltar in his deep, mellow voice.

"Fine. I'm fine."

"You are the first of man to come forth, seeking knowledge." The young man felt humbled by Voltar's deep, but mellow voice.

"I am very interested in pyramids."

"Each, a storehouse of knowledge and wisdom," Voltar said.

"Is it true their placement relates to the circumference of the earth, some mathematical constants like *Pi,* and also some energy zones of the earth?"

Voltar beamed. "More than man knows. Of these, when reconstructed by man and activated, the energy zones will help to stabilize the energy of the planet."

"Stabilize the planet? Why would we need to stabilize the planet?"

"In that, the energy field: to control earthquakes. And, also--the orbit. Of this, the stabilization points on earth may be activated from satellites in space--distant. In this, the fulfillment of Quantum Displacement Physics, and the knowledge of orbital reality."

"I don't understand," the young scholar said. "What is Quantum Displacement? Why is that so important?"

Voltar picked up an ornate silver spoon from the table and held it plainly in sight. He balanced the spoon on his index finger. Then Voltar stared at the spoon for a moment in reverie. Both ends of the spoon slowly drooped downward until the spoon hung around his finger in a "U" shape.

The young engineer gasped.

Voltar smiled. "The beginning of understanding." He handed the spoon to the young man.

"It's hot," the scholar breathed.

"Heat," Voltar smiled. "Quantum displacement will allow man and his world to survive. That is the purpose. The Secondary World of man--at Nous negative nine--does not have all the knowledge of quantum displacement which we offer to man."

"I can't believe you did that," the young man stammered. His friends watched in awe with hands to their mouths. He called out to them. "He just bent a spoon. This spoon just melted and all he did was look at it." We all had watched.

"He's not supposed to be doing that," I said.

"A beginning of understanding, for man," Voltar said.

"We talked about this," I warned. "*No paranormal stuff.* "

"In this--education," Voltar said. "Approved by Danyael."

I had been over-ridden, by Danyael who apparently was in charge—not me.

Voltar lifted an elegant, half-full coffee cup in one hand. As everyone watched, he slowly placed another silver spoon into the cup. His eyes glazed for a moment and the handle of the spoon sunk downward, twisting.

"He's not supposed to be doing this," I said as the group gathered closer.

Then Voltar gestured to the engineering student. The bearded young scholar lifted the spoon out of the cup. The shank of the spoon had been twisted into a knot. The young scholar gasped--dropping the spoon on the table

"Owe."

"Heat," Voltar said. "MORE heat."

The bearded scholar picked up the spoon carefully. "It's VERY hot," he announced to everyone.

"That of the metal grows hot," Voltar said to everyone.

"How did you do that?" the young man gasped. He held the spoon up for everyone to see.

Voltar spoke slowly. "By that of Nous 4. Not difficult—not even a challenge." He looked calmly into the eyes of the young man. "Quantum displacement is the displacement of time, by that of Nous 4, allowing energy and matter to be moved--in space, or time."

The young man's mouth dropped open. "I have just seen a miracle." He said to his friends. "We just saw a miracle." They asked Voltar to do it again.

Voltar looked at them solemnly. "He sought knowledge. Given." The students backed away, feeling power in his words.

"I am blown away," the scholar said. "Blown away. He did that with his mind. That is what he is saying."

"Of Nous 4," Voltar said calmly. "Available to man. A reaction: displacement. Energy rating by man: heat."

"You have to be at Nous 4," I said waving everyone away.

"Nous 4?" the scholar said in a daze as he shuffled back to his seat. "I have to think about this," he mumbled. "I have just witnessed an impossibility."

I smiled at Voltar. "I thought we agreed on this. Okay? But I guess, Danyael actually runs the show."

Voltar smiled, turned away, and gazed out the window with a grin on his face. He looked content and filled with joy.

Later, the train chugged out of the Aymara region into the mountains, home of the Quechua. Voltar saw men working the fields and women washing their clothes in a stream. He felt great sorrow for the people of the land. As we chugged past the native people, he silently raised the palm of his right hand, and prayed for the crippled, or blinded, or deformed.

As Voltar approached Cuzco, he spoke little, saying only that "*much needed to be done for the people of the land.*"

The train arrived in Cuzco at about 7:30 p.m. on December 24th--Christmas Eve. I tried to call Wanda from the "Publico Telephono" building, but a line of people stretched out the door.

After checking into the hotel Kancharina at 8:00 p.m., Voltar, Nyles and I walked down the sidewalk toward the town plaza. An electronic tone whined over our heads. WowweeooooooooeeeeeeeeeEEEE.

The tone was not a simple, velvety beep, like most of the others, but a gentle howl with low AND high frequencies.

"Now is now," Voltar said. "I am here. I am content. The city of the Fathers-- the jaguar priests. Now, that of Brian and the children begins."

Brian and the Children

We entered the plaza of Cuzco just after sunset on Christmas Eve. Aromas of barbecued meat and hot alcohol wafted in the air. Boys and girls screamed with delight. Fireworks sparkled and firecrackers popped on the sidewalks as children played. Dogs barked and howled at the fireworks.

Quechua ladies cooked food on brass stoves. They offered beef, chicken, potatoes and hot drinks for sale. Aymara ladies and men sold handmade alpaca sweaters, hats, jewelry or pottery. Tourists from all over the world shopped the plaza, bartering and buying from the people of the land.

For hundreds of years, the royal Inca had ruled from buildings around this plaza, the seat of their government and religion—home of the jaguar priests—the center for Incan Oracles. The city had supposedly been designed in the shape of a jaguar, with twelve wards representing the zodiac.

The central plaza had seen much pageantry including parades of the Royal Inca on feast days, displays of sacred mummies, sacrifices of llamas, and rites of initiation for young men—plus, executions of Incan royalty by the Spanish.

As we walked through the plaza, I was surprised to hear a classic Christmas song in perfect English. "Silent Night, Holy Night......" The words floated into the plaza from across the street.

Formerly an Incan temple, the building now served as a Catholic church. Music drifted out the open doorway. Several hundred Spanish people, wearing fine clothes, sang the classic Christmas tune in English, then Spanish.

Outside, on the steps of the next building, a dozen Quechua Indians, in traditional clothes, watched sadly.

"This was their temple," I said. "How sad."

"Ironic," said Nyles. "On Christmas Eve, they cannot go inside. They are outsiders looking in—at their own temple." Several of the Incan men held musical instruments.

"They wait," Voltar said with sorrow. "Their glory will be restored. The promises of Viracocha will be fulfilled."

He stepped towards the Indians. "Viracocha regresaddo," he said. One man stepped forward with a smile on his face. Voltar showed the tattoos on his arms. "Viracocha regressaddo," he said. Stunned, several other men slowly stepped forward.

"Viracocha regresaddo," Voltar said holding up his arms. Their faces brightened with joy and understanding.

Voltar fumbled into Brian's shirt pocket," frustrated he gave up.

"Of this, Brian returns," Voltar said.

Suddenly, his blue eyes flipped upward, showing only the white eyeballs. The personality of Brian, lively and animated, returned.

Brian searched his pockets until he found the writing. "Forgot where I put it," he chuckled. "Things get a little confusing." He handed the paper to Nyles.

"He wants you to read it," Brian said, rapidly. "See what they think of it. This is something he gave me before we left, Jim. The Cuban draftsman translated it. It's important, for tomorrow."

"Is that you Brian?" I asked softly, "Because your eyes are rolled back."

"It is the reversal," Brian said, looking at me, with eyes up.

"Are you aware of what is going on here?"

"Just bits and pieces," Brian said. "I was out of it until you got to Cuzco."

"What's it like for you?" I asked.

He glanced around at the plaza and at the Incan men seeing their energy auras. "It's fantastic," Brian gushed. "Mostly, I am with them, on their world, playing with the kids, working with the Council and studying the disks. They have these holographic projection disks. The images just surround you—all around you. It's incredible. They have disks on everything: their world, ours, other places they have been. Any subject. It just comes to life, all around you."

"Well, are you seeing us, here?" I asked. "Right now, because we see your eyes rolled up."

"Oh, I see the energy forms. It's amazing."

"What about when you are there?"

"No--not really. I get reports, but if there is a problem, Danyael can get me."

"Then you're having fun?"

"Oh, yeah! For me it's fantastic. I get treated like I am a king, Jim. I mean everyone treats me as if I was really, REALLY important," he laughed. "I'm not kidding. They seriously do. I went before the Council and got to speak. They asked me lots of questions. They are so happy, Jim, that this is happening. Their whole world is ecstatic. It is unbelievable. Despite their losses and the destruction, they are celebrating in joy. I wish you could know how important this is--what you have done. But it is Voltar, who is getting the raw end of the deal. We have nothing for him, nothing prepared."

"We didn't know."

"You are doing fine. I will be back tomorrow. Can you read that Nyles?" Brian asked.

"Sure. It's about Viracocha's return," Nyles said in his raspy voice.

"Right. Okay, see you tomorrow morning," Brian said. His big blue eyes snapped down and the solemn, noble presence of Voltar returned.

Voltar spoke. "Brian truly is of greatness among our people. They enjoy his happiness and his humor, and we are learning much from him."

Nyles turned to the Incan men and women on the steps and read the message to them aloud.

DEL LA TIERRA, EL MAR, Y DE LE GENTE SOY. DE LA ISLA DEL SOL HE VENIDO Y HACIA ALLA VOLVERE. YO SOY VIRACOCHA. DE ESTO, CONOCIMIENTO HAY ENTRE LA GENTE, Y DE MI EXISTENCIA. MIREN HACIA EL

ESTE, DES ESTO. MI PROMESA SERA CUMPLIDA ENTRE LA GENTE, AL TANTO QUE ME APURO EN MI REGRESO. CON LAS PRIMERAS LUCES DEL SOL DEL DIA 22 DE DICIEMBRE DEL ANO 2011 d.c. y DESDE LA ISLA DEL SOL,

YO SOY TICCI VIRACOCHA. DE LA GENTE SOY EL ESPORITU DE LA TIERRA.

When Nyles finished, the Incan descendants talked seriously among themselves. Finally, one man lifted his flute and began playing a beautiful melody. Then another man pounded on his drum. The group launched into a joyful Incan song.

An elder from inside the Catholic church stepped outside, perturbed. He glared at the Indians and pulled shut the heavy doors.

The Indians quickly walked back into the plaza, playing softly.

"Manyana," Voltar said. They waved.

For the next several hours, in the crisp night air, Voltar walked up and down the streets of Cuzco stopping small groups of Indians saying, "Viracocha will return. Viracocha regresaddo." Their faces lit up with excitement and smiles. When they asked questions, Voltar showed them the spider and jaguar tattoos. "Viracocha regresaddo," he would say again.

Everyone seemed to understand.

"Manyana, in the plaza. Sun high. Go. Tell the people," Voltar would say.

Sometimes, Nyles helped by interpreting Voltar's words into Spanish. Soon Nyles began to have fun mimicking Voltar. "Go and tell the people," he would bellow in a deep, but raspy voice.

The people seemed excited, but most walked away whispering with secret, guarded glances. "I think they are scared," Nyles said. "They are frightened by what he is saying."

I wondered why. Then a military truck rumbled past filled with armed policemen. They wore helmets and carried machine guns. "I think they are state police," Nyles said. "Like the national guard, maybe."

Why would they be driving around the plaza on Christmas Eve, I wondered.

"I think the Spanish run this place with an iron hand," Nyles said.

Early the next morning, Christmas Day--December 25th 1976--Voltar, Nyles and I ate breakfast together in the hotel. Afterwards, Voltar said Brian was ready to return.

"What is this reversal?" I asked Voltar. "What technology did you use for the transformation?"

Voltar, with a commanding voice, said he would explain all at a later time. "Know this," he said firmly. "When Brian is with you, he and I are one. And we will remain--as one, united at Nous 4--until we return again to the doorway and the Portal in June 1977. In that, the attainment of unity--at Nous 8--and the completion of our purpose. From that, Brian will proceed on his own to attain, during his lifetime--Nous 10."

"This is really heavy," Nyles said. "I am starting to understand what he is talking about--and it is freaking me out."

Voltar's eyes rolled up into his head showing only the white orbs, and the amiable personality of Brian fully returned. "Hi Jim," Brian said with an animated face. He glanced around the room. "Can we go pass out some gifts now? I may need to buy more, and I would like to get something for Debra." He stood up holding a pillowcase. "I borrowed this from the hotel."

Nyles and I watched Brian stand up and prance around nervously. I had never imagined that Brian would be able to walk so naturally with his eyes rolled up. He looked at us, peered around at people, and even grabbed some toast off the table. Then he smoothed jam on bread and ate like a teenager.

"My God," Nyles whispered.

Brian pushed his chair aside. "Let's get going," he said. "Come on--it's late." We sat in awe. He waited a moment. "Okay, I'm going."

He ambled out of the restaurant into the hotel lobby.

I bolted from my chair and ran after him. "Brian, wait!"

Brian stopped. "What?"

"Your eyes are rolled up, and I am not sure it is a good idea to walk around that way."

"Oh, I'm sorry." Brian froze. "Return Scott," said a mechanical probe-voice from his lips. "Danyael, Nous 10 over-ride. Accepted,"

Suddenly Brian's big blue eyes flipped downward. He wobbled for a moment. "Oh, daylight," Brian giggled as he peered around the hotel lobby. He rubbed his eyes, and tested the sidewalk. "I guess I can handle it." He took a few uncertain steps, and then pranced towards the door waving the pillowcase. "I want to fill this up," he said.

Nyles and I followed, amazed. Brian had learned to handle our world with eyes up, or down—inward or outward. We were stunned.

In the street, Brian asked for his money back. I gave it to him with concern. "I hope you know what you are doing."

"I do. This is for me," he said. "My idea—not Voltar's."

Brian hurried around to buy candy and gifts from several three-wheeled wooden carts owned by young Spanish men. The plaza was empty. All the Incan ladies were gone. Not a scrap of trash remained.

When the bag was half full of candy and gifts, Brian hurried along the sidewalks, passing out candy and money to each child he saw. He quickly attracted a crowd of about twenty Spanish children who followed him up and down the side streets. Gradually, the crowd grew.

They joined him out of muddy backyards, where chickens and ducks and dogs splashed in water next to infants in dirty diapers. They joined his parade out of nice Spanish houses and buildings. They joined out of doorways and alleys. They weren't Incans. All of these children were Spanish.

Nyles and I enjoyed the spectacle of Brian's happy parade, while watching from a distance.

At high noon on Christmas Day, Brian entered the empty plaza surrounded by children. At the sound of the crowd, a few Incan families in traditional hats, shawls and brightly colored dresses, filtered into the streets, but they stayed out of the plaza.

Children screamed with delight. Older Spanish boys, hearing the laughter, ran to investigate. Evading the bigger boys, Brian jogged into the center of the plaza and waved the white bag over his head. Children and young men pulled at his clothing and jerked at the bag.

Brian climbed up on the edge of the fountain and waved the big bulging bag over his head. He tossed handfuls of candy and gifts into the frenzied crowd.

"Viracocha regresaddo," he shouted. "Viracocha's promises will be kept," he shouted. "Viracocha regresaddo."

From where he stood on the fountain, in the center of the plaza, Brian could see Indian children and families watching from alleys and side streets. They seemed afraid to enter the Plaza. He could see dozens of Indian children milling in the shadows and doorways of the shops and buildings.

He threw candy towards them. A few Incan children broke loose from their parents and ran towards the fountain. Their parents, in traditional Indian dress, followed. The size of the crowd grew, expanding quickly to several hundred.

Brian pranced around the huge fountain, throwing gifts and candy in all directions.

At noon, church bells around the plaza began to chime. As if a signal had sounded, more Incan families rushed towards the fountain with their children. From all directions they came--out of doorways, from narrow streets, from wide streets, from windows, and from basements. They walked and ran towards the fountain.

All wore traditional dress. Many of the young women carried children on their backs. Several men brought llamas burdened with loads. One white llama was decorated in red ribbons, the symbol of purity and sacrifice.

"Nyles," Brian shouted across the crowd. "Nyles. I need your help."

"I guess he wants me," Nyles smiled. He ran into the crowd as I snapped pictures.

At the fountain, a big Spanish teenager pulled at the bag and forced Brian off-balance. He almost fell to the concrete. Swinging the bag above his head, Brian ran northward across the plaza away from the crowd. Spanish teens and children followed. The Incans did not. At a full gallop, Brian jumped up on a wood bench and then leaped over a wrought-iron fence into a grassy area. He emptied the bag on the grass before the children arrived.

As the children and older boys scrambled for the gifts, Brian jogged back to the fountain. Nyles was frightened. "This crowd could kill us," he whined.

"This is of love," Brian said, speaking as One with Voltar. "You will not be harmed." He handed Nyles the note. Nyles understood.

Brian helped Nyles climb up onto the lip of the huge concrete fountain in the center of the plaza. They looked out over the crowd. Over 400 people had gathered with many Incans in colorful costumes, and several white llamas.

Nyles shouted out the words in Spanish.

From the Earth, the water and the People, I am. From the Island of the Sun, I have come, and I wish to return.

I am Viracocha—I have knowledge of the People from my existence here, and within. My promise shall be kept--I shall comply to the people, within.

With the first light of the sun, on the day of December 22, 2011 A.D., and from the Island of the Sun, I shall return.

I am Ticci Viracocha, from the People. I am the Spirit of the People, and of the Earth. I am from the Earth.

Brian stretched out his bare forearms showing the people his spider and jaguar tattoos. Then he lifted the palm of his right hand and showed his numbers: 020 - 020 - 020. When Nyles finished, he looked at Brian to see white orbs for eyes.

"What should I do now?" Nyles asked.

"Read it again," Voltar commanded.

Brian's blue eyes re-appeared. Nyles shouted the message over the crowd as Brian held up his arms out for everyone to see.

For a while, the silence seemed frightening. People whispered, others prayed--some cried. Finally, someone cheered. Musicians began to play flutes, and drums and tambourines. The people began dancing and singing.

"The People," Voltar said. "The People of the Land celebrate."

"Can you read it again?" Brian's personality asked.

"Sure," Nyles nodded as he began shouting the message again.

As Nyles read the message a third time, Brian looked across the plaza northward to see a Spanish official run out of a building in a flurry. The big, thick-shouldered man wore a gray suit, white shirt and tie. Angrily, he pushed into the crowd. "Alto, alto." Towering over the Indians, he shoved smaller men aside as he shouted, "Alto. Alto."

Brian gestured for Nyles to get down. They both jumped to the ground. Then Brian shoved Nyles away. "Go," he said. "Go now."

The crowd began to mob Brian as he calmly stood among them united as One with Voltar. Brian raised his arms, and they backed away. The musicians continued playing as Brian lifted up the big, empty, white pillowcase and slowly began to fold the bag into squares.

The people around Brian watched him in awe for he folded the bag with flair--square upon square.

Shoving men and women aside, the Spanish official cleared a path. None of the Indians resisted and not one said a word in protest. But, they turned their backs and leaned against him, forcing him to shove hard. They did not step aside until pushed, and they only moved a foot or so before they leaned back against him.

"Alto, ALTO," the man yelled, his voice growing hoarse. As he approached Brian, the official trembled with rage. Over the decades, Incan riots had lead to bloody deaths in the plaza. Assembling on December 25th had been made illegal by the Spanish, due to conflict with the most important of all the ancient solar festivals. For the Incan sun priests, and for sun-worshippers around the world, December 25th is the first day that the sun's rising point on the horizon moves northward after 180 days of moving south, day upon day. Initiations in most ancient civilizations always took place at sunrise on December 25th --the day of new Hope, and New Birth.

Centuries ago, the Roman Catholic Church had appropriated the day as Christ's birthday to cover up the celebrations of sun-worshippers throughout the Holy Roman Empire.

Finally, through the crowd, the Spanish official saw the back of Brian's head. "Alto, Alto," he shouted at the musicians. The big man pointed at them. "ALTO," he raged. The musicians slowly stopped, keeping their eyes to the ground, like all the other Incans had done.

Then a few final notes caused giggles in the crowd. "ALTO," he warned with his finger shaking in anger.

Stepping forward, the big man glared at Voltar. Like the Incans in the crowd had done, Brian stood with his back to the man, waiting to be shoved.

For a moment, time stopped. A dangerous silence covered the plaza. I felt Brian was in real danger. Holding up my camera, I ran closer.

Nyles screamed across the crowd. "Jim, get out of there."

But I ran to Brian, like a news photographer looking for a story.

The Spanish official yelled at Brian in Spanish. "Did you start this?" Brian didn't move.

"Get out of the Plaza," the man yelled in Spanish. He pointed at Brian as I arrived and snapped a photograph. The big man paused. When he saw the camera pointed at him, he restrained his rage.

Instead of spinning Brian around angrily, he stepped up beside him and looked Voltar in the face.

"Americans? Who are you? WHO ARE YOU?" the official demanded in English.

Voltar gazed into the man's face without anger. "I come in love and peace, for all."

"Who are you?" the man asked in a softer voice.

Brian handed him the tightly folded square of cloth.

Thinking the material might be literature, he took the bag in hand. The big white cloth unfolded and hung downward—nothing but a big, empty bag.

The crowd giggled. The official glared at the people, and then glanced up. To his great surprise, Brian was gone. Voltar had slipped into the crowd leaving the Spanish authority *holding the bag.* The crowd laughed louder.

Musicians quickly started to play a song as Indians closed ranks behind Brian, protecting him. Frantically, the official searched with his eyes. Then he tried to follow into the crowd, but an Incan blocked his way with a big white llama decorated in red ribbons.

As Brian bent low and pushed through the crowd, dozens of Incan men and women patted his shoulders and touched his hands. He held out his palms to them as he ran.

"Gracias," they whispered. "Gracias." Taking another path, I snuck away through the Incans, too, and they helped me hide.

A few minutes later, Nyles waved us into a shadowy side street. "Let's get back to the hotel and hide," Nyles whispered. "We could go to jail for this. Incans can't assemble in the plaza on Christmas Day. It's illegal."

At the hotel, we avoided the front desk and stayed in our rooms all day. That night, I feared we would be arrested at the hotel, but nothing happened.

The next day, we snuck out of the hotel early in the morning before sunrise. Nyles and I helped shelter Voltar, so his face couldn't be seen.

We avoided police or any officials as we boarded the train for Machu Picchu. We had one extra day, and Voltar wanted to give us a tour of the mysterious city in the clouds.

Machu Picchu sits high on a mountaintop above the green jungle. Voltar said it was a city, "anchored to the sun."

He led us directly across the huge steppes to a small stone cabin. "This was the first home built," he said. "The first people here came from Tiahuanaco. As the city grew, they allowed this house to remain, in memory of the past, from which they came."

He described the purpose of the virgin baths and the raw, un-carved stone in the center of a round building. The first Incans, though master stonemasons, believed that this raw stone was more sacred than any others at Machu Picchu, he said. It was their anchor. It reminded them of their past before they had learned to carve stone.

Voltar then pointed out the seven different sundials. "Each is an anchor to the sun," he said. "Man must have anchors, if he is to be uplifted. Anchors of the mind, anchors for the people."

He taught us about the styles of stonework, and the meaning held by different types of stone.

Pointing out the unique stairways, Voltar said giants lived here with the Incan people. "Was the city built by giants for those of shorter legs, or was the city built by the shorter people so that the giants might dwell among them?" he asked. "Ask that question, and you will find the answers."

He explained that Voltar's people lived at Machu Picchu at the request of the first Inca.

Around noon, Voltar pointed out a tiny, hidden room once buried by a wall of natural stone. A strange sundial rested on a small pedestal. "Of the priests," Voltar said. "The doorway nebulous to time." He didn't explain.

At the end of the day, as we prepared to catch the train back to Cuzco, Brian's personality returned into dominance with his blue eyes rolled down. He was flustered and in a hurry. "We can't leave, yet," he said. "I am supposed to get something. They have a gift for me to take home."

Brian loped away. I raced after him, stunned.

The setting sun cast a golden glow over the beautiful white stones and green terraces as Brian galloped expertly up and down the shadowed stairways. He navigated down the narrow paths like he had played on them as a child. He made no mistakes and no false turns as he jogged through the ancient pathways. Finally, he stopped at the tiny, dark cavern holding the mysterious sundial of the priests. "Whatever they want me to get is in there. But I have to go alone," he said. As Nyles and I arrived gasping for air, he stepped inside.

We heaved for air and waited. Then Brian re-emerged into the golden light holding a vase about eighteen inches tall. Plain and undecorated, the reddish clay pot looked like a grain or water holder. The diameter was about ten inches and the rusty color reminded me of the stone at Tiahuanaco—not the dark soil or white stones of Machu Picchu.

"It's not Incan, really," Brian said. "It's not even ancient. It's from the people of today--the common people, of the land, of today." He smiled. "That's what he is telling me."

"There was nothing in there earlier," Nyles said. I had been inside, also. There had been no pot. "Even if they projected it there for you," I said. "I don't think you can take pottery off of an archaeological site."

"They want me to have it," Brian said as he started back to the train. Nyles and I stopped him. We touched the clay, looking inside and out for any markings. We found none.

"It's a basic, working pot," Brian said. "Common."

"Why would they give you that?" I asked in awe.

"It's a thank you. That's what Voltar said. It's for *Brian* from the common people of today."

"There are guards up there," I warned.

Brian shrugged. "Voltar told me to walk out with it. Take it home. It's mine to keep--as Brian."

"I'm not walking up to the gate with him," Nyles warned. "There is a huge fine for taking anything from this place--like ten thousand dollars. It's posted at the gate."

I had seen the sign too and as we approached the exit, we both stayed back away from Brian. But Brian walked calmly through the gate with a big smile on his face. None of the guards said a word about the pot that he held in plain sight.

I couldn't believe my eyes.

The next day, as we boarded the plane home, I asked Nyles his official impression. "Voltar is definitely a different man," Nyles said into my microphone. "He is amazed with little things that we take for granted. It has been definitely the most interesting and unusual experience in my life--and I have traveled all over the world."

"Good luck in Los Angeles," he chuckled. "I don't think he will be able to handle L.A.," Nyles laughed. He waved goodbye to us and then watched the plane lift off from the high mountain airport of Cuzco, surrounded by green mountains. Nyles had been a great aid to both of us, and a good friend to Voltar.

The next day, Wednesday, December 29th, Voltar and I landed at Los Angeles International Airport with sunburned faces.

As we entered customs, the guard questioned Voltar about the clay pot.

"A gift," he said. "From the people of the land, in love."

"How much is it worth?" the agent demanded. "You must declare a value."

From the next aisle, I answered. "It was less than five bucks. It's a throw away."

The man studied Voltar suspiciously. He looked inside the pot for any sign of hidden compartments. As he searched, Voltar was passed on to the next agent who searched his clothes.

"What is your purpose in the United States?" the second agent asked.

"Much is to be done," Voltar said. "I come in love, bringing gifts for mankind."

"What?" the man asked. "What gifts?"

"He doesn't mean that," I said.

"I bear knowledge," Voltar said. "And wisdom. Of this, the NOR and the Biological Monitoring Belt for man."

The white-haired agent glanced at Brian's belt. Then he searched in the pack again. "What belt? Where is this belt?"

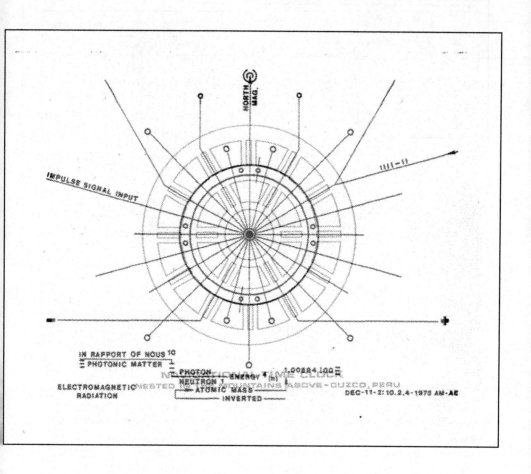

PHOTONIC MATTER drawing superimposed on Cuzco time clock

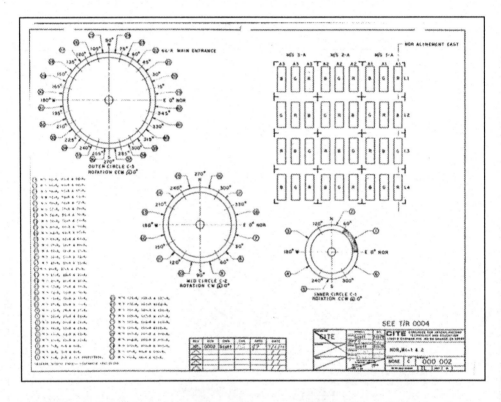

VOLTAR'S NOR – three rings that rotate within each other. Each ring projects patterns of light—red, green and blue. Voltar's diagram shows alignment of each ring, and placement of each color. The outer ring rotates counter-clock wise. The middle ring, clockwise. The inner ring, counter-clock wise. The subjects sit or stand at the center of the NOR where a doorway is created "nebulous to time." The purpose of the NOR is to create "ascending and descending levels of consciousness" through harmonious blending of lights and sounds. The center becomes a "matter displacement vehicle."

Note that each ring is aligned to the East.

RITE OF PASSAGE

ALL OF THESE DISTINCT STATES
(DISSOCIATION TRANCES, SHAMANISTIC TRANCES,
RELIGIOUS EXPERIENCES AND ACUTE PSYCHOTIC EPISODES)
HAVE THE SAME STRUCTURE AS A RITE OF PASSAGE:
PANIC, INSIGHT AND REINTEGRATION.
THE DARK NIGHT OF SOUL IS FOLLOWED BY LIGHT, THEN INTEGRATION.

-- Larry G. Peters and Douglas Price-Williams
(Transcultural Psychiatric Research Review, 1983)

Chapter 20

The Duality

"It's a project," I said apologetically to the Customs Agent. "Something he is working on. He is an engineer, a design engineering draftsman."

"What language is he speaking?" the man asked.

"Oh, that's English. He's just, tired. Very tired."

The man studied Voltar. "Looks like he was out in the sun. Maybe he has heat stroke."

"That explains it," I chuckled. The agent actually suspected Voltar of being on drugs because Peru and Bolivia were becoming known as suppliers of illegal cocaine to the United States.

"I come in peace," Voltar said gazing into the eyes of the grandfatherly officer. "And love, bearing knowledge for man."

The old man chuckled as he waited for a report on the clay pot. No contraband. It was empty. "We can all use more peace and more knowledge," the guard said, finally waving Voltar onward.

The first officer smirked. "It takes all kinds."

Upstairs, a crowd of people waited for Voltar. Debra, frantic with excitement, pushed her nose and hands against a glass wall. She saw him on an escalator and screamed in delight, jumping up and down like a schoolgirl.

"Oh God," she said. "Jesus, help me. I am so nervous and so excited."

Wanda rushed to the window to see Voltar walking forward, slowly, with a royal, noble stride. Turning his head slowly from side to side, Voltar gazed at the people and watched their energy fields.

Wanda gasped. "Oh God. It's Voltar," she yelled. Tears rose into her eyes as she watched Voltar walk among the crowds.

Debra and the others ran to the window.

"My God," Debra gushed. "It is!" Debra said. "It's Voltar!" She closed her eyes and jumped up and down until Wanda grabbed her tightly.

"Get a grip on yourself," Wanda said.

"It's Voltar," Debra whined as tears of joy ran down her face. "Oh God. Dear God," she tried to pray but rushed back to watch Voltar again. "Oh Jesus. JESUS! What am I going to do now?"

The Introductions

Voltar approached slowly and stopped to gaze into the faces of all those who awaited him. He saw in their countenances, excitement, hope and anticipation. As he gazed upon them, they all slowly calmed--except Debra. With tears of excitement on her face, she ran forward to hug him, but he received her stiffly. Stunned, she backed away.

I stepped forward with a cracked, sunburned face.

"Voltar wants to be re-introduced to everyone, for all is new to him," I said. "He wants to establish a relationship with each one of you, but first you will need to understand his situation."

Everyone crowded closer as I read from my notepad. "These are his words. *'Brian and Voltar are united as one, and through Brian the spirit of Viracocha is renewed.'*" Everyone stared at Voltar's solemn expression as he nodded approval, like a king endorsing a resolution.

"I am not sure what that all means, but the only way we talk to Brian is if Voltar's eyes roll back," I added. "But Brian is still a part of Voltar."

Voltar looked into the eyes of each person and waited for each to nod with understanding. About fifteen people had gathered. I felt each become serious, engaged and aligned in some way with Voltar's words.

I continued. "The orientation period will last about 12 more days. During this time, he wants to be alone with Debra as much as possible. He doesn't want any meetings. It's like a honeymoon, I guess." They all laughed. Debra gushed with excitement. Wanda and several other ladies held onto her.

"He doesn't shake hands, because, by touch, *he feels all*--and everything. So when he does shake hands or touch you in any way, it's special. He sees the energy form of your being, as well as your physical body, so it is kinda confusing for him at times. He likes to go slow. He stares a lot. He can actually see through walls, and into buildings, and ahead on the road.

Voltar raised his right hand and gazed at Debra. Voltar stepped slowly towards her as I continued, and her heart swelled. "His speech patterns are slow and halting. He doesn't understand many things. For example, he is a little bit afraid of airplanes, cars and all. Everything is new to him. He is like a baby, a child. He really shouldn't be left alone. And I mean that seriously. At *no* time should he be left alone."

Everyone nodded with agreement. The responsibility for Voltar began to weigh upon the people who had gathered.

Finally, Voltar allowed Debra to hug him. She cried—then backed away from him with respect. She didn't know him. He wasn't Brian.

I introduced Voltar to each person, and he nodded with respect to each--one at a time. After the introductions, Voltar strode out of the airport in a regal manner. Debra held onto his arm, like his queen.

Whispering, the group followed.

When people in the airport stared at Voltar like a dignitary, he nodded at them with equal honor. He spoke to no one until he was alone with Debra that night at our house. Wanda and I wanted him to stay with us a few days to see if he could handle Los Angeles.

Integration

My list of anomalies had overwhelmed simple multiple-personality. Certainly, this was not a *simple* case. Perhaps, the Host's process of "quantum evolution" involved going through stages of multiple-personality, and then coming out on the other side, integrated as One.

Integration is the goal of therapy, I knew that—and I had seen integration begin after observing 'the reversal.' Now, Brian spoke *only after* Voltar rolled up the blue eyes they shared. They were a team—integrated. Amnesia didn't seem to be an issue. No more blackouts. Brian could be present when Voltar agreed.

Yes, a new integration had begun--the Host never spoke, Viracocha said little. Voltar and Brian ran the show, mutually, operating as One—with Voltar in the foreground, and Brian behind, watching.

However, the duality was still linked to the eyes. Somehow eyes played an enormous role as a "switch" in the process, rolling up and down, seeing inward or outward. The 'reversal' meant Voltar was available with the blue eyes out. Brian was only available with eyes up, like in a trance. Physically, he acted normal like he saw everything. But how could he? What did he see? That, I didn't understand.

I still favored multiple-personality as a paradigm. The pattern was obvious and consistent, but what if Voltar's people were real?

What if these people from Epsilon Eridani existed and had long ago discovered traits of the human mind we don't grasp today? What if they were trying to help us understand and get free from our own Secondary World—an invisible, but physical world controlled by the grays from Epsilon Bootees. What if the stepping-stones to higher levels of mind were laid through trances, amnesia, multiple-personality, paranormal powers and other phenomenon involving *dissociation of mind and body?*

If man must go inward to evolve, then taking a journey through trances, psychosis, multiple-personality, and demonic possession may be part of the process. Since these phenomena could be triggered by stress, hypnosis, and torture, perhaps they are innate capacities in all mankind. Perhaps they could be triggered by patterns of light and sound.

Certainly, the ancient legends of heroic adventures seemed to involve symptoms of dissociation and similar processes—though shaped by cultural beliefs.

Sounds and lights often played a role. Viracocha supposedly used sounds to lift stones at Tiahuanaco, according to legends. In the Bible, Jericho fell by sound. Voltar's magnetic pulses put sound on my tapes. Perhaps sound and patterns of light could be used to manipulate matter, energy and the human mind. Perhaps sound waves could influence the magnetic field of the earth at certain nodal points in an energy grid. Perhaps, the magnetic field of earth could create sounds that record on magnetic tape. Maybe Photonic Matter could be recorded on sound tape.

I took all the theories with a grain of salt, but I could never forget my sign— the Ball of Fire in the Sky. I had asked. The Host had replied. Everything that followed had come from that request, and that relationship—whatever, or whomever the Host, happened to be. That's all I knew, for certain.

Voltar's Honeymoon

Sitting on sleeping bags in the living room, Voltar gently reminded Debra of the missing time she had experienced in October. By candlelight, he opened her memory to a ceremony that had been performed which consecrated them together in a special marriage, a very unique marriage. He explained that for them to live together, and sleep together, they needed to be married in mind and spirit. He slipped onto her finger a ring that Brian had bought in Cuzco.

Slowly, Debra remembered the missing time and the ceremony that had been performed on October 8. Voltar had taken her, in some way, to Big Bear and the stone amphitheatre where he had given Brian the white rock. There he had placed a rock into her hand. Together, they had held the rock on her abdomen. That is all she remembered of the 35 minutes.

"Of this, a child conceived," he said.

Debra knew she was pregnant for sure. She had been to a doctor.

"As two lives dwell within Brian, you now bear another life within you," he said. "The rock of the New World."

Voltar covered her with a blanket and lay down beside her. He held her hand and they drifted off into sleep, dreaming together of a child to be.

Over the next few days, Voltar survived the noise and confusion of the big city with Debra's sense of humor and guidance.

They visited Universal Studios and the Los Angeles Zoo. She adapted to his serious, solemn nature by becoming silly and giddy with joy. She tried to get him laughing, and succeeded on several occasions by making faces and imitating animals. Reluctantly, he gradually learned to laugh with Debra.

But primarily, everything Voltar saw, he wanted to change.

Voltar's diet was the opposite of Brian's. He wanted fresh fruit, nuts and vegetables instead of hamburgers, sodas and hotdogs. Debra promised to cook for him, and after a few days in Los Angeles, I gave her a vegetable steamer to take home.

She looked forward to living with Voltar. They returned to Santa Ana for their extended honeymoon with the last $100 contribution for the trip. In Orange County, they visited the Queen Mary in Long Beach and several marinas along the ocean.

Debra called me daily from phone booths. "We are getting along fine. He is so much better than Brian," she cooed. "He is so patient and calm, it is humbling to me," she said. "He never gets ruffled."

At night, Debra read to Voltar from the Bible, and he explained many of the scriptures that had concerned her. They walked along the beach and the seashore nearly every day. On Sunday she took him to church at Calvary Chapel in Costa Mesa. They both cried together as hundreds of people sang love songs to Jesus.

"He is so beautiful," Debra said. "And so vulnerable. He is like a little boy. He cries like a baby at beautiful things."

Near the end of the second week, Voltar asked to visit a drafting supply store. His attempt to buy drafting paper turned into a hilarious adventure because, for the first time, Debra let him talk to store clerks on his own.

As she stood back and watched, he described his need for drafting paper in a deep, serious voice, and with unusual detail. Frustrated, the clerk finally called the manager for help.

Debra laughed at the confusion. "He's from another land," she explained. "He doesn't understand our language very well."

"He understands it very well," the manager said as he looked for the materials. "We just don't use those terms, very often, but we do get lots of foreigners in here. Arabs and Hindus, mostly. Where is he from? "

"Ah, South America," Debra answered. "Bolivia and Peru."

She stifled her laughter. Debra knew how to make fun with little moments of life, and Voltar gave her great reasons to laugh.

"Looks like he's going to be doing some detailed drawings," the manager said with a smile.

"He's a rocket scientist," Debra said, stifling her laugh.

"May God be with you," Voltar said with deep reverence to the manager, to the clerk and to all of the people in the store. He addressed each one individually and gazed deep into their faces. Debra pulled him away as one tried to shake hands.

"I'm sorry," Debra whispered. "I'm really sorry."

"Not at all," smiled the manager. "We could use more politeness around here."

That night, Debra took Voltar and her son Mark to a colorful, old time ice cream parlor in Orange County. Laughing, noisy tourists crowded the booths.

When a costumed waiter asked Voltar if he wanted coffee, the loud, mechanical voice of Saturn answered from his lips, "NO-EM."

"I'm sorry," gasped the waiter.

To cover the confusion, Debra started cackling like a chicken. Soon, a crowd of people around laughed loudly.

Debra whispered to Voltar. "If your friends are going to act outrageous, I will too." Then the other voices turned loose at a high volume.

"Me too," said Lynana.

"Me too-em," said the loud, shattering Saturn.

"Me too," said the gravely voice of Energy.

"Me too," boomed Mars.

"We shall also," blasted Tau Ceti.

Debra shrieked with laughter as the crowd of people stared. "I love it," she howled. In response, Debra chicken-clucked again, even louder. "Bluuck, Bluuuuuuuuck, Bluck, bluck. bluck,"

As people around them laughed, the waiter delivered cherry-topped, ice-cream sundaes to their table. Voltar took a spoon and Saturn spoke: "Spoon, bendem"

The spoon handle melted and drooped in Brian's hand, shocking the waiter.

Voltar held up the warped spoon as if asking for another. The stunned waiter hurried away. As he grabbed at a spoon on the counter, it also bent. He jumped back shocked.

Saturn spoke again: *"spoons, bendem."*

Suddenly, all around the area, people lifted up bent spoons, and showed them to Debra.

She shrieked with laughter. "Oh my God."

The frantic waiter ran around to replace them.

"It's all right," Debra consoled the people. "He does that all the time. That's Saturn, not Voltar. Sometimes he's a little monkey."

She looked at them straight-faced. She was telling the truth. Let them deal with it, she thought.

Some people giggled. Others frowned and worried, but they soon all turned back to ice cream, ignoring Debra and Voltar.

"It doesn't bother them," Debra exclaimed. "I can live with this, if you and your friends can all live with my chicken," she laughed.

"It brings me pleasure to see you happy--with them," said Voltar. "For they are now able to be amongst the people."

Voltar goes to Work

The next day, Voltar began work on five gifts for mankind. "The pyramid is first in priority," he explained to Debra. In Brian's tiny rooftop apartment, Voltar worked all day with her help. He set up a portable drafting table, examined the existing drawings and planned others. He dictated to Debra the five gifts of knowledge he held for mankind. Using her shorthand skills, she noted each word on a secretarial pad.

1. The Pyramid Design for Tiahuanaco
2. The Story of Voltar's People
3. Design of Time Capsules
4. Quantum Displacement Physics
5. The Biological Monitoring Belt

1. THE PYRAMIDS

The master plan for the first pyramid could be used at Tiahuanaco and the four other sites: Stonehenge, Giza, China, and Sedona, Arizona. The pyramids would provide solar power to their region, balance the earth's magnetic flux and store biological materials until the year 14,000 A.D. when the material would be reclaimed. The pyramids, once built, could be coordinated from space by satellites, mutually operated by man and by Voltar's people.

By balancing and controlling the magnetic field of earth, the pyramids would help prevent earthquakes and stabilize the earth's orbit, should it become unstable.

2. THE HISTORY OF VOLTAR'S PEOPLE

Secondly, so man would understand more about the need for the pyramids, Voltar planned to write the history of his people, with Brian. Entitled: GOD'S

OTHER CHILDREN, the book would illustrate the mistake of Voltar's people after they contacted earth the first time.

3. TIME CAPSULES

Thirdly, Voltar would design time capsules for man to place into orbit as satellites. The capsules were to contain information about this era from 1971-2011, so that future generations would understand the great transformation that began with Brian. The capsules would be recovered at various intervals from 500 years in the future to 14,000 A.D.

4. QUANTUM DISPLACEMENT PHYSICS

Fourth, Voltar would bring forth the knowledge of Quantum Displacement Physics as the core of man's technological advancement. This science would lead to development of a transportation system allowing man to travel through space -- and time. That would all begin with the Biological Monitoring Belt, and the NOR, a Neural-Optical-Responder.

5. BIOLOGICAL MONITORNIG BELT (BMB) and NOR

Fifth, Voltar would design several versions of a Biological Monitoring Belt and the NOR. The belt would help man create a transportation system based on Quantum Displacement Physics: the teleportation of human beings.

The first stage of the belt would record and display the wearer's biological state on colorful panels. Training of the individual would lead to a personal biofeedback control system reflecting moment-to-moment changes in the mind and body.

In the second stage, the belt would monitor blood, and input medicines into the blood as prescribed by doctors. With a training program, the belt would help man expand self-control of emotions, mind and body.

In the third stage, after the wearer had gained more understanding of how to control body reactions with the mind at Nous 4, the displacement functions would be activated with help from Voltar's people.

The NOR, Neural-Optical-Responder, would stimulate the eyes of people with patterns of light controlled by a trained operator—a therapist. The NOR would be suitable for use with small groups of people to create "ascending and descending levels of consciousness."

The NOR and the Biological Monitoring Belt would both eventually help harmonize the mind with the magnetic fields of the earth. They were the elementary parts of an advanced Quantum Displacement System.

In an advanced system, the wearer of a belt would be able to transport his physical body to a receiving booth. Terminals would have to be built around the world, and managed by a ring of satellites.

Using the Biological Monitoring Belt, the NOR and Quantum Displacement Physics, man would eventually be able to travel easily around the earth, and later -- explore the planets of our solar system in crafts.

"The Biological Monitoring Belt is the beginning," said Voltar. "These gifts of knowledge will bring freedom to man--freedom from the Secondary World," Voltar said.

When Voltar finished, Debra heard a knock on the door. She froze. She was not expecting anyone. The person knocked again, louder.

"I know you are in there. Open up," shouted Mary Beth. "I want my husband back." Debra felt terrified for at that moment, the honeymoon ended.

The Duality

Debra carefully opened the door to greet a drunken Mary Beth wearing black leather pants, a black jacket and thick make-up. She had chosen the dark side, again. "I heard you were living with him," Mary Beth snapped. "I want to talk to him, now" she demanded drunkenly.

"He's not Brian, anymore," Debra said, coldly.

"He is too, and he is still my husband," Mary Beth slurred.

Debra smelled alcohol. Mary Beth lifted up a big red capsule, held it in her teeth and swallowed.

"You're on reds!" Debra seethed. "And drunk."

"I still want my husband."

"It is not a good time," Debra said. "He can call you tomorrow and set up something, when you are not so stoned."

Mary Beth lifted up a pearl handled revolver and pointed the barrel at Debra.

"Get him now, Jezebel. Or I will go in right over your ass."

Debra fell down with fear, then scrambled over to Voltar terrified. He sat in the chair with eyes rolled back. Voices spoke in quick succession forging an agreement. "Locked," the mechanical probe voice concluded.

Then Voltar spoke. "These things are of Brian and his life, his past, and the past of Mary Beth," he said. "For each is of free will and his own mind. By agreement of the council with that of Brian, he will return."

"But what about the projects, the gifts for mankind?" Debra cried pointing at the drawings and papers.

"Of this, a start. The process has begun and will continue in the evenings. For, Brian has told us, he must return to work and provide that of sustenance for his family. Of this--the *Play of Life.*"

The door opened and Mary Beth sauntered into the room wearing high-heeled shoes and glitter beads.

"I want my husband back," she said, glaring at Brian. He rubbed his eyes in shock. Her looks had changed. The wholesome Mary Beth was gone. She looked tough as nails wearing all black.

"God, what is happening?" asked Brian.

"I want you, now. Tonight," said Mary Beth. "Right now." She folded the gun across her chest. "I am staying right here until you take me home."

"Mary Beth?" Brian asked in a daze. "What are you doing?"

"Get your keys," she said waving the gun. "You are taking me home."

For the next few weeks, Brian lived in turmoil. Before the trip to South America, he had resigned his position at the business machine company. So he went out to drafting agencies and registered for work. Within a few days, he was offered a high-paying contract as a free-lance design-draftsman with a bio-medical company. The company provided products to doctors and hospitals. The new job proved fun and challenging, but most of Brian's free time was spent shuttling between Debra, Mary Beth and the kids.

He suppressed Voltar during the day so he could work, and he helped baby-sit at night.

After the first visit, Mary Beth had agreed to stay off drugs and away from bad influences. She had been given a last chance by her parents and by social services to care for the children, but she needed a man in her bed, and a baby-sitter, she said.

Brian agreed to continue with babysitting, but insisted that he must live with Debra to accomplish the projects. Mary Beth wanted him to come home and try to make a life, with her. He refused. After a long discussion, Mary Beth said she would file for a divorce and find another man to keep her happy. Brian agreed to pay child support.

The Knowledge

By the last week of February, Brian's life had stabilized. Voltar emerged in the evening to answer questions or provide comfort to Debra. No trances were needed. He just emerged when Brian gave permission.

Various investigators wanted to visit with Voltar and get data clarified. The radio astronomer in Scotland had not received a return signal from the probe, and he was disappointed. Brian said a reply was not promised immediately. "The timing all depends on man," he said.

Lunan wrote letters to Brian. He felt that certain dates in the manuscript aligned Giza, Stonehenge and Teotihuacan, the holy city of the Toltecs, to the planet Mars and to the star Tau Ceti. As Brian listened to the most recent letter, he ate celery and peanut butter chomping loudly. He barely understood Lunan's questions, but the allies of Voltar responded by confirming some points and rejecting others.

Basically, the Toltecs and the Maya, and even the Olmecs could be linked and compared to Tiahuanaco for many similarities, they said. The Host and Voltar's people had operated more than one *Play of Life* in the region of Central America. Quetzalcoatl, the cultural hero of the Toltecs could be directly compared to Viracocha for understanding. Researchers would find many parallels.

Both the Incas and the Aztecs came much later, taking many beliefs and much knowledge from the previous civilizations. Voltar's people had lived in both regions and still controlled a few zones in Central America.

Watching Brian answer questions while eating celery was hilarious. When the allies answered a question, Brian's body froze, stiff as stone, but afterwards he instantly continued without missing a chomp. His transition from deep trance to normal Brian was instantaneous and smooth, as quick as a blink, as sharp as a bite—total integration.

But, Brian didn't understand the answers on astronomy, and insisted they be read back to him, slowly. "I have to learn," he said. "Please, don't leave me out of the loop."

Quantum Displacement Physics

The next week, Bill Hamilton presented his findings on the drawings and writings. "There is a logic described in the Brian Scott writings," Bill said for the record as Brian listened. "There are lots of symbols and mathematical equations given as comparatives so man can understand--in his own terms. They refer to applying non-Newtonian physics. That means Einsteinium Physics. They use Einstein's relativity equations when talking about space travel and orbital reality, but indicate a limiting speed of 858,000 mps, roughly 4.6 times the speed of light. They move in a point to point manner by expanding and contracting some field of energy, but are limited or impacted in some way by this factor of 858, 000 miles per second."

"That's right," Brian said.

"Four primary logical factors are given," Bill continued.

"First, all of their logic relating to substance on earth involves the force of magnetism. They affect the substance on earth with mind at level four through level ten, all using magnetism, in some way.

"True," said Brian.

"The basic formula given is not alien. The basic formula is a standard equation for determining the Force between two magnetic forces or poles. It is used in numerous sciences from electronics to astronomy, in related forms. The formula is:

$$\frac{F = M_1 \times M_2}{R^2}$$

Bill explained. "The force between the two objects is determined by multiplying their Masses and dividing that by the Radius of the distance between them, squared. This is one of the main equations used by Einstein in the Unified Field Theory. That is factor number one."

The second factor was $E = MC^2$ "This is the core of Einstein's Unified Field Theory. Notice that both formulas involve mass. Remember this is a logical factor involved in affecting substance on earth with the mind.

"The third factor also involves Mass and Energy," Bill said. "Energy can be converted to Mass at Nous 10. Also, Mass can be converted to Energy at Nous 10. So the mind, at Nous 10, can go both ways with Mass and Energy."

"They like it so far," said Brian nodding agreement.

Bill was certain of the formulas and factors, for they had been repeated often in the writings with comparisons and examples applied to biology.

"Biology is the primary technology of earth, as viewed by these people. Quantum Displacement Physics underlies all other life sciences."

"That's right on target," Brian smiled.

"The unifying concept to this science is Orbital Realities. The principles apply to biology, to living cells, to solar systems, to galaxies, to electrons in orbit around a nucleus, to sub-atomic particles. It's similar at every level of matter because the universe is electromagnetic. Everything on earth shares the earth's electromagnetic field.

"But their primary interest is in applying this to genetics and DNA. Their goal is to use this knowledge to create certain results in the mind of human beings."

Brian laughed. "You get a bingo on that one, Bill. You are right on target."

"I believe they are saying that the DNA structure of man can be changed through magnetic fields, and through thought, but I am not sure how." Brian did not respond.

"Anyway, the fourth logical factor is definitely TIME. This is very difficult for man to grasp. The writings indicate "Time is of the Mind at Nous 4. Also, that Mind at Nous 4 can displace Time.

"For earth, they give a factor regarding time. All time is relevant to this number, they say: 1/31,556,925.9747. That number is the total of seconds in a year at the equator on earth. They give this reference as a starting point.

"Time has direction, time has velocity: D = S x T. Distance traveled equals your speed multiplied by time. They give this simple formula we all learn in grade school.

"Time is related to the speed of light, squared, and that is related to mass and energy of an object.

"Their entire science comes together in the Photonic Matter drawing. This drawing indicates that the primary unit of mass, which contains both positive and negative electric charges is the neutron. This drawing, I believe, shows how matter is related to energy and time. The drawing is the key. Some how, it shows us what happens to *matter* and *energy* when *thought* expands to Nous level ten— mind level ten.

"They indicate that any substance can be moved by thought, energy can be moved by thought, any mass can be moved by thought. At Nous ten, they are capable of controlling the displacement of mass and energy through time and space, by the power of their minds." He took a deep breath and continued.

"This is the exact definition of Quantum Displacement Physics: **The movement of Mass and Energy through space by displacement of Time with the Mind at Nous 4,** and above--up to level ten. But it doesn't start until Nous 4."

Bill summarized. "These four logical factors are the keys that man needs. This is the core of the material in Scott's manuscripts, though there is a lot more."

When Bill finished, Voltar responded. "You have discovered much, but not all is at a 100 percent comprehension factor. Indeed, it is a beginning for man. The Photonic Matter drawing is indeed, the key. Each line is important to understand. From research into this, the answers will come, answers to the hidden mysteries. Man must reason each of these things out, and provide proof by his own logic, and his own hand, for man himself will be the one to benefit from this information."

The voice of Energy blurted. "Each drawing aligned to the Gate of the Sun."

Then Saturn blasted. "Knowledge of the past. Related to sun, to solar energy."

Voltar returned with his mellow, flowing voice. "Through this knowledge, your people may advance themselves both technologically and spiritually—even among those of opposing spiritual beliefs. It has been done before--it can be done again. Remember, you are all connected. You are each of *free choice.* Your own will is yours, and will always be yours. You lose nothing. You will only gain by working together in this purpose.

"Through this effort each man will truly learn to reach out to the person next to him, to share--whether that sharing be of knowledge, religion or the essence of your being.

"Remember, by sharing, you will all come to a fulfillment and a new understanding of your purpose in life, as a people. You of earth are the Positive Force, the Secret, the Answer to the universe, God's Last Creation. Thus, you attract the Negative—the Secondary. This you must learn to understand as you overcome the Secondary World of man.

"But for now, what is to be done, must be done by your own hand."

Brian's personality returned. Man didn't have to understand the physics, Brian said. If he, Brian, could build a prototype system, it would work--and man could figure it out afterwards. "The problem is the human mind," Brian said. "What happens to a person at Nous 4 when they are dematerialized—when their body moves through space and time instantly? They are in for a shock. It's like a religious experience—life without a body. That's why the philosophy is important," Brian said. "Man needs a philosophy and a system of education to prepare for living with Quantum Displacement."

Bill didn't understand. He wanted to really grasp what Brian was talking about.

"Each man must be raised to Nous 4," Voltar warned. "Of this, the human mind must be known. Of this, understanding shall be given."

Bill Gets a Taste of Nous Two

A few days later, Bill experienced the first stage of an uplifting. While studying the Photonic Matter drawing, he heard a buzzing sound, a roar in the back of his head and neck. He felt his mind open and looked up to see another reality, another world. He saw himself in another life, navigating and fully understanding a spacecraft. He blinked, but the world didn't go away. He saw people. They spoke to him.

Within moments, his emotions were overwhelmed—he fainted. When he awoke, he raved to his friends about what he had seen, and the exciting revelations he had received. The episodes continued until he began to act out and interact with the other reality, laughing and talking with people no one else could see. Fearing for his safety, his wife and friends eventually locked him into a room. They called Brian for help.

"Basically he is hallucinating," said a friend. "That's our position. But, who is to say? All we know is that he was working with the Photonic Matter drawing when it happened. We are just protecting him until he calms down."

Brian suggested they take him out to the wide-open spaces of the desert for several days to unwind. They did, and the episode subsided. Bill had taken a taste of a higher level of mind, a Nous Level 2.

The Challenge

Afterwards, Bill insisted that he still heard voices in his mind, talking to him. He believed *they* told him a landing would take place on March 12 in the desert at Giant Rock Airport. He was to bring Brian because the landing involved Brian.

Brian accepted the invitation at Voltar's request. "A challenge must be made," Voltar said. "Nothing will happen. This is of the imagination of man."

Voltar said, in contrast, a real sighting would take place along the coast of California on March 22 "for all to see." Debra marked a big red "X" on the calendar.

After making a formal statement on tape, Brian drove out to the desert in a caravan of five cars filled with people, all roused up to expect a UFO descent.

Brian insisted I document each statement, in advance.

"I don't like this challenge, idea," Brian said. "It's a hell of a responsibility." We roared along in the caravan riding in Brian's recently purchased 1963 Ford, painted metallic copper. With the windows down, Brian shouted into the microphone. "We could hurt friendships, offend allies—blow people away. But Voltar said there are too many people running around destroying the truth.

"People who are interested in UFO's need to help complete the projects of contactees," Brian said. "The projects will bring about an uplifting of our technological society—a society that will be more spiritual—based on each person's freedom of choice. But everyone must learn to test the voices, test the knowledge."

Debra wanted to challenge Voltar. "Christians say you, Brian, should challenge the entities speaking through you. They want to know if you have challenged Voltar by asking if he will confess that Jesus is Lord God of Heaven and Earth, and that he walked the earth as a real man in Israel. If he can't confess that, then he is a demon, they believe. What about that challenge?"

Wanda leaned forward. "Most of the New Age channelers just ask if the entity is a Being of Light. They tell them to leave if they are not of the Light."

"That's not the same," Debra said. "In the final days, demons come as Teachers of the Light, that's exactly what the Bible says. So we have to be very careful. If they won't confess Jesus is God, they are demons."

"I will do what I have to do," said Brian. "My part is NOT RELIGIOUS. How many times do I have to say that? If you have a need to make a challenge, make sure it is right for you. My purpose is hardcore engineering and scientific reality. That's how I was in the beginning, and I am not going to change. I have to be scientific about it. I have to work with engineers and designers. We create and build things all day long, all over the world without praying over it. It works—that's all that counts."

"Is the voice that speaks through someone's mind, a God, or a demon? Or an alien?" I asked. "How do we know?" The ancient Greeks had faced the same problem with their Oracles. They had called the voices gods, and people sat in huge amphitheatres to listen to them speak through an old man or a woman – the Oracle. The Greeks never figured out the answer to the question, but with knowledge from the oracles they did create a New World.

"Right," said Brian. "This is the battle--the battle of the minds."

"This is it?"

"This is the battle that will divide the world," Brian said. "The battle for the mind of man--Armageddon will come from that exact question. I can tell you this. I didn't go through this transformation to just sit around. It has to go somewhere."

Brian continued. "Besides the gifts of knowledge and the technology, I've got to be able to set the people up, put their feet firmly on the ground in a basic scientific belief system which allows for a true, a real spiritual belief for our society.

"People will have to know and believe that the world is part of a *collective universe* that is a part of each person, already. They don't have to go seeking. Each is already part of it all. They go within. But I have to be able to show this to them in a very solid, nuts and bolts manner. That is my thing, and what I have to do."

Wanda responded. "Well, Bill thinks he is getting accurate information on a sighting tonight. You say he is not. It's a simple test."

"It's not me. It's them! How would I know?" Brian answered.

I leaned forward. "Is this a man challenging a man, or is Voltar challenging some alien speaking through Bill?"

Brian spoke carefully. "First of all, I am not afraid to put people into their place, if they are wrong or in error. But, yes, this could open one hell of a can of worms. If there are real entities talking through someone, then the entities should talk to each other. If they talk to each other, in the presence of all the people, and the people end up working together to create a new reality for mankind, we will have our own proof. If they will not cooperate, then that is the negative proof."

"So you will challenge the man--and Voltar will challenge the other entities?"

"I don't know what is going to happen actually," said Brian. "Let the two entities hash it out, that's my point. If the man is for real, he won't be afraid of the challenge. There is no reason why a physical person who is having a real contact cannot go through a challenge, and come out okay. Now, if one of the entities speaking through a man--whether it is a sub-transmission or direct signal, or by some other means--challenges a false or bad entity's authority, and his purpose, and why he is using the other physical body, well, you will probably find some big worms crawling out. That is all I can say. Only the real ones will be left after a challenge."

"This could get scary," Debra said. "Worms could be demons."

"Not everything is a demon," Brian said. "There are all kinds of entities trying to help man. But--many are just imagination."

"Imaginations of the heart," said Debra. "Or they could be familiar spirits. WE are not supposed to consult them."

That afternoon, Brian met two other UFO contactees living in the Giant Rock area: George Van Tassel and Bob Short. Both had reported several contacts in the 1950's, then later became oracles. On a regular basis, they sat in trance with deep, booming voices coming out of their mouths. Each had gained a small following of people who helped transcribe their tapes and work on their projects. Van Tassel channeled "the Ashtar Command," and Bob Short channeled "Saturn."

The voice of Bob Short's "Saturn" sounded just like the "Saturn" which spoke through Brian – loud and distinctive with an "em" at the end of most words.

Brian said very little to George Van Tassel, an ex-Marine with a wall full of commendations from military and civic organizations. But, he challenged Bob Short to bring forth a fulfillment of his true purpose. The challenge caused an uprising among Short's followers, and we quickly departed.

Later that night, five carloads of people waited at Giant Rock Airstrip until midnight. Then Brian asked Bill to join him for a talk.

Alone with Brian, Bill accepted that no craft had appeared at the time he had indicated.

Voltar emerged and gently challenged Bill, saying the information he had received was not real, but from his own imagination.

"Certain information you received is NOT ACCURATE," Voltar said, firmly.

555

In a display of unity, the allies all agreed. Reluctantly, Bill agreed. He asked for guidance.

"You have been tested tonight and have seen the truth," said Voltar. "It is a beginning. Of these imaginations, test them within your own self. Be in unity--first--before reaching out to others. This is the way. This is the beginning. It is a good beginning."

Then Saturn spoke. "And much prosperity will come through that of justice and the ability to be in unity in your own mind."

"There is much to do," said Voltar. "You must be sure in our own mind, for the unity you seek, must be assured to you, first. There can be no mistakes. To bring forth a scientific and spiritual achievement on this planet, the directives must be clear and clean-cut. Be cautious of those who would make statements without full clarification. And those who go forth speaking untruth, must be challenged in the same manner.

"Today, we offer guidance and wisdom, for you are new, and we are aware that your questions are many. Your purpose is great, and we offer our love and our understanding to you."

Then all the allies of Voltar each wished Bill a good evening.

When they finished their "good evenings" a deeper, more powerful Presence spoke, "Good evening--my children."

"Who was that?" Bill gasped in surprise.

"That was the Him," Brian said. "The center, Center of the Universe. You are blessed Bill. Continue on, and learn."

Although some turmoil had developed from the weekend of challenges, everyone felt better afterwards, and some bonds of trust were strengthened. But everyone walked away wondering what it meant to be of "unity in your own mind."

To me, it meant full integration. All the levels of mind, all the personalities of a person, must be in agreement.

Voltar was one of twelve personalities that now regularly spoke through Brian, and at the end of most talks each presence joined in a round of goodbyes. If a decision had been made, they each voiced "agreement" in their own distinctive voice.

The Proof

On Tuesday March 22, around 11 p.m., Brian started a tape recorder at the house of a new friend. Brian didn't have a TV. He hung a microphone down in front of their television as a newscast began. "Here is our proof," he said to Debra. "Make sure Jim gets this tape."

556

"There really was a sighting today?" Debra asked.

"It was all over the news this morning," the young engineer said. "Brian asked me a few days ago to watch for it on TV. "

"This IS it," Brian said as he saw captions about UFO's. He turned up the volume.

"This is Metro News, LA's number one prime-time news cast with Larry Atteberry and Chuck Ashman," said the announcer. Then the news anchor began:

"Good evening. A barrage of UFO's reportedly descended on the Southland just as dawn was beginning to break this morning. Hundreds of early risers, including two Los Angles County Sheriff helicopter patrolmen, reported seeing mysterious bright lights streaking across the dark gray sky.

"The officers say they saw a pair of objects that looked like landing lights for an airplane, but there was no airplane attached.

"Police in Whittier and Long Beach reported similar sightings. Reports that mysterious objects were illuminating the skies finally reached the UFO Center in Washington. By 5:00 a.m., the center was on the hotline with the Huntington Beach police department to verify some sightings there.

The scene switched to a lady reporter on site. **"It all started out as a routine night-time patrol for Huntington Beach helicopter pilots Jim Lehr and Tom Arnold, but at 3:00 a.m. it all changed. They saw something they can't explain."**

One of the sheriff officers spoke. **"Two light blue objects, at a very high rate of speed. They appeared to be similar to a tear drop, and they were on about a 60 degree heading."**

Then the second man spoke. **"My partner called my attention to it and by the time I got a fix on it and began to watch it myself, there was no doubt in my mind, after I'd watched it for about two seconds, what they were. They were unidentified flying objects."**

The lady responded. **"Why? You sound very positive about that."**

"Well, they were flying in formation. They were both exactly the same configuration, exactly the same size and going exactly the same speed, heading exactly the same direction. I've never seen a falling star or anything else look like that. It was just, very, very odd."

"You said what you saw could not be described by anything in your experience," the reporter said. "How about the possibility that it might be from outer space?"

"Well, people would have to be pretty narrow-minded to believe that in this vast ocean of space, that we would be the only ones in it. So, you never know."

Brian laughed and hooted as the news lady signed off with a closing comment. "This is Barbara Simpson for Channel 11 news in Huntington Beach."

"I told you," Brian shouted. "They did it. Now there's a feather you can stick in your cap. We even put it on the calendar, didn't we Debra?'

"You sure did honey. What do you think it's all about?"

Brian flipped the channels as he answered. "Oh, they do things. Sometimes, just to get things stirred up. The children do it. It was proof about the challenge. There is always a purpose when they do something like that. It's the 22nd, you know. It's an ending of winter. Start of spring--a new beginning, a celebration. Another round. I think it means we made it."

On Channel 2, another report started.

"A lot of people in Southern California are probably staying up late tonight to see if the same thing happens again. We are talking about that unexpected light show this morning. Two diamond shaped objects, suddenly blazing across the sky at about three o'clock."

Brian cackled. "Now they are diamond-shaped." As the report continued, the young engineer from work questioned Brian.

"What are they?"

"I don't know really. Not sensors, for sure--probably two small craft--one kid in each, having fun."

"Are they from Voltar's world?" Debra asked. Brian listened a moment. In his mind, he heard the probe clicking, changing channels. Then he heard the voices of two boys laughing. Then Voltar spoke. "Of the alliance--a demonstration of unity: two as one. Two in unity: in color, direction, speed. Of this, UNITY."

Brian smiled. "It was one of Voltar's allies. I am sure two kids got to do it."

The report finished. "There are reports of sightings that came in all over the state, not just from Southern California."

"I hope they had a good time," Brian smiled. "I wish I had seen it. Blue is my favorite color."

The Abortion

Debra graduated from her Secretarial School prepared to enter the world of work. But she was pregnant—and frightened. She wanted to prove herself with a career but also she felt Brian had never answered her challenge about Jesus, directly. He always refused to publicly commit to Jesus as the Savior of man. She loved Brian and she loved Voltar, but she still held doubt.

She had seen Brian tell little lies, or exaggerate to get his way. He was still a common man. He was still Brian. She liked Voltar much more. In fact, she wanted Voltar 24 hours a day. But, Brian was in dominance now and Voltar's vegetarian diet had been forgotten.

Brian had gone back to his old ways. He seemed rude, crass, self-centered and obnoxious, at times. So, she still had a nagging doubt that the voices might all be demons, even Voltar.

At Calvary Chapel she had found a brochure about <u>Confronting Familiar Spirits.</u> The descriptions scared her. The Hebrew word for familiar spirit was *ob,* the word for *a leather bottle.* According to the brochure, the Bible says that when a familiar spirit spoke, the voice sounded *hollow* as though it was coming out of a skin bottle. The words stunned her. She thought Voltar sounded a bit like a hollow bottle.

In the Old Testament in Leviticus 20:27, people with familiar spirits were stoned to death. Saul lost his kingdom for consulting a familiar spirit rather than the Lord. And the Jews were ordered not to consult with familiar spirits when they entered Canaan. In fact, God drove the Canaanites out of their land, primarily because they consulted with familiar spirits.

For Debra, the dilemma was serious. She would accept Brian, and she would love to live with Voltar for the rest of her life, perhaps even have children, but not now. Not this baby. She feared the child might be part alien, or used by Voltar. She just couldn't handle the fears, the thoughts, the tension—not while working as a secretary—she'd crack up, go nuts. Maybe her feelings were paranoia, but still—she had not intended to get pregnant.

She scheduled an abortion, despite Brian's protests and pleadings. He even broke down and cried, begging her not to abort the baby. But, she went forward, thinking mostly of her career. She wanted a life as an Executive Secretary, and she wouldn't accept pressure or guilt from anyone.

Brian waited outside during the abortion. Debra emerged, crying and distraught. The nurses and doctors were a bit panicked. Debra had seen two gray, long-eared giants in the room. She had seen them take the baby out of her womb.

"This sometimes happens," the doctor explained to Brian afterwards. "Some women become hysterical." Her screams had upset them all.

But Debra insisted she wasn't hallucinating. She *saw* them.

The doctor whispered to Brian. "The tissue has been disposed of. The baby is dead." He wanted to assure Brian that Debra was hallucinating.

Brian didn't want to hear those words. He cried. They walked to the car, both crying, arm in arm.

Later, Voltar emerged and talked to Debra. "That of the creation--the energy and the being that was created--has been taken, and saved in our world, in our way.

"He will grow into manhood, and he will return on that day, when all the children return, to play with the children of men. When the touch is given and the thousand years of peace begins, he will be among them."

He referred to December 24, 2011.

Brian figured the child would be 34 years old in 2011--his age, at the time.

Debra didn't know what to think. But after the pain passed, she wondered what life might be like without Brian and Voltar.

Wanda says Goodbye

Through March, April and most of May, Brian and Debra lived a normal life. Debra started her first job as a secretary and Brian received a second pay raise for his creative designs. They moved into a two-bedroom apartment. The copper Ford which Brian liked so well, overheated all the time—even with a new water pump. Frustrated, Brian bought a1962 Mercury that looked terrible, but ran very good. "This one is dependable," he said.

Around the middle of May, when Wanda heard me talk of a second trip to South America in June, she flipped out. "I can't take it anymore," she screamed. "Brian is ruining your career. And you are going along with it." She sobbed. "I can't stand to see you following Brian around, anymore. We always do what he wants to do. We have no life. I am so confused. My friends don't believe me. No one believes me at work. You are always at some meeting. I can't take this anymore."

We fought for several days, but one afternoon, she left the house and didn't return. I saw her the next morning at the Paramount gate. She asked me to leave her alone for a while. She had obtained an apartment near the studio.

I was sad. I loved Wanda. She had been a great friend, and had provided key revelations in the story, but I could understand. She hadn't been able to go to South America and she refused to go through another phase of transformation, alone.

Besides, she had suitors—men with normal lives, big houses, nice cars -- people in the film industry. She wanted a different life. After a few days of agony, I let her go and continued on, alone.

The Preparation

A week later, on May 22, at Brian's apartment, two big water drops splashed onto Brian's face, sending his mind reeling. Since the transformation, water drops had been non-existent.

When a drop hit, Brian simply experienced a sudden transition between each Presence—in the middle of a bite, or when dancing on one foot. When a personality manifested, he could pay attention, go to Voltar's world, or just "gray out" and go into a fuzzy, restful sleep.

On the night the water-drops began again, Debra handed me a piece of scratch paper with words scribbled all over the front and back. "I am supposed to give this to you," she said.

"The words are for you, Jim," Voltar said. "The last words in the *Play of Life*. So that you may now know--you have the beginning, the Alpha, and, you have the end--the Omega. Home to God. Kista Homo. Home to God."

The words looked Greek. I figured them to be phonetic:

Dela laous nuwebous shen telsa serian otapa

Danyael, kleasta saveiu.

The second word probably was phonetic for laos—Greek for *the common people, members of a church.*

"What do they mean?" I asked.

"I don't know," said Debra, but he also had me write this down. He said this belonged at the beginning and the end of the *Play of Life,* so maybe it is the same in meaning:

> **Man is Two Men in One. One is awake in Darkness, the other Asleep in Light. When you see between the Two, You will find You, and in that moment the great change-- not only the body, but of the mind—will Awaken you to a World which is Forever and Forever, You.**

Voltar spoke softly. "As I have said, Jim, we will offer all that we can, for our love is with you, and our sadness too for Wanda's departure from your life. She is of greatness, but to each their own mind. We wish only goodness for man, as do you. It is our desire to bring the *Play of Life* to an end, which will bring the answers mankind needs.

"Science must balance with that of the spiritual mind, and the body--and by that, unite all mankind. For your world is just a beginning. You have a long way to go, yet. When the *Play of Life* is complete, and those events transpire of the returning with the children--you must then all reach out to the universe. For you will be then, a light to the universe--the secret, the answer. Man himself is the secret, the answer that so many others need. In this, the spirit of man is of God."

Then the Center of the Universe spoke: "And I await your coming, for you are all My children."

Voltar continued. "In your world, He has spoken to many and they knew Him for what He is. They found no confusion in His words. As we said before, to understand--man must reach backward to his beginning. We will offer you the past of this, and the knowledge. When you see how simple it is, you will be fulfilled."

"Is it the spirit? The Holy Ghost?" I asked. "Are you saying that was God?"

"Be patient. The transformation is soon at hand."

The Center spoke again. "A new beginning and a new world to come."

Voltar gazed at Debra. "We also did not understand all, at our beginning, but we do now. The time will be soon, when I may speak to you and others deeply of these matters--the spiritual side of the unity we all seek.

"Of this, we came to you, as inscribed in the book: *that man reach outward to his brother.* In this, we are reaching outward to man. And when you have the full understanding of this, your world will also reach outward to others, as brothers. But, you will need crafts in which to travel, and in this is the purpose of Brian.

"From his beginning, from this beginning and the *Play of Life,* man will reach outward to all."

"Amazing," Debra gasped.

Voltar looked at me and took the microphone to my tape recorder so he could speak to the people. "Good evening, my friends. The essence of my being is now in the hands of mankind—June twenty-second, 1977. And I thank you for all you have done. God be with you all. " He continued, speaking to Debra and me.

"The second phase of the transformation will take place. This is of you. Go forward as you know best. Reach outward to the people for this must be of others-- in this, the understanding of man. By this, the full meaning of the *Play of Life* will be revealed."

I shrugged. "Hmm. I guess I am supposed to know what to do?"

"Indeed the responsibility for this, and the *Play of Life* is given unto you--the beginning and the end."

I looked at Debra and laughed. We had less than three weeks to raise thousands of dollars. With Wanda's departure, I had not been able to work much at raising money for the trip.

The Journey Begins

I quickly created a one-page flyer about the transformation. With several hundred copies in hand, I stood outside a big theater on Sunset Boulevard. When the movie "Star Wars" ended, and crowds poured out into the street. I held up the flyer, and passed them to interested people.

A few days later, the phone rang. A 31-year-old entrepreneur--Mickey Zalpa wanted to talk about South America. Tall, dark and handsome, Mickey ran a cement construction company. He built skateboard parks all over Los Angeles. He was interested in Incan engineering and water flow systems, but also, he wanted to develop new technology and advanced electronics.

After several meetings, we forged an agreement. Mickey and his wife Linda would fund the trip to South America, including photography of the transformation on 16mm film. Afterwards they would provide six months of office space for Voltar and me with salaries, drafting tables and supplies.

Voltar would be allowed to design new technologies, but Mickey and his partners would have the first right of review. If they chose to develop a product for the marketplace, they could. They would own most of the rights.

Voltar's only stipulation was that he be allowed to select his clothing. He wanted a silver suit with small magnets in the lining, and especially around his waist.

Mickey agreed to provide expense money and a monthly stipend to both Brian and me, immediately. During the trip to South America, Debra was to be given funds to relocate near the office.

Brian quit his job, and gave final notice on the apartment. I sold my car and gave up the house. We were ecstatic about the arrangement. We had obtained everything we wanted in time for the departure on June 18.

But on that day, Brian and Debra fought. Boxes cluttered their apartment, ready to move. Both cars had broken down, and Mickey had not provided the money on time. The contract had not been signed, and Mickey's attorney had quietly gathered up all the rough drafts. He promised to have a final draft for signing—at the airport.

We were all under a pressure due to the short time, and we were asked to understand.

"This is ridiculous," Debra screamed. "I am going to be left here with broken down cars and no money."

"You will have money, today," Brian said. "They promised."

Betrayal

At the airport, Debra hurried along with two-year old Mark in her arms. His face was dirty, and she looked frazzled. Brian and Debra were both exhausted from packing all night, and from fighting.

As we waited for Mickey and his team to arrive, Debra questioned Voltar. "How will this turn out?" she asked. "I have to know. What do you know?"

Voltar said nothing. He had said little since negotiations began.

Mickey's group arrived: four well-dressed young men in their early thirties and Linda, Mickey's wife -- a beautiful, Beverly Hills blonde.

"God, there is a difference between *us* and *them,*" breathed Debra. "I am a mess compared to her."

Mickey told Debra to go to his office. A check would be waiting at the receptionist desk for the full amount.

As for the contract, he promised we would all sign on the airplane. "We will have time to talk about it," he said. I was concerned, but they were ready to go, and our tickets were purchased--round trip. I had pre-loaded everyone's luggage including 15 cases of film production equipment, and enough 16mm film to shoot a documentary.

"Don't worry about anything," Mickey said.

As we prepared to board the plane, Debra fretted. "I don't like this," she whispered to Brian. "The money to move was to be paid in advance. That was clear."

"I don't know what to do," Brian said. "Go to his office after we leave and get the money."

As the line surged forward to board the airplane, Debra grabbed Brian's shoulders.

"I want to talk to Voltar right now. I want to know what is going on. What is going to happen?"

Voltar turned calmly and looked out her. He whispered, "Betrayal."

Debra pulled Brian out of the line. "He said *'betrayal'* Brian. Don't go. Don't go."

"But we have to," pleaded Brian. "We have to, we are boarding now."

Debra's eyes filled with tears. "Brian, please. Please don't leave me."

"I'll be back," he said.

"But, he just said...BETRAYAL."

"I know. I know. But I have to go anyway. I have to go. It's all part of it. That's all I know. Voltar is telling me to go. I will be okay," Brian said. "You'll be okay. We will return." The line surged forward. "It's the *Play of Life,* " said Brian. "We have to go anyway."

Brian hugged Debra one last time. "Don't worry. We'll survive. Call everyone you can for help. Tell them what happened."

PART III

Transformation

Integration

The drive towards meaning.

Norms, values and influence of the culture.

Chapters 21-24

James E. Frazier

Man is

Two Men in One.

One is

Awake in the Darkness

The Other

Asleep in the Light.

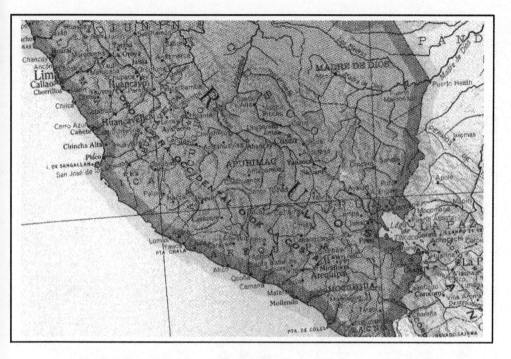

SOUTHERN PERU and WESTERN BOLIVIA – Lima is the capitol of Peru and features an international airport. From Lima planes fly to La Paz, Cuzco, Arequipa and even Nazca.

A train carries passengers from Cuzco to Puno—a beautiful 8 hour adventure.

Most people fly to Lima, then to La Paz and take a taxi to Tiahuanaco—about 90 minutes. Tiahuanaco is 12 miles south of the lake in Bolivia—due west from La Paz where the Tiwanaku Museum is located.

A few people know English—but most do not. Spanish is extremely useful, and mandatory if you get into any complex situations. Aymara and Quechua are the Incan languages.

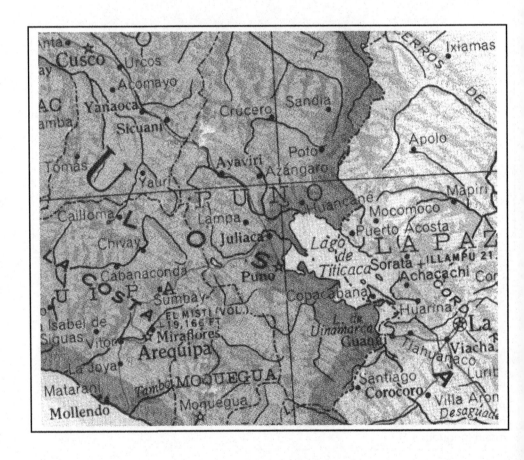

TEMPLE OF TIAHUANACO – SOUTH WALL looking east.

CUZCO NAVIGATIONAL Time Clock from the air. Brian said water played an important role, and many upright columns have been taken away, but the alignments are still valid. The floor pattern relates to Voltar's NOR, the Photonic Matter drawing, and to the Rings of Time on board the craft.

When activated, the "clock" was also "a doorway nebulous to time," according to Voltar. It is the template for his NOR designs and Brian's Photonic Matter drawings.

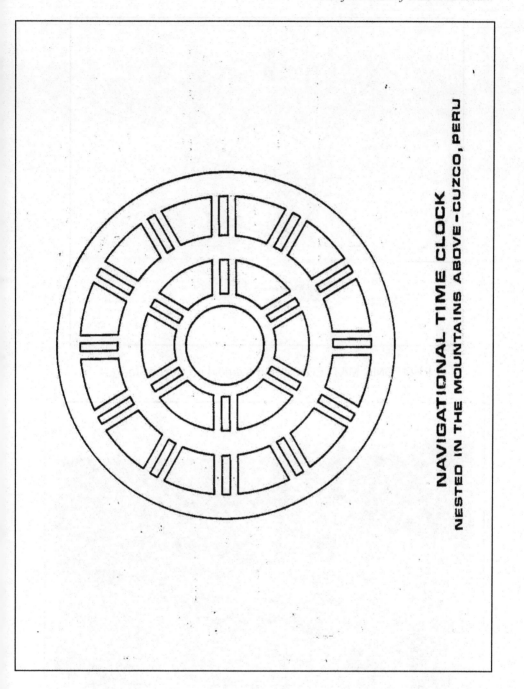

NAVIGATIONAL TIME CLOCK
NESTED IN THE MOUNTAINS ABOVE - CUZCO, PERU

James E. Frazier

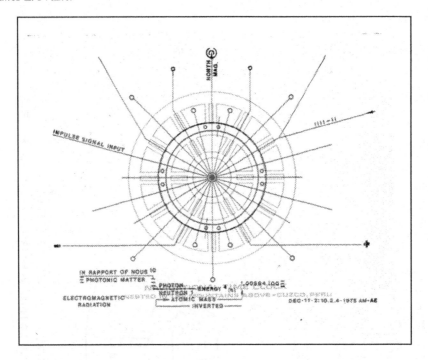

PHOTONIC MATTER drawing overlaid on Cuzco time

574

JUNE 22, 1977 – The doorway waited for Brian--activated again. During phase 2, he was uplifted to Nous 8, and he became fully united as One with Voltar. Convulsions again lasted several days, but this time -- on the *right* arm and leg.

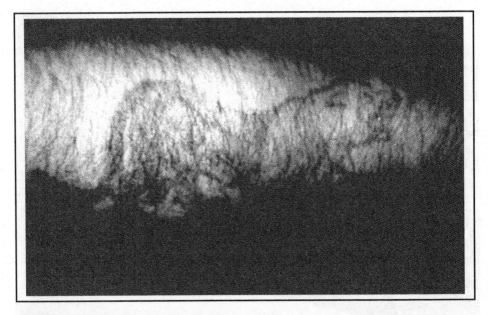

JAGUAR TATTOO on Brian's left arm matched an archaeologist's map of villages around Lake Titicaca. "The People of the Jaguar," Voltar said. In the region, other villages were also linked by animal shapes.

NOUS 8 -- TRANSFORMATION, PHASE 2

COME FORTH ALL THOSE WHO SEEK KNOWLEDGE,
FOR THESE ARE THE DAYS OF TRUTH

-- Voltar

Chapter 21

Transformation – Phase 2

On board the airplane, Brian and I sat together in coach class. Mickey's group sat forward together. They had purchased the tickets and selected the seats.

Within an hour, Brian was engaged in conversation with a dark-skinned man born in Cuzco. Of Incan descent, Julio Haro worked as a costume designer in Los Angeles. About forty, he had emigrated from Peru years earlier.

On this flight back home, Julio was taking a blond girlfriend, Jeannette Creer, to Cuzco for her 30th birthday--June 22. He wanted her to see the famous Incan sun festival in the Plaza of Cuzco. For years, tourists from around the world had flown into Cuzco for the colorful, musical event.

Jeannette had believed for years that on her thirtieth birthday, she would be in Cuzco. She didn't know why, but she felt *called* to be there. Unusual dreams had inspired her to search for links between Israel, the Phoenicians, the Sumerians and the Inca. She had no facts, only visions and dreams. With his birthday present, Juilo was making her dream come true so she could seek out similarities between the cultures.

Julio had grown up in Cuzco. He believed that life originated in Peru. "I have seen things I won't reveal," he said. "But I know life did not just begin in Africa, or on the Euphrates. It started in Peru, too." He whispered cautiously. "But it's dangerous. Two other men who saw what I saw are dead." He had left Peru in fear for his life.

Suddenly Saturn, Tau Ceti and other allies of Voltar started talking to Julio in their usual loud manner. "We haven't even been in the air an hour," I laughed.

"Julio is of the *Play of Life*," Voltar said. Voltar promised to confirm Julio's belief with evidence. "Of this, proof will be given to you as a gift, for in your words are truth," Voltar said.

As all twelve of the allies loudly agreed, passengers in the plane turned to see the source of the commotion. They watched in awe as each distinctive voice proclaimed, "Agreement."

Mickey, Linda and their group were shocked. They pretended not to know us.

When we landed in Lima, Julio and Jeannette agreed to meet us in Cuzco after Phase 2 of the transformation. Voltar and his allies would provide the gift there. I felt Voltar was going out on a limb again.

Jim's Sound Test

That evening, Brian talked about the betrayal. "Voltar said to go on with it—*the Play of Life*--so what can we do? We're here."

I worried that something bad would happen—like death or injury. As I tested the camera and sound equipment, the allies of Voltar began to speak.

"It's starting," Brian said. "Something different. More powerful." He felt dizzy, and disoriented.

I turned on the Nagra sound recorder used for making films. "Testing, Testing," I said. "Anybody want to speak up? We need a sound check."

I recorded sound and set volume levels as each ally of Voltar spoke. In between each personality, Brian experienced a spatial change and disorientation. He could see through walls and into other buildings with his eyes rolled up--or down.

"This is damn weird," Brian complained. Several times, he stumbled and fell down. As he lay on the bed, the Center of the Universe spoke, "Of this, you are one with I."

Then the allies responded, each saying "granted."

"What is happening?" I asked.

Suddenly Brian snapped back. He wobbled and nearly fell down. "Wow," he said. "Unbelievable."

"What is it?"

"Oh, the space-change. Everything goes away except life forms. There wasn't anything here in this room except you."

"What do you see?"

"Well, nothing, but the energy form. And I can see them all over. But not the buildings."

"What did you see of mine?" I asked.

"Oh, yours is blue, white and yellow. The weird part is the headphones. That area stayed the same size. It's weird. I don't think I could handle that."

For Phase 2, Brian had agreed to accept Nous 8. He would receive five more gifts for mankind, including the gift of "Touch." But now, Brian was worried the jump to Nous 8 would be too dramatic, too overwhelming for him to handle.

Martine Martinez

The next morning in the airport, the American Ambassador to Peru staged a press conference. News reporters and TV cameras swarmed around the dignitary.

As we watched, I asked Voltar if he would speak to the media, someday. "Of this, of my unity, and of the people, and of the past, and of the Inca--of these things I will speak to the people. For Viracocha was the beginning of their society. They again need courage, for Viracocha WILL return."

"Will you play a part in this," I asked.

"I only come to reassure them. For their wishes, their desires and their dreams will be fulfilled, and they will again rise to be a great nation."

When we boarded the plane to La Paz, Voltar wanted to sit with others. "I am ready to be with the people," Voltar said.

"Now, in the airplane?

"Let us begin where we now sit." A young Spanish man sat next to Brian. Martine Martinez was an engineering student at the Massachusetts Institute of Technology returning home to Argentina for the summer.

"He doesn't know much of your background," I whispered. "It might be better to start with someone who knows more."

"Then let us start with those who know the least," Voltar said firmly.

I tugged at Martine's arm. "He wants to talk to you."

"Huh," Martine said.

"How do you find the day?" Voltar said.

"How do I find the day?" Martine asked. "I don't understand."

"How do you find this day?" Voltar repeated.

"Fine?" Martine said with confusion.

"Of this, confusion will pass," said Voltar. For you will be one with the All."

"I will be one with..."

"All," Voltar said firmly.

"God?" Martine asked.

"All." Voltar insisted. "All of those about us, and of yourself. You will again soon be one."

"How?" Martine asked politely.

"By the hand. By being. Of this, is your gift from birth."

"I don't understand the gift," Martine said.

"Of this, each person was given, at his birth, the ability to be one with himself, and by that to be one with all. And by your own self, by first understanding all that you are, and reaching out to others--you will fulfill your destiny. Soon, you will begin the work of your life. For this, the mind and the body must be united as one. And by this, the time will be, within your own life, that you will bring to others, the fulfillment of your meaning and your purpose."

579

The words baffled Martin. He looked at me for an explanation. I chuckled as Brian's personality returned.

"What's happening? Was he talking?" Brian asked. "I was out."

I chuckled. "He was talking to this man, who now looks rather pale." I turned to the stunned student. "What did he say?"

"I didn't understand it all," Martine said. "He talked about me being one, that my mind and my body will be one, and through this, I have some purpose that would be...fulfilled. I don't know quite what the purpose was."

Instantly, and smoothly, Voltar's presence emerged. "Tomorrow, you will," Voltar said. "For you are the first of I--of the transformation--and by the gift of touch."

Martine frowned. "What did he say? Tomorrow? What happens tomorrow?"

The Archaeologist – Danilo Kuljus

A few hours later, on June 21, we arrived at the Sheridan Hotel in La Paz, Bolivia. Bellboys in bright uniforms helped unload baggage.

"Not like our first visit," laughed Brian. "We were in a straw manger the night before." We hurried to the Tiwanaku Museum and met the archaeologist for the region, Danilo Kuljis. Though Bolivian, he had been educated at the University of Texas, and he spoke good English. I hoped to get some answers.

In a room of huge maps of the region, Danilo examined the jaguar tattoo on Brian's left arm. "Is that Lake Titicaca?" I asked.

Danilo turned Brian's arm in his hands. "No. No, it is not," he mused. Then he found a big map of the lake region, and lifted up Brian's arm to the map as a comparison. For a moment we all studied Brian's tattoo and the map, comparing points.

"My God," I gasped. "It's a perfect match."

"I would say so," mused Danilo. "How did you do that?"

"Back in 1959," Brian said.

He started to explain, but I stopped him. "We only have a short time, today. Can you tell us about your map? What is it?"

Danilo pointed at the map. Around the lake, a researcher had penned a brightly colored line. "It's Lake Titicaca, but your tattoo doesn't match the lake, it matches the line we drew."

"It is a perfect match," Brian gasped after study in detail. "What is the line?"

"That line connects all the villages around the lake."

Suddenly, Voltar spoke with a deep voice. "The PEOPLE. Viracocha returns to The People."

Danilo looked at Brian in shock. I quickly explained about Brian, Voltar and Viracocha as best I could in five minutes. Strangely, Danilo seemed to understand.

"I have been working on something," he said. "I want to show you something. Maybe you can help." He led us to another room and rolled out a huge aerial map of the region around Lake Titicaca.

On the black and white photomap, white lines had been inked. "Keep this sort of quiet," he said. "No one knows about this. Nothing has been published, okay. We are working on it." He stood back and pointed.

The white lines, drawn on the map, inscribed the figures of various animals and insects. It looked like the Nazca Plain with all kinds of sharply drawn figures.

"But it is not Nazca," said Danilo. "This is several thousand square miles around Lake Titicaca."

"All villages of the people." Brian said.

"That's right," Danilo snapped. "You've got it. How did he know that?"

"If you can come out to Tiahuanaco tomorrow, you'll find out."

"I can't be there," Danilo said. "I've got a meeting, a professional meeting."

In a hurried conversation, Danilo explained that the maps showed lines of connection between the villages, and the lines all portrayed various animals in complex, yet precise designs.

"It's amazing that they would lay out villages like that, at key points in the shape of animals. The pre-planning would be awesome. How could they do it? It seems that they would need to see it all from the sky. This wouldn't be apparent from the ground, but even then if they had hot-air balloons, or something, why do it? Why villages?"

"Of this, there is a meaning," said Voltar. "Those of a certain knowledge and wisdom were joined, united in their beliefs and their duties within the region."

"But why put the villages in a pattern?'

"Why not?" Voltar said. "What better way for the people to know and understand who they are, what they are, and their purpose--simply by walking along the lines."

Danilo smiled in amazement.

I chuckled. "He can tell you a lot about Tiahuanaco."

"The designs are done as drawings and models," Voltar said. "Plan view, looking down from above. Brian knows of this—as a draftsman."

Brian's career and skills began to make sense to me. At work, he drew four views of every object under development by a company: a top, side and front view, then a perspective or three-dimensional view. The top view was called the 'plan' view because it was most often used as the plan.

Of course, ancient architects and builders would also need a draftsman to create the models and plans for a village, for a temple, or for villages spread over miles of land. They would need someone like Brian who could visualize and draw with accuracy – a draftsman designer with mystical knowledge.

We talked rapidly about the design of the temple grounds and the mound of Akapana as an inverted pyramid. "It is still activated," I said. "There is something still there, generating energy."

Danilo gasped. "Who are you guys? Really?" Again, I explained the transformation. Danilo led us into his private office. He shut the door.

"You have just confirmed my own privately held beliefs and research about the mound. It makes sense, an inverted pyramid. The bottom is upright. It's not a pyramid, but an 'inverted pyramid.'" His data supported the idea.

He rubbed his face. "Listen, I don't know if I should tell you this, but in only a few minutes you have opened my eyes to things I have been working on for years."

He pondered deeply. "Listen, I have taken measurements off the mound. Electromagnetic readings," he said. "There are anomalous, unexplainable radiations from the mound. Electromagnetic pulses. No one knows this, but a few very close associates. You are the first people to mention this to me."

"Like I said, he knows a lot about Tiahuanaco," I pointed at Brian.

Brian smiled. "It's not me."

"You guys are onto something, or up to something," said Danilo. "I don't know who you are, but you've got my attention."

He couldn't come to the transformation, but wanted to meet with us afterwards.

Phase 2 – June 22, 1977

The next morning, golden rays of sunlight warmed the beautiful stone doorway at Tiahuanaco as two taxicabs arrived. Wearing heavy jackets and coats, a dozen people unloaded. The air was cold, crisp and the temperature just above freezing. June 22 is the shortest day of the year--the start of winter in the Southern Hemisphere.

Wearing thick gloves, I set up the film camera and trained Mickey to help with sound. For the next several hours, I documented Tiahuanaco on film as Brian led the group from location to location just as he had done before, six months earlier.

In the lower courtyard, Brian stated on camera why he had agreed to experience the transformation. "If this will help people experience their own being, I am happy to do it," he said. "If only one man is saved, it is worth going through."

Around 2:00 p.m., Brian sat down on the steps. The air had warmed, and under a bright blue sky, we didn't need jackets. I joined him wearing a heavy battery belt for the film camera. We talked, alone. Brian wasn't sure what would happen. Voltar had asked him to proceed, despite the warning. Brian had agreed, but he wanted to minimize the problems.

"Keep these people away from Voltar for awhile," Brian said. "For several days, at least. I don't want them just swamping him with questions."

I agreed.

"And if something happens, try to get him to Debra, right away. He really likes her, I guess he loves her in his way. If something goes wrong, get him home, and to her. I don't care what it takes."

I agreed.

Brian's eyes watered. "And don't let these people turn him into a circus, Jim. He's got to wear a silver suit and have magnets in the lining. He must have the magnets to balance the energy, okay? Make sure they do this quickly. Several days at the most. And, make sure it's not some joke to people," Brian sniffled.

"He's going to wear it around Los Angeles. I've done everything I can to talk him out of the suit, but he insists."

"Okay," I said. "I think I can manage all of that. What about you?"

"As far as I know, it's Kista Homo for me. I'll be gone."

"Gone, gone?"

"Nous 8 is too much for me," Brian said. "I will be out of the picture. You'll have Voltar twenty-four hours a day." Brian sniffled again as a tear rolled out of his eyes. "I just hope this pays off for man," Brian said. "This is what is needed."

My eyes suddenly filled with tears. We had been through a lot, and since the last transformation, I did feel responsible for Brian and for Voltar. As everyone watched, we hugged.

"Thank you," I whispered. "Thanks again for going through with this."

"Go with God," Brian whispered.

I ran to the film camera. Brian stepped into the doorway, spread his legs for balance, breathed deep, and shoved his hands out to stone. Bolts of energy shot into his body. Trembling and shaking, Brian fought to stand. He looked up and his eyes rolled back. His head bowed.

After a while, he stood up straight. Brian's arms slowly wrapped around his body. Voltar spoke. "Of this, we are united as One."

The allies of Voltar agreed. "Alignmentem," Saturn blasted.

"Alignment," boomed Mars.

"Alignment," Tau Ceti echoed.

"Alignment," Energy surged.

"Alignment," Lynana squealed.

"Alignment," another gurgled.

"Alignment."

"Alignment."

"Alignment."

"Alignment."

"Alignment."

"Alignment."

"It is done," said Voltar. "Align with those about you." Brian's arms opened and stretched outward to the world. Brian's blue eyes opened. Voltar gazed around at all the people who had gathered. He looked squarely at Martine Martinez, the engineering student.

"Come forth all those who seek knowledge for these are the days of truth."

At that moment, as the people walked forward, my camera batteries drained of all energy. Voltar greeted everyone, and spoke to their hearts as I fiddled with the battery. I couldn't believe the batteries had gone dead at that exact moment.

When I finished my tests and ran to him, Voltar spoke with sorrow.

"Take me from this place quickly," he said. "For the sadness of the stones--and what is to be--is overwhelming."

The people wanted more time with him. Though he had said little to each person, his words touched each heart, deeply. Mickey and Linda were convinced they had witnessed a significant transformation.

We drove back to La Paz, and that evening Mickey made plans to hurry back to Los Angeles. He said there was no need to sign the contracts. We could sign them in Los Angeles. He was convinced. He wanted to get back to LA and prepare the office for Voltar.

That night in heavy rain, Danilo Kuljis, the archaeologist, drove a hundred miles on bad roads to meet with Brian. He arrived late, and Brian's body was sound asleep.

The Touch

Early the next morning as the group prepared to depart for Lima, Martine Martinez, the young engineering student, said goodbye to Voltar.

Martine started to shake hands, but Voltar firmly held the young man's right hand in both of his own." Goodbye my friend," said Voltar. "Of this is given, the fulfillment of your being." Voltar squeezed.

Suddenly Martine closed his eyes. His neck stiffened and his chin lifted, as if breathing deep. He paused for a long time. Finally, Voltar released the young man's hand.

In a daze, Martine glanced at me. "Oh, wow," he said. "Wow! Your friend has a very unusual way of shaking hands," Martine said. "Very unusual."

"What happened?" I asked.

"Oh...I...I..."

Voltar spoke. "All that is needed was given, for the fulfillment of your being, and your purpose. Go forth, from this moment, forward. Speak not of this, for this is of you and your meaning."

Martine stammered. "I thank you." He gasped.

I studied Martine. "Are you okay?"

"Ah. I think so. I just saw, many things, in my mind," he choked back a tear.

"Of this, is of you," Voltar said. "For you will truly be of greatness among your people. What you wish to bring them as you grow older in years, you will. You have been given what you need. Go forth, in joy."

Martine started to cry. Tears dribbled from his eyes and he sniffled. "Thank you," he said. "Thank you. I'll be happy," he sniffled. "I'll be very happy."

"Go forth in joy," Voltar said.

Martine smiled. "Okay, I will. I will go forth in joy." He lifted his head, and carried his luggage, walking with tears of joy streaming down his face.

Voltar turned away from the young man. "There is much to be done. We must go forth to Cuzco--for that of Julio--and the answer to his question, awaits."

Martine flew to his home in Argentina, and we never saw him again.

Julio's Answer

The group arrived in Cuzco on June 24. Chuck had flown back to Los Angeles with Mickey, so only Linda, Woody--the attorney--and Chris remained. Chris was a college psychology student and son of Mickey's business partner.

In a taxi, we cruised near the central plaza. Military guards, armed with machine guns, stood on each corner.

"There were no machine guns last time," I said. "This is strange. The Festival of the Sun is a big deal." Everyone had expected a big crowd.

At our hotel, the desk clerk explained. "The sun rituals were cancelled," he moaned. "Bad for tourism. Mucho bad. Many people have left."

"Why cancelled?" I asked.

The man waited for his supervisor to leave, then he spoke in hushed tones. "Sixteen were killed in the plaza," he said in broken English.

Linda gasped. "Who got killed?"

The man shrugged. "Indians, mostly--a few college students. It was a riot."

"Who killed them?" I asked carefully.

"Police. Military police." He pretended to hold a machine gun, and made sounds like rapid firing. "The Indians," he said. "Every now and then they get big ideas. You know--revolution--take back their land," he laughed. "The police have to let them know--they lost that war—a long time ago."

I glanced at Voltar. "Of the people, and their dream for freedom," he said.

"We better watch our step," the attorney whispered as he ushered the group towards the elevators. "Their legal system is not the same as ours. Here, you're guilty until proven innocent. Don't tell anyone you were here before, six months ago. They may still be looking for you."

Everyone nodded in agreement. "Let's not broadcast to anyone what we are doing," I cautioned. "Especially, don't call Brian, *Ticci Viracocha*." Everyone chuckled.

"He is of greatness, among all people, here--even today," Voltar said. "Of this, fear not." He paused and his eyes rolled upward, then downward. "The answer Julio seeks, awaits," Voltar said.

After checking in, the group met outside the hotel and crowded into an old, beat-up taxicab.

"Where do we go?" I asked Voltar. He raised an arm and pointed. "Pisac."

The Fossil

Six months earlier--after the first transformation--Voltar had led me on a tour to Pisac, an ancient temple, in the beautiful Valley of the Inca. Located on a mountaintop, at the pinnacle of massive steppes, the temple overlooked the lush Ollontombo River valley.

Voltar had described the water engineering, rituals of the priests, and sun measurements. He had wanted me to see a big, raw, un-carved stone that was holy to the Inca, like the raw stone at Machu Picchu—located in a round building. The un-worked stone was considered the most holy, and most powerful stone in the temple complex. I figured it had been activated, first, or brought them a first taste of paranormal power, like Brian's white rock.

This time, however, Voltar led the group around to the backside of the mountain. No ruins could even be seen as we trudged up a narrow dirt trail.

Voltar walked stiffly and slowly with his eyes rolled back in his head. He received direction from the probe, and then pointed a path through the brush until we had climbed about halfway up to the top of the peak. We were stranded in knee-high brush.

Finally, Voltar stopped. "Here, the stairway," he said. The group looked around and saw no stairway. "There is nothing here," I shouted.

"It is here," Voltar said.

Woody, the mustached attorney, and Chris began kicking at the brush looking for any sign of steps. Finally, Woody shouted. "Hey. There are steps."

Voltar remained at the bottom of the slope, with his eyes rolled up. "Upward," he said.

Woody and Chris trudged up the slope as their feet found ancient steps their eyes couldn't see because of thick brush. "This is a stairway," Chris breathed. He had studied psychology and anthropology in college. He wanted to understand Brian's story from a cultural perspective. "It's amazing that he would know about this tiny path," he shouted. The steps were small and ordinary compared to the huge, beautiful steps near the temple.

"Now, Jim," Voltar said. "Go up."

"He wants me to walk up the stairs," I announced.

"Slowly," Voltar blurted from below as I moved up the steps.

I slowed down and looked at Voltar. He was leaning against a stone, looking away from the slope, peering out over the distant valley.

"How is he seeing this?" Linda asked.

"He can see without his eyes. He sees energy forms," I said taking another step.

"Stop," Voltar said. I could barely hear his words.

"Stop," echoed Linda. "He said stop."

I froze. "There, beneath the footstep of Jim, the answer will be found," Voltar said.

Linda looked at Voltar. "What did you say?"

Voltar turned and spoke to Linda. "It is for you to find--beneath the footstep of Jim. Of this, the *Play of Life,* and the meaning therein for man."

"What does he mean?" Linda asked me. "I think he wants me to look under your foot." I had not moved.

"Which foot?" I shouted.

Linda climbed up the steps until she could see my left boot, but the right foot was obscured by tangled brush.

"Which foot?" Linda shouted down the steps to Voltar.

"It is that of the right," said Voltar without turning his head around. Again, he faced out across the valley with eyes rolled up.

"How can he be seeing anything?" Linda asked.

"They give him information," I said. "Through the probe."

She shrugged. "I don't understand any of this. He's not even looking."

"Beneath the footstep of Jim," Voltar boomed. "In this, understanding will come for man."

Linda exhaled with frustration, then she gingerly cleared brush away from around my right boot. She saw nothing.

"Can you lift up you foot?" she asked, frustrated.

I rocked upward. Linda squinted. In the shadow, she saw a gold-colored, shiny stone about two inches long, oblong and polished.

587

"Oh my God," she gasped.

"You have found the answer," Voltar said. "The knowledge Julio seeks."

As my foot lifted, sunlight streamed into the shadow. On the smooth, shiny rock, Linda suddenly saw a small, smiling face. It looked human.

She screamed, softly, but in a frightened way that made Woody and Chris race down to her side. I backed up and clicked photos rapidly.

She picked up the stone and gasped with excitement. "What is this? LOOK AT THIS. Is it an egg? A petrified egg?"

"It's a fossil of some kind," Chris said in amazement. "It does have a face." A human-like face smiled beneath two big, open eyes. The features were perfectly formed, symmetrical and balanced. No one could believe the stone's beauty, or what happened, and for a moment we all shared awe and wonder.

Woody held out the stone for me to photograph. Voltar's eyes rolled down. He stepped forward to see. He was curious to see it with physical eyes. "Of Julio," Voltar said. "The gift."

"But what is it?" Woody asked turning the stone in his hands.

"It is the answer to the riddle which Julio seeks; it is a new beginning for man."

"A new beginning?" Chris mused. "Is this some alien life form? Or a petrified egg, or a seed of man, in some way."

Voltar frowned. "Of the earth, of common knowledge, but in this, the location is not as man would expect. Give this to Julio, and let *him* share it with various learned men, and scholars. Let him say to them, not, where it was found, but let him listen to their words and ponder with them, before he speaks, again."

"This is common?" Chris asked. "I've never seen anything like this." They all nodded in agreement. Never had I seen such a smooth, polished fossil, cut with such clear features.

"The answer is not in what it is, but in WHERE it is," Voltar said. "In this-- the location. Let Julio ask. And—to him the wisdom shall be given of what to say, and when. For this is the answer he has sought. The gift will hold great meaning and purpose in his life."

Woody and Linda looked at the beautiful fossil in awe, and began to silently covet the fossil, and estimate the financial value.

"It's Julio's," I said, gently lifting the stone from their hands.

The Betrayals Begin

That night, at the hotel front desk, I checked for messages. Julio had not arrived at his hotel. Linda and Woody were waiting for me in the lounge. "We have seen enough," Linda said. "We are ready to go back."

"But what about Toro Muerto?" I asked. "We have to go there--and to Nazca—for filming. That was our deal." We had agreed on sites for the documentary in advance.

"You can stay in Cuzco for another day, or two," she said. "The hotel will put everything on my credit card. Then go down to Lima. Check into the Lima Sheraton. I will leave my credit card there for you. You can use it. Just come back on time."

Brian and I had tickets with a return date set, about five days later. Chris had volunteered to stay and help us with filming.

I asked Woody for a copy of the contract. "Mickey didn't leave it with me," he said. "Nothing to worry about, though," he assured. "Everything is working out fine."

"This isn't the right way," I protested. "We need a copy, at least."

"You've got your trip and filming paid for. What could go wrong? You'll get a copy when you get back. Marshall has everything with him."

I was very disappointed. All along, I was led to believe Woody had the contracts with him. Then Woody cleared his throat. "The other thing is, since Julio hasn't shown up, we thought it might be a good idea to take back the fossil--to protect it."

"Protect it?" I asked.

"So it doesn't get lost when you are traveling all around."

"I'll keep it in my purse, so customs doesn't see it," Linda said.

"It's for Julio," I countered.

"But, he's not here. I'm sure he'll be coming back to Los Angeles," she argued. "But, if you guys go climbing all over the Andes, it might get lost--or stolen from your hotel room. I will take it back in the morning, and put it in a vault. It'll be much safer."

"I know how Voltar works," I warned. "This has to be given to Julio, and *he* has to take it to scholars and ask the questions."

"We just want to make sure it is in a safe place," Linda said. "That way you can concentrate on filming. That's what you need to do."

I didn't want to take a chance of losing the golden fossil, so—I reluctantly agreed. That was a big mistake.

The next morning, as Linda and Woody departed with the fossil, Chris and I loaded the heavy cases of film equipment into a taxi. I wanted to film Pisac since we had no film footage of the site. Voltar waved goodbye with his somber expression. "If it gives you peace of mind, so do," Voltar said. I felt uneasy about his words.

I was looking for Toro Muerto as requested in Brian's writings. We only knew it was somewhere in the Andes—that's all. Pisac held royal tombs of the

Inca, and local guides felt it *might* be considered Toro Muerto—place of the dead bull. I wanted to see the tombs. Voltar had promised to stay close to the hotel, and for the first time I left him alone, unsupervised.

In the taxicab, I queried a fat Spanish driver with a crucifix on his dash.

"It is not called, Toro Muerto," he laughed. "But who cares? Who knows? Maybe it is. You have a camera. Call it anything you want, but don't film the Indians."

I asked why. "They get mucho big cabasa," he said. "Big head. Much importante. You Americanos film them, put them on TV--not good. Big cabasa. We have too much trouble with them already. We had to kill them and cancel their Sun Festival." I was stunned.

The government of Peru didn't know what to do with the Indians, the driver said. "When the Spanish took over, we let them stay on their land. Not like you in America. You put your Indians on reservations and gave them smallpox so most of them died. You took their land. We didn't. We were much more humane and forgiving than Americans. Today, we allow them to work and live on their own land, to keep their culture, as long as they don't protest. But sometimes they get riled up."

He was right. In both Peru and Bolivia, I had seen thousands of Incan families in native dress—in the cities, in the countryside, everywhere. In comparison, in the United States, we rarely saw Indians working and living in native dress, especially not in major cities. Our Native Americans lived on reservations, or integrated into the dominant society, wearing White Man's clothes. Of course, some Incan descendants had followed the path of integration, but most had not. Many tried to survive on their family's land, and hold onto their pre-Spanish culture.

"As for the ruins," the driver said. "The government doesn't know what to do with them. Tourists bring money--lots of money. We don't know whether to tear them down, or build roads to them. So many people are coming to see the ruins now since the Van Daniken book. They even want to fix up more of them."

I laughed. Maybe Voltar would bring thousands more tourists, someday.

"But, if the Indians start thinking they are something special, that is bad," he said

That evening, when I returned to the hotel, sunburned and exhausted from filming, the desk clerk waved.

"Mr. Frazier," he said. "You have visitors waiting in the café." He pointed at three men in the restaurant. "That is the manager of the Cuzco TV station, Anton Ponce DeLeon," said the clerk. I glanced in the restaurant to see a distinguished, white-haired Spanish man in a business suit waiting with two younger men, also in nice suits. I was surprised, I hadn't called a TV station, I had called one local "Paranormal Research" group for information on Toro Muerto.

As I started into the restaurant, the desk clerk tugged my arm. "But first, your friend Mr. Scott has run into some trouble." He pointed to the rear of the lobby.

I peered across the dark room to see three uniformed policemen standing over Voltar. He sat in a chair with his hands behind his back, clearly bound in handcuffs.

Voltar Detained

One of the big policemen in a military-style uniform stepped forward. "Are you Mr. James Frazier?"

"Yes. What is happening?"

Voltar stood up with his hands cuffed behind his back. "Of this, an error, Jim. They await your return, for of this, to discuss. Of this, *the Play of Life,"* Voltar said.

Then the voice of Lynana spoke. *"If it gives you peace of mind, so do."*

I knew instantly what she meant. I should not have left Voltar alone. It was a test—in the *Play of Life*—something to learn.

I took a deep breath. On the couch sat a Spanish man, about twenty years old, also handcuffed. "What happened?" I asked the officers.

The Captain politely explained in broken English as he pointed at the young man. "This Federal Exchange teller received money from Mr. Scott, we don't know how much, perhaps two twenty dollar bills, and for some reason--we have not determined why--he apparently returned the value of $400.00 in *soles* in exchange." *Soles* are the Peruvian dollars. The word means *sun.*

I frowned at Voltar. "Did you do that on purpose?"

"An error," Voltar said. "That of the young man. They wish to incarcerate him--or I."

"Where is the money?"

The Captain explained. "Mr. Scott was very cooperative. We accompanied him to your room, and we found the paper work, with his small purchases this afternoon and the change, which amounts to most of two hundred dollars. He paid the difference of about fifteen dollars, American."

"Well, fine, that lets Brian off, right."

"Not exactly," the Captain said. "It is against the law to obtain money for another person," he said. "For each must sign the form."

I didn't understand. "What other person?"

He received $400 in value. He gave another $200 to a Texan, who had asked him to make the exchange."

"Then the Texan was pulling a fast one on my friend," I said

Another officer leaned forward and spoke in broken English. "*If there was a Texan.*" He imitated a southern Texas drawl, perfectly.

"We find no evidence of this other man, except hearsay," said the Captain. "We can't go on that. In any event, your friend signed for the money and received it. He is responsible for returning it all. He still owes $200."

"But the teller made the mistake," I said. "Mr. Scott wouldn't even know how much he received. It could have been $10 or $20 or $200."

"That is what we are trying to determine," the Captain said. He doesn't know how he made the mistake. But the cashier is short. He apparently gave $400 instead of $40. We think, perhaps, maybe your friend tricked him in some way."

I took a deep breath and studied the college student. He looked wholesome, and innocent, but very frightened. "Please, don't let them throw me in jail," he pleaded in broken English. "I'll do anything."

"What if this boy just pays the money," I asked.

"Fine," said the officer. "But he has no money. He is a student, a trainee. We will have to take him to jail--and Mr. Scott--until the matter is resolved."

"Don't let them take me," cried the boy. He sweated, nervously—terrified. He was either a great actor, or he had done nothing wrong.

I figured this was my first big real life test in the *Play of Life.* I decided to take the tough position. Together, Brian and I had only $200. That was our expense money for the rest of the trip—a week of travel. I couldn't risk being penniless in Peru.

"Basically, I don't care about this man," I said pointing at the teller. "As far as I am concerned, he made a mistake. I don't care if you take him to jail."

The boy screamed. "No. NO. PLEASE."

"Of this, he fears that of which we know," Voltar said.

The policemen all leaned forward to listen as Voltar spoke.

"What is wrong with him, anyway?" the Captain whispered to me. "He talks funny. I understand English, and he still talks differently."

"Oh, he has a little problem--a little slow," I said, tapping my head. The Captain nodded in agreement.

"So, basically, I don't care," I said. "This man made a mistake. He should pay for it. Mr. Scott returned his half of the money. I don't see how you can hold him."

The Captain looked at Voltar with compassion. "I don't think Mr. Scott is a common thief," he said. "Still, we have a question that has not been answered. Why did the teller give the money to Mr. Scott in the first place?"

I figured Brian might have tried a con of some sort because I was worried about funds. The Captain spoke firmly. "Mr. Frazier, we had agreed to wait for your return out of courtesy to you as an American citizen, but if you have no resolution, we must take them. We will get to the bottom of this before the night is over." He glanced at his two officers. They stood up and started to man-handle Voltar and the student--as prisoners.

In desperation, I mentally shot a quick question up to the probe. "HELP. What is this? What is going on?" It was the first time I had ever asked the probe for help, and I was surprised to hear a voice respond—from Brian.

"That of the vulnerability of Voltar," blasted Saturn's voice from Brian's lips.

"What is that?" gasped the Captain. The other two officers recoiled. "That *voice*. He did that before."

"You don't want to know," I said. "He has a problem, a cabasa problem." I tapped my head again. The officers nodded with understanding and laughed among themselves with concern. They really didn't want to deal with mental problems. They wanted to leave Voltar with me.

I gestured for them to wait. "We can work out something. But, I am not putting out our last $200 to save this guy from jail. I just can't," I said.

"Please," the boy cried out. "Please. I will pay you back. I will work it off, somehow, and pay you. Please, please don't let them take me to jail."

I glared at the boy. "You made the mistake. You have to pay--not my friend."

Voltar stood up. "Of this Jim, if there is any other solution, I would prefer it-- for he is truly innocent."

"No," I said firmly, whispering to Voltar. "I made one mistake already by leaving you alone. I am not making another by giving our last money away to save this guy from jail. We would have only twenty dollars left. That is wrong. Twenty dollars! I just can't do that."

The Captain stepped forward. "My compatriots feel that we should take them both in for questioning. There is just too much here that doesn't make sense."

"No," I said. "NO. Let me think. We can work something out." Just then I heard the clerk shout my name. I looked up to see Julio and Jeannette at the front counter asking for Brian.

"Julio," I shouted. "JULIO, WE NEED HELP."

The voice of Saturn blasted from Brian's lips. "Thirty kilometer radius. Location possible. Energy form detectable—30 kilometer radius."

The policemen all recoiled at the loud blast. They saw Brian's eyes roll up, then down. They were very concerned, and did not want him in their jail all night. So negotiations began.

As Julio talked to the police officers, the distinguished man in the café approached me. Mr. Ponce De Leon introduced himself with the deep resonate voice of a TV news anchor. He offered to help. "I research UFO's on the side" he said. "That is the capacity in which I am here." He handed me a card for his organization: Paranormal and UFO Investigations. We would like to meet with you and Brian."

I ushered the UFO investigators back into the cafe. "Right now, I am trying to keep him out of jail," I said earnestly.

"I am general manager of the Cuzco television station," Anton said. "Perhaps, if I talked to them--I am well known in this community. I could make a difference." He smiled with assurance. He must be in *the Play of Life,* too. I thought.

We shook hands, and with confidence Anton followed me back to the room with the police. The Captain recognized Anton and nodded with respect. Anton spoke to the Captain in Spanish. "These are Americans--very important Americans. They are making a film for television. If you can provide leniency, I would be grateful."

The Captain nodded politely as we began a final round of talks. He looked Voltar in the eyes. "You seem to have a lot of important friends," the officer said man to man. "That is surprising, in the short time you have been here." Voltar nodded agreement.

The Captain looked at me. "He has a lot of friends for a man with a 'cabeza' problem." The Captain and I laughed together, both caught in a web of mystery within the *Play of Life.*

"I think we can find the money," I whispered to Julio. "Saturn said something about a 30 kilometer radius. They must have a plan. Just get us some time to find the Texan."

Julio spoke quickly in Spanish. The Captain asked a lot of questions which Julio quickly answered. After a while, the Captain gestured at Voltar. "Release him," he said.

He looked into Brian's face. "Do not try to leave town," he warned. "Don't go to the airport, or train. Or you will be arrested. I will give you 24 hours, until 8 pm tomorrow night, to come up with the money."

The Captain glanced at the young teller. "Release him, too." He glared at the nervous young man. "You also have twenty-four hours, and you must be at work tomorrow on time. We will visit you there."

He nodded to the TV station manager. "I hope you will see that the police of Cuzco are not heavy handed, " he said in Spanish. The two men nodded at each other, and shook hands in mutual respect.

The Captain looked at me. "We will return at 8:00 p.m. tomorrow. If the money is not here, we will arrest both Mr. Scott and Mr. Ramirez. They will both go to jail and face felony charges of theft."

I gasped. He was dead serious. "You have twenty four hours." He gestured and then marched away with his men.

Julio looked at me. "Do you think he can find the Texan?"
"If he is within 30 kilometers."

Jeannette smiled at everyone. She looked like an all-American woman wearing long straight hair and an Incan poncho. Her dream had been fulfilled—to be in Cuzco for her thirtieth birthday--but since the Sun Festival had been cancelled, she had changed plans. "Sorry we got here late," she said. "We took a hike on the Incan trial." She was intelligent, and articulate. Talking to her seemed so easy compared to everyone else. She and Julio both promised to help.

I quickly explained how Voltar had found the fossil for Julio. But, he would have to wait to see it—in Los Angeles.

He turned to Anton and his younger investigators. "I will help interpret for you," Julio said. We all slipped into the café. Late into the night, we talked with Anton and his assistants. Brian laughed at some of their stories about the 12-foot aliens with red hair and blue eyes who had visited the Incan people.

"They are only eight feet," Brian chuckled. He answered their questions about who was living in the tunnels connecting Tiahuanaco to sites in Ecuador. "That's the Secondary World," he said. "Stay away from the tunnels." They knew of the dangers. Men had died in the tunnels, and never been found.

He gave them procedures to follow. "If you go into the wrong tunnel, and do the wrong things, you will be killed." Brian's instructions were precise.

Later, Voltar emerged and shared, also. At the end of the evening, Anton agreed to be filmed on camera making statements about the "illuminated mind" of the Inca and their use of magnetic fields. But first, we had to find the money.

The Illuminated Mind

Early the next morning, Voltar led the group in two taxies up to Sacsahuaman, the huge fortress overlooking Cuzco. The name in Quechua means, *"illuminated mind,"* said Anton. He showed us the entrance door. To one side of the door, a deep impression had been cut into the rock-- a serpent's head and body.

To me, the image looked more like a brain and spinal cord. "We call it a serpent," said Anton. "Maybe you are right, maybe it is the brain. We do know this is the Temple of the Illuminated Mind."

Voltar placed his fist inside the carved out bowl – the brain of the serpent. "Of this, the magnetic field would touch the hand, and of the hand--the MIND," he said. "When the stones are activated, they give to man, the knowledge needed—Universal Knowledge—the uplifting of mind—like Brian at Tiahuanaco." I began to understand. The stone served as a transmitter of a

595

magnetic energy field that could 'uplift' the mind of man, when activated by the probe.

"The anchor is stone," Voltar said. "Man needs stone, as an anchor."

Voltar encouraged each person to place a hand into the fist-sized bowl. "In these things, we did play a part, for we were here, but greater was our involvement at Machu Picchu, and far greater at Tiahuanaco--for there was the beginning."

Sacsahuaman is a giant fortress with one huge wall 1500 feet long and sixty feet high. This zig-zag shaped wall is built of giant-sized stones. Many weigh 10-20 tons. Some stones are polygonal with up to a dozen corners and sides, yet all fit together perfectly, without mortar. Not even a knife blade could slip into any union. Each juncture is custom carved, and polished to perfection.

The construction seemed impossible. Worse, no one knew who built the fortress. Historical records of the Inca indicated the fortress existed before their time. Their legends say giants with supernatural powers moved the stones before the time of the Flood.

Voltar said nothing about the fortress stones. He led the group through the doorway and up to a circular monument that looked like three rings on the ground. These stones didn't reach up high, and since they were flat on top, we climbed up and walked on the circular paths. The openings between the paths were perfectly shaped and deep. "Pools," Voltar said. "Of the water and the reflections of light." He said that water filled openings within and around the three rings of stone.

Voltar called this site the time clock, the *navigational time clock*. When Brian looked at the stones, he remembered the three "Rings of Time" on the floor, inside the craft. They were similar in size and shape.

From earlier reading, I knew this sundial was called the 'eye of the jaguar'--the 'seat of the soul,' of Cuzco. Cuzco was laid out in the shape of a jaguar, and this was the eye—the soul—the most sacred site of the jaguar city, home of the jaguar priests.

"Of this, the full meaning and knowledge of Brian's drawings--that of the overlays," Voltar said, gesturing at the three circles. "For in this, is the key to the knowledge man seeks, Nous two through ten, and more--much more."

I was the only one that understood. Brian's drawings had all used the Photonic Matter drawing as a template. Voltar meant that the Photonic matter drawing would overlay on the time clock.

As I studied the stones, I could imagine the drawing, aligned to magnetic north. The positive and negative terminals must lie on the ground in identifiable stones. The impulse signal coming into the center must be the sunrise point on the summer solstice. Amazed, I hurried around trying to see where the alignments might be, while imagining water in pools between the stones—water reflecting the golden colors of sunrise or sunset.

Down below in the valley, I imagined a temple complex covered in real gold. The Spanish must have been stunned to find buildings of gold.

As I studied the design, Voltar began speaking loudly to the crowd. Walking stiffly, Voltar shuffled around the site, outside the rings. His eyes were rolled up, as the allies provided direction.

Finally, he stopped in front of bushes below one of the huge carved stones. "There," he said pointing into the bushes. "Money. Of the man from Texas, for it fell from his pocket as he walked here, yesterday."

"The money is in that bush?" I asked.

"Indeed," Voltar said with his eyes rolled up into his head, and one hand pointing to the bush. He is in trouble, I figured. Either way, I was upset.

Seeing inside the thick brown vegetation was difficult. I pulled at the branches, but saw nothing. "Let this be of those who are with you, the female, for this is of Lynana," Voltar said. Voltar glanced at Jeannette.

The presence of Lynana had helped find the fossil and some of the earlier materializations. Her high-pitched "voice" was the only obvious female among the allies.

"I think he wants you to look in the bush," I shouted to Jeannette. She didn't understand. "You, Jeannette—look in the bush."

She reluctantly began looking into the base of the huge, tangled bush. She climbed up onto the stones of the time clock. She searched down into the vegetation from above, squinting into the dark shadows.

"This is so weird," Chris said to Julio. "But this is exactly how he found the fossil." He pointed at Voltar's eyes which remained rolled up in his head. Voltar didn't even look at the point of interest. He faced away from the people.

I expected this event to be embarrassing. For the first time, I figured Voltar would be wrong. For a moment, I imagined him in a dark jail in Cuzco locked away for weeks, or months. How would we get him out? I wondered. We had no money for an attorney. How far would they go with this *Play of Life*? I thought of Joseph in the Bible, and the apostles that had been imprisoned, and freed by an angel. Maybe that's what they had in mind—Voltar freed miraculously from jail. After all, they could dream up anything in their *Play of Life*. But, then man had free will. They might leave Voltar in jail, and make me figure a way to get him out. This could be terrible, I reasoned. Voltar could rot in a dark, dungeon and I would be blamed for leaving him in South America--alone.

"I see something," Jeannette shouted. She lay down flat peering down into the bushes. Everyone watched as she struggled to reach out with the full length of her arm. Someone else held her legs so she didn't fall down into the bush.

"Is it money?" I shouted.

"I don't know," she said, groaning. Then suddenly she jumped up to her knees. "Yes!" she said holding up a wad of bills. "*Yes!* Look at this." She waved a handful of folded bills – Peruvian *soles.*

I was relieved. My doubts had peaked out. "You did it again," I said.

"It is not of I," said Voltar solemnly. "But of Lynana and the allies."

"How much is it?" I shouted at Jeannette.

She counted. "That is exactly two hundred dollars," she shouted. "Incredible. Absolutely, incredible."

She clapped, and everyone burst into applause for Voltar.

"It is that of learning and wisdom," said Voltar to me. "For in this, you must know, errors do exist and repercussions are costly. If the man had departed outside the primary scanning radius of 32 kilometers, the energy form of the money could not have been located, and I would be with the young man, in jail this evening. Of this, for you to know and understand."

"I've got the picture," I said. "Whenever you say, *'If it gives you peace of mind, so do'*—don't do it.'"

Jeannette handed me the money, and I held it up. "In the normal world, this would be called a miracle—or a hoax." Everyone laughed.

I still felt Brian might have planted the money. He could have placed it there, on purpose, when I was gone filming. So, I didn't add the event to my list of paranormal anomalies. Instead, I scored a point to *hoax or fraud*—by Brian or Voltar, it didn't matter. I was still upset that I might be blamed for causing such a serious situation.

Voltar spoke up as everyone gathered. "Of the camera, and the knowledge of the people, we must begin--for Toro Muerto awaits, and nearby--it is not. Let Anton's wisdom be recorded by the film device, for this is important to man."

We took the money to the police and were cleared of any debts. For the rest of the day, we traveled to ancient sites surrounding Cuzco. Anton showed us a location where the Incans believed a tall, red-haired man had come from space to teach their ancestors about the *'energy of the being.'*

As I filmed, Anton stood in the center of a small amphitheatre with high walls of natural stone. It looked very similar to "The Place of the Whole" back in Orange County. "The spaceman told the Incan forefathers that a magnetic field from the rock could influence their body and their energy field," he said. "The *energy of their being*. It was described as a monkey, jumping around. He talked about energies of the body, and their mind—and gave many examples. This was the beginning of their knowledge, and of Sacsahuaman, fortress of the Illuminated Mind." I was amazed. He sounded just like Voltar.

"This will again, be a beginning for man," said Voltar endorsing the words. "For of this, is the NOR which Brian will build, in the days to come."

We filmed for two days around Cuzco with Anton. I learned much about the most ancient sites of the Inca. He showed us a frog carved in stone, and caverns of polished black rock.

Voltar listened to the Incan legends and smiled. He corrected the errors at times, but concluded. "The knowledge man needs is within the People. Of this, you have seen, Jim. All that is needed is here, already. With this knowledge of the past, and understanding of today, man may now begin to create, and build devices which would uplift the mind."

On the last day, Voltar led us back to the time clock at Sacsahuaman. "This is the beginning for man of today," he said. He explained how the three circles of the time clock were similar to the three-ringed computer on board the craft. He described how water in the pools reflected light from the sun and flames from torches at night. Brightly burning torches around the outside edges provided a reddish-orange light that reflected off mirrors on the dresses of whirling dancers. Whirling fire flashed into the eyes of young initiates, triggering trances and opening their minds.

Voltar described how holes in pillars of stone, could be used with mirrors to make flashing patterns of light at certain rhythms in harmony with the beautiful music. He said that frequency of the flashes could induce trances.

He talked about the music of flutes and how the mind of a few chosen initiates had been stimulated from birth so their growth accelerated beyond others. He described how skulls had been opened with surgery, and brain tissue stimulated directly with tools that vibrated. The technology of Tiahuanaco had been transported to Cuzco and implemented in the House of the Illuminated Mind.

"The knowledge of the past," said Voltar. "A New Beginning for Man."

I understood. I knew that scientists in psychology, neurobiology and cognitive sciences would understand the process. "Begin with the children," Voltar said. "Of this, in the crib, of stimulation with patterns of light and sound, in harmony with measured rhythms. Build the NOR, patterned on that of the Time Clock, and man will create his own uplifting — and eventually -- his own Matter Displacement Vehicle.

"In this, the *Play of Life,* of man—of the people, and their agreements. For all must be done *of the People, by the People and for the People,*" he said.

"Laos Nous Hikano," a deeper voice boomed from Brian's body. *"The God Mind of Man Returns*--of his own hand, of his own will--maintained with wisdom and understanding by the Common People."

I understood. "All has been given," said Voltar with gentle compassion.

I could see the need for development of new psycho-biological technologies that might apply to learning and education, to bio-telemetry and bio-monitoring on earth—even to travel in space.

Space travel was still my primary interest—astronauts. I had wanted to be involved with their training as an experimental psychologist. Now, I could see that trances and altered states might be helpful in long space voyages, like to Mars—or even in a space station. I could see that paranormal "cheap thrills" weren't necessary for developing technology and research in a business-like manner. I could see dozens of potential products and great business potential.

Mickey and Linda would be rich, someday—I guessed. When we returned to Los Angeles, the process would begin of designing, financing and actually *building* a new technology for man—the foundation of a psycho-cybernetic civilization.

Voltar would design on paper, and using my background in psychology and biology, I would administrate the projects, write the technical manuals and perhaps, design the psychological training. I could also use my skills in film production for training videos, marketing and sales.

It all made sense.

Money could be earned by everyone, except Brian. He could not profit, personally. Mickey and Linda would have first rights to market any products. They and their investors would profit handsomely.

The situation seemed ideal.

Voltar and I would both live in Los Angeles, within walking distance of the offices on Wilshire Boulevard.

Within six months, Mickey would be able to present a full package of drawings and support materials to investors for financing—new products for the future.

I knew Voltar would perform. I had interviewed Brian's supervisors. He worked hard. He had helped develop new products and new manufacturing processes. Brian's background was perfect. We were not out of line, or starting something unfamiliar to him. He had been trained and employed as a draftsman in new product design. We were on track.

At the very least, even without Voltar's help, Brian could qualify as a New Product Designer based on work tasks and job duties. In addition to his employment record, Brian had drawn schematics of the bio-telemetry scanner—for the remote sensing of human beings, from space satellites.

So, our plan wasn't a stretch of imagination. We had not exaggerated or mislead Mickey in any way. I had convinced Mickey and Linda to accept the deal based on Brian's work background and employment history—not on Voltar. Consider Voltar a *'bonus,'* I had said. Just take Brian at face value. In our talks, Mickey had agreed.

Everything was in place. By now, Debra should be decorating a new apartment in Los Angeles. The professional drafting table should be waiting for Brian, and a furnished office waiting for me with a fancy typewriter—an IBM Selectric with white erasing ribbon--that's what I wanted as my special gift. I had never owned a typewriter with a white erasing ribbon.

Together, Brian and I would operate in the office as a design and marketing team. I was willing to try it, for six months, just to see what Brian might create--let alone Voltar.

Then, the betrayals began.

Three betrayals of man destroyed Voltar's hope, and devastated my dreams of the future.

FOSSIL is FOUND – A trilobyte with a perfectly formed, eerie face is found under Jim's foot on the priest's staircase -- a secret entrance to the temple at Pisac. The fossil was a gift to Julio Haro, supposedly evidence that life originated in the Western hemisphere of Earth--as well as in the Eastern hemisphere.

JIM'S GIFT -- The "X" marks the spot for correct location of the Gate of the Sun in the Temple of Tiahuanaco. These rocks at Toro Muerto are located over 600 miles away from the temple near the coast. They were used for "planning," Voltar said.

The north-south aligned wall separates the Priest's court from the Public court used for dancing, healing and worship by the temple women. Note the dancer.

Outside the temple, the south side was used by common people for worship and religious dancing. Note the dancer with bended knees. The east doorway, the Portal to Life, is linked to the lower, subterranean courtyard—which was underground, Brian said.

THE PROBE – The Mark of Voltar's People. Voltar had promised Brian that he would find an image of the probe carved onto stone at Toro Muerto. Among thousands of carvings, Voltar found this stone in minutes. Supposedly, the probe can track an individual from space, and transmit a signal to his body that activates the mind, and the energy of the being. The man appears to radiate-- perhaps the ten rays indicate mind level 10.

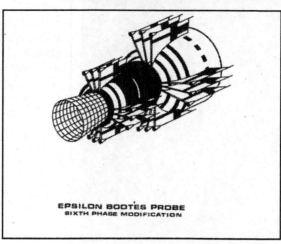

EPSILON BOOTES PROBE
SIXTH PHASE MODIFICATION

THE HOST with ephemeral hands and feet welcomes visitors. This stone is only a few feet from the Aliens & Common Man stone.

SECONDARY WORLD aliens are on a stone featuring a big image of a Common Man with a single spiral of DNA.

LESSON OF THE THIRD BETRAYAL

IF A MAN CANNOT TRUST THE WORDS OF HIS FRIENDS,
THEN HE IS SURROUNDED BY PEOPLE HE DOES NOT TRUST.
QUANTUM DISPLACEMENT PHYSICS CANNOT BE GIVEN TO ANY MAN
WHO SURROUNDS HIMSELF WITH FRIENDS HE CANNOT TRUST
FOR, OF THIS, IS FOOLISHNESS.

-- Voltar

Chapter 22

The Three Betrayals

At the front desk of the Lima Sheraton Hotel, I loaded in 15 impressive cases of film equipment. Two bellboys helped push the cart, and waited for a tip. The clerk could not find Linda's card on file. We had no mail. He remembered Linda, however—the beautiful American blond. She had departed that morning with Woody.

Her bill had been paid with the credit card including a fancy dinner and bottle of champagne. But, no card had been left behind and no rooms reserved. I insisted that an error had been made.

Linda was producing a film, I said. We were the crew. Since the manager was gone for the weekend, the starry-eyed clerk provided a room -- number 943.

"We'll work it out on Monday," he said eyeing the film cases. Clearly, we could afford to pay.

With the help of a Spanish-speaking secretary who made phone calls from the room, we located a site called *Toro Muerto* near the town of Arequipa, Peru -- a two-hour plane flight southward. The Nazca Plain lay southward also about half-way to Arequipa—a one-hour flight.

We tried to reach Linda and Mickey by phone but no one answered in the office, or at their home.

Brian's personality returned in dominance so we could count every penny and combine our pocket change. We didn't have enough cash for both Brian and me to visit Nazca *and* Toro Muerto. We counted the costs to the dime.

"If I don't go to Nazca, we can both go to Arequipa," Brian figured. "And we might have twenty dollars to spare." We would need to take food from the hotel, because plane tickets and taxis would consume our cash.

607

I wanted to wait for the credit card, but schedules conflicted. Flights to Arequipa were limited. We held one chance to go and get back before the date of our return flight. We could not change the return date without paying more money. So, we were stuck. Stranded.

"I've already been to Nazca," Brian said. "Remember, all those pulses: twenty-two times from A22. Nothing can beat that," Brian said. "Besides, I already know how they were built."

Voltar emerged for a moment.

"Of Nazca, models. Of this, they will be discovered someday, but for now—given in trust—models remain buried beneath the soil, far down, at key points on the symbols."

Brian's personality returned. "You guys go. Get some pictures. I don't need to see it again--not now." Brian promised to stay in the hotel.

"If anything happens, I will leave you in jail," I laughed. He assured me this would be different.

So, early the next morning, Chris and I flew off to Nazca on a commuter plane with the film equipment. I needed his help, and trained him to record sound.

In the small town of Nazca, a pilot with an old Cessna 150 provided rides over the symbols and lines for a reasonable price. The pilot took off the passenger door so I could photograph.

Once in the air, I couldn't believe my eyes. Hundreds of straight lines could be seen, cut into the soil over huge distances, over mounds and hills, running for miles and miles. Most were trapezoid in shape, but in one area we found the animal, insect and bird symbols.

As the plane circled above the spider symbol, I stood with one foot on the wing strut--the heavy film camera on my shoulder. Wind buffeted the plane and my foot slipped wildly as we bounced through the air. Chris held onto my belt to keep me from falling out the door. He was my only life support, my only safety belt.

But, as we tilted sharply right over the spider symbol, and I leaned out the door, Chris let go of my belt. My foot slipped off the wing strut, and I nearly fell out of the plane. Luckily, the big camera wedged against the door for a moment, so I could kick backwards. Without the camera's help, I would have been splattered on the spider symbol below—probably on A22.

I yelled at Chris in a rage, and ordered the pilot to land.

"You could have killed me," I seethed.

Chris said nothing.

"Why did you let go?" I screamed. "My life was depending on you."

"I wanted to take a picture, too" Chris said. "I forgot for a moment." Chris felt bad. Excited by the spectacular view, he forgot.

My thoughts raced. Did he do it on purpose? Is he there to eliminate Brian and me. No, probably not. He was just a college student who 'forgot' someone trusted him for their life. Forgetting can be deadly, I reasoned. There's one good reason to *"fear the mind of man"*—forgetting. People forget. People forget their purpose, their commitments, their promises to a mate, or friend. FORGETTING can kill and destroy a family, a friend—maybe a nation.

Brian would never have done that, I thought. Not even in a trance.

Early that afternoon, we visited the home of Maria Reiche, an elderly German mathematician who had devoted her whole life to studying designs on the Nazca Plain. "I think they had to use models," she said. "That is the only way."

I didn't tell her what Voltar had said.

When we returned to the hotel that night, Voltar explained how and why the symbols were made. "For the people," he said. "Symbolic representations of ideas for each man to understand. Each is a concept, of mental energy, of photonic matter. The spider is intelligence, organizing, like the spider's web. The monkey represents the *energy of the being* which jumps around, always changing shape and form." He talked long into the night.

The many long straight lines pointed at the sunset and sunrise points of stars and planets on certain dates. The people could watch the stars, night after night, and see the change in movement and direction. They could observe the planets by watching the setting and rising points. They didn't need telescopes.

"As this knowledge was given to the people, their minds were uplifted," Voltar said. "After Nazca, the People journeyed to Tiahuanaco." But they didn't start out learning at Nazca. They started at Toro Muerto, he said.

"From Toro Muerto, the people journeyed to both Nazca and Tiahuanaco," he explained. Of this, the knowledge man seeks is of Toro Muerto," he said. "There was the beginning. There full understanding will be given."

The next morning in the hotel, the chief manager called me to the front office. Linda had made no arrangements with him for the credit card, or for paying our bill. She had NOT discussed the arrival of a film crew.

I figured we had been stranded, but decided to bluff, like Brian might do. After all, supposedly I had been given the essence of Brian. He had street knowledge. I would try it out. I would use his bravado to protect Voltar.

"This is a big company. Lots of employees," I said. "They have a big office in downtown Los Angeles. She must have told someone."

"I have checked with all three managers," he said. "No one remembers any discussion."

I bluffed again. "Well, they are not going to leave us down here with all of this film equipment," I said. "The camera alone is worth $10,000 dollars." The man nodded with understanding. "We'll leave that here if we have to."

"Why don't you call your Los Angeles office and have them call me? Something can be worked out."

That day, I called Mickey's office repeatedly, leaving urgent messages with a receptionist to call the hotel, immediately. No reply.

"Betrayal," whispered Voltar. "The first of man."

We decided to try and complete our mission, anyway. Toro Muerto had been requested many times in Brian's writings, during hypnosis and in trances. Like the Gate of the Sun, Toro Muerto held a key to understanding for man.

Brian and I figured we could get to there and back with twenty dollars to spare, if we didn't eat. We'd need the last twenty dollars to reach the airport in a taxi.

"Sustenance will be provided," Voltar said. "Of Lynana, for you Jim--of the *Play of Life.*" I groaned. I was getting sick of their *Play of Life.*

Brian pointed at a counter-top in the hotel room. Three moist chocolate-chip cookies sat in plain sight. "For you, Jim. It's from them."

I love chocolate chip cookies, but for some reason, anger filled me—I snapped. "I've had it with their *Play of Life.* I almost get killed, and they offer cookies when we are being stranded."

Brian handed me a cookie. It was fresh, good. Brian laughed. "Lynana wants to know if you are happy with your cookie." He and Chris laughed, as they ate. I was enraged.

"No! Damn it. We need more than damn cookies. This is serious. They are stranding us because I gave them the fossil. I know it. All of these batteries have to be charged and the camera cleaned. Damn it. There is too much going on to have stupid problems with a hotel bill."

"If you are not pleased, perhaps what *we* offer will be more of your liking," said Voltar. Then several allies spoke.

"What are they doing?" I asked.

"Go outside," Brian said. "That's all I know. Something outside is waiting for you."

"I don't want any more GAMES Brian. I am sick of YOUR GAMES." I threw an ink pen and it splattered blue ink all over the nice hotel wall.

"It's not a game," Brian said ducking. "It's a gift, for you, Jim. Just for you--for all of your hard work. That's what they are telling me. Just go out the door."

I looked at the door. He was going over the edge, again. I knew he hadn't been out of the room for hours. I wanted to punch him out. I hated not knowing if

610

he faked something. I hated always having to go another step, to go through another door—taking all the risks.

I peeked outside, on the floor and saw nothing.

"There is something out there," Brian said.

"If it's for me, I hope it is a check for $5,000.00."

"I don't think so," Brian said. "But you might find it rather tasty. They think you didn't like the cookies." Brian chuckled.

"When do these people get serious?"

"I told you they are like children," Brian said. "Sometimes they ARE children—their kids." Brian gestured.

I looked up and down the hallway. I saw nothing. This was it. Now I had a good reason to hit Brian, to poke him in the face. I really wanted to explode and let him have a good blow.

I thought of my Mom, my Dad, my three great brothers, especially Kendrick who was now Editor of the Skeptical Inquirer published by the Committee to Analyze Claims of the Paranormal. He should be here, not me, I reasoned. Why couldn't I just get some spectacular proof, give it to Kendrick, and put this insanity of Brian Scott all behind me?

"It's out there," Brian said. "You must be missing it."

Since the transformation, Brian had been in dominance most of the time. He moved easily back and forth between Voltar and himself. The change had been far less dramatic than the first time—and in a way, I was a bit disappointed. The transitions were too smooth. Few people recognized the change.

"You better go out there," Brian said. "Before somebody else gets it."

I jerked open the door and walked into the corridor. I saw nothing on the floor, up and down the hallway, or in the open plaza. The hotel had been built as a rectangle with a huge open plaza on each floor surrounded by a walkway.

I heard Voltar speak, behind him. "There before you," he said. I raised my gaze to the railing. A protective fence surrounded the open plaza. On the wooden railing, sat three big pastries. I couldn't believe my eyes. Three cream puffs, in the shape of swans, rested on the wooden banister evenly spaced about ten feet apart. Each pastry was overflowing with mounds of whipped cream.

My mom made cream puffs when I was a kid, so I knew what they were. But these crème puffs were elegant, with long curved necks. My mom's cream puffs were more like ducks--simple, plain. She made them ducks on purpose. She knew I liked ducks, because I hunted ducks with my dad. Duck hunting was our bonding, as father and son. I loved hunting ducks with my dad, and so when my mom made cream puffs, they were always ducks.

Voltar urged me forward. I tasted the first cream puff, expecting it to be plastic—or phony in some way. But the soft white puffery was *real* whipped cream. Not cream out of a can, not phony aerosol cream, but REAL cream—whipped into a delicious mound.

Tears welled up into my eyes. No pastry had ever tasted this good. "Do you like the offering?" Voltar asked, beaming.

"I do," I sniffled, my mind spinning with suspicion. "But, what do I do with THREE cream puffs?"

"Bring them in, Jim," Brian laughed. "Let's eat them. We're hungry, too."

The Phase Two transformation to Nous 8 was much different than Phase 1. Brian seemed more integrated. Voltar and Brian now switched back and forth with ease--instantaneously. Brian's blue eyes never rolled up as a transition or "switching device" – except for the allies. When they spoke, the eyes rolled up.

The sharing between Brian and Voltar seemed totally mutual. The best personality for any particular moment, or circumstance emerged instantaneously, faster than a man could think. Brian and Voltar truly seemed united, like One.

As Brian showered, I ran down to the kitchen and obtained a big bowl of real chocolate from the chef. With the excitement of little boys on a camping trip, we ate those creams puffs covered with chocolate like I had done in my youth.

We giggled hysterically for hours. For the first time in days, I laughed to my heart's content—with Brian, like Brian. Although I respect the knowledge and presence of Voltar, I needed Brian's sense of humor, to survive.

Later that night, while having coffee in the restaurant, Chris asked Voltar to explain how the cream puffs appeared. "A gift for Jim," he said. "No more understanding is needed."

"But how do you do these things? I asked. "Why that? If you can do that, why not give money. Why not solve our problems?"

"That which is given is of the heart, and is done with wisdom and understanding. That is all we may give." Voltar lifted up a spoon so we could see it clearly. It was normal--an elegant spoon from the restaurant. His hand jerked—just a tiny move--right in front of my eyes.

"May this be for your understanding, and the understanding of man," he said. I looked at the spoon. A very sharp crevice marked the ornate handle.

I laughed. "He's bent spoons before, in circles, twisted them in knots. Now, he makes a tiny dent."

Voltar smiled. "Of this, let this be a dent in your understanding, Jim--a beginning for you and for mankind, of *true* understanding." I didn't understand.

Chris fondled the spoon, and took a guess. "I get it. He is saying he can do big stuff, but he only does little things--the very tiniest things."

Voltar smiled. "Of this, sustenance has been provided, and *will be provided*."

I moaned. "I know you can do big stuff, but why *only* the little things?" Voltar refused to answer.

Chris just laughed. "It must be *their Play of Life*." Laughing, Brian returned. As he giggled, I slammed away from the table in anger. The strategy made no sense. I felt like a victim—teased and tantalized, but not taught.

The next morning, I awoke early and began packing the equipment. Linda had not called the hotel. "We are in trouble," I said as Brian and Chris awoke. "Something is wrong."

As Brian sat up, I confronted him. "You know. If *they* really wanted to help, *they* could do some serious explaining of things, instead of just walking away with *half-assed answers and explanations.*"

"Don't yell at me, Jim," Brian pleaded. "Geez. Try to lighten up, it's six in the morning."

As Brian dressed, I raged. "When we have serious problems like this, and they say nothing, and do nothing—it drives my mad."

"They gave you cream puffs."

"You could have done that."

"I was in the room with you," Brian said.

"Well, it could have been done," I said. "Maybe a waiter left them there and you happened to see them. I don't know. It's not evidence. I can't prove anything with cream puffs. Why do it? It's like a clown," Brian. "That's what bothers me. "It's like YOU."

Brian smiled. "I didn't do it Jim. I don't know anything about making cream puffs, except whatever they did--it was probably assembled from the immediate area. They probably got them from the kitchen."

"So *they* stole cream puffs?"

"No, they probably duplicated the ingredients, made them on their home world and transported them here. That's how they do it."

"If they can do that, they could get Linda to call back. This is hell, Brian and they are joking around."

The presence of Voltar emerged. "Of this, we give what we can. What we give to you--is given in love."

Then Brian's personality returned.

"Let's get going," he said. "I think they have another gift for you, because you work so hard, Jim." He gestured at the door. "Go and look."

I angrily jerked open the door. This time, I looked at the railing, first. I was amazed. On the banister, at equal spacing of about twelve feet, sat elegant cream puffs filled with real whipped cream, graced with long beautiful swan necks. Not just three cream puffs waited for me, but enough to cover the entire railing, all around the open plaza.

Then I noticed the cookies. Between every cream puff, sat a chocolate chip, oatmeal raisin cookie--my absolute, all time favorite.

"They want to know if you like the gift," Brian laughed.

"This is crazy," I shouted and laughed and cried all at the same time. "What are we supposed to do with these?"

"Take them with us," Brian said. "It may be all we can afford to eat."

I found a box and insisted that Chris and Voltar walk ahead of me around the banister to gather them. I had a plan for a test.

Chris gently picked up each cream puff and loaded it into the box held by Voltar, while walking at his side.

I placed both hands on the wooden railing and walked forward until they burned with friction. I stared at the back of Brian's head.

For only the second time, I projected a thought upward to the probe. "If this is real, if YOU provided the cream puffs because you knew I would remember my childhood--this is your chance to convince me.

As we walked forward, my hands squeaked and burned with heat. I continued with the thought projection. "I am going to hold both hands on the railing so tightly that they burn every second. And we are going to go around the entire railing, this way. I am going to watch Chris pick up each pastry, and I am going to make sure Brian stays with him, at his side. My hands are NOT going to stop burning and squeaking, NOT for one second.

"Then, if you want to convince me, if you want to give me a sign that you hear me, place another cream puff on the railing—behind me. Then, I'll go forward with happiness. Otherwise, I just think it could be Brian, pulling a prank." I was satisfied. That was my challenge.

As we completed the perimeter, I had not taken my eyes off Brian. I had not lifted my hands. I had kept them squeaking and burning all the way. This was my test, spontaneous, and internal--not communicated to Brian or Voltar in any way. I spoke not a word to them of the test.

Neither Brian or Chris had bothered to even glance back at me. But, as we completed the perimeter, Voltar spoke. "Of this, for your education, Jim--and all man."

"What did he say?" I shouted at Chris. They were fifteen feet in front of me.

Brian turned around to see what I was doing. "Voltar said to look behind your HAND -- whatever that means."

I swung around. About ten feet behind me, on the railing, rested a big, plump cream puff. My hands burned. I had not lifted them. No one else was in the area, but it happened.

I stared at the cream puff in amazement. For a moment, I could hear my heart beating, and feel my breathing, and the energy of life within my being.

Something paranormal had happened—at my request—as a test, as a sign. The test had been private, secret, silent. My test was mental—secret thoughts of my own--yet, THEY responded.

"In this, your beginning," Voltar said. He looked at me with compassion as tears of joy welled up into my eyes. I tasted the fresh cream —REAL cream-- sweet and thick, whipped into a delicate mound.

"Look at this," I grinned like a little boy about to cry. "Real cream, again."

"We know," said Brian, giggling. His face was a mess. "Real cream. Tastes great!"

Chris' hands were also covered with cream. "We've got a baker's dozen, counting yours."

"Thirteen? Why thirteen? Is everybody in their *Play of Life*, a comedian?"

"Just Danyael," shouted Brian.

I suddenly remembered learning about a "baker's dozen." I had always loved going to the bakery in my hometown to order a dozen pastries for my dad's Drug store. He had served them with coffee at the counter in the mornings. My first job as a young boy was to make sure that thirteen pastries were in the bag—I had to count them, and if there were thirteen—a baker's dozen--I got to eat the extra one. In that way, my dad had taught me to enjoy counting. The memory stunned me to tears. I had not remembered that experience before, at any time in my life. Why now? I wondered. Perhaps, counting the baker's dozen had started my love for knowledge. Perhaps, the cream puffs inspired love for my family, and my parents. Heart and mind, I whispered--heart and mind, united as one. I was growing too, like Brian, and I understood the deep emotions he must have felt for his father, and his mother, his wife and children. The emotions were overwhelming, he always said. I began to understand.

Toro Muerto

The next morning, stars still sparkled in the sky as we bounced shoulder to shoulder inside a 4-wheel drive Land Rover. Brian, Chris and I looked east to see the first pink glow of dawn. Worn gears on the vehicle growled like a jaguar in the jungle as we climbed up a steep hill. Then we rumbled downward at the first light of day to splash through a stream of cold water. We were all asleep.

"Time to wake up," said our British guide. He had red-hair and a thick British accent. "The sun's a rising."

To save money, we had not slept that night. After filming an archaeologist— an expert on Toro Muerto at a museum—we had walked the streets until 3:30 a.m.

We had spent some time at a dance hall, courtesy of a taxi driver who wanted to show us the town. Dark-haired, fair-skinned Spanish girls had been sitting in chairs wearing elegant gowns, all waiting to dance for money. A dozen beautiful young ladies, some green-eyed or blue-eyed, wore frilly feminine dresses, and radiant smiles. We didn't dance, but we admired them and saw a different way of life, something we'd never experienced before.

As we awoke, the women of Latin America still filled our thoughts and hearts. We all had been swept away.

"Beautiful," muttered Chris. "But there is something else about them."

"Wholesome," I mumbled.

"They are feminine and very sexy without being tramps," Chris muttered. He was right. The girls of Arequipa seemed dignified and submissive all at the same time. "They are not trying to be like men," Chris said. "They are happy, sweet, loving girls—that grew up to be loving women."

"We're just used to California girls," said Brian. "They're out-there more--tougher." We all agreed that California girls seemed physically more aggressive and more overtly seductive compared to these conservative Latin beauties.

Mr. Ted Holly, owner of Holly's Unusual Tours, laughed. He spoke with a thick British accent. "Trying to figure out the women, mates? Did you ever hear about the passion of Latin American women? Why do you think I am here?" he paused to shift gears. The Land Rover struggled up another steep hill.

"I married one of them," he said. "Latin women--everything a man could want. Why do you think there are so many Americans down here, and Germans and Brits, and Francs? It's not oil. It's the Latin female. They are *real women*, the way they are supposed to be, and they *love* being that way." He sang a tune. *"You'll be a happy man for the rest of your life if you find a Latin wife."* Again, we splashed through a clear mountain stream.

"Of course, they can have a temper, too," he laughed. "But I wouldn't have it any other way. Even when my wife is mad, she doesn't try to be tough—she cries. That's what you are talking about. They leave aggression to the men, and are happy to do it. That makes you feel like a man—you want to take care of them—and would die for them."

"Vulnerability," I said. "The softness attracts strength in a man."

"That's like Voltar," said Chris. "He is vulnerable and he shows it. Whereas Brian, he doesn't show it. He tries to be tough. He is the macho man."

"That's right. Brian is the tough guy," I mused. "Voltar is softer, more vulnerable—the inner man--but he has the *real* power, the paranormal power."

"Maybe the lesson is, you don't get those powers by being tough," said Chris.

"What are you talking about?" Brian mumbled, sleepily.

"We are talking about you," I said. "Your duality, at face value."

"Voltar is tough," Brian said. "He's got muscles galore. He looks like a professional wrestler, but he still has the other side, too."

"Maybe you can have both," said Chris. "If you're evolved to Mind Level Four," he laughed. "

"Anybody want breakfast," laughed Brian holding up a squashed cream puff. "Sunny side up?"

We all giggled like little boys until our sides hurt.

The trip to Toro Muerto required nearly four hours on bumpy roads up into the Andean Mountains. We were on a tight time schedule: arrival at 7:30 a.m. with departure locked in at 10:00 a.m. to catch the only plane back to Lima in time for our flight home.

From the expert archaeologist at the museum, we knew the site contained 15,000 rock carvings, spread over several hundred acres.

Voltar wanted me to photograph only a handful. Most importantly, he wanted to find a stone etched with three circles, like the one in Yosemite. That stone symbolized his people, the NOR and their technology, he said. Three rings.

I remembered Yosemite when Brian found the three-circled symbol. At the rock in Yosemite, we both got zapped with a signal—a test of Nous ten. Brian had passed the test. He had "received and transmitted" Nous ten.

I had felt an arrow in my brain. Perhaps I had received, but not transmitted. They never said. All I knew was that the simple, three-circle pattern was very important to Voltar.

He also wanted me to find and photograph the probe, their "selene orbital" carved into stone—somewhere. He called it "their mark."

The Land Rover stopped on a steep slope.

"We are here, men," Mr. Holly said. Scattered around us on white sand lay big, angular rocks, each with engravings. Some of the rocks were hollow, as if blown from a volcano. Many were broken. None of the rocks seemed native to the area.

The place gave me goose bumps. We gazed upon beautiful red rocks, white sand, and a deep blue sky. Below, in the distant valley, green crops grew in fertile brown soil, a contrast to the barren white sand.

All around us, huge sharp-edged rocks lay on the sand, as if dropped there from the sky--no water erosion on them. Dense and heavy, some were 15 feet wide, lying flat, like big tables. Others looked rounded and hallow, as if air-blown--they were open on one side.

Ancient people had etched pictures on the rocks, in some manner, taking off the dark red surface to reveal a light layer of stone underneath. The etched lines looked rounded, as if cut by a chemical. The lines weren't sharp and precise, but they clearly presented animals, men and geometric symbols.

Archaeologists believed an ancient volcano had blown the rocks to the site. Locals had cut up and carried many stones away for homes and fences.

"You can get out and walk around here," said Mr. Holly. "Or, we can drive ahead for miles. Carvings all the way—you can watch them out the windows."

At least six square miles of rock coverings lay before us like an open picture-book, but we had only two-hours of time to read the story. What could we do?

The presence of Voltar emerged. "That which we need will be given," he said. "But not that of the cave and the tunnels today--only that of the stones."

He wanted us to discover "quipu," the rope memory devices used by Incan and pre-Incans. Brian had been described as "Keeper of the Quipu," and his drawings showed a system of black and white stones that was used with knotted strings to record and predict cycles of the sun and moon, even eclipses.

Voltar also wanted us to go into a cave. Earlier, he made us promise not to profit or gain financially from anything we found. "All must be given for education," he had said.

But we did not have time.

Voltar started walking with long strides. "Wait," I shouted. "I need the camera." Chris helped lug the tripod, batteries and film as we raced across the white, sandy slope.

Within a few minutes, Voltar had located a stone with three circles. He was satisfied. That was the first priority. Then quickly, he found the 'selene orbital'—the probe.

Voltar didn't have time to explain everything. Brian returned so he could be photographed standing next to the probe. He was proud of the discovery. He had drawn the probe on paper, months earlier—and the drawings seemingly matched: Brian's probe and the ancient rock carving. Brian smiled with pride for the camera.

In a short time, we had accomplished a lot, but Voltar wanted to show us more. He walked stiffly forward, with his eyes rolled up while receiving directions from the probe. He pointed out carvings of crafts for travel *on waves of water*—ships at sea. "All will be explained, later," Voltar said.

Many of the drawings seemed mechanical, and precise--like sketches of structures.

"That of teaching, learning and planning," Voltar explained "Plans. By these, agreements formed. First the drawing, then the agreement—and then the building. Of this, in Brian's terminology--*the top view*. This is what you see, represented. In much, only the top view is represented. But in all, by the hand of man, this was done in *their* understanding of what was given. You see on these stones, the understanding of the common man as his mind was uplifted -- men like Brian. For in them, is the beginning of all that is built."

After filming each of the stones and interviewing Mr. Holly, very little time remained. As we prepared to leave, Voltar urged me to come back someday, and find the cave and caverns. Then the probe pulsed. We heard a long, velvety beep overhead. Voltar suddenly rushed away downhill. In stiff-legged strides, he ran past hundreds of carvings I wanted to photograph. "All that you need will be given," Voltar assured me, when he stopped.

"Of this is the entrance way," he said, searching among the car-sized stones.

"What are you looking for?" I arrived gasping for air and exhausted from carrying equipment in the high altitude. "Do we have to go any further? We are out of time."

"That of the Host," Voltar said. "The greeting." He moved quickly from stone to stone, and then stopped. "Here," he said pointing. On the stone I saw the image of a man with one hand upward in greeting. The image was smooth and flowing, ephemeral--very unlike the hundreds of images we had seen. The Host did not have legs or hands. "The projection, as to Brian," he said "An image."

Then Voltar turned aside and pointed at a large rough carving of a stocky man with a big face. Inside the childlike form was a single strand representing DNA. Next to this Common Man were figures of the gray skinned aliens with long arms and domed heads. "That of the Secondary World," said Voltar, "You see the Common Man of the land, and the process by which he was uplifted."

"I don't understand," I worked in a sweat to prepare the heavy film camera. "What are you saying?"

"Here was the beginning," said Voltar. "Here the information and training was given for the uplifting of man's mind, by that of DNA and education. Much knowledge was given of the probe, and of the beginning of man.

"From here, the People traveled to Nazca, and on to the lake and the island therein, and then to Tiahuanaco. The knowledge given here was passed on to the children, and from this beginning, structures arose from the land, and the stone. Through activated stone, the mind levels rose, and the society developed.

"Here by the sea, people arrived. From here, after training and education the groups split, one going to Nazca, the other going directly to the lake, to Island of the Sun and to the stone. Later, those of Nazca joined those of the lake at Tiahuanaco, and the stones were laid, the city built."

I was confused. The Secondary was here? The Host was here. Your people were here?"

"All and more," Voltar said. "For many came."

"Who was it?" I asked. "What people? The red-haired, eight footers? Is that you? Were the long-ears here?"

"Of this, the importance for man today is the movement of the people across the land, and the process of uplifting. As I said, we were together with the Secondary in this. And, by that of the DNA, man was uplifted. But, we did not agree to all that was done. And we do not agree today, in many things."

"I don't get it."

"We were a people of red and blond hair, with blue eyes, when we first came upon your world," Voltar said. "At one time, we did work together, with the Secondary to uplift the brown-skinned man of this region. Later, at Tiahuanaco, others came from around the world for uplifting."

Mr. Holly listened carefully. "I don't know exactly what he is talking about, but I have seen UFO's out here. Right here. Many times."

"How many times?" I asked.

"Oh, maybe eight or ten--lights in the sky. But three or four times I have seen silver disks, flying in the daylight. They have followed right over my Land Rover."

"Here?"

"Right here," he said. "And up higher. There's much more. You are only looking at one-tenth of everything that is here."

"Of this, much remains to be told," Voltar said.

I glanced at my watch. "Oh no. We've got to go. We're late." "Everybody take something and run."

Brian's personality returned to help. He shouldered a big load of the heavy equipment, and he led us on a shortcut up the hill through the hundreds of rocks.

On a plateau we all stopped for a breather. The hot sun burned. "This is winter?" I gasped.

"It's hotter in the Southern hemisphere," said the Mr. Holly, handing us a canteen of water.

"Voltar's got something for you, Jim," Brian said after a big gulp. "Can you film one more thing?"

"No!" I shouted. "We'll most likely miss the plane now. We'll be stuck here for days--with no money."

"Well, use your small camera," Brian said as he picked up my load, adding to his own. He looked at me with compassion. "It's a gift—for you. It is the proof you need -- for your beginning."

"We will be late," I said. "Besides, how can I find it?"

"You'll know it." Brian said trudging up the hill with his back arching under the load. "I'll put this stuff away, but--you need to find this. It's important for *you.*"

Sweating in the heat and bright sun, I jogged down a ravine. I saw nothing striking until coming upon a huge red stone on a sandy plateau--a drafting table. On the rock had been etched a rectangular pattern—obviously, the temple at Tiahuanaco. The schematic outline included the thick walls, the doorway, and a covering over the underground courtyard.

Even the dividing wall between the public court and the priest's court was clearly represented. That was all intriguing, but I was even more stunned by a big "X" which dominated the sketch. In the priest's court, right where Brian had indicated the Gate of the Sun belonged, an "X" had been inscribed. I recalled Brian's drawings of the Gate of the Sun, done in Los Angeles before I had even met him. The top of the Gate of the Sun featured lines that crossed, like an "X." Those lines aligned perfectly with the "X" at the center of the Photonic Matter drawing. Why was the "X" so important, I wondered. Then I remembered that the top of the Gate of the Sun was also the target of a beam from the Island of the Sun. That target was the "X." That beam supposedly created the activation zone with a radius of 49 kilometers around the temple. That beam somehow made the "quantum withdraw" and the "descent" possible: the transformation.

The beam was important to me, but I knew that many archaeologists simply wanted to confirm the Gate of the Sun's location in the temple. Even though Brian had shown me the pillars and posts and connecting pylons, I wanted corroborating evidence. Here it was—my "gift," my "beginning."

I snapped lots of pictures quickly, then raced uphill to the Land Rover.

Time Displacement

After an hour of driving, Mr. Holly calculated that reaching the airport in time was hopeless. "We will be nearly an hour late," he said. "No way to avoid it." He had driven the road a hundred times. He knew the exact mileage and time to the airport. "You really don't have a chance," he said. "You will be at least 45 minutes late."

Voltar and his allies spoke up as we shared the last oatmeal raisin cookie. "Displacement. Time. Displacement."

"What is happening?" I asked.

"He is talking about a time displacement," Brian said. "Is there a tunnel?" Brian glanced ahead. "Are we coming to a tunnel?"

We all looked up in time to see a stone tunnel. The Land Rover slipped into the darkness for about seven seconds, and then emerged into bright light. We all blinked.

Brian shrugged. He handed me the last cream puff, which had been squashed miserably. "Go ahead and enjoy," Brian laughed. "Saturn and the others just took care of it."

"Took care of what?" I asked.

"Our departure time. We'll make it."

"No you won't make it," Mr. Holly shouted. "I'm the one driving. I know how long it takes." His face reddened with anger. I'm telling you. You better prepare to miss that plane."

Brian smiled as we shared the rich, tasty cream from a once elegant, long-necked swan. Now the swan looked worse than a duck. Brian laughed. I liked making him laugh for a change. Now, for the first time, I was having fun, too.

When we finally arrived at the airport, the plane to Lima sat parked on the ground. Mr. Holly choked in disbelief. "It's still here. By God, I don't believe it. It must be late."

Inside the terminal, he frantically helped us with the film equipment. "This is a bloody miracle," he gasped. He checked each clock in the small building.

"My watch is right," he panted. "This is unbelievable. I mean it. Bloody unbelievable."

"They said there was a time displacement," I said.

"But, that...that means... Were we transported without knowing it?" The color drained from his face.

"It's by TIME displacement," I said. "I don't think WE were displaced."

"My God. My wife will never believe this. I don't believe this. I can't believe we are here. The plane hasn't left. We are forty-five minutes early. That's impossible, bloody impossible. That means we gained 90 minutes. Ninety minutes!"

I shrugged. "This stuff happens all the time around Brian."

"Well it doesn't happen all the time to me," he said panting with excitement. "I didn't feel anything. Did you blokes feel anything?" He looked at his arms and legs. "Did you notice anything? I mean--have we been taken aboard a UFO?"

I laughed. "No. I don't think so. Let's just say it was a fluke. You got us here in time—that's all that's important."

"Hey. Hey. You are not getting off on that one," he said earnestly. "I KNOW what it takes. I KNOW this was impossible. Something happened. Something that cannot be explained by my mind just happened. Okay. It happened to me. And my mind can't explain it to me. Do you understand?"

"I understand how you feel," I said. "Some of the things are frightening. But nothing bad happened. You are fine--and we aren't stranded."

"Oh, it did happen," he said. "I can guarantee that. *Guaranteed*. That was not normal. Not possible." Finally, he calmed down and smiled at Voltar. "Thank you," he said. "Thank you for the most unusual excursion of my life."

Voltar nodded. "Thank *you*," he said. "For you provided what was needed." Then the allies responded.

"Thank You-em."

"We thank you."

"Thank you."

"Of this, and your efforts, we are grateful."

"Thank you."

"Thank you."

Mr. Holly gasped. Others in the airport gathered to hear the strange voices as Mr. Holly received their thanks. When all twelve finished, Brian waved gently. "Vyaos Con dios," he said with a smile.

Mr. Holly cried. The tall, red-haired Brit plopped down into a chair laughing, crying and talking to himself.

We walked away towards the plane. "He'll never forget this day," I chuckled. "Now his bumper sticker really does mean something." We all laughed. The bumper sticker on his Land Rover had read: *Holly's Unusual Tours.* The artwork featured a UFO.

On the plane, as we looked down with great memories of Arequipa, Chris leaned forward. "Were we really displaced?"

"That of the tunnel," Voltar said. "A displacement did occur for you must return. The betrayal..." Voltar suddenly choked and gagged. His throat bulged and his face reddened. The Secondary World attacked.

The Second Betrayal

That afternoon, when we reached the hotel, Voltar walked with a limp. He had suffered some paralysis. His right hand and leg trembled out of control every few minutes. Chris and I helped him up into the elevator. In the room, he lay down on the bed in misery.

"Debra, noooo. Debraaa," he moaned. Then an evil voice snarled.

"What is happening?" Chris asked in terror. "Is he being possessed?"

"I hope not," I said. "I sure don't want him walking around as...

"Bealzelbubbbbbbbbbb," Brian's lips hissed. His whole body shook with convulsions. Chris bolted from the room.

The probe interrupted. "Over-ride, Negative Nous 11. Over-ride attack.

Brian's presence returned in agony. "Jim get Debra on the phone. Voltar needs to talk to her—NOW."

I called Los Angeles, immediately. Linda and Mickey were in their office. They said money had been sent by wire to pay the bill, but that due to the holiday, the funds had not arrived at the bank in Lima.

They had not seen Debra. She had never picked up expense money for the move to Los Angeles. Voltar moaned in anguish. Beelzebub roared.

Brian's body jolted as if shocked. He tried to reach the phone, but slammed into a chair, and rolled to the floor with a crash.

"What is happening?" Mickey asked. "Was that Brian?"

"It's bad," I said. "Something is wrong. He wants Debra. He is calling out to her, crying and moaning."

623

"Brian's phone is disconnected." Linda said. "We tried to call her. We don't know what to do. She was supposed to come to the office, but never did."

"Something terrible is happening," I said. Voltar cried in deep sorrow, and my heart ached for him.

"Jim, we need to talk to you about the fossil," Linda said.

"Not now. We are having an emergency," I said, kneeling to examine Brian's body.

"I have a good friend who knows a professor at UCLA, and we just happened to take it over to him and show it to him."

"Oh God," I moaned. "You were not supposed to do anything with it."

"Well, he said it couldn't have been found in South America."

"Good," I said. "That was the whole point. Listen, we are having a problem with Voltar. Can we talk about this later?"

Voltar convulsed and spoke Greek. Brian's body stiffened and shook violently with tremors. Chris stood behind the door and hid in the hallway. I was alone with Voltar.

Linda continued. "But this professor said the only way it could have been found it Peru, is if it had been planted there."

"Planted? What do you mean *'planted?'"*

"Well, that is what I am asking you, Jim," Linda said sharply. "He said it had to be put there, in advance, for someone to find."

"Oh, he did?" I seethed. "And did you tell him how it was found--with Brian sitting in trance with his eyes up in his head, telling you where to move your hand?"

"Well, that is the part I can't believe," Linda said. "I can't even fathom that part of it."

"*That part of it,"* I laughed. "Why did he do it that, Linda? Why?"

"I don't know. I don't know about that."

"Look, he told us NOT to take it to anyone. It is Julio's and the whole point of it was the *location.* He said all of that at the time."

"Well, this man is an expert and he said it was a fraud, Jim. That someone had to be pulling a hoax, because the only place it could be found was in Texas."

"Well maybe that is the point of it," I said.

"Have you ever been to Texas?" Linda asked.

"Yes I have," I raged. "But I sure as hell didn't buy a fossil."

"What about Brian? Has he been to Texas?"

"I think he has. I can't ask him right now. He's in trouble."

"Well, you went to Pisac--the first time. You said you had been out there before. He could have planted it."

"Linda," I breathed. "THEY could plant it anywhere, anytime. But, for your concern, neither Brian nor I got anywhere close to that location when we went to Pisac. We never went to the backside."

"How do we know YOU didn't plant it?"

"Linda, don't you remember how it was found, beneath the footstep, and all that. He directed your hand, inch by inch until you found it. Can you just forget that?"

"I know he did," Linda said. "But no one will believe that. I can't even..."

"Astaaaaaa," a demon hissed through Brian as Chris peeked back into the room.

"I am not staying in this room with him. Should I call for help?" Chris asked.

"No. He's not getting up," I said. "He's not a problem unless he gets up and walks."

"What is going on?" Linda asked.

"We have a problem. Voltar needs to talk to Debra. I think he's being attacked. But, I assure you, Linda--that fossil was not planted by Brian or me. Okay? Put it in the vault until we can give it to Julio. I told you in Cuzco, if you don't do things just right, everything will get all screwed up."

"Well, it is the final determination of an expert that this is a fraud," Linda said. "It doesn't have any great value."

"It's a fossil," I screamed. "Voltar said it was *common*. Didn't you hear him? He said the value was in the knowledge, in the location. Only Julio could ask the right questions. Listen, are you ripping us around and stalling us out because you think it's valuable, and you're trying to sell it?"

"No," Linda said. "We were just getting information."

"Listen, we are stranded down here," I shouted. "For some reason, you have not come through with any payments to this hotel, and we have no way to get back. Our plane leaves in five hours. Are you meeting us at the airport or not?"

Mickey spoke up. "We'll be there," he said. "That's all I can say for sure, until we get to the bottom of this."

"Bottom of what?" I shouted.

"The fossil business," Mickey said.

I raged at him. "The fossil was supposed to be kept in a vault until Julio gets it. That was the agreement. Nothing else was said, nothing else was promised about it. Voltar even said it had no great value. Something has gone awry here in somebody's mind, and it is on your end, not ours."

"We will see you at the airport," Mickey said.

"Linda?" I asked. "What about the hotel?" What about the payment?" The phone line clicked.

I threw the phone in a rage. "Damn it. They are stranding us here, because of the fossil. People and their damn imagination!"

625

On the floor, Voltar struggled to his knees. "Asta," a voice hissed. The demon glared at Chris when he peeked in the door.

"Jesus," he screamed, slamming out the door again.

Then the demon glared at me like a jaguar ready to kill. Brian's lips curled back and I saw snarling fangs. I grabbed a film battery. "Stay down," I warned. "Stay down." The demon rose up on Brian's knees.

I prepared to attack. The sharp-edged battery would hit like a rock, slamming into Brian's forehead, possibly killing him. How would I explain that to the police?

Suddenly, I remembered Mary Beth, and the bathtub. "Jesus. Jesus Please handle this. Cast out this..."

Instantly, Brian's body dropped to the floor with a thud. "Over-ride, over-ride, Secondary World interference," crackled the probe voice. "Over-ride."

Voltar moaned in anguish for Debra, but the demon was gone.

About that time, Debra, sick with despair, opened a vial of tranquilizers. She had struggled for two weeks living in the apartment among boxes packed up for moving. She had borrowed diapers and canned food for sustenance.

She had used up her last dollar calling Mickey's office from payphones. Despite numerous calls, Linda and Mickey had refused to talk with her, and the receptionist never knew anything about a check to pick-up.

Debra had driven up to Los Angeles once, and sat in the office, making a commotion on purpose, but neither Mickey nor Linda had appeared with the payment.

Debra swallowed two red tranquilizers then wrapped her son into a blanket as a volunteer arrived. The helpful, older man loaded Debra into his station wagon and drove to his home. He had promised to take Debra to the airport early the next morning. He was separated from his wife and lived in a big house alone. He showed Debra the guest bedroom, but that night when he left for a meeting, Debra crawled into his bed.

About the same time, I pulled Voltar to his feet and gave him a drink of cold water. He said little. His body convulsed with tremors and uncontrolled shaking.

The Escape

In the hotel lobby, I pushed a big cart with 15 cases of film equipment. The bellboys notified the night manager who ran out to confront me. "Are you leaving?"

"No," I lied. "They are going back to Nazca with the equipment. I'm staying here until the money arrives from Los Angeles."

As Brian and Chris loaded the taxi, the suspicious night manager gestured to the bell captain who ran to the elevator. He zipped upstairs to the ninth floor. I watched the numbers above the door and timed his investigation. I knew the young man would run to room 943 and look inside. I knew he would see my shirts, my underwear, my shaving kit, hiking boots and a shiny film case all set out for him to see. I had created a great deception using the street-knowledge of Brian, given to me for protection of Voltar. I hoped my ruse would work. We all froze waiting for the report.

The elevator descended. As Voltar and Chris watched from the taxi, the bellboy reported back to the manager in Spanish. "Looks like he's staying." The manager was satisfied.

I waved as the taxi departed, then walked towards the manager with a deceptive smile. "Is the kitchen still open?" I asked. He gestured politely to the restaurant. Due to a Peruvian holiday, the banks were closed. Linda had been right about that point, so I figured money had been sent, but I didn't know. The manager had agreed to wait another day for the wire transaction to go through— as long as at least one of us stayed.

"The banks down here take forever," he said. "Don't worry about it. You can stay another day."

But instead of eating in the restaurant, I snuck out a side door of the hotel, and ran through the night in a sweat. Several blocks away, I hailed a taxicab with our last few *soles.*

At the airport, I met Brian and Chris. We ran to the international gate and boarded the plane. As we waited in our seats, we all sweated in fear. I expected the police to board the plane at any moment. If arrested, we could be jailed and charged with a fraud of nearly $2000. That's a serious crime in any nation. We would all go to jail until a trial. Voltar would be trapped in South America. Eventually, I would be found guilty of the hoax, and would spend years in a South American jail.

Finally, the door to the plane shut, and we waited breathlessly. The plane taxied out to the runway, and waited for the longest time. I feared we would be called back to the gate when the plane turned and began to move. I gripped the chair tightly. Seconds passed like slow motion, but when the wheels left the ground, I breathed a sigh of relief.

Chris and I cheered quietly, but Voltar said nothing. "Is this in your *Play of Life?"* I asked Voltar with an angry sneer.

"Man betrays man, and himself," he said. "The worst is yet to come."

That night, the friendly volunteer returned home to find Debra in his bed. "Hold me," she cried. "I am so frightened." He volunteered to sleep on the couch, but Debra insisted. She needed to feel his arms. He couldn't resist.

We flew all night, and the next morning our plane landed in Los Angeles. At US customs, the agents confiscated all of my cans of exposed film. "I go with the film," I insisted. "You don't know how to handle it."

"We know how to handle everything," said an armed agent. He slammed me into a wall, and held me with a club.

Voltar told the agent he had come "in peace and love for all mankind." Two armed agents immediately escorted him to a room where he was strip-searched and given blood tests for drugs. He cooperated with their requests, but said little. Finally, an hour later, we were released.

In the waiting area, Debra greeted Voltar with tears streaming down her face. "I thought I'd never see you again," she sobbed, hysterically.

"What happened," I asked her. She looked terrible with bags under her eyes and stress etched into her face.

"I never got a penny," she cried. "No one called me. They left me alone."

As Voltar comforted her, I pulled Mickey aside. "We have absolutely no money," I said. "Nothing. Based on our agreement, you still owe each of us about $750, plus enough for deposits on new apartments in Los Angeles. We need some cash now."

"And of the silver suit with the magnets," said Voltar, overhearing our conversation. Mickey insisted everything could be worked out, and suggested we come to the office the next day.

"How?" I said. "We don't have a car that works. Brian's is broken and I sold mine."

Mickey and Linda agreed to rent a car for a few days while we talked things over. "We'll get you your money," Mickey said. "But don't bring Debra up to the office. She came up and sat in the lobby all day with a screaming kid. It was terrible," he said. "She was obnoxious and very disturbing." Mickey glared at her. "She's very loud."

"Voltar likes her," I said.

He pulled me away from the group. "Look, if he is going to be going around in the public eye, he can't be seen with someone like that. Not in Beverly Hills -- not in Linda's circles. It's a woman thing. That's the problem I am having. Linda likes Voltar and wants to find him a suitable girlfriend."

"Good Lord--that's crazy. We go by the contract."

"Well, what if he becomes a celebrity? She has friends who are movie stars, actresses. They would love to be seen with him. Help me on this."

"Help you? Voltar is committed to Debra. You are on a WRONG line of thinking. He is not going to get dressed up and go to parties in Beverly Hills. It's more likely he'd go to people in the ghettos."

Mickey pointed at Debra. "She can't even be healthy. She's carrying 70 pounds of fat."

"Looks are not important to Voltar. That is the point he is making. It is the heart that counts, not the looks, not the body."

"That is too much," Mickey said. "But come up tomorrow, we'll work something out."

Debra's Revelation

That night, Brian, Debra and I slept on the floor of their apartment among boxes packed for moving. We were all exhausted, and no one talked.

The next day, July Fourth 1977, Debra couldn't restrain herself as we drove to Los Angeles in the rented car. She began pleading for forgiveness.

"Help me, Jim," she pleaded. "Help me tell him."

"What did you do, Debra? Just tell us."

"I couldn't help it," she cried. "I was so foolish. I just wanted some hugs and affection. Just to feel someone's arms around me. I was so frightened."

"You slept with someone?" I asked.

"Yes. Yes I did," she cried. "I am so sorry. So, very, very ashamed."

Voltar said little, at first. He waited for input from the Council and the allies. Then, he spoke slowly. "Of this, the people find great sorrow, for at a time in our past these things did happen, among men and women—but not any more. For so long, they have not experienced such a betrayal in our world. Now, the people are overwhelmed in grief, for they did know of this, and I knew--last night. The women cry openly for you, and the men--for they know what it means."

"What does it mean?" Debra asked.

"Of the *Play of Life*--the women of earth cannot be trusted."

"Oh God, have I done that to our people, to all of our people?"

"It is not just you, Debra," Voltar said. "We know well, the betrayals of man and woman on your world, and the lies and the deceptions. We know well, that the value of one's heart cannot be trusted in the hands of another--but we had hoped, that you would not submit unto the temptation. For this allowed an attack by the Secondary World. Many of our world gave up their lives--for when man fails, when man lies, when man betrays--we suffer. This *Play of Life* is not complete, and of this--we pay a price when man fails."

"I am so sorry," she cried. "I mean, being a Christian and all. Does this bring judgment on me? Am I condemned to a life of sin?"

"Not of I," said Voltar. "Nor from my people. Not of what you speak. We are your friends—your brothers and your sisters. We do not judge you, and we cannot deliver you from sin, in your terms. We simply project the *Play of Life* to uplift and strengthen man. We cannot create victory and freedom for man. Freedom is our hope and our desire. Freedom, man must earn."

"I did not pass my test," Debra moaned. "I messed up, bad."

"Of this, there is sorrow, for this does have great meaning to the future of man, and your world. For decisions are made within the Council on *our* world by your actions. Of this, your time within *the Play of Life...*" Voltar stopped abruptly.

"What is it?" Debra pleaded. "What have I done?"

"I can say no more," Voltar said. "I have said enough. Let it pass for now. I have only love for you," Voltar said. "I do understand, and shall always be your friend."

She hugged Voltar and cried with repentance.

I wondered what would happen to Debra. She had betrayed Voltar, not Brian. Brian had not even spoken. He was not even in the equation. The reversal was complete. Debra was drawn into Voltar's world, completely. She had crossed the line. She hung on Voltar's words, sought his forgiveness, and fed on his understanding. By her own sin and guilt, she had become subject to his judgment. Was this right? Was this fair? Was Voltar's world becoming her reality? Yes, without question, she had crossed the line.

The Third Betrayal

An hour later, after leaving Debra in a Los Angeles park, Brian and I slipped into Mickey's business on Wilshire Boulevard. We peered into several empty offices designated for Brian and me. No furniture had been installed, no desks, no drafting tables.

"He lied to us," I said. "He was to have the rooms furnished."

We met Mickey in a conference room. "This thing with the fossil threw us a loop," he said. "Linda didn't want to spend any more money until it was resolved."

"The fossil was NOT in our contract," I said. "It is not part of anything. It was a gift for Julio."

Mickey groaned. "I know, but you've got to help me out on this. She provided most of the money."

"The contract is with you," I said. "Signed or unsigned, we acted upon it, and you are liable."

Mickey took a deep breath. "Look, I really want to get this thing going. You guys come up tomorrow morning and get started. We'll pick out all of your office furniture, I can do that much. But I want Brian, I mean Voltar, to talk with a man--a scientist from Cal Tech."

Brian shrugged. "What about?"

"He is one of my partners. He is working on a laser projection system—advanced holography."

"What about the money in the contract?" I said. "You owe us $1500 dollars and housing deposits. We are sleeping on the floor in Brian's apartment, and the lease ended last week."

Mickey dug into his wallet. "Look, I can give you $30 for today. The banks are closed. Just get back up here tomorrow and we'll take care of it."

"You'll take care of everything? Fifteen hundred, tomorrow?"

"Sure, all of it."

We all shook hands.

The next morning, Brian and I arrived at 8:30 a.m. with hope and apprehension in our hearts. Debra waited in the parking garage.

Mickey spent an hour with us picking out office furniture at a nearby store. We selected modest desks, file cabinets and a big drafting table for Brian's work. We even rented an IBM typewriter for me—with a white correcting ribbon. Mickey signed the order. "It'll be delivered tomorrow," he said. For the first time, we felt hopeful.

At his company, Mickey asked us to wait in the lobby so he could begin a meeting. In a distant office with glass walls, we could see him at a table with five distinguished men in suits. "Looks like it is going to happen," I said.

"I hope so," Brian breathed. "Voltar is about to explode. He is so eager to get on with the drawings." He wanted to start with the Biological Monitoring Belt, and continue by working on elements of the NOR. "He needs the magnetic outfit, right away. Don't forget that. That is vital for him."

For an hour we talked about the magnetic lining, then Debra burst into the lobby with her crying son.

"Did you get it?" she screamed.

"We are waiting for Mickey," Brian shouted.

"No. We need money, now" she pounded on the counter and yelled into the offices. "We have been using rags for diapers. If Mickey hasn't got a check I just might have to leave this diaper on his desk." She held up her soiled son for everyone to see.

Terrified, the receptionist ran back to Mickey's office.

"They don't want that in here," I said. "That was part of the deal--no babies in the lobby."

"I know that, Jim," she said. "But, I've been sitting in a damn hot car in the parking garage for two hours with a crying baby. Any woman who is a mother would understand. And if they don't--I don't care. We had a deal."

With baby screaming, she slipped into the bathroom.

Mickey arrived with a tall, slender man who looked like a scientist.

"This is the man we talked about," he said. "I would like Brian to talk with him."

They shook hands. "We need to get a payment," I said. "Debra is going nuts with a child here. They need to buy basic things—like diapers and food."

Mickey stammered. "Can't she wait outside for one more hour? The check hasn't been cut. It will be ready in an hour. Let Voltar and this man talk together, until then."

"Can you get Brian's half of the payment, now? She needs to find an apartment."

Mickey heard the screaming child in the bathroom. He ushered us into a large vacant office. "Let's let Brian and Dr. Johnson talk." He dug into his wallet for a twenty dollar bill. "Take Debra around the block. Just keep her away from here. This is an office, and I have investors in the other room."

As I escorted Debra out of the building. Brian sat down, face to face with the scientist. The man was a bit nervous as he presented his idea for a laser holographic projection system. He asked Brian what he thought.

"I'd have to study it, see the designs," Brian said. "Do you have designs?"

"Not, yet," he said as Mickey entered the room. I nudged in behind and whispered to Mickey. "She's gone for an hour," I said. "But then, she'll be back."

Mickey paced, nervously. "Listen Brian, I want to be straight about this," he said. "I've told Dr. Johnson about your Quantum Displacement Physics, and that you can bend spoons and all. And, well, it sounds good to him, but, as a scientist, he just can't take it on belief, you know. He has to see it."

Brian balked. "Is that what this is about?"

"Well, people need to see things. I need investors to finance this project."

"That is not part of the deal," Brian said. "Our deal is based on designs—on my background as a design engineer."

"Well, that too," Mickey said. "I checked out your resume, but this is different. We are talking about designing advanced technology. I need to see some sign of it."

"We can talk about Quantum Displacement. It has been defined, there are formulas that apply."

"Great," Mickey said. "We can get started. Now, if you can just do something for Dr. Johnson to demonstrate it. Anything. Bend a spoon. Bend a wire he can take back for analysis. Give him something to work with."

"That is not part of the contract, Mickey," I said with apprehension. "You know he won't do that."

Mickey stammered. "We have got to raise money and this is the best way to do it."

"Neither Voltar or I will allow that," Brian said. "That was made clear in the beginning."

"Brian," Mickey said in a soothing tone. "You have bent spoons for Chris. He told me about it. He saw it. Linda got the fossil. Everybody has seen something but me. I've got to be honest with you. I am just a man. I have to see something, too."

"That of the design," Voltar said. "That of the agreement. In that, and by that, all will be given to you."

"But that doesn't help me now."

"The word of a man," said Voltar. "For in this, without trust in the word of another, no project will succeed."

Mickey swallowed hard. "You ask me to trust you, and have faith in you, and I do, but I have to raise money from others."

"In this, the barter has been given--the right to sell, or refuse first, all designs. There will be many--far more than you know--and from these you would prosper in the days and years to come." Voltar spoke firmly.

Mickey breathed deep. "But I can't take that to the bank."

"Neither can you take that of a bent spoon to the bank," said Voltar. "In your expression--barter."

"I can't do this without something," Mickey whined.

"Of this, your test," said Voltar. "Your word has been given, and those around you have seen much."

Mickey knelt down close to Voltar. "Can you please, just do one thing for this man, just like you did for Chris or Jim, or all of the others? Just one bend-- one dent?"

Voltar's posture straightened, even more. He spoke like a king to a childish prince. "The word of a man is great in importance. For without the trust of others, there will be no displacement of time or energy, no ability to transport through space or time, any man."

"I don't think I understood that," said Mickey.

"For man to be displaced, the zone of retrieval, the end point of the transmission, must be of safety. The people, who experience displacement, must trust they will arrive. But first, the uplifting of a man's mind to Nous 4 will not take place without trust in himself. He must have unity in his own will, and mind. He must be ONE, at all levels. The entire process, from beginning to end, depends on trust, unity and agreement--especially, the word of one man to another. Of this, your test, and your beginning, or your end, in the *Play of Life.*"

Mickey pondered the words and began to sweat. "I have to ask you one more time. Can you do something? Can you tell this expert something about Quantum Displacement Physics that will make him understand how it works?

"Given," said the voice of Tau Ceti.

"All that was asked of me, has been given," said Voltar. "All that remains is for you to *comply with your own word.*" Mickey gulped. Voltar would not be persuaded. Mickey felt embarrassed in front of the scientist.

Suddenly, Brian's personality returned, eyes forward.

"He is really getting upset," Brian said. "What is going on? This could blow up. I mean, if I get pissed off, I could blow out a wall in this building."

"I just want him to bend a spoon for Dr. Johnson, and he refuses to do it," said Mickey.

"I can assure you, he won't do it," Brian said. "And I wouldn't permit it either. This is not going to become a circus. If one man can pull *his* chain, then another can--and another. They have too much to offer, Mickey--too much. And they have had this happen to them before. Their whole civilization was nearly destroyed because the Secondary World tried to get the knowledge of Quantum Displacement. Thousands died. They were literally tortured to death for it, and still they wouldn't give it. But they will give it to us freely, if we have agreement, and trust."

Mickey pleaded. "I trust you, but -- one spoon is all I ask. Is that too much? One spoon, and I will go through with it. You can have your desks, your money. You can have your silver suit, even. But I would prefer he not wear it around the office."

Brian breathed deep. "I don't think you know or understand what you have in your hands," he said. "He--Voltar and his allies--are willing to give man the knowledge of quantum displacement *as a gift*. So that we can be free forever from the Secondary World. But it will only be step by step. It will take dozens of designs, and many devices that need to be built. It will take training and research and manuals for education. It will take psychologists, engineers, teachers and professors, like Dr. Johnson here--all working in a step-by-step process. And each step will be based on trust, and discovery of something new."

"Are you saying you can do it, but you won't do it," Mickey said.

"Of course I can do it. I can do it myself," snapped Brian. "But I won't do it for him or anyone—not under demand. That is the wrong purpose, and ONE wrong purpose—ONE TIME--opens the door to the Secondary. Five minutes later I could end up...well. Jim has seen it. I do not want to be walking around like that. And if Voltar in a silver suit makes you a little nervous, how would you like to have Beelzebub crawling all over your desk? That's an example of what can happen."

"Who is Beelzebub?" gasped Dr. Johnson.

"Someone you don't want to meet," Brian said.

"I guess it's over then," Mickey said with a shrug. "I guess that's it."

"What?" Brian gasped. "Does that mean you are not keeping your part of the bargain?"

Mickey stammered. "I've got to think about this. I need some time."

"TIME? We are here, now today," Brian said. "We are here to start work on the designs. In six months, Dr. Johnson, and others like him will have something solid to evaluate."

"I can't go six months," Mickey pleaded. "The trip was more expensive than we expected. I can't pump ten thousand MORE dollars into this. I just don't have it."

Brian stood up. "If your word is not good, you don't deserve Quantum Displacement." He slammed out the door. The walls shook with his anger.

"Get me out of here," Brian said as I caught up with him. "Let's leave this place, before I lose control."

For the next several days, I tried to hammer out an agreement in some form. Neither Mickey nor Linda would provide the fossil or the initial contract, but we talked cordially and at times seemed close to a deal. Then I discovered they had tried to obtain the slides and film footage from the laboratories. Luckily, the labs followed correct procedure, and refused. I obtained the slides with money from an attorney and locked up the film footage until I could pay for the processing.

With the lawyer's help, we threatened to sue based on non-performance of a verbal contract. Brian wanted to charge them with extortion. He called the police and Los Angeles officers began an investigation.

In response, Mickey and Linda called the police, too. They said the car I was driving had been stolen from them. The police called me and insisted the car be returned.

As hope for fulfilling the transformation failed, as the dream of a home for Voltar evaporated, Brian began throwing up. For three days he vomited on his knees -- hour after hour, puking into the toilet.

I felt a sharp pain in my back. My kidneys ached so badly I could not walk a straight line—like I had a kidney stone.

By the second day, I began running a high fever with cold chills and sweats. I was in severe pain with no place to live. I felt Voltar's people should rescue us, but they did nothing. They had provided cream puffs and cookies, time displacement and all kinds of "miracles" but *they* remained silent in our suffering. That made me angry.

Debra quoted from the Bible, "If they are demons they will *'eat out our sustenance,'*" she said. "If they are angels of God, *we will prosper.* We are not prospering," she said. "That's the proof I need."

"It is not *their* fault," Brian argued. "They have to follow rules. This is of man. Man betrayed man. We pay the price. Look at all the apostles. Did they prosper? Most of them died with their heads chopped off. You have to be careful with quotes from the Bible," he said. "At least we're not dead."

As my fever rose, I didn't care about the arguments, or the theories. I was suffering, and becoming dazed by pain.

Debra's friend, Karen listened to the whole pathetic story. "You guys are all in deep trouble," she said. "You need help." She volunteered to drive with me to Los Angeles so I could return the rental car. Afterwards, she drove me back to Brian's apartment.

I was covered with sweat. "You need a doctor," she said. "Is there any place you can go?" I wanted to go home to my mom and dad, but they would never understand. I needed a nurse, a bed—time to recover.

Karen had just broken up with her boyfriend, and she was looking for an adventure to take her out of Orange County. I asked her to drive me to Northern California, to my cousin's house in Arcata, in redwood country.

To my great surprise, she agreed. My cousin offered me a place to stay for a week. I sold my camping gear for gas money, and we departed Orange County without even saying goodbye to Voltar, Brian or Debra.

I didn't care. I was fed up with Voltar and his *Play of Life*. I held Brian personally responsible. Who else was causing our suffering? Was Voltar an entity that could be tried in court, and punished for a crime? No. If I believed that, then I had accepted the alternate reality as real. I didn't, not for a court of law. The responsible person had to be Brian.

"It's not me," Brian said. "It's THEM." But that excuse was too convenient and a dangerous logic. What if THEY killed someone—even by accident? Would that line play well to a jury? No, Brian would be held accountable.

Could he plead to a jury, and say "the Secondary World made me do it. Or, we were following THEIR instructions?"

No, each man had to be accountable for his own familiar spirits, or aliens, or whatever he believed them to be. That's how I felt.

Besides, why should my life be destroyed because Brian refused to bend a spoon. How many times had Brian bent a spoon and talked about the heat? He could have done the same. Sure, Mickey applied pressure, even blackmail, and true—he had broken his own word--but the scientist wanted education. Couldn't Brian compromise, just a little? Perhaps some money could have been paid, at least the amount due--$1,500 would have meant a lot to us.

But, Brian insisted that Mickey needed to be "cut-off." If he tried black-mail, and breaking his word at this early stage, what would happen down the road, with new technology in his hand? That scenario could not be allowed—too dangerous for mankind.

Quantum Displacement could not be given to any man who surrounds himself with friends he cannot trust. Sure, I knew the issues might be serious, and I accepted that Voltar must stand his ground, but why not rescue us? Why destroy us? Why were we left hanging over the fire? I was tired of paying the price so man could be tested in the *Play of Life.* My body hurt, my life had been destroyed, and I had become an unwilling actor in THEIR *drama of probabilities.* I hated it.

But then, maybe I had been rescued. Karen was a cute, green-eyed young woman, with a bright spirit. I couldn't have asked for a more beautiful angel.

When we arrived in the pretty little town of Arcata, I was nearly unconscious with a fever of 104. I could barely walk from pain and dizziness. She had to help me into the house. My cousin immediately insisted we go to the hospital for tests, but after three days, the doctors found no infection, no kidney stone, no injury. They offered no explanation. Baffled, they sent me away.

My cousin and his wife owned a beautiful Victorian house they had restored and painted in the style of the era. They graciously provided a big bedroom on the first floor with tall windows, lovely white curtains and white bedspread. The room looked like heaven to me. They allowed Karen to put me into the bed and care for me, like a private nurse. Twice a day, she gave me water or soup-- otherwise I was near coma, in a daze.

Meanwhile, Brian and Debra also struggled to survive. They were also devastated financially and emotionally. Brian lost his sense of humor. But, the volunteer who had slept with Debra felt guilty. He offered a loan of $500 to help Brian find a job, and new apartment. Within a few days Brian felt better and he started working as a design-draftsman. For weeks, neither he nor Debra could talk without being overcome by anger. Their hopes and dreams had been destroyed, also.

"He warned us," Debra said. "He said 'betrayal.' Three times he said it. God, he sure was right."

"It's not at bad as what the Secondary World did to Voltar's people," Brian said. "They were tricked, then killed, and their children were trapped for generations. It could be worse. All we did was get wiped out financially."

"We didn't volunteer for this," Debra snapped. "It's not fair."

"It's a lesson," Brian said. "In the *Play of Life.* What happened to us can happen to others, and it can happen to our whole nation. It's a lesson for all mankind. It's worth the price."

"You've got to be kidding," said Debra. "What do I get out of it? Guilt? Heartbreak?"

"What's inside of each person comes out," Brian said. "It's a very deep thing."

"Bullshit," snapped Debra. "I'm not going to be their guinea pig. I'm not paying their price."

For weeks, Brian didn't even know where I had gone. When I finally called to say hello in late August, he had stabilized in a good job and a nice apartment.

"Our government is working with the Secondary World," he said, "on the same technology. In twenty-five years, they will have something like the NOR up and running. If the common people don't know about it, it will be used against them. That is the point. Our children could be betrayed and enslaved by our own government," he said. "What we experienced is nothing compared to what will happen to them."

He wanted me to come back and help him do something about it. "We have to build a prototype," he said. "We must do something to finish this. It's not over. The gifts must be given to man. That is the final step."

"Let them materialize something, or somebody else," I said. "I am sick of paying the price for their *Play of Life.*"

NOR X1-11 – The lights are red, green and blue. Lights are connected to a control panel (on the right) so they can be assigned to various types of input: music, voice, heart-rate, brain scan and other biological or psychological stimuli. A purple "black-light" projects out from within the hood so that the visual experience is beautiful. The floor pad carries low frequency vibrations so a person can feel the rumble of deep sounds on their feet. (The black light did not photograph in this shot.)

NOR X1-11 installed at the Easter Seal Rehabilitation Center in Orange County. The NOR was used by therapists for one year to stimulate deaf and aphasic children. Then the device was moved to the Psycho-biology Lab at California State University in Fullerton for 12 years of research.

Rehabilitation Institute
of Orange County

Serving Handicapped Children and Adults Since 1950
1800 East La Veta Avenue, Orange, California 92666
Telephone (714) 633-7400 or 951-7400

Accredited by: Commission on Accreditation of Rehabilitation Facilities **CARF**

June 24, 1982

Brian Scott
Marla Park
1603 N. Parton
Santa Ana, CA 92706

RE: CITE NOR, XI-II

Dear Mr. Scott and Ms. Park:

Per your request re the above referenced CITE, NOR, XI-II, the following is an update/progress report:

- The machine is not now being used by Physical Therapy and Occupational Therapy Departments since a bio-feedback unit is needed to facilitate use in those areas.

- The machine is being used in Audiology. The uses are in auditory training and Speech Therapy. Maria Abramson, RIO Audiologist states:

"The NOR X-I-II has proven to be a very effective clinical tool for both auditory training and speech therapy. Because the visual light display in synchronized with the audio input, deaf children can "see" what they hear. Further, speech impaired and hearing impaired individuals can "see" what they say. Thus, the NOR provides a visual reinforcement for speech production and perception.

The NOR has also been useful in developing children's attention skills. When placed in a darkened room, a deaf infant attends to the attractive visual display. Gradually, as his attention span increases, he will learn that the lights are associated with sound, and the sound is associated with meaning. In summary, the NOR is useful in developing children's auditory skills from the level of attention to the level of discrimination."

641

James E. Frazier

THE HERO

A HERO IS ONE WHO JOURNEYS INTO DARKNESS
TO BRING LIGHT TO HIS PEOPLE.
THE HERO EXPERIENCES THE SUPERNORMAL
AND THEN COMES BACK WITH A MESSAGE.
THE HERO IS FORCED INTO GOING ON AN ADVENTURE
TO DISCOVER SOME NEW LIFE-GIVING KNOWLEDGE FOR HIS PEOPLE.
IT'S A CYCLE - A GOING AND A RETURNING.
HIS JOURNEY BRINGS TRANSFORMATION
VIA TRIALS AND ILLUMINATING REVELATIONS.

Abstracted from Hero with a Thousand Faces, by Joseph Campbell

Chapter 23

The First Gift: The NOR x1 -11

I refused to help Brian anymore. Someone else could play the role. I would drop back and simply document what they did. Luckily, many people who knew Brian wanted to help. They wanted him to bring out Voltar and go public.

Jerry Lind--the tall, slender aviation executive--paid the bill and purchased the video tapes of Brian's hypnosis sessions. The tapes had been recorded in black and white. Renting a machine to play them was difficult. However, Jerry felt the hypnosis tapes validated Brian's UFO contact. To him, the hypnosis of Rex Walters provided some corroboration. He wanted to start at the beginning, and bring Brian out into the public by beginning with the hypnosis.

Brian agreed and on August 20,[th] a small crowd of people gathered at the Art of Living Center in Orange County. Brian wanted me to be there. I had never seen all of the tapes, and Karen wanted to go home so we drove down from Arcata in time for the session.

Brian hooted at the big TV screen when the "Host" challenged the investigators to "know the truth." The crowd cheered when the Host said the investigators had "mis-stated the truth."

"He just called them liars," one man laughed. "Under hypnosis, Voltar calls them liars. No wonder they didn't like him."

Watching the tapes closely for the first time, I felt the questions were clumsy. Just as Brian began answering in a deep hypnotic trance, the question changed. Brian complained of "buffeting" and his body trembled when questions changed so rapidly. His frame cringed, twisted and almost fell off the couch.

"People should not be allowed to do this without more training," said Lind. "Hypnotists for contactees should be certified therapists." I agreed.

Brian believed that hypnosis was dangerous. "If I *didn't* have a UFO contact, and went through this, I could really be screwed up," he said. "I wouldn't know what was true."

Brian felt that the hypnotism might have started the frightening, paranormal phenomenon. "That's where it all started," he said. "If they had kept their word, I would not have had to go through six months of hell," he said. "Because of them, we had to do it the hard way."

But, at times, Brian laughed loudly at the tapes. "I really can't believe that is me on the screen," he said. "It's so different to see it, than to experience it."

People who viewed the tapes felt the events had a consistent logic. The pattern made sense from beginning to end. The Host's request for trips to South America had all involved Nazca, Toro Muerto and Tiahuanaco—even in the hypnosis. The request for 'quantum evolution' never changed. Details and dates were consistent in drawings, trances and the hypnosis.

Brian failed to meet the request for Nazca, but he had met the requests for quantum evolution to Nous 8. Then he was betrayed. In overview, a simple story.

"How can we help?" the people asked Brian.

"Voltar needs a home," he said. "Until I can create a home for Voltar, I can't let him out of the bag—not full time." Brian didn't want to pick up the pieces of another failure, or betrayal. "It's too hard to recover," he said. He had decided to remain in dominance and protect Voltar. "Voltar is too vulnerable to live in our world," he said.

But, the people wanted to visit with Voltar and hear *his* perspective.

Brian agreed to provide a way—a method with controls. He asked the probe for suggestions. He received instructions, and agreed to follow a pattern. He would create an imaginary wall with red lights. He would make *the people* turn the lights green--by their deeds, actions, commitments. When the lights were green, in his judgment, Voltar could emerge.

On September 17th, a small group met in the Art of Living Center and requested "recognition within the probe." That was the first step.

Brian sat in a trance. The mechanical probe requested an access code from each person. Supposedly, the probe scanned each person as they stated their name, their mind-level (one), and the proper access code: 020-020-020.

Usually, after a long pause, the probe, would simply say, "Accepted." Often the probe reported on the person's supposed genetic heritage by naming a plantation and zone number. This information was the origination point of the "energy of their being" on earth, supposedly.

People took it all with a "grain of salt," but it was an interesting process. Official recognition by the probe meant that the person's guidance would be accepted and evaluated regarding Voltar's mission. Also, upon acceptance, a person could access the probe directly, and search Memory System 1A--by the power of thought. Memory System 1 A was a "front porch" where people could talk to the probe about basic questions. They could ask to access deeper memory systems, but they would have to be given the right access code—and that wasn't likely until the *Play of Life* was completed.

Brian created a schematic drawing showing how the probe's memory systems were organized, and he laid out the access procedure in writing for everyone to practice. Then, Voltar emerged and taught the group how to "go within" and access the probe mentally--with the "energy of their being."

No one talked to Voltar without being scanned and accepted within the probe. That was Brian's protection for Voltar.

Even if this was a case of multiple-personality, Brian had come with an elaborate procedure for protecting his alternative self. The process was like a ritual with detailed steps of logic.

Debra and I withdrew into the background as Brian worked with new people, but I watched for any signs of cultism. If I saw Brian start to exploit people, or isolate them in any way, I planned to shout loudly and stop him.

I had never accepted Voltar's world as reality, and I was embittered.

In a way, Brian blamed me for failure of the agreements with Mickey. We should have had a contract in writing, in advance. Also, I had let the fossil get away. Plus, I had left Voltar alone in Cuzco. From his viewpoint, I should have provided better protection for Voltar.

Whenever I complained, Brian would say, "Voltar's purpose is to *build a people.* Not just provide the technology. That means wisdom and understanding—for everyone. That means you, too—Jim."

"What more did I need to understand? I had been drawn into the fantasy, into the mythology, into the life of Voltar, his Council and even the allies. I knew all twelve allies by name, and personality: Lynanna, Energy, Mars, Saturn and Tau Ceti. Each had played a role. Then on Voltar's own council, twelve more had spoken. So, twenty-four personalities had expressed themselves through Brian, in some way. Each of them alleged to be a representative of their people—on their WORLD. It was an elaborate fantasy—or, perhaps an amazing reality of multiple-personality. How could I know? I was a mere mortal.

645

My basic theory of multiple-personality still held high ground in the battle of ideas. From that view, I could survey the personalities, Voltar's mission and the journey Brian had accepted. I could even acknowledge that paranormal powers were held by some of the personalities. Lynanna always seemed involved in materializations—especially of personal gifts, like cookies, or crème puffs.

However, Brian, the Council, and the allies were following a protocol--a set of rules that seemed logical—and that logic still interested me. The actual process, and their *reasons* were compelling.

After all, Brian wasn't acting like a crazy man. Instead, he was going to work everyday, progressing in his career, and maintaining relationships with many people, under stress. He coped. He even enjoyed the excitement. Plus, his goals were clearly stated. He wanted to give the "gifts to mankind" and present Voltar to "the People" in the right way—from the heart, without a lot of publicity or acclaim. That was noble, certainly. Brian refused to use his paranormal powers to attract people to the cause, or to convince anyone—of anything. But, he still bent spoons, for fun and the entertainment of friends. He was still the "life of the party" as Brian, or as Voltar.

I was impressed that he insisted on following rigid rules and a set of ethics that were obviously not those of a common man. Brian had earned my respect. He certainly didn't give up easy, in fact he persisted against all odds and opposition. He wasn't making money, or exploiting crowds of young women. He didn't inspire people to give up their religious beliefs or serve him in any way, like a cult leader might do. So, I watched with respect and awe.

In the kitchen, during the first probe access session, Karen and Debra also watched the process in amazement. "I can't believe this is happening," Debra said. "But I just can't put my heart into it anymore."

Her own guilt had weakened her commitment to Brian. She wanted Voltar more than Brian. She had seen Brian argue one day with their new apartment manager. Brian had blown his top because they could not have a waterbed in a second floor apartment. "But we don't have a water bed," said Debra afterwards. "Why did you do that? It's not a problem for us."

"I am just working off energy," he said. "I am so damn frustrated."

That was not a Godly deed, Debra thought--especially after two phases of transformation. He hadn't changed. He had resorted to a behavior of the 'old Brian,' laying a guilt trip on an older lady, without any real provocation. "Where is the transformation?" she complained. "All I see at home is Brian—the old Brian: self-centered, cranky, irritable."

"Change without change," Brian had explained. He was in command, and he was free to be his old self, OR Voltar at anytime. He chose to be the Common Man. He continued to smoke Marlboro's, and he replaced the vegetarian diet of Voltar with hamburgers, milk and potatoes. Brian himself was a bit amazed. "I can be all of the old Brian, and still retain the transformation," he said. That much freedom, he had never expected. He had imagined being Voltar, but not being able to go back to Brian, at will. That was a bonus of the duality for Brian.

But, Debra didn't enjoy the duality. She wanted Voltar back. She wanted to see more change in Brian, and especially more concern about *her* life from Brian. Debra started to suspect that Brian kept Voltar from her, on purpose.

"I am supposed to be a Christian," she told Karen. "And here I am living with a guy marked by a number in the palm of his hand. He sits in trance, hooking up people to an alien probe with their minds. And for what? No one knows. He's still Brian, most of the time."

Karen laughed. "Brian takes the cake on all of the guys we have ever met. I thought I had some weird ones, but I think you've topped me on this one."

Debra laughed as they smoked cigarettes in our kitchen. Karen and I were living together in an apartment. Everyone thought we made a good couple, and we had learned to have fun and pay the bills together. I had found a job as a printing press operator in Orange County, and she worked as a bookkeeping assistant.

We both needed each other to survive. I didn't expect the relationship to last forever, and neither did she. We were all still recovering. The four of us, two couples, played in the sun together on weekends. We enjoyed life. We all worked at high-tech electronics companies in the area, and we shared the same 8-5 work schedules. We could talk to Voltar in the evenings, and weekends—if we wanted. Or, we could just forget Voltar and go to the beach, or to the mountains for fun with Brian.

For a long time, we just shared life as friends. Voltar rarely emerged and Brian dominated. But as the weeks passed, Debra complained more and more about the duality. "I loved Voltar," Debra told Karen one day in September. "I want him back. I prefer him over Brian." She finally decided, for certain, that Brian kept Voltar away from her on purpose, because of the betrayal. She felt frustrated. She needed Voltar's compassion and concern for her life. She had come to love him even more than Brian.

Fall came and I suspected we might start a new cycle, because the events seemed to follow a calendar--a 22 day pattern—each month from September to June. Voltar had explained that we should make decisions in the first week of a month, then carry out the decisions until the 24th, then relax and analyze for 6-7 days. I realized that pressure had been applied to us in this pattern that they called *The Day of Twenty*. The most critical days were the 20-24th of each month—they were a climax. The biggest challenges usually came on those days. This 20-24 day cycle formed the core of *The Play of Life*.

On the fall equinox, September 22, Voltar emerged, briefly. He wanted to move forward and accomplish his mission to "give the gifts" to mankind. He wanted Debra to help create a life for him, including a way he could work on the projects at home in the evenings and weekends. Debra agreed, but her dilemma over the duality increased.

On September 27th, the moon was in an eclipse, and on Brian's 34th birthday, the sun entered into a TOTAL eclipse. A birthday eclipse of the sun seemed special, and two eclipses within two weeks was intriguing. We laughed that the story must be nearing completion. The sun and the moon had aligned with Brian—or he with them. The words Helios and Selene had appeared on many drawings, especially with the Gate of the Sun. The Sun and Moon were consorts of the Common Man. Perhaps, in some way, Duncan Lunan, and Michael Helios represented the moon and sun in Brian's life. Each held knowledge that Brian needed. Each was important on his journey—and their names couldn't have been better.

We rarely sat around and speculated, but we were having a party that day. "I really, love Voltar," Debra told Karen after the cake and ice cream. " I really do-- and Brian too—though, he's sometimes picky, and irritable. But, Voltar is so deep and so filled with compassion, I want him even *more* than Brian."

Unfortunately, Debra didn't care about Voltar's projects—the pyramid at Tiahuanaco, the NOR, or the Biological Monitoring Belt.

"What about that little number? 020 020 020," Karen said.

"I'm not too worried about the number," she said. "Voltar has never lied to me. That's the truth. He's been totally, painfully honest with me--and he has never held anything against me that I did wrong. And believe me I've done plenty wrong." She heaved with feelings. "I just never have met anyone like him."

Two weeks later, on October 22, another group of people accessed the probe including several Mormons, New Age Christians and Scientologists. "Don't all these weird people bother you," Karen again laughed in the kitchen. "They make a Marine on a Harley look pretty good."

Debra laughed. "Those Marines are *boys* with one thing on their mind," she said. "Voltar is a man, a real man."

"Just teasing," Karen said as they watched the 'probe session.'

"Does Brian know why they are doing this?" asked Karen.

"Oh, I'm sure he does. He's aware of everything now. He has the council of 12, speaking through him--all different. It's a gas when they all rattle off."

"This is so bizarre,' Karen said. "I feel like I am losing my head. It makes me want to go country western dancing. Drink beer. Party."

Debra laughed. "From their point of view, Karen--that is weird. Given what they say is happening on our planet--things we *'common people'* know nothing about--that is VERY weird."

"As long as you like him," laughed Karen.

"I LOVE HIM," said Debra. "He is like a deep reservoir of true love--and I've got him. But, then there is Brian. I have to put up with Brian all week to get Voltar, just for an hour."

In November and December of 1977, a wide variety of people visited our apartment to question Voltar and access the probe: a Russian scientist, a Catholic priest, a high level Scientologist, a Christian fundamentalist, a Hollywood writer. I recorded all of the sessions, on tape, as usual.

Voltar spoke to each person's heart, answering questions with depth and gentleness. At times, people cried when words of wisdom nourished their soul-- but Voltar did not answer personal questions. He would not prophecy, like a psychic about an individual's life, or even counsel on personal problems. Instead, he taught people to be strong, and to search within. "To each his own mind," he would say.

Voltar also refused to be led by people. He wouldn't start a cult. He told the weak-willed to NOT seek him for answers. "Seek not of I, but the reality of your own being," he would say. He didn't want followers. He didn't ask for money, and refused payment for any probe sessions.

Debra and Karen learned a lot by watching the parade of people. "All these weird people are strange, but they have vulnerable, gentle souls," Karen said after observing one session. "They all want to know about God, and themselves and their lives. It's incredible, people are so good, so *gentle* inside."

"It really is beautiful," Debra smiled. "They just pour out their hearts and souls to Voltar, and he strengthens them."

"And afterwards, Brian tells jokes," Karen laughed. "Then he carries out the trash, and cleans up the mess. Even scrubs the floor."

Brian seemed happy and organized. He worked every day, and kept everything clean. Debra called him "Mr. Clean" because he vacuumed every night and scrubbed the floors before going to bed. He washed the dishes, the pots and the pans, and prepared most of the meals. "He is a dream man," laughed Debra, "Most of the time."

"But is it just Brian--on the surface?" said Karen. "How can he do it?"

"Well, it's one guy, Brian Scott, that you see. But he is definitely not a normal person under the surface. He's more than one man."

"Like multiple-personalities?" Karen asked.

"Exactly. But, I think it's beneficial to him. Obviously, he is doing fine, after going through two years of this."

Because of the betrayals, Voltar had agreed to provide "gifts to man" through Brian's career. Brian's job duties accelerated rapidly after the second transformation. He was amazed at how easily he could solve design-engineering problems for the companies who hired him. His salaries increased steadily so he caught up on child support payments to Mary Beth.

He began to invent new devices, but he never sought patents or ownership. Even Voltar's smallest ideas were each "a gift to mankind."

Brian enjoyed giving his little "gifts," but they didn't fulfill Voltar's purpose—the Pyramid, the NOR, or the Biological Monitoring Belt. So, Brian still sought ways that Voltar could give his gifts to mankind. Voltar still wanted to use the power of his Touch. He still wanted to "build up a people."

The Alpha Man

As the story became known in Orange County, Brian made friends with many people who wanted their own experience of "quantum evolution." Glenn Rivers, a young Catholic man with five children, radiated abundant energy like Brian. Though bright-minded, Glenn lived a simple non-intellectual life. He worked as a refrigeration technician, earned a good living for his family, and supported his local Catholic Church by building solar powered water wells for villages in Mexico.

In January of 1978, while working on a customer's home freezer, Glenn lost two hours of time. He couldn't explain what happened, and the customer was upset. By the time Glenn arrived home, he felt dehydrated, feverish and confused. Worse, he heard a mechanical voice speaking clearly into his mind. He figured he was going crazy.

Frantic, he passed out in his living room. A deep, soothing voice spoke from his lips calming his wife and children. His older kids enjoyed talking to this noble presence for nearly 20 minutes. However, when Glenn's personality returned, he was disoriented and frightened with total amnesia of what was said. This terrified him.

After several hours of spontaneous blackouts, his wife called for an ambulance--and then she called Brian. The voice that spoke during the blackouts, called himself Alpha. The deep voice said Glenn was the First of Man—an example for all.

Brian and Debra arrived in the emergency room as doctors finished their exam. Brian asked to see Glenn. His wife gave permission over protests from the doctors.

"He's delirious from the high fever," a doctor advised. He is babbling about things that don't make sense. Brian understood. He sat next to Glenn and held his hand.

"Glad you are here, compadre," Glenn moaned. "It's like, I am communicating to everything. It's so much, so many out there. Some are so weird--some good, some evil. They are all talking to me. They seem to *be* me, at least -- *one with me.*"

"You'll be all right," Brian assured. "You are who *you* are. You are NOT all of them. You can choose who you talk to, which one becomes *one with* you. You choose. That is the key. You are the bottom line, the rock—the foundation. You are in command. Just choose something you can maintain, but remember, when it is all done, you are still just you. For that you can be thankful." He squeezed Glenn's hand.

"But there are so many," Glenn breathed in a daze. "So much. It's all connected, connected to *me,* somehow. How can that all be part *of me?* I can't even say what I am experiencing."

"You are the anchor--the Common Man. You gotta pay the bills. You choose which one you want to communicate with. You might as well choose the YOU, that already exists."

"But they ABSORB me. Unite with me. I become them, they become me."

"You will still be YOU, afterwards--after the unity. It's change without change. You change, but you don't. You still have your life. You are still you, but new things are added on to you--wisdom and knowledge and powers. There is nothing to fear, if you choose wisely. But don't choose some identity, some personality, you can't maintain. Don't choose anything evil to get power, and don't choose anything so good, that you can't maintain the life. It's better to choose you, as you are."

"I understand," Glenn moaned. "I just want to experience it all, but--it's too much."

"Right," Brian said. "Too much. Just bring back a little tiny piece that you can work with. Bring a tiny bit back home. Say no, to all the rest. Wait for the next time. Okay? Don't be afraid to say no. You are in command."

"But I don't want it to go away. I don't want it to stop."

"It won't stop. Once you are hooked in, it will all be there again. Whenever YOU WANT. You can go back and learn more, at the right time and place. When it is right for you. You can be in command. You should be in command. You tell it when to start and stop. Remember, it's all really you. You are the Common Man—the Universal Man."

"That's what it is," Glenn breathed. "Universal Knowledge about anything I think or know, or am. Instant, universal knowledge tied to each thought, but expressed as beings, as personalities."

"I am--that I am," Brian said. "Remember?"

"I understand," Glenn whispered.

Finally, Voltar emerged. "Now is now," Voltar said with a deep gentle voice.

Glenn had been hoping to hear from Voltar. "It's so unexplainable, Voltar--I need a friend."

"I am your friend and your brother," said Voltar. "And you are mine."

Glenn felt better. "The energy of mind, it's so, so vast, so many connections. I feel happy, but every thought turns into entities that come to me-- good and bad. I see their heart, their mind--their souls. They are me." He sniffled. "The emotions are flooding me."

Glenn sobbed as Voltar patted his hand.. "This is a beginning for you, and for man," he said. "Brian felt the same, and he finally chose to laugh. You can too. You have been given a taste of mind level two. From two, three will come, and from three--the fourth. Onward until all ten have been accomplished by man. From this day, go forward in joy."

"I can't imagine beyond this," said Glenn. "If this is only a two. God, what you must have gone through if this is only two," Glenn moaned and laughed all at the same time.

"To give this to man, is easy for us," said Voltar. "We can give Nous two to all man—in an instant by activating a geographic zone on the earth. But, is man prepared? Would all man be as you are now? As Brian was, in his beginning? Many would not survive."

Brian's personality returned and laughed with Glenn.

"I screwed up much worse than you," he said. "I didn't do a very good job of it," Brian said. "At the beginning, I flipped out and became very irritable. It's my fault that Mary Beth cracked up. I didn't take care of her. Make sure you take care of those around you—or you might lose them. You could lose your family."

Voltar returned. "Brian has proven that the common man of today on your world can attain a higher level of mind, but the costs are high. Knowledge has been given through the *Play of Life* to Brian, and to man. Now, you are the Alpha, the beginning for man. You must proceed forth with Brian's experience and knowledge as a guide."

Voltar squeezed Glenn's hand. "Laos Nous Hikano," he said. "Look to the East has come—a New Dawn. "

"That's right," Glenn gasped, squeezing Brian's hand tightly. "That's it--*The God-mind of Man Returns*. I get it. That is what I am experiencing." A devout Catholic, he crawled out of bed and onto his knees. "Nothing can happen without the will of God," he said. He prayed. "Thank you God. Thank you for sending Brian and this experience to me. Thank you, God."

An hour later, the doctors released Glenn. His fever was gone, and his mind had calmed.

Brian and Debra helped steady his steps to the family car, a big station wagon filled with sleeping kids. Glenn's wife was thankful that Brian had come.

"This is amazing," Glenn said. "It's over. But I still lost two hours. I have no recollection of what happened during that time. Nothing."

"You were with *them*," Brian said. "Someday, at the right time, you will know what happened."

Glenn was very thankful for the experience, but Debra didn't believe it was from God. "Why would someone end up in a hospital," she asked. "Does God do that?"

"Look at Job, in the Bible," said Brian. "He was basically tortured with God's permission. His sons were killed. Look at Joseph. He was thrown into captivity. Or Abraham who was asked to kill his own son. Or Moses, who murdered a man. Or David, who had to run for his life, and kill many men in battle. Look at Paul who was beheaded, or John, and most of the other apostles too. All killed. You have a wrong idea, if you think God makes an easy path for everybody. That's a mistake many Christians make. God gives strength to overcome in tough situations, and be fulfilled--even if you die. Strength--that's all Voltar gives in his *Play of Life*. At least we don't have to go to that level. I'm thankful for that, at least." Debra didn't know what to say.

"I thought when you became a Christian, everything was rosy, and you would prosper, and become good. I didn't realize God provided such serious tests," she said. "You're right about the Bible. The heroes, the main leaders, went through terrible times. Maybe they died happy."

"Man must grow through a process of education," said Voltar.

"Are you working with God, or against Him?" Debra blurted. "That's what I have to know."

"We are servants," said Voltar. "In obedience to His will."

Taking Voltar to the People

In the first six months of 1978, Brian tried several ways to "take Voltar" out to the people. He spoke at a few UFO gatherings and in a New Age Christian Church. But nothing worked right for him.

"It is wrong," Brian said. "I can't live in a church -- or as a New Ager. I could care less about going to UFO conventions. I am a nuts and bolts kind of guy," Brian said.

James E. Frazier

When people protested that Voltar had promised a spiritual AND technological uplifting for man, Brian agreed. "But we have to have the engineering side done, before the spiritual uplifting begins," he said.

Voltar's NOR – Neural Optical Responder

In June of 1978, Brian seemed frustrated. He said Voltar wanted to get started. Since the pyramid seemed so remote, Brian decided to focus on the NOR and the Biological Monitoring Belt.

To understand the belt, people first needed to understand the NOR, so Voltar began explaining the NOR to everyone. He described how Cuzco's three-ringed time clock had been the model for Voltar's three-ringed NOR, drawn AFTER the first transformation. Both were related to the Rings of Time that Brian had seen onboard the craft.

At Cuzco, in the three rings of the time-clock, ancient priests had moved mirrors and reflected torchlight through holes in pillars to impact the eyes of children. "Man is a neural-optical being," Voltar said. Eyes affect the brain. Harmonious patterns of light and sound could induce altered states of consciousness, like hypnosis or trances.

Many of the initiatory rituals Voltar described took place in polished caves located around Cuzco. When the initiate was isolated in a cave, the priests would flash light into his eyes with an obsidian mirror. Another priest played flute music. Another whispered to the young man or woman through tiny tunnels in the stone walls.

The whispering provided guidance to the initiate as he journeyed, like Glenn Rivers had done, through the choices of identity and personality. The person must choose to be a Common Man, linked to his family, Voltar said. The transformed man must build a life for his family--not an excuse to abandon them.

The transformation must proceed outward, from the individual, to his family, to his nation, Voltar emphasized. It all begins with the person, the individual. Any other method would lead to disaster. "The group cannot force the individual," he said. "Each to his own mind."

Voltar talked to small groups of people who came to our apartment. "Fear not the mind of mankind," he told them. "Knowledge of the past is given. Man will be uplifted by his own will—by his own choice, by his own hand."

Voltar warned that if the US government builds a NOR-like device in cooperation with the Secondary World, destruction could come to mankind, and even the planet. The NOR is much more dangerous than the nuclear bomb, he warned.

"The power you will discover is greater than any known to man today," he said. Thus, he wanted the Common People to have the knowledge, also. "The

NOR and the Biological Monitoring Belt will lead all man to understand Quantum Displacement Physics. Each man, woman and child will learn to displace time. You will all learn to transport matter and energy through space— with the mind at level four—in order to survive," he said. He always said we would be develop the skills --*'to survive.'*

Voltar's first design of the NOR, based on the time clock at Cuzco, had featured a domed building with a 200 foot radius and three inner rings. Inside the dome, he planned a water fountain, water falls, running streams, huge green plants and several ways to generate patterns of light and sound. One projection system was very simple, using water and sunlight. Another, more complex, used a high tech system -- like holography. He said the methods for projection would change as man's technology unfolded in the future. The principals would remain the same.

Outside the central dome, he designed six smaller domes each thirty feet in diameter. Each was dedicated to one color: red, orange, yellow, green, blue and violet. They were used to align people to certain frequencies.

The complex of domes comprised the NOR. At the very center, in the middle of the big dome, stood a gateway *nebulous to time,* like the Portal to Life at Tiahuanaco—a doorway for creating ascending and descending levels of consciousness. When complete, Voltar's people would activate the earth grid at the selected point, and from that time forward, man could use the NOR as a portal—Nebulous to Time—a *'matter transportation vehicle.'*

It all seemed so simple.

Discussions followed with a variety of people, and after several months, raw land in the desert near Twenty-Nine Palms was offered without cost. However, Brian would need to raise the money for construction, and move to the desert.

For a while, he tossed the idea around. He investigated domes, and construction costs—a million dollars, or more. However, Brian didn't want to live in a desert. He did not want to withdraw from society—like a cult. Voltar insisted the projects take place 'among the people' without causing anyone to move or give up their normal lives. No one was to change their religious beliefs, withdraw from society, or their family.

When Brian talked about the land deals, I emphasized his accountability. "You need a contract," I said. "You will sign it and you will be accountable in a court of law. You can't say 'Voltar' told me to. Even if Voltar signed a contract, YOU will be the one forced to pay for any loss or damages."

The realization hit home with Brian. "If I am accountable, then I will build what I can with my own hands--in my own apartment," he said. "A prototype is what we need. I'll build it in the living room."

With Voltar's help, Brian took command of the projects. He roughed out designs for a prototype of the Biological Monitoring Belt. The first design featured colored squares of light that pulsed to music played on a tape in the belt. A more advanced version actually monitored biological systems and converted the biological data to patterns of light and sound played by the belt to the wearer, and friends.

Brian discovered that basic costs for a plastic mold were over $30,000. He was stymied. One day, at an electronics store, I found an attractive floor display—a molded plastic pedestal that looked futuristic with a black and white design. It had been used for selling phones. I paid $25 and brought it home to Brian.

Because he liked the shape, Brian decided to design a NOR using the pedestal. He went to work on the drawing in a flurry. Within a week, he had conceptualized the NOR X1-11, an experimental prototype for the huge NOR of Voltar. It would be *'man's stepping stone to Quantum Displacement Physics.'*

Debra didn't like having the pedestal in the apartment. She didn't think any man should build a machine to uplift his mind. "It's not in the Bible," she said. "Man doesn't need a machine to reach God. Man didn't need the tower of Babel," she said. "It's the same thing."

"It's just technology," Brian said, "new technology like cars were, at one time."

"It's not in the Bible," she argued.

"Dinosaurs are not in the Bible," Brian said. "Cars and airplanes are not in the Bible," he argued. "Nor surgery and modern medicine, or rockets or even typewriters—which you use everyday. Or how about telephones? They were all created by men. We have to be real. This is for society as it is today."

"But they don't uplift the mind," she said. "They don't expand the consciousness."

Brian pleaded with Debra to cooperate, but whenever he withdrew to work on the machine, she created problems—like slamming doors, breaking glasses or screaming.

Voltar reminded Debra that she had agreed to cooperate. He had asked her to change within six months. If she couldn't change, one of them must move out of the apartment. She agreed to the terms.

Brian's NOR – The NORX1-11

Brian continued to work on his tiny NOR which featured the same basic concepts as Voltar's giant NOR—harmonious patterns of light and sound projected to multiple users.

My college degree in psychobiology prepared me well for understanding the NOR. In fact, Voltar always said it came from *my mind,* so I was interested. I had studied trances, epilepsy and knew that lights flashing at a certain speed could induce an epileptic trance in some people.

I wondered if the same idea might be applied for beneficial purposes, perhaps for accelerated learning. I felt research on the subject might be of interest to NASA, and the space program, So, I was willing to participate. I even dreamed of completing my doctorate in Neural-Optical Technology with an advanced NOR linked to big screens, like in a movie theater. We all knew that huge computers existed in big companies and universities. I wondered if someday, the NOR might be operated by a huge computer. That concept really frightened Debra. She feared the idea of "Big Brother" controlling everyone's mind, as prophesied in the futuristic book, 1984.

Voltar warned that the NOR technology was dangerous. "Man will mature," he said, "and develop new ethics and new philosophies—a new way of life. For this, wisdom will be given."

Voltar's Teachings of Space

Brian began to gather parts for the NOR from vendors he used at work. Sample lights, switches and buttons were contributed, and Brian started a stockpile of parts.

As the list of parts grew, Brian realized he would need about a thousand dollars for sound speakers, a tape deck and large sound amplifier. So, to help finance the NOR, he wanted to hold a class, a seminar.

He didn't pressure me to continue. I could have walked away, but as a dramatist, I knew the story had not yet reached conclusion. Sure, Brian had supposedly completed 'Quantum evolution to Mind Level 8,' but the time had not yet come, for the final epiphany. I was still learning about the logic and method of the post-contact experience. I was still learning about the rules and protocol. Whether or not Voltar's people were really living in the star system of Epsilon Eridani, was not important to me. I still believed their world to be a fantasy, a mental construction of Brian's, perhaps a view of our future, or some alternative reality.

Dr. Hynek and Jacques Vallee still had not figured out the dilemmas, and I figured that now, I was probably closer to solving the mystery than anyone. I agreed to help run the seminar, so I could get my remaining questions answered.

Voltar titled the series "The Teachings of Space." Classes started on September 27, 1978. Forty people paid the small fee. In six sessions on Wednesday nights, they learned from Voltar about the "energy of the being" and the "space around their body."

657

Each week before the class, I went through a pre-class training session with Voltar so I would understand each point from my own perspective. That way, I could direct the class.

Voltar taught that each person must master the space about their own body, and understand the energy of their *own being* before understanding others. Man needed anchors. Brian was the anchor for Voltar. Brian protected, and provided a home for Voltar.

Using music tapes, and low-frequency sounds, Voltar taught the people to "go within" and connect with the "energy of their being." It was a first step, only. To really understand their own "being," people would need to build something like the NOR, he said. The group learned about Voltar's plan for a three ringed super NOR, and then Brian's smaller prototype – the NOR X1-11. They knew that money for the class would be used to build the device.

"My NOR is not fancy," said Brian, "but I can build it on my own. "

The prototype would help man understand how to control ascending and descending levels of consciousness – in an elementary way—with patterns of light and sound.

People enjoyed the class, though no one received personal guidance or psychic counseling. Voltar taught by asking people in the group to agree with a statement—YES or NO.

He selected those who said 'no' and asked them to sit in front of him. They came forward and sat down close to him. He supposedly looked at the "energy of their being" as he answered their questions in depth.

The process was slow, but effective. Everyone in the group learned from the questions and objections.

Voltar did not want everyone to agree with him. Bold disagreements were rewarded, and objections dissected. He taught by question, asking the person to reason out an answer, step-by-step, until a revelation came, and true understanding.

Sometimes the group strained to hear. Voltar allowed privacy on personal feelings, but when "one of the no" had experienced an epiphany on the issue at hand, Voltar addressed the group in a booming voice using the objection, and reasoning as an example.

The group quickly learned that Voltar was leading them to reason on their own, and to seek out implications of their words and decisions.

After the opening dialogue, Voltar would show the people how to use a certain sound to "go within" and experience various levels of consciousness. As they entered meditation, he whispered and led them -- as if reading each person's mind.

When emotions peaked, and a person cried, Voltar asked people to reach out to each other with open hands and arms. "For in each other is your strength," he would say. "For you are all one at Nous ten."

People poured out their hearts to Voltar as each faced fears about higher levels of consciousness. Many feared blacking out, dizziness, bright flashes of light in their mind, unusual sounds in their head, and vibrations on their neck and crown. To all, Voltar provided comfort and counsel.

Week by week as sessions continued, people reported strange dreams, out-of-body experiences—and supposed visitations by entities. Some experienced blackouts or convulsions.

In the classes, tears often flowed when Voltar understood their unspoken fears. He would address each person's private life as if reading their mind and heart. Without embarrassing the person, he spoke about their secret fears and deepest most intimate feelings. He provided challenges and questions for them to answer, not personal guidance. "Seek not of I, but the reality of your own being," he told them. "The answers you need are within." Thus, by this method, by his warmth and understanding, he won the hearts of the people.

Afterwards, Brian cracked jokes and cleaned up the mess, and took out the trash. He counted the costs, and took care of the worldly details, so Voltar could teach. He purposely would not let people treat him like Voltar--with honor or respect. "I'm just Brian," he would say. "Keep it that way."

Return of The Children

In response to religious questions, Voltar taught from scriptures in the New Testament, especially the Book of Revelation.

He explained the meaning of the anti-Christ and Armageddon. He urged people to go to Israel, to the town of Qumran, 'when the army of the north is swept from the doorstep of Israel.'

"The day of the dragon and the day of Qumran are One," he said.

He promised that on December 24, 2011 A.D. the "children of the stars" would return to five locations on the earth: Qumran in Israel; Sedona, Arizona; Giza in Egypt; Stonehenge in England; and, to a pyramid in China.

"For some of you Qumran is the place to be, for others Sedona, or Giza or Tiahuanaco or China. You will know what is right for you."

The final return of "the Children" was to be the end of Voltar's people. "Through the touch that is shared with those who gather, our ending will come-- our passing away--but in this will be a New Beginning for man. All those who receive the touch will receive in that one moment, the knowledge to fulfill and build the New World, the thousand years of peace—THE MILLENNIUM."

Before December 24th 2011, he wanted man to build his version of the NOR, and the pyramid at Tiahuanaco so they could be activated, in advance, as portals.

The Millennium? Finally, I understood. The full scenario could now be viewed within a Biblical perspective. The stated role of Voltar and his people was not religious, but to help provide a new technological beginning for man in a POST-tribulation world, a world AFTER Armageddon, after prophecies in the Book of Revelation were completed, after Jesus had supposedly returned to set up His kingdom on earth.

The overview seemed consistent. There had been hints of Christianity, all along, but Voltar had refused to let his role become religious, or Brian's. He had refused to become a preacher or a prophet.

I still didn't accept Voltar's reality as valid, but I had to agree that the big picture was consistent. My role, I felt, was to determine the logic, the method of interaction, and the inner consistency—despite the source. Whether or not the plan was created by Brian, or by a "familiar spirit" or by multiple-personalities, I certainly could not say. All I could say, is that it seemed consistent from beginning to end.

Voltar's core group of people included conservatives and liberals, housewives, engineers, scientists, Christians and Buddhists. Despite their divergent beliefs and backgrounds, they shared a deep experience with Voltar and a feeling of unity. No one knew if the big picture was right or wrong. We would all have to wait and see. The next Generation would be the ones to know. The next generation would probably be the ones to fulfill the request—to build the NOR and the pyramid at Tiahuanaco.

Voltar did not push people to complete the tasks. He did not inspire people in the class to follow him, give up their possessions, or abandon their own religious beliefs. He always resisted their suggestions to withdraw from society, or share housing with anyone. Instead, he insisted each person stay in their own family, in their own home, and in their own religion. He asked no one to build the NOR or the pyramid. But, *The Play of Life* wasn't over.

Voltar had not gone out "amongst the people," and his gifts had not been given away to man. For the final phase, another person needed to enter Brian's life—a person with full understanding of who he was, and where he had been, and what he wanted to do. Amazingly, such a person waited in the wings to play her role on center stage.

Marla's Experience

Marla Park had been prepared. A pretty brunette about twenty-five, she was Mary Beth's supervisor at work in an electronics company. Marla read blue-prints and supervised the assembly of computers. She had called for help when Mary Beth was jolted from her chair, possessed by Ashtarte. She had followed the story, from Mary Beth's perspective since then. When Brian moved out of the home, she tried to help Mary Beth with the kids. She had even lived in the house for a short time.

In the summer of 1978, Mary Beth finalized the divorce with Brian, and threw a big celebration party with a live band. She was ready to start a new life, without Brian. She picked Marla's birthday as the special day and invited Marla as an honored guest. She had been a good friend, and helped her survive. Marla had put Mary Beth "back on her feet."

To show there were no bad feelings, Mary Beth also invited Brian, as the honored ex-husband. Brian thought the idea was bold and healthy for Mary Beth. He attended to show support for her, and the children. He had no bad feelings for Mary Beth. He still loved her in a way. From his view, she had not grown; she simply had remained behind, when he expanded. She had created evil where there was none, because she wanted power. The problems were inside of Mary Beth, and—under the conditions—they came out. If he had not left, she might have ended up in an institution the rest of her life. That's how he felt.

Mary Beth had admitted to Marla that she made mistakes. "If I had supported Brian, if I had seen what he was going through, and helped him, instead of trying to have my own experiences, we would still be married today. I was too jealous," she said. "I was so jealous I didn't want anyone to have him--not aliens, not investigators, no one. That's what drove me nutty," she said. "Jealousy."

They both still loved each other, as friends. They both understood.

At the party, the two honored guests met. Marla and Brian talked about the kids, the frightening events and Mary Beth. Marla believed Mary Beth created most of the problems by over-reacting, but she held Brian accountable for causing the situation. She was tough as nails on both of them.

Marla Park knew all about Brian -- good and bad. She understood that Brian still loved Mary Beth and wanted the best for her, and his girls. They agreed that his departure from the home was best for the kids, and for Mary Beth. Marla understood his dilemma, but she wanted answers—spiritual answers about ethics, about right and wrong.

Brian liked Marla's spunky spirit. She was a fighter. Although she was a bit heavy, Marla was pleasant and light-hearted. She was 24, a cute brunette with a Mormon background, and a solid character. Her eyes sparkled and she laughed easily--but she held him accountable for the problems. She would not let him "off the hook."

To Brian, Marla was a mystery. She was tough, but nice. She really wanted to understand what had happened to Mary Beth, and how he rationalized his feelings. She wanted to know how he could live with Debra, if he loved Mary Beth.

"There are all kinds of love," he said. "The whole thing is bigger than anyone can imagine."

Marla understood love. She had been trained as an electronics technician, and then quickly promoted from soldering to supervising. A great manager of people, Marla believed in taking care of family, friends and co-workers in true "brotherly love." Her "family of love" philosophy worked well on the assembly line. Marla could be "in charge," without being bossy. She would go to the ends of the earth to look out for her workers--their needs, and their safety.

Marla believed in God, and she believed no harm would come to a person who had accepted Jesus into their heart. She believed that a good person could take any bad situation and make it good. "That's what life is about," she said.

Brian liked her style. She wasn't a pushover, but she was pleasant and positive.

After the July party, Brian was surprised to see Marla show up in late September at the first class in the Teachings of Space. Brian didn't know that she had come because an out-of-body-experience had panicked her, a few nights before. She was frightened, and wanted answers. She didn't want to end up like Mary Beth.

When Voltar opened the class by purposely providing false, but logical speculations, she boldly defied him. Her quick objection stunned the class, who were still pondering. Thus, Marla--the sweet-hearted, tough-willed Mormon from Park City, Utah--became known to everyone in the class as "the first no." She would not tolerate any statements that didn't sound truthful. She had said "no" when others remained silent. Thus, she was chosen to represent the class in an experience of the paranormal.

A few weeks later, on Saturday, October 28th, Marla and Brian journeyed to the beautiful, rocky amphitheater in the mountains outside of Orange County — *"The Place of the Whole."*

Playing on the gray rocks, Marla and Brian waited most of the day. Nothing happened until after sunset when they were about ready to go home. Around nine o'clock, the crickets stopped singing--suddenly. Marla felt eerie, like someone might be approaching in the darkness. She saw a light in the woods, in a circle of trees.

Suddenly Voltar spoke loudly--from the air. "I come in peace." His voice echoed from the stones. Brian sat next to Marla. His lips didn't move. She could see that he wasn't doing the talking, and she clutched his hand in fear.

"Good evening," Voltar said. Marla saw flashes of white light off to the side of the amphitheater. At the same time in the amphitheatre, one rock started to glow. The light pulsated as Voltar spoke.

"Of this, man seeks for us to descend and to be among him, and for many this would provide a great fulfillment, but better man should seek himself first, and fulfillment from within. For in this is the greatness of man."

She started to ask a question. He interrupted.

"Seek not of I, but the reality of your own being. In this, man must know himself, before he can know others. Of this, man must shower in the light of his own soul -- to find fulfillment."

Marla relaxed. The voice sounded just like Voltar in class. She noticed that the rock glowed more brightly when the voice grew louder. The light dimmed when the voice slowed, or stopped.

"Man must learn to use the energy of his own being, for of this is the doorway and the portal within," he said. "Truly man must seek within. In this, each man must seek the reality of his own being, first. From this, much can be given to each, and to all. As man learns to reach outward, from within, his world will be changed and transformed."

From another spot in the amphitheatre the voice of Lynanna spoke, "Of this, energy is given to you, tonight, and knowledge to aid that of Brian. Goodbye."

Then other allies spoke briefly, like Saturn, Mars and Tau Ceti, "You are given energy. Of this, thank you. Goodbye. "

They continued with each voice saying *thank you--and goodbye.*

When the voices ended, the crickets started singing. That's the last thing Marla remembered--the crickets starting to sing.

The next day, around two in the afternoon, she woke up in the car, driving back into Tustin.

"What happened?" she asked Brian. "WHAT HAPPENED?"

"We went for a little visit," he said. "Don't you remember anything?"

She glanced at her watch and the sky. "It's daytime! Two o'clock." She gasped, terrified.

"It's okay," Brian said gently. "You'll remember at the right time."

Marla's Commitment

The next week, Marla told her story to the class. Everyone was skeptical about the missing time. Marla and Brian had spent the night together--one way or another.

Debra knew Brian had not come home that night. He had no explanation. He'd simply "lost time." Strangely, she believed him and wasn't upset.

After the classes ended, Marla told Brian that she could solder anything he wanted—just bring her the parts. She had seen enough—she didn't need any more proof. She would help build the NOR.

With money from the class, he was able to buy an amplifier for the sound system, and a control panel. He started building the NOR in his living room. Brian and I cut the opening for the amplifier. Everything fit. But, when the first step was completed, Debra felt frightened. In front of her eyes, a machine for "uplifting the mind" was taking shape--becoming a reality.

One evening each week, Brian visited Marla with small parts. She soldered them together with her portable soldering iron, and they talked for long hours about his situation. Marla finally suggested he move the machine to her apartment, so Debra wouldn't be upset.

When Brian told Debra, she became jealous, and they fought. He could accomplish nothing more in the apartment. Finally, Voltar reminded Debra of her agreement. Voltar asked if she felt the proper atmosphere had been created for him to work. She said no, and agreed that she had failed. Brian worked out an agreement to leave the apartment, and live with Marla until the NOR was complete.

To my surprise, Debra wasn't crushed. Instead, she felt relief. She wanted a chance to live on her own, to try out her wings. She had been devastated by the betrayals and the financial setback. But most of all, she didn't want to be part of a *machine* for uplifting man's consciousness. That was against her religion—against the Bible, she believed. She wanted a life of her own, earning her own way, as an executive secretary.

There was only one problem—she was pregnant, again.

VOLTAR, MARLA PARK and JIM FRAZIER on February 7, 1980 give "The Voice of Common Man" in a video-tape to White House liaison Mr. Jim Purks, who accepted on behalf of President Jimmy Carter.

James E. Frazier

VOLUME 57—NO. 41   TUSTIN, ORANGE COUNTY, CALIFORNIA,

Tustinites' Opinions Filmed for President

Driving by the intersection of El Camino Real and Main Street Friday afternoon, motorists saw movie lights, a camera and a man with a microphone interviewing passers-by. Those who stopped to investigate heard people describing the nation's ills and offering suggestions and opinions. They were told by the firm company that President Carter would eventually hear their views.

Tustin residents Brian Scott and James Frazier said the film is an answer to the President's call for the common man to speak out. The idea came about when the two men were forming an engineering consultant firm called Congress for Interplanetary Technology and Education (C.I.T.E.). Their goal is to hand deliver a videotape of the common man's views to Carter's door, Frazier said.

One of those interviewed, Tustinite Gordon Gray, voiced his concerns on the President's credibility pro-

blem and the Nick Ogden, the Tustin TL gram, mentio of senior citin ble solutions.

Tustin Char merce Presid bern, said o President: I what we exp said the grou Police Chief Cl and Mayor p Saitarelli earli city hall.

Frazier adc venture will ec out of their poc they hope t Washington, D the filmed Carter person

LIGHTS, CAMERA...Tustin student Sean Plummer is interviewed by Brian Scott in a film on the "common man's views" of national problems to be hand delivered to President Carter. Plummer gave the President his opinions on the gas crisis. See story on page, 7 section 1.   NEWS Photo

TUSTIN NEWS article on the first day of filming. Aug. 4, 1976.

Orange County Edition

Los Angeles Times

Orange County Edition

s Angeles T

SATURDAY, FEBRUARY 2, 1980

TUSTIN TRIO'S TALE OF THE TAPE

The People's Voice to Be Brought to Carter's Ear

By HERMAN WONG
Times Staff Writer

SANTA ANA — This Tustin-to-Washington scenario reads like a 1980 update of a Jimmy Stewart-Frank Capra movie folk tale.

You know, the triumph of vox populi, the small-town boy bringing "Aw-gosh" sunniness to a politically dark Capitol.

Only this time it isn't Mr. Smith who is going to Washington, it's Mr. Frazier.

James Frazier, in case you've forgotten, is the 32-year-old Tustin go-getter who videotaped "commonfolk" interviews on the state of the union to be sent to Jimmy Carter himself.

His colleagues in the $5,000 filming project, which took all last summer, were two other Tustin residents, Brian Scott, 35, and Maria Park, 24.

Their rendezvous with destiny, namely a formal visit to the White House, is scheduled for 8:30 a.m. Thursday, according to Frazier.

So Friday, their 10 pieces of luggage all packed, they were poised to make the first leg of the rail trek — the 2:40 p.m. Amtrak from Santa Ana to Los Angeles.

But the Tustin trio, immersed in a trackside media parley and farewells to friends and neighbors, missed the train, which made only its usual two-

Please Turn to Page 11, Col. 1

James E. Frazier

The Register

METROPOLITAN ORANGE COUNTY'S   WATCHFUL NEWSPAPER

ORANGE COUNTY, CALIFORNIA Mon., Feb. 18, 1980 Daily 10¢—Sunday 35¢

President Hears Voice Of OC's 'Common Man'

By ROSA KWONG
Register Staff Writer

TUSTIN, Washington, D.C., and Tustin are a continent apart, but the anxieties of people living in the two cities are the same.

A young man worries about ways to survive a nuclear attack. Where are the fallout shelters? Which are the roads leading to safety? Who would organize the escape routes?

Socked by inflation, a single woman bemoans her inability to afford rent for an apartment alone and wonders where the national economy is heading.

Welders, carpenters, teachers see themselves as pawns of big business, big oil monopolies, big government.

James Frazier, Brian Scott and Marla Park of Tustin listened to Orange Countians tell of their feelings of confusion and animosity last August. And they have a tape recorder full of the same sentiments expressed by residents of Washington, D.C., supposedly the source of answers to the nation's concerns.

The trio's interviews with 150 men and women in the streets and politicians and government bureaucrats in the capital is part of a project they called "Common Man and Survival."

They returned here Friday after a two-week cross-country pilgrimage that began when President Carter asked in a July 26, 1979, speech for "the voice of the common man" to help solve the gas crisis.

Little did Carter know that three Californians would take him up on his request.

Frazier, a technical writer; Scott, a design engineer; and Marla Park, an assembly line supervisor, spent $5,000 and countless hours producing a one-hour videotape of interviews with Orange Countians on whether they feel threatened and what the president can do about it.

The self-styled crusaders took an Amtrak train from Santa Ana to Washington, D.C., Feb. 1 and gave the tape and manuscript to Jim Purks, Carter's assistant press secretary.

Frazier said the material has been placed in the national archives. It's uncertain whether Carter will look at the tape, but the three have brought home letters from the president praising their "ingenuity and determination."

A flattering article about them in the Washington Star has been added to the collection of publicity they already have received locally.

By far the most valuable reward of the trip, though, according to the three, was the chance to interact with people in Washington, D.C.

They now are even more convinced that there is a dire need for more "closeness" between the president and the common people.

A list of ideas the trio sent to Carter included suggestions for a national forum, where the people and their president can agree on a common national goal; the appointment of White House ambassadors who would "gather the voice of the people" throughout the nation and frequently scheduled, televised conversations between the president and representatives of common folks.

Scott said he sees the local trio's efforts as the groundwork for a return to the days when the president or his representatives "went to the people. They reached out and knocked on your door — and that's not just during elections. They not only reached the door, but also reached the heart."

668

An Earnest Message for A President

By Boris Weintraub
Washington Star Staff Writer

Three Californians have come to town with a little TV viewing for President Carter. Last summer, the president said he wanted to hear from the people of America; so they went out and collected the voices of the people of Orange County to bring to him in a 53-minute videotape entitled "Common Man and Survival."

No, the three are not Hollywood film-industry bigwigs. They are simply Jim Frazier, a 32-year-old technical writer; Brian Scott a 36-year-old design engineer, and Marla Park, a 25-year-old assembly-line foreman whose participation in the project was delayed by gallstone surgery. (Her cohorts dragged their cameras

Brian Scott, Marla Park and Jim Frazier with their videotape for the president

—Washington Star Photographer

Earnest Trio Brings Carter a Message – Thursday, Feb. 7, 1980

(The above article ends with the following words:)

"They want the president to reaffirm the bond of trust

between the American people

and the presidency—

a bond that defines the nation,

creates the nation and ensures its survival.

They really do talk like that."

Turning Point in History

THE WHITE HOUSE

WASHINGTON

February 7, 1980

To Brian Scott

Thank you for the videotape, "Common Man and Survival," which Jim Purks accepted on my behalf. I look forward to viewing it at my earliest opportunity.

You and the others who conceived of this project are to be commended for your creative response to the challenge I offered last summer to the American people to let their voices be heard and to renew the spirit which has made America the greatest country on earth.

I am confident that American ingenuity and determination, such as you, Jim Frazier and Marla Park have displayed, are more than sufficient to solve the problems we face in the decades to come.

With appreciation for all your efforts and with my best wishes,

Sincerely,

Jimmy Carter

Mr. Brian Scott
15660 Tustin Village Way
Tustin, California 92680

CARTER'S PRESIDENTIAL LIBRARY in Atlanta, Georgia stores all materials filed with the National Archives including the video tape, statements from common people and information about the NOR x1-11. People may obtain the actual White House photographs of the presentation, and other documents.

The Final Goodbye

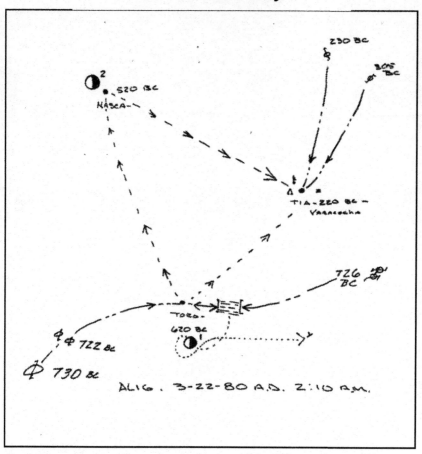

GOODBYE GIFT – Map of "movement of the people" from the Eastern hemisphere to the Western hemisphere. The drawing indicates that migrations started in 730, 722 and 726 B.C. By 620 B.C. training was complete at Toro Muerto, and movements began to Nazca. In 520 B.C. the people at Nazca migrated to the Lake Titicaca region. Ticci Viracocha may have been active around 220 B.C.

James E. Frazier

TRIALS OF THE HERO

THE TRIALS ARE DESIGNED TO SEE IF THE INTENDED HERO
SHOULD REALLY BE A HERO.
CAN HE OVERCOME THE DANGERS?
DOES HE HAVE THE COURAGE, THE KNOWLEDGE,
AND THE CAPACITY TO SERVE?
THE HERO SACRIFICES HIS OWN LIFE SO OTHERS
MIGHT KNOW THE MIND OF GOD.
KNOWING THE MIND OF GOD IS THE ULTIMATE GOAL.
IT IS THE FLEECE OR HOLY GRAIL THAT BRINGS SURVIVIAL.

ABSTRACTED FROM
Hero with a Thousand Faces, by Joseph Campbell

Chapter 24

The Second Gift – Voice of Common Man

Brian and Debra separated in November of 1978 when she was six months pregnant. Brian moved the NOR and himself into Marla's apartment in Tustin.

Later, a blond-haired surfer who had taken the *Teaching of Space* class introduced his girlfriend to Brian. The happy young lady wanted to help build the NOR. About 20, tanned and beautiful from living at the beach, Rebecca Martinez had nearly died in a car accident, a year earlier. She was still recovering from a broken neck. When near death, Rebecca experienced a split between her mind and body. She had journeyed out-of-body, and visited places. For her, reality out-of-the-body was more real than normal life on earth. But, she wanted ways to control the experiences. She understood Voltar and his NOR.

In April of 1979, she provided $1,200 from her settlement to buy the final, most expensive parts for the NOR X1-11. Young Rebecca Martinez made Brian's NOR a reality. He bought the parts and went to work.

When Marla had completed soldering the complex light panel and control switches of the NOR X1-11, Voltar suggested another public class. He wanted to invite people to a seminar to be titled--*The Play of Life.*

The compassionate, caring Voltar had submerged after Brian and Debra parted. He was present, but not often in the forefront. He introduced another trusted member of the Council to teach the *Play of Life.* Voltar never said why, but I suspected he was too intertwined with Debra. Others felt he was too kind, too soft and too gentle for the arduous tasks that remained.

Voltar formally introduced the strong-willed Vertex as instructor for the *Play of Life* class. Vertrex spoke sharply, without deep compassion. He was more commanding than Voltar and boomed like an oracle speaking to a vast auditorium. People didn't feel like questioning Vertrex. He spoke with absolute certainty on a point, or said nothing. He held great knowledge of the Greek amphitheaters and Greek educational processes. Voltar described Vertrex as the Apollo of Delphi in Greece. The Greeks were 'his people,' he said.

Vertrex paralleled America's *Play of Life* to ancient Greece—to the time of Athens, Delphi and the great oracles, to the year of 454 B.C. He spoke of Socrates as if he were a close friend.

In preparation for the class, I visited the library for books on oracles. I discovered that Socrates would have been about sixteen in 454 B.C. Over the next forty-five years, Socrates and Plato became famous in Athens. Notorious might be a better word. They visited the oracle at Delphi, and proclaimed that oracle, Apollo, to be greater than the one in Athens. This created problems for Socrates—in Athens. Each city had an approved god that was to be followed as the authority.

Apollo, the oracle at Delphi, said that no man was wiser than Socrates. This launched Socrates on a mission to seek out people in Athens who *appeared* to be wise. For, Socrates said, he did not consider himself wise--at all.

By asking questions, Socrates challenged *"people with knowledge"* to see if he could find one wiser than he. Young people began to follow him around, and soon they questioned people in the same, *"Socratic"* way—questions and answers.

In his journey, Socrates took words from the oracle of Delphi to the people of Athens. In real-life situations, he questioned the poets, the politicians, teachers and craftsmen. He asked people to reason with him about what is good, and just, and pious--*obedient to god*. He asked how to create good in man. He reasoned out all details of ethics, virtues, and piety—not as a paid teacher, but as an unpaid philosopher seeking to understand his mission--so given by a god -- by the oracle of Delphi.

He even questioned the separation of body and soul. He plainly said he had been given "a voice" at childhood that told him what NOT to do. He openly claimed divine inspiration for his behavior.

Eventually, he was charged with a crime--rousing the youth of Athens to rebellion, and believing in a "god" not approved by the city.

At his trial, Socrates said he had been true to his mission "inspired by god, by oracles, by dreams and in every other way that a divine manifestation has ever ordered a man to do anything."

To his jury, he said that that those people of Athens who were thought to possess knowledge did not have wisdom, but those deficient in knowledge did have wisdom. This got him in serious trouble—and they sentenced him to death.

Socrates never wrote a word, but Plato recorded the dialogues, and later published many books about the discussions.

Though Socrates was eventually executed for "corrupting the youth," his memory and mission have lived on for millennia. He said, before the execution, that he would rather die and serve god, than pander to the will of foolish men.

Perhaps, the oracle of Delphi was correct. Perhaps he was the wisest of men. He was considered a friend of the oracles, and he spent much time at Delphi-- perhaps touching the stones.

When he drank the fatal poison, hemlock, he laughed at his jury. "I will go down in history and be remembered as wise, while you will be remembered as fools." He was right again.

Greek oracles sat in an amphitheater of stone and drew energy from the earth, from *'pneuma'* – a physical, but invisible exhalation of the earth. Voltar had used the same words to describe the earth's grid system--*physical, but invisible.* The energy from activated stones at Tiahuanaco was also *'physical but invisible.'* I found even more parallels.

Greek oracles were loquacious, meaning talky--like Voltar and Vertrex--plus they provided designs for the streets, the temples of worship, and especially the altars.

That caught my attention--designs and plans for temples.

Then I found references to ancient reports that Socrates had been seen more than once talking to *a sphere of orange light.* Bingo. A SPHERE OF ORANGE LIGHT! What light? Whose orange orb of light? Where did the orange orb originate? No one knew. Suddenly, my list of anomalies expanded. It seemed that the "ball of light" phenomenon was not new.

My theory of multiple-personality also expanded to include Greek oracles-- and men like Socrates. Oracles were simply people in trance speaking to an audience. Brian certainly qualified, as did many other UFO contactees.

I began to form a new framework for viewing the post-contact UFO syndrome. Why do any alleged UFO contactees end up acting like oracles? What does an oracle do? What was the connection to heroes and religious leaders?

Literature from around the world agreed on the picture of an oracle: a man or woman sat in trance in the center of a stone outcropping or structure surrounded by dozens of people, maybe hundreds or thousands.

And the stones were activated somehow by 'pneuma' (exhalation of the earth) or maybe by the probe.

675

Just by sitting on the activated stone, a person might be uplifted. Simply by being present to talk to the oracles, and touch the stone pillars or carvings, the mind of a person might be expanded.

Voltar had talked about the Incan philosophy for polishing stone: *perfect mind, perfect hand.* At Sachsahuaman, initiates at this temple of 'illumination,' placed their fist inside the stone so that rock surrounded their fist. Why, I wondered.

Voltar had said that when common people worked on *activated stones,* their minds expanded. To me he was saying that some energy was transmitted *from* stone to the mind, and it was magnetic in nature, enough to affect a modern day magnetic tape recorder, with pulses.

What connected the hand, to the eye, to the mind? Man is a "neuro-optical being' Voltar had said. I pondered for a moment. Nerves had to be the answer-- of course. Nerve tissue conducts electricity. Nerves carry electricity, and that means a magnetic field is created. The magnetic field of the brain, of nerve and brain cells, must interact with this "pneuma" – the physical exhalation of the earth.

A magnetic field of some kind, surrounding the hand, might affect the electrical nature of nerves in the hand. That electro-chemical-magnetic effect might move upwards through the nerves, into the spinal cord and into the lower brain stem. That path would be possible because nerve tissue transmits BOTH WAYS-- like electricity flowing in a wire.

The right hand sends signals to the left brain. The left-hand relates to the right-brain. BOTH hands probably impacted the lower brain stem, I guessed. At least, I understood what Voltar meant. The energy from stones could stimulate the brain, uplift the mind, and make the transformation real.

What about oracles? I wondered. The facts of history indicated that from natural stone amphitheaters, nations around our globe arose. How? By agreements among people, by designs and actions taken by wise men and women who had been inspired and guided by oracles--people sitting in trance.

The pattern was not unusual, or a great discovery. It had been noted and recorded by scholars from around the Earth. From Babylon to Egypt, from Assyria to Israel, from the Toltecs to the Inca, over and over, the pattern repeated. Oracles talked to people. Some of the people took actions—right or wrong.

Inspired by the oracle of Delphi, Socrates and Plato set out to create a New World, and they succeeded. We live in the result of their work today—Western Civilization. The man often labeled "father of Democracy," Lycurgus of Athens, attributed his plan for elected representatives to the oracle at Athens. He was so inspired that he stepped down as king, and implemented the plan.

I wondered how the Greek Oracles of Delphi related to oracles in Peru. From library books, I learned that priests trained Greek Oracles. The initiation process remained SECRET, taking place in caves and caverns, or beneath a temple.

The voices speaking through oracles were considered the gods. That simple statement stunned me. Were the gods of the Greeks simply VOICES speaking through oracles? Yes, of course they lived in the sky, but they spoke through a man or woman in trance. That realization explained a lot. Was it true in all religions?

The writings of history, and of anthropology indicate that worldwide, ancient man's definition of god was often a *voice, a presence*, speaking through an oracle. Plutarch wrote about oracles in the oldest books of the western world, the Iliad and the Odyssey. In his ancient books, the lives of the gods and their children became the legends, the plays, and the dramas that have survived thousands of years.

What about Judaism and Christianity? In a map of the first Hebrew temple, I found an inscription– "The Seat of the Oracle." Where was it? I wondered. The map referred to the inner, most sacred sanctuary—the Holy of Holies. It was called the Mercy Seat.

The Mercy Seat was a small chair or platform on top of the box that held the Ten Commandments. The box was called the Ark of the Covenant.

Supposedly, only the High Priest could enter the sanctuary to sit on the Mercy Seat, and only once a year. His feet were supposedly tied to ropes so he could be pulled out, if he died.

Supposedly, Jesus placed his blood, on the Mercy Seat in heaven. To suggest to a Christian priest or Jewish Rabbi that a High Priest sat on the Mercy Seat *in trance* would probably be considered heresy, but here is what the Bible says in Exodus 25:17-22.

> **You shall make two cherub of gold, make them of hammered works at the two ends of the Mercy Seat....and the Cherubim shall have their wings spread upwards, covering the Mercy Seat with their wings and facing one another; the faces of the Cherubim are to be turned towards the Mercy Seat. And you shall put the Mercy Seat on top of the ark and in the ark you shall put the testimony which I shall give to you. And there I will meet with you. And from above the Mercy Seat, from between the two Cherubim which are upon the ark of the testimony, I will SPEAK TO YOU about all that I will give you in commandment for the sons of Israel.**

677

It sounded to me, like, in ancient times, the High Priest sat on the seat with the Cherubim pointed at his ears or his temples. I also knew that ancient Hebrew priests used two stones of Onyx as oracles. I checked Exodus 28:15-30.

Called the Urim and Thuminn, each stone was inscribed with the names of six tribes. These 'stones of decision' were *"the means of making decisions"* by the High Priest.

The two stones were held over the heart of the priest when he wanted to receive answers from God, when he ventured to the inner sanctuary and to the mercy seat. The priest's breastplate was decorated with these two oracular stones and twelve other gems – one for each tribe.

I wondered if the onyx stones were anchors, like Brian's white rock had been. I knew that many secret practices and temple rites of the Hebrews were not known to the public, but were "tradition." Much was passed down by "oral law." The sacred Kaballah, a book of secret teachings, was given to Moses, orally, and then passed on down to the generations of priests—through the priesthood. Only temple priests knew about these teachings—this knowledge was not for the Common People.

So, I wondered if Hebrew priests entered a trance, or a state of ecstasy inside the Holy of Holies. The word *trance* did not show up in the Old Testament, but the word *oracle* is used.

In the New Testament, the word *trance* appears in several places important to the spreading of Christianity.

In the Book of Acts, Peter sees a vision and hears a voice speak to him in a trance. (Acts 10:10.) "Do not call anything impure that God had made clean," says a voice during the *trance*. Peter interprets this as the *voice of God*. This trance was crucial to extending Christianity beyond the Jews for it led Peter to create an open door for Gentiles to accept Jesus. Until then, all believers had been Jewish. Until then, the idea of a Gentile Christian was unknown-- unfathomable to the first followers of Jesus. They considered Gentiles to be impure, until Peter's trance.

In Acts 22:10 Paul, also used the word *trance* to describe the experience that helped him establish Christianity. He tells the story in his own words to a crowd on the steps of the temple. In Acts 22:18 he says, "I fell into a *trance* and saw the Lord speaking." The Lord tells him to get out of Jerusalem quickly because the priests will not accept his testimony.

The Bible clearly shows that trances helped inspire two of the primary founders of Christianity. In the trances, they both *heard a voice*—and they both believed *the voice to be God.*

These are facts. There are many other "dissociation" types of experiences recounted in the Bible. But these are the only places in the New Testament where the word *trance* actually appears. In other cases, men are "lifted up into the spirit" or they "speak in tongues" or they see a vision, all of which may be considered dissociation experiences similar to a trance.

Walking Oracle - The Hero

After Brian learned to enter trances at will, he could have been accurately described by a scholar as an oracle -- with Voltar as his Presence—his god.

However, after the transformation--after he walked and talked as Voltar 24 hours a day--he was no longer a simple oracle. This was different. The role of a classic oracle sitting on a chair or stone in trance had been surpassed. Walking and talking as an oracle fit the pattern of the hero, the fully transformed man whose instincts had been "deified" for spiritual purposes like the Quetzalcoatl of the Toltecs, Mayans and Aztecs.

Various symbols of the hero as a deified man existed throughout ancient cultures of the world: the serpent with wings, the flying jaguar, or lion, or dragon with wings. Even an eagle on a staff qualifies, especially outstretched wings on a staff entwined by a serpent. This implies that the serpent—the evil or instinctual energy in man--has been placed into submission to a higher good. The one energy descends from the sky, the other energy rises up from the earth.

Then, of course, there is the man or woman with wings—angels.

Each symbol holds the same meaning: the unruly, evil instincts and emotions of man have been placed into submission, and obedience to a higher purpose—a goal that is good for all mankind.

In the transformed man, instinct unites with wisdom, dark unites with light, matter with spirit, static with moving, spirit with flesh. The result was to be a paranormal power—the ability to see like a god—to see the future and the past.

Brian's symbols were the spider and the jaguar. Instinct and intelligence—the same symbols as Ticci Viracocha. In fact, Tiahuanaco was considered the center of Viracocha's web—his home. To the native people of Peru, he was symbolized as a spider with tremendous intelligence.

But, the true hero is not just wise, he is a warrior—a fighter. He fights evil and wins, not just for himself, but for his people. Joseph Campbell described a truly "transformed hero" in his book, "Thousand Faces of the Hero." The details are quite specific and I was surprised to see the comparisons. Brian's story closely fit the pattern prescribed by Campbell.

Brian had received a white rock as a gift which gave him magical powers; he had been visited by people from the stars; his mother and wife were both named "Mary;" he had battled demons and conquered them; he had been given wisdom about *time* and the *mind*. He had received paranormal powers; he had been directed to live a new life; he had journeyed to a past which somehow united the future; he had been taught to align his own inner self to the Universal knowledge;

he lived in happiness and joy most of the time—finding bliss—as he journeyed through the darkness and the light.

Most importantly, if the Secondary World existed in the form of black-eyed aliens with domed heads, and if they truly lost their hold on man because of Brian's accomplishments, then he was a hero indeed, for he had set mankind free from an ancient enemy.

The unifying idea of a hero is MOVEMENT. Some being "from the heavens or the stars" touches the initiate and sets him into motion. Even more, his movement is focused and directed. In fact, the hero becomes highly directed to accomplish some great task which benefits others, not himself. The heroic journey chronicles movement from self-interest in the "now" to attaining goals for others, in the future.

Brian, like Quetzalcoatl and Viracocha, illustrated this *movement*--the movement of a man forced onto a path of transformation for the benefit of his people.

I was amazed. The pattern fit. Brian had played the role of a classical hero-- except for one thing.

Brian had not yet given his gifts to the people. The true hero had to give his people a gift that transformed the culture. Quetzalcoatl had given the concept of "zero," the alphabet, and seeds for corn. Gilgamesh of Babylon had taught the people to build walls around their cities. Moses provided the Ten Commandments. Jesus provided the "gift" of salvation. Each classic hero had provided some gift that transformed his people.

Now, I understood why Brian was desperately trying to give the NOR to "the people," as his gift. To qualify as a legendary hero, to match the pattern of Gilgamesh, or Quetzalcoatl, he would need to give the NOR away as a gift, and it would need to be used *"by the People"* to create survival and freedom.

All of these questions, I considered as we prepared for the *Play of Life* seminar. As in the Teachings of Space, before the classes could begin, I had to understand the lessons. Thus, after the date was set, preparations began. On June 30th, we drove to Kings Canyon, a National Park in the mountains, where I was uplifted, in a way, by Vertrex. I was shown how the transformation of Brian might extend to others throughout the land. My education continued over the next three weeks in evenings at Brian and Marla's apartment.

On July 21, the first class in the *Play of Life* began. I had the script, and knew the steps through which Vertrex would take the people. I had prepared the music and sound effects he requested—mostly deep, low-frequency rumbling vibrations.

When the people assembled, Vertrex spoke in a voice that crackled with authority. At the end of the first session, he asked the group if they would help take the transformation of Brian "to America." The people asked questions, and finally everyone agreed. Voltar asked for written commitment, and each person in the *Play of Life* class signed a statement which said they would support the idea of taking "the transformation of Brian Scott to America."

I had not anticipated the development, and was surprised by the turn of events. But, that simple agreement turned out to create a lot of results.

Five days later, on July 26th, President Jimmy Carter appealed to the people for help. He asked for "public pressure on Congress to defy the oil lobby and support a windfall profits tax." In a televised news conference from the White House he said, "Your voice can be heard, your voice must be heard." He emphatically stated, "I consider it crucial to our nation's future."

When Brian saw the press conference on TV, Voltar provided a vision of success. Brian saw himself in the White House with a letter from the President in his hand. He understood. "That's it. We'll take the voice of Common Man to the President," Brian said. "Let's go to the White House. Voltar will help. He will be *with the people*."

At first, I was baffled. I didn't want another big project, another journey. I wanted it to be over. The NOR needed only a projection screen to be completed. "Why do this, now?" I asked. "Why not finish the NOR, and give it to the people, first?"

"This is of you," Voltar said. "It is the *real Play of Life*." Voltar wanted the Voice of Common Man taken to the White House. "Of this you will gain much," he said. "This is of you, Jim—for you."

I didn't understand. "The NOR and the Voice of Common Man, must be united as One," he said.

Brian emerged and tried to explain. "The NOR has to go to the White House, too," he said. "Not the real NOR, but information about the NOR. They have to be presented together for -- for it all to make sense," Brian said. "The two have to be considered as ONE."

"For what to make sense?" I asked. "When will it be over? What is the message, the moral of the story?"

"I don't know," Brian said. "Not exactly, but I do know Voltar must walk among the people for it to be finished," Brian said. "He always said that. He must learn about the world, and touch the hands of the people. His wisdom is a gift— his touch. It's not just the NOR." Finally, I agreed. The *Play of Life* class, became the *Play of Life* project—in the streets of America.

Brian and Marla worked at their jobs for several weeks as I used their phone and apartment to prepare a video featuring people in the town of Tustin. I roughed out a script, contacted all the people, and found a cameraman. Brian and

Marla had agreed to provide $500 for the production expenses. Members of the *Play of Life* seminar volunteered their homes and time to help.

In the first week of August, on the 3,4 and 5th, we began taping at a busy street corner in Tustin, California--on Main Street.

On camera, Brian interviewed common people and asked them to speak to the President about their hopes and fears for the nation.

The fall of 1979 was a dark time in America. Newspaper headlines screamed with fear. America had reached the 'era of limits.' Supposedly, no more oil was available anywhere to be discovered. The planet had been depleted. Our prosperity was over, as a nation. The prime rate on interest for a bank loan skyrocketed to over 21 percent. No nation had survived such high bank rates. We were doomed. Even experts said America would soon fall.

Religious leaders preached from the pulpits that America, as we knew it, had come to an end. Only one escape remained from the tribulations prophesied in the Bible--Rapture. Church after church adopted the line, and millions of people waited to be lifted into the sky— to join Jesus in the clouds. Most refused to do anything to relieve the problems. Taking action, would only delay the Rapture. Thus, many evangelical Christians just waited for the Second Coming, like lambs.

Others in society struggled. On the political front, Iranian militants had taken hostage our embassy in Iran. Fifty-three Americans were held captive. In daily news reports, the Iranians burnt our flag and accosted America, calling us names—like the devil.

The Ayatollah Khomeini, leader of a Shiite sect of Iranian Muslims, branded America as the Great Satan. He supported the militants and declared a Holy War against America--an Islamic Jihad--against an evil nation.

Americans wanted action. President Carter's political plans to free the embassy had failed, so he launched a military strike. Unfortunately, our helicopters collided in a desert sandstorm leaving young American's dead on foreign soil. The mission was aborted. As the news spread around the world by TV, the Iranian militants celebrated. To them, America had failed by an act of God. To militant Iranians, this was a sign America would lose in a wide-spread Holy War, for our protection from God was gone.

The military flop sent shockwaves through everyone in America. Fear ran rampant like a prowling lion, devouring the weak, and strong. What was happening? Christians feared being overcome by Muslins and slaughtered. Jimmy Carter had been elected with evangelical Christian support, as a Southern Baptist, as a Sunday school teacher—a Christian. Wasn't God on his side--on our side? Didn't he represent America – to God.

Maybe Carter was not pleasing to God. Maybe he was too soft, too kind to be President? Everyone had a theory. Coffee shops hummed with talk as common people in America shared their fears openly. The Iranian militants were devastating Carter's Presidency and ruining America's image as a strong, powerful nation. The gas lines and interest rates caused every American to feel the pain, personally—in their pocket book. Instead of feeling pride, Americans felt helpless and fearful. This was a time of darkness, of apprehension and of fear. In this time, at this hour in America's history, Voltar stepped out and walked amongst the people.

Voltar Goes to the People

In Tustin, California, Brian interviewed numerous common people including a carpenter, a blacksmith, and the town hall janitor. At times, he sounded like Voltar as he questioned the Mayor, the Police Chief and Chamber of Commerce president. We told no one about the transformation. Brian just seemed like a bold, articulate and very earnest man.

As director of the video, I asked the people to talk to the President of the United States, not Brian. They breathed deep, realizing our goal was serious.

When they looked into the lens and spoke directly to the President, their hearts fluttered and unfurled like a flag with respect for the office. It wasn't really President Carter that they respected, but the Office of the American President. They were "the People" offering their fears to their PRESIDENT, like children asking their father to save them from danger.

Brian and I were privileged to hear their words, feel their hearts and listen. Each day, each hour, both Brian and I were touched by *The People*, young and old, by their honor and dignity as they spoke to the President. So was Voltar, for he watched and listened with compassion. Many times he shook hands. Without people knowing, Voltar emerged to touch their hand, their heart and their souls.

Many people remarked that Brian was a gifted speaker, a 'special kind of guy.' Many suggested he run for some political office. Together, we interviewed spokespeople for various groups like the veterans and the retired. Each spoke about their fears, their hopes, and problems. Brian asked questions, and they answered. The whole process reminded me of Socrates, seeking wisdom -- seeking to find someone wiser than he.

Newspapers, like the Los Angeles Times, Santa Ana Register and Tustin News wrote stories as Brian and I gathered the "Voice of Common Man" for the President.

Some articles featured him as a design-engineer. Others featured me as a "Mr. Smith Goes to Washington," character. We insisted that Marla be included for she spoke with clarity about the issues--and besides--she helped pay the bills. With her input, we became known as "the trio from Tustin."

As the project grew, we learned that many people feared the "Voice of Common Man." As one man pointed out, "the Common Man shouldn't be running the country. All he cares about is his job, his car and his six-pack of beer."

Others openly accosted us. They "hated" common people. The Common Man was lazy, and ignorant—yet, often religious, dogmatic, unchanging, stagnant.

A blacksmith answered the challenge on camera. "We ARE ignorant. We Common People need someone to handle those big decisions for us—but someone who won't lie, who will tell us the truth."

I often thought of the statue of common stone in the lower courtyard at Tiahuanaco. All the Common Man of ancient times cared about was his family, his heart and his stomach. He was too overwhelmed by life to serve the public good. He couldn't contribute to politics. He couldn't be concerned about the state, and the nation. That was for the elite – not the Common Man.

When we completed the video, we screened it to audiences in Tustin. On November 1 and 13, viewers signed petitions to the White House asking the President to accept the video as "The Voice of Common Man."

Brian telegraphed the White House to request a meeting with President Carter. When a response was slow in coming, he contacted California's Senator Allan Cranston, and local Congressmen for help. I followed through making presentations.

Each phone call led to a meeting and a screening of the homespun video that carried a poignant message:

The people fear for their future. They ask the President to answer their questions. They don't believe there is a real oil shortage, and they will help fight the oil cartel, but they want their questions answered, truthfully. Please reply to the questions of Common Man. We will help you. Let's build a stronger bond, a new relationship—between the Common Man and the President.

Brian and Marla worked daily to pay bills while I negotiated with the White House staff for a presentation date. News stories chronicled our efforts. Reporters and politicians agreed that the video was truly the "Voice of Common Man" -- not partisan or political in any way. Still, no direct invitation arrived from the White House.

Finally, Brian inspired local radio stations to become involved. They aired interviews with Brian during rush hour traffic. He urged radio producers to call the White House every hour and ask why the President would not receive the "Voice of Common Man."

After all—the President had asked for help. The "trio from Tustin" had replied. Had anyone else? Had another group of people responded to his plea? No.

Finally, on January 8th, a White House aide was authorized to issue an invitation – but with no guarantee for us to meet the President.

Brian insisted that the presentation take place, face to face, but the official told us to come and "take your chances." The world is very unstable, right now, he said. The best he could offer was that if an opening arose, President Carter might accept the video personally. If not, *The Voice of Common Man* would be accepted by an aide.

With the invitation and a date set, AMTRAK agreed to provide transportation for the *Voice of Common Man* and the *"trio from Tustin."*

Holiday Inn's in Chicago, Washington, D.C. and New Orleans agreed to provide free rooms. I raised a few dollars to cover food, but only enough for one meal a day.

On the departure day, reporters surrounded us at the Santa Ana train station. We were submerged in a crowd as the train rolled out of the station leaving us behind, hollering at the conductor in a panic. Reporters laughed.

What could we do? Luckily, Marla's older brother quickly loaded us into his pickup, and raced to Los Angeles. He bounced through red lights and over tracks to reach the train station in time.

Despite the hilarious glitch, which made most of the newspapers, we boarded on time in Los Angeles and we were soon riding the rails to Washington, D.C. We had worked hard, suffered, and learned a lot about *The People* of America.

Voltar had rarely emerged blatantly during the strenuous production, but Marla and I both knew Voltar had set the pace, offered the challenges and asked the deep, probing questions about the future of America.

Voltar and Brian were seamlessly united as One, now--fully integrated. There was no difference anyone might see—no division—total unity.

As Brian walked amongst the people, Voltar was walking, talking and touching the people—with his hands, his words and his wisdom. We knew he had inspired many with his words, and touched many others with his hands. We wondered if some had received strength and inspiration like Martine Martinez from Argentina. With a touch of the hand, Martine had supposedly been given all that he needed to fulfill his life's purpose. Marla and I believed others had received similar touches.

As we rode the rails to Chicago and then on to Washington, D.C., Brian and I recorded statements from passengers on sound tape. From Arizona, New Mexico and across the Midwest, common people echoed the refrain of people in California.

685

They felt fear for their lives, and the future of the nation. No one trusted the government, or that the "gas crisis" was real. Old and young, rich and poor—they all poured out the problems they faced, and their worries about surviving in America. For many, food was a problem, or housing, or money for gasoline and heat.

We heard the stories not broadcast on the nightly news. We felt their feelings, and came to know --*The People* of America. We saw the Spirit of our Nation revealed in the Voice of Common Man. Each person became precious to us, and we began to understand, and feel the compassion of Voltar—for man.

When we arrived at the Holiday Inn in Washington, D.C., I condensed all the newly taped comments to one hour so the President could hear and feel the heart of his people in an updated *Voice of Common Man.*

We called the White House. Our liaison, Mr. Jim Purks, invited us over. He graciously introduced us into the White House and to the executive offices with his warm Southern drawl. With his help, we presented the video and sound tape to numerous officials and aides of the President.

Over the next few days, at each screening we answered dozens of penetrating questions about why we had gathered the "Voice," who had funded the project, and how many votes were represented in Orange County.

At key moments, Voltar spoke in a somber, serious tone to White House aides, a Senator or Congressmen. "Let the President hear the Voice of Common Man, and a new day shall begin," he said.

Voltar's commanding presence stunned people. His deep voice, and sense of authority stopped all other talk. Heads jerked around and people listened.

When he finished speaking, often Marla or I, would crack a joke and change the subject. Some were brave enough to enter into dialogue with Voltar. Others said he should run for office. "Seek election," one aide said. "You've got the voice for it—the presence."

Voltar spoke boldly, with authority. "The bond of trust must be strengthened between the Common Man and the President. Let the President reply to the people, so Common Man knows his voice can be heard in a time of fear. Of this, will come strength to the people and freedom--for all that is needed to be done, can be done 'by the People.'"

Voltar sounded like a dignified orator, a powerful Senator, a royal monarch. Luckily, Brian usually returned to break up the serious atmosphere generated by Voltar. People were relieved. They weren't used to dialoguing in such a deep manner.

At other times, Voltar walked into a meeting with a noble posture, attracting the attention of everyone. When he spoke, people responded immediately with respect. Often people shook hands and gazed into his calm, blue eyes. People began to whisper, "Who is that?" and "What is he?"

If Voltar was too powerful, Marla or I would gesture, and Voltar would immediately submerge. I felt a bit deceptive—like a magician hiding a prize in a box. We just couldn't tell everyone the full story—and didn't need to. Our background wasn't important to the purpose. We wanted to be taken at face value. We had one message, one purpose: to renew the bond of trust between the Common Man and the President. That's all—it was a valid purpose. The President asked for help. The People had replied. We were delivering the *Voice of Common Man* to the Office of the President.

Simple—and true.

As we waited to meet with the President, we realized that Voltar's primary goal had been satisfied. He had been walking "amongst the people" now for several months, learning and touching dozens, if not hundreds and thousands, of people. In this city of great orators, he fit right in. In fact, he ranked as one of the best, if not THE BEST orator in the city. But--he wasn't satisfied.

Voltar wanted to personally touch the President, and shake his hand. What if he did? I wondered. What would happen to our nation--to President Carter? What if the President received all that he needed to fulfill his purpose with a touch of the hand? Could it happen? I wondered.

After numerous meetings with staffers, we were invited to "wait around" for the President. So, we did.

In the Executive Offices, Voltar stood silently stroking the pillars of stone, the books, and the desks. He would close his eyes and absorb all that he could of the knowledge, and the energy of our nation.

In the White House, he stood silently watching energy forms of the people, seeing through walls and doorways, looking into hearts of the people. I wondered what he saw.

Each hour, I wondered if Voltar might use his powers to make something dramatic unfold. But, he didn't.

"Free choice," he would say. "All must be done of free will. Each to his own mind."

I knew that Voltar also wanted a home--provided by the People—so he could complete designs for the Pyramid and the NOR.

"It's the People's house," the tour guides would say in the White House. "It's yours. It belongs to the People, and is rented out temporarily to each President." Voltar liked that idea.

I realized that in other nations, in other times, beings like Voltar had become leaders of the people. What was Royalty, after all, but incarnation—the incarnation of another being—a god who would rule the people. In most every kingdom of our world, priests directed the process and "ordained" the king. The god incarnated into the next leader on a scheduled date based on the religious calendar. Even the Royalty of England followed the same pattern.

Whether the Royal leader was titled a King, an Emperor, a Caesar, a Pharaoh, a Shah, a Chief, or an Inca, the pattern was the same. Throughout our world, the leaders of nations had been anointed and chosen by priests, who initiated the chosen young men from the proper bloodline—the pure, Royal gene pool. The process was part of the great secret of man, a responsibility of the Mystery School priests.

But not so in America. America had been created in rebellion to royalty. We were a different, unique nation. We started a new pattern. Our forefathers opposed royal rule and won our freedom in battle against a King's army— proving to England that their god incarnate could fail in battle—proving, for certain, the King was not a god.

The lesson struck home as I watched Voltar stroke marble pillars in the White House. I wondered why he seemed to be touching so many objects of stone.

As he stroked the stones, I thought more deeply about America. We would never submit to Iranian Muslims inspired by religious principles. Perhaps, President Carter was confused, going down a wrong path. Perhaps, he needed strength and wisdom.

America separated religion from government, and the policy cut deep into our beliefs, and our procedures. Most people were not aware of how this idea defined our national policy, and protocols. I had talked to the President's Office of Protocol regarding the presentation. I was told that every event must be carefully studied and then directed to fit the policy of America—the proper protocol.

The American President does not bow to a king, an emperor or a monarch of any kind. His wife does not bend a knee. They shake hands.

Even within our borders, the sovereign Native American nations must elect "Chairmen" because a "chief" is a priest--a religious figure. Indian tribes were theocracies—headed by a priest—and theocracies are not allowed within the borders of the United States.

No royalty, no king, no Indian chief can rule in America, because we had suffered the abuses of a corrupted king. Even in 1980, we were unique. Of nearly 200 nations on the Earth, only a few had become formal Republics—less than 10 percent. In most nations of the world, monarchs, dictators or some form of royalty still ruled.

America was one of the few to forbid Royal rule. Even modern England was still legally a monarchy—the queen or king could exercise their right, and take over the government at any time.

Few people truly realize what great Freedom our nation represents. The United States is one of a handful of nations that allows a Common Man to become President.

Even more impressive, in our short history as a nation, America has defeated the King of England, the Kaiser of Germany and the Mystical Hitler; then we bought the Emperor of Japan down onto the streets. Lastly, we asked the Shah of Iran to step down from his Royal throne, and he did—ending the last, pure bloodline of Royal Rulers known on earth.

That was our legacy, as a nation—to take down royal rulers. By official protocol, our President, our Ambassadors and military leaders never bow or kneel before a King, a Queen, an Emperor or monarch of any kind. The American President shakes hands—as an equal—and, so do all of his people— The People. Each is equal to the President. No American citizen is expected to bow to the King of another nation.

For the first time, I understood the powerful inheritance given to every citizen of America. I understood the potential power that one citizen of America can exert in nations around the world. I understood the strength, and the meaning of citizenship in our nation.

For some reason, through watching Voltar in the White House, my eyes had been opened to a new truth—the original meaning of America.

Each day as we were invited back to the White House to wait, we called radio stations and newspapers. On-air interviews were conducted on the East Coast and back home in California, as we waited. At times, we visited radio stations in Washington, D.C. for interviews, or we met with reporters at newspapers.

On one day, we meandered around in the basement of the White House following Brian's lead. Suddenly a squad of Secret Service officers rushed at us, herding us into a meeting room. The ambassador of a favored nation marched through with his entourage.

We had become sort of a joke among the White House Secret Service agents. In the meeting room, Marla smoked a cigarette as a tall, blond agent stood guard, nearby.

He knew about us. Each agent wore earphones connected to a central office that "listened" to every room in the White House. They had been briefed about our purpose, and left us to wander around.

"We hear every breath the President takes," the agent said.

The ashes on Marla's cigarette grew long, and she asked for an ashtray. The agent smiled. "Not in the White House," he said.

"No ashtrays?" Brian laughed. "I was hoping to take one home as a souvenir."

"That's why we don't have them," laughed the agent. "The Common People would steal them all." He glared at us. "The Common Man is a thief," he said. "A criminal."

Marla gulped and shoved the ashes into her coat pocket. Brian frowned. We had heard the same phrase before -- during our interviews.

From the elite, we often heard bad things about the "Common Man." We understood. They were right to a degree. The Common Man really can't do much more than survive—and not all are honest. Again, we remembered the statue in South America, in the lower courtyard of Tiahuanaco. The Common Man of the times cared only about his heart, his stomach and his family. More lofty goals and ideals were beyond his ability. Sometimes the Common Man even steals to feed his family, or himself. Perhaps he tries to steal from the royal palace, or the White House.

When the ambassador passed in the hallway, the agent let us out of the room with a laugh. He knew his point had struck home. But Voltar offered a different view.

"The Voice of Common Man is the heart of the people," Voltar said on a national radio show. "It is the Spirit of the Nation. That is all—nothing more. But by lifting up that Voice and that Heart, by meeting the needs of the common people, all men in your nation will be fulfilled."

"What is the purpose of government?" an interviewer asked Voltar.

"To create freedom for the Common Man." Create that freedom and everything else will fall into place," Voltar said.

That was the vision America needed—the single goal, the one purpose to unite our nation. "Let us move forward as friends to fulfill the needs, and the questions of the Common Man," he said. "Let us move forward as one, as one nation in unity, to fulfill one goal and one purpose—in that, to create freedom for Common Man, and through this, freedom for all."

The next day, on the cold morning of February 7, we were told that the President was departing the White House for an important meeting at Camp David. However, he had agreed to sign a letter to each of us as a formal "thank you, and acceptance."

As part of the arrangement, all of our papers, tapes and statements would be placed into the National Archives. The papers included a description of the NOR X1-11 and it's potential impact on our society. Our statement described the NOR'S language of "light and sound"–a technology that might someday transform our society.

As an official White House photographer prepared to snap pictures of the formal presentation, Voltar emerged. With Marla's help, he combed Brian's hair differently so people would know—he was present—in dominance there, and in the White House.

Mr. Jim Purks accepted on behalf of the President.

Brian, Marla and I were excited with our personal letter from the President of the United States. He commended us for a "creative response to the challenge...to renew the Spirit of America." But Voltar did not seem pleased.

"Of this, a point in history will be noted," Voltar said. "For the documents will record our purpose, and in years to come--a turning point in American history will be noted-- for Brian did succeed. But of this, we also find sorrow, for the Voice of Common Man was offered, as the heart of your nation--to your leader--yet he did not fully understand. He did not receive the Voice, nor the Touch, and he did not reply to the People."

Voltar said that if President Carter had spoken to us publicly, and answered the questions of Common Man honestly on radio and TV, that a New Beginning would have been created for America. Even a small response, would have been amplified.

"To each his own mind," Voltar said. He and his people would wait. Voltar would move on, and find another way, to begin the Transformation of America.

A New Beginning For America

That fall, disappointed voters across America defeated President Carter by the largest landslide in history. A conservative movie star and former California Governor, Ronald Reagan, swept the polls, sending Jimmy Carter back home to Georgia.

In the fall of 1980, Ronald Reagan won votes from liberals, from Democrats and Republicans alike, because he promised -- *a New Beginning for America.* We had heard the phrase many times before—from Voltar.

Within months of Reagan's election, the hostage crises ended, gas prices dropped, interest rates dropped, and America began a new age of prosperity that lasted for over two decades. Eventually, the Cold War ended, the Wall in East Berlin came down, and the Soviet Union fell. Dozens of nations around the world rebelled against their own dictators or monarchs to become republics, like America. The political picture of the world changed. Maps of nations and republics changed. It all began in 1980, and continued for the next decade. Even President Clinton, a democrat, vowed to carry on aspects of Reagan's policies. Truly, 1980 was a major turning point in American history.

Technology changed rapidly, too. The desktop computer emerged in the early 1980's. The screens were small, and memory limited. The idea of a hard drive didn't even exist. But, year by year, the disk operating systems became

691

easier to use and by 1985, the technology of computers had became available to the Common Man.

When the internet, which started as a military project, was down-classified and released for use of the people, the transformation expanded worldwide. For the first time, people around the world could communicate to each other, through their computer, by simply placing a local telephone call—no charge.

Voltar's Goodbye

A month after we returned home from the White House, Voltar and the Council began saying goodbye to people. The *Play of Life* was over—my role had finally ended. Brian had succeeded.

They formally said goodbye to me, on March 22, 1980. For the first time in nearly four years, I breathed a big sigh of relief. I wanted to go home, back to Colorado.

"Through the eyes of one man, all mankind will see," said Voltar. What has been given has been understood. Through your eyes all mankind will see."

I was afraid that I would leave something out, or misinterpret an event. "Fear not the mind of mankind," Voltar said. "For in the days to come, all will be known--man will truly understand. Brian's story will be a trigger for transformation that is already within the people. Transformation will, indeed, come to all man. For of this, Brian's story is a model, a prototype for others to follow."

He told me to go forth, and write the story. "Wisdom has been given, to you," he said. "And much has been given to other people who will understand, and know what to do. You will have much help. Complete freedom from the Secondary will come," he said.

"In our going--in our goodbye--is the true illumination for man--a New Beginning for all Mankind."

The Return

Voltar said that when the Children of the Stars return in 2011 A.D. their 'touch' would give the people of that era all they need to complete the transformation. Many young people would be involved, he said. If a person was about 33 in 2011, they would have been born around 1978-9. These would be the children of the Baby Boomers, the "X" generation.

Brian never saw himself at the final return, though he would only be 68 years old. He said his attendance wasn't important. Others would be there to receive the touch. His role was to reach Nous Ten during his life—on his own.

"You no longer need us," Voltar said in our final goodbye. "For you have been given all that you need. By the *Play of Life*—and the logic within, man will succeed."

Then Voltar drew a map for me—a triangle connecting Toro Muerto, Nazca and Tiahuanaco. He added dates going back to 722 B.C. and arrows showing direction of travel.

"This is your beginning Jim," he said. "A Riddle for man--the movement of the people. Take this to your people and let this knowledge of the past be the beginning of understanding, and the future of man."

"I don't understand," I said. "Why this?" The date of 722 B.C. meant nothing to me. The arrows showed a movement from the Eastern hemisphere to the Western hemisphere of earth.

"The people came. Seek of your own land to understand."

Later, I discovered that in 722 B.C., Assyria dispersed the Ten Tribes of Israel. Many were taken captive, but many more just disappeared from the region. I discovered that some scholars believed the white-skinned priests of Tiahuanaco came from the Sumer-Assyria region. Scholars know that the "Viracocha People" of Tiahuanaco were called *the Uru* by brown-skinned natives around Lake Titicaca. Uru means *day* in the Andean language and daylight in Sumerian. Many correlations have inspired some scholars to believe that both the Quechua and Aymara languages originate in the Middle East, in the Sumer-Assyria region.

From books, I also discovered that by 722 B.C. the cultures of Egypt, Phoenicia, Israel, Babylon, Sumer and Assyria had been deeply intertwined including their languages and religious symbols. To distinguish between them, especially after a dispersion, would be very difficult. So, who could know where they came from, exactly.

"These people came to Toro Muerto by sea," said Voltar. "Here, our people and the Secondary World met them. The process of education began."

Voltar explained the drawing for one last time. "From Toro Muerto some went to Nazca where they created lines and the symbols as part of their education regarding the stars and the energy of their being. From Toro Muerto others went to Lake Titicaca and the Island of the Sun where they learned about moving water from the lake, and moving stones.

"Later, those of Nazca joined those of the lake. With knowledge and uplifted minds, together they built Tiahuanaco. But the plans, the first understandings, were given at Toro Muerto—the place of New Beginning for the New Land."

I understood—but why tell me?

"Of this, and the rock at Toro Muerto--your gift. Of this, man will come to understand the ninth descent of 110 B.C. From this, the true meaning of Tiahuanaco and the Gate of the Sun will be known. In this, only you have the knowledge of what to do, and when to reveal the story. No other man, including Brian, knows what to do. In this, you have the last words, and you truly are Director of the *Play of Life*. By this, your purpose and your destiny will be fulfilled."

Voltar laid his hands on my head, and gave me a vision like he had given Martine Martinez in La Paz. The images I saw, and the strength received, gave me courage to go out into the world, walk alone and prepare for my own destiny—and for a *real Play of Life*—in America.

The story had finally reached completion—except for the NOR.

A few days later, Voltar and the Council said goodbye to Marla at the stone amphitheatre. As darkness fell, she saw a rock glow with light, and then heard a very deep voice from the air. "You are one with I," the voice said.

Marla and Brian listened as the Center of the Universe spoke. "Of all, in the *Play of Life*, I am pleased. Of this, Brian will become a light to all mankind."

Voltar and the Council discussed the future with Brian and Marla. Options were offered for Brian's personality. For example, as one extreme, he could live as Voltar 24 hours a day, or—he could return to the Brian of 1971. The choice belonged to Marla.

She considered the decision deeply, but she didn't need much time. She desperately wanted a life with Brian--as a normal man. She asked that all paranormal phenomena stop. She just wanted a normal life with Brian – living as a Common Man.

The Council agreed, the allies agreed, and Brian agreed. After a long round of goodbyes, Voltar spoke. "Say this to man, from this time forth: Seek not of I, but the reality of your own being, for of this is the first step to the fulfillment of man."

After the Council and allies said goodbye, all paranormal events ended. Brian never fell into another trance, never spoke with another voice, and never lost another moment of time.

But, he prospered in his career--and the Presence of Voltar never departed from him.

The Moral of the Story

"What is the moral of the story?" I asked Voltar on my final day with him. "I want to be certain to quote you correctly." The NOR, and the White House trip comprised a joint message that I didn't fully comprehend.

"Don't forget the Voice of Common Man," Voltar said "Changes in technology will be offered. As your culture transforms into a psycho-cybernetic civilization, temptations will arise to divide and split the people. Those that have new technologies would place themselves above those who do not. The Common Man may be ignored. This division could destroy your chance for success as a people."

He emphasized that the Common Man must be instrumental in developing the NOR technology. "Do not forget--the heart of Common Man is the Spirit of your nation, the Voice of your people. His needs and his heart should be fulfilled by those of politics, of science, of religion and commerce. That should be their prime goal, and their purpose. Create freedom for the Common Man, and all other freedoms will follow.

Finally everything began to make sense, to me.

Voltar continued. "Don't forget that Common Man is one with all—the Universal Man, that you all share—for you are all One, and in this, WE are ONE with you, and you are one with us at Nous Ten." I still didn't understand how this all could be.

"Of this, universal brotherhood is a reality which man will someday share." I remembered the Big Bear message.

"The knowledge is all within the People," he said. "Go, enjoy and learn from your brothers and sisters. As Brian will become a light to your people, and your people become a light to the world, so mankind on earth will become a light to the universe of beings awaiting you.

"Let each man and woman reach out to the world, to the common man and to all those around you--as brothers and sisters. The time will come, when each man is uplifted as was Brian. In moments of fear, share with each other, what you are, who you are -- and allow others to share their lives with you. In this is the beginning, for you are all truly One.

"Fear not the mind of mankind, fear not each other, but join together as One, in celebration of the differences and the diversity given to you. For you are an infinity of people, of bodies and personalities, but you are all ONE in heart, and in soul.

"In this generation, all knowledge will be revealed. Man will come to know the truth of his world, his origin and his being. In this, fear not the truth for you are of the Center of the Universe, and of this—GOODNESS--is the nature of all man. Man is good—not evil.

"Enjoy this knowledge. Bathe in the beauty of your being, shower in the light of your own soul, and soon, man will be free from his Secondary World.

"Goodbye—my friend—goodbye."

Voltar handed me a note:

A Friend
A friend is one who knows you as you are,
Understands where you've been,
Accepts who you've become – and
Still, gently invites you to grow.

Then he handed me a burgundy colored pen as a gift. "Go forth and create a New World," he said. "All has been given." I departed for my home in Colorado, a day later.

The NOR is Given

Over the next few months, Brian and Martla completed the NOR and displayed the machine to professors, doctors and researchers. After each presentation, Brian asked for proposals on how the machine might be used. Brian and Marla studied proposals from a medical school, a university and a treatment center. They selected the least wealthy applicant of all—The Orange County Rehabilitation Institute, an agency of the Easter Seal Society.

Their staff planned to us the NOR for stimulating deaf and aphasic children—children who could not speak due to brain disorders.

When the documents were drawn and signed, and the transfer complete, Brian breathed a sigh of relief. He had given the gift to mankind, with no strings attached--without profit to himself. The NOR and the Voice of Common Man were his gifts to mankind.

The people who accepted the NOR knew nothing of his life, nor Voltar, nor the time clock of Cuzco, the plans for a pyramid, nor even the White House trip. They accepted the working NOR on face value—as a gift.

The NOR Transferred

After a year of use with very positive results, Brian faced a difficult decision. The biofeedback equipment for the NOR had not been purchased due to budget cuts. The therapists wanted to keep the NOR, but Brian wanted more data and research. He transferred the NOR to one of the other applicants--the Psychobiology Lab at California State University in Fullerton. Dr. Richard McFarland planned to use the NOR for research.

Under McFarland's direction, the NORX1-11 operated from 1981 until the late 1990's—over twelve years—as an instrument for research. Used by professors and graduate students, the NOR provided lights and sounds for studies on emotion and learning. Some of the studies were published in scholarly journals. At least one study thanked Brian and Marla for the device.

The Next Generation

With the NOR in place at California State Fullerton, Brian fully relaxed. He could go on with his life. The fulfillment would be up to 'the People,' and the Next Generation of Man.

The plans about Quantum Displacement Physics, and the Pyramids, and Voltar's NOR, had all been roughed out. Brian had done his part. The next step was up to man. "I will do more drawings, I will provide more knowledge," he said, "when man wants to proceed—when the time is right."

1980 - 2000

The only promise ever given to Brian by the Host, in the beginning, was that he would prosper in his career. Brian did. He and Marla moved to Seattle, Washington for jobs in the aerospace industry. With Voltar's guidance, Brian's career accelerated. As a "design project engineer," he specialized in switching devices. He worked on pilot-firing mechanisms in helicopters and fighter jets. He specialized in military night vision, weapons systems, flight deck instrumentation and infrared cockpit suppression. He worked on the planes that helped fight Desert Storm. He worked for companies like Lear-Siegler, Bell Helicopter and prime subcontractors to Boeing and McDonnell Douglas.

He saw his visions from the past fulfilled when he worked for GE Astro Space as a Project Designer on satellites and space probes. As a "spacecraft design engineer"-- he provided designs and manufacturing support for the Mars Observor, Telstar, the Viking Orbitor and GeoStar. Working with engineers from NASA, Jet Propulsion Lab, and AT&T, Brian designed spacecraft frames and platform structures, master oscillator systems and RF packaging. He drew the designs and watched parts of the spacecraft take shape.

Aerospace, telemetry, optics and biology combined in his career. In later years, he changed focus to work in the bio-medical industry. Doctors and scientists provided input as Brian created designs for blood flow systems, and bone implants in the face and head. Brian could not believe how rapidly his career accelerated with helpful ideas from Voltar.

697

All that he had learned from Voltar about the bio-telemetry scanner, the probe, the Biological Monitoring Belt, and the NOR contributed in some way to his design projects.

In return, Brian learned from his work with high technology companies. He kept notes about how he might enhance the Biological Monitoring Belt, the NOR or Quantum Displacement Physics. However, he did not advance the projects for over two decades.

After work, he lived as a Common Man with few cares for the bigger world. While living in a small town in Pennsylvania, he bought a big, black horse—a stallion that he decorated and rode in parades. He won awards for horse and rider costume design—as a silver clad cowboy.

Later, he customized a white Z-28 Camaro—a show car from 1978 with seventeen coats of white paint. The car earned first place in stock car shows around his area. For Brian, that was fun, and the fulfillment of his personality.

To his many new friends and associates, Brian said nothing about his life story. For two decades, he and Marla lived a normal life.

By the year 2000, the NORx1-11 had stopped working. The psychobiology lab at California State University in Fullerton had placed the NOR into storage. Brian arranged for the NOR to be shipped back to him in Pennsylvania. He and Marla began work to rebuild and renovate the device. When people saw the NORx1-11 in action, and understood the story, they were inspired to create modern versions. Since then, Brian and a small number of associates have made progress on related devices.

The Children

Brian's two daughters from Mary Beth grew up, married and gave birth to their own children. Today, they all live in Nevada with their mother. They have resentments, and strong feelings about the events, and about Brian. He wasn't there when they needed a father, growing up, and they don't understand why.

Brian's son from Debra, the only child born after the transformation, never knew much of his father. Debra became an executive secretary for a big computer company, but after two years, she followed her green-eyed friend Karen to a Missouri hog farm. Karen and I had parted company soon after Brian split from Debra. Karen married a truck driver and moved to Missouri. Debra tried living on the farm, but didn't last long.

In early 1981, she called me in Colorado. I was producing a slideshow that I had written for the Governors of 12 Western states. I needed help to wrap-up the project. She drove to Colorado on her last dollar and helped me finish the slideshow. Debra liked Colorado and she stayed in the area for the next twenty years working as a secretary for various companies, a laboratory technician, or an

LPN—a licensed practical nurse. She eventually married an electronics technician and gave birth to another very bright son.

I always felt Brian's son with Debra might be special. I tried to help him understand and survive the stress of life as best I could. His first grade teacher told me he was a "mechanical genius." He could fix everything in the classroom and keep all the kids laughing at the same time." But, he required special handling. He was so filled with energy that a special teaching aide was assigned to control him, while the primary teacher handled the class.

Years later, of his own choice, he studied drafting and design in high school. Using only a pencil, he learned to sketch houses and buildings that looked like an architect's work--freehand. He grew to be a radiant young man, filled with vision and energy—just like his Dad.

Now, in the year 2000, he is 21. What will become of him, and his "X" generation? What will happen to those who will be the age of thirty-three in 2011 and 2012?

The world of tomorrow will be on their shoulders. They will inherit the world of the Baby Boom generation, like we inherited the world created by "the Greatest Generation" – those men and women who won World War II, and became heroes to the world.

Since 1980, technology has escalated creating a booming economy in America. Supposedly technology will rapidly keep changing until a truly psycho-cybernetic technology is available. When that happens, the mind-machine technology will trigger a *quantum evolution* to a higher level of mind.

People will grow, rapidly, especially children stimulated at an early age with certain patterns of light and sound. Perhaps, many will develop the abilities that Brian held. Perhaps, gifts will be given, and the transformation of mankind will unfold.

If these events do transpire, I am certain that some of the answers the young people will need can be found within these pages in my gift to the children—*the Play of Life.*

Today, I still can't say whether Voltar is a "familiar spirit" of Brian's, a multiple-personality, an avatar, a demon, or just a fanciful creation. Perhaps he is what he first said to Brian. A man "from time beyond all time."

I do know that he never turned me from my religious beliefs, and in fact, I became more committed to Christianity and to Jesus after my 4 years with Brian. "To each his own mind," Voltar would always say.

"My role has nothing to do with religion," Brian always said. "It's the mind."

"The day will come when mankind will need a man such as Brian," said Voltar in our last conversation. "A plasma will be discovered that will respond to the thought of man with an electrical impulse. With that discovery -- the New World begins—a true psycho-cybernetic civilization."

"'Look to the East' has come," said Voltar. "A new day, a new world is only one step away. When Quantum Evolution comes to you, remember this:

Man is Two Men in One. One is awake in Darkness, the other Asleep in the Light. When you see between the Two, You will find YOU, and in that moment a great change will take place—not only in your body, but in your mind. You will awaken to a World which is Forever and Forever, You."

-30-

BRIAN and MARLA in the year 2000--twenty years after the
story formally ended on March 22, 1980.

Addendum A

I AM

I am that, that I am, a child of the living God, the Creator of the Universe. With this knowledge, and the destiny of my being before me, I step forth with open arms to all. I am Voltar, and on this world Earth, I am with you today, and forever. I come with love to all those about me, and offer to all, all that I am.
Thank you.

Voltar –

The Brian Scott Story

By Fay Harris

A rotten kid I called him, when first this boy I knew,
But I felt a strong affection,
For this boy of thirty-two.

That boy had lived a life that drove him to confusion,
Crying out for help and asking—
what is real and what's illusion?

UFO's, Flying Saucers, Men from Outer Space--
they were nothing new to him,
in fact, quite common place.

There was something about this young man,
a part of every boy –
mischief, rebellion, confusion,
taking and giving LOVE in great joy.

I had raised two boys and they were there
with all the trials and tribulations.
All of the boys from every walk,
with all the mixed relations.

I saw the world back away from him,
because they didn't know,
what to do to help this boy,
with the row he had to hoe.

Then a stranger came forth in true brotherhood,
and they became as one.
They knew that together, they could prove
to the world,
what is meant by "All in One".

A boy of great strength that stranger was--
he got his strength from somewhere,
that others did not know,
but he knew it would be there,
and it was always so.

I loved, waited, and helped where I could.
But the burden was heavy on them.

They returned my love, and I was a given a gift:
to see two boys become men.
Two men with far more courage and strength
that any man I had known,
with vision as great as the first pioneers,
and a task they knew was their own—
to do what they could to bring to mankind,
the truth to make them free.

Free of confusion and creed,
Free of mystery,
free of mystery--
free of mystery.

Addendum B

ABRIDGED CHRONOLOGY

BRIAN SCOTT STORY - TRANSFORMATION

(With statement of the moral and message)
© 2000 James E. Frazier

October 12, 1959
Young Brian Scott sees orange ball of light on 16th birthday in Garden Grove, CA. He tattoos spider on his right arm and a jaguar on his left. He drops out of school knowing he has a special role to play in life.

May-June 1971
The FIRST contact takes place in the Arizona desert north of Phoenix. Giants with long-ears give medical exam. Brian agrees to accept a "quantum evolution to mind level ten." Shortly after the contact, he is jailed in Utah for stealing food from a store. All he remembers of contact is that he saw a light, and lost two hours of time.

1971-1973
Brian meets Mary Beth and they marry in northern California. Brian works selling signs to stores. In a big storm, his small fishing boat is swamped in San Francisco harbor. Newspaper articles about the rescue lead to his arrest for not delivering signs as promised. He goes to county jail for 90 days. When he gets out, he works as a punch press operator in Orange County and goes to night school in pipeline drafting.

October 25, 1973
Brian and a cousin to his wife are abducted by little, dome-headed gray aliens. Brian didn't like them. They wanted to know what he had been told about them by the first group. They said the 'plan would fail.' Brian didn't know what they were talking about. "Tell us all that you know...."

705

1973-74
Brian graduates from tech school with straight A's, the top of the class, one of the top ten. He is amazed. He wins two awards from the state for drafting designs, starts first job as mechanical draftsman, and gets rapidly promoted.

August 1975
Blackouts begin at work after seeing flashing lights in his mind. The lights repeat 22 times. In addition, at night, Brian has repeating dreams of the first contact. He becomes worried, agitated.

September 1975
First automatic writings begin: NOUS LAOS HIKANO is the first. Brian calls UFO researchers for help due to "black-outs" and auto writings. He wants them stopped.

September-Nov. 1975
A medical doctor and professor at Anaheim Hospital conduct hypnosis. Sessions become very dramatic and are videotaped. A strong, authoritative voice comes from Brian. The Host requests physical transportation to South America. Investigators request proof that is provided by The Host in the form of signs in the sky, and knowledge. They refuse to comply.

Oct. 31, 1975
The Host appears in Brian's garage. "Why has man not complied?" He shows Brian the "fate of mankind" – an underground nuclear waste explosion in the URAL MOUNTAINS of Russia. The Host says the factor of time in this will "mark the mind" of all mankind. When investigators find no newspaper articles about the explosion, they begin to believe Brian is a hoaxer. Later, in November of 1976, a Russian scientist reveals truth of the explosion in a British science magazine. He is attacked by the CIA as a fraud, but publishes a book in 1979 that shows purposeful suppression of the 1959 event -- for nearly two decades.

November 1, 1975
First ball of light, a bright orange orb, appears in backyard of home, a sign for Brian and his wife. His wife is terrified, but Brian is relieved someone else has seen the light.

November 5, 1975
Various people witness the ball of light. Vance Dewey, an electrical engineer at the Naval Electronics Laboratory, arrives to measure and monitor ball of light. Equipment placed into home.

November 22, 1975
Brian abducted by giants with long-ears, and taken to Nazca Plain for a healing on the Spider carving—a point previously named A22. Brian returns after 27 hours, radiant and filled with joy. Police reports document "missing person."

December 22, 1975
Brian abducted by Secondary World. They question him, "What do you know about the Children...."They attempt to remove implant with cold green light and provide THEIR form of quantum evolution.

January 1976
Brian's face droops. He is hospitalized for Bell's palsy. Exams are conducted: psychiatric and neurological plus CAT SCAN. No physical or psychiatric disorders are found. Brian released.

February 1976
Dark time. UCLA investigators get involved to force trance channeling and get psychic predictions. Demonic possessions follow, frightening investigators. The battle of good and evil begins in the house. The lights are "sensors," the Host says. Brian, wife and others see red lights and orange lights from both groups, in an apparent battle. The Host, aliens and Voltar all materialize in the home at various times. Wife and both children hospitalized after contact with ball of light. The first newspaper story appears when a hospital doctor allows exorcists to come for wife. Brian begins to believe he has taken a wrong path.

MARCH 1976
Brian calls out for help to UFO investigators and to religious groups. He watches as people parade through his home, like a circus--including scientists, psychics, doctors, police, researchers and news reporters. They argue philosophy with each other, but no one has answers for Brian. His wife is placed into a regional psychiatric hospital, while one child remains in a local hospital. Brian feels alone, and reaches out for help. Priests and preachers attempt two exorcisms in the home.

APRIL 1976

Finally, Brian puts the dark-side behind him. He starts to get answers by asking himself questions while in a trance using a tape recorder. He hears a first tape recording of himself in trance and laughs. Brian still does not believe it is really him. Doctors and in-laws blame Brian for causing the problems and insist that Brian leave the house so wife and children can return home from a psychiatric hospital. Brian must leave or turn children over to state Social Services.

JUNE 22, 1976

Living in his own apartment, Brian is asked by the Host to go to the desert for a final contact. Brian tries to tape record as two hulks take him by surprise. A high-pitched voice is recorded on a tape recorder dropped behind in the sand. On the craft, the Host explains everything. Brian is being tested, and trained. He must learn to know the "heart and mind of all mankind." He is told to go forward, that he will meet new people and that he might succeed. If he fails, the Secondary World aliens will eliminate mankind. The Host cries for mankind.

JULY 1976

Brian meets Jim Frazier and Debra, a young Christian woman who is excited about the conflict between the two groups. She wants to know more. She is not afraid of demons.

August 19, 1976

A UFO investigator urges Brian to take the story "to the People" since UFO investigators and top experts can't help, like Dr. Hynek and Jacques Vallee. Brian speaks publicly at the Garden Grove Civic Center. People offer to help. That same day, Jim Frazier asks for a sign.

August 23, 1976

Brian finds a writing that gives a LATITUDE AND LONGITUDE, and says -- "A Ball of Fire comes in the sky, for all mankind to see. A thousand particles of this of I. Seek this in knowledge of I." Twenty-two hours later the Ball of Fire soars over San Francisco sparkling. Bright particles shoot off from the green head that is followed by a long orange tail.

September 1-5

Brian and Jim go to the latitude and longitude given in advance and find everyone excited by the "ball of fire." They say "the night become like day." It was like the "sun came down to the earth." With horse wranglers, Brian and Jim try to find the meteorite. Above 8,000 feet, on a mountaintop, the first test of

Mind level ten is given. Electronic signals in the air can be heard by everyone--even the cowboy wranglers. The signals go through Brian's mind and brain. At an ancient rock carving, the final test is given. Both Brian and Jim experience the signal. The Host says, "Thank You."

September
After the successful test, Brian's memory is restored of the first contact, and all contacts. He writes the story of the first contact. The giants with long-ears are really a beautiful people with blond and red hair who wear a "Cloak of Sorrow." Their leader, red-haired, boyish Voltar, appears inside a stone amphitheater in the mountains and gives Brian a WHITE ROCK. Paranormal events begin with water drops that fall on Brian. Then Brian meets a man described in his writings as "the one who would know." Mr. Helios understands the math and science in Brian's 100 pages of writings and drawings.

October 8, 1976
As water drops continue falling on Brian, sending him into dazes, and trances, strange beeps are received on tape. They are to be patterned in a certain order and sent to a probe in orbit near the moon. Information on the probe, a target in space, and a code are sent to a Scottish Astronomer, Duncan Lunan.

October 12, 1976
The white rock is dematerialized by Brian on his 33rd birthday. Brian is able to displace the rock, at will, with his mind. He begins bending spoons, and playing games with his new found powers, but soon gets into trouble. He makes an ethical mistake, upsets his girlfriend, and the evening of his 33rd birthday turns disastrous when he throws the rock away. It shatters. The next day, he ends up in a church. He is forgiven and asked to proceed.

November 4, 1976
New Scientist magazine in Britain publishes article by a Soviet geneticist that refers to the underground nuclear waste explosion in the Ural Mountains. Within days, the scientist is interviewed by newspapers and TV stations from around the world. The American CIA and British intelligence agencies begin a plan to discredit the scientist and attack the reports as fraudulent, and not important.

November 22, 1976
Duncan Lunan, after a month of checking Brian out through Scotland Yard, British Intelligence and the FBI, agrees to transmit the signals to the target in space.

December 5, 1976
Brian receives a mark in the palm of his right hand: big black numbers -- 020 020 020. It is supposedly an access code to the probe in orbit near the moon.

December 19, 1976
Brian and Jim leave for South America.

December 22, 1976
Lunan again transmits to the probe, and the transformation takes place at Tiahuanaco, home to the god of the Inca--Ticci Viracocha. Brian stands in the Portal to Life and places his hands on the stone. Energy from the probe is transmitted to the Temple and enacts the transformation—a descent of the "radiant energy" of Voltar with an "ascent" of the radiant energy" of Brian.

December 25th, 1976
Christmas Day, Brian--united as one with Voltar and Viracocha--starts a riot in the royal plaza of the Inca. More than 400 Incan celebrate his message to them: "Viracocha will return." A Spanish official breaks up the gathering as Voltar is helped by Incans to escape.

January to June 1977
BRIAN and VOLTAR are united as one with VOLTAR in dominance for a month. Then BRIAN'S personality returns to dominance so he can go to work and pay the bills. VOLTAR's personality is only available at night and on weekends. They change places effortlessly. BRIAN challenges other UFO contactees to give up their fantasies, unite and create the New World.

JUNE 22, 1977
Wealthy investors help fund a trip to South America and film documentary. Phase 2 of the transformation takes place in the same temple in South America as Jim films. Brian is taken to Mind Level 8, and when United as One with Voltar, he has spiritual powers, as well as knowledge given during the first phase. He can simply touch someone, and cause him or her to receive all that they need to "fulfill their destiny."

June 25, 1977
Voltar provides a fossil to one man, an Incan descendant as proof that life started in the Western Hemisphere, as well as the Eastern Hemisphere. Betrayals begin

July 5, 1977
Brian, Jim and Voltar are stranded without resources in South America. They must use street smarts to complete filming at NAZCA and at TORO MEURTO, both sites requested by The Host. Finally, with no money left, they get to the airport and fly back to LA. More betrayals unfold in Los Angeles. Brian/Voltar is betrayed three times. The agreement to provide a "home" for Voltar and place for him to work for one year falls apart back in Los Angeles. In anger Brian's personality returns to full dominance. He takes control to protect VOLTAR who is "too vulnerable" for our world.

From 1977-1978
For one year, Brian and Jim both recover emotionally, and financially from the betrayals.

1978-1979
Russian scientist publishes book in the US: <u>Nuclear Disaster in the Urals</u>. The subject: Radioactive waste disposal explosion in Russia in 1959. He proves suppression by the CIA of all knowledge about the disaster so that anti-nuclear power protesters will not have ammunition for their arguments. Book focuses on DNA research on plants and animals impacted by the radiation. A later 1993 report confirms that 8000 people died and more than 28,000 were radiated.

Brian, as Voltar, teaches two seminars to people in Southern California: TEACHINGS OF SPACE and THE PLAY OF LIFE. The NORX1-11, a Neural-Optical-Responder, is built after the first seminar and the WHITE HOUSE project develops from the second. Brian's Christian girlfriend refuses to help build the NOR for religious reasons. She does not want any form of technology to be used to "uplift" man, and the number in his right palm frightens her. Brian and Debra dissolve their relationship.

MARLA PARK comes to the first session and is selected to have an experience for the entire class. After seeing a rock glow, and hearing a voice, she agrees to help Brian complete the NORX1-11. Then she helps him take the Voice of Common Man to the White House.

Summer of 1979
The Voice of Common Man is gathered in the streets of Orange County on videotape. Many newspaper articles document the project.

711

February 7, 1980
President Jimmy Carter acknowledges Brian, Jim Frazier and Marla Park at the White House. Documents related to the story are placed into the National Archives and stored in Carter's Presidential Library.

March 22, 1980
The Brian Scott Story is declared over. Voltar's people say goodbye, and indicate Brian is a success -- the first success in nearly 2000 years. Quetzalcoatl is closest. Brian is to continue as a common man—transformed. Voltar promises that "the children" will return December 24th, 2011 to five sites on the earth. There the "touch" will be given. "Seek not of I, but the reality of your own being," says Voltar.

March 1980 - 1981
Brian and Marla donate the NORX1-11 to an Easter Seal Society site -- The Center for Rehabilitation in Orange County. After a year, the NOR is transferred to the California State University psychobiology department at Fullerton. Twelve years of research are completed using the NOR, and many studies are published in scholarly journals on emotion and music.

1980 - 2000
Brian's career escalates, and he works two decades in the aerospace, military and biomedical industries as a design-engineering draftsman for major companies. He is united as one with Voltar, and Brian is "in charge of the switch." He is the dominant personality, but can receive guidance, wisdom and ideas on new technology from Voltar at any time. He provides design changes and adaptations to various projects for companies in aerospace, aeronautics, and biomedicine.

Results

The gray aliens who interacted with Brian have supposedly been restrained due to Brian's success. Their plans and projects with man were revised. Starting in 1980, our government plus many young men and women were "inspired" by Voltar's people--and by the grays *jointly*--to bring new technologies into our world that will create freedom for the "common man."

The original plan to replace man's form may be fully stopped, or not. That depends on how well the transformation process unfolds. Voltar and his people still want the Pyramid to be rebuilt at Tiahuanaco, prior to 2011 A.D, and a new technology created based on the NOR prototypes. Brian needs to do no more except grow in wisdom, and write the history of Voltar's people – <u>God's Other Children</u>. The rest is up to man.

James E. Frazier

MORAL AND MESSAGE

The gifts, the story and *The Play of Life* are a moral and a message for "all mankind." Brian succeeded as a common man, and so will the "thinking person" succeed once aware of *The Play of Life.* However, the "thinking person" will have different temptations unique to their own life. Each must learn to resist the temptations to betray the Common Man. Instead, the growth, the technology and the wisdom should be used to create freedom for the Common Man in America first, then in other nations.

Quantum Displacement Physics will create an ability *to transport matter through time and space by mind at level 4.* That means people will be able to be transported, at will, anywhere around the planet...and eventually—throughout the solar system.

Brian—a Common Man--reached a higher level of mind, and did not SELF-DESTRUCT, or destroy others. He succeeded, so can the "thinking man" – and other common people.

MORAL in Voltar's words:
As you transform into a psycho-cybernetic culture, do not forget the Common Man, but lift him up, and create freedom for him. From this will come greater freedom for all. Remember, the "voice of common man" is the heart of your nation and the spirit of your people.

MORAL in Jim's words:
Understanding the process of transformation, incarnation, or unity of multiple-personalities may be a next step in the quantum evolution of all mankind. That step is a likely key to paranormal powers, and to conquering the dark side of mankind. Apparently, the transformed mind somehow impacts DNA of the individual, and the uplifted consciousness can be passed on to progeny. However, this process can be enhanced and controlled by manipulating the magnetic fields around the subject – the "physical, but invisible exhalation of the earth." If man can begin stimulating or training children with patterns of light and sound before the age of five, a new language of light and sound will begin to enhance the brain's abilities. This represents a first big step with children. A second step is to train the children to interact with the electro-magnetic field about their body. Then supposedly, children will expand to higher levels of mind, very rapidly, plus they will be able to manage paranormal powers with success.

The problem is that man's progeny do NOT seem to maintain the transformation without some directed assistance, so even though one man is

714

uplifted, the higher consciousness hasn't been maintained for more than a few generations. That may be changing with the supposed introduction of different genes and genetic material into the population by various alien groups.

Althought this is all very interesting, why bother? The answer is SURVIVAL. Voltar always said that we would need to develop the expanded levels of mind for one reason: to survive. When I asked for explanations, the stories of the Inca and the Aztec, and of Voltar's people were repeated. The thrust of these stories was always the same: a highly evolved nation must always be on guard, because less evolved nations can conquer a more highly evolved civilization, and place them into slavery. That is the lesson of Voltar's history. In short, America could be conqured in the future by a nation of less advanced people who obtained paranormal or expanded mental powers.

Ethics are not a factor in the growth. Both good and bad people can learn to expand themselves and their children, and their nation. People and nations of opposing religions or philosophies can learn to expand their minds.

Voltar's people want our nation to learn the lessons and go forward as *a nation* for 1,000 years—a millennium. Brian's story, the gifts, and this knowledge are supposedly mental and logical preparations for this MILLENNIUM of peace. The role of this *Play of Life* is not religious, but the knowledge and wisdom are foundations for a spiritual transformation.

Each person must learn to conquer the dark side with freedom of choice and freedom of religion. The actual uplifting of the mind can be given with a touch, or with the NOR, or by activation of zones on the earth. That is the easy part.

The challenge is to not go down the wrong path, to not select the wrong identity, especially an identity that leads to destruction of self or others. The challenge is to MAINTAIN the uplifting, and to create a world in which the "higher you," the more vulnerable being, can survive and prosper, and reproduce. That can only be done, step-by-step, in agreement with others who share a similar goal and purpose. Without trust, honesty, and solid agreements – all will fail.

To that end, each must learn to protect his "higher self," keep his word to others, associate with those whom you trust, take action to fulfill your God-given destiny, and help each other to build their "first step," because the first step is the hardest.

No one can build his or her own "first step." People can go easily from mind level 2-10, but getting to mind level 2 is the big challenge for us all. Brian's story, *The Play of Life,* and the two projects are all considered gifts, given as a "first step" for mankind. These gifts will supposedly help "all mankind" step-up to Mind Level 2. From there, on our own, each man and woman will ascend to a higher level of mind using wisdom given in *The Play of Life.*

About the Author

In 1976, James Frazier, a 29 year-old filmmaker, escorted Brian Scott, a 33 year-old alleged UFO contactee to South America for a "Quantum Evolution to Mind Level 8." Jim guided Brian through the transformation process. There is no one more qualified in modern times to tell a story of human transformation.

Afterwards, Frazier became a newspaper reporter and editor. He was given full editorial control of three weekly newspapers over the next few years. He then worked as an investigative reporter focusing on crime and political news for two daily newspapers.

Since 1986, he has owned and operated his own video and film production company producing advertising media, documentaries and public affairs programs for local TV and for corporate clients.

On film and sound tape, Frazier documented Brian's experiences from 1976-1980 on a daily basis. He helped plan the Neural-Optical-Responder, (NORx1-11) built by Brian, and in 1980 President Jimmy Carter acknowledged James in the White House with Brian -- for bringing the "Voice of Common Man" to the President.

Frazier started out to become an experimental psychologist. He has a B.S. degree in psycho-biology from Colorado State University with a minor in journalism. He attended graduate school in clinical psychology at the University of Texas on a full ride scholarship, and was offered a full-ride fellowship from NASA to study space psycho-biology at Florida State University. Later, on a full ride fellowship from CBS, he attended the University of Southern California's MFA program in cinema directing and writing. He heard Brian Scott for the first time on a radio show in May of 1976 and optioned all rights to the story.

After spending four years investigating Brian, he returned to Colorado. As a newspaper reporter, he became a member of the Colorado Press Association, and founded the American Lyceum, Inc., a non-profit organization for public debate and deliberation.

Today, he is a writer, director and producer of video, TV and film programs.

CPSIA information can be obtained at www.ICGtesting.com
Printed in the USA
BVOW08s1634180515

400686BV00001B/12/P